PROBLEM-SOLVING AND
ARTIFICIAL INTELLIGENCE

PROBLEM-SOLVING AND ARTIFICIAL INTELLIGENCE

JEAN-LOUIS LAURIÈRE

Translated by Jack Howlett

Prentice Hall

New York   London   Toronto   Sydney   Tokyo   Singapore

First published in French in 1987 by
Eyrolles, Paris

English edition first published 1990 by
Prentice Hall International (UK) Ltd,
66 Wood Lane End, Hemel Hempstead,
Hertfordshire, HP2 4RG
A division of
Simon & Schuster International Group

Printed and bound in Great Britain by
BPCC Wheatons Ltd, Exeter

Library of Congress Cataloging-in-Publication Data

Laurière, Jean Louis.
   [Intelligence artificielle. English]   •
   Problem solving and artificial intelligence / J. L. Laurière;
translator, J. Howlett.
     p. cm.
   Translation of: Intelligence artificielle.
   Bibliography: p.
   Includes index.
   ISBN 0-13-711748-5 : $40.00
   1. Artificial intelligence. 2. Problem solving. I. Title.
Q335.L3813 1989
006.3—dc19   88-35465
                                       CIP

British Library Cataloguing in Publication Data

Laurière, J. L.
   Problem solving and artificial intelligence
   1. Problem solving. Applications of artificial intelligence
   I. Title II. Intelligence artificielle 006.3

   ISBN 0-13-711748-5

2 3 4 5 94 93 92 91 90

CONTENTS

ABBREVIATIONS

AAAI   American Association for Artificial Intelligence
ACM Computing Surveys
            Journal of the ACM.
AFCET   Association Française de Cybernétique et d'Etudes Techniques.
AFIPS   American Federation for Information Processing Society.
AI   *Artificial Intelligence* (Journal, published by North Holland).
CACM   Communications of the Association for Computing Machinery.
CAD   Computer Aided Design.
CAO   Conception Assistée par Ordinateur.
CS   *Cognitive Science* (Journal).
ECAI   European Conference on Artificial Intelligence.
IEEE   Institute for Electrical and Electronic Engineers.
IFIP   International Federation of Information Processing.
IJCAI   International Joint Conference on Artificial Intelligence.
JACM   *Journal of the Association for Computing Machinery.*
MI   *Machine Intelligence.* Collection of articles in 9 volumes published by Elsevier.
MIT   Massachusetts Institute of Technology, Cambridge, USA.
OPN. RES.   Operations Research (Journal).
RAIRO   *Revue d'Informatique et de Recherche Opérationnelle*, published by Dunod.
SIGART   Special Interest Group in Artificial Intelligence (ACM).
TSI   *Technique et Science Informatique.* (Journal, published by Dunod).

INTRODUCTION

My feeling that a book such as this was needed probably began in my schooldays: like all my fellow students, I absorbed the contents of the lessons in physics and mathematics, while continually asking myself – but what's the use of all this? In physics, the relationship with reality should have been obvious but we never got to believing this – too many things remained a mystery and, besides, the new teacher would tell us that the model described to us the previous year was wrong. So we saw physics as a strange game played by adults. It was different with mathematics, for here we respond both to the pleasure of finding an elegant proof and, equally, to the beauty of the abstraction. However, this pleasure became spoiled by a deepening feeling of being tricked: we are being continually fed with definitions and proofs, presented as though these were revealed truths, but the reasons for these were never given and most of the proofs seemed to spring from the teacher's chalk as though by magic. How could anyone ever have linked together all those lines of the proof and foreseen how the wonderful conclusion in the last of them would follow from the first? And, above all, there was the thought – what use is all this?

What became clear later, after several years of 'real' life, was that it is of no use at all – or, at least, of no direct use; the subjects are chosen arbitrarily and just put into the school timetables. Their real purpose is to transmit something more important – how to learn to understand, to learn to solve problems; in fact how to learn to learn. Strangely enough, the need for this is never openly acknowledged and the subjects are scarcely ever taught. There is a kind of intellectual terrorism that classes a large fraction of schoolchildren as 'no good at mathematics', when their only failing is that they have not understood something that has never been said to them. Others get by because at an early stage they have caught on to the implied rules of the game, whilst still others just learn everything by heart.

Well, a field of research has now come into being in which the prime aim of the workers is to understand how an information processing system, whether human or machine, is able to assimilate, analyse, transform and generalise what it is taught and, as a result, deal with actual situations and solve problems. This is what is called Artificial Intelligence. It is the eldest child of information science and is concerned with all those intellectual activities of mankind that cannot be studied by any method known *a priori*; its field can therefore be defined as 'everything that hasn't been done so far in information science'. If information science is the science of information processing then artificial intelligence – AI in what follows – is concerned with all those situations in which this processing cannot be reduced to a simple and precisely defined method, that is, to an algorithm.

There are innumerable examples of such situations, including such mundane ones as reading a book – this book, for example. Here, for instance, the character written as I can be interpreted by our visual system as an upper case letter I, as lower case i or as an absolute value symbol, according to the context; it is even worse with handwriting, for, for example, the three written words all use (differently) the same written symbol: how does our cognitive system resolve these ambiguities? This typifies one of the key problems dealt with in AI. Others are the recognition of human faces – which are less easy to characterise formally than simple letters; understanding of text – not just of isolated words such as 'tube', 'main', 'useful'); understanding of speech – spoken, that is, with no written form available; theorem-proving and problem-solving; choice of the next move in a chess game; timetable construction; answering intelligence tests; devising an architectural plan; producing a medical diagnosis; analysis of a journal paper. All these have been the objects of recent studies, and in many cases impressive progress has been made.

Chapter 1

ARTIFICIAL INTELLIGENCE

The subject of Artificial Intelligence – AI – is concerned mainly with the acquisition and representation of knowledge, in all its forms; and researchers in AI have as their objective not only the construction of new theories but also the design and implementation of programs that are to be as general as possible in their scope.

We commence this study by looking at the role played by what we may now call classical information science, or *informatics*. We shall see later why, and in what way, the aims and methods of AI diverge from those of that subject and lead to a fundamental reappraisal of the whole field.

1.1 THE STATUS OF INFORMATICS

Informatics is used in two different ways:

1. As an aid to modelling. This is simply an extension of the use of mathematics with emphasis on the part played by time and on processes that evolve over time. After a mathematical solution to a problem has been found, this is put into the form of a program that can be executed by a computer.
2. As a means for testing hypotheses. By its very nature a computer is impartial and perfectly reliable, so it is the ideal machine for testing ideas.

Thus informatics, and AI even more so, has special links with linguistics, psychology and logic; three disciplines that relate to cognitive phenomena, to understanding and to reasoning. Further, these are links in both directions. On the one hand, linguists, psychologists and logicians now program the models they construct – and biologists, medics and mathematicians are tending to do the same; on the other, AI researchers are taking these models and attempting to deduce from them software for solving real-life problems.

There are especially close relations between AI and the cognitive sciences, for one simple reason: apart from the computer the only reasoning tool that we have is our own brain, and it is extremely difficult, maybe impossible, to study this objectively because the introspection will always vitiate any such attempt. Thus the computer is a unique aid in the study of reasoning.

A consequence of this is that AI ranks with the revolutionary achievements of Copernicus and Darwin in calling into question the place of Man in nature; here it is his monopoly of intelligence that is being questioned.

1.2 ARTIFICIAL INTELLIGENCE

AI is a science with a history covering some 30 years. Its aims are to reproduce what we understand as intelligent reasoning and actions in artificial devices, almost always in computers. The essential difficulties are of two types:

1. We ourselves do not really know how to achieve most of our activities. Thus we do not know the precise method – the algorithm, to use the informatics term – we use in order to understand a piece of written text, to recognise a face, to prove a theorem, to construct a plan of action, to solve a problem, to learn something, ...
2. Computers have nothing approaching our ability in this way; they have to be programmed afresh, from the start, for every new task and the programming languages that we have enable us to express only the most elementary concepts.

From two points of view AI is seen as an experimental science. It involves experiments made with computers in which models, expressed as programs, are tested and refined with the help of many examples; and experiments with human subjects – usually the researcher himself – aimed at finding models for human intelligence, so as to understand this better.

We shall now give a more precise definition of AI and its scope, and follow this with a short history in which we indicate the driving forces that have acted on the researchers. We conclude this first chapter with a review of the present methods, the results obtained so far and the tasks ahead.

1.3 DEFINITION AND SCOPE OF ARTIFICIAL INTELLIGENCE

1.3.1 Definition

Any problem for which no algorithmic solution is known is a problem in Artificial Intelligence.

By *algorithm* we mean an ordered, precisely specified sequence of operations that can be executed by a computer in a 'reasonable' time – of the order of a minute or an hour. Thus we have no algorithm for playing chess, for although any game involves only a finite number of possible situations, to examine them all would take thousands of years. Equally there is no algorithm for making a medical diagnosis, summarising a piece of text or translating from one natural language to another.

1.3.2 Scope

The fields in which we operate without having any well-defined method are very varied but have two notable characteristics in common:

1. They all concern symbolic information – expressed by letters, words, signs, drawings. This contrasts with the numerical processing traditionally associated with computers.
2. They always involve some element of choice: in fact, to say that there is no algorithm to deal with some situation is to say that at some stage a choice has to be made between several possibilities, with no certain rule for making that choice. This fundamental non-determinism, with consequent freedom of action, is an essential feature of AI.

The first problem encountered by AI researchers is that of capturing information. Existing hardware and software technologies are far from rivalling the human organs of sight, taste, smell, production or understanding of speech and physical manipulation of objects.

1.3.2.1 Pattern perception and recognition

An information processing system receives its information from its sensors. In our case, of our five senses the eye, with the visual system, is certainly the most important. In artificial systems cameras and lasers are used for input to 'image processing' and 'scene analysis' programs, and microphones for sounds.

The subject of coding and processing signals is known as pattern recognition. This is something that has to be done by automated information processing systems, but we are a long way from knowing how to solve the problems that arise here, even when the information is already coded and stored in the computer. Workers in AI are concerned particularly with the problems of understanding and reasoning that logically follow the pattern recognition stage.

1.3.2.2 Mathematics and automatic theorem proving

As we have seen, symbolic – that is, non-numerical – information is of especial importance in AI; and for this reason the first work was done in the fields of mathematics and games. Both these had well-established formalisms and both were regarded as strongholds of human intelligence; so they provided excellent material for tests.

The fallout from AI research, and the social implications, will soon become important. Several disciplines will be affected: psychology – AI has to concern itself with the human brain; logic; linguistics; biology – models for transport of information by the genes; informatics – advanced operating systems, database querying; medicine – aids to diagnosis; and perhaps above all, teaching in all subjects – the level of detail required in AI programs has revealed gaps in traditional teaching and shown that not enough is being taught in certain fields.

1.4 HISTORY OF ARTIFICIAL INTELLIGENCE

The computer may not be indispensable in the building and testing of the models used in AI research but it certainly provides the most powerful aid, and has made the rapid development of the subject possible. In 1954 Newell embarked on his project to write a program that would play chess well, based on a method already suggested by Shannon, the father of information theory. Turing, one of the first information scientists, had improved Shannon's method and had simulated it by hand. Shaw and Simon of the RAND corporation became associated with Newell's project and brought in as collaborators a group of psychologists in Amsterdam, led by de Groot, who had studied the methods of the great chess masters. A special language for manipulating symbolic information by computer, using pointers and linked lists, was developed at RAND: this was IPL-1 (Information Processing Language 1, 1956), the forerunner of LISP (McCarthy 1960). The first known AI program was LOGIC THEORIST, for working with propositional logic, which gave its first demonstration on 9 August 1956.

The Newell, Shaw and Simon chess program was shown for the first time in 1957. It has the structure of LOGIC THEORIST and embodies the concepts of 'goals to be attained' and 'heuristics' (from Greek ευρισκω, to find, meaning here a rule that enables a choice to be made in the absence of a firm theoretical basis). This work led to the idea of the program GPS (GENERAL PROBLEM SOLVER), which solved problems by a process of setting goals and analysing the differences between the current situation and the goal aimed at; GPS could range from puzzles such as the 'Towers of Hanoi' to the formal integration of algebraic expressions.

Interest in AI then began to spread among information scientists and soon papers were written that have become famous, for example by McCarthy, by Minsky and by Simon. Gelernter (1963), working in geometry, claimed that a program could perform better than its creator. As an illustration to support this his program proved the equality of the base angles of an isosceles triangle ABC (with $AB = AC$) not by the classical method of drawing the altitude from A but by considering the triangles ABC, ACB – from the congruence of which the result follows at once. Another program, Feigenbaum's EPAM (Elementary Perceiving and Memorizing Program) simulated psychological situations.

Some success in handling natural language was achieved very early on in work on extracting information from databases, for example in BASE-BALL (Green *et al.* 1961), which could answer questions about baseball matches; and STUDENT (Bobrow 1964) solved problems in algebra, stated in English.

There were great expectations for computer translation from one natural language to another. Many teams worked on this, believing that all that was necessary was a combination of syntax analysis with a dictionary; but this approach failed, and received severe criticism in, for example, the reports on AI by Dreyfus (1972) and Lighthill (1973). Several years had to pass before it was seen that automatic translation is not an isolated problem but necessarily involves that of *understanding*.

A new type of logical processing, based on the systematic manipulation of *reductio ad absurdum*, was developed by J. Robinson (1965). This made it possible for many problems to be expressed formally and handled by the machine; it has been used for theorem proving (Slagle, Green, Kowalsky), for checking programs (King, Waldinger) and for manipulating objects (Nilsson, Fikes). It formed the starting point for the novel programming language PROLOG, developed by Colmerauer in 1971 – see Chapter 3.

AI research has always proceeded in step with the development of computer languages and systems of continually increasing generality, bringing programming continually closer to our normal way of reasoning and to our normal vocabulary. LISP and PROLOG have been mentioned already; other important ones are PLANNER and QA4, which help in setting goals and formalising deductive processes in problem solving;

MACSYMA and REDUCE, for formal manipulation of mathematical expression; the TMS for handling uncertain information and checking for consistency.

Workers in robotics make use of the results of AI research as they appear, for the purpose of controlling systems that are either fixed in position or able to move about in a real world. Here they meet also all the problems concerning sensors: and the solutions of the problems of camera vision, and of detecting boundaries (Gussman, Waltz, Winston) and hidden objects in a complex universe are becoming steadily better. However, at this stage in the history (1968) the AI researchers were working only with very restricted universes – games, geometry, integral calculus, simple building blocks, short sentences on a limited vocabulary. The aim was always the same, to reduce the rate of combinatorial explosion, and for this they reduced the amount of exhaustive enumeration needed by applying 'common sense' and using heuristic arguments and numerical evaluation functions.

A sensible person will not attempt to use anything more ambitious than such methods; but even with these, many programs have been written, for universes of many different types, that rival the average human performance – the present microprocessor game players, for example for chess, draughts, reversi, Bridge, Go, are in this class. But there is still the challenge of matching the expert's performance.

1.5 ACHIEVEMENTS

The beginning of the 1970s was a turning point for AI research, for two reasons.

First, all these working in the field had gradually become convinced that all the programs so far written lacked a vital component: a deep knowledge of the field with which they are concerned. What distinguished the expert from the man in the street was the former's experience – the knowledge accumulated over the years. This led to the realisation that to improve the performance of an AI program it was not sufficient to change the heuristics or adjust some numerical coefficients, but that better reasoning mechanisms, and symbolically expressed experience, had to be provided.

Second, an explicit, consequential problem was raised: how can such knowledge be given to the program when the programmer himself does not have it?

The answer to this question is obvious: the program itself must get this knowledge from the expert. Thus the researchers were led to provide their programs with capabilities not available through the standard programming languages: for example, to assimilate a piece of information such as 'In

Paris today, 10 February, the weather is fine', to store this and to use it when, but only when, it was sensible to do so. This raised the need for a separation of the statement of a fact from that of the way in which that fact is to be used; programming languages, in contrast to this, allow only the expression of executable instructions. This new property is essential because the expert who is supplying the knowledge will do so as a series of isolated facts and will not be able to say in advance at what point this can be taken as complete.

Research into problem solving and understanding of natural language converges towards the central question of how to represent knowledge.

Many programs based on these ideas appeared around 1970. The first of these was DENDRAL, for inferring chemical structures from mass spectrometer data. This was developed at Stanford under the influence of the Nobel prizewinner Joshua Lederberg who continually contributed his knowledge to the program until it contained several thousand basic facts. DENDRAL was one of the first *expert systems*; the facts it contains are expressed in the form of disjointed rules in the expert's own language. It has performed strikingly well and is now sold by the manufacturer along with the spectrometer.

Of course, the ideal situation is that the program itself deduces the rules from the information given to it – that is, that it learns. This was achieved by the DENDRAL team with METADENDRAL; by means of repeat simulations and with the help of a few general rules giving the ways in which molecules could be fragmented, this program inferred in succession the special rules, first for each chemical bond and then for each substance. By this means it has been possible to investigate some chemical groups that had been little understood, and to report this in papers in the international chemical journals.

Another name to be mentioned is that of Terry Winograd, the author of SHRDLU (1971). This is a robot system that conducts a dialogue in English and so manipulates a set of cubes; it does not simply concern itself with the syntax of the statements but, because of the semantic and pragmatic knowledge it has concerning its universe of blocks, really understands their meaning. It can resolve ambiguities, such as deciding the noun to which a pronoun refers, understand metaphors, justify its behaviour and give an account of its actions. In addition, it shows that thanks to the robot, it can handle the real world effectively.

The general picture is that AI has now reached the operation stage. Whilst there are only a few hundred full-time researchers throughout the world – of whom about a hundred are in France – the results they are achieving affect all of us. The media are always telling us of these achievements and promising the 'intelligent machines' of tomorrow; but this is difficult research and progress is bound to be slow. Those who work in the field know that, far from producing magic formulae (in the form of algorithms), the task is to gather together, step by step, bodies of specialised knowledge and experience and put these onto the machines.

A difficulty in this is that for the most part this information is not there, simply to be picked up: it has to be acquired by long discussions with the experts, to reveal what they have learned subconsciously over the years, and languages and methods of knowledge representation have been developed specially to help in this. Although more information has to be collected and input than is contained in a dictionary or an encyclopedia, this is not an impossible task with the tools we now have available; but it calls for great staying power. Fortunately it is fascinating, for it leads to a better understanding of the human mind and human intelligence – the real subject of the study is mankind. It is perhaps not too much to say that when the work is finished, the next century's AI programs will be able to run on today's machines.

Chapter 2

REPRESENTATION OF PROBLEMS

This chapter provides an introduction to, and a plan of, the rest of the book.

2.1 INTRODUCTION

We are conscious of the existence of a problem when we want to achieve something but cannot see immediately just how to set about doing so.

The word 'problem' is derived from the Greek '$\beta\alpha\lambda\lambda\epsilon\iota\nu$', meaning 'to throw'; so a problem is something thrown or set before us – interestingly enough, the words parabola, hyperbola, symbol have the same derivation. Apart from the problems we meet in everyday life, the first that are put to us are those set in our primary schools, which, like all those put to us throughout our schooldays, are characterised by being stated in a conventional language with all the information given that is necessary to reach the solution. The language most often used is that of mathematics, and this leaves a very strong mark on us: differences in level of understanding of this language, of the rules that its use must obey and of the implications behind these rules can very soon bring about a sharp distinction between the young scholars, classifying them as having either an 'analytic' or a 'geometric' mind. Later in this chapter we give a brief sketch of the history of the language of mathematics, with the aim of showing that the subject is far from simple, that it has taken Man several thousand years, and much trial and error, to develop the concepts and tools that we now use and that the adventure is certainly not ended.

However, most of the problems that we meet outside school or university do not come with 'everything given'. They arise unexpectedly; mostly they are only incompletely stated; very often they are put to us by some other person who uses a variety of means for conveying information to us and

various representations of the real world, by voice with different inton-
ations, gestures or drawings. Natural language is the prime choice here and
from the point of view of solving problems has at least four basic defects: it
is incomplete, redundant, ambiguous and grammatically incorrect.

2.2 NATURAL LANGUAGE

Taking first the incompleteness of natural language, it is clear that in any
normal dialogue much of the information is not stated explicitly, the two
speakers being assumed implicitly to have the same fund of knowledge of
the subject under discussion; if this condition is not met, complete mutual
misunderstanding can result – this in fact is the source of many of the
difficulties that arise in information science. The use of check lists and
formal specifications is an attempt to overcome this defect of natural
language.

The defect of redundancy is currently exploited in a positive way, to
emphasise those features that seem important to the problem-setter, but
there is no guarantee that the essential difficulties of the problem reside in
these features.

Without the ambiguity it would be just impossible for us communicate;
but as with incompleteness, incorrect resolution of an ambiguity can result
in a complete misinterpretation of the problem. Finally, grammatical
incorrectness, especially of spoken language, although very evident is,
paradoxically, the least serious defect for our present purposes.

2.3 STATING A PROBLEM

Whether it is a question of a textbook problem, a personal experience or
that of a third person, the first essential is to gain a complete understanding
of what the problem really is; and this means stating it in a form that is
complete and without any ambiguities, that is, to find a representation in
which everything is given. Here the possibility of a form different from that
of written or spoken language arises, that of graphical representation, for
our visual system is a very powerful tool for capturing and processing
information.

A problem is not fully understood until a representation has been found
in which all the essential elements are given without redundancy or
ambiguity, so that the universe within which the solution lies is completely
specified: very often this stage reveals most of the main difficulties of the

problem. When this has been done, much of the pragmatic and semantic content of the problem has been expressed formally and the problem has become both more abstract and purer; we say that we now have a *closed statement*.

2.4 CLOSED STATEMENTS

The most general form in which a problem can be stated mathematically can be written:

Given a set X find all those of its points x that satisfy the set of constraints $K(x)$.

A classical example is the problem put by Binet to the calculating prodigy Inaudi: find all the integers x such that $x^3 + 84 = 37x$.

Two things should be noted in connection with this form of statement:

1. Giving the space X generally means giving simultaneously, but implicitly, the structure of X and the legal operations that can be performed on its members. Thus the knowledge of X is a vital compression of information.
2. The first closed statement found can usually be transformed so as to take into account the constraints $K(x)$, thus restricting the space to be searched and giving a better representation of the problem. It is by making a sequence of such transformations that the problem is solved, the final closed statement giving the solution directly.

There are two main variants of the closed statement, as follows.

Variant 1. The universe of the problem consists of an initial state, S_0 say, a final state S_1 and a finite set of operators Oab by means of which we can go from state S_a to state S_b. The problem is to find a path from a given S_0 to a given S_1.

An example is the '15s Puzzle' of Sam Loyd (Fig. 2.1).

$$S_0 = \begin{array}{|c|c|c|c|} \hline 2 & \square & 6 & 7 \\ \hline 12 & 9 & 10 & 3 \\ \hline 15 & 5 & 1 & 8 \\ \hline 4 & 13 & 14 & 11 \\ \hline \end{array} \qquad S_1 = \begin{array}{|c|c|c|c|} \hline 1 & 2 & 3 & 4 \\ \hline 5 & 6 & 7 & 8 \\ \hline 9 & 10 & 11 & 12 \\ \hline 13 & 14 & 15 & \square \\ \hline \end{array}$$

Fig. 2.1.

Oab = the state S_a can be changed by moving one of the adjacent numbers (sliding a tile in the actual puzzle) into the vacant square, resulting in the state S_b.

A solution is a sequence $(Oab, Obc, ..., Otu, Ouv)$ with $S_a = S_0$, $S_v = S_1$. The set of constraints is expressed by the law of succession of the operators: the state resulting from any one is the initial state for the next.

Variant 2. This is the traditional mathematical form:

Given the hypotheses $H(x)$, prove $C(x)$

For example: prove that for all positive integers n

$$\sum_{i=1}^{n} i^3 = \left(\sum_{i=1}^{n} i \right)^2$$

This reduces to the first variant if we put $S_0 = H(x)$, $S_1 = C(x)$, but there is the important difference that the operators for transforming one state into another are not given: the art of the mathematician lies in finding those that are of use in attacking the particular problem. It can happen that the 'conclusion' $C(x)$ is not given explicitly, for example the problem could be stated simply as 'Find $\sum i^3$'. This leaves an ambiguity, for the criterion is now subjective; it is reasonable to expect that a 'simpler' expression than the given statement is required, but simplicity of expression is not a rigorous mathematical concept.

2.5   STAGES IN PROBLEM-SOLVING GENERALLY

It seems that generally the human mind, when confronted with a problem, goes through seven key stages in reaching in a solution:

$E1$ Absorb and understand the statement.
$E2$ Make some immediate inferences, so far as possible.
$E3$ 'Play with' the situation.
$E4$ Reflect, let things mature.
$E5$ Look for a better representation, frame a closed statement.
$E6$ Find a partial solution and return to $E2$, or a complete solution.
$E7$ Check the validity of the solution; generalise.

Let us consider these in turn.

The first stage $E1$ involves our physical senses as information receptors, with sight and hearing playing a key role. An important consideration is that we have only a moderate capacity for immediate memorisation (see

Chapter 7, psychological studies) and this makes it difficult, even impossible, for us to absorb long statements.

$E2$ makes calls on our general knowledge to do the following:

1. To supply missing information.
2. To summarise long statements by means of forms that are more appropriate and more easily handled, for example drawings, graphs, algebra.

Since 1962 simple programs based on 'key words' have been written that can solve problems, stated in English, in kinetics and probability (Bobrow 1964, Gelb 1971).

With humans at least, $E3$ is crucial. It involves, first, returning to $E1$ and $E2$ to make sure that nothing is missing and that no serious error has been made in interpreting the problem; to find the nub of the situation, see where the real difficulty lies.

$E4$ is also basic. Here we have to clear our minds of all those facts that are related to the original formulation of the problem but irrelevant to the solution process, so as to let the right operators come to the surface. One way is to put the problem aside for a time and do something else; our minds are so programmed that 'forgetting' provides an excellent climate for the pursuit of old ideas and the encouragement of new ones, and this self-distraction from the problem in hand is a great help towards finding a solution.

$E5$ is the stage at which the closed statement of the problem should be reached – that is, the complete, unambiguous and non-redundant form. The difficulty of the problem can now be assessed more precisely – the extent of the space X to be searched, the complexity of the constraints $K(x)$ and the number of legal operations are good indicators of this.

The aim in $E6$ is almost always to find a better representation for the problem, meaning one that requires a smaller space to be searched. A new closed statement having been found, the cycle is repeated from $E2$ onwards.

$E7$ marks the end of the solution process properly speaking. However, it can be useful to return to $E1$, and perhaps to discuss the solution arrived at with the originator of the problem, to check this solution against the original statement and its behaviour in limiting cases, and to judge which are the critical parameters. It can be interesting also, and perhaps important, to see if the method used can be generalised to other situations:

1. Can the problem be generalised, keeping to the method found?
2. Are there other problems to which the method applies?
3. Are there other methods for solving the same problem?

To illustrate part of this process, consider the application of stage $E1$

(understanding the situation) and $E2$ (immediate inferences) to the following four simple problems (see Figs. 2.2–2.5).

The first is a well-known optical illusion and shows that our visual system is continually and actively interpreting the image before it. This is made still more clear by the second picture which can be interpreted variously, possibly after turning the page around, as a house, a sentry box or a bar cut to a corner at one end.

Fig. 2.2 Necker cube: how is this to be interpreted?

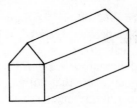

Fig. 2.3 What object(s) does this represent?

Fig. 2.4 Pass four straight lines through these nine points without lifting the pencil.

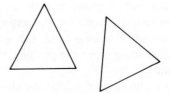

Fig. 2.5 Form four equilateral triangles with six matches.

Figure 2.4 shows how our cognitive system can, on occasion, restrict arbitrarily the space to be searched: if we look for a solution within the square formed by the nine points we shall not succeed, for there is none; but no such constraint is imposed, and there is the simple solution of Fig. 2.6. For Fig. 2.5, two conditions might be assumed but are not in fact stated, so we can allow that (a) the matches may cross and (b) the solution may not be in one plane. There are then the two possible solutions of Figs. 2.7 and 2.8.

In the following example only natural language is used:

> A cruel king locked up in a dungeon a young girl who refused to marry him. When after a year she still kept to her decision he had her brought into the forecourt of his castle and made her this offer. 'I will pick up two pebbles, one white and one black, and hold them hidden, one in each hand, and you shall choose either hand as you wish. If it holds the white stone you shall go free, if the black you shall marry me.' The girl accepted this offer with great trepidation, and her fear turned to panic when she saw the king surreptitiously pick up two black stones. What can she do?

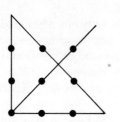

Fig. 2.6 Solution to Fig. 2.4

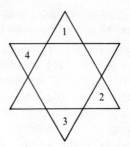

Fig. 2.7 Plane solution to Fig. 2.5

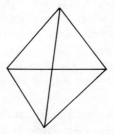

Fig. 2.8 Non-plane solution to Fig. 2.5

This problem – stated, for example, by Edward de Bono in his *Lateral Thinking* – illustrates again how a wrong specification of the universe to be searched can lead to there being no solution. Actually, the constraint expressed by 'I will pick up a black stone and a white one' rebounds nicely on the king. The girl takes the stone from one of his hands and drops it on the ground, among all those lying there. 'I'm so sorry' she says 'but it doesn't matter – the stone in your other hand will tell us the colour of the one I picked.' This being of course black, she is free.

These simple examples show that stages 1 and 2 are generally closely overlapped. They also illustrate the fact that when no solution can be found to the problem as it has been supposedly understood, the search for a solution will reveal the true problem and an unnecessary constraint can be removed.

A different situation, but one that arises fairly often, is that we cannot make any immediate inference; it is a matter of 'all or nothing' and the solution is revealed only after subconscious effort. This is what Martin Gardner calls the 'Ha-Ha effect', and here is an example.

You are alone in an empty room in which there are two identical bars of iron, identical except that one is magnetized and the other is not. They are solid,

heavy and unbreakable and no other material is available to you. How do you
find which is the magnetized bar?

This statement of a problem is in some ways the only one of its kind. We are
in a bad way here; the number of operators – that is, of actions open to us
– is very limited and the temptation is to throw up our hands and say that
either there is no solution or that if there is it must be very far-fetched. In
fact, the solution is very simple: the reader should pause for reflexion before
continuing.

Rather as in the problem of the girl and the king, it is a question of
destroying a symmetry; here the solution is purely physical and the only
manipulable objects are the two bars. Now magnetic attraction is completely symmetrical with respect to the two bars, and so gives no indication
of which is the attractor and which the attracted – except at one point, the
mid-point of the magnetised bar, which point cannot be magnetised. The
solution therefore is to hold one of the bars, call it A, at right-angles to the
other, B, and present one end to the mid-point of B; if there is no attraction
then it is B that is magnetised, but if there is attraction then A is
magnetised.

To illustrate stage $E3$ – 'play with the situation', which as we have said is
crucial – we take the following very simple example which can convey the
idea of an elegant solution. What could be simpler than to prove Pythagoras's Theorem by playing with ruler and set-square?

The theorem concerns a right-angled triangle and it is natural to view the
set-square as this triangle; let c be its hypotenuse and a, b the other two
sides. We can construct $a + b$ by placing the setsquare on the ruler in two
different ways, and thus construct a square of side $(a + b)$ in two different
ways, as shown in Fig. 2.9.

If the area of the set-square is T, the construction on the left shows that
the area of the large square is $a^2 + b^2 + 4T$, and that on the right shows that
it is $c^2 + 4T$, from which it follows that $a^2 + b^2 = c^2$.

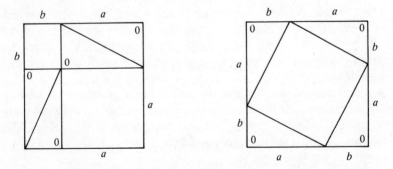

Fig. 2.9 Two squares of side $a + b$ for proof of Pythagoras's Theorem.

2.6   A COMPLETE EXAMPLE

The following example reconsiders the steps just described in arriving at a closed statement of a problem and then at a solution:

A chess board of 100×100 squares is completely covered by $10\,000$ black pawns. We play a game in which the only legal move is to change, in a single row or column, all the black pawns to white and all the white to black. Is it possible in a finite number of moves to leave 1990 white pawns on the board?

This statement in natural language is easily understood; however:

1. The answer is not obvious.
2. 'Playing with the situation' is not easy – 100×100 boards are not common.

A natural first step, to get a grip on the problem and make some inferences, is to reduce the complexity by taking smaller values of the parameters: thus we might try playing on, say, a 4×4 board, or better on an 'abstract' board whose dimensions are left unspecified. Whatever we decide, one thing always follows: white pawns appear after the first move. This removes an oddity that may have been noticed on first reading the statement of the problem – to speak of white pawns makes sense only after the first move. It also follows, and will be seen from play on a model board:

1. The result of two consecutive moves on the same row or column is as if no move has been made.
2. The order in which the moves are made is immaterial. Operating first on row $R1$ and then on row $R2$ gives the same result as operating first on $R2$ and then on $R1$, for the two have no pawns in common; and similarly for two columns. If a row and a column are concerned, these have only one pawn in common, at their intersection, and this is returned to its original colour after the pair of moves, whatever the order.

It is worth noting that this second deduction, whilst it may seem obvious to an adult, is not so to a young child. It corresponds to Piaget's fourth stage in the development of intelligence and is not firmly grasped until after about the age of 10.

3. The position of any row or column played is immaterial: the problem concerns only the number of black (and therefore of white also) pawns left on the board, and not their position.
4. It follows from the first two deductions that we need consider only rows or columns played 0 or 1 times: the order being irrelevant, any sequence of $2n$ moves is equivalent to no moves and any sequence of $2n + 1$ is equivalent to 1 move.
5. If follows from (3) that we can group all the rows that have been operated

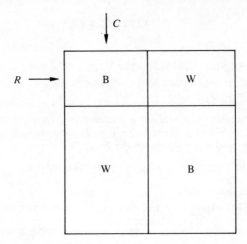

Fig. 2.10 The chess board, with black and white pawns.

on once at the top of the board and all the columns at the left; this divides the board into four rectangles, as in Fig. 2.10. The rectangles at top left and bottom right are filled with black pawns, because the first have been changed twice (from original black) and the second not at all; and the two other rectangles are filled with white pawns, having been changed once.

6. All that we need to know are the numbers R of rows and C of columns that have been changed once.

7. The board of Fig. 2.10 has a row/column symmetry: if (R, C) is a solution then so is (C, R), by rotation through $90°$

8. The board also has a symmetry about its centre: if (R, C) is a solution then so is $(100 - C, 100 - R)$. This is perhaps not so obvious; it can be checked by substitution in the equations derived below.

None of the above assertions have really been proved. It would be very difficult to give formal proofs because the starting point, the statement of the problem in natural language, is formally incomplete and ambiguous and we have made use of our pragmatic knowledge and our visual system in pursuing the argument. However, here and with all problems this is an essential stage that has to be gone through in order to arrive at a closed statement with everything expressed formally and accepted as the true statement of the problem.

Constructing the formal statement is now easy; this is entirely in terms of the numbers R and C of rows and columns, respectively, that have been changed. The number of white pawns in the top right rectangle is $R(100 - C)$ and in the bottom left rectangle is $C(100 - R)$, so the total is

$100(R + C) - 2RC$ and if this is to be 1990 we must have:

$$100(R + C) - 2RC = 1990 \tag{1}$$

which is the required closed statement.

It is immediately obvious that it is impossible to obtain an odd number of white pawns by this process. Further, it is now easy to generalise the problem, for if the board is of side $2p$ and the required number of white pawns is $2n$ the equation is:

$$p(R + C) - RC = n \tag{2}$$

It is now clear that:

1. The essential difficulty lies in solving equation (2) in integers.
2. The equation revives certain memories of conics: $xy - ax - by - c = 0$.
3. What makes it awkward to find a solution is the mixture of linear and quadratic terms in R, C.

We can now argue as follows: A conic has two axes of symmetry and its equation becomes much simpler if their intersection, the centre of symmetry, is taken as origin of co-ordinates; we can therefore hope to remove the linear terms from our equation by a change of variable $R = r + k$, $C = c + k$, with k chosen suitably.

The equation in (r, c) is $p(r + c + 2k) - (r + k)(c + k) = n$
i.e.

$$2kp + p(r + c) - k(r + c) - rc - k^2 = n$$

and if we take $k = p$ the term $(r + c)$ vanishes and we have

$$rc = p^2 - n \tag{3}$$

where

$$r = R - p, \quad c = C - p$$

It is of no accident that the appropriate choice for the change of variables is $k = p$; it follows from the existence of symmetry about the centre of the board.

Without equation (3) we now have a third universe to be searched for the solution. The left side is the product of two integers and therefore the right side must be decomposable into integer factors that are compatible with the side of the board. For the problem as given this is:

$$50 \times 50 - \tfrac{1}{2} \cdot 1990 = 1505 = 5 \times 7 \times 43$$

Since $p = 50$, we must have $-50 \leqslant r, c \leqslant 50$ and the solutions are:

$$r = 5 \times 7 \quad c = 43, \quad \text{i.e.} \quad R = 85, \quad C = 93$$
$$r = -5 \times 7, \quad c = -43, \quad \text{i.e.} \quad R = 15, \quad C = 7$$

So there are two ways in which 1990 white pawns can be obtained.

For any given values of p and n the possibility of a solution depends on the factors of $p^2 - n$, and we can see that for our 100×100 board there will be numbers of white pawns that cannot be created. For example, if $n = 1984$, $p^2 - n = 2500 - 992 = 2 \times 2 \times 13 \times 29$ and we find that one or other of r, c always exceeds 50, so no solution to the real problem exists.

If $n = p^2$ then $rc = 0$, so either r or c is zero and the other is arbitrary; that is, either R or C is 50 (for the 100×100 board) and the other is arbitrary. Put otherwise this states that if exactly 50 rows or columns are changed the only possible number of white pawns created is 2500.

All problems of this type can be solved by the same method, including the case when the board is not square but is rectangular. In Chapters 3 and 6 we shall consider other methods for finding integer solutions of algebraic equations, as for example equation (1) above.

The following section gives a way of going about solving a problem that is proposed by George Polya in his *How to Solve it* (1956).

2.7 HOW TO SOLVE A PROBLEM

You must do these, in this order:

A. Understand the problem. What are the unknowns? What are the data? What are the conditions that have to be satisfied? Are these conditions sufficient to determine the unknowns? – insufficient? – redundant? – inconsistent?

Draw a figure. Find suitable notation. Distinguish between different parts of the conditions – can you formulate these?

B. Devise a plan. Find the relation between the data and the unknowns; you may need to consider some subsidiary problems if you cannot see this immediately. In the end you must arrive at a plan for the solution.

Have you met the problem before? – or the same problem in a different form? Do you know of any related problems? – a theorem that might be useful?

Study the unknowns carefully and try to think of a problem with which you are familiar and which has the same or similar unknowns: here is a related problem that you have solved – can you make use of the method? if not, could you do so if you modified the problem now facing you?

Can you state the problem differently? – in a completely different form? Look at the definitions again.

If you cannot solve the problem given, try to solve a related problem. Can you think of one that is easier to attack? – a more general one? – a more particular one? – an analogous one? Can you solve a part of the problem? Suppose you keep only some part of the conditions and ignore the rest: how far does this determine the unknowns, and how could they vary? Can you deduce anything useful from the data? Can you think of other data that would enable you to determine the unknowns? Can you change the unknowns or the data, or both if necessary, so that you can solve the problem and the new unknowns and data are close enough to the originals?

Have you used all the data? – all the conditions? – taken into account all basic concepts that are involved in the problem?

C. Put the plan into action. In putting your plan into action, check every detail in turn. Can you see clearly that all the details are correct? – can you *prove* that they are correct?

D. Study the solution obtained. Can you check the result? the reasoning? Can you get the result by a different method? Can you see it at a glance? Can you use the result or the method for another problem?

2.8 A LITTLE HISTORY OF MATHEMATICS AND MATHEMATICAL TEACHING

Before the start of the known history of mathematics there is a long prehistorical period of which we have only traces going back some 4000 years. Young children and the higher animals, in their perception of the world, are aware of two fundamental abstract entities, number and form; and from these have arisen the two fundamental sciences, arithmetic and geometry, respectively, which for long have been held distinct. Originally, Man had only a limited capacity for numbers; members of primitive societies still cannot distinguish between two sets of objects when the numbers are almost equal, and can scarcely count – saying, for example, 'one – two – many'. There is still a trace of this in French, where *trois* (three) has the same derivation from Latin as *très* (very or many).

2.8.1 Notation through the ages

The universe around us was studied by the most ancient civilisations, who made observations of the cycles of the heavenly bodies; we know, for example, that the Sumerians were already using a lunar calendar in about 3000 BC. This led to the idea of using symbols to represent numbers: thus unity was represented by the moon and the succeeding numbers by a series of moons written side-by-side. The need to make accounts and to write these down led to the use of abbreviations for the sake of convenience. A single vertical or oblique stroke came to be used for unity in Phoenicia, Syria, Nabatea, Ancient Greece, Southern Arabia and India; and sets of 5, 10 and 20 were abbreviated to special symbols, possibly derived from their names. All these systems were additive, that is, the number thus encoded was the sum of the representing symbols.

The Babylonians are distinguished by having invented the sexagesimal system, in which the basic symbols represented 1, 10, 60 and then 600, 3600, 36 000 and so on. This system has come down to us through astronomy and we still use it for measuring time and angle. Several civilisations conceived the idea of using letters of the alphabet to represent numbers, a system that led to the attribution of special senses to certain numbers – the so-called cabalistic calculations. The number corresponding to a certain letter now depends on the position of that letter in the written word, and from this the need to indicate 'nothing' became felt. The origin of the zero symbol is still obscure; it certainly exists in some Indian texts of the sixth century, where it has the form of a point or dot, and in some Greek astronomical writings it is represented by the letter 'o', the first letter of the Greek word $ουδεν$, 'nothing'.

The form we now use for the figures in our decimal system came from western India (gouzratie form) via the Arabs; but it was not until the thirteenth century that it was adopted in Italy by the Florentine merchants, and until the sixteenth century that it came into general use. There is a record of this journey in our words 'cipher' and 'zero' and the French *chiffre*, all of which are derived from the Arabic *sifr*, meaning zero.

It was the invention of printing in 1440 that finally fixed the forms of the ten-digit symbols. The use of the point to express what we now call real numbers did not become common until the seventeenth century. The four operations of arithmetic were known to the ancient Egyptians but their methods for showing these were often very inconvenient; both they and the Greeks placed two numbers side by side to indicate addition and used an inverted ψ for subtraction. It was the copyists of the Middle Ages who abbreviated the Latin *et*, for addition, to what became ' + ', and the practice of using a horizontal stroke to separate the weight of a vessel empty (the tare weight) from its weight filled led to the use of ' − ' to denote subtraction; but against this Marcel Cohen in his outstanding book *La grande invention de l'écriture et son evolution* (Paris, Klincksleck, 1958) gives + and − as abbreviations for 'plus' and 'minus'. Our present signs for multiplication and division appeared only in the seventeenth century, when equality was shown by the symbol ∞, used by astronomers to mean the constellation Taurus; but the Latin *aequalis*, written in full, was also in use then and was abbreviated progressively to 'ae' and finally to ' = '. The symbol ∞ was used to denote the number 1000; in 1660 John Wallis elevated it to the meaning of 'infinity', this concept not having existed before then.

Why, you may be asking, discuss all this? There are two reasons. First, simply to give some feeling for the fact that it has taken Man several thousand years to domesticate number, and that science as we know it has existed for only a few hundred years. Mathematics was not built in a day and, what is more, its beginnings are not far back from us: is it surprising, then, that a schoolchild should find the subject difficult?

The second reason in that the question of representing concrete or abstract objects lies at the heart of artificial intelligence. Representing something requires first that one knows how to distinguish it from others and is conscious of its importance and of its practical value, which implies that its properties have been studied and expressed in some manipulable form. In a word, to represent is to understand. Whilst biology is now beginning to explain how hereditary information is represented in the genes of living creatures, neurology and psychology are still very far from being able to explain how knowledge is coded and organised in our brains; it is not impossible that AI research may lead to some clues.

But to continue: since Euclid in the third century BC, geometers have known how to represent abstract objects by means of letters. Pappus of Alexandria (third century AD) and then Diophantus (fourth century) gradually developed a similar notation for the unknown numbers of a problem and it was Francois Viete (*Maître des Requêtes* to Henri IV), in the sixteenth century, who first used this notation systematically in his *Ars Analytica*, which thus became the precursor of our modern algebra.

In Viete's writings we find expressions such as:

$$\frac{H \text{ in } D - F \text{ in } D}{F + D} \qquad aequebitur \ A$$

Here the first letters of the alphabet, A and D, represent the unknowns, the word 'in' means 'multiply' and the two expressions above the line are to be added – our present linear notation had not then been developed; in modern from this would be written:

$$\frac{ay - by}{b + y} = x$$

Viete knew how to manipulate such expressions; he deduced '$F + D$ is to $H - F$ as D is to A', from which he was able to solve the equation.

In the seventeenth century Descartes normalised and extended this notation, and the popularisation of ' + ', ' − ', '*', '/' and the use of the letters at the end of the alphabet to denote unknowns are due to him: 'x' in Arabic is the initial letter of the word *sayc*, meaning some unspecified object. Thus it was Descartes who brought about the abandonment of the old signs derived from Greek and Hebrew in favour of those we now use; and it was he who by laying the foundations of analytic geometry finally united the science of numbers and the science of figures, and so established the fundamental unity of mathematics. This unity will be deepened in future centuries.

Indices and exponents did not appear until very late. Euler (1707–1783) was still writing $x * x * x$ for x^3. Evariste Galois (1811–1832) was the first to use subscripts; but Jordan, and even Hilbert, at the beginning of the present century, were reluctant to use them and continued to write in a heavy and almost unreadable style in which the alphabetical order of the letters was used to imply indexing. Functional symbols were introduced by Leibnitz and John Bernoulli and the summation sign Σ by Euler.

Functional notation experienced many vicissitudes and there is still no unanimity. The notation still confuses a function f, as a function, with its value $f(x)$ at a point x and a shift of $+a$ is still written $T(+a)(f)$ instead of $T_{+a}(f)$. The lack of an adequate symbolism results almost always in the derived function being confused with its value at a point and the situation is even worse with partial derivatives. Further complications arise when we wish to consider an expression as a function of a particular one of its several variables: thus in a problem in mechanics or physics we should write $y(t)$ when regarding the position of a point or body as a function of time t, $y(x)$ when as a function of a space variable x and simply y for a general indication. Such notation should not be allowed, for it is inconsistent and incomprehensible to the young student. But it has to be recognised that it is not practable to provide a special symbol for every different functional dependence.

To overcome this difficulty, Church proposed the λ-notation, in which the symbol λx, say, before an expresssion means that the expression is to be considered as a function of x. Thus $\lambda x(ax + b)$ indicates a linear function of x. This gives a very elegant resolution of the difficulty and was used by McCarthy in 1960 for defining the programming language LISP.

Notation for symbolic logic was developed over a long period. In 1891 Peano used ϵ to indicate 'belonging', inclusion being denoted by α or $<$ and by $\subset$ by Hausdorff in 1920 – this last being the symbol used today, although it may or may not include equality, according to the taste, or national custom, of the author. Peano's symbols $\cap$, $\cup$, $\supset$ for set intersection, set union and logical implication, respectively, have finally prevailed over other proposals, but the last of these is, confusingly, the inclusion symbol reversed – so that one could write: if $E \subset F$ then $(x \in E) \supset (x \in F)$. Hilbert used the arrow $\rightarrow$ to denote implication, but this in turn is used to denote a mapping of one set on to another and also for re-writing of expressions; so the Bourbaki school has preferred $\Rightarrow$, a symbol now is common use. However, in this book we shall use the Peano symbol $\supset$, which is what the logicians use.

In an effort to put logical reasoning on a formal basis Euler (1707–1783) had the idea of using circle-like diagrams to represent sets, what we now call Venn diagrams (John Venn 1834–1923). C. L. Dodgson ('Lewis Carroll') (1832–1898) proposed another type in which the duality between a set and its complement is preserved, and which is used now in Boolean logic.

Other logical symbols are $\wedge$ and $\vee$ for 'and' and 'or' respectively, clearly influenced by $\cap$ and $\cup$. Negation is sometimes indicated by $-$, sometimes by a horizontal bar over the set symbol (e.g. $\bar{S}$) and sometimes by $\sim$; but since all these are used with other meanings Heytinj in 1937 proposed $\neg$, which we shall use.

The existential quantifier $\exists$ is again due to Peano. Russell and Whitehead in 1903 added the universal quantifier, which they represented simply by putting parentheses around the variable thus quantified; it was only in 1920 that the now-current symbol $\forall$ was adopted. Finally, G. Frege in 1940 saw the need for a symbol to denote affirmation and used $\vdash$; thus:

$$\vdash A \text{ means } `A \text{ holds' or } `A \text{ is a theorem'}$$

The famous French school of mathematicians which, under the pseudonym Nicolas Bourbaki, has published the long series of monographs *Eléments de mathématique*, has brought about agreement on the use of many of these symbols and has introduced several others, for example $\Rightarrow$ already mentioned and C for the complement of a set; also many others for use in group theory. It is the insistence of the Bourbaki series on clarity, simplification and rigour that has given it its influence, aided by the many translations into other languages. However, the effect on the style and spirit of mathematics as it is now practised has resulted in a steadily increasing difference developing between the syntax of a natural language and that of a formal language. Thus where in the former separators would be used, such as 'and', 'or', 'because', the mathematician would prefer symbols for grouping such as the various kinds of brackets; and the equality sign, used to denote the identity of two objects, becomes a separator of special importance. Some confusion can result from this; for example, one can read in current mathematical writing statements such as:

$$`\text{for all } y = ax + b$$

in which the symbol y is used in two senses, and which should be written:

$$`\forall y, \; y = ax + b$$

meaning 'whatever y, there is an x such that $y = ax + b$'.

There is in fact some confusion between the $=$ sign used with its true meaning as above and that used as an operator. Thus the basic identities

$(a - b)^2 = a^2 - 2ab + b^2$ are really rules for re-writing, as are $x + 0 \to x$, $x.1 \to x$. The sign is also used to denote a definition, such as $\tan x = \sin x / \cos x$; or for abbreviations, e.g. put $u = (ax + b)/(x^2 + 1)$, or x_1, $x_2 = (-b \pm \sqrt{\Delta})/2$ where in the subsequent algebra u and x_1, x_2 will then be used as entities.

There are other ambiguities that find their way into mathematics from natural language. Thus when defining a group G one first postulates that for all g belonging to G there is an e such that $ge = g = eg$, and then writes:

$$\forall g, g \in G, \exists g^{-1} \in G \quad \text{and} \quad g^{-1}g = gg^{-1} = e$$

This is a striking misuse of the mathematical language, because the g quantified universally in the first part of the statement has no relation to the g of the second part. Misuses of this type can lead to difficulties when programs for automatic theorem proving are being written.

In general, great care must be taken over the quantifiers when translating natural language statements into formal mathematics. Thus in 'a right-angled triangle, one angle is a right angle' the first 'a' is universal and the second is existential; the verb 'is' sometimes indicates a definition, sometimes a property and sometimes belonging; and 'or' can be sometimes inclusive, sometimes exclusive – 'black or white'/'more or less' – corresponding to two different mathematical situations.

At a very early age children are taught pseudo-mathematical rules such as '2 times 2 equals 4', 'plus times minus equals minus'; this is risky, and when unexplained can create mental blockages exemplified by stories such as

Teacher: What is the next integer after n?
Pupil: 'o'
Teacher: Suppose q is the integer ...?
Pupil: But q isn't an integer, it's a letter.

and what should be the reply when told 'give the set of letters x such that x is a vowel'? – the set is empty, for x is a consonant.

What must be appreciated, then, is that the passage from a natural language statement to its equivalent in a formal language is not an easy matter; it is the essential first step in the attack on any problem in mathematics or a physical science, and workers in operational research, who often have to represent complex situations, speak of it as 'modelling'. Mathematical language itself is not without its faults, with its conventions and unstated implications: x, y, z usually imply unknowns, i, j, k, l, m, n, p, q integers, r, s, t reals, $\alpha, \beta, \theta, \phi$ angles, f, g, h functions; whilst certain letters, for example e, π, i are taken to stand for specific numbers. It also repeats some of the bad habits of natural language, so that a 'Lie group' is no more a group than a 'dark horse' is a horse. Thus the student has to learn to read with an understanding of these features and fill in the gaps for himself.

This brings us to the history of mathematical teaching.

2.8.2 Teaching mathematics

The Greek Schools of Socrates (fifth century BC), Plato (fourth century BC), Aristotle (fourth century BC), Euclid (third century BC) are justly famous, and Euclid's *Elements of Geometry* is still regarded as a model of clarity and rigour. In about 290 Pappus of Alexandria published his great *Collection*, a handbook to Greek mathematical sciences, and Diophantus his *Arithmetic* around 370. After the great work of the Greeks, science in Europe stagnated for centuries and it was not until the Italian Renaissance that research and teaching came to life again.

Mathematics remained for long the preserve of an elite. In the colleges it was taught by the philosophers, whilst methods for calculation were developed in certain specialist schools, such as those in France for architecture, astronomy, navigation and the military arts. The French Revolution, with its spreading of public education, started the teaching of the exact sciences on the route to the status it now has – as well as bringing about the simplification that resulted from the metric system. In 1794 Lakanal and Monge created the Ecole Polytechnique and in 1808 the Sorbonne – which had been a theological college since its foundation by Robert de Sorbon in 1227 – established a chair in 'Higher Mathematics'. Ever since then the teaching of mathematics in our schools and colleges has been oriented towards the entrance competitions to these institutions.

Thus the schools are teaching a set programme of mathematics, rather than how to do mathematics. Very few writers indeed have taken an interest in more active, as opposed to the usual passive, methods of teaching, to the phenomenon of discovery, to inductive reasoning, to the way the thought process works, to *heuristics* – from Greek ευρεκιον, 'to find', with the meaning here of encouraging the pupils to find out for themselves the things we want to teach them. There is a need to study the technical and cognitive aspects of the teaching process and to make a full evaluation of these. An attempt to avoid the disadvantage of the standard pedagogical methods was made by Celestin Freinet in 1940, who started a school in which collaborative working in groups was advocated.

It is very rare for a mathematician writing a book or a paper to explain how in actual fact an important result was arrived at – one might even say that everything is done to hide this. Mostly, the reasoning is presented in the opposite order to that of the original, usually inductive, process; heuristic arguments are removed from the proof, representations are changed and encoded, new concepts and constructs are simply shot into the argument. Many teachers are very well aware of these problems, but there is no simple solution; the introduction, not well received, of 'modern mathematics' was an attempt to deal with some of them. It is precisely the heuristic method that is important to AI research in all fields of application.

2.9   NOTATION AND REPRESENTATION

In daily life our minds operate not on the real physical world but on *models* of this, captured and conveyed to us by our perceptive senses – sight, hearing, smell, taste, touch. This model is *represented* somehow in our nervous system by means of the neurons and synapses, but how this information is encoded, stored and later accessed is almost completely unknown. According to Konrad Lorenz the representation is essentially a visual image of the outside world; thus the higher apes acquired 'intelligence' because, to survive in a hostile environment, they had to foresee the actions they should take and to 'reflect' on their situation. Our current language bears many traces of the influence of spatial relations on our thought processes – see, grasp, understand; level, plane, depth; clear, obscure: it is space that acts as a reference frame for all abstract relations. This is very much a human characteristic, and abstract relationships are not innate; children acquire these only gradually and do not grasp the concepts of physical invariants until after a long period of learning: according to Piaget the constancy of weight or volume of an object is not appreciated until the age of about 13–14. However, this abstract representation of the world gradually leads the individual to the ability for pure thought, needing no physical support and divorced from all immediate actions.

The representations that we use, for written text, drawings, music, mathematicial statements or other, are essentially graphical; and in this book mathematical notation will play an essentially important role.

2.9.1   Mathematical notation: objects and operators

All the notation systems in general use consist on the one hand of symbols representing *objects* and on the other of *operators* representing actions to be performed on single objects or groups of these. Thus in the expression $x + y - 1$, the symbols $x, y, 1$ are objects and $+, -$ are operators. Every operator acts on, or links, a specified number of objects: thus $+, -$ each link two objects and are called *binary* operators, as are $*, /, \cup, \cap, \vee, \wedge, \supset$; but $\sqrt{\ }$, log, ! (factorial), sin act on a single object and are *unary* operators;

and the summation symbol Σ represents a *ternary* operator, the three objects being the general term to be summed, the set over which the sum is to be formed and the symbol representing the sum. The **if ... then else ...** of programming languages are also ternary operators. Generalising, an *n-ary operator* is one that acts on n objects. An n-ary operator followed by its n objects is called a *well-formed expression* or *term*; and such an operator is said to have *weight n*.

A well-formed expression can itself be regarded as an object, and in turn can be related to others by an operator in the same way as an object can be related to other objects; finally, a term can be defined as an n-ary operator followed by n terms. This definition, which defines a term by means of other terms, is what is called *recursive*; it makes sense only because there are terms from which the process can start, that is, objects.

Among the objects of which a term consists there will in general be some that can be replaced by other objects or by terms, and others that cannot be so replaced; the first are *variables*, the second *constants*. Thus in the expression $\sin^2 x + \cos^2 x = 1$, the x can be replaced by any term whatever but neither the operators sin, cos nor the objects 2, 1 can be changed. These concepts will be dealt with in more detail in Chapter 3, on Formal Systems.

2.9.2 Linear notations

The invention of printing led to the writing of mathematical expressions on lines, which in western cultures were to be read from left to right. Given this convention, there are three possibilities for what are called linear notations: an operator can be written before, after or between the terms on which it acts. All three are in use, with three corresponding notations.

By far the most commonly used notation is what is called *infix*, in which the operators are placed within the terms. To make expressions written in this way easier to read, various types of bracket have had to be added, such as (.), [.], which are *not* part of the basic symbolism. Writing these brackets is tedious, so the tendency is to insert them only in order to resolve a possible ambiguity or to break up over-long expressions. Further, there is an agreed hierarchy among the operators, so that, for example, $a - b + c$ is interpreted as $(a - b) + c$ and not as $a - (b + c)$. Associativity and commutivity of certain operators, especially $+$, $*$, are implicit in most writing and $2*x*y$ is written for $x*2*y$ or $x*y*2$; and the multiplication operator $*$ is usually omitted.

There are several strange features in this notation; for example, unary operators can be written on any of three levels, with many variants $-$ $\sin A, \dot{B}, C', \mathrm{d}D/\mathrm{d}t, E^+, \bar{F}, G', |H|$ $-$ and the operator $-$ is both unary and binary. Thus this form is far from being clear and rigorous.

Logicians prefer a purer notation in which each operator is written before the terms on which it acts, the *prefix* or Polish notation due to Lukasiewicz. With this the infix form: x operator y becomes: operator x y, whilst operator z remains unchanged. No parentheses are needed and the principle operator for any term appears at the head of that term; the notation is more concise than infix and after a little practice is found to be pleasant to use.

As examples, the expression $(p \supset q) \supset p$ of infix notation becomes $\supset \supset pqp$ and

$$\log(y + \sqrt{y^2 - b/\sin x}) \quad \text{becomes} \quad \log + y\sqrt{} - \uparrow y2/b \sin x$$

There is the following fundamental theorem for prefix notation, due to Rosenbloom:

A sequence S of symbols in prefix (Polish) notation is a well-formed expression if and only if:

1. *rank* $(S) = -1$;
2. *rank (sub-expression on the left of S)* ≥ 0;

where rank is defined by rank (operator) = weight (operator) -1
rank (empty sequence) $= 0$
rank (n-ary symbol) $= n - 1$
rank (variable) = rank (constant) $= -1$
rank (S1 concatenated with S2) $=$ rank(S1) + rank(S2)

The proof is straightforward and proceeds by induction on the number of symbols in S. An important corollary is that the theorem provides an algorithm for finding the location in an expression of the end of a term that begins at any given location.

Applying the evaluation of rank to the above expression T we have:

	log	+	y	$\sqrt{}$	$-$	$\uparrow$	y	2	/	b	sin	x
symbol rank	0	1	-1	0	1	1	-1	-1	1	-1	0	-1
sum	0	1	0	0	1	2	1	0	1	0	0	-1

giving rank $(T) = -1$.

For the term starting with the exponentiating symbol $\uparrow$ we have:

$$\begin{array}{cccc} \uparrow & y & 2 & / & \ldots \\ 1 & -1 & -1 & 1 & \ldots \\ 1 & 0 & -1 & & \end{array}$$

so this term ends at the symbol 2 – it is y^2.

NB:

1. In this process, variables and constants are equivalent to operators of rank -1.

2. The theorem applies to infix notation if the expression is fully parenthesised, with each opening bracket counting as a binary operator
   (weight 2, rank 1) and each closing bracket counted as a constant (rank
   -1); other ranks are unchanged.

   Thus for a binary operator O, the successive ranks in (aOb) are
   $1, -1, 1, -1, -1)$ with sum -1.

The third form is *postfix* or reverse Polish notation; in this, as the name
implies, the operator is placed immediately after the term(s) on which it
acts: so

$$x \text{ operator } y \text{ becomes } xy \text{ operator}$$
$$\text{operator} \quad z \text{ becomes } \quad z \text{ operator}$$

and the previous expression T becomes:

$$y \; y \; 2 \uparrow b \; x \; \sin / - \sqrt{\ } + \log$$

This form is particularly convenient for evaluating an expression and for
this reason is the form used most commonly in electronic calculators; it is
also used by many compilers in programming languages, which translate
expressions input in infix notation into postfix form. The evaluation can be
done in a single pass through the postfix expression from right to left.

As an example, let us evaluate the same expression T for $x = -\pi/2$,
$b = 80$, $y = 1$.

$$
\begin{array}{llllllllll}
y & y & 2 \uparrow & b & x & \sin & / & - & \sqrt{\ } & + & \log \\
1 & 1 & 2 \uparrow \\
& & \quad \hookrightarrow 1 & 80 & -\tfrac{1}{2}\pi \\
& & & & \quad \llcorner\!\!\longrightarrow -1 \\
& & & & & \quad \hookrightarrow -80 \\
& & & & & \quad \rightarrow 81 \\
& & & & & \quad \rightarrow 9 \\
& & & & & \quad \rightarrow 10 \\
& & & & & \quad \rightarrow 1 \qquad \text{(logs to base 10)}
\end{array}
$$

2.9.3 Two-dimensional notations

In leading to the linear form of notation typography imposed constraints
that resulted in this form not reflecting visually the true structure of the
expression. In effect, it put all the symbols on the same footing, although
we usually know that this is not so and that some are what are called
terminal symbols – variables or constants – and others are not. The true
situation is that each operator acts directly on a given number of known

terms, and this can be represented exactly by a diagram of the type:

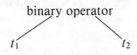

or, more generally, for an *n*-ary operator:

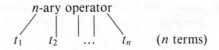

Diagrams (graphs) of this type are called *trees*; they correspond well to our own envisioning of the structure of an expression, as is illustrated by the tree representing the above expression T, given in Fig. 2.11.

It should be noted that the three linear notations are in fact contained within the tree form. Thus:

1. Prefix form is given by traversing the tree from top to bottom and from left to right, evaluating each symbol as it is encountered.
2. Postfix form is given by making the same traverse, evaluating a symbol only when it is met for the last time.
3. Parenthesised infix form is given by projecting the graph on to a horizontal line and adding parentheses to make the different levels clear.

As we have already emphasised, any representation is of value only in so far as it helps some processing of the expression to be performed. The processes generally performed in mathematical work are:

- Substitute one term for another.
- Combine two terms.
- Remove a term.

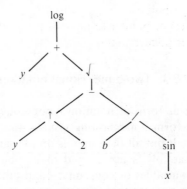

Fig. 2.11 Tree representation for $T = \log(y + \sqrt{y^2 - b/\sin x})$.

to which correspond, respectively, very simple operations on the graph:

● Move a branch.
● Make local modifications to the terminal symbols (the *leaves*).
● Delete a branch.

In contrast, with the usual infix notation we have to be continually rewriting the original expression, line after line.

2.9.4 Representation in the machine

Modern computers have very large memories that can be accessed very quickly; we can take advantage of this and free ourselves of many restrictions by putting the tree representation of an expression in a machine memory. We can do this by constructing a table in which all the variables and operators of the expression are listed, showing for the operators the operands on which they act.

For each symbol we give three items of information: its name, its 'daughter' on the left and its 'sister' on the right, the daughter being the first symbol of the corresponding term. Thus the entry (Fig. 2.12):

Each (S, L, R) line would have an identifier, probably a numerical index; the full table for a complete program could be of considerable size.

In any actual case the daughter (a) and the sister (b) can themselves be trees; the entries L, R are then not a, b themselves but *pointers*, that is, indices showing where in the table these are to be found, and therefore the relevant operands. The terminal symbols (leaves) of the tree are the variables and constants of the expression and have no daughters, shown by setting $L = 0$.

Thus for the index i the entries in the table are:

$S(i)$ name of the symbol
$L(i)$ daughter of $S(i)$ or pointer to this
$R(i)$ sister of $L(i)$ or pointer to this

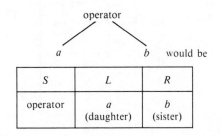

Fig. 2.12.

and the tree is traversed by following the pointers; it will be clear that there is no requirement that the consecutive terms of an expression are given in any particular order, say of increasing indexes: the pointers give the order in which they are to be used.

The entry (S, L, R) forms a *list* and the complete table is a *list structure*; list structures are much used for manipulating symbolic expressions by machine.

Figure 2.13 gives the list representation for the expression T.

	..	..	..
112	log	113	0
113	+	119	0
	..	..	..
119	y	0	121
120	*	140	218
121	`	135	0
	..	..	..
135	−	136	0
136	↑	255	137
137	/	138	0
138	b	0	139
139	sin	140	0
140	x	0	0
	..	..	..
255	y	0	256
256	2	0	0
	..	...	..
431	t	433	0
432	−	431	0
433	/	434	0
434	π	0	435
435	4	0	0
	..	..	..

Fig. 2.13.

Comments on the list representation

1. The expression itself is referenced by the *head of the list*, that is, the index of its first symbol. Thus in Fig. 2.13 the reference for T is 112.
2. Very often the entry S is not the actual name of the symbol but a pointer to an entry in a *dictionary* where the name is to be found.
3. The system can be extended, if necessary, to deal with operators of order greater than 2; thus + can be generalised to $+xyzt$, standing for $x + y + z + t$ (the sister of x is y, of y is z, of z is t).
4. The basic operation of substitution of a variable by a term is particularly easy in this representation. Thus if in T above we wanted to change x to $(t - \pi/4)$ all we need to do is change the pointer $L(139)$ to a place in the table where this can be found or computed, as in Fig. 2.13. If $L(139)$ is the only pointer to x then the line 140 becomes *dead*, for it cannot be reached from any point in the program.
5. There is nothing to prevent there being several different pointers to the same location, but this is *not recommended*. Thus if at some stage y were also to be changed to $(t - \pi/4)$ it would be better to have a second entry for this latter for that substitution, because there is nothing to say that x and y will always be treated identically.
6. During list processing the number of deal locations can easily overwhelm the available storage, so these need to be identified so that they can be used for new entries. This is done by means of a special program called a *garbage collector*.

2.10 GRAPH MODELS IN ARTIFICIAL INTELLIGENCE

In AI we are concerned with automatic handling of situations where we have no algorithms. In this section we shall study three major fields: theorem-proving by computer, automatic solution of problems, understanding natural language; and with all three a basic interest will be the ways in which knowledge can be represented and used. If any of our activities merit the description 'intelligent' it is doubtless because they make use of reasonable representations of the world around us, with processes of unification of observations and abstraction of concepts.

2.10.1 Knowledge representation and automatic proof

In mathematics as in other fields we are concerned with two levels of representation: the first is of *objects* that are to be manipulated, such as mathematical entities, formulae, expressions; the second is of *knowledge* about these objects, including relations among them, theorems, proofs.

We now give some comments on these levels and on the role of the diagram and then some examples.

A. Representation of objects. Diagrams play a fundamental role in geometry; and computer programs that prove geometrical theorems, find loci and generate ruler-and-compasses constructions in plane geometry also use a figure, represented in the machine by a graph.

B. Representation of knowledge. Neither books nor more than a few mathematics teachers explain *how* one finds a proof. In actuality the mathematician goes about this in three stages – see Pastre 1978a, Polya 1962, Merialdo 1979:

1. Understand what is to be proved; that is, translate the statement as given into some personal representation.
2. Prove the theorem thus expressed, using whatever knowledge can be brought to mind, also expressed in this personal form.
3. Translate this incomplete proof into a rigorous one by recasting the arguments into standard formal mathematical language.

This process is shown in Fig. 2.14. It is very difficult to go directly from (I) to (IV) because the guiding lines developed in stage 2 are not available. Of course we have little idea of the personal forms used by mathematicians in this process but some studies of this have been made and as a result some

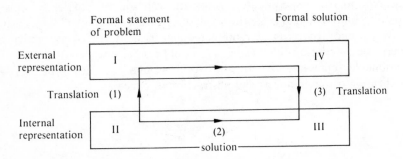

Fig. 2.14.

procedures have been programmed that seem to be equivalent to the mathematician's method.

C. The role of the diagram. A diagram is above all a means for summarising information and provides a convenient aid to memorising the essential elements of a problem (and the relations among them). Thus if two elements x, y are linked by a number of relations $R_1, R_2, ..., R_k$ this is conveniently shown as in Fig. 2.15, which is a convenient way of expressing the written statement (see Bundy 1973, Pastre 1978a)

$$xR_1y \wedge xR_2y \wedge \cdots \wedge xR_ky$$

A combination of a diagram with certain simple processing algorithms can be used to work efficiently through a chain of deductions. Thus for a transitive binary relation such as $=$, $\subset$ or $\in$ a diagram such as Fig. 2.15 translates:

$$xRy \wedge yRz \quad \text{into} \quad x\underline{R}y\underline{R}z$$

from which immediately follows:

$$x\underline{R}z$$

With a diagram it is easy to jump over 'obvious' steps in an argument and so to short circuit a proof; also the elimination of false sub-goals is helped – if a relation is not checked in the diagram it must be false and there is no point in wasting time in proving this. The inverse also is true: the diagram can be an aid to discovery. If it shows that some relation holds then we may be able to find a formal proof – we have all used this method at times for finding geometrical loci.

Further advantages arise in revealing symmetries between variables and pointing directly to other situations that are equivalent to the one under consideration; and particularly in geometry in guiding the introduction of new elements when these are needed to complete a proof.

To sum up, a diagram, together with the appropriate algorithms, takes into account the relevant structure of the concepts that are being studied, that is, their semantics; whilst a mere listing of the formal properties of

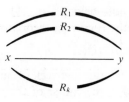

Fig. 2.15.

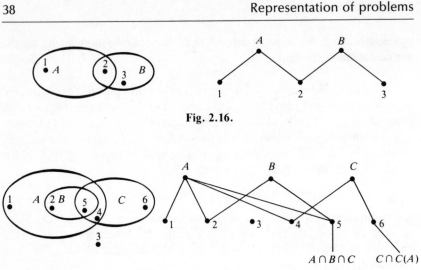

Fig. 2.16.

Fig. 2.17.

these concepts, which is all that (most) books give, describes only their syntax.

D. Example. D1 – topological representation of sets (Merialdo 1979). The usual mathematical representation is the Venn diagram; this is easily converted into a graph (Fig. 2.16). Here the letters represent the sets and the numbers atoms, that is, representative elements of sub-sets; an empty sub-set would not be shown on the graph. Relations of belonging, inclusion and equality are displayed very compactly. As with Venn diagrams, it is easy to give simple algorithms for adding further sets, forming an intersection, enforcing equality, checking inclusion, finding the complement of a set. Thus a set B is included in a set A if and only if for every arc joining the node B to an atom there is also an arc joining the same atom to node A. This is illustrated in Fig. 2.17.

For a set A let $\bar{A}$ denote its closure (the smallest closed set containing A), $C(A)$ its complement (the set of all elements of the universe under consideration that do not belong to A) and A^* its boundary: $A^* = \bar{A} \cap \overline{C(A)}$. There is the following theorem:

Theorem T1. $A^* = (\bar{A} - A) \cup (\overline{C(A)} \cap A)$.

Figure 2.18 illustrates the relation between A and its various derived sets, and only the graph is used in the course of the proof. We have

$$A \subset \bar{A} \quad \text{and} \quad A \subset \overline{C(A)}$$

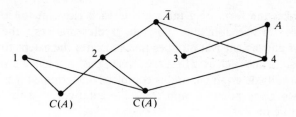

Fig. 2.18.

Then

$$A^* = \bar{A} \cap \overline{C(A)} \quad \text{(in the diagram, atoms 2 and 4)}$$
$$\bar{A} - A = \text{atom 2} \quad \text{and} \quad \overline{C(A)} \cap A = \text{atom 4}$$

and the theorem follows.

A program has been written for the IBM 4331 that will generate this proof; as any mathematician would expect, it efficiently handles problems involving larger numbers of sets, and in fact has produced proofs of over a hundred theorems in naive set theory and topology, each in a time of the order of a second.

D2 – A problem in geometry (Buthion 1979). Given a circle c and two external points A, B construct a line d through A such that its intersections C, D with c are equidistant from B.

It is practicable for us to reason about this problem without a diagram; suppose we have solved it, and the solution is as in Fig. 2.19. The program also works from the diagram, constructing and naming the two essential elements, the line d and the mid-point I of CD. For the program the

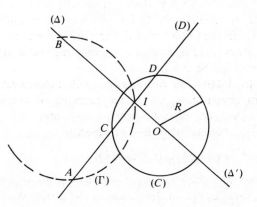

Fig. 2.19 A problem in geometrical construction.

diagram takes the form of a table giving each element, together with its type, degree of freedom and possible 'representatives': the degree of freedom of an element is a number that indicates the extent to which it is determined – a line such as d here that has to pass through a given point (A here) is partially determined, and is completely determined if it has to pass through two given points – and the representatives of a line are all the points that lie on it.

For our problem, an entry in the table will be, initially:

name of element	type	degree of freedom	representatives
Δ	line	1	B, I

The problem is to determine the line d completely. The program considers the triangles BCD, OCD which by construction are isosceles: OI and CI are both right bisectors of CD and are therefore the same straight line, so the lines labelled Δ, Δ′ on the diagram coincide. This is expressed by the program as:

Δ	line	0	Δ′, B, I, O

I is therefore a point on the known line BO. Further, the angle AIB is a right-angle and therefore I lies on the circle of diagram AB. This circle also is completely determined and therefore the point I, and its intersection with the known line BI, is determined. The required line d is then the line through A and I.

D3 – properties of functions (D. Pastre 78). Pastre's program DATE, which works rather like a mathematician, has proved about 150 theorems in naive set theory, direct and inverse (images) functions, congruences, order relations and ordinals. One theorem is as follows:

Theorem T2. *Let $f: A \to B$, $g: B \to C$, $h: C \to A$ be three mappings. If of the three functions $k1 = h \circ g \circ f$, $k2 = f \circ h \circ g$, $k3 = g \circ f \circ h$ any two are surjections and the third is an injection, then f, g, h are all bijections.*

The program has to show, in particular, that if $k1$ is an injection and $k2$, $k3$ are surjections then h is a surjection. This is one of the most difficult of the six results that have to be established in order to prove the theorem; the program makes use of the diagram given in Fig. 2.20. If $x1$ is an arbitrary element of A we have to find an x in C such that $h(x) = x1$. To do this the program constructs points $x2$, $x3$, $x4$ as shown, such that:

$$x2 = f(x1), \quad x3 = g(x2), \quad x4 = h(x3)$$

Since $k3 = g \circ f \circ h$ is a surjection (given), there is an element $x5$ of C such that: $k3(x5) = x3$; DATE constructs points $x6$, $x7$ related to $x5$ by

$$x6 = h(x5), \quad x7 = f(x6)$$

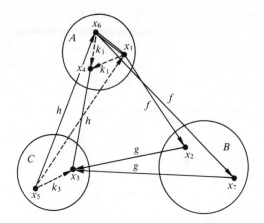

Fig. 2.20 One of the graphs used by DATE to prove Theorem T2.

From the construction it knows that

$$g(x7) = x3$$

and

$$k1(x6) = k1(x1) = x4$$

But since $k1$ is by hypothesis an injection, $x1$ and $x6$ must coincide; so a point $x5$ has been found such that $h(x5) = x1$, which is the required result.

The above three examples illustrate the different roles a diagram can play as an aid to reasoning, and in particular how it allows new objects to be introduced in a natural but controlled manner.

2.10.2 Graphical representation in automatic problem-solving

One very general method of attack on problems is to break down the goal to be attained into a set of sub-goals, which together satisfy the conditions of the original problem; so that if each sub-goal, taken separately, can be attained the given problem is solved. However, it is possible that any of a number of methods may be used in order to attain any particular sub-goal, and each method will give rise to its own sub-goal; so the first sub-goal will be attained if any one of this set of subsequent sub-goals can be attained. Thus the search for the solution can be represented by a tree having an 'AND–OR' structure as that shown in Fig. 2.21. The tree makes it possible to visualise the effort required to solve the problem, whether by

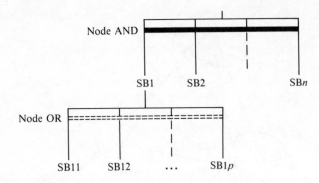

Fig. 2.21.

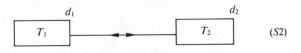

Fig. 2.22.

Fig. 2.23.

human or machine means. The limiting case – the rarely-met ideal – is that the tree reduces to a single branch; the solution process is then one of steady linear progression with no unfruitful deviations, and we say that we have an *algorithm*.

The objects that have to be processed in many real-life problems, in operational research for example, are graphical in nature. Thus if the problem is to find the optimum routeing for a postal package from a given source to a given destination the data object is the graph of the links, whether by rail, road or air, between the various centres. Again, if the problem is to minimize the total execution time for a set of tasks with constraints on the relative time orderings, it is convenient to summarise these constraints graphically, for example as a PERT chart. For example, a diagram such as Fig. 2.22 expresses the fact that task T_1, requiring $d1$ units of time, must be completed before T_2, requiring $d2$, can be started; whilst Fig. 2.23 means that T_1, T_2 are mutually exclusive and cannot be executed simultaneously.

We have an illustration here of the basic importance of all mathematical modelling: that a variety of different problems may reduce to the same model, so the modelling reduces the variety to a small number of basic problems. Here, problems whose constraints are solely of the type of $S1$ above are all equivalent to finding the longest path through the graph of tasks; if the constraints are solely of the type of $S2$ the problem is one of graph colouring.

2.10.3 Graphical representation and understanding natural language

The first attempts at computer understanding of natural language, undertaken with the aim of automatic translation and documentation, were based on syntactic analysis of sentences and word-for-word equivalences. It is now clear that such an approach is inadequate and that if a program is to 'understand' a piece of text it must be given the kind of semantic information that is found in a dictionary, and in addition a large amount of pragmatic information that describes our behaviour as humans and the world in which we live.

The first syntax-analysis grammars, the 'context free' grammars of Noam Chomsky, were readily represented by re-write rules. But it soon became clear that in order to resolve ambiguities, for example those arising from pronouns, the analysis had to be interrupted at the level it had reached and descent made to a lower level to study some related problem, returning later to the point of interruption.

What are called transition graphs or Augmented Transition Networks (ATNs) (Woods 1975) are now normally used for simultaneous syntactic and semantic analysis. The vertices of such graphs can represent either words or semantic families or further graphs, so the representation is essentially recursive. An example of their use is a program due to Chichetchi (1979) for electric circuit problems, in which the data are given in the form of Fig. 2.24. The graph would recognise a sentence such as: 'The frequency of the voltage V is 50 Hz.' It will be seen that certain words are ignored and that others could have been omitted, Hz for example, without affecting the analysis. Any sentence that corresponds to a route through the network is

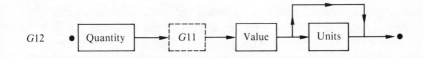

Fig. 2.24.

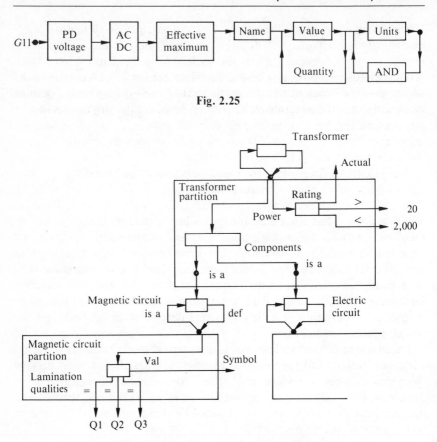

Fig. 2.25

Fig. 2.26 Partitioned semantic network.

accepted *a priori*. G11 is another graph, giving the various possible characteristics of an electric current (Fig. 2.25): This would recognise 'the voltage *V* is 10 volts', or 'the effective AC PD is 80 volts and the current is 80 amps'. As such a piece of text is recognised by a system of this type it is translated into an internal form in which all the information relevant to that text is summarised. This internal representation is often called a 'semantic network' (cf. Cordier 1979, Lopez 1979, Simmons 1973). It is empty at the start of the analysis and is added to, modified and corrected as this proceeds; the items of information that it contains can be certainties, others that are only probable and yet others that are conditional on something else.

Lopez gives the representation for a transformer shown in Fig. 2.26, in a computer aided design (CAD) program. The vertices are grouped in 'spaces', shown in frames in the diagram, containing related conceptual units or sub-sets of related items of information.

2.11 FINDING THE RIGHT REPRESENTATION

This is almost always a crucial step in the attack on a problem. There are many cases in which our immediate impulse is to operate on the physical presentation of the program just as we see it; this removes the need for any abstract model, but has the disadvantage of leading to unfruitful trial and error activities, with no possibility of generalising the idea that has led to the solution and so applying it to other problems.

Consider as an illustration *the four knights problem*. The chessboard and the movements of the pieces have fascinated very many writers and have been made the subject of many problems; this particular one is, given two black and two white Knights in the positions shown in Fig. 2.27, to find the minimum number of moves necessary to interchange their positions. The standard knight's move is implied, that is, two squares horizontally and one vertically, or inversely. The first impulse would be to try some moves with real pieces on a real board, but this is soon seen to offer too rich and too detailed possibilities and to make too little use of the symmetries of the problem. Seeking a more general representation we might think in terms of the co-ordinate plane, but we see that the need to take account of quantities having values ±1 and ±2 in order to represent the movements leads to a clumsy notation. Further reflexion then shows that it is the movements, and only these, that are important: the board itself is of scarcely any importance, the moves are defined in terms of related squares and the physical representation can be changed so long as these relations are preserved (cf. the Rubik Cube). Here we are concerned only with a 3 × 3 board; let us label the squares as in Fig. 2.28.

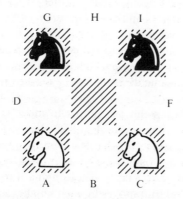

Fig. 2.27 The four knights problem.

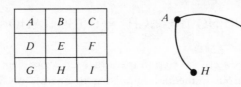

Fig. 2.28 Labels for the squares, and the two possible moves for a knight at A.

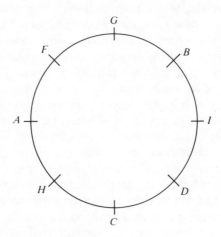

Fig. 2.29 Path of knight A.

The knight at A can move either to F or to H; from H it can either return to A or move to C, and continue to D, then to I, then to B, then to G, then to F and from there to A again, having visited every square except E. We can show this path as points on the circumference of a circle as in Fig. 2.29 which is clearly more pleasing to the eye. The square E does not appear in this diagram, as is reasonable because it cannot be reached from any of the other squares and does not form part of the problem. All the other squares are represented, so the same diagram can be used to represent the paths of all the other knights.

In this new formulation the problem is to move the knights round the circle so that the black knights at A and C change places with the white knights at G and H, remembering that at any move a knight moves to one or other of its neighbouring positions. The solution is then obvious: all that is needed is to give the diagram a half-turn, bringing A to I and C to G, G to C and I to A. This requires four moves by each knight, 16 in all, and this is the minimum (Fig. 2.30).

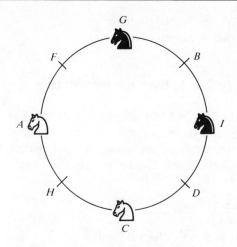

Fig. 2.30 *Solution of the four knights problem.*

2.12 THE LANGUAGE LISP

The importance of symbol manipulation in AI is such that in 1956 Newell, Shaw and Simon invented a language IPL (Information Processing Language) with which they could manipulate lists; IPL is one of the ancestors of LISP – LISt Processing Language – designed by John McCarthy at MIT in 1960. Among all the programming languages that have been produced so far, LISP has a unique style and flavour; many AI programmers swear by it alone, especially in the USA where the standard form is now what is called COMMON LISP (Steele 1984). It is regrettable that LISP has not made more headway in the general information processing world, for it is rigorous, concise and attractive.

LISP automatically provides the means for representing the tree structures of which we have already spoken; as this lies at the heart of symbol manipulation, which in turn is of first importance in AI work, it is not surprising that many AI programs are written in LISP. However, once the ideas of lists have been absorbed, these can be programmed easily in any of the high level languages, for example FORTRAN, PL/1, Pascal, Ada, and so on.

The following account of LISP falls into the following sections:

1. Basic elements of the language.
2. Representation and machine evaluation of lists.
3. Further functions, iteration.

4. λ-notation, properties related to objects.
5. New constructions, F expressions, macros.

2.12.1 Basic elements of LISP

Syntax. Expression used in LISP are called *S-expressions*, abbreviated to
S-exp. An S-expression can be an *atom* or a *list*. An atom is any string of
alpha-numeric characters with certain exceptions given below; a list is a
body enclosed in parentheses. The formal Backus–Naur definition of the
syntax is as follows.

$\langle$S-exp$\rangle := \langle$atom$\rangle \mid \langle$list$\rangle$
   $\langle$list$\rangle := (\langle$body$\rangle)$
   $\langle$body$\rangle := \langle$nil$\rangle \mid \langle$S-exp$\rangle \mid \langle$S-exp$\rangle\langle$body$\rangle$
   $\langle$atom$\rangle :=$ alphanumeric string without spaces (blanks) or any of the
            special characters (,), ., ;, '

where *nil* is the empty list, the list containing no elements.
    Every S-expression is a properly parenthesised collection of atoms, e.g.

((KING QUEEN) ((ROOK) (KNIGHT) BISHOP)) PAWN)

Elementary functions. As in all programming languages, some of the
pre-defined atoms are functions whose arguments are the S-expressions that
follow the functional symbol. But since the argument can itself be a
function that also has to be evaluated, the evaluation process must be able
to distinguish between a value *L* and an S-expression that has been given the
symbolic name L. This is achieved by preceding the symbol with an
apostrophe, thus 'L, or written out (QUOTE L): the apostrophe inhibits the
evaluation and causes the S-expression L to be taken just as it is.
    A name is given to an S-expression by use of the function SETQ:

(SETQ$\langle$atom$\rangle$ '$\langle$S-exp$\rangle \rightarrow \langle$S-exp$\rangle$, not evaluated

where the arrow $\rightarrow$ means 'is evaluated to'.
    In general, where an S-expression is entered into the machine it is
evaluated immediately, e.g. (SETQ G 'F) $\rightarrow$ F and the result is attached to
$\langle$atom$\rangle$, e.g. G $\rightarrow$ F.
    There are two basic functions, CAR and CDR, for manipulating
non-empty lists:

(CAR$\langle$non-empty list$\rangle$) $\rightarrow$ first sub-expression of the list, without its
                  parentheses

Thus

 (CAR '(A B C)) → A
 (CAR '((A)B) → (A)
 (CAR 'A)   → error, because A is not a list (no parentheses)
 (CAR '( ))   → error or nil, according to the dialect used
 (CDR⟨non-empty list⟩) → what remains of the original list, together
            with its parentheses, after the CAR has been
            removed

Thus

 (CDR '(A B C)) → (B C)
 (CDR '((A)B) → (B)
 (CDR 'A)   → ( ), by convention
 (CAR(CDR '(A B C)) → (CAR '(B C)) → B

This curious notation, CAR, CDR, is of historical origin: in the first implementation of LISP, on the IBM 7094 machine, these functions made use of what were called the address and the decrement register respectively and therefore stand for 'content of address register' and 'content of decrement register'.

 CAR and CDR and various combinations of these are very useful functions; there are the standard abbreviations:

 (CADR S) ≡ (CAR(CDR S))

e.g.

 (CADR '(A B C)) → B
 (CADDR S) ≡ (CAR(CDR(CDR(CAR S))))

and so on.

 A third important function is CONS, which reassembles what CAR and CDR have separated:

 (CONS⟨S-exp⟩⟩list⟩) → ⟨list⟩

e.g.

 (CONS 'A '(B C)) → (A B C)
 (CONS 'A NIL) → (A)

and for any S-expression S,

 (CONS(CAR S)(CDR S)) = S

We now give the standard machine representation of LISP objects and the algorithm for evaluating S-expressions.

2.12.2 Representation and evaluation

For a LISP interpreter the memory locations are organised into linked pairs, and any member of each pair except for atoms may contain a pointer to another address. If we represent the pointer by an arrow, the diagram on the left in Fig. 2.31 corresponds to the physical situation on the right. The two pointers play the roles of the first son and the first brother of that memory location (the 'father') respectively; thus the instruction (SETQ LI '(A B)) gives the structure of Fig. 2.32. Conventionally, Ø indicates the absence of a pointer, atoms are indicated by a special mark.

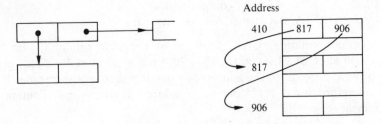

Fig. 2.31.

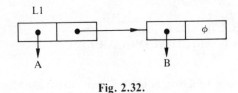

Fig. 2.32.

Then:

(CAR S) is what is pointed to by the first son
(CDR S) is what is pointed to by the first brother, put in parentheses

To retrieve an S-expression from such a representation we must first follow the left-most vertical pointers to the greatest depth and then the corresponding horizontal pointer, writing an opening parenthesis (each time a vertical pointer reaches a cell that does not contain an atom, the atom itself when the cell contains an atom and a closing parenthesis), when the cell contains Ø. Nothing arises from the horizontal pointers. Thus Fig. 2.33 corresponds to the list 'L2: ((A) (B))

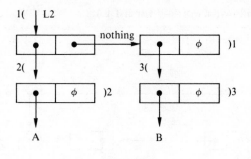

Fig. 2.33.

Further, the interpreter is at all times keeping a record of the list of available memory cells whose head is *d* (Fig. 2.34):

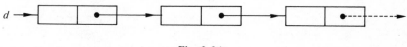

Fig. 2.34.

Thus for a form such as (SETQ L3(CONS ′C L2)) we have:
if the atom *C* does not exist yet, the pointer corresponding to *d* is moved on one step and *C* is created; then a horizontal pointer (the brother point) from *C* to the head of *L2* is created, giving the following (Fig. 2.35):

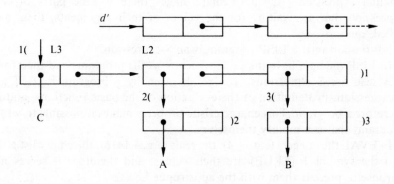

Fig. 2.35.

We have the following wording for list L4:

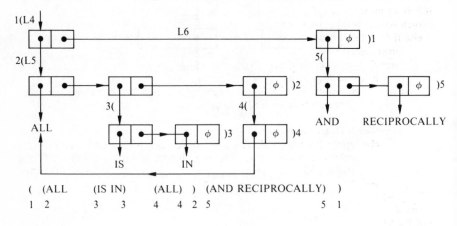

Fig. 2.36.

Evaluation of a list. This is performed by the function EVAL, and the principle is shown in Table 2.1: of course, it uses the internal represent-ation, so the parentheses as such do not enter into the procedure.

An *execution* of a LISP program is an evaluation of every S-expression that has been input; each expression is traversed by first following a sequence of 'son' pointers to its end, then the last 'brother' pointer encountered and the 'sons' to which this leads, and so on until a terminal value can be calculated. The steps are then retraced, returning to the original expression. At intermediate stages there will be parts of the expression that are waiting for the values of their arguments; these are called 'quasars'.

NB (important): a LISP program is an S-expression.

In LISP the data have the same structure as the programs and therefore they also are S-expressions. The result given by a program is itself an S-expression, by definition of the evaluation of the basic functions, and is therefore a program. This characteristic property makes it possible to write programs that can modify themselves.

In EVAL the integers (e.g. − 4), the reals (e.g. 3.1416), the empty list NIL and the symbol T (TRUE) are their values, and therefore it serves no purpose to precede them with the apostrophe '.

Table 2.1 Principle of LISP evaluation by function EVAL. S1 is the first 'son' of the expression S, S2 is the set of brothers of S1 in S. It is assumed that 'L has been written out as (QUOTE L).

---

if S is an atom
  then return ← value of S
  else if S1 = QUOTE
    then return ← S2
    else S1 is a function if not there is a coding error
      if S1 requires some special processing:
          : do not evaluate certain arguments and/or accept certain variable
          :arguments, e.g. AND, RPLACA, ...
          :
      then perform this processing
      else apply EVAL to all elements of S2 successively and return these
          values recursively, once they have been found; finally return ← S1
          (EVAL S2)
      end if
    end if
  end if
end EVAL

Examples of evaluation

  (CAR '(A)) → A
  (CDR '(A)) → NIL
  (CAR 'A) → error
  (CDR 'A) → NIL by convention
  (CAR '((A))) → (A)
  (CDR '(A(BC))) → ((BC))   : note!
  (CAR '(CDR(A B C))) → CDR   : the ' inhibits evaluation
  (CAR(CDR(A B C))) → error   : A should be a function

EVAL can be called by its name:

  (SETQ A 'B) → B
  (SETQ B 'C) → C
  A   → B
  B   → C
  (EVAL A)   → C

The following (Table 2.2) are more difficult; the numbering of the parentheses will be obvious.

Table 2.2.

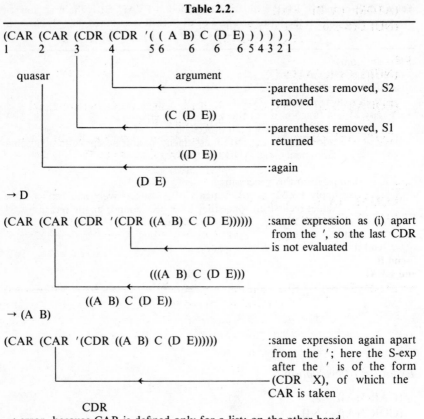

(CAR (CAR (CDR (CDR '((A B) C (D E))))))
1   2   3   4   5 6   6   6   6 5 4 3 2 1

quasar   argument
                                                    :parentheses removed, S2
                                                    removed
                          (C (D E))
                                                    :parentheses removed, S1
                                                    returned
                          ((D E))
                                              :again
                    (D E)
→ D

(CAR (CAR (CDR '(CDR ((A B) C (D E))))))   :same expression as (i) apart
                                            from the ', so the last CDR
                                            is not evaluated

                    (((A B) C (D E)))
                  ((A B) C (D E))
→ (A B)

(CAR (CAR '(CDR ((A B) C (D E))))))   :same expression again apart
                                       from the '; here the S-exp
                                       after the ' is of the form
                                       (CDR   X), of which the
                                       CAR is taken
          CDR
→ error, because CAR is defined only for a list; on the other hand,
(CAR '(CAR (CDR (CDR((A B) C (C E)))))) → CAR

2.12.3 Other functions

2.12.3.1 Predicates, taking the value T or NIL

ATOM⟨S-exp⟩ → T iff the value of S is an atom or a function
                  → NIL otherwise

e.g.

    (ATOM 'A)   → T
    (ATOM NIL)   → T
    (ATOM 'CAR)   → T

(ATOM '(A B) → NIL
(NULL⟨S-exp⟩   → T iff the value of S is NIL
               → NIL otherwise
e.g.
    (NULL(CDR 'ATOM))   → T

    (EQUAL⟨S-exp1⟩⟨S-exp2⟩   → T iff the values of S1, S2 are equal
                             → NIL otherwise
    (EQ⟨S-exp1⟩⟨S-exp2⟩   → T iff the two values are the same list
                                and occupy the same cells
                             → NIL otherwise
e.g.
    EQUAL '(A B) '(A B)) → T   but
    EQ '(A B) '(A B))   → NIL because the list (A B) has been
                                created twice and the same instances will be
                                in different cells

    (AND⟨S-exp⟩*)   :the * means that the argument can be any number of
                    S-expressions; these are evaluated from left to right in
                    turn and if any gives NIL this is returned as the value
                    of AND; otherwise the value of the last S-exp is
                    returned
    (OR⟨S-exp⟩*)   :as for AND except that the first value found that is not
                    NIL is returned; otherwise NIL
    (NOT⟨S-exp⟩) → T iff the value of S is NIL
                  → NIL otherwise

2.12.3.2 Functions

Conditional expression – choice between possibilities. This is made with the
aid of COND, which is not actually a function. The syntax is:

    (COND(⟨t1⟩⟨a1⟩)
         (⟨t2⟩⟨a2⟩)
         ...
         (⟨tn⟩⟨an⟩))

Here *t* means 'test' and *a* means 'action', and the number of (*t*, *a*) pairs is
arbitrary. When the LISP interpreter encounters this expression it first
evaluates the S-expression *t*1; if this gives any non-NIL value it then
evaluates *a*1, returns this value and skips over all the remaining pairs. If
*t*1 evaluates to NIL it moves to *t*2 and so on until either a non-NIL value for
t is found or the list is exhausted, when NIL is returned.

It is permissible to omit the *a* from any pair; if *ti* is the first non-NIL value encountered and *ai* is not given, then the value *ti* is returned.

Functions for constructing lists. CONS is such a function; others are APPEND and LIST, defined as follows.

(APPEND⟨list1⟩⟨list2⟩ ... ⟨listn⟩) → list consisting of list1, list2, ... listn

the first level parentheses having been removed from the component lists, e.g.

(APPEND '(A) NIL '((B)(C))) → (A(B)(C))

(LIST⟨S-exp1⟩⟨S-exp2⟩ ... ⟨S-expn⟩) → (S-exp1 S-exp2 ... S-expn)

but here all the parentheses are retained; further, LIST, in contrast to APPEND, can have an atom as an argument, e.g.

LIST '(A) NIL '((B)(C))) → ((A) NIL ((B)(C)))
(LIST 'A NIL)   → (A NIL)

Functions for operating on lists.

(LENGTH⟨S-exp⟩) → number of 'first level brothers' in S, e.g.
LENGTH '((A B)C(D))) → 3
(REVERSE⟨S-exp⟩) → the S-expression formed by taking the 'first
                                        level brothers' of the given expression in reverse
                                        order
e.g.

(REVERSE '(A(B C)D)) → (D(B C)A)

(SUBST⟨S-exp1⟩⟨S-exp2⟩⟨S-exp3⟩) → the result of substituting in S3
                                                          all occurrences of S2 by S1: the
                                                          value of S2 must be an atom
e.g.

(SUBST 'A 'B '(A B C)) → (A A C)

(MEMBER⟨atom⟩⟨list⟩)   → NIL iff the value of ⟨atom⟩ does not
                                        occur as a first order brother in ⟨list⟩
                                   → otherwise, the complete sub-list starting
                                        with the first occurrence of ⟨atom⟩
e.g.

(SETQ M '(A B(C D)E))
(MEMBER 'F M) → NIL
(MEMBER 'C M) → NIL
(MEMBER 'B M) → (B(C D)E)

(RPLACA⟨list⟩⟨S-exp⟩) → replace CAR('⟨list⟩) by S in ⟨list⟩

e.g.

    (SETQ G '(A B C))
    (RPLACA(CDR G) 'D) → (D C)

RPLACD is the corresponding function acting on the CDR of the first
argument.
RPLACA AND RPLACD have side effects on the original list: thus after
the above RPLACA, G → (A C D)

2.12.3.3 Numerical functions

To maintain consistency with the preceding, these are written in Polish
(prefix) notation. The meaning will be obvious.

    (PLUS 2, 3) → 5:

PLUS can have any number of arguments, so, e.g.,

    (PLUS 1 2 3 4 5)   → 15
    (DIFFERENCE 5 2) → 3
    (TIMES 4 5)   → 20
    (QUOTIENT 8.2)   → 4

most LISP interpreters accept +, −, ∗, / for the four basic functions.

    (MAX 5 8 7 6)   → 8
    (MIN 5 8 7 6)   → 5
    (ADD1 6)   → 7
    (SUB1 6)   → 5
    (SQRT 16)   → 4
    (EXPT 2 3)   → 8
    (MINUS 3)   → −3
    (ABS −3)   → 3

Function can be combined, e.g.

    (MAX(MIN 2 4 6)(MAX 3 5 2)) → 5
    (ATOM(PLUS 1 2 3)) → T because (PLUS 1 2 3) → 6 which is an atom.

There are the following predicate for numerical arguments N1, N2:

    (LESSP N1 N2)   → T iff value N1 < value N2
    (GREATERP N1 N2) → T iff value N1 > value N2
    (ZEROP N1)   → T iff value N1 = 0

and the following function:

    (REMAINDER N1 N2) → remainder when value N1 is divided by value
N2

In the above, the system gives an error message if N1, N2 are not numerical; an S-expression can be tested to find if it has a numerical value by the predicate

(NUMBERP⟨S-exp⟩) → T iff value ⟨S-exp⟩ is numerical

2.13.3.4   Iteration: MAPCAR and APPLY

(MAPCAR '⟨function⟩⟨S-exp⟩ → the S-expression resulting when the
                                      argument ⟨function⟩ is applied to
                                      every element of S

e.g.

(MAPCAR 'ADD1 '(4 8 3)) → (5 9 4)

⟨function⟩ must of course be a function known to the system; and since it is applied to one element of the ⟨S-exp⟩ at a time it must have only one argument.

(APPLY '⟨function⟩⟨S-exp⟩) → the   value   resulting   from   applying
                                    ⟨function⟩ to the value of S

e.g.

(SETQ A '(4 5 8 1)
(APPLY 'PLUS A) → 18

The need for APPLY arises because, for example, writing simply (PLUS A) would give an error message since PLUS expects numerical arguments.

   The two functions together provide an elegant method for performing the same operation on all the elements of a list.

2.12.4   LAMBDA expressions, relating properties to atoms

2.12.4.1   Definition of LAMBDA atom

The LAMBDA notation, devised by Church in 1930, enables us to use a function locally without needing to give it a name:

((LAMBDA(X)⟨S-exp1⟩)⟨S-exp2⟩) → value of S1 when all occurrences
                                      of X have been replaced by S2

In this definition,

   X is the *variable*

S1 is the *body* of the LAMBDA function
S2 is the *argument*

e.g.

((LAMBDA(X)(EQUAL X 'PEN) 'PEN) → T
(MAPCAR '(LAMBDA (i) (∗i i i)(1 2 3 4)) → (1 8 27 64)

Note that in the second example an apostrophe must be placed before LAMBDA.

2.12.4.2 Properties: PUTPROP, GET

The concepts of arrays and indices do not enter into LISP. The attaching of a property to an object, and referring to the value of this property, is done with the aid of the function PUTPROP:

(PUTPROP⟨atom1⟩⟨list⟩⟨atom2⟩) has the effect of assigning the property whose name is ⟨atom2⟩ to the object ⟨atom1⟩ and giving it the value of ⟨list⟩, e.g.

(PUTPROP   'PETER(JOHN   JAMES)   'CHILDREN) → (JOHN JAMES)

which by means of pointers assigns the 'children' John and James to Peter.
GET is used to find if an object has a given property:

(GET⟨atom1⟩⟨atom2⟩) → NIL iff ⟨atom1⟩ does not have property
⟨atom2⟩
→ otherwise, value of property ⟨atom2⟩

e.g.

(GET 'PETER 'CHILDREN) → (JOHN JAMES)

2.12.5 Constructing new functions

New LISP functions can be constructed with the aid of the function DEFUN, the syntax of which is:

(DEFUN⟨atom⟩(⟨p1⟩⟨p2⟩ ... ⟨pn⟩)(S-exp)

where ⟨atom⟩ is the name to be given to the function, the pi are the formal parameters or bound variables that enter into it and S is the body of the function. As an example, let us use DEFUN to construct two simple functions, LENGTH and REVERSE, as though these were not already available.

(DEFUN LENGTH (L) (COND((NULL L)0): if L is NIL then → 0
                           (T(ADD1(LENGTH(CDR L)))))
                                    : else add 1 to LENGTH(CDR L)
                 → LENGTH

(DEFUN REVERSE (S) (COND((NUL S)S): if S is NIL then S
                           (T(APPEND(REVERSE(CDR(S))
                           (LIST(CAR S)))))))
                 → REVERSE

Now consider some applications of DEFUN.

(i) Union of two sets (i.e. the set of all elements of at least one of the given sets). We assume that the sets are represented by lists of LISP atoms; calling these E, F the result (UNION E F)) will be in F.

(DEFUN UNION(E F)(COND((NULL E)F)((APP(CAR E)F)
    (UNION(CDR E)F))
:if the first element of E is an element of F we take no action and continue to the next element. APP is a function defined below
:if not, add this element to F and continue with the next
(T(UNION((CDR E)(CONS(CAR E)F)))))
 → UNION

The function APP(A X) of two arguments, the atom A and the list X, returns T if A is in X and NIL otherwise. It is defined as follows:

(DEFUN APP(A X) (COND((NUL X)NIL) :NIL if X is empty
                     ((EQUAL A(CAR X))) :T if A is the first element
                                            of X
                     (T(APP A(CDR X))))) :if not, continue with the
                                            next element
      → APP

e.g.

(UNION '(A B C D E) '(Z U B D Y) → (E C A Z U B D Y)

(ii) Generation of a numerical sequence. We construct a LISP S-expression that forms a program to generate the sequence of integers u_n defined by:

$$u_{n+1} = u_n/2 \quad \text{if} \quad u_n \text{ is even}$$
$$= 3u_n + 1 \quad \text{if} \quad u_n \text{ is odd}$$

given any initial value u_1. We call this PIMP (u).

```
(DEFUN PIMP (u)
      (PRINT u)
      (COND ((EQUAL u 1)              NIL): stop if u = 1
             (ZEROP (REMAINDER u 2) (PIMP (QUOTIENT u 2) : case
                                       u even
                T                     (PIMP (ADD1 (TIMES u 3)))))))) :
                                       case u odd
   → PIMP
   (PIMP 17) → 17  52  26  13  40  20  10  5  16  8  4  2  1
```

(iii) Pattern matching. We construct a function FILTER that will compare two strings of characters; this is a special case of the *unification* algorithm that we shall meet in Chapter 3.

The strings are E and F, where F is a pattern against which the expression E is to be matched; they are compared character by character from left to right, but F may contain the special characters $+$, $*$ which have the following effects:

- if $+$ is encountered in F, any character in the corresponding position in E is accepted; e.g. (FILTER '(A + B) '(A B C) → T;
- If $*$ is encountered in F, any number of characters in E are accepted; e.g. (FILTER '($*$C) '(A B C)) → T.

```
(DEFUN FILTER (F  E)
       (COND((AND (NULL F)(NULL E))   T): F and E both empty
             ((OR(NULL F)(NULL E))    NIL): one of E, F empty
             ((OR(EQUAL(CAR F)(CAR E))
                (EQUAL(CAR F) ' +))
                        (FILTER(CDR F)(CDR E))): + case
             ((EQUAL(CAR F) '*)
                (COND((FILTER(CDR F)(CDR E)
                      ((FILTER F(CDR E)))))
                (T    NIL)))                    :* case
    → FILTER
```

No 'action' expressions are given in the last COND, which means, as explained in the definition of COND, that the result returned is the value of the first non-NIL 'test' expression encountered: in the first case the $*$ is skipped over as though it were a $+$, in the second we move one further step along E without moving along F and apply FILTER again − the $*$ has 'absorbed' the character. Thus:

(FILTER '($*$ B K + M $*$ Z) '(B A O B A B K L M Y Z) → T

(iv) Use of LET. This enables values to be assigned to identifiers, which values can be used later as arguments in expressions; in particular, LET makes it possible to avoid computing the same quantity several times. The syntax is

(LET ((name1 S-exp1)
      (name2 S-exp2)
          ...
      (namen S-expn))
      ⟨expressions⟩*)

→ values of the expressions, in which the names have been replaced by the value of the corresponding S-expressions.

Example – HCF of two given numbers

(DEFUN HCF N1 N2)
        ((LET((M (REMAINDER N1 N2)))
        (COND((ZEROP M)N2)
             (T   HCF N2 M))))))

2.12.5.1 The functions FEXPR, MACRO

The name FEXPR is used to denote a function whose arguments are not evaluated, but simply made into a list; this is used in conjunction with DEFUN with the syntax

(DEFUN ⟨function name⟩ FEXPR(parameter(s))⟨function body⟩)

e.g.

(DEFUN PRINT FEXPR (P) (PRINT P))
→ PRINT
(PRINT THIS SENTENCE)
→ (THIS SENTENCE)
→ T

The functions QUOTE, SETQ, COND are of FEXPR type.

MACRO enables new functions to be defined and evaluated: the body of the new function is first translated, and is then evaluated. The syntax is:

(DEFUN ⟨function name⟩ MACRO (parameter(s))⟨body⟩)

As an example, let us construct the classic **if** ... **then** ... **else** ... The parameter is the list (IF TEST ACTION1 ACTION2); the expressions TEST, ACTION1, ACTION2 will not be known when the function is called so we use the instruction SUBST to place them in a COND, for eventual evaluation.

```
(DEFUN IF MACRO (X)
        (SUBST (CADR X) 'TEST
        (SUBST (CADDR X) 'ACTION1
        (SUBST (CADDDR X) 'ACTION 2
                '(COND(TEST  ACTION1)
                     (T      ACTION2))))))
→ IF
```

We should recall here that (SUBST x y z) substitutes x for every occurrence of y in the expression z. Here SUBST acts on the entire program, so this MACRO defines in effect a transformation of a program by the program itself.

2.13   GRAPHS

Generalising the representation of an expression by a tree leads to the idea of a *graph*. A graph G is a set X of objects, called *vertices* (or *nodes*), pairs of which are related to a binary relation R; this is denoted by $G = (X, R)$.[1] The relation R is given by the set of linked pairs of vertices, e.g.

$$X = 1, 2, 3, 4, 5$$
$$R = (1, 1), (1, 2), (1, 3), (1, 4), (2, 4), (3, 4), (3, 5)$$

If R is symmetric, as is assumed in Fig. 2.37, the pairs are non-oriented and are called *edges*; but if the order in which the vertices is taken is important then they are called *arcs*. The most natural interpretation of a graph is a diagram of links between points; examples are telephone or road networks – which are usually non-oriented – and electrical networks – usually oriented, with the directions given by the current flows.

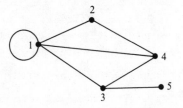

Fig. 2.37 Example of a graph.

1. In what follows, R can also denote the relation that links the two members of each pair.

Definitions

> A graph $G' = (Y, V)$ is a **partial** graph of $G = (X, U)$ iff $Y = X$ and $V \subset U$.
> It is a sub-graph of G iff $Y \subset X$ and $V = U - W$ where $W = \{(v, w)\}$ and
> either v or w or both are in $(X - Y)$: that is, some of the vertices, together with
> all their arcs incident on them, have been removed.

> If $u = (x, y)$ belongs to U, x is called the **initial end-point** of u and y the
> **terminal end-point**; x is a **predecessor** of y and y is a **successor** of x.

> **The degree** of a vertex is the number of its neighbours, that is, of vertices that
> are either its predecessors or its successors.

> A **path** from one vertex a to another b in G is a finite sequence of vertices
> $c_1, c_2, ..., c_n$ such that $c_1 = a$, $c_n = b$ and all (c_i, c_{i-1}) belong to U. If the
> graph G is not oriented it is sufficient that either (c_i, c_{i-1}) or (c_{i-1}, c_i) belongs
> to U, and the path is then called a chain joining a and b.

> A **circuit** or **cycle** is a closed chain, i.e. the end point b coincides with the
> starting point a.

If there is a chain from any vertex a to any other b, the graph is said to be
connected; if a path, it is *strongly connected*.

Applications. Very many situations can be represented by graphs, apart
from those of the types already mentioned. Graphs can be used to model
many types of communication, but also parenthood relations, material or
information flows, chemical formulae and symbolic expressions in general;
trees are only special forms of graphs. The familiar graphs of functions are
simply examples of the special case in which the set of points concerned is
specified by $(x, f(x))$.

Chapters 4, 5 and 6 give many examples that illustrate the usefulness of
graphs and the power of the models they give rise to.

Chapter 3

FORMAL SYSTEMS

3.1 INTRODUCTION

The aim of formal logic is to provide a theory of valid reasoning; it is concerned with the form of the reasoning process and not with any content, so that in any chain of formal reasoning the elements of the discourse can be replaced arbitrarily by any others wherever they appear, without affecting the validity. In the classical syllogism, generally attributed to Aristotle but in fact due to William of Occam (1349):

> **S**: all men are mortal
> Socrates is a man
> therefore Socrates is mortal

the two occurrences of the words man, mortal, Socrates can be replaced by any other words and the reasoning remains formally valid. Thus a simple means for reasoning about this reasoning is to substitute symbols for these words, so constructing the abstract model for this process:

> if all x are y
> and if z is an x
> then z is y

The syllogistic method of reasoning was invented by Aristotle and it is in his writings that we first meet substitutable symbols, later to be called variables.

However, variables alone are not sufficient to formalise the whole process of reasoning as it is conducted in natural language: link words such as if, then, or, and, because, therefore, ..., and verbs such as is, belongs to, implies ... play essential roles. These express the process of the reasoning and cannot be replaced by anything else; thus in the above syllogism if the second 'if' is replaced by, for example, 'or', the reasoning is no longer valid. These non-substitutable symbols are called operators.

It is important to realise that the relation between a natural language statement and its expression in logical formalism is not invariant. Thus 'or' can mean either 'one or other but not both' – the exclusive or – or 'either or both' – the inclusive or; and 'is' can convey any of the concepts of equality, inclusion and belonging to. Different symbols must therefore be used to express the different meanings of the same word; this illustrates one of the important aims of formal logic, that of removing ambiguities and enabling the steps in a chain of reasoning, the *inferences*, to be studied one by one and their validity to be established rigorously.

Formal logic was originally an integral part of the teaching of the great philosophers such as Aristotle, the Stoics, Avicenne, Abelard, Kant and Leibniz; later it became more technical and more mathematical, and with Boole, Venn and de Morgan results began to be developed that were directly usable in other fields, thus realising Leibniz's dream of the construction of a 'universal language'. We can see here the differentiation of formal reasoning in written arguments from spoken; logic developed originally as a theory of valid verbal argument. But is was first with Frege, then Peano and finally in the monumental *Principia Mathematica* of Russell and Whitehead (1913) that it broke completely free from spoken language and became a discipline in its own right with its own nomenclature; and this led to the raising of a number of serious questions:

1. Is it not just arguing in a circle to study logic itself and therefore to reason about its formalism?
2. To what extent can mathematics, taken as a whole, be based on logic?
3. How can an argument in formal logic, the symbolism of which is devoid of meaning, be legitimately applied to a situation in the real world?

Since the time of the classical Greeks the geometrical arguments of Euclid's *Elements* have been regarded as a model of rigorous deductive reasoning; and it was only in 1882 that M. Pasch drew attention to certain tacit assumptions contained in them, such as that of the existence of a point between two given points.

In 1895 Hilbert proposed a programme of study that would lead to basing the whole of mathematics on a set of explicitly stated axioms, in which nothing would be tacitly assumed about the entities that were to be manipulated but everything would be put into the axioms themselves. However, in 1931 Gödel, in his famous, brilliant and fundamental theorem, showed that this was intrinsically impossible and that there are essential limits to what can be proved within a formalism. The importance of Gödel's type of approach, which concerns the theory of a theory, or *metatheory*, will be emphasised throughout this chapter and referred to many times in the rest of the book.

3.2 DEFINITION OF A FORMAL SYSTEM

A *formal system* (abbreviated to FS) is a set of purely abstract data items, having no relation to the outside world, that define the purely syntactic rules according to which a set of abstract symbols can be manipulated – rules, that is, into which no considerations of meaning (semantics) enter. Such a system consists of the following:

1. a finite *alphabet* of *symbols*;
2. a procedure for forming *words* of the system;
3. a set of *axioms*, all of which are words;
4. a finite set of *deduction rules*, by means of which a further set of words can be deduced from a given finite set. These are of the form:

$$U_1 \& U_2 \& \dots \& U_p \rightarrow W_1 \& W_2 \& \dots \& W_n$$

where the U_i and W_j are words of the system and the arrow $\rightarrow$ means that the set W_j can be deduced from the set U_i.

3.2.1 Supplementary definitions

A formal system is sometimes called an *axiomatic* system, or a *theory* or simply a set of formulae; and the alphabet, assumed finite, a *vocabulary*. A distinction is made between constants, variables and operators, as will be illustrated in the example in Section 3.2.3 below.

The procedure for forming words ((2) above) defines the syntactic structure or *grammar* of the words, which are *well formed* strings of symbols; this is distinct from (4), which defines the deductions that are allowed by the system.

A *proof* in the system is a finite sequence of words M_1, M_2, ..., M_r in which each M_i is either an axiom or a word that can be deduced from the preceding M_j, $j < i$.

A *theorem* is a word t for which there is a proof such that $M_r \equiv t$; this is expressed by $\vdash t$. Every axiom is a theorem, by definition.

The deduction rules are also called derivation or inference rules; in principle they enable arbitrary words to be distinguished from theorems. Thus we have the sets

$$(\text{theorems}) \subset (\text{words}) \subset (\text{strings of symbols})$$

where in general strict inclusion is implied.

The rules are of two types. On the one hand are those that act on words taken as complete entities and cannot be applied in any other way; these are called *productions*. On the other are those that can be applied to any part of a word that is itself a word of the system, and these are called *re-writings*. Thus with the usual mathematical notation the rule:

$$x < y \,\&\, y < z \text{ leads to } x < z$$

is applied to the complete words x, y, z; it is a production (with two antecedents) and 'leads to' can be abbreviated to ' $\rightarrow$ '. The rule $x - x = 0$ can be applied to any sub-expression; this is a re-write, expressed by $x - x \mapsto 0$.

The rules can of course be applied only in one direction, from left to right. We must know that both $a \mapsto b$ and $b \mapsto a$ before we can re-write in either direction at will – as is the case, for example, with those striking identities we meet in school algebra – and when this is so we must be careful, in a proof, not to argue in a circle.

In the fully general case the only restrictions on the sets of axioms and of the words (U), (W) entering into the deduction rules is that they are recursively enumerable; but in all that follows we shall assume that they are finite.

3.2.2 A universally applicable rule: substitution

In any formal system, in order to apply a rule to a word M we must first make M and the left side of that rule identical. To achieve this we can perform any *substitution*(s) we wish on either of these expressions, where by substitution is meant the replacement of every occurrence of a variable by any word whatever provided that the word does not contain the variable in question.

3.2.3 Examples

1. The formal system, JP, is defined as follows:

1. Alphabet: $(a, b, \Box)$.
2. Words: any sequence consisting solely of symbols of the alphabet.
3. Axioms (one only): $a\Box a$.
4. Rules (one only): $c_1 \Box c_2 \rightarrow bc_1 \Box bc_2$

c_1, c_2 are not symbols of the alphabet of JP and serve simply as intermediaries in the formalisation of the rule; they can be replaced by any sequences of the symbols a and/or b. By convention we say that:

$\Box$ is an operator (non-substitutable)
a, b are constants (non-substitutable)

An obvious way to generate the legal words of JP – that is, the words that can be constructed by means of the given rule – is to apply the rule in every possible way to the given axiom; this gives

$$a \square a$$
$$ba \square ba$$
$$bba \square bba$$
$$bbba \square bbba, \text{etc.}$$

It is clear that, for example, $baab \square abba$ is not a legal word. We shall return to this system in §5 below.

2. The formal system DH. In his wonderful book *Gödel, Escher, Bach: an Eternal Golden Braid* in which he traces through some 700 pages the ideas of recursion and self-reference in logic, Gödel's theorem, information science, the extraordinary drawings of Escher and the fugues, canons and improvisations of Bach, Douglas Hofstadter sets the '*MU* puzzle' in his first chapter. He defines the following formal system:

1. Alphabet: M, I, U.
2. Words: any sequence consisting solely of letters of the alphabet.
3. Axioms (one only): MI.
4. Rules: $R1$ $mI \rightarrow mIU$ (production)
   $R2$ $Mm \rightarrow Mmm$ (production)
   $R3$ $III \rightarrow U$ (re-writing)
   $R4$ $UU \rightarrow$ (re-writing)

As with the c_1, c_2 in the first example, m here is not a member of the alphabet of the system and can be replaced by any word whatever.

$R1$ being a production rule, it can be applied only to a theorem whose last symbol is I; thus given the theorem $MIUMIUMI$ we could deduce $MIUMIUMIU$. Similarly, given the theorem MUI we could use $R2$ to deduce $MUIUI$. $R3$ enables, for example, $MIIIUM$ to be replaced by $MUUM$. $R4$ means simply that any pair UU can be deleted, e.g. $MMUUUUM$ becomes MMM. Thus we can use the system to derive:

1. MI axiom;
2. MII R2 applied to (1);
3. $MIIII$ R2 applied to (2);
4. $MIIIIU$ R1 applied to (3);
5. $MIUU$ R3 applied to (4);
6. MI R4 applied to (5).

Hofstadter puts the question: is MU a theorem of this system?

I leave the reader to play with the system, and to try to answer the question.

3.3   IMPORTANCE OF FORMAL SYSTEMS: DECIDABILITY AND INTERPRETATION

3.3.1   Decidability

Given any formal system, the first and most natural question that comes to mind is, can the machinery be operated in reverse? – that is, is it possible to say of a given word of the system whether or not it can be derived from the axioms by means of the rules? In other words, is the word a theorem or a non-theorem? – non-theorem being a word that can be *proved* not to be a theorem.

What is needed here is a deterministic procedure that will always give an answer to the theorem–non-theorem question in a finite number of steps: this would be called a *decision procedure* and if one exists for a given FS that system is said to be *decidable*. Figure 3.1 illustrates the situation; the difficulty is that such a procedure does not always exist, and indeed does not exist for such a simple and fundamental system as the first order predicate calculus which we consider in Section 3.5 below. The essential reason is that whilst it is possible to enumerate the theorems, even if they are infinite in number, because they are obtained by applying the rules in all possible ways and combinations to the axioms, there is no method for enumerating the non-theorems. The effect of this is to cast doubt on the method of exhaustive search for deciding whether or not a given word is a theorem: if no decision has been reached after some number of steps, one cannot tell whether the given word is a non-theorem or the system is non-decidable.

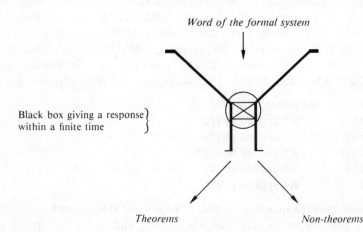

Word of the formal system

Black box giving a response⎱
within a finite time   ⎰

Theorems   *Non-theorems*

Fig. 3.1 Decidability of a formal system.

The general statement is that the set of theorems of a formal system is not necessarily recursively enumerable.

3.3.2 Interpretation

Formal systems are not constructed arbitrarily, but as models for certain mathematical realities.

An *interpretation* of a formal system is a relation set up between the system and something in the world outside: this attributes a *meaning* to every symbol of the system, as a 1–1 correspondence between each symbol and some object in this external world, to be understood in the ordinary sense, and as such can be judged as true or false.

It is worth noting that here we have come round in a circle in our mathematical development. Initially, the mathematician has studied the real world and has constructed an abstract representation of this, a formal system; he has then proved a number of theorems in this system, working only with the abstract properties – the one system could be a model for any number of real situations; and finally he returns to his starting point by interpreting these abstract theorems in terms of objects and properties of the real world.

For any given formal system it will always have been arranged that there is at least one interpretation in which every theorem translates into a true statement. A system is the more significant, the more such interpretations it has, for then a single proof in the system gives all the more true statements about the real world. Modern mathematics, through the theory of categories and that of models, is therefore becoming interested in formal systems of greater and greater generality.

3.3.3 Truth and provability

It follows from the definitions given in the preceding paragraphs that there is a fundamental distinction between the concepts of truth and provability: they belong to quite different universes. There is no a priori reason why a statement that is true in the ordinary sense of the word corresponds to a provable word of a given formal system: the fact that a statement is true does not guarantee that it can be proved.

The relation between truth value – TRUE (T) or FALSE (F) – and provability – THEOREM (Th) or NON-THEOREM (NTh) – can be displayed as the four possibilities of Fig. 3.2. A given word is either a theorem or a non-theorem and its interpretation can be judged to be either true or false. The two cases at the top of the diagram present no difficulties.

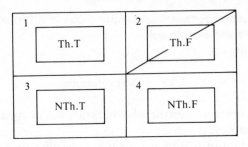

Fig. 3.2 Provability and truth values.

Case 1, where the word is provable and its interpretation is true, is clearly straightforward; and in case 2, where the word is provable but its interpretation is false, the interpretation is clearly of no interest and this case can be eliminated. Thus for any given formal system we should retain only those interpretations for which all theorems are interpreted as TRUE. This deals with the theorems but we now have to consider the non-theorems, cases 3 and 4. We should like to associate every non-theorem as FALSE, always – that is, to eliminate case 3; but this is not always possible. However, it is so for the most commonly used systems, including propositional logic which we study in Section 3.4.

Thus the most awkward situation is that of case 3, non-theorems of the system that are true for certain interpretations; and as we have seen, we cannot say that such situations cannot arise. The famous Fermat last theorem, that if x, y, z, n are all integers, the equation $x^n + y^n = z^n$ has no solution for $n > 2$, may be true in the normal arithmetical interpretation, and computer calculations have shown it to be true for all values of n up to several tens of thousands; but this is not a proof and the theorem may not be provable within the present axiomatic system of arithmetic. And to make matters worse, se shall see in Section 3.6 that there are formal systems for which the class NTh-T (case 3) is non-empty for *every* interpretation.

We know that the general problem of deciding whether or not a given string is a word of a given formal system has no solution, but we may wish to investigate a particular case and the question then arises, how should we go about this so as to arrive at an answer as quickly as possible? Blind search is inefficient (and likely to be defeated by the combinatorial explosion) so we must make all possible use of the properties of the system itself. For example, if a certain constant A appears neither in the axioms nor in the rules it cannot appear in any theorem and therefore we need not consider any strings containing A. Or if no rule can generate a word of greater length (measured by the number of symbols it contains) than the word to which it is applied, we need consider no string longer than the longest axiom. In this second case we can be certain of arriving at a decision within a finite number of steps, because if L is the length of the given string and n the number of symbols in the alphabet, the number of cases to be examined is L^n, which is finite.

We now illustrate the importance of using such a *metatheory* by considering again the two simple systems introduced previously; and then the two classical systems, propositional calculus and first-order predicate calculus. It was studies of this type that led the great mathematicians Church, Gödel, Tarski and others in the 1930s to some very general results concerning formal systems, which we shall touch on later.

3.3.4 Examples of proof

(i) The system JP. This has one axiom and one rule

$$a \square a$$

and one rule

$$c_1 \square c_2 \rightarrow bc_1 \square bc_2$$

from which the theorems

$$ba \square ba, \qquad bba \square bba, \qquad bbba \square bbba \dots$$

can be derived successively.

It is obvious that all theorems of this system will be of the form:

$$b \dots ba \square b \dots ba$$

where the symbol b is repeated some number p times on the left and the same number of times on the right. We can abbreviate this to:

$$b^p a \square b^p a$$

where the convention is that b^p represents a string of p consecutive symbols b and b^0 represents the empty string. This convention introduces a meta-notation, because the operation of raising to a power is not an operation of the original system: we have in fact brought in the reasoning of a higher level formal system, arithmetic.

The need to distinguish between a language and a meta-language arises in other situations, giving rise to known difficulties when natural languages are used, e.g. the definition of the grammar of a language in a text in that same language. This distinction is of fundamental importance for compilers, which are computer programs that translate other programs into the machine's language. The Backus–Naur Form (BNF) for defining a programming language is in fact a formal system that specifies the expressions that are allowed in the language. Thus:

⟨program⟩ ≔ ⟨instruction⟩ | ⟨program⟩ ⟨instruction⟩

(a program is either an instruction or a program followed by an instruction)

⟨instruction⟩ ≔ *⟨comment⟩ | ⟨line⟩ | ⟨label⟩ | ⟨label⟩⟨line⟩
⟨comment⟩ ≔ blank | ⟨letter⟩⟨comment⟩

and so on; as one proceeds through the definition, all the terms in angle brackets are defined.

Returning to the system JP, we see that we now have a decision procedure: the string to be tested must start with some number, p say, of successive symbols b, which must be followed by an a and this followed by the symbol □; then there must follow the same number p of successive symbols b and finally an a. If the string passes this test it is a theorem, otherwise it is not.

Consider now some interpretations of JP.

Interpretation 1. Let a represent zero, b the concept of successor in the set of integers and □ equality in this set. The axiom is then interpreted as $0 = 0$, which we consider TRUE; and the successive theorems become $1 = 1$, $2 = 2, \ldots p = p$, all of which are TRUE. The statement $1 = 2$ would have to arise from $ba□bba$ which is a non-theorem of the system; in our interpretation it is clearly FALSE. Thus we have a 'correct' interpretation of JP in ordinary arithmetic, with the correspondences Th ↔T, NTh ↔F and classes 2, 3 empty.

Interpretation 2. Let a represent the proposition 'Socrates is mortal', b the negation of what it precedes and □ the identity of two propositions. The axiom is then

'Socrates is mortal' is identical to 'Socrates is mortal'

which we should consider a true statement.

The first theorem derived, $ba□ba$ is

Socrates is not mortal is identical to Socrates is not mortal

which again we should consider true: and it is important to note that we should consider the statement of identity true, whether or not the statement of Socrates's mortality were true.

However, the word $bba□a$, which is not a theorem of the system JP, has the interpretation:

'The negation of the statement that Socrates is not mortal' is identical to the statement 'Socrates is mortal' and this again we should consider true: so we have a non-theorem of the system with a true interpretation − that is, the class NTh-T is not empty; and this true statement could not be the interpretation of any theorem of the system.

(ii) For a second example we take the system DH defined above, with the rules:

$$R1 \; mI \rightarrow mIU \qquad R2 \; Mm \rightarrow Mmm$$

$$R2 \; III \rightarrow U \qquad R4 \; UU \rightarrow$$

and the single axiom *MI*, with the problem of deciding whether or not *MU* is a theorem. The start of the tree of derivations from *MI* is shown in Fig. 3.3; let us consider the general process. First, since the production rules *R1*, *R2* do not change the first character of any word they act on, the system will generate only words beginning with *M*; so it is not impossible that *MU* is a theorem. The next observation is that if *MU* is to be derived from the axiom *MI* then at least one *I* has to be deleted in the process, and this can be done only by means of *R2* and/or *R3*, as *R1* and *R4* have no effect on the number of *I*s. But any application of *R2* will double this number whilst *R3* will reduce it by 3. Therefore to reduce the number of *I*s to zero, *R3* must be applied either once to a word containing three consecutive *I*s or several times in succession to one containing a number that is a multiple of 3; and as *R2* can generate only numbers that are powers of 2 this is impossible, so *MU* cannot be generated and is therefore not a theorem of DH.

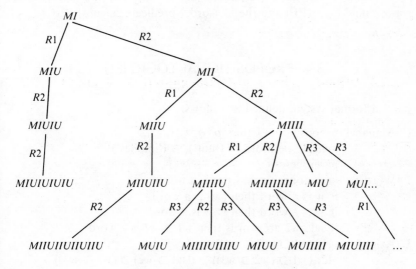

Fig. 3.3 Derivation tree for MU.

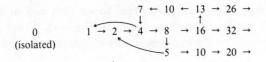

Fig. 3.4 Abstract representation of the system DH.

Notice that we have obtained this result by using another formal system, that of arithmetic. The process can be written, so far as the number i of Is is concerned, as:

axiom: $i = 1$
$R2$: $i \rightarrow 21$ one application of $R2$
$R3$: $i \rightarrow i - 3$ one application of $R3$ ($i > 3$)
goal: $i = 0$

and the numbers of Is that can be generated is as shown in Fig. 3.4. The system cannot generate any word having a number of Is that is a multiple of 3, so M, MUU, $MIIIU$, etc., cannot be theorems.

Another way of arriving at the result is as follows. As before, let i be the number of Is at any stage, and $j = i$ (mod 3). R3 leaves the value of j unchanged, so we need consider only the effect of $R2$, which gives $i \rightarrow 21$.

Now $2i$ (mod 3) $= (3i - i)$ (mod 3) $= -i$; so as the process starts with $j = 1$ the only values that j can take are $+1$ and -1, and the required value 0 is impossible. This is summarised by $j \equiv i$ mod 3, $j = \pm 1$.

We now describe two important formal systems that are greatly used: propositional logic (PL) and the first-order predicate calculus (PrC).

3.4 PROPOSITIONAL LOGIC (PL)

This is a formal system defined as follows:

1. Alphabet: propositional letters p, q, r, s, t, ...
   logical operators $\neg$ ('not'), $\supset$ ('implies')
   parentheses (,)
2. Words: any propositional letter is a word
   if w is a word then (w) is a word
   if w is a word then $\neg w$ is a word
   if $w1$, $w2$ are words then $w1 \supset w2$ is a word
3. Axioms: $A1$: $(w1 \supset (w2 \supset w1))$
   $A2$: $(w1 \supset (w2 \supset w3)) \supset ((w1 \supset w2) \supset (w1 \supset w3))$
   $A3$: $(\neg w2 \supset \neg w1) \supset (w1 \supset w2)$

4. Rules: there is only one rule, the *rule of detachment* or *modus ponens*: if ($w1$) and ($w1 \supset w2$) are theorems then ($w2$) is a theorem; or formally, ($w1$) & ($w1 \supset w2$) → ($w2$)

This system models the usual process of logical reasoning; from the start it has been used with the interpretation that the propositional letters can represent any statements whatever and that ¬, $\supset$ represent negation and logical implication respectively. Neither the axioms nor the rules presume any special role for the propositional letters, which are regarded as completely interchangeable; thus if ⊢ ($p \supset \neg q$) $\supset$ ($r \supset s$) then equally ⊢ ($t \supset \neg s$) $\supset$ ($q \supset r$), for example. Any *renaming* of any letter is allowed and for this reason the letters are called *free variables*: there are no constants in PL.

Certain other symbols are used with this system, in particular ∧ for logical AND and ∨ for logical OR. These are defined in terms of the PL operators by:

$$w1 \wedge w2 \text{ is equivalent to } \neg(w1 \supset \neg w2)$$
$$w1 \vee w2 \text{ is equivalent to } \neg(\neg w1 \wedge \neg w2)$$

Logical identity, written ≡, is defined by:

$$w1 \equiv w2 \text{ is equivalent to the word } (w1 \supset w2) \wedge (w2 \supset w1)$$

These further definitions add to the richness of PL. The reader will see, on reflexion, that the system expresses the normal processes of deductive thought; in particular, the three Aristotelian principles can be formally established:

identity: ($p \supset p$)

excluded middle: ($p \vee \neg p$) (i.e. every word is either a theorem or a non -theorem)

non-contradiction: ¬($p \wedge \neg p$) (i.e. no word can be both a theorem and a non-theorem)

As an example of calculating with PL let us establish the first of these. If in the axiom A1 we write p for $w1$ and ($p \supset p$) for $w2$ we get:

($p \supset ((p \supset p) \supset p)$) which is therefore a theorem, $T1$ say

If we make the same substitution in $A2$ and p for $w3$ also we get a second theorem $T2$:

$$(p \supset ((p \supset p) \supset p)) \supset ((p \supset p)) \supset (p \supset p)))$$

The first word of $T2$ is simply the theorem $T1$, so applying *modus ponens* we get:

$$\vdash ((p \supset (p \supset p)) \supset (p \supset p) \qquad T3$$

and since $(p \supset (p \supset p))$ is itself a theorem, by $A1$ with $w1 = w2 = p$, a second application of *modus ponens* gives:

$$\vdash (p \supset p), \text{ as required} \qquad T4$$

Other fundamental theorems can be established by similar arguments; for example:

$$p \equiv \neg\neg p$$
$$\neg(p \vee q) \equiv (\neg p \wedge \neg q)$$
$$(p \supset q) \equiv (\neg p \vee q)$$

The third of these shows that proving $(p \supset q)$ is equivalent to proving $(\neg p \vee q)$; this is the principle of proof by *reductio ad absurdum* – cf. the Resolution Principle of Section 3.10.

As with the systems JP and DH considered previously, several meta-theorems are easily established for PL; for example:

$$p \rightarrow \neg^{2k} p \ (k \text{ any positive integer})$$
$$(p \& q) \leftrightarrow p \wedge q$$
$$(p \supset q) \& (q \supset r) \rightarrow (p \supset r)$$

The & here is a metalinguistic symbol and is not a word of PL; it is the same & as appears in *modus ponens*. It is not identical with the $\wedge$ of PL: $(p \supset q) \& (q \supset r)$ means that we have two theorems, $(p \supset q)$ and $(q \supset r)$.

Such metatheorems are useful, indeed indispensable, for shortening proofs and they enable new deduction rules to be established. To take an example, analogous to the theorem $(p \supset (q \supset r)) \supset (q \supset (p \supset r))$, which in PL is trivial if p, q, r are propositional letters, we can establish the much stronger result that:

$$(P \supset (Q \supset R)) \supset (Q \supset (P \supset R))$$

holds for *any* words P, Q, R of PL; which becomes a new deduction rule.

Suppose $(P \supset (Q \supset R))$ has already been established as a theorem of PL. We can make this coincide with the left side of the axiom $A2$ by substituting P, Q, R for $w1$, $w2$, $w3$ respectively and then by *modus ponens* we have $(P \supset Q) \supset (P \supset R)$ as a new theorem, say T. Substitution of T in $A1$ gives $(T \supset (w \supset T))$, where w is any word; and as T is a theorem, a second application of *modus ponens* gives:

$$(w \supset T), \text{ i.e. } (w \supset ((P \supset Q) \supset (P \supset R)))$$

Using $A2$ again, with $w1 = w$, $w2 = (P \supset Q)$, $w3 = (P \supset R)$ and applying *modus ponens* a third time, we get:

$$(w \supset (P \supset Q)) \supset (W \supset (P \supset R))$$

If we put $w = Q$ in this theorem, the left side becomes the axiom $A1$ and therefore, by a fourth application of *modus ponens*, we have:

$$(Q \supset (P \supset R))$$

which establishes the result.

Important note: notation. With a certain amount of misuse of language we can express the theorems compactly in the form:

$$H \Rightarrow C$$

meaning that the hypotheses H imply the conclusion(s) C. This is instead of the correct formal form $H \& H \supset C \rightarrow C$, and the symbol $\Rightarrow$ is a kind of concatenation of the $\supset$ of PL with the $\rightarrow$ of meta-PL, and includes modus ponens.

Much work has been done on PL since Aristotle and in 1910 Russell and Whitehead finally put it on a rigorous foundation and proved many results. Interestingly, their system rested on not three but four axioms and it was not until 20 years later that Lukasiewicz showed that one of these could be deduced from the others and was therefore redundant. It is the resulting 3-axiom system that we have given here; this involves two operators ($\neg$ and $\supset$) but it can in fact be based on a single operator, the 'Sheffer stroke |' defined by:

$$p \mid q \equiv (\neg p) \vee (\neg q) \qquad \text{[i.e. 'NAND' } - \text{ not } (p \text{ AND } q)]$$

J. Nicot showed in 1917 that in terms of this operator PL can be based on the single axiom:

$$(p \mid (q \mid r)) \mid (s \mid (s \mid s)) \mid ((t \mid q) \mid ((p \mid t) \mid (p \mid t)))$$

One writer on this subject comments: 'This illustrates what one has to pay in terms of complication and length if one wishes to use only the one connector. It can be proved that all the theorems of PL as we have defined the system can be proved with the aid of this single operator and this single axiom.'

3.4.1 Interpretation of PL

A fully rigorous and general interpretation of PL can be based on the 2-element set $B = \{0, 1\}$, where 0 and 1 play the roles of TRUE and FALSE respectively, together with the two functions:

$$C \text{ ('complement' defined by } C(x) = 1 - x$$
$$T \text{ ('true') defined by } T(x, y) = 1 \text{ iff } (x = 0, y = 1)$$

Let ϕ denote an application of propositional formulae in B with the properties:

$$\phi(\neg p) = C(\phi(p))$$
$$\phi(p \supset q) = T(\phi(p), \phi(q))$$

The second equation gives the rather counter-intuitive result that if $\phi(p)$ evaluates to 1 and $\phi(q)$ to 0 then $\phi(p \supset q) = \phi(1, 0) = 0$, i.e. FALSE $\supset$ TRUE is TRUE.

A word w of PL is said to be *valid*, or is a *tautology*, if and only if $\phi(w) = 0$ for every application ϕ that has the above two properties.

It is easy to show that the three axioms of PL are tautologies: for $A1$, for example:

$$\phi(w1 \supset (w2 \supset w1)) = T(\phi(w1), \phi(w2 \supset w1))$$
$$= T(\phi(w1), T(\phi(w2), \phi(w1)))$$

so if $w = (w1 \supset (w2 \supset w1))$, $\phi(w) = 0$ if $\phi(w1) = 1$ or $T(\phi(w2), \phi(w1)) = 0$. If $\phi(w1) = 1$, $\phi(w) = 0$ by definition. If $\phi(w1) = 0$ then by definition of T, $T(\phi(w2), 0)$ cannot be 1 and therefore $\phi(w) = 0$. Thus $\phi(w) = 0$ whatever the value of $\phi(w1)$, which means that $A1$ evaluates to TRUE for all interpretations ϕ and is therefore a tautology.

Further, if $(w1)$ and $(w1 \supset w2)$ are both tautologies, then since $\phi(w1 \supset w2) = T(\phi(w1), \phi(w2)) = T(0, \phi(w2)) = 0$, $\phi(w2)$ cannot be 1 and must therefore be 0; so $w2$ also is a tautology. This shows that the *modus ponens* rule is consistent in all interpretations.

The argument can be continued by induction on the length of the words deduced from the axioms (and therefore of arbitrary length), to give the following meta-theorem:

MT1: *every theorem in propositional logic is a tautology.*

The interpretation class defined above makes PL isomorphic to classical Boolean algebra with the addition of the operators $\lor$, $\land$ and complementation; from this a second important meta-theorem can be established:

MT2: *every tautology is a theorem in propositional logic*

An immediate consequence of these two meta-theorems is that *PL is decidable* but there is still the problem of finding an actual decision procedure.

3.4.2 Decidability of PL

In 1921 Emile Post proved the following:

A formula F is provable in PL if and only if it is valid, that is, is true in all interpretations.

Propositional logic is therefore:

- *non-contradictory*: formulae F and $\neg F$ cannot be proved simultaneously;
- *complete*: all theorems are valid words, and conversely;
- *decidable* (or *resolvable*).

Because all theorems of PL are tautologies, that is, propositions that take the value TRUE for all possible values TRUE (0) or FALSE (1) of all their variables, there is a decision procedure. This makes use of *truth tables*: for the elementary operators these are what intuition would suggest, as shown in Fig. 3.5. We see that in the interpretation we have used $p \supset q$ is FALSE only when p is TRUE and q is FALSE. In effect, $p \supset q$ is equivalent to $\neg p \vee q$; the normal interpretation of the symbol $\supset$ as 'implies' is rather unfortunate, since $(p \supset q)$ and $(\neg p \vee q)$ are TRUE if p is FALSE – a result sometimes stated as 'a false proposition implies anything'. The result does not accord well with the normal use of 'imply' in the language, and the interpretation has led to some difficulties.

The truth table method was established by Post in 1932; it is based on the result that for a word in PL to be a theorem it is necessary and sufficient that is has the truth value 0 for all possible truth values of its variables. As an example, Table 3.1 gives the truth table for the word:

$$(p \supset q) \supset ((q \supset r) \supset (p \supset r))$$

showing that this is a theorem. This coincidence of theorems with TRUE

for $\neg$

p	1	0
$\neg p$	0	1

for $\supset$

p	1	1	0	0
q	1	0	1	0
$p \supset q$	0	0	1	0

Fig. 3.5.

Table 3.1 A truth table for the word $(p \supset q) \supset ((q \supset r) \supset (p \supset r))$.

p	q	r	$q \supset r$	$p \supset q$	$p \supset r$	$(q \supset r) \supset (p \supset r)$	$(p \supset q) \supset ((q \supset r) \supset (p \supset r))$
0	0	0	0	0	0	0	0
0	0	1	1	0	1	0	0
0	1	0	0	1	0	0	0
0	1	1	0	1	1	1	0
1	0	0	0	0	0	0	0
1	0	1	1	0	0	0	0
1	1	0	0	0	0	0	0
1	1	1	0	0	0	0	0

interpretations is not, however, general: the system JP considered previously provides a counter-example.

The fundamental result, that PL is decidable, is a theorem of a metasystem that we have not developed; it is established by a process of recurrence on a sequence of meta-meta- ... systems, which we shall not go into here.

Post's result is remarkable in that it brings PL into coincidence with our normal logical reasoning processes and shows that these, at least in part, can be formalised and reduced to purely symbolic schemas. It was precisely here that the greatest difficulties were expected in the great programme for the formalisation of all mathematics proposed by Hilbert in 1885; and after they had been overcome, with such rigour and such elegance, it was later, in connection with the formal theory of arithmetic, that new difficulties arose.

3.5 FIRST-ORDER PREDICATE CALCULUS

The very first example given in this chapter, starting 'All men are mortal', cannot be expressed in propositional logic: the statement brings in a *quantified* variable, (all) men, and the quantifier 'all' conveys the concept of *universality*, expressed formally as:

every x that has the property 'man' has the property 'mortal'

A formal system capable of expressing this must be richer than PL; the propositions p, q, r, ..., can no longer be considered as entities in themselves but must involve parameters that refer to specified individuals, and in such a system the above statement is written:

$$(\forall x)(\text{man}(x) \supset \text{mortal}\,(x))$$

where 'man' and 'mortal' are *predicates* and x is a quantified or *bound* variable, the *universal* quantifier $\forall$ meaning 'for all' or 'whatever'.

In the formal system called the first-order predicate calculus (PrC) the predicates themselves are not quantified. It is defined as follows.

1. Alphabet. constants: $a, b, c, d, \ldots$
variables: $t, u, v, w, x, \ldots$
predicates: $A, B, C, D, \ldots$
quantifier: $\forall$ ('for all ...')

2. Words.   As for PL but with the addition that a *weight k* is assigned to each predicate and $A(x_1, x_2, \ldots, x_k)$ is a word iff the weight assigned to A is k
$((\forall x_1)A(x_1, x_2, \ldots, x_k)$ is a word in which
x_1 is a *bound* variable
x_i, $i \geqslant 2$, is a *free* variable

3. Axioms.   The three axioms of PL and additionally
A4: $((\forall t)B(t)) \supset B(u)$ (axiom of *particularisation*)
A5: $((\forall t)(w_1 \supset w_2)) \supset (w_1 \supset (\forall t)w_2)$ where w_1, w_2 are any words of PrC and t is not a free variable in w_1.

4. Rules. $(w_1) \& (w_1 \supset w_2) \to w_2$ (modus ponens)
$w_1 \to (\forall t)w_1$ (generalisation)
where t is a free variable in w_1.

Axiom $A4$, also called the axiom of specification, plays a fundamental role; the variable t is said to be *instantiated* by the variable u, and u becomes a free variable.

As in PL the symbols $\vee$, $\wedge$ and $\equiv$ are used and there is a second quantifier, the $\exists$ ('there exists ...'); $\forall$ and $\exists$ are related by the identity:

$$(\exists x)B(x) \equiv \neg((\forall x)\neg B(x))$$

Any formal system whose axioms include those of PrC is said to be of first order; the many such systems that have been constructed are variants of PrC in which one or more further axioms and/or rules have been added.

As already stated, the term 'first-order' means that the quantifiers $\forall$, $\exists$ can act only on the predicate variables, and not on the predicates themselves; 'second-order' would mean that the predicates could be quantified, and higher orders would bring in predicates of predicates and so on.

As an example of a proof in PrC, consider the following:

for any predicate D of weight 2, $(\forall y)(\forall x)D(x, y) \supset (\forall x)(\forall y)D(x, y)$

Putting $t = y$ in A4, the left side of this relation becomes:

$$(\forall y)(\forall x)D(x, y) \supset (\forall x)D(x, y)$$

and then, with $t = x$:

$$(\forall x)D(x, y) \supset D(x, y)$$

From A5 we have:

$$D(x, y) \supset (\forall y)D(x, y)$$

and

$$(\forall y)D(x, y) \supset (\forall x)(\forall y)D(x, y)$$

Finally, the meta-theorem $(A \supset B) \& (B \supset C) \rightarrow (A \supset C)$ can be proved to hold for PrC just as for *PL*, so the result follows.

The following important PrC theorems can be proved similarly:

$$(\exists y)(\forall x)D(x, y) \supset (\exists x)(\forall y)D(x, y)$$

$$\neg((\forall x)(\forall y)D(x, y)) \supset (\exists x)(\exists y)(\neg D(x, y))$$

$$\neg((\exists x)(\exists y)D(x, y)) \supset (\forall x)(\forall y)(\neg D(x, y))$$

$$(\forall x)D(x) \supset (\exists x)D(x)$$

3.5.1 Gödel's first theorem, the 'completeness' of first-order predicate calculus

Gödel proved the following in 1930:

> *The theorems of first-order predicate calculus coincide exactly with the logically valid formulae, that is, with the formulae that are TRUE in all interpretations.*

This is the analogue for PrC of Post's theorem for PL; but unfortunately, for reasons that will be explained in Section 3.6.3, it does not lead to a decision procedure.

3.5.2 The formal system of arithmetic

In 1899 Guiseppe Peano expressed arithmetic as a formal system; his system is an extension of PrC by the introduction of a special constant and the addition of four new operators and nine new axioms, as follows.

Constant: 0 (zero – the only constant of the system)
Operators: s (successor) (weight 1)
$\quad\quad\quad\quad$ $s(0)$ is denoted by 1 and $s(n)$ by $(n + 1)$
$\quad\quad$ + (plus)
$\quad\quad$ * (multiplied by)
$\quad\quad$ = (equal: this plays a special role in the new axioms)
Axioms:$\quad$ A6$\quad$ $(\forall x(x + 0) = x$
$\quad\quad\quad\quad$ A7$\quad$ $(\forall x)(x*0) = 0$
$\quad\quad\quad\quad$ A8$\quad$ $(\forall x)\neg s(x) = 0$

A9 $(\forall x)(\forall y)(x + s(y)) = s(x + y)$
A10 $(\forall x)(\forall y)(x*s(y)) = x*y + x$
A11 $(\forall x)(\forall y)(s(x) = s(y)) \supset (x = y)$
A12 $(\forall x)(\forall y)(x = y) \supset (s(x) = s(y))$
A13 $(\forall x)(\forall y)(\forall z)(x = y) \supset ((x = z) \supset (y = z))$
A14 $(A(0) \& (\forall u)(A(u) \supset A(s(u)))) \supset (\forall u)(A(u))$

The last axiom, called the axiom of complete induction, formalises the process of reasoning by recurrence. Notice that a number of very basic relations are not given as axioms, but have to be derived from these; for example:

$$(x = y) \supset (y = x), \qquad \text{and } x + y = y + x$$

This formalisation of arithmetic is of the greatest importance. We have in effect assumed it earlier in this book, for it underlies the meta-theorems we have used implicitly in our discussion of the system JP and DH. Let us now look more closely at the relations between those systems and arithmetic.

JP was defined by

> axiom (A): $a\square a$
>
> rule (R): $u\square v \rightarrow bu\square bv$

with u, v any strings whatever of the characters a, b.

The symbols a, b, $\square$ of this system are merely *codes* that can be replaced by any others, for example by 1, 2, 3 respectively; and with that replacement the axiom is 1 3 1 and the rule states that 'if the string u followed by 3 followed by v is a theorem then so also is the string 2 followed by u followed by 3 followed by 2 followed by v.'

However, the operation 'is followed by', which acts on the symbols of this system, has a corresponding operation in arithmetic: in ordinary decimal arithmetic, the number 'x followed by y' is formed by multiplying x by the appropriate power of 10 and adding y to the product. More precisely, if y is a number of n decimal digits, that is, can be written as:

$$\sum_{i=0}^{n-1} c_i *10^i \qquad \text{where } c_{n-1} \text{ is not zero}$$

the number 'x followed by y' is simply $x*10^n + y$.

To express the rule in these terms, suppose u, v are numbers with m, n decimal digits respectively; starting on the right, the number '2 followed by v' is $10^n*2 + v$ and is of $n + 1$ digits. '3 followed by 2 followed by v' is then $10^{n+1}*3 + 10^n*2 + v$, of $n + 2$ digits. This has to follow '2 followed by u', which is the number $10^m z + u$; so the final number generated by the rule is

$$(10^m*2 + u)*10^{n+2} + 10^{n+1}*3 + 10^n*2 + v$$

Thus the rule R has been completely arithmetised and in this interpretation of the system states the following: if u, v are any decimal numbers of m and n digits respectively, and if

$$10^{n+1}*u + 10^n*3 + v$$

is a theorem then

$$(10^m*2 + u)*10^{n+2} + 10^{n+1}*3 + 10^n*2 + v$$

is a theorem. If we take $u = v = 221$, so that $m = n = 3$, from the theorem 2213221 we get, by applying the rule,

$$(10^3*2 + 221)*10^5 + 10^4*3 + 10^3*2 + 221$$

and the result that 222132221 is a theorem.

The conclusion is that the study of the system JP can be reduced to that of a sub-system of formal arithmetic.

We can treat the system DH similarly. If we replace the symbols M, I, U by 2, 1, 0 respectively the axiom becomes 2 1; and if we write the rule R3 in the form $uIIIv \mapsto uUv$ and take u, v as before as decimal numbers of m, n digits respectively, this becomes: if

$$u*10^{n+3} + 111*10^n + v$$

is a theorem then

$$u*10^{n+1} + v$$

is a theorem. Thus DH also can be embedded in formal arithmetic.

The result is that the proofs of theorems and meta-theorems in JP and DH can be reduced to proofs in formal arithmetic; and of course, any formal system so arithmetised can be given an arithmetical interpretation. For example, if in the arithmetised JP we interpret

'1' as the ordinary digit 1
'2' as 'successor'
'3' as ' = '

the theorem 222132221 interprets as the 'true' statement '4 = 4: we have closed the loop.

The type of process we have just described contains the germ of the idea that led finally to Gödel's second theorem.

3.5.3 Gödel's second theorem: the incompleteness of arithmetic

Any formal system can be arithmetised: in particular, propositional logic, predicate calculus – and formal arithmetic itself. The idea behind Gödel's proof is suggested by this strange piece of self-reference; it leads to an arithmetical variant of the 'paradox of the liar' due to Eubulides of Miletus, dialectician of the Megarian School (fourth century BC, founded by Eucleides the companion of Socrates). The statement of the 'paradox' is:

Epimenides the Cretan says 'All Cretans are liars'

Statements of this kind have been put forward as criticisms of Aristotelian logic; they do not fit into the syllogistic mould, and were much discussed by the Stoics and their followers. Actually, there is no paradox: if we assume that Epimenides is a liar then what he says is false; the negation of his statement, which is therefore true, is that there is at least one Cretan who is not a liar, and there is nothing contradictory about this. The classical error here is to interpret the negation wrongly and thence to deduce the paradox.

After the ancient Greeks there was a long period in which no new results in logic were obtained; the subject had to wait until first Leibniz and later the modern logicians took up their work again, systematised it and embedded it in the general body of mathematics. And all this led finally to Gödel's second theorem: there are words w in formal arithmetic such that neither w nor $\neg w$ can be proved.

In the proof we shall give of this theorem we make use of the work of Jean Ladrière in his '*Les limitations internes des formalismes*' (Nauwelaerts & Gauthier Villars 1957) and that of Douglas Hofstadter in his *Gödel, Escher, Bach*. But first let us recall a result that must have influenced Gödel, the 'diagonal process' of Cantor, who in 1873 proved that the set of real numbers is not enumerable. Considering only the real numbers between 0 and 1, Cantor started with the assumption that these are enumerable and therefore can be listed in some order, say $a_1, a_2, \ldots a_n \ldots$ They are infinite in number but the assumption of enumerability means that any real number between 0 and 1 appears somewhere in this list.

Cantor's next step was to represent each number as an infinite decimal, e.g.

$$a_i = 0.a_{i1}a_{i2} \ldots a_{ij} \ldots$$

the a_{ij} all being integers 0, 1, ... or 9. The list is thus:

$$0.a_{11}a_{12} \ldots a_{1n} \ldots$$
$$0.a_{21}a_{22} \quad a_{2n}$$
$$\vdots$$
$$0.a_{n1}a_{n2} \quad a_{nn}$$
$$\vdots$$

The final step was to construct a number b:

$$b = b_1 b_2 \ldots b_n \ldots$$

such that for all i, $b_i = a_{ii} + 1$, or $a_{ii} - 1$ if $a_{ii} = 9$. This number does not appear in the list: it differs from a_1 in the first decimal place, from a_2 in the second, ... from a_n in the nth.... But it is a real number between 0 and 1, thus contradicting the hypothesis and proving that the reals cannot be enumerated.

The essential idea in the 'diagonalisation' is that every integer k is used in two ways: to specify the position of a real number in the list and of a digit in the expansion of each number as an infinite decimal. Closely related to this procedure is a paradox due to J. Richard (1907), consideration of which will take us closer to Gödel's method.

Richard's paradox. This depends not on the concept of 'truth', as does Eubulides's, but on that of definition.

Consider the defining of an integer – in some natural language – English, for example; any integer can be specified unequivocally by a finite set of symbols – letters, digits, punctuation symbols – and clearly there are many different ways of specifying any given number. Let us adopt the convention that we always select the shortest specification, meaning the one with the least number of symbols.

Now consider the sub-set S of integers whose shortest specification requires fewer than 100 symbols. This is a finite set because there is only a finite number of permutations of 100 symbols, and since all the members of S are integers there will be a least member. Call this L. L can then be defined as 'the least integer than can be defined in fewer than 100 symbols'. But this definition uses fewer than 100 symbols, so we have a contradiction. The paradox is related to the circularity of our definition.

The first stage in Gödel's proof is the coding in numerical form of all the statements of formal arithmetic; this is followed by the construction of a 'paradoxical' statement, leading finally to the famous theorem: there is a statement $E*$ in formal arithmetic which is such that neither $E*$ nor $\neg E*$ can be proved in formal arithmetic.

3.5.4   Basis of Gödel's proof

The essential idea is to construct an expression that itself confirms that it cannot be proved. This is done in three stages:

1. Setting up a 1:1 correspondence between the system of formal arithmetic and the integers: this is called Gödelisation.

2. Constructing a certain property $(A(x)$ about which one does not know whether or not it is a theorem of formal arithmetic.
3. Substituting for x in $A(x)$ the integer corresponding to $A(x)$ itself.

We now look at these in turn: it is convenient to abbreviate 'the system of formal arithmetic' to FA.

(a) Gödelisation of FA (giving GFA). We shall how FA can be arithmetised; when this has been done every theorem is coded by an integer, every number can be interpreted as a theorem and every theorem can be understood in two different ways – as a theorem in FA and as a theorem *about* theorems in FA; that is, as a meta-theorem corresponding to the proof of a theorem. This last is equivalent to the important statement: FA contains its own meta-system.

To be more specific:

1. As we have seen in previous cases, we can specify a way to associate each symbol u of FA with a unique integer; this is called the Gödel number for u, written $G(u)$.
2. If U is any string of symbols (u_i) we can assign to this a Gödel number $G(U)$ with the aid of a function f, giving $G(U) = f(G(u_i))$.
3. Since any proof Δ consists of a sequence of theorems, (U_j) say, and every theorem U_j itself consists of a string of symbols constituting the axioms, rules and substitutions used in its proof, a Gödel number $G(\Delta) = f(G(U_j))$ can be assigned to any proof.

Thus any argument in FA can be translated into a calculation with the integers, and in particular the symbol manipulation required by a proof reduced to such a calculation. More precisely, to any statement such as 't can be proved in FA' there corresponds a unique determinate number that we shall denote be Dem (t). All this is equivalent to the statement

The formal system meta-Fa is contained in the set of integers $\mathbb{N}$ *which is itself contained in an interpretation of FA i.e. meta-FA* $\subset \mathbb{N} \subset$ *FA.*

and FA is in the position of a natural language for which there is nothing to prevent it from being used to discuss itself.

A suitable choice of the function f makes the relation between Δ and $G(\Delta)$ injective, that is, such that different Gödel numbers correspond to different theorems. Gödel's first step is to code each symbol by a prime, as in Table 3.2. A formula U consisting of the q symbols u_i, $i = 1, 2, ..., q$, is then coded by:

$$G(U) = 2^{G(u_1)} * 3^{G(u_2)} * 5^{G(u_3)} * \cdots * p_q^{G(u_q)} \qquad (p_q = q\text{th prime})$$

A proof Δ consisting of the sequence of r formulae $U_1, U_2, ..., U_r$ is then

Table 3.2 Arithmetisation of the alphabet of FA.

u	$=$	0	$*$	$+$	1	σ	$\supset$	$\neg$	$\vee$	$\wedge$	$\forall$	$\exists$	$($	$)$	$\equiv$	x	y	$\cdots$
$G(u)$	2	3	5	7	11	13	17	19	23	29	31	37	41	43	47	53	59	$\cdots$

coded by:

$$G(\Delta) = 2^{G(U_1)} * 3^{G(U_2)} * 5^{G(U_3)} * \cdots * p_r^{G(U_r)}$$

Conversely, the process can be reversed and by decomposition into prime factors – which, by the fundamental theorem of arithmetic, can be done in only one way – a unique theorem can be associated with any given number. This general statement is true only in a theoretical sense, because the numbers become much too great to be manipulable practically; but the essential point is that the possibility exists.

For example, suppose we have found that a given number has only the prime factors 2 and 3 and in terms of powers of these is:

$$2^{1981027125 \, * \, 2^{53}} * 3^{1981027125 \, * \, 2^{11}}$$

This shows that the proof of the corresponding theorem Δ is in two stages, the first corresponding to the number $1981027125 * 2^{53}$ and the second to $1981027125 * 2^{11}$. Factorising these gives:

$$2^{53} * 3^5 * 5^3 * 7^2 * 11^3 \quad \text{and} \quad 2^{11} * 3^5 * 5^3 * 7^2 * 11^3$$

and therefore the numbers correspond to the sequences of symbols coded by:

$$53, 5, 3, 2, 3 \quad \text{and} \quad 11, 5, 3, 2, 3 \text{ respectively}$$

which interprets to:

from the word $x * 0 = 0$ can be deduced the word $1 * 0 = 0$

and from a purely arithmetical number we have derived a meta-theorem in FA.

(b) Gödel's Lemma. This 'Gödelisation' of FA gives the system we call GFA, to every axiom and every rule of which there corresponds an arithmetical operation. Thus it is possible, by a wholly systematic procedure, to find if a given number T corresponds to a proof of a theorem of FA, which theorem itself corresponds to a number t. We say that two such numbers form a conjugated pair. Therefore Gödel's lemma says that the statement 'T and t are conjugates' can itself be expressed as a number in

GFA; that is, there is a Gödel number, $D(T, t)$ say, that represents this statement.

This brings us to the crucial point in Gödel's proof. Suppose A is a statement in GFA that contains a free variable; any term whatever can be substituted for this variable, in particular the statement A itself. The GFA statement A is a number and, analogous to Cantor's diagonalisation procedure and Richard's paradox, this plays two different roles: here the original statement A and the term that is substituted in A. Let us call this process substitution-* and denote it by S^*, and write $S^*(A, n)$ for the statement that n is the Gödel number obtained when the operation substitution-* is performed on A:

$$S^*(A, n) \Leftrightarrow n \text{ is the *-substituent of } A$$

Gödel now constructs a statement, not known to be either a theorem or a non-theorem, that contains this substitution S^*; the statement, e, is:

$$e \qquad \neg((\exists T)(\exists t)D(T, t) \wedge S^*(F, n)) \qquad \text{with } F \text{ a free variable}$$

(c) Final substitution. Let E be the Gödel number corresponding to this statement e; since F is a free variable we can apply substitution-* and replace F by E; and denoting by t the *-substituent of E we get:

$$\neg((\exists T)(\exists t)D(T, t) \wedge S^*(E, t))$$

Call this e^*, and let its Gödel number be E^*. Interpreting e^* we have:

1. There is no pair of numbers (T, t) such that T is the number of the arithmetised proof of the arithmetised theorem t, and also t is the *-substituent of E^*, i.e. $S^*(E, t)$ does not hold. But since S^* is a transformation like any other, it can be expressed in terms of the alphabetical symbols $+, *, /$, etc., and therefore by a Gödel number; so a number t exists. Therefore, perhaps, it is the number T that does not exist, and whatever the case a new interpretation of e^* is required; the first possibility is (2) below.
2. There is no proof arithmetised to T of the theorem t where t is the *-substituent of E; this may be because t is not in fact a theorem, leading to the further interpretation of (3) below.
3. The statement whose Gödel number is the *-substituent of E is not a theorem of GFA; but this gives a contradiction, because, by construction, e^* is the *-substituent of E and t is simply the number E^* itself. There is therefore the final interpretation.
4. e^* is not a theorem of GFA.

Thus the statement e^* is simply saying:

I am not a theorem

from which one of two things follows:

- either e^* is a theorem, but then FA is self-contradictory because we have proved both e^* and $\neg e^*$
- or e^* is not a theorem, in which case the contradiction disappears: but then what e^* says is true but cannot be proved.

It follows from this second conclusion that there are regions of *unattainable truths* in the system; and so, having proved that $\neg e^*$ itself cannot be proved, we have arrived at Gödel's second theorem:

If formal arithmetic is not self-contradictory then it is incomplete.

which means that, rejecting the self-contradictory possibility, there is at least one statement e^* such that $\nvdash e^*$ and $\nvdash \neg e^*$, where '$\nvdash t$' means 't is a non-theorem'.

The conclusion that arithmetic is either self-contradictory or incomplete must extend to all formal systems that include the axioms of arithmetic; and further, the proof shows that the absence of self-contradiction cannot be proved by the methods of the systems itself. The situation is summarised in Fig. 3.6.

Notes on this section. We have given a sketch of Gödel's proof because the principle on which it rests is at one and the same time rigorous, fundamental and hard to grasp. The proof touches on the hidden, but intrinsic, limitations of those systems, not especially powerful, for manipulation of symbols that include numbers. It is not easy to follow at a first reading, and the reader will probably need to go back to the list of principles at the beginning of Section 5.3; there may be some consolation in recalling that its validity was, initially, attacked by many mathematicians – Ladrière quotes 'refutations' by Pereleman, Barzin and Kurzynski.

It might be thought that the intrinsic limitations would be removed if either e^* or $\neg e^*$ were added as an axiom to FA; but in fact this would serve

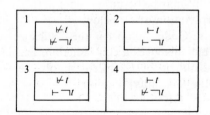

Class 1: non-empty undecidable statements			Class 2: empty if the system is non- self-contradictory
1 $\nvdash t$ $\nvdash \neg t$		2 $\vdash t$ $\vdash \neg t$	
3 $\nvdash t$ $\vdash \neg t$		4 $\vdash t$ $\nvdash \neg t$	Classes 3, 4: symmetrical, no difficulties

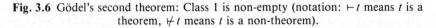

Fig. 3.6 Gödel's second theorem: Class 1 is non-empty (notation: $\vdash t$ means t is a theorem, $\nvdash t$ means t is a non-theorem).

no purpose, for the same process would then show that a new proposition, e^{**} say, could be constructed which was undecidable.

3.6   THEOREMS ON THE LIMITATIONS OF FORMAL SYSTEMS

Gödel's theorem was the first great limitation theorem to be discovered and has had tremendous repercussions in mathematics and in the philosophy of science. It is not, however, the only theorem of this nature; we now state two others, due to Tarski and Church respectively, that are of great theoretical and practical importance.

Tarski's theorem (1935)

> *There are formal systems for which in every interpretation there are true statements that cannot be derived from the axioms.*

The 'interpretation' of a formal system was defined in Section 4.3. Tarski's theorem is the semantic counterpart – that is, as concerns interpretation – of Gödel's; briefly, it states that not all that is true can be proved, or, to put it another way, the concept of truth cannot be formalised. The theorem does not say that it is always the same true statements that cannot be proved, whatever the interpretation, but that in every interpretation there is at least one word that is always interpreted as TRUE but is not a theorem of the system.

The concept of interpretation enters into both Gödel's and Tarski's theorems. This is self-evident for Tarski's; Gödel's proof involves the normal interpretation of the symbol $\neg$ (negation), and also the postulate of non-contradiction (both t and $\neg t$ cannot be derived simultaneously – for otherwise, as is easily shown, every word is a theorem and the system is of no interest).

Church's theorem (1936)

> *There are formal systems that are undecidable; in particular, first-order predicate calculus is undecidable.*

This is a strictly syntactic theorem; of the three it is the most fundamental. It is saying that there are formal systems for which it is not possible to construct a procedure that will separate the theorems from the non-theorems. Another way of stating this is that certain formal systems are non-resolvable, or are not recursively enumerable. Naturally one would like to avoid the need to use such systems, but in fact it is impossible to do so because, as Church has shown, first-order predicate calculus itself is undecidable; and the more powerful system of Russell and Whitehead's Principia Mathematica is, *à fortiori*, undecidable also. Tarski has shown that the theories of groups, of rings and of fields are all undecidable, but that projective geometry and the theory of closed real fields are decidable. Further, it can be proved that first-order predicate calculus is *semidecidable*, meaning that if *t* is in fact a theorem there is a finite process that will establish this.

All the proofs just referred to depend on the definition of a decision procedure. Church stated that the idea of an *effective* or *computable* procedure was identical to that of an *algorithm*, that is, a recursive function: this is 'Church's thesis'.

Independently of this work, Turing in 1937 formalised the concept of a 'machine' and reduced the problem of decidability to that of determining whether or not an ideal machine would halt within a finite time (see Section 5.2). The two approaches were finally seen to be equivalent, giving the result that in general there is neither a recursive function nor a program for a Turing machine that will decide whether or not a given word is a theorem of a given formal system. In particular, the halting problem for a Turing machine is undecidable.

The consequences of these limitation theorems can be compared to the effect on physics of the Heisenberg uncertainty principle – interestingly, established several years earlier (in 1927) by means of quantum-mechanical arguments. This states that certain pairs of physical properties are linked in such a way that whatever the precision to which either can be measured separately, there is a lower limit to the product of the precisions to which the two can be measured simultaneously: so if the precision of one measurement is increased that of the other is decreased. This lower limit is a universal constant, Planck's constant h; if for example the position s and the momentum p of a particle are measured with precisions Δs, Δp the relation is:

$$\Delta s * \Delta p > h$$

Philosophers and information scientists such as J. R. Lucas, E. Nagel and J. R. Newman have used the limitation theorems to emphasise the limitations of symbol-manipulating machines – that is, of computers; and they deduce, rather too quickly to my mind, that man is inherently superior intellectually to the machine. Similar arguments are still heard, and there are people who use them to condemn all work on artificial intelligence. But what in fact the Gödel, Tarski and Church theorems (Table 3.3) are saying is simply that certain problems cannot be solved by the methods of mathematics as we know them, and the consequential limitations apply to us just as to the machines – to the mathematician just as to the program. And the discovery of these theorems around 1930 did not bring mathemati-

Table 3.3 The theorems of limitation for formal systems.

Gödel: At least one word w exists such that neither w nor $\neg w$ can be proved.

Tarski: In every interpretation there are true statements that cannot be proved.

Church: There is no algorithm that will separate theorems from non-theorems.

cal research to a stop − far from it: some problems may be impossible to solve but others are worth attacking. Further, it is a new line of research to find which problems are especially difficult and why: it is still to be decided whether, for example, the Goldbach conjecture or Fermat's 'Last theorem' are provable or undecidable. It was not until 1970 that Yuri Matiyasevich proved that Hilbert's Tenth Problem − to construct a finite procedure that finds the integer solutions, if any exist, to any given algebraic equation − posed with 22 others in 1905, is undecidable.

Another illustration is provided by the famous four colour problem: what is the maximum number of colours needed to colour a map so that no two regions having a common boundary have the same colour? F. Guthrie in the middle of the last century conjectured that the number was 4, but 120 years elapsed − during which many unsuccessful attacks were made − until Appel and Haken, at the University of Illinois, proved this − with the essential help of a computer. We discuss this problem in Chapter 5.

The lesson to be learned here is: if a problem seems hard, first make sure that it is not one of a class known to be undecidable; if it is not, do not give up too quickly.

3.7 THE UNIFICATION ALGORITHM

The algorithm that we shall describe in this section is a response to the question 'How can we apply a theorem to an expression?' This algorithm is completely independent of any particular formal system, and for any given theorem and expression it works steadily through the two in an order that is fixed in advance, with no back-tracking and no choice to be made during the process; its complexity is a linear function of the total number of substitutable variables in the theorem and the expression together. We have in fact used this algorithm implicitly in the preceding paragraphs in obtaining some proofs in different formal systems.

Mathematicians seem not to make use of this algorithm, even in works on logic. Its discovery in 1966 by Jacques Pitrat in the work for his thesis, and independently by J. A. Robinson, resulted in a sudden jump in performance in theorem-proving programs. It is of fundamental importance in artificial intelligence.

3.7.1 The problem

Given a theorem T, which can be a re-write or production rule:

$$T: \quad H \quad \mapsto \quad C$$
$$\text{(hypothesis)} \quad \text{implies} \quad \text{(conclusions)}$$

and an expression E, the problem is to find if H and E can be made identical: that is, to *unify* H and E by a sequence of substitutions for the free variables. If this can be done then, by *modus ponens*, making the same substitutions in C will give a new form for the expression E resulting from the application of the theorem T.

Example 1. The classical algebraic identity:

$$(a + b)^2 = a^2 + 2ab + b^2 \quad I_1$$

considered as a convenient abbreviation of a re-write rule, states: 'If an expression is the square of the sum of two terms it can be re-written in the form of the square of the first term, augmented by twice the product of the two terms and augmented again by the square of the second term.'

Suppose we have the expression E_1

$$x^2 + (y + \sqrt{3})^2 \quad E_1$$

We have long been familiar with the way to make the term in parentheses coincide with the left side of I_1: the simple substitution of y for a and $\sqrt{3}$ for b will unify $(y + \sqrt{3})$ and this left side.

Example 2. Similarly, the well-known trigonometric re-write rule:

$$\sin^2 u + \cos^2 u \mapsto 1 \quad I_2$$

can be applied to the expression:

$$\sin^2 3x + \cos^2 3x \quad E_2$$

to show that this also is identical to 1. But of course the process fails for:

$$\sin^2 3x + \cos^2 x \quad E_3$$

It fails also for:

$$\cos^2 3x + \sin^2 3x \quad E_4$$

because we must first apply the theorem of the commutivity of the operator $+$, i.e.

$$a + b \mapsto b + a$$

Applying this to E_4 gives E_2 again and I_2 can then be applied.

Example 3. The unifications required in the above examples are particularly simple, but this is not always the case. The question of what substitutions to choose arises; there may be several different ways in which the coincidence can be brought about, and some of these may result in formulae that are merely particular cases that can be deduced from a more general form. As an example in propositional logic, consider the expression:

$$(p \supset (q \supset p)) \qquad E_5$$

which, by the first axiom of PL, is a theorem, and the meta-theorem:

$$((P \supset Q) \supset R) \to (Q \supset R) \qquad T_1$$

We give first a set of substitutions that is non-optimal; this, as we shall see, results in a new expression that is correct but is uninteresting because it is too specific.

Recall first the basic rules of the process: in PL the propositional letters $p, q, r, \ldots$ and the words $P, Q, R, \ldots$ are free variables and in any formula every occurrence of any one of these can be replaced by the same term provided only that that term does not contain the variable substituted. To bring T_1 and E_5 into coincidence we can try some tentative substitutions: thus the substitution that changes Q in T_1 to q gives:

$$((P \supset q) \supset R) \to (q \supset R) \qquad E_6 \; [Q/q]$$

and if in E_5 we change p to $P \supset q$ so as to unify the first components of E_5 and E_6 we get:

$$(P \supset q) \supset (q \supset (P \supset q)) \qquad E_7 \; [p/(P \supset q)]$$

This substituted form of E_5 will coincide with the left side of the substituted form of T_1 provided R is changed to $(q \supset (P \supset q))$; and then, analogously to the previous examples, the required result is given by the corresponding new form of the right side of E_6:

$$(q \supset (q \supset (P \supset q))) \qquad E_8 \; [R/(q \supset (P \supset q))]$$

However, we shall see that the unification algorithm gives the result:

$$(p \supset (q \supset (P \supset p))) \qquad E_9$$

without any trial-and-error whatever; and this is clearly more general, E_8 being the weaker result obtained by putting $p \equiv q$ in E_9.

The unification algorithm is of two-fold importance: it provides a direct and systematic process of substitution for bringing two arbitrary formulae into coincidence, provided that this is theoretically possible, and the result so obtained is the most general possible.

3.7.2   Principle of the algorithm

The expression E and the theorem T are scanned in parallel and unified step by step, and only essential unifications are performed. If the process reaches the end of the hypothesis part of T then the unification has succeeded and the result is the conclusion part C modified by the same substitutions; if not, this is a check and the unification is not possible.

There are several points to be remembered. In any expression it is only the free variables that can be substituted, that is, variables not quantified by either $\forall$ or $\exists$; and the only substitutions allowed are the replacement of a free variable x of E or H by a term t of E or H, with the single restriction that the term t must not contain the variable x. It is because of this restriction that, to avoid any ambiguity, the first step is to rename the variables of E or of H so that no variable name is common to both.

Substitutions are made only when they are indispensable to progress in E and H simultaneously, and only such substitutions are made. No symbols other than names of variables can be substituted, neither operators such as $+, *, \supset, \sin \ldots$ nor constants such as $1, 2, \pi, \ldots$; unsubstitutable symbols must be encountered simultaneously in the same places in E and H for the unification to be possible.

The basic idea of the algorithm is related to a process for scanning an expression: principle operator first, then each of the sub-terms that it applies to, starting on the left and working towards the right; the same rule applies to each sub-term in turn, principle operator first and then sub-sub-terms from left to right, and so on until either a variable or a constant is reached. Representation of an expression as a tree is well adapted to this process, as is shown in Fig. 3.7. This is what is called 'depth first' scanning; we defined two indices, e and h:

e: index for the symbol currently being scanned in E
h: index for the symbol currently being scanned in H

The scanning process for the unification is one of recurrence, as follows:

having unified E and H up to but not including e and h, an attempt is made to bring e and h into coincidence.

There are four possibilities at each such step, since each of the symbols indexed by e and h can be substitutable or not. If a substitution has to be

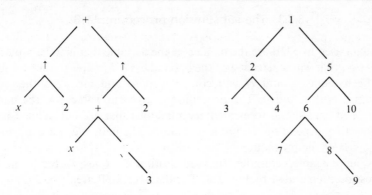

Fig. 3.7 Tree representation of $E = x^2 + (y + \sqrt{3})^2$, with scanning order.

made this is done by means of a specific procedure called SUB, which we
now give.

Table 3.4.

---

procedure SUB
               DATA: v free variable
                          t term
                          e, h index in E, H
               RESULTS: FALSE if substitution is not possible
                                 TRUE otherwise; then new E, H, e, h
               SUB ← TRUE
               SCAN H starting at the beginning
                      if current_symbol $= v$ **then** SUB ← FALSE
                          RETURN (case of failure 1)
                      end if
               end SCAN
e ← index__term__following__term__beginning e
h ← index__term__following__term__beginning h
(the parts of E and H already treated are no longer relevant so e and h must be
updated; we know that the first parts of E, H are identical)
               SCAN E starting from e
                      if current_symbol $= v$ **then** <u>replace</u> current symbol by t
                      end if
               end SCAN
               SCAN T starting from h
                      if current_symbol $= v$ **then** <u>replace</u> current symbol by t
                      end if
               end SCAN
               store substitution (v, t)
end SUB

3.7.3 The substitution procedure: SUB

The data used by SUB are the name v of the variable that is to be replaced, the term t that will replace it and the two indices e, h. After the substitution has been made, E and H will coincide up to and including the terms beginning with e and h. The procedure is given in Table 3.4; the names underlined correspond to elementary functions that are not defined here, because they depend on the implementation. The indices e, h are advanced at the end of the procedure.

As an example, consider the substitution of $(y + \sqrt{3})$ for x in the expression represented by Fig. 3.8. The data for SUB are:

$$v = x \qquad t = y + \sqrt{3} \qquad e = 3 \qquad h = 1$$

The procedure goes as follows:

SCAN H the current symbol is not v, so substitution is possible
$e \leftarrow 4$ (index of next term in E)
$h \leftarrow 5$ (index of next term in H)

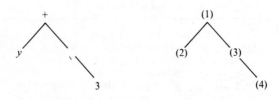

Fig. 3.8 Representation of t $y + \sqrt{3}$.

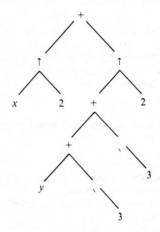

Fig. 3.9 New form of E after substitution.

SCAN E   starting from $e = 4$ the current symbol x is met again at
              index 7 and is replaced by t; E then becomes as in Fig. 3.9
SCAN (T)   this has no object at the moment

At the end of SUB x has been replaced only in the useful part of the
expressions; the first parts are assumed to have been unified already.

We now describe the unification algorithm itself.

3.7.4 Body of the unification algorithm (Table 3.5)

Table 3.5.

---

procedure UNIFICATION
    DATA: E expression $T = (H, C)$ theorem (hypothesis, conclusion)
    RESULTS: TRUE, new E, new C list of substitutions if successful
                FALSE otherwise
                $e \leftarrow$ head__of__expression of (E) $s(e) =$ symbol in e in E
                $h \leftarrow$ head__of__expression of (H) $s(h) =$ symbol in h in H
    SCAN in parallel E, H starting at e, h
        while $h \leqslant$ last__expression of H
      if $s(e) \neq s(h)$ **then**
              (if these symbols are already equal the scan continues)
              (first, the two cases in which $s(e)$ is an operator, constants being
              considered as operators here)
            if $(s(e) =$ operator **then**
                if $s(h) =$ operator **then** UNIFICATION $\leftarrow$ False
                    RETURN (case failure 2)
                    else $t \leftarrow$ term beginning at e in E
                    ($s(h)$ is a free variable for which t is substituted)
                    SUB $(s(h), t, e, h)$
            end if
            else (case in which $s(e)$ is a variable)
            if $s(h) \neq$ operator **then** SUB$(s(h), s(e), e, h)$
            (variable/variable: simple name change)
                else $t \leftarrow$ term beginning at h in H
                SUB $(s(e), t, e, h)$
            end if
            end if
            if SUB = FALSE **then** UNIFICATION $\leftarrow$ FALSE RETURN
            end if
        end if
    end
                UNIFICATION $\leftarrow$ TRUE
                RETURN list of substitutions
                (the new expression E is the conclusion C of T, with the substitutions
                made)
end UNIFICATION

3.7.5 Finiteness of the unification algorithm

The procedure stops when it reaches the end of H; E can be longer than H if T is a re-write rule. But since the sub-trees of both E and H can grow we have to prove that the procedure is indeed finite.

At the start the total number of substitutable variables in E and H is of course finite; and in the course of the process:

- No new free variable is created.
- Each substitution, which replaces a variable by a term that does not contain that variable, can only reduce the number of variables to be dealt with.

The process must therefore converge, with a number of substitutions not exceeding the original total number of free variables.

Some examples:

1. E: $a + b$
   T: $x * y \rightarrow y * x$
   case of failure 2: operators cannot be unified

2. E: $\sin^2 a + \cos^3 a$
   T: $\sin^2 x + \cos^2 x \rightarrow 1$
   case of failure 2: operators = constants

3. E: $\log_{\sqrt{}} a - \log_{\sqrt{}} 2 * a$
   T: $x - x \rightarrow 0$
   check 1 (in SUB)

In (3), the first step is to substitute $\log_{\sqrt{}} a$ for x, so that T becomes $\log_{\sqrt{}} a - \log_{\sqrt{}} a \rightarrow 0$; the operators log and $\sqrt{}$ are identical in E and T but for unification we should have to replace a by $2 * a$, and this is forbidden.

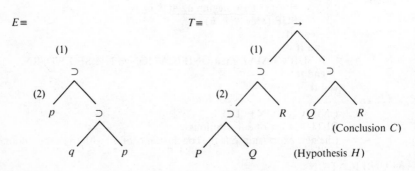

Fig. 3.10 Unification in propositional logic.

4. This is the example from PL already studied:

E: $(p \supset (q \supset p))$
T: $((P \supset Q) \supset R) \rightarrow (Q \supset R)$

Tree representation, as in Fig. 3.10, makes it possible for the progress of the algorithm to be visualised. The first symbol in both E and H is the operator $\supset$ so we can progress down both trees. In E we meet the variable p at the same time as we meet the operator in H, this operator indicating the start of a term t; we *must* therefore change p to t, and t is the sub-tree shown in Fig. 3.11.

The next symbols we meet are the operator $\supset$ in E and the variable R in H; the process continues as shown in Fig. 3.12. Thus we have succeeded with the unification; returning to the original notation, the expression E has been changed to F where:

$$F \equiv (Q \supset (q \supset (P \supset Q)))$$

as a result of the substitutions $p/(P \supset Q)$ and $R/(q \supset (P \supset Q))$; or in other words, the expression E and the hypothesis H of theorem T have been unified to:

$$(P \supset Q) \supset (P \supset (P \supset Q))$$

so as to give the expression F. Normalising, we can say that from E and T

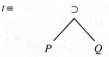

The symbols already examined are replaced by points:

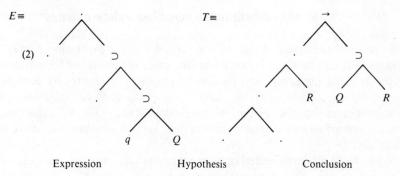

Fig. 3.11 Unification of Fig. 3.10 (continued).

The substitution of t for R with:

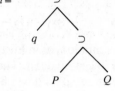

leads eventually to the traversing of H and gives:

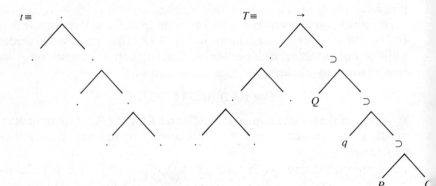

Fig. 3.12 Unification of Fig. 3.10 (end).

we get:

$$(p \supset q) \supset (r \supset (p \supset q)) \rightarrow (q \supset (r \supset (p \supset q)))$$

of which the result obtained by the tentative process of Section 7.1 is a special case.

3.7.6 Non-substitutable variables: indeterminates

So far we have assumed that all the variables in the expression E play the same role; this however is not always the case. Whatever the formal system that is being used, all the variables of the theorem T are, by definition, substitutable, because at the start these are quantified universally and become free by the axiom of particularisation. On the other hand, situations arise in which the 'variables' in E are not substitutable, as we now explain.

The basic principle underlying unification is that only free variables may be substituted, that is, variables not quantified by ∃ or ∀. It is not uncommon for an expression to be written with unquantified variables that are not in fact free, simply in the interests of conciseness, for example when an expression is being manipulated for computation. Thus in the expression $3x^2 + 4x + 6 = 0$ the 'variable' x is certainly not free. Variables entering in this way are more constrained, and there can be interdependencies between them; so it is no longer permissible for them to be replaced by arbitrary terms. This gives a third case – 'failure 3' – in which unification is impossible.

As we have said, the variables of any theorem are free, or 'dummy variables'; those of an expression are in general bound variables and in such a case we speak of *semi-unification*. For example, in algebra there is the legal rule for simplification:

$$T \equiv a + (b - a) \mapsto b$$

If we wish to apply this to an expression such as:

$$E \equiv x + y$$

the first substitution, changing a to x, is valid, giving:

$$T_1 \equiv x + (b - x) \mapsto b$$

but a second substitution that would change y to $(b - x)$ is not allowed because the context – such as the solution of an equation in x and y – links the two 'variables' x, y together. If in fact there was some reason to insist on making this substitution the transformation 'y changed to $(b - x)$' could be given as a condition linking the variables x and y, to hold throughout the solution of whatever was the problem in hand; and E could then be simplified to b, and b treated as a free variable.

To take a second, more specific, example, for the real numbers there is the rewrite rule:

$$T \equiv e^z * e^z \mapsto e^{2z}$$

Let us use this to simplify the expression (an equation):

$$E: e^{x-3} * e^{2y-3} = e^2$$

Making the first substitution $z/(x - 3)$, T becomes:

$$e^{x-3} * e^{x-3} \mapsto e^{2(x-3)}$$

and the second substitution $x/2y$ unifies E and the left (hypothesis) side of T, giving the conclusion $e^{2(2y-3)}$; but in reaching this we have implicitly added the condition $x = 2y$.

If we used this conclusion to solve the original equation we should get: $e^{2(2y-3)} = e^2$, i.e. $2(2y - 3) = 2$ so $y = 2$ and therefore $x = 8$; but the equation can be solved directly without using T:

$$e^{(x-3)+(2y-3)} = e^{(x+2y-6)} = e^2, x + 2y = 8$$

This is clearly the general solution, of which the result obtained by unification is only a particular case. The symbols x, y are related by the equation E and are not substitutable in the normal sense. If there is a need to substitute certain terms for them then the corresponding implied conditions must be noted and brought into any consideration of the solution obtained.

The lesson to be learned is that one must beware of the false free variables that commonly enter expressions. They must not be substituted without a subsequent checking of the validity of the substituting, for otherwise false paradoxes are easily created.

3.7.7 Unification in action

The unification algorithm we have just described can be used systematically in various mathematical contexts – arithmetic, algebra, trigonometry, logic, formal differentiation and integration; and it is easily extended to cover the rules for deduction from a set of hypotheses, $H1 \,\&\, H2 \,\&\, ... \,\&\, Hn \rightarrow C$. In any application the algorithm is called into play for each relevant general theorem of the field of the problem, for each special theorem given for the particular problem and for each sub-expression of the main expression being processed. The general procedure is as given in Table 3.6. The process stops when no theorem can be applied to any expression. What Table 3.6 gives is of course only the principle: the process shown can be extremely inefficient in practice if the set τ contains many theorems. Also in practice some rules may, logically, take priority over others and, further, the final result obtained may vary with the order in which the theorems are taken. If the need is to manipulate the expression ε so as to arrive at a result given in advance it is likely to be necessary to make several trials, taking the theorems and/or sub-expressions in different orders. Thus the general procedure has to be used intelligently, with the context always in mind.

Table 3.6 General unification procedure.

READ τ (set of production or rewrite rules for the field of the problem, forming the data for the general UNIFICATION procedure)
READ ε (expression to be processed)
REPEAT FOR every theorem T of τ
          REPEAT FOR every sub-expression E of ε
                    UNIFICATION (E, T)
          end REPEAT ON E
end REPEAT ON T
WRITE ε

There is also the possibility that the process may not terminate, and this arises in particular whenever τ contains a pair of rules of the form:

$$x - x \mapsto 0 \quad \text{and} \quad 0 \mapsto x - x$$

These can cause the process to go into a loop and the same thing can result from a single rule such as:

$$x + y \mapsto y + x \quad \text{or} \quad x * y \mapsto y * x$$

which can start an unending sequence of oscillations between pairs of successive terms; or again with sets of any number of rules, such as:

$$u * (v/w) \mapsto (u * v)/w$$
$$\tan x \mapsto \sin x/\cos x$$
$$(u * v)/u \mapsto v$$
$$\sin x \mapsto \cos x * \tan x$$
$$\text{which will loop on } \sin x$$

We can get over this difficulty by recalling how we should deal with the situation by hand; there are two parts to the solution, a procedure for *normalisation* of the expression and one for *inhibition* of certain theorems.

Normalisation. The application of certain rules is governed by a condition that prevents them being used a second time when that would destroy the effect of a first application. For the commutivity of multiplication, for example, the condition is expressed as:

$$y * x \quad x * y \quad \text{can be invoked only if} \quad \text{mass}(x) < \text{mass}(y)$$

where mass (expression) is a numerical function that gives the stardard order for the variables of the expression. This corresponds to the convention that when working by hand we normally write $2 * a$ rather than $a * 2$ or $x^4 y^2 z$ rather than $z^4 x^2 y$.

Inhibition. The successful application of certain rules results not only in changes that will help the unification but also inhibits temporarily the use of other rules related to the one just used. For example, $x - x \mapsto 0$ and $0 \mapsto x - x$ inhibit each other, and $\tan x \mapsto \sin x/\cos x$ inhibits the two rules:

$$\sin x \mapsto \tan x * \cos x, \quad \cos x \mapsto \sin x/\tan x$$

Conversely, it is possible for the application of certain rules to reactivate rules that have been inhibited. This can be the case when it is judged that an application has changed the expression sufficiently for there to be no risk of return to a previous state.

NB: A different, but often more expensive, method for avoiding loops is

Table 3.7 Rewrite rules for algebra, for simplifying expressions.

$-0 \mapsto 0$	$T0$
$0 + x \mapsto x$	$T1$
$0 * x \mapsto 0$	$T2$
$1 * x \mapsto x$	$T3$
$-(-x) \mapsto x$	$T4$
$x * (-y) \mapsto (-x) * y$	$T5$
$-(x * y) \mapsto (-x) * y$	$T6$
$x * (y * (-z)) \mapsto (-x) * (y * z)$	$T7$
$z * (x + y) \mapsto z * x + z * y$	$T8$
$x + (-x) \mapsto 0$	$T9$
$x + x \mapsto 2 * x$	$T10$
$C1 * x + C2 * x \mapsto (C1 + C2) * x$	$T11$
$x * (y/x) \mapsto y$	$T12$
$x * (y/z) \mapsto (x * y)/z$	$T13$
$(x/z) + (y/z) \mapsto (x + y)/z$	$T14$
$x/1 \mapsto x$	$T15$
$x/x \mapsto 1$	$T16$

to delete any new expression that is found to be identical with one already obtained.

With the inclusion of these two loop-avoiding procedures, normalisation and inhibition, the unification algorithm provides a means for automatic manipulation of formal expression. Table 3.7 gives a set of rewrite rules with which all the manipulations employed in 'simplifying' and algebraic expression can be performed by machine. $C1$, $C2$ are arbitrary constants and x, y, z free variables. All re-arrangements take account of the 'masses' of the terms (see text) and obey conventions such as: constants are placed before variables, $-x$ after $+x$, x before y, etc.

3.8   USES OF UNIFICATION

I cannot feel sure that at this stage of my presentation of the unification algorithm I have convinced you of its full richness. You may very well be saying to yourself, this is all very fine, it's neat and rigorous, but it's still only a piece of mathematics and applies only to well-defined formal systems. Well, that isn't so; let me take a very different type of example to open your eyes.

3.8.1 Problems concerning analogies

You know about these intelligence tests that all people applying for jobs are now put through. Figure 3.13 is an example: a set of geometrical diagrams is given, labelled as shown, and the question is: which is the diagram X such that C is to X as A is to B? This is to ask, what is the analogy between A and B that is also the analogy between C and X? What has to be done is to see if we can 'unify' Figure C with the left side of the 'theorem' $A \rightarrow B$; we shall see later that the result of the unification is indeed one of the three suggested answers.

However, just what does '$A \rightarrow B$' mean? A can be described simply as a collection of shapes, linked by certain relations just as an algebraic formula is a collection of variables linked by certain operators. Thus we have:

$A \equiv$ (point, triangle, rectangle) **and** (rectangle **inside** triangle)
  and (point **outside** triangle)
  and (point **outside** rectangle)

The words in bold specify the relations, and their meanings are self-evident; those in lower case correspond to the variables. Similarly for B:

$B \equiv$ (rectangle, triangle)   **and** (rectangle **left of** triangle)
  and (rectangle **outside** triangle)

A   B   C

1   2   3

Fig. 3.13.

There is also the relation of scale; if we refer all sizes to those of A we can add to the description of B:

$$\textbf{and (scale } \text{rectangle} = 2)$$
$$\textbf{and (scale } \text{triangle} = 1)$$

The theorem T is now simply:

$$(\text{desription of } A) \rightarrow (\text{description of } B)$$

with:

$$A \equiv (\text{point, triangle, rectangle})$$
$$\textbf{and } (\text{rectangle } \textbf{inside} \quad \text{triangle})$$
$$\textbf{and } (\text{point} \qquad \textbf{outside } \text{triangle})$$
$$\textbf{and } (\text{point} \qquad \textbf{outside } \text{rectangle})$$

$$B \equiv (\text{rectangle, triangle})$$
$$\textbf{and } (\text{rectangle } \textbf{left of} \quad \text{triangle})$$
$$\textbf{and } (\text{rectangle } \textbf{outside } \text{triangle})$$
$$\textbf{and (scale } \text{rectangle} = 2)$$
$$\textbf{and (scale } \text{triangle} = 1)$$

The description of C is:

$$C \equiv (\text{circle, triangle, point})$$
$$\textbf{and } (\text{point} \qquad \textbf{outside } \text{triangle})$$
$$\textbf{and } (\text{triangle } \textbf{inside} \quad \text{circle})$$
$$\textbf{and } (\text{point} \qquad \textbf{outside } \text{circle}$$

and the question becomes: can we unify the description of A with that of C?

Let us work through the unification algorithm by hand, noting first that the order of the sub-expressions is not significant: any relation in A can be unified with any in B without reference to where these occur in the two descriptions. Further, we can change the names of the variables so as to make the most general possible substitutions in T: it happens in this case that certain variables in A and C have the same names, but in fact there is no reason why the 'triangles' of A and B should have any association with the 'triangle' of C. So the statement of $T \equiv (A \rightarrow B)$ becomes:

$$A \equiv (a, b, c) \qquad\qquad\qquad B \equiv (c, b)$$
$$\textbf{and } (c \textbf{ inside} \quad b) \qquad\qquad \textbf{and } (c \textbf{ left of } b)$$
$$\textbf{and } (a \textbf{ outside } b) \qquad\qquad \textbf{and } (c \textbf{ outside } b)$$
$$\textbf{and } (a \textbf{ outside } c) \qquad\qquad \textbf{and (scale } c = 2)$$
$$\qquad\qquad\qquad\qquad\qquad\qquad \textbf{and (scale } b = 1)$$

There is the implied assumption in this new description that the actual forms of the objects A and B are not significant, and that it is only the relations between them that count.

We can now start to unify the descriptions of A and C, following the order in which relations appear in C. The relation 'point **outside** triangle' can be made identical to 'a **outside** b' by simply writing 'point' for a and 'triangle' for b in A. We can see at this stage that there is another possibility connected with the second occurrence of the relation **outside** in A and with the fact that the ordering is irrelevant: the unification of 'point **outside** triangle' of C with 'a **outside** c' of A; but let us put this on one side for the moment and consider only the first possibility. The proposed substitutions give for A the new description:

$A \equiv$ (point, triangle, c)
    and (c **inside**   triangle)
    and (point **outside** triangle)   (unified with the first relation of C)
    and (point **outside** c)

The next relation in C is 'triangle **inside** circle' for which only one unification is possible, that concerning the relation 'c **inside** triangle' of A. But here we come up against the third type of check to the progress of the algorithm: in order to identify the two expressions we must in the one part change c to 'triangle', which is possible, but in the other, and simultaneously, change 'triangle' into 'circle', which is not allowable because, as has been pointed out before (see Section 3.7.6), in many contexts, including C here, the variables of an expression cannot be taken to be independent. The 'circle' and 'triangle' of C cannot be unified because in this diagram they are interdependent and in fact behave like constants.

Thus we must take up the second possibility, which we can express by:

           unify 'point **outside** triangle' in C
           with ' a **outside** c ' in A

If now we substitute 'point' for a and 'triangle' for c the theorem $T \equiv (A \to B)$ becomes:

A (point, b, triangle) $B \equiv$ (triangle, b)
    and (triangle **inside** b)   **and** (triangle **left of** b)
    and (point   **outside** b)   **and** (triangle **outside** b)
    and (point   **outside** triangle)[*]   **and** (**scale** triangle = 2)
                                     and (**scale** b = 1)

where the [*] marks a relation already unified.

The relation 'triangle **inside** circle' of C can be unified with 'triangle

inside b' of A in only one way, substituting 'circle' for b; this gives:

A (point, circle, triangle) $B \equiv$ (triangle, circle)
   and (triangle **inside** circle)* **and** (triangle **left of** circle)
   and (point   **outside** circle)   **and** (triangle **outside** circle)
   and (point   **outside** triangle)* **and** (**scale** triangle = 2)
                                 and (**scale** circle   = 1)

The remaining relation of C is 'point **outside** circle', which is identified immediately with the second relation of A.

If we now apply to C the theorem $T \equiv (A \rightarrow B)$, that is, apply the same transformations to the expression C as those that enable us to go from A to B, we get a description D which is that of B transformed by the substitutions that have unified A and B, that is, a/point, b/circle, c/triangle:

$$D \equiv \text{(triangle, circle)}$$
              and (triangle **left of** circle)
              and (triangle **outside** circle)
              and (**scale** triangle = 2)
              and (**scale** circle   = 1)

The scale factors relate again to the diagram from which we start, C here.

All that remains to be done is to see if this description corresponds to one of the diagrams of Fig. 3.13, and this again can be done with the aid of the unification algorithm because it is a question of identifying two descriptions. It is, however, a trivial application because no substitutions are allowed, the 'variables' (of C in this case) being effectively constants. There is a solution here, diagram 3.

We could have saved time in this search by using the fact that both A and C have only a single relation of the type 'x **inside** y'; if we start by unifying these relations we find we must make the substitutions c/triangle, b/circle and so necessarily a/point; and hence the result.

3.8.2 Comments on geometrical test problems of this type

I suspect that although we are not consciously aware of it we do in fact use a unification type of procedure in responding to such tests. Several questions arise, however. First of all, the human eye, backed by the visual system, is a wonderful information processing device that enables us to go easily and immediately from a diagram to a geometrical description of the type just given. The same is not true, at least not at present, of a computer equipped with one or more cameras; and here lies the whole problem of 'pattern recognition'.

A second point is that there is an implicit assumption in the treatment just given that there is a single standard description of objects and their relations; but in fact the relation 'triangle **left of** circle' could equally well be written 'circle **right of** triangle' and the same possibility arises whenever a relation has an inverse, e.g. **inside/outside, above/below.** This requires changes to be made in the body of the algorithm to take account of all the substitutions that are possible; and with long expressions the number of equivalent descriptions grows exponentially and can become very great.

This second point relates to the efficiency of the unification algorithm and what we may call the pertinence of the descriptions, and here the problem of 'parasitic' information arises. It is always possible to add more detail to the symbolic-language description of a diagram, the limit corresponding to an exact copy of the diagram as drawn; thus for diagram A above we could say not simply that the point is outside the triangle but that it is also on the left and near the top of the diagram; whilst in C, in contrast, it is on the right and in the middle. We can see that unification in this detail cannot succeed and that to make it succeed we must return to our previous description. Here the information giving the exact positions of the points can be taken as being non-pertinent, as is justified *a posteriori* by the absence of any reference to the points in the final descriptions of B and D.

A further comment concerns the languge in which these descriptions have been given. This is not fixed. There is no standard adopted by all users, as perhaps is the case for ordinary mathematics; it is neither as rigorous nor as well formalised, and consequently the vocabulary can always be extended to take account of new properties – for example:

line type	(continuous, dashes, dots ...)
colour	(black, white, grey ...)
orientation	(e.g. with respect to an axis of symmetry)

and with such extensions to the language more complex diagrams can be handled automatically, as for example those of Cattell's IQ tests shown in Fig. 3.14.

Tests based on sequences of numbers, letters or dominos are often more difficult and made so because:

1. The set of possible replies is usually not given.
2. Several different unifications are usually admissible and therefore there can be several logically acceptable answers.

A few examples are shown in Fig. 3.16.

For these reasons a whole set of data is given in such tests and the general

Fig. 3.14.

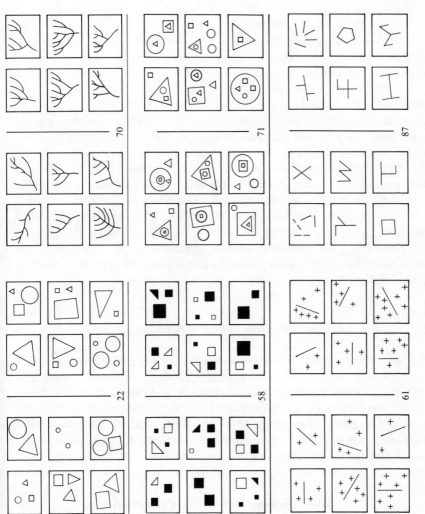

Fig. 3.15.

3	7	16	35	74	?				
U	D	T	Q	C	?				
1	4	7	11	14	17	41	?		
691	602	513	424	355	?				
2	4	5	6	4	3	4	4	4	?
13	50	27	26	55	14	111	8	?	
B	E	I	N	T	?				

Fig. 3.16

form is $U1 \rightarrow U2 \rightarrow U3 \rightarrow \cdots \rightarrow Un \rightarrow$. The hope is that the ambiguities can be reduced by progressively eliminating possible transformations, leaving only those that are valid for every link in the chain from $U1$ to Un; in the end one has to choose among several possibilities. There are always of course an infinite number of curves through a finite number of given points, and here the points correspond to the data items and the curves to the relations that have to be found. The tests devised by the Russian mathematician Bongard are of this type (Fig. 3.15), and it is mainly because of the ambiguities that the use of such tests for measuring 'Intelligence Quotient' ('IQ') has been and still is criticised so strongly. In the end some criterion of 'simplicity' – always subjective – has to be applied in order to select between legal transformations.

3.8.3 Use of unification for automatic proof

We have now reached the stage at which we can write an efficient program to prove several theorems in some simple formalisms; this will serve as a test-bench for more sophisticated programs such as for example those based on the Resolution Principle (Section 3.10), or in connection with expert systems (Chapter 7). One thing always has to be done before the unification algorithm can be made to run on a real machine: the local parts of the search tree for the problem in hand must be eliminated.

3.8.4 Siklóssy and Marinov's method

A feature of some rewrite rules is that they can give a right-hand member of a relation to which the same rule can be applied again. Such rules are called *expansive*; they can generate an infinite sequence of formulae, so their use must be limited by some means or other. For example, in logic the rule $p \mapsto \neg\neg p$ is expansive. With the help of the unification algorithm itself the program can of course become aware of whether or not a rule, provided as data, is or is not expansive.

Rules such as $x + y \mapsto y + x$ which, applied twice in succession to the same expression, leave it unchanged are called *pseudo-expansive*; they cannot lead to an infinite search. Laurent Siklóssy and Vladimir Marinov suggest that expansive rules should be used only when there is simply no alternative and that they should be triggered at most once at the current level of the search, the full search. When this has been done the search is performed over the non-expansion rules. In 1971 they obtained remarkable results compared with what could be done by hand; we now give two examples of proofs with the simple heuristic, independent of the particular field, of discarding expansive rules.

Example 1 – propositional logic. Given the six rules:

$$R1 \quad p \wedge q \mapsto q \wedge p;$$
$$R2 \quad p \wedge (q \wedge r) \mapsto (p \wedge q) \wedge r;$$
$$R3 \quad p \wedge (p \supset q) \mapsto q;$$
$$R4 \quad \neg q \wedge (p \supset q) \mapsto \neg p;$$
$$R5 \quad \neg\neg p \mapsto p;$$
$$R6 \quad p \mapsto \neg\neg p;$$

we are to prove the theorem:

$$T: (s \supset \neg t) \wedge t \mapsto \neg s$$

Initially the expansive rule $R6$ is disregarded and the search proceeds systematically; expressions already encountered are not developed afresh and are marked *dead*. The conclusion represented by the theorem to be proved is used only as a test for when to stop, the search in fact being carried on blindly.

The tree for this search is given in Fig. 3.17, where the nodes are numbered in the order in which they are reached – the search is breadth first, with all derivations that are possible, at the same level and for the same expression, being performed before descending to the next lower level.

Only the rule $R1$ can be unified with the starting expression H (node 1). A second application only gives H again and $R2$, $R3$, $R4$, $R5$ cannot be applied. $R6$ is therefore triggered for one level only; it is unified with H in three different ways to give the three expressions of nodes 2, 3 and 4; $R1$ is now applied to each of these, followed by R at node 7, which gives success.

For the sake of simplicity we have not given all the possible unifications in this proof; the propositional letters have not been treated as substitutable variables and the applications of $R6$ to the expression $(s \supset \neg t) \wedge t$ has not been considered.

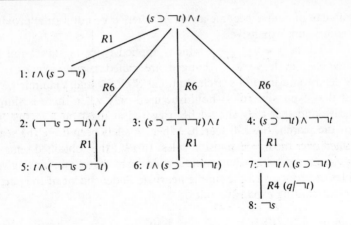

Fig. 3.17.

Example 2 – elementary group theory. Given the following six rules:

$$S1 \qquad a + b \mapsto b + a;$$
$$S2 \qquad a + (b + c) \mapsto (a + b) + c;$$
$$S3 \qquad (a + b) - b \mapsto a;$$
$$S4 \qquad a \mapsto (a + b) - b;$$
$$S5 \qquad (a - b) + c \mapsto (a + c) - b;$$
$$S6 \qquad (a + b) - c \mapsto (a - c) + b;$$

the following theorem is to be proved:

$$T1: (a + b) + c \mapsto a + (b + c)$$

The reader should attempt the proof for himself: the given rules – which are all that can be assumed – represent a severe restriction of our basic knowledge, and progress is not easily made. Rule $S1$ is marked by the system as pseudo-expansive and $S4$ as expansive; further, the system makes implicit use of the following meta-theorem: so long as $S4$ is not triggered the connective – does not appear and only $S1$ and $S2$ can be applied. The proof is shown in Fig. 3.18; it will be seen that the goal is reached in eleven steps in which only $S1$ and $S2$ are used.

The more important theorem:

$$T2: (a + c) - (b + c) \mapsto a - b$$

can be deduced from the same six rules; the proof now requires 351 steps – but only a few seconds of machine time!

We certainly cannot claim that the method we have just described will ever produce any really important mathematical results; nevertheless it is

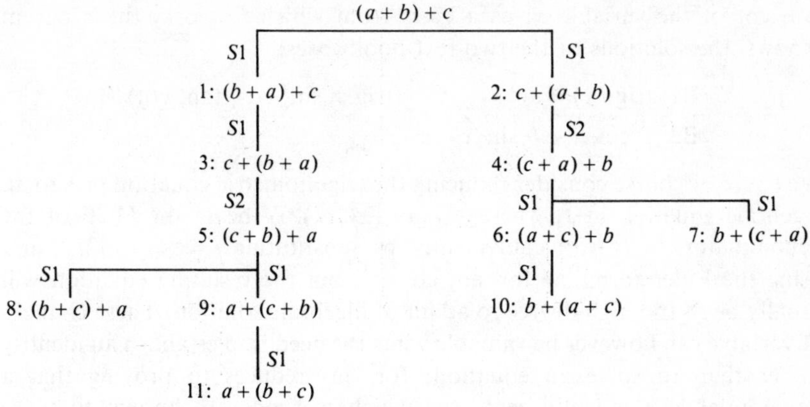

$$(a+b)+c$$

S1 | | S1

1: $(b+a)+c$ 2: $c+(a+b)$

S1 | S2

3: $c+(b+a)$ 4: $(c+a)+b$

S2 | S1 | | S1

5: $(c+b)+a$ 6: $(a+c)+b$ 7: $b+(c+a)$

S1 | | S1   S1 |

8: $(b+c)+a$ 9: $a+(c+b)$ 10: $b+(a+c)$

S1 |

11: $a+(b+c)$

Fig. 3.18.

basically capable, in contrast to many others, of finding new theorems – all that is necessary is to let it run. It shows very clearly the power of the computer as a symbol manipulator, the longest proofs taking only a few seconds. Thus it acts as a valuable sub-program in systems for which symbolic proof is not the main goal – for automatic program construction, for example – or for establishing intermediate results in fields outside that in which the main proof is being attempted; this corresponds to a mathematician who specialises in topology consulting a textbook on analysis for help with unfamiliar calculations.

An improvement of this enumerative method of Siklóssy and Marinov is based on the separation of the rules into two classes, 'obligatory' and 'non-obligatory' respectively, the first corresponding to the standard processes of normalisation and simplification of expressions, the second containing the 'dangerous' – in particular, expansive – rules. The improvement involves, among other things, a more careful consideration of the process of triggering these non-obligatory rules; later we shall describe two theorem provers that make use of these ideas.

3.8.5 Solution of trigonometric equations: the PRET program
(Grandbastien 1974)

The input to this program is a set of statements of the form:

$$P(\text{trig }(x)) = \text{constant}$$

where $P(\text{trig }(x))$ is a polynomial in the trigonometric functions sin, cos, tan, cot of the variable x; as a basis from which to work, the program 'knows' the solutions of the two text-book cases:

> B1: trig $(x) = c$ (trig $\equiv$ sin, cos, tan, cot)
>
> B2: $a \cos x + b \sin x = c$.

We could of course consider reducing the trigonometric equation in x to an algebraic equation in t, where $t = \tan (x/2N)$, N being the HCF of the denominators in P – or equivalently, by substituting $t = \exp (ix/2N)$ and using the Euler formulae for sin, cos etc; but the resulting equation will usually be of too high degree to admit of algebraic solution. These changes of variable can however be valuable when the need is to establish an identity rather than to solve an equation, for this reduces to proving that a polynomial is identically zero, for which methods are known that are independent of the degree.

The essence of the method used by PRET is keep B1 and B2 in mind as goals and to operate on the given expression so as to bring it continually closer to one or other of these forms. The general procedure is an iteration of three stages:

1. Apply the obligatory rules so far as possible.
2. Apply a suitable non-obligatory rule.
3. Choose the most promising of the expressions obtained.

These general rules must be made more precise. Consider first stage 3: by construction, the search is over a tree, each node, representing an expression, giving rise to a number of descendants; if each of these latter has been derived from its parent expression by the application of a different rule the lines of descent are labelled OR. Since all of these are equivalent expressions solving any one of these equations will give the solution of the parent equation. This is illustrated in Fig. 3.19. If the parent expression has been resolved into factors, then if the right side of the equation is zero the several equations obtained by equating each factor to zero can be solved separately. This gives a number of sub-problems which are labelled AND, as shown in Fig. 3.20.

Now at every step in the solution process a choice has to be made of the expression that the program will handle next. PRET makes this choice with

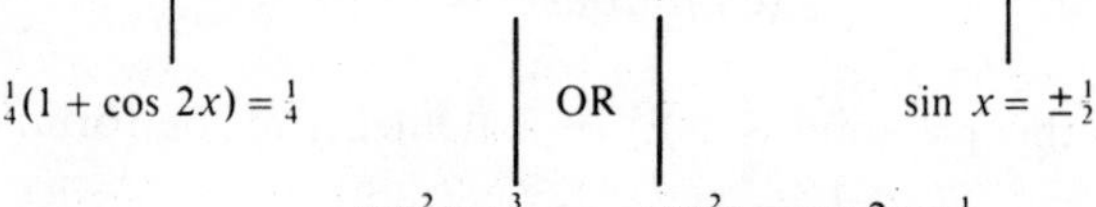

$$\sin^2 x = \tfrac{1}{4}$$

$$\tfrac{1}{4}(1 + \cos 2x) = \tfrac{1}{4} \qquad\qquad \text{OR} \qquad\qquad \sin x = \pm\tfrac{1}{2}$$

$$\cos^2 x = \tfrac{3}{4} \qquad\qquad \cos^2 x - \cos 2x = \tfrac{1}{4}$$

Fig. 3.19 OR node in a proof.

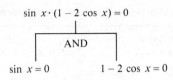

Fig. 3.20 AND node in a proof (all solutions are required).

the help of a certain evaluation function applied to the descendants of the last OR node; this function is a measure of the complexity of an expression, defined here for an expression e by

$$C(e) = \text{number of first-level factors}^{[1]}$$
$$+ \text{number of different arguments}$$
$$+ \text{sum of the powers that differ from 1}$$

PRET's rule is to choose the expression for which $C(e)$ is least.

This is a very simple measure of complexity but it suffices for the purpose, for $C(e)$ increases very quickly if the expression is badly chosen. If this happens PRET abandons that branch of the tree and chooses another node.

Next consider stage 1, the application of the non-obligatory rules. These are rewrite rules and are ordered; the program applies them wherever it can. A complete list is given in Table 3.8 in which, except for (a), *trig* denotes either of the trigonometric functions sin, cos, as before. This set has been arrived at by experiment, observing which rules do not always work very satisfactorily either because they complicate the expression (as with (g)) or because they take one further from the goal (as with (c)) or because they are expansive in tendency (as with (i) and (j)).

Finally, stage 1 falls into three parts. PRET first tries to break the problem down into a number of sub-problems by factorisation and so creating an AND node; if this does not succeed it next tries to simplify the expression by a change of variable; and if this also fails it standardises the expression by unification, applying the obligatory rules, which fall into ten groups, in the order given in Table 3.9. When a particular goal has to be attained a table gives the only transformations that need be considered.

Over 100 problems of this type have been solved by PRET, each needing only a few seconds on the CII 10070 machine. We now give two examples.

Example 1.

$$\sqrt{3} \tan x - 4 \sin^2 x = 0 \tag{i}$$

---

1. e.g. in $3xy^2 + 4(z + t)$ there are five first-level factors: $3, x, y^2, 4, (z + t)$.

Table 3.8 Non-obligatory rules in trigonometry.

(a) trig $u \pm$ trig v	$\mapsto 2.\text{trig } (u + v)/2.\text{trig } (u \pm v)/2$
(b) sin $2x$	$\mapsto 2 \sin x \cos x$
$\quad$ cos $2x$	$\mapsto 2 \cos^2 x - 1$
(c) sin $u.\sin v$	$\mapsto \frac{1}{2}(\cos(u - v) - \cos(u + v))$
$\quad$ cos $u.\cos v$	$\mapsto \frac{1}{2}(\cos(u - v) + \cos(u + v))$
(d) trig $(u + v)$	$\mapsto f(\text{trig } u.\text{trig } v)$
(e) trig α_u	$\mapsto f(\text{trig } \alpha u)$
$\quad \sin^2 u$	$\mapsto \frac{1}{2}(1 + \cos 2u)$
$\quad \cos^3 u$	$\mapsto \frac{1}{4}(\cos 3u + 3 \cos u)$
(f) trig$(-u)$	$\mapsto f(\text{trig } (u))$
$\quad$ trig$(\pi \pm u)$	$\mapsto f(\text{trig } (u))$
$\quad$ trig$(\pi/2 \pm u)$	$\mapsto f(\text{trig}) (u))$
$\quad$ trig$(\pi/4 \pm u)$	$\mapsto f(\text{trig } (u))$
(g) trig $(2x)$	$\mapsto f(\tan x)$
(h) $\sin^2 x$	$\mapsto 1 - \cos^2 x$
$\quad$ sin $x \cos x$	$\mapsto \frac{1}{2} \sin 2x$
(l) tan u	$\mapsto \sin u/\cos u$
(j) sin $u/\cos u$	$\mapsto \tan u$
(k) $\cos^2 u$	$\mapsto 1/(1 + \tan^2 u)$

Table 3.9 Obligatory rules in trigonometry.

(a) Development (rewrite rule)

$$(a + b)^n \mapsto \text{binomial expansion}$$

(b) Elimination if radicals (production rule)

$$\sqrt{a} = c \mapsto a = c^2$$

(c) Replacement of a sum by a product

$$\sin u + \sin v \mapsto 2 \sin(u + v)/2.\cos(u - v)/2$$

(d) Factorisation (rewrite rule)

$$a^n - b^n \mapsto (a - b).(\text{polynomial in } a, b)$$

(e) Elimination of the cotangent if the expression has only a single argument

$$\cot x \mapsto 1/\tan x$$

(f) Elimination of the tangent if the expression has only a single argument

$$\tan x \mapsto \sin x/\cos x$$

(g) If the sine and cosine appear with only odd powers, division by $\cos^r x$ so as to arrive at the form $P(\tan x) = 0$

(h) If the sine and cosine appear with only even powers, substitution $\sin^2 x \mapsto 1 - \cos^2 x$ so as to arrive at the form $P(\tan x) = 0$

(i) If the expression is symmetrical in sine and cosine, substitution $x \mapsto x + \pi/4$

(j) If there are any denominators, reduce to a common denominator.

No factorisation is possible and no change of variable is helpful, so Rule 3.9(f) is applied, to eliminate the tangent; this gives:

$$\sqrt{3} \sin x / \cos x - 4 \sin^2 x = 0 \tag{ii}$$

5B(j) is then applied, and since $\cos x \neq 0$ we have:

$$\sqrt{3} \sin x - 4 \sin^2 x \cos x = 0 \tag{iii}$$

PRET now returns to stage 1, detecting the factor $\sin x$:

$$\sin x(\sqrt{3} - 4 \sin x \cos x) = 0$$

leading to two sub-problems, marked AND in Fig. 3.21:

$$\sin x = 0 \qquad \text{which is trivial} \tag{iv}$$
$$\sqrt{3} - 4 \sin x \cos x = 0 \tag{v}$$

(v) is now the new expression to be considered. The obligatory rules (3.9) do not help here, but of the non-obligatory rules 3.8(h) applies:

$$\sin x \cos x \mapsto \tfrac{1}{2} \sin 2x$$

giving the expression:

$$\sin 2x = \sqrt{3}/2 \tag{vi}$$

and the problem is solved.

Example 2.

$$\sin(n + 1)x + \sin(n - 1)x - \sin 2x = 0 \tag{i}$$

None of the rules of 3.9 is triggered by this expression, but 3.8(a) gives:

$$2 \sin nx \cos x - \sin 2x = 0 \tag{ii}$$

The complexity of (ii) is $4 + 3 + 0 = 7$, whilst that of (i) is $3 + 3 + 0 = 6$;

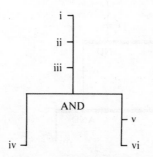

Fig. 3.21 Tree for the solution of $\sqrt{3} \tan x - 4 \sin^2 x = 0$.

however, the same rule can be used to group the terms in two other ways, and thus PRET generates simultaneously:

$$2 \sin \tfrac{1}{2}(n - 1)x . \cos \tfrac{1}{2}(n + 3)x + \sin(n - 1)x = 0 \qquad \text{(iii)}$$

$$2 \sin \tfrac{1}{2}(n - 3)x . \cos \tfrac{1}{2}(n + 1)x + \sin(n + 1)x = 0 \qquad \text{(iv)}$$

which both have the same complexity as before, 7.

PRET now considers the application of 3.8(b) to the original expression; this gives:

$$\sin(n + 1)x + \sin(n - 1)x - 2 \sin x \cos x = 0 \qquad \text{(v)}$$

with complexity $5 + 3 + 0 = 8$.

No other rule of 3.8 can be applied so PRET returns to the first-obtained expression of minimum complexity, that is, to (ii); 3.8(b) can be applied to this, so PRET now obtains:

$$2 \sin nx \cdot \cos x - 2 \sin x \cdot \cos x = 0 \qquad \text{(vi)}$$

which is immediately factorisable, giving:

$$2 \cos x(\sin nx - \sin x) = 0 \qquad \text{(vii)}$$

We have now reduced the original problem to the two sub-problems:

$$\cos x = 0 \quad \text{(viii)} \qquad \text{and} \qquad \sin nx - \sin x = 0 \qquad \text{(ix)}$$

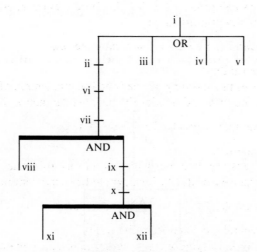

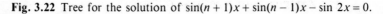

Fig. 3.22 Tree for the solution of $\sin(n + 1)x + \sin(n - 1)x - \sin 2x = 0$.

and applying 3.9(c) to (ix) we get:

$$2 \sin \tfrac{1}{2}(n-1)x \cos \tfrac{1}{2}(n+1)x = 0 \qquad\qquad \text{(x)}$$

and the problem is solved. The tree is shown in Fig. 3.22.

3.8.6 Problems in integer arithmetic: the PARI program
(Bourgoin 1978)

The mathematical knowledge built into this program is organised into a number of specialised modules and the basic approach is to manipulate a given problem so as to reduce it to a form that one knows how to solve. PARI will accept any expression involving integer variables; it consists of six modules, each of which can handle a particular type of sub-problem, and which play roles corresponding to those of the 'obligatory' rules of the previous section.

Module 1: 'product = constant'.
Uses the decomposition of a number into prime factors, and criteria for divisibility.

Example: $x.y = 5 \Rightarrow (x = 5, y = 1)$ OR $(x = 1, y = 5)$.

Module 2: 'congruence'.
Handles linear equations, operating in a purely combinatorial manner and basing its approach on congruences with respect to the small primes, $2, 3, 5, 7, 11$. It derives the conditions that the unknowns must satisfy.

Example: $5x = 2y + 1 \Rightarrow x$ must be odd.

Module 3: 'divisibility'.
Bases its reasoning on the fundamental lemma of Gauss: if a is prime to b and divides the product bc then a divides c.

Example: 3 divides $7z \Rightarrow$ 3 divides z.

Module 4: 'equations'
Is able to find particular solutions to linear equations by successive trials (the ideal would be to use continued fractions).

Example: $7x - 5y = 11$: a particular solution is $x = 3, y = 2$.

Module 5: 'generalised Euclidean divisibility'
Computes symbolically the quotient and remainder when one polynomial is divided by another.

Example: $x^2 - 2x + 1$ divided by $x - 3$ gives
$$x^2 - 2x + 1 \equiv (x - 3)(x + 1) + 4.$$

Module 6:   'recurrence'
Given a recurrence relation and an initial value can find the general term.

Example: $u_n = 3u_{n-1} + 4$, $u_1 = c \Rightarrow u_n = 3^{n-1}(c + 2) - 2$.

These modules use 'service programs' to normalise the expressions, carry out substitutions and incorporate the results found into the current relations. The ultimate goal is to give the solution, either completely in some explicit form or as a simple condition that characterises it, or to show that no solution exists.

At each stage in the procedure the adequacy of each module for the problem at that stage is judged with the aid of a set of six triplets, each of which measures, for the corresponding module, its relevance, the difficulty in applying it (taking into account the number of variables and the maximum degrees to which they appear) and the expected resulting cost for the rest of the problem. There are criteria for deciding, from these measures, which module to apply.

Example 1. Find two primes p, q such that $p^2 = 8q + 1$.

The 'divisibility' module is the one that best fits the requirement $p^2 = 8q + 1$: it treats the problem as an equation in q and re-states it as a divisibility problem:

$$8 \mid p^2 - 1, \text{ where we use the notation } a \mid b \text{ to mean '}a \text{ divides } b\text{'}$$

The 'congruence' module takes this relation but adds nothing new, p and q being already known to be both odd since they are primes (and the possibility of either being 2 is eliminated immediately). However, this module is the best candidate for a direct study of the original statement of the problem and working modulo 3 gives:

$$(p \bmod 3)^2 \equiv 2(q \bmod 3) + 1 \qquad (\bmod 3)$$

There are three cases to consider:

1. $p \equiv 0 \bmod 3$. Since p is prime it can be only 3; then $9 = 8q + 1$, and $q = 1$. Thus a solution is $p = 3$, $q = 1$.
2. $p \equiv 1 \bmod 3$. The equation is then $1 \equiv 2(q \bmod 3) + 1$ and hence $q \equiv 0$ mod 3, and since q is prime, $q = 3$; then $p^2 = 8.3 + 1 = 25$, so $p = 5$: but this contradicts the assumption $p \equiv 1 \bmod 3$, so this case cannot arise.

3. $p \equiv 2 \bmod 3$. Then $4 \equiv 2(q \bmod 3) + 1$ and again $q \equiv 0 \bmod 3$, so $q = 3$. Hence again $p^2 = 25$ and $p = 5$, which is now consistent with the assumption, so $p = 5$, $q = 3$ is a solution.

No other cases can arise, so the only solutions are $(3, 1)$ and $(5, 3)$.

Example 2. Find all the positive integers x and n such that:

$$\frac{5x^3 - 6x^2 + 7x + 8}{x^2 - 3x + 4} = n$$

'Euclidean division' is favoured here; applying that module we get the identity:

$$5x^3 - 6x^2 + 7x + 8 \equiv (x^2 - 3x + 4)(5x + 9) + 14x - 28$$

The problem requires that the quadratic divides the cubic without remainder, so it must divide $14x - 28$; the 'divisibility' module now forms the new condition

$$(x^2 - 3x + 4) \,|\, (14x - 28)$$

and 'Euclidean division' is invoked again to give the new identity:

$$14(x^2 - 3x + 4) \equiv (14x - 28)(x - 1) + 28$$

Since $x^2 - 3x + 4$ divides $14x - 28$ it must also divide 28; so we have now

$$k.(x^2 - 3x + 4) = 28$$

with k some integer.

The module 'product = constant' now takes over, testing the values ± 1, ± 2, ± 4, ± 7, ± 14, ± 28. PARI finds the solutions for the 12 corresponding second-degree equations: for example:

$$k = 14 \text{ gives } x^2 - 3x + 4 = 2, \text{ so } x = 1 \text{ or } 2$$
$$k = 7 \qquad\qquad\qquad = 0 \qquad x = 0 \text{ or } 3$$

The complete set of solutions is $x = 0, 1, 2, 3, 5$; however, PARI's method of reasoning is not by a sequence of equivalences but by a sequence of necessary conditions: each potential solution is checked against the original expression with the result that $x = 3$ is eliminated, leaving only $0, 1, 2, 5$ as true solutions.

Example 3. Find all the integers n such that $\sum_{i=1}^{n} 2i = n(n + 1)$. The 'recurrence' module is called. It first checks that the relation holds for the case $n = 1$: $2 = 1 \cdot (1 + 1)$. It then substitutes $n + 1$ for n, as an attempt to prove that if the relation holds for a value n it holds for $n + 1$. Separating out the term on the left corresponding to $n + 1$, the problem is to find if the following relation holds:

$$\sum_{i=1}^{n} 2i + 2(n + 1) = (n + 17)((n + 1) + 1)$$

As it has assumed that the relation holds for n it can use the original expression as a rewrite rule for the sum term on the left, getting:

$$n(n + 1) + 2(n + 1) = (n + 1)(n + 2)$$

as the relation to be tested; and since $n \neq -1$, so that $n + 1 \neq 0$, this is trivial: $n + 2 = n + 2$. So the result is proved by induction to hold for all positive integers n.

Some problems solved by PARI are as follows:

1. Find integers a, b such that $a \mid b$ and $a \mid b + 1$.
2. Prove the identities:
   (a) $\sum_{i=1}^{n} (2i - 1)^2 = n(2n - 1)(2n + 1)/3$;
   (b) $\sum_{i=1}^{n} 4(i + 1)(i + 3)(i + 5) = n(n + 1)(n^2 + 13n + 52) + 60n$;
   (c) $\sum_{i=1}^{n} i^3 = (\sum_{i=1}^{n} i)^2$;
   (d) $nr^2(n + 1)(2n + 1) + 6arn(n + 1) + 6na^2 - \sum_{i=1}^{n} (a + ir)^2 = 0$.
3. For the sequence defined by $u_1 = 3a + 2$, $u_{n+1} = 3u_n + 2$ show that the nth term can be wrtten $u_n = ab^n$
4. Find the integer solutions of the equations:
   (a) $2x^3 + xy + 7 = 0$;
   (b) $p(100 - q) + q(100 - p) = 1978$;
   (c) $x^2 + 8z = 3 + 2y^2$.
5. For what values of x does $x^2 + 8kx - 3k^2$ divide

$$4x^4 + 35kx^3 + 5k^2x^2 - 65k^3x + 21k^4?$$

6. Prove the following congruences:
   (a) $(10k + 7)^{10} + 1 \equiv 0 \pmod{10}$;
   (b) $(6k + 1) \cdot 2^{6k+1} + 1 \equiv 0 \pmod{3}$.
7. Show that 5^{2n} and 2^{5n} have the same remainders when divided by 7.
8. Find x such that $5 \mid 4x^2 + 1$ and $13 \mid 4x^2 + 1$.
9. Show that if both p and $8p^2 - 1$ are prime then $8p^2 + 1$ is composite.
10. Show that the equation $p^2 + q^2 = r^2 + s^2 + t^2$ has no solutions such p, q, r, s, t are all primes greater than 2.
11. Find all the positive integers n such that $n + 1$, $n + 3$, $n + 7$, $n + 9$, $n + 13$, $n + 15$ are all prime.

All the programs so far described confine themselves to proving a stated theorem or solving a stated problem. The mathematician, however, does not work in this way; he does not know in advance what theorems he is looking for and he has no built-in criteria to tell him when to stop. What guides him is 'intuition', that kind of higher-level knowledge that enables him both to direct his searches in promising directions and to simplify the work by short-circuiting stages of unimportant detail. Another way to put this is to say that he is guided by a metatheory.

There are programs that use metatheory; we now describe one of the first, due to Jacques Pitrat (1966).

3.9 PITRAT'S PROGRAM IN PROPOSITIONAL LOGIC

3.9.1 The hierarchy of metatheories

A theorem is a statement in a formal system, and a metatheorem is a statement about the theorems of a formal system. This is important in two respects:

1. On the one hand, it enables proofs to be shortened by avoiding the need to repeat intermediate stages that can be taken for granted; and makes possible the direct passage from a tree structure such as that on the left in Fig. 3.23 to the linear derivation shown on the right.
2. On the other, it provides a better global view of the search, focussing on the important choices and avoiding confusing the situation with unimportant partial results.

Metatheorems can be manipulated with the help of a second formal system, in which, however, one must take care to distinguish, by using a different notation, the new operators. Thus *modus ponens*, a derivation rule with which new theorems can be generated, is also a metatheorem that can be written:

$$p.\ p \supset q \rightarrow q$$

meaning: 'if p is a theorem and $p \supset q$ is a theorem then q is a theorem'; and

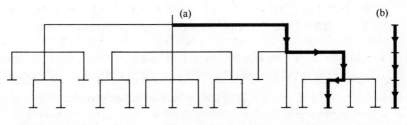

Fig. 3.23 (a) Tree-structured derivation (b) Linear derivation.

the symbols '.', '→' are the counterparts in the metalanguage of '∧' and '⊃' respectively.

Metatheorems can be proved within a formal system. Thus we have shown that in PL from any theorem of the form $P \supset (Q \supset R)$ we can deduce, by *modus ponens* and substitutions, the new theorem $Q \supset (P \supset R)$. This is a metatheorem of PL:

$$P \supset (Q \supset R) \rightarrow Q \supset (P \supset R)$$

which clearly can be applied to many statements in PL.

A convenient different way to construct metatheorems is to use meta-metatheorems, of which the following is an example:

if, given a, b can be deduced; and if, given b, c can be deduced; then given a, c can be deduced.

This is a meta-metatheorem that expresses the transitive property of deduction, which is so valuable in many systems; to write this we need a metalanguage with new symbols for implication and conjunction, and here we shall choose ':' and ' ⊶ ' respectively. In this notation the statement is:

$$a \rightarrow b: b \rightarrow c \multimap a \rightarrow c$$

It seems legitimate to provide a program with general meta-metatheorems of this type, which are used by all mathematicians.

Unfortunately, there are also important meta-metatheorems that are specific to particular formal systems; for example, $p \supset q \multimap p \rightarrow q$ is not legal in all logical systems because it involves an operator, '⊃', which is not necessarily part of the language of every system. In general, any meta-metatheorem that involves an operator of the original formal system will be specific to that system. Thus we need a means for proving meta-metatheorems, and for this we define meta-meta-metatheorems, at which level the generality is such that it is valid for all mathematics now known. Thus the statement:

if $a.b \rightarrow c$ is a metatheorem then $a \multimap b \rightarrow c$ is a meta-metatheorem.

is a meta-meta-metatheorem that holds universally.

3.9.2 The metatheories of Pitrat's program

The axiomatics of Pitrat's program are different from those of propositional logic; the program uses the following eight general metatheorems:

1. $a \cdot b \rightarrow c \multimap b \cdot a \rightarrow c$ commutativity of antecedents
2. $a \cdot a \rightarrow b \multimap a \rightarrow b$ simplification
3. $v \rightarrow a \multimap a$ v a variable that does not appear in a

4. $v \cdot a \to b \mathrel{-\!\!\circ\!\!\to} a \to b$ as (3)
5. $a: a \to b \mathrel{-\!\!\circ\!\!\to} b$ *modus ponens* for metatheory
6. $a \to b: b \to c \mathrel{-\!\!\circ\!\!\to} a \to c$ trasitivity of deduction – 1st form
7. $a \to b:$
    $b \cdot c \to d \mathrel{-\!\!\circ\!\!\to} a \cdot c \to d$ transitivity of deduction – 2nd form
8. $a \to b:$
    $c \cdot d \to a \mathrel{-\!\!\circ\!\!\to} c \cdot d \to b$ transitivity of deduction – 3rd form

These metatheorems are in fact used by mathematicians, although not explicitly. In addition, the program 'knows' five meta-meta-metatheorems which enable it to prove other meta-metatheorems that will apply specifically to some theory; and for these we use a further new notation: '!' for conjunction and '$\mathrel{-\!\circ\!\circ\!\to}$' for deduction. In this meta-meta-metalanguage the new theorems are:

1. $a \cdot b \to c \mathrel{-\!\circ\!\circ\!\to} a \mathrel{-\!\!\circ\!\!\to} b \to c$
2. $a \cdot b \to c \mathrel{-\!\circ\!\circ\!\to} v \to a \mathrel{-\!\!\circ\!\!\to} v \cdot b \to c$ v not in a, b, c
3. $a \cdot b \to c \mathrel{-\!\circ\!\circ\!\to} c \to v \mathrel{-\!\!\circ\!\!\to} a \cdot b \to v$
4. $a!a \mathrel{-\!\!\circ\!\!\to} b \to c \mathrel{-\!\circ\!\circ\!\to} b \to c$
5. $a \to b!a \to b \mathrel{-\!\!\circ\!\!\to} c \cdot d \to e \mathrel{-\!\circ\!\circ\!\to} c \cdot d \to e$

The notations for the four language levels are given in Fig. 3.24. These statements enable important results in formal systems to be established quickly. They are used by Pitrat's program in conjunction with the unification algorithm, which undertakes the task of making the (meta)*-theorems that are to be proved coincide with the left sides of these given statements; thus if the validity of the word:

$$p \cdot p \to p \wedge q$$

has been proved in some particular theory, (iii) enables the meta-metatheorem:

$$p \wedge q \to r \mathrel{-\!\!\circ\!\!\to} p \cdot q \to r$$

to be deduced.

If the program is to have any inventive powers it must be able to answer two fundamental questions:

1. How are interesting or important results to be identified?
2. How are attempts to be made?

	Language	M-language	MM-language	MMM-language
Conjunction (AND)	$\wedge$	,	;	!
Implication	$\supset$	$\to$	$\mathrel{-\!\!\circ\!\!\to}$	$\mathrel{-\!\circ\!\circ\!\to}$

Fig. 3.24 Notation for different language levels.

Selection of results. When using these M-, MM- and MMM-theorems the programmer is soon faced with a combinatorial explosion of elements to be stored; three general principles are incorporated into the program with the aim of avoiding this:

1. A statement is the more interesting the fewer the symbols it involves.
2. A production is the more interesting the closer the antecedent is to the consequent. Recall here that a production is a rule for derivation, that is, an M^*-theorem with one or more antecedents.
3. It is better to spend time deciding what to retain than to waste it later in fruitless trials.

Productions are treated separately for the simple reason that very few are needed. A very strong discipline must be enforced so as to avoid storing different versions of one general form or implicitly duplicating, because of transitivity, what is already known: thus if we already have $a \rightarrow b$ and $b \rightarrow c$ there is no point in recording also $a \rightarrow c$ because the program can easily obtain this. On the other hand, derivations that lead to a simple result from something more complicated should always be retained.

The interest of a production is evaluated in terms of what is known already and what new results it may lead to: certain results regarded as unimportant in the early stages of a study may later prove worth recording, some considered very important to a given system may be discarded in the study of another. At any one time the program stores only the simplest productions, meaning those with the fewest operators and the fewest propositional variables.

Theorems present a more difficult problem because whilst productions, by definition, consist of antecedents and a consequent that can be compared, a theorem is merely a string of symbols of the language in question. In this program the interest of a theorem is measured by the sum of the interests of the productions it can generate, plus a decreasing linear function of the numbers of its unary and binary operators. In reality, however, the interest lies not in this but in the number of possible interpretations of the formal system; and this is only partially treated by the relations set up between language and metalanguage in the study of the productions generated by a theorem.

3.9.3 Choosing attempts

Initially the only attempts will start from the results of maximum interest in the sense defined above. If what is to be considered is a theorem, all productions are applied that simplify an antecedent, and therefore increase the interest. If it is a simplifying production, it is applied to all the theorems that have been stored and to all the complicating productions, taking the latter as antecedents. If it is a complicating production, it is applied to the simplifying productions and also to the productions with several antecedents. Not all possible trials are made because the program records with each statement tests in which it has already been involved and does not take these up again.

Clearly, the selection criteria are rather superficial; however, since not all the results will be stored the demands on both machine time and store capacity stay within acceptable limits.

Results. The program has worked with six different theories, due to Russell, Lukasiewicz, Hilbert and Bernay, Sheffer, and has rediscovered all the important theorems, in some cases giving novel proofs. It uses all the meta-levels provided and is able to work in conjectural mode; in this latter case, when it is to prove a precisely-stated result, it has to adopt rather different strategies because it has to invert its production rules so as to go from the conjecture towards the axioms. In all cases the program succeeded in proving, unaided, theorems that the mathematician who submitted them had been unable to prove. An impartial judgement here is that of Lukasiewicz: 'One must be very expert in performing such proofs, if we want to deduce from the three axioms of logic the law of commutation: $(p \supset (q \supset r)) \supset (q \supset (p \supset r))$, or even the law of simplification: $p \supset (q \supset p)$'. Both these deductions have been performed by Pitrat's program.

Example of a proof by the program

Axioms:	$(p \supset (q \supset r)) \supset ((p \supset q) \supset (p \supset r))$	T1
	$p \supset (q \supset p)$	T2
	$(\neg p \supset \neg q) \supset (q \supset p)$	T3
Production:	$p \cdot (p \supset q) \to q$	M1

In describing how the program works we shall use its own notation, prefix Polish. It first uses two of its *MMM*-theorems to obtain two *MM*-theorems from *M*1, as follows:

$$\supset pq \;\dashleftrightarrow\; p \to q \qquad MM1 \;(M1 \text{ and (i))}$$
$$p \to \supset qr \;\dashleftrightarrow\; p \cdot q \to r \qquad MM2 \;(M1 \text{ and (ii))}$$

Thus for example MM2 is obtained from (ii) and M1 by taking $p \supset q$ for a, p for b and q for c and using the commutivity of '.' given by (1). The result of the substitution is

$$(v \to \supset pq) \;\dashleftrightarrow\; (v \cdot p \to q)$$

Table 3.10. Proof of the theorem $(\neg p \supset p) \supset p$.

$T2 + MM1$	$p \to\ \supset qp$	$M2$
$T3 + MM1$	$\supset \neg p \neg q \to\ \supset qp$	$M3$
$T3 + MM1$	$\supset p \supset qr \to\ \supset\ \supset pq \supset pr$	$M4$
$M4 + MM2$	$\supset p \supset qr \supset pq \to\ \supset pr$	$M5$

This MM-theorem is obtained from the production $M5$:

	$\supset p \supset qr \multimap\ \supset pq \to\ \supset pr$	$MM3$
$T2 + MM3$	$\supset pq \to\ \supset pp$	$M6$
$T2 + M6$	$\supset pp$	$T4$
$M2 +$	first antecedent of $M5\ \supset pq \supset rp \to\ \supset rq$	$M7$

These MM theorems are obtained from the
production $M7$:

	$\supset pq \multimap\ \supset qr \to\ \supset pr$	$MM4$
	$\supset pq \multimap\ \supset rp \to\ \supset rp$	$MM5$
$T3 + MM5$	$\supset p \supset \neg q \neg r \to\ \supset p \supset rq$	$M8$
$T2 + MM4$	$\supset\ \supset pqr \to\ \supset qr$	$M9$
$M4 + M9$	$\supset p \supset qr \to\ \supset q \supset pr$	$M10$
$T4 + M10$	$\supset p \supset\ \supset pqq$	$T5$
$T5 + M4$	$\supset\ \supset p \supset pq \supset pq$	$T6$
$T6 + MM1$	$\supset p \supset pq \to\ \supset pq$	$M11$
$T6 + MM5$	$\supset p \supset q \supset qr \to\ \supset p \supset qr$	$M12$
$T1 + M9$	$\supset\ \supset pq \supset\ \supset rp \supset rq$	$T7$
$T7 + MM1$	$\supset pq \to\ \supset\ \supset rp \supset rq$	$M13$
$T7 + M10$	$\supset\ \supset pq \supset\ \supset qr \supset pr$	$T8$
$T8 + MM1$	$\supset pq \to\ \supset\ \supset qr \supset pr$	$M14$
$T2 + M14$	$\supset\ \supset\ \supset pqr \supset qr$	$T9$
$T9 + MM5$	$\supset p \supset\ \supset qrs \to\ \supset p \supset rs$	$M15$
$T1 + M15$	$\supset\ \supset p \supset qr \supset q \supset pr$	$T10$
$T10 + MM4$	$\supset\ \supset p \supset qrs \to\ \supset\ \supset q \supset prs$	$M16$
$T3 + M9$	$\supset \neg p \supset pq$	$T11$
$T11 + MM4$	$\supset\ \supset pqr \to\ \supset \neg pr$	$M17$
$M14 + M17$	$\supset pq \to\ \supset \neg q \supset pr$	$M18$
$M18 + M8$	$\supset \neg pq \to\ \supset \neg q \supset rp$	$M19$
$M19 + M11$	$\supset \neg pq \to\ \supset \neg qp$	$M20$
$T4 + M20$	$\supset \neg\neg pp$	$T12$
$T12 + M3$	$\supset p \neg\neg p$	$T13$
$T13 + M13$	$\supset\ \supset pq \supset p \neg\neg q$	$T14$
$T14 + M8$	$\supset\ \supset \neg pq \supset \neg qp$	$T15$
$T15 + M13$	$\supset\ \supset p \supset \neg qr \supset p \supset \neg rq$	$T16$
$T16 + M12$	$\supset\ \supset \neg p \supset \neg qp \supset \neg pq$	$T17$
$T17 + M16$	$\supset\ \supset \neg p \supset \neg qq \supset \neg qp$	$T18$
$T18 + MM1$	$\supset \neg p \supset \neg qq \to\ \supset \neg qp$	$M21$
$T12 + M21$	$\supset \neg p \neg\ \supset \neg pp$	$T19$
$T19 + M3$	$\supset\ \supset \neg ppp$	$T20$

and hence, on normalising,

$$p \rightarrow \supset qr \leftrightarrow p \cdot q \rightarrow r$$

which is *MM2*.

We now give part of the derivation tree that leads finally to the striking theorem $(\neg p \supset p) \supset p$: Table 3.10. To achieve this purely automatically the program constructs 5 *MM*-theorems, 21 *M*-theorems and 20 theorems, using the methods described above: note the important results *T4*, *T7*, *T8*, *T9*, *T11*, *T12*, *T13* and *T15* obtained in the course of the derivation.

The program has proved other theorems in this axiomatic system, and theorems in other systems; details are given in Pitrat 1966.

3.10 THE RESOLUTION PRINCIPLE AND THE PROLOG LANGUAGE

3.10.1 Resolution

In 1930 Jacques Herbrand presented in Paris a mathematical thesis in which he gave a new and original method for proving theorems in first-order logic. The underlying principle is one is seeking to prove that a conclusion C follows from a set of hypotheses $H1, H2, \ldots Hn$, that is, to establish the theorem:

$$H1 \wedge H2 \wedge \cdots \wedge Hn \supset C \qquad (T)$$

it may be simpler to show that the formula:

$$H1 \wedge H2 \wedge \cdots \wedge Hn \wedge \neg C \qquad (F)$$

(i.e. the negation of the conclusion added to the set of hypothesis) is self-contradictory. This will be achieved if it can be shown that F is a non-theorem of the system, for example containing a sub-expression of the form $p \wedge \neg p$; in other words, it will suffice if a counter-example for F can be given. Herbrand gave a constructive procedure (the so-called 'resolution' procedure) that will achieve this in a finite number of steps whenever T is in fact a theorem. We now describe this.

3.10.2 Herbrand's theorem

The proof that F is a contradiction depends on the interpretation of the negation symbol $\neg$. Herbrand's theorem ensures that this contradiction can always be established in a finite number of steps, whatever truth values are given to the functions that enter into the hypotheses and the conclusion.

Definitions
Let us agree to work only with certain disjunctive expressions Ci called clauses:

$$Ci = (Li1 \lor Li2 \lor \cdots \lor Lin_i)$$

and let F be written as a conjunction of clauses, $F = \land\, Ci$; we shall see later that any first-order formula can be put into this standard form. The quantities j, k, called literals, do not contain any of the symbols $\land$, $\forall$, $\exists$, $\supset$. Let E be the set of clauses of F and G_0 the set of constants appearing in E; we now define recursively G_i, for all integers i, as the set formed by the union of G_{i-1} with all the terms $f_k(t1, t2, ..., tm_k)$ where f_k is a function of the m_k arguments t_j, $j = 1, 2, ..., m_k$ and t_j is a term of G_{i-1}; and put:

$$G(E) = \bigcup_{i=0}^{\infty} G_i$$

The set $G(E)$ is called the Herbrand universe of E.

The Herbrand base $B(E)$ of a set of clauses E is the set of all atomic formulae of E: that is, of formulae that contain at most one predicate or one predicate preceded by $\neg$. Herbrand's theorem is proved with the aid of a tree A of the elements of $B(E)$ such that:

1. E is the root of A;
2. every vertex of A is a subset (possibly instantiated) of E;
3. no path starting from the root contains both p and $\neg p$, where p is any formula.

Assigning truth values to formulae built with $B(E)$ thus reduces to choosing a path through the vertices of A, and a contradiction is established when it is found that (3) cannot be satisfied. It follows from Herbrand's theorem, stated below, that this will always be the case when E is inconsistent, that is, contains a contradiction.

Herbrand's theorem (1930)

> *A necessary and sufficient condition for a set E of clauses to be inconsistent is that E contains a finite set of fully instantiated sub-formulae that is inconsistent.*

The critical set of sub-formulae can be constructed by means of a tree, with the aid of a very simple procedure derived from the following fundamental result:

Resolution theorem

> Let $F1$ be the formula, in standard form
>
> $$C1 \wedge C2 \wedge \cdots \wedge Ci \wedge \cdots \wedge Cj \wedge \cdots \wedge Cm,$$
>
> $$\text{where } Ci = (p \vee Li), \; Cj = (\neg p \wedge Lj)$$
>
> and $F2$ *the formula*
>
> $$F2 = F1 \wedge (Li \vee Lj)$$
>
> Then if $F2$ *is contradictory, so also is* $F1$.

Proof. It suffices to show that $F1 \rightarrow F2$. The case $Li \equiv \emptyset$ is trivial, for it then suffices to show that if $E2 = Lj$ is contradictory so also is $E1 = p \wedge (\neg p \vee Lj)$, and the Ck for k different from i and j do not enter the argument.

Since in first-order logic we have

$$(\neg A \vee B) \equiv (A \supset B)$$

it follows that

$$E1 \equiv p \wedge (p \supset Lj)$$

and hence, by *modus ponens* and the metatheorem

$$p \cdot q \leftrightarrow p \wedge q, \; E1 \equiv Lj$$

and the result follows.

The case $Lj \equiv \emptyset$ is treated similarly, using the fact that $p \equiv \neg\neg p$:

$$E1 \equiv (p \vee Li) \wedge \neg p (\neg\neg p \vee Li) \wedge \neg p = (\neg p \supset Li) \wedge \neg p$$

and hence

$$E1 \equiv Li$$

and it follows that

$$F1 \rightarrow F2$$

In the general case $E1$ has the form

$$E1 \equiv (p \vee Li) \wedge (\neg p \vee Lj)$$

and as before

$$p \vee Li \rightarrow \neg Li \supset p \text{ and } \neg p \vee Lj \rightarrow p \supset Lj$$

Thus

$$E1 \equiv (\neg Li \supset p) \wedge (p \supset Lj)$$

and by the theorem

$$(a \supset b) \wedge (b \supset c) \rightarrow a \supset c$$

it follows that

$$E1 \rightarrow \neg Li \supset Lj$$

i.e.

$$E1 \rightarrow Li \vee Lj$$

and hence

$$F1 \rightarrow F2$$

Thus $F2$ can be deduced from $F1$, so the clause $(Li \vee Lj)$ has no effect on the deductibility of $F1$; therefore if $F2$ is contradictory this must be because $F1$ was already contradictory.

Further, the process of successive 'resolutions' established in this way is *complete*, that is, if a formula E is contradictory this will be shown by resolution in a finite number of steps: this is the result guaranteed by Herbrand's theorem.

The clauses $Ci = (p \vee Li)$ and $Cj = (\neg p \vee Lj)$ are called the *parent clauses* of $Li \vee Lj$, which is called the *resolvant*. Of course, if Ci and Cj contain variables, as will usually be the case in first-order logic, a common literal p must be found by unification; this can be given by several different unifications, so that a tree of formulae has to be constructed in order to carry out the proof – that is, to establish the contradiction.

Examples of resolution

1. Propositional logic. Let $F1 \equiv \neg s \wedge q \wedge (p \vee \neg q) \wedge (\neg p \vee s)$. This is a conjuction of four clauses which we can write $C1 \wedge C2 \wedge C3 \wedge C4$. A first resolution of $C1$ and $C4$ gives the resolvant $C5 \equiv \neg p$ and a second with $C2$ and $C3$ gives $C6 \equiv p$. Resolution of $C5$ and $C6$ gives an empty resolvent, therefore the original formula $F1$ is contradictory; thus by adding $\neg s$ to the left side we have proved that:

$$q \wedge (p \vee \neg q) \wedge (\neg p \vee s) \supset s$$

2. First-order logic. Let x, y, z, t, v be variables, a, b, c constants and P, Q, R any predicates; and let $F1$ be the expression

$$F1 \equiv P(x, y) \wedge Q(t) \wedge R(v) \wedge (\neg P(a, z) \vee \neg Q(b) \vee \neg Q(c))$$

Unification leads to three substitutions and correspondingly three resolvents:

$$S_1 = \{x/a, y/b\} \text{ gives } F2 = \neg(Q(b) \vee \neg Q(c)$$
$$S_2 = \{t/b\} \qquad\qquad F2' = \neg P(a, z) \vee \neg Q(c)$$
$$S_3 = \{t/c\} \qquad\qquad F2'' = \neg P(a, z) \vee \neg Q(b)$$

Here again, $F1$ will be shown to be contradictory if Li and Lj are found to be both empty, that is, if a resolvent shows an internal contradiction. This is so for $F2$ and the second clause of $F1$: the substitution

$S_3 = \{t/b\}$ gives $F3 = \neg Q(c)$ which with the same clause and
$S_4 = \{t/c\}$ gives the resolvent $F4 = \emptyset$

which establishes that $F1$ is contradictory.

3.10.3   Practical organisation of proofs by Herbrand's principle

If the standard form for a clause is taken to be a sequence of conjunctions there is no need to preserve the $\land$ symbols. To generate the tree it is then sufficient to maintain the clauses stacked one behind the other; at a resolution the resolvent is added at the top of the stack, without removing its parent clauses, in such a way as to preserve the possibility of other substitutions (in example 2 just above, in which case the resolvent $\neg Q(b) \lor \neg Q(c)$ is put at the top of the stack after the substitution $S1$ has been performed – see Table 3.11). Only one occurrence of any clause is retained, and a resolvent $C1$ is not retained if it is less general than a clause $C2$ that is already stored – that is, if there is a substitution S such that $S \cdot C2 = C1$, for example if $C1 = Q(a)$, $C2 = Q(t)$. Further, it follows from the commutativity of the operator $\land$ that the order of the clauses in the stack is immaterial.

Table 3.11 Storage of the tree
for the proof

$\neg P(a, z) \lor \neg Q(b) \lor \neg Q(c)$
$R(u)$
$Q(t)$
$P(x, y)$

The number of literals in a resolvent is two less than the sum of the numbers in the two parents; thus it is greater than that in either except in the case where one of the parents has at most two literals. The contradiction is established only with two *unitary* parent clauses, that is, with each having only a single literal.

3.10.3.1 Putting an expression into normal conjunctive form

All that we now have to do is to show how this can be done for any expression in first-order logic. Six steps are necessary, as follows.

1. Putting into 'prenex' form. In this form all the quantifiers are brought to the head of the expression. The operation separates the quantifier symbols from the variables to which they apply and does not seem very natural; the operators do not commute so their order must be preserved exactly. It may be necessary to rename the quantified variables, using the theorem:

$$(Q1x)A(x) * (Q2x)B(x) \rightarrow (Q1x)(Q2y)(A(x) * B(y))$$

where $Q1$, $Q2$ each denote either $\forall$ or $\exists$ and $*$ denotes either $\land$ or $\lor$. Conversely, factorisation is allowed:

$$(\forall x)A(x) \land (\forall y)B(y) \rightarrow (\forall x)(A(x) \land B(x))$$

Example. The initial formula E:

$$(\forall x)(P(x) \supset ((\exists y)(P(y) \lor \neg R(a, x, y)) \supset (\forall z)(\neg S(y, z))))$$

becomes after this operation:

$$(\forall x)(\exists y)(\forall z)(P(x) \supset ((P(y) \lor \neg R(a, x, y)) \supset (\neg S(y, z))))$$

2. Elimination of existential quantifiers. The idea of this is due to the mathematician Skolem (1927); it is a recognition of the fact that any variable that is quantified existentially is really a function of the universally quantified variables on which it depends, that is, in whose range it lies. There is thus a process called *skolemisation* in which each existentially quantified variable is replaced by a new function and the corresponding quantifiers removed; applied to the expression E above this gives:

$$(\forall x)(\forall z)(P(x) \supset ((P(f(x)) \lor \neg R(a, x, f(x))) \supset (\neg S(f(x), z))))$$

3. Elimination of universal quantifiers. Since all the variables that remain in the formula are now universally quantified, the quantifiers can be taken as implied; thus E can be written:

$$(P(x) \supset ((P(f(x) \lor \neg R(a, x, f(x))) \supset (\neg S(f(x), z))))$$

If at this point there are still some existential quantifiers at the head, they too are removed: instantiations of the associated variables should be found which satisfy the formula.

4. Elimination of the symbols $\supset$ and $\leftrightarrow$. For this, the theorems

$$A \leftrightarrow B \mapsto (A \supset B) \land (B \supset A)$$
$$A \supset B \mapsto (\neg A \lor B)$$

are used wherever necessary. The formula now becomes:

$$(\neg P(x) \lor (\neg (P(f(x)) \lor \neg R(a, x, f(x))) \lor \neg S(f(x), z)))$$

Thus three operators only are needed to express any formula of predicate calculus.

5. *Reduction of the scope of the negations.* The theorems

$$\neg(A \vee B) \rightarrow (\neg A \wedge \neg B) \quad \text{and} \quad \neg(A \wedge B) \rightarrow (\neg A \vee \neg B)$$

enable the scope of the negation symbols $\neg$ to be progressively reduced until they each act on only a single predicate. With this, E is written:

$$(\neg P(x) \vee ((\neg P(f(x)) \wedge R(a, x, f(x))) \vee \neg S(f(x), z)))$$

6. *Putting into conjunctive form.* In this final stage the operator $\wedge$ is brought to the head everywhere so as to give the form:

$$C1 \wedge C2 \wedge \ldots \wedge Cn$$

in which the clauses Ci contain only the connectives $\vee$ and $\neg$; this is achieved by using the distributive theorems:

$$A \vee (B \wedge C) \rightarrow (A \vee B) \wedge (A \vee C)$$
$$(A \wedge B) \vee C \rightarrow (A \vee C) \wedge (B \vee C)$$

E is now written:

$$(\neg P(x) \vee (\neg P(f(x)) \vee \neg S(f(x), z)) \wedge (R(a, x, f(x)) \vee \neg S(f(x), z))))$$

and finally:

$$(\neg P(x) \vee (\neg P(f(x)) \vee \neg S(f(x), z)))$$
$$\wedge (\neg P(x) \vee R(a, x, f(x)) \vee \neg S(f(x), z))$$

The stack of clauses before resolution is shown in Table 3.12, where the unnecessary parentheses have been removed from the disjunctive expressions. The various stages in this process do not necessarily have to be performed in the order given here; for example, the removal of the quantifiers can be left to the end.

J. A. Robinson, in 1963, was the first to put Herbrand's proposed processes into a form in which they could be carried out by a computer.

Table 3.12 Normal conjunctive form, with stack of clauses for resolution.

$$\neg P(x) \vee R(a, x, f(x)) \vee \neg S(f(x), z)$$
$$\neg P(x) \vee \neg P(f(x)) \vee \neg S(f(x), z)$$

3.10.4 Examples of proofs by Herbrand's method

We give first an example of a complete proof that can be obtained with Robinson's implementation of Herbrand's principle; we shall comment later on the rather unfamiliar nature of the proof. The problem is to prove the following:

'a hand is a part of a man'

We need a binary predicate $A(x, y)$, say, that states 'x is a part of y'; and an expression that expresses the transitivity of the relation, that is:

$$A(x, y) \wedge A(y, z) \supset A(x, z)$$

which we put into normal disjunctive form:

$$- A(x, y) - A(y, z) + A(x, z)$$

in which $- P$, $+ P$ are written for $\neg P$ and P respectively, for any predicate P. This is the notation of the language PROLOG and enables the symbol $\vee$ to be omitted from the clauses.

With the constants h, a, b, m denoting hand, arm, body and man respectively the hypotheses for the problem are $A(h, a)$, $A(a, b)$ and $A(b, m)$; to which, for the purposes of the proof, we add the negation of the desired conclusion, that is, $- A(h, m)$. Thus the program starts with five clauses, implicitly linked by symbols:

C1	$- A(x, y) - A(y, z) + A(z, x)$
C2	$+ A(h, a)$
C3	$+ A(a, b)$
C4	$+ A(b, m)$
C5	$- A(h, m)$

We give only those resolutions that lead most quickly to a contradiction; the tree actually constructed by the program consists of many more clauses, with many more paths. The resolutions preformed are given in Table 3.13. The last resolution gives the empty clause, showing that the set of hypotheses is inconsistent; since C1–C4 are known to be true, C5 must be false and therefore the theorem $A(h, m)$ is proved.

Now let us take a second, more complicated, example:

'if in a group the square of any element is equal to the unit element, the group is commutative'.

Here we need a predicate to express the fact that the product of any two elements (as defined by the law for the group) is equal to some element of

Table 3.13

Parent clauses with numbers of literals unified	Substitutions	Resolutions
$C5 + C1.3$	$\{x/m, z/h\}$	$C6 - A(m, y) - A(y, h)$
$C6 + C2$	$\{y/b\}$	$C7 - A(b, h)$
$C7 + C1.3$	$\{x/b, z/h\}$	$C8 - A(b, y) - A(y, h)$
$C8.1 + C3$	$\{y/t\}$	$C9 - A(t, h)$
$C9 + C4$	ϕ	$C10$

the group, say:

$$I(x, y, z) \text{ iff } x \cdot y = z$$

The properties of the unit element are then expressed by:

$$+ I(e, x, x) \quad \text{and} \quad + I(x, e, x)$$

The variables x in these two predicates are of course independent and would be quantified separately; in the proof we write them $x1$, $x2$ so as to avoid any confusion during the unification; as already stated, care should always be taken, before performing any resolution, to rename variables so as to differentiate between those that are quantified independently – this is the 'separation of variables'.

Let $i(y)$ be the Skolem function that gives the inverse of any element y, then:

$$+ I(i(y), y, e) \quad \text{and} \quad + I(y, i(y), e)$$

where again the variables y are independent and should be separated.

We have to express the associativity of the product law. This is done in two stages; take first the left associativity:

$$x \cdot (y \cdot z) \mapsto (x \cdot y) \cdot z \tag{LA}$$

The only predicate concerning equality at our disposal is I, and to make use of this we have to introduce some intermediate steps. If $x \cdot y = u$, $y \cdot z = v$ and $x \cdot v = w$ the law LA states that then $u \cdot z = w$ also; that is

$$I(x, y, u) \land I(y, z, v) \land I(x, v, w) \supset I(u, z, w)$$

Using the identity $(A \land B \land C) \supset D \to (\neg A \lor \neg B \lor \neg C \lor D)$ to put this in normal disjunctive form we have:

$$- I(x, y, u) - I(y, z, v) - I(x, v, w) + I(u, v, x) \tag{LA}$$

Similarly we have the right associative law:

$$- I(x, y, u) - I(y, z, v) - I(u, z, w) + I(x, v, w) \qquad \text{(RA)}$$

The property given for the group is:

$$+ I(x, x, e)$$

and the result to be proved is:

$$(\forall x)(\forall y)(\forall z)((x \cdot y = z) \supset (y \cdot x = z)),$$

the negation of which, since

$$\neg(A \supset B) \mapsto \neg(\neg A \vee B) \mapsto \neg\neg A \wedge \neg B \mapsto A \wedge \neg B$$

can be written

$$(\exists a)(\exists b)(\exists c)(a \cdot b = c) \wedge (b \cdot a \neq c)$$

The elements a, b, c are treated simply as constants in what follows and the proof of the stated property consists in showing that such constants cannot exist. The negation itself can be expressed as a pair of clauses:

$$+ I(a, b, c) \quad \text{and} \quad - I(b, a, c)$$

The essentials of the proof by successive resolutions are given in Table 3.14.

3.10.5 Comments on the proofs

Although these proofs may not seem very natural they are easily restated in familiar notation. For the first, working back from the conclusion, we have:

$$(\forall y)h \in y \supset y \notin m$$

$$a \notin m \qquad \text{('an arm is not part of a man')}$$

$$(\forall y)a \notin y \supset y \notin m$$

$$b \notin m$$

and the conclusion follows.

Many other resolutions can be performed, with many paths leading to the empty clause. It is a disadvantage to have a system of clauses with a single predicate because this increases the number of possible resolutions. Thus in the second proof it will be seen that the clauses $C3$, $C4$ concerning the inverse $i(x)$, given as hypothesis, are not used: all the many steps involving resolutions with these clauses have been deleted − over 100 steps were needed to produce Table 3.14 and the program would have been less cumbersome without $C3$ and $C4$. The first important step is $C12$ which

Table 3.14 Proof of commutativity in a group where $\forall x\, x, x = e$ using Herbrand's method.

C1	$+ I(e, x1, x1)$
C2	$+ I(x2, e, x2)$
C3	$+ I(\mathsf{l}(y1), y1, e)$
C4	$+ I(y2, \mathsf{l}(y2), e)$
C5	$+ I(x3, x3, e)$
C6	$- I(x4, y4, u4) - I(y4, z4, v4) - I(x4, v4, w4) + I(u4, z4, w4)$
C7	$- I(x5, y5, u5) - I(y5, z5, v5) - I(u5, z5, w5) + I(x5, v5, w5)$
C8	$+ I(a, b, c)$
C9	$- I(b, a, c)$

Parent clauses	Substitutions	Resolutions
C5 + C7.1	$\{x5/x3\ y5/x3,\ u5/e\}$	
C8 + C10.1	$\{x6/a, z6/b, v6/c\}$	C10 $\quad - I(x6, z6, v6) - I(e, z6, w6) + I(x6, v6, w6)$
C11.1 + C1	$\{w7/b\}$	C11 $\quad - I(e, b, w7) + I(a, c, w7)$
C9 + C7.4	$\{x5/b, v5/a, w5/c\}$	C12 $\quad + I(a, c, b)$
C5 + C13.1	$\{x3/b, y8/b, u8/e\}$	C13 $\quad - I(b, y8, u8) - I(y8, z8, a) - I(u8, z8, c)$
C14.2 + C1	$\{z9/c\}$	C14 $\quad - I(b, z9, a) - I(e, z9, c)$
C15 + C6.4	$\{u4/b, z4/c, w4/a\}$	C15 $\quad - I(b, c, a)$
C12 + C16.1	$\{x10/a, y10/c\}$	C16 $\quad - I(x10, y10, b) - I(y10, c, v10) - I(x10, v10, a)$
C17.1 + C5	$\{x3/c, v11/e\}$	C17 $\quad - I(c, c, v11) - I(a, v11, a)$
C18 + C2	$\{x2/a\}$	C18 $\quad - I(a, e, a)$
		C19 $\quad \square$

states that it follows from the hypotheses that $a \cdot c = b$; this serves as a lemma and the search then takes a new direction to arrive at C13: $((b \cdot y = u)\, (y \cdot z = a))\, (u \cdot z \neq c)$, a partial clause that seems rather strange. Then

$$C16: x \cdot y = b \supset x \cdot (y \cdot c) \neq a$$
$$C17: a \cdot (c \cdot c) \neq a$$

and the contradiction follows since $c \cdot c = e$. Notice that in this resolution multiplication on the left by c has been performed without any special 'invention' by the system.

3.10.6 Strategies

There still remains the problem presented by the combinatorial explosion in the resolution process: how to choose the clauses and literals to be unified so as to get to the empty clause as quickly as possible. As usual, there is no general solution; what to do depends on the context. However, workers in this field have in fact defined some strategies for these choices that do not involve the context, achieving this by restricting the number of possible resolutions. It is important not to sacrifice completeness in imposing these restrictions, that is, not to lose the guarantee that by one means or another a proof will be established in every case. The following are some of these strategies.

Unit strategy. One of the parent clauses always has only a single literal. This strategy clearly is not complete because the process must come to an end as soon as the set of clauses no longer contains one with a single unifiable literal. The above proofs could be obtained with this strategy.

Input strategy. One of the clauses is either one of the hypotheses or the negation of the conclusion. This strategy is not complete. An example is the first of the two proofs just given.

Set of support strategy. One of the parent clauses is either the result to be established or a clause derived from this; the process starts by assuming the desired result and tries to work back to the hypotheses, forbidding all resolution within the given initial set. This strategy is complete but is lengthy because introduces a structure of lemmas that is not always efficient.

Linear strategy. One of the clauses is the previous resolvent and the other is either one of the ancestors of this or an input clause. This, which is an improvement over the input strategy, is complete and is one of the most efficient.

Other strategies have been proposed, and descriptions can be found in the literature. Note that a combination of two of the above strategies will give one that is more restrictive and which is not necessarily complete even if both of the originals are complete.

There remains the problem of choosing the literals in the parent clauses when several unifications can be made. In general, the literals are ordered in some way and the program chooses the first pair that lead to success; when the enumeration of the literals is transmitted from the parent clauses to the resolvant what is called *lock resolution* is obtained, which is both complete and efficient.

3.10.7 Importance and limitations of resolutions

Proof by resolution, being systematic, is powerful and attractive; many papers on 'automatic proof' using this method have been written since

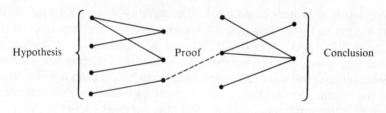

Fig. 3.25 Schematic for proof by resolution.

Herbrand's work and Robinson's implementation in 1965. A very specific result follows from the impossibility of defining a strategy that will apply in all circumstances: with any given set of clauses the computer will produce a proof either very quickly or not at all. The program rapidly becomes clogged as the number of clauses increases, so the problem is to formulate a criterion for deciding when to stop the run, for there are two risks to be avoided: (1) Explosion of the number of clauses (2) Premature abandoning of the run when a proof would in fact be reached.

The importance and originality of resolution can be summed up in two properties:

1. Processing of the AND/OR tree, normally necessary in any proof, is eliminated. The standardised form of the stack of clauses plays this role and a very simple form of processing, choice + unification, can be specified.
2. The hypotheses and all the intermediate clauses play the same role. The process advances in two directions simultaneously, from the hypotheses towards the conclusions and inversely, and the proof is achieved when the two paths meet. This is illustrated in Fig. 3.25.

At the same time, the method suffers from the major disadvantage that, by its nature, it is limited to proving given theorems; it cannot be used to conceive, and then prove, theorems, as does a mathematician. Further, if the method is given a conjecture that is not a theorem it can develop an infinite tree. Thus resolution is an excellent method that is both simple and systematic, but which, unfortunately, can be applied in only a limited number of circumstances characterised by the proof not being very deep and the number of potential resolutions being small.

3.10.8 The PROLOG language and applications of resolution

In 1972 Alain Colmerauer, with his team at Marseilles, developed a problem-solving system based on the Herbrand–Robinson method. Problems are put to this system in the form of predicates and expressed in the language PROLOG; thus PROLOG can be regarded as a declarative programming language in which only the definition of the problem is stated.

Since the user will want an explicit solution to his problem it is important that the system provides this, and the proof by refutation that resolution provides is not sufficient. Green in 1969 has suggested adding to the set of input clauses a predicate related to the conclusion:

$$\neg \; \text{conclusion}(x) \quad \lor \; \text{output}(x), \quad \text{or} \quad \text{conclusion}(x) \quad \land \; \text{output}(x)$$

so that the instantiation of the variable x gives the solution explicitly, the system finally outputting the instantiated value of x. We now show how PROLOG does this.

Consider the problem of contacting someone over the telephone. The data can be expressed in terms of four predicates, T, V, A, J, with meanings:

$J(p, n)$ person p can be reached by telephone number n

$A(x, l)$ person x is at location l

$T(l, m)$ location l has telephone number m

$V(y, z)$ person y is visiting person z

The starting condition is V(Peter, John).

We need now to express some useful properties of these predicates. If y is visiting z and if z is at location e then y is at e: this is clause $C2$ below; and if p is at location l and l has telephone n then p can be contacted by telephone number n: this is clause $C1$.

In PROLOG the symbols are omitted in the interior of a clause and, as explained in Section 10.4, negation is indicated by the minus sign, $-$. PROLOG performs the separation of variables automatically at successive resolutions. All the clauses that relate to the same conclusion predicate (which will be preceded by a $+$ sign) must be given in succession in the data. Further, only Horn clauses are allowed in PROLOG, that is, clauses having only a single positive literal, which is placed at the head. The following clauses therefore are input to PROLOG:

$C1 + J(x, m) - A(x, l) - T(l, m)$
$C2 + A(y, e) - V(y, z) - A(z, e)$
$C3 + A$(John, office__John)
$C4 + V$(Peter, John)
$C5 + T$(office__John, 654-3210)
$C6 - J$(Peter, n) $-$ output(n)
PROLOG responds: $n = 654$-3210.

The resolutions performed, given below, are not seen by the user. The strategy employed is set of support with lock resolution, PROLOG developing the search tree depth first, starting from the goal clause (the only negative clause), and taking the other clauses in their natural order. The literals are examined systematically from left to right. At each new resolution preference is given to the previous resolvent: that is, backtracking is built into the interpreter.

$C6 + C1.3$ $(x/\text{Peter}, m/n)$ $C7$: $- A(\text{Peter}, l) - T(l, n) - \text{output}(n)$
$C7.1 + C2$ $(y/\text{Peter}, e/l)$ $C8$: $- V(\text{Peter}, z) - A(z, l) - T(l, n)$
                                    $- \text{output}(n)$
$C8.1 + C4$ (z/John) $C9$: $- A(\text{John}, l) - T(l, n) - \text{output}(n)$
$C9.1 + C3$ $(l/\text{office\_John})$ $C10$: $- T(\text{office\_John}, n) - \text{output}(n)$
$C10 + C5$ $(n/654\text{-}3210)$ $C11$: $- \text{output}(654\text{-}3210)$

The predicate *output* having become the only literal, the system prints out the response.

PROLOG's response to a problem may be not simply a constant but possibly a formal variable, as in the following example: '($C1$) if x is the father of y and if z is the father of z then z is the grandfather of y; ($C2$) everyone has a father. Who is the grandfather of t (t arbitrary)?'

The formal statement of this is:

$C1 + GP(z, y) - P(x, y) - P(z, x)$
$C2 + P(p(u), u)$
$C3 - GP(v, t) - \text{output}(v)$

which leads to the resolutions:

$C3 + C1$ $\{z/v, y/t\}$ $C4$ $- P(x, t) - P(v, x) - \text{output}(v)$
$C4 + C2$ $\{x/p(u), u/t\}$ $C5$ $- P(v, p(u))$ $- \text{output}(v)$
$C5 + C2$ $\{v/p(u), u/p(t)\}$ $C6$ $- \text{output}(p(p(t)))$
        output: $p(p(t))$

These examples indicate the richness of the system and the possibilities for application wherever the tree for the proof is not too extensive. One important application is to querying a database: if the need is to extract items having specified attributes, the language of this logical system provides all the power one could wish for framing the appropriate questions, and a PROLOG-type system can then immediately get the responses.

Another application is to the control of a robot. The robot has to solve 'in its head' a problem put to it and then formulate a plan of action; the same methods will enable it to record for itself the plan, built by resolutions. It may need to 'walk', for example, to move some object, to climb on to a box in order to reach some bananas hanging from the ceiling:

for this problem let $E(x, y, z, s)$ be the predicate which expresses: the state s is defined by the robot being at x, a box at y and the bananas at z. Then define as follows:

$M(x1, y1, s1)$ the state reached when the robot, starting from state $s1$, goes from $x1$ to $y1$

$P(x2, y2, s2)$ the state reached when the robot, starting from state $s2$, pushes the box from $x2$ to $y2$

$G(s3)$ the state reached if the robot, starting from state $s3$, climbs on to the box

$A(s4)$ the predicate which expresses the fact that the robot, starting from state $s4$, can reach the bananas

a, b, c the initial positions of the robot, the bananas and the box respectively (state $s0$)

The initial clauses are:

$C1 + E(c, y, c, M(t, c, s)) - E(t, y, c, s)$	the robot can walk to the box
$C2 + E(v, y, v, P(x, v, w)) - E(x, y, x, w)$	push the box
$C3 + E(x, y, x, G(s)) - E(x, y, x, s)$	climb on to the box
$C4 + E(a, b, c, s0)$	(initial state)
$C5 + A(G(z)) - E(b, b, b, G(z))$	take the bananas
$C6 - A(w) - \text{output}(A(w))$	(negation of the goal)

PROLOG solves this problem without difficulty but needs 50 unifications. The result can be reached more quickly using the following strategy: starting from the goal, never use the same clause twice in the same branch of the tree and always use only the previous resolvent and a clause from the initial set. Adopting this strategy the process goes as follows.

$C5 + C6 \ \{w/G(z)\}$

$C7 \quad - E(b, b, b, G(z))$
$\quad\quad - \text{output}(A(G(z)))$

$C7 + C3 \ \{x/b, y/b, z/s\}$

$C8 \quad - E(b, b, b, s) - \text{output}(A(G(s)))$

$C8 + C2 \ \{v/b, y/b,$
$\quad\quad\quad s/P(x, b, w)\}$

$C9 \quad - E(x, b, x, w)$
$\quad\quad - \text{output}(A(G(P(x, b, w))))$

$C9 + C1 \ \{x/c, y/b, M(t, c, s)\}$

$C10 \quad - E(t, b, c, s)$
$\quad\quad\quad - \text{output}(A(G(P(c, b, M(t, c, s)))))$

$C10 + C4 \ \{t/a, s/s0\}$

$C11 \quad - \text{output}$
$\quad\quad\quad (A(G(P(c, b, M(a, c, s0)))))$

Starting from its initial position the robot moves (M) to the box at c which it pushes (P) to b, under the bananas; all it then has to do is to climb (G) on to the box.

Chapter 4

CLASSICAL METHODS FOR PROBLEM-SOLVING

There are four main ways for finding the solution to a given problem, that is, to exhibit an object belonging to a set known to satisfy the constraints explicitly imposed. These are as follows:

1. The application of an explicit formula that gives the solution.
2. The use of a recursive definition.
3. The use of an algorithm that converges to the solution.
4. The application of certain other processes, in particular trial and error, involving enumeration of cases.

When it is available the first method is undoubtedly the best: the formula, found and proved in advance, gives the solution in all cases. Examples are finding the zeros of a second degree polynomial, the day for any given date, the current in an electrical circuit; and it is a prime aim of mathematics to find such explicit solutions for as many problems as possible.

When there is an explicit solution the complexity of the problem is measured by the computational effort needed to evaluate the formula, which by definition can involve only a finite number of symbols and operations, whatever the parameters of the problem, that is, whatever the scale of the original problem. Thus the complexity is constant, independent of this scale, that is, $O(1)$. Here we are taking the complexity of each operation, such as $+$, $-$, $/$, $*$, to be independent of the number of digits in the operands, so that the complexity of the evaluation is proportional to the number of operations.

4.1 EXAMPLES OF SUITABLE ALGORITHMS

Example 1. Compute the sum of the first n integers. There is a known closed formula for this, of constant complexity and requiring one addition, one multiplication and one division:

$$\sum_{i=1}^{n} i = (n*(n+1))/2$$

Example 2. Compute the sum of the squares of the first n integers. Again there is a known formula:

$$\sum_{i=1}^{n} i^2 = (n*(n+1)*(2n+1))/6$$

Example 3. Compute the sum of the cubes of the first n integers. This suggests that a whole series of problems will follow, for which explicit formulae for the solutions will not always be known. But this is where information-science takes over from mathematics: there is no fatal disadvantage in not having a formula so long as a computational process can be defined that will give the solution in a finite number of steps. But now a new question arises: if a formula is replaced by a process, how many steps will be needed to give the solution? Answering this is the aim of this chapter.

It often happens that the statement of a problem provides an implicit computational formula that gives the solution by a recursive approach, repeatedly referring to itself. Thus the sum $S(n)$ of the first n integers is defined recursively by:

$$S(n) = S(n-1) + n$$

with

$$S(1) = 1$$

which is a process that can be expressed in any good programming language:

```
procedure S(n): sum of first n integers
  if n ≠ 1 then S(n) ← S(n − 1) + n
           else S(n) ← 1
  end if
end S
```

To compute $S(5)$ an information processing system calls the procedure S with the formal parameter n equal to 5; 5 is different from 1 so the system knows that it must add 5 to the value of $S(4)$, which it must therefore compute. It now calls S again, recording in a 'stack' that when it has found $S(4)$ it must add 5 to this so as to get the value required; we can represent this as

+   5 $S(4)$

The next call organises the computation of $S(4)$, giving:

+   5   +   4 $S(3)$

and so on until:

+   5   +   4   +   3   +   2 $S(1)$

When it calls $S(1)$ the system can compute the value by an explicit formula: $S(1) \leftarrow 1$. It then has no more need for stacking and can empty the stack, working backwards, to get the result. Clearly, the process is strictly equivalent to the iteration schema:

$$S \leftarrow 0$$
repeat for $i \in [1; n]$
$$S \leftarrow S + i$$

The complexity in each of these cases is $O(n)$, because that is the order of the number of additions that have to be made. The algorithms are easily extended to find the sum of the squares, or more generally the pth powers, of the first n integers; in the general case exactly $n - 1$ additions and n raisings to the pth power are needed.

Algorithmic technique, considered generally, consists in constructing algorithms of acceptable complexity for all problems for which an explicit formula for the solution cannot be found; and a very good particular method is to go straight to a recursive expression, which is often easily and quickly obtained and is always concise and elegant. When the complexity of the algorithm proves to be too great it is the task of the information scientist, starting from the recursive formulation, to construct a succession of more direct formulations until a process of acceptable complexity is reached. The theoretical complexity, which is what is being discussed here, is not very different from what is felt by a user at a terminal: so the theoreticians' efforts to reduce complexity are made in response to a very real practical need.

Example 4. Fibonacci numbers – computation of $F(30)$. These are defined recursively by:

$$F(n) = F(n - 1) + F(n - 2)$$
$$F(2) = F(1) = 1$$

They were introduced by Leonard de Pise, son of Bonacci, in 1540; they characterise many natural phenomena – for example, in population growth $F(n)$ is the number of individuals at time n – and occur in many branches of mathematics – for example, in the proof of the impossibility of there being a solution of Hilbert's tenth problem concerning diophantine equations.

A. Explicit formula. If we assume $F(n) = x^n$, x must satisfy $x^2 - x - 1 = 0$, so $F(n)$ is a linear function of the nth powers of the quadratic: if the roots are α, β then $F(n) = A\alpha^n + B\beta^n$ where A, B are some constants. With the given initial values the formula, due to F. Binet, is:

$$F(n) = [(1 + \sqrt{5})^n - (1 - \sqrt{5})^n]/(2^n \cdot \sqrt{5})$$

However, we may not know this; and further, the formula is quite complicated, as is made clear if one tries to compute even $F(3)$ by hand, and more so for $F(10)$. And even so the problem is not completely solved, for an algorithm for evaluating the formula has still to be specified: should the expressions $(1 \pm \sqrt{5})^n$ be expanded by the binomial theorem, or not? should $\sqrt{5}$ be manipulated as a formal symbol or numerically with its value $2.236068...$ to d decimals, and if the latter, what value should be taken for d? The value obtained for $F(n)$ should always be an integer, but it is clear that with a pocket calculator, and even with a large computer, this will not be so – so to what 'nearest' integer should the result of the computation be rounded? And how can we be absolutely certain that we have the correct result? So let us consider other methods.

B. Recursive formulation. This is given immediately by the statement of the problem:

procedure $F(n)$:   compute the n'th Fibonacci number
        if $n > 2$ **then** $F(n) \leftarrow F(n-1) + F(n-2)$
               else $F(n) \leftarrow 1$
      end if
   end

But here a new difficulty arises. Suppose we attempt a stack-like process, analogous to that for the sum of the integers; for the start of the calculation of $F(30)$ we have:

```
+   F(29)   F(28)
+   F(29)   +       F(27)   F(26)
+   F(29)   +       F(27)   +       F(25)   F(24)
    ...
```

and so on, until we get to the only two values known explicitly:

```
+    F(4)   F(3)
+    F(4)   +    F(2)   F(1)
```

Starting at this end of the stack, the appropriate substitutions are made and the system works backwards to get $F(3)$, and then has to start the process again for $F(4)$. Since the only known results, for $F(2)$ and $F(1)$, are both 1, the total number of additions needed to compute $F(n)$ is the number of units in $F(n)$; and since $F(30)$ is 832040, that is the size of the stack for this evaluation. So brute-force recursion is not a viable method; the complexity is in fact $O[F(n)]$, which, as the explicit solution shows, increases exponentially with n, and we must find a more 'reasonable' method.

C. Iterative algorithms. The recursive method is computationally very costly because the recursion goes to great depths; the way to reduce this cost is to avoid the need for continual repetition of the same calculation by transforming the process into one of iteration. We do this by assuming the problem solved – up to a particular point: that is, that we know the solution up to and including a certain value, i say, of n; from which we deduce $F(j)$ for at least one other value j.

What we are doing here is setting up a recurrence relation. We have found $F(1)$, $F(2)$, ..., $F(i)$, with $i = 2$ initially; if $i = n$ the problem is solved; if not, the formula $F(i + 1) = F(i) + F(i - 1)$ that defines $F(n)$ enables us to take the process one stage further, at the end of which we have $F(1)$, $F(2)$, ..., $F(i)$, $F(i + 1)$. It is clear that the values $F(1)$, $F(2)$, ..., $F(i - 2)$ do not enter into this determination, the only information necessary for continuing the recursion being the triplet $[i, F(i), F(i - 1)]$; if this is known, the succeeding triplet can be deduced:

$$[i + 1, F(i + 1), F(i)] \equiv [i + 1, F(i) + F(i - 1), F(i)]$$

Thus we have simplified both the recurrence relation and the computing schema and in addition have the required iterative algorithm.

We do not need to store the complete vector $F[1 : n]$; all we need is two consecutive values, say $u = F(i)$, $v = F(i - 1)$; the process of going from $[i, u, v]$ to the next triplet $[i + 1, u + v, u]$ is as follows:

$i \leftarrow i + 1$	new value of i
$w \leftarrow u$	save the old value of u
$u \leftarrow u + v$	new value of u, from the definition
$v \leftarrow w$	new value of v = old value of u

With the initial values and the termination criterion as stated, the complete algorithm for this method is as follows:

> **procedure** Fibonacci n
> $\quad i \leftarrow 2; u \leftarrow 1; v \leftarrow 1;$
> $\quad$ **repeat while** $i \neq n$
> $\quad\quad i \leftarrow i + 1; w \leftarrow u; u \leftarrow u + v; v \leftarrow w;$
> $\quad$ **return** u
> **end**

The complexity now is clearly $O(n)$ instead of the previous $O[F(n)]$: there are $n - 2$ steps, each requiring 1 test, 2 additions and 4 assignments. A 'good' algorithm must be of polynomial (i.e. less than exponential) complexity, and this is what we have achieved. The algorithm is entirely acceptable.

Designing an algorithm is not always so simple a task; the structures that have to be manipulated are often more complex than numbers or common arithmetical expressions. In the next section we show how the method just discussed can be developed so as to deal with some more complicated examples, still leading to a polynomial algorithm. Subsequently we shall give a list of all the problems that have been completely solved up to the present time; there are problems that have not been solved, and which, it seems, will always resist solution: it does not seem possible to find 'good' algorithms for these (see Section 4.4).

Example 5. Sorting numbers by comparison. Sorting into some specified order a set of randomly-assembled elements is a problem that arises very frequently in information processing; the elements can be ordinary numbers, of any origin, but need not be: all that is necessary is that there is some order of precedence – alphabetical, for example. There is of course no explicit formula for the solution here, so a process has to be defined that will arrange the elements in the required order, for example in decreasing numerical order if the elements are numbers. The basic operation is one of comparison; in numerical terms, given any two elements a, b to decide whether or not a is greater than b. We must first find a theoretical lower bound number of such comparisons needed to sort a given set.

A set of n elements can be arranged in $n!$ different orders. A sequence of t comparisons can be represented by a tree, as in Fig. 4.1, and can distinguish between 2^t arrangements, each corresponding to a leaf of the tree. It follows that t comparisons will suffice to put an initially randomly arranged set of n elements into any specified order provided that:

$$2^t \geqslant n! \tag{1}$$

Stirling's formula states that for large values $n!$ is of order $n^{n+1/2}$, so, taking logarithms, we have as the lower bound of the number of com-

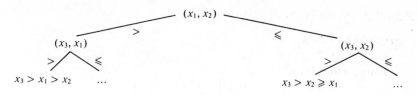

Fig. 4.1 Tree of tests for a sort.

	1	2	3	4	5	6	7	8
	20	7	84	75	45	78	30	9
$k = 3$	84	7	20	75	45	70	30	9
$k = 6$	84	78	20	75	45	7	30	9
...	...							

Fig. 4.2 Sorting by simple comparisons, $O(n^2)$ algorithm.

parisons needed to sort n items into a given order:

$$t = O(n \log n) \tag{2}$$

Let us now see how a sorting algorithm might work. The most obvious method is to find the largest element, put this at the head and repeat the process until all have been dealt with; this can be expressed as follows:

repeat for $i = 1$ **to** $n - 1$
  $k \leftarrow i$ {the first $i - 1$ elements have been sorted}
  repeat for $j = i + 1$ **to** n
    if $x_k < x_j$ **then** $k \leftarrow j$
  end repeat j
  interchange x_j, x_k
end repeat i

The inner loop involves $n - 1$ tests at each cycle, giving a total of $(n - 1) + (n - 2) + \cdots + 2 + 1 = n \cdot (n - 1)/2$ for the sorting of n numbers initially in random order; so the complexity is $O(n^2)$. Figure 4.2 illustrates the process.

A better algorithm can be devised by taking advantage of the information that is available at each step but is not used in this process, which at each step ignores the results of all preceding comparisons. One way to reduce the number of comparisons is to replace the inner loop (on j) by a 'tournament': elements are compared in pairs, e.g. (x_j, x_{j+1}), $(x_{j+2}, x_{+3})\ldots$, then the 'winners' compared in pairs and so on; for the numbers of Fig. 4.2 this goes as in Fig. 4.3. This method reduces the number of tests needed to find

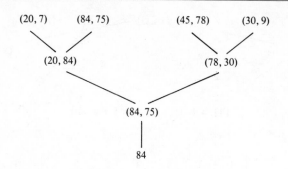

Fig. 4.3 'Tournament' process for sorting, $O(n \log n)$ algorithm.

the maximum and provides information for continuing the search. The depth of the tree is clearly of the order of $\log_2 n$ – by (1) above, or simply by noting that the number of elements to be compared is halved at each step – and in the worst case the total number of comparisons needed is n times the number needed to search a tree of n elements, that is, $n \log_2 n$, and this, by (2), is the best possible. When this type of sorting process is implemented on the computer careful attention has to be paid to the way in which the numbers are stored and how the exchanges are made between numbers already sorted and those not yet sorted. This is important, because the tree is not given initially and has to be constructed; it is developed progressively, going through an intermediate 'heap' structure, that is, one in which all the descendants of a node are smaller than that node.

A final comment here is that sorting is an example of a non-trivial problem for which we can give an optimal polynomial algorithm.

Example 6. Finding the shortest route between given points of a network. This is a problem we meet in our daily lives when we plan journeys by road or rail – or try to solve certain mathematical puzzles. Suppose we wish to go from location 1 to location 6 in the graph of Fig. 4.4 by the shortest route, the various point-to-point distances being as shown. This is to state the problem in terms of physical distances, but it is only a particular case of a much more general problem; the numbers attached to the arcs of the graph could equally well represent the costs of travel between the pairs of points, and more generally the nodes of the graph could represent the states of a system and the numbers the values of any function concerning the transition from one state to another; consequently the numbers are also called, more generally, the 'values' of the arcs of the graph.

Clearly, it will in general be impracticable to attempt to solve the problem by enumerating all the possible paths from the starting point to the goal; also, if all the values are positive, as is the case for physical distances, only 'elementary' routes need be considered, that is, routes in which no link is

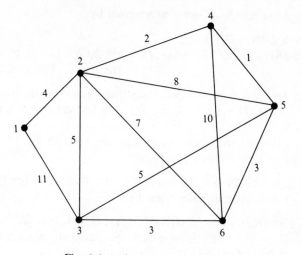

Fig. 4.4 A shortest-route problem.

travelled more than once. The natural approach is to use an iterative process to develop a sequence of minimum distances from the starting point, 1. If we consider first the neighbours of 1, that is, the points linked to 1 by a single arc, and continue in the same way, we can be sure that when we have reached any given node we know the minimum distance from there to 1 and that therefore we shall never need to back-track. In other words, at each stage the set of vertices of the graph has been partitioned into two sub-sets S and S^* such that:

1. for all verticies in S^* the minimum distance to 1 is known;
2. this is not known for any vertex in S.

Initially S^* contains only the starting point 1. A vertex is transferred from S to S^* when it can be shown that no path not already examined can give a distance shorter than the shortest of those known at that stage. Thus in this example we can first reach 2 and 3 from 1 in one step; since the distance to 3 is strictly greater than that to 2, the distance 4 between 1 and 2 is necessarily the shortest to 2, whatever paths (unknown at this stage) might be taken between 3 and 2.

In order to construct the algorithm for this problem we express this reasoning as follows (this holds for any arc values, provided these are positive);

let $D^*(i)$ = distance from vertex 1 to vertex i, $i \in S^*$

$\quad D(i)$ = shortest known distance from 1 to i, $i \in S$, *at a given stage*

$\quad L(i, j)$ = distance for the arc (i, j)

At every stage the sets S, S^* are characterised by:

if $i \in S^*$ then $D(i) = D^*(i)$
else $i \in S$ and $D(i) = \min[D(k) + L(k, i)]$ where $k \in S^*$, $(k, i) \in U$,
                                                   the set of all arcs of the graph

The distance $D(i)$ given by this process is then the minimum from i to 1.

Initially $S^* = \{1\}$, $D^*(1) = 0$, $D(i) = \infty$ for all vertices except i, which are therefore in S.

With this notation the above argument for vertices 2 and 3 can be generalised to give the following proposition:

let $j \in S$, where $D(j)$ is the smallest of the $D(i)$; then for $i \in S$,
$D(j)$ is the shortest distance from 1 to j.

Thus for $j \in S$, $D(j) = \min_i[D_S(i)] \Rightarrow D(j) = D^*(j)$: that is, if this condition is satisfied – as it must be for at least one value of j at each step – it is correct to transfer j from S to S^*.

To prove this proposition we must show that there is no path from i to j that is shorter than the one that we already have and of which the distance $D(j)$ is recorded. For this, consider the situation of Fig. 4.5: w is a path from 1 to j, w_1 the part of this path that goes from 1 to k, the first vertex on w that does not belong to S^*, and w_2 the remainder of w. The length of w is the sum of the lengths of w_1 and w_2. By construction the length of w_1 is greater than or equal to $D(k)$, which at this stage is the minimum distance from 1 to k, and by hypothesis $D(k) \geqslant D(j)$. Further, the length of w_2 is positive, so the length of w cannot be less than that of $D(j)$. Thus the vertex j can be put in S^*, and the process can be repeated until it ends after $n - 1$ iterations where n is the number of vertices. The resulting algorithm is as follows, where U is the set of arcs of the graph.

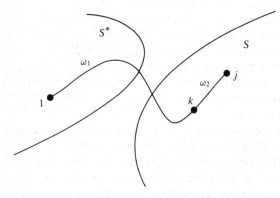

Fig. 4.5 Proof of the algorithm: the path w.

(initialisation) $0 \to D(1)$; $[2, 3, ..., n] \to S$
do $\forall i \in S$: **if** $(1, i) \in U$ **then** $L(1, i) \to D(i)$ **else** $+\infty \to D(i)$
while $S \neq \emptyset$ **repeat choose** $j \in S$ **such that** $D(j) = \text{Min } D(i)$, $i \in S$
$$S \leftarrow S - \{j\}$$
        do $\forall i \in S$ **and** $(j, i) \in U$
$$D(i) \leftarrow \min[D(i), D(j) + L(j, i)]$$
      end repeat
end

With the example of Fig. 4.4 the process goes as follows:

initialisation:
	1	2	3	4	5	6
D	0	4	11	∞	∞	∞

step 1 $S = \{2, 3, 4, 5, 6\}$ $j = 2$, min = 4
        $(2, 3) \in U$, $D(3) = \min(11, 4 + 5) = 9$
        $(2, 4) \in U$, $D(4) = \min(\infty, 4 + 2) = 6$
        $(2, 5) \in U$, $D(5) = \min(\infty, 4 + 8) = 12$
        $(2, 6) \in U$, $D(6) = \min(\infty, 4 + 7) = 11$
step 2 $S = \{3, 4, 5, 6\}$ $j = 4$, min = 6
        $(4, 5) \in U$, $D(5) = \min(12, 6 + 1) = 7$
        $(4, 6) \in U$, $D(6) = \min(11, 6 + 10) = 11$
step 3 $S =$
        $(5, 3) \in U$, $D(3) = \min(9, \ 4 + 5) = 9$
        $(5, 6) \in U$, $D(6) = \min(11, 7 + 3) = 10$
step 4 $S = \{3, 6\}$ $j = 3$, min = 9
        $(3, 6) \in U$, $D(3) = \min(10, 9 + 3) = 10$
step 5 $S = \{6\}$ $j = 6$
end

The result is that the distance from 1 to 6 by the shortest route is 10.

It should be noted that in this algorithm the order in which the vertices are transferred from S to S^* depends on the existence of arcs in the graph and also on the values they carry; without any change in the graph structure, a change in the values can alter this order.

The algorithm gives, simultaneously, the shortest distances from the starting point (here, 1) to all the other vertices, at least if the process is not stopped as soon as the goal vertex (here, 6) has moved into S^*, which can occur before the end.

We can compute the exact number of elementary operations needed by the algorithm. Since each arc links precisely two nodes of the graph and each stage in the updating of $D(i)$ involves the vertex that has last entered S^* and one vertex of S, each arc is dealt with precisely once; so if there are m arcs altogether, by the end of the process this updating will have required m additions and m comparisons. Further, if the set S is represented by its characteristic vector the determination of the vertex transformed from S to S^* by finding the minimum of the $D_n(j)$ requires $|S|$ comparisons, and therefore for the complete process $\Sigma_{k=1}^n (n - k)$, that is, $n \cdot (n - 1)/2$. So the total requirement is of the order of $n^2 + m$ comparisons. Since the operations of addition and comparison take comparable amounts of time, and since in any graph $m \leqslant n^2$ (because an arc joins only two vertices), we can say that the complexity is $O(n^2)$.

This algorithm was first given by Moore in 1957, and later by Dijkstra in 1959. Variations have been given by Dantzig (1960) and by Whiting and Hillier (1960).

In the example we have given the arcs joining the vertices can be traversed in either direction; however, the context can be such that only one direction is allowed, in which case the graph is said to be oriented, and the direction is shown by an arrow. If for the arc (i, j) the allowable direction is from i to j then i is called the predecessor of j and j the successor of i. All the above treatment remains valid for an oriented graph because the concept of direction has not entered into the argument; it does, however, enter in the next example.

Example 7. A task-ordering problem. In an automobile assembly plant the work is broken into a number of tasks, for each of which the time needed is known. The physical circumstances impose certain ordering relations among these tasks, that is, some cannot be started until others have been completed. With the times and the relations as given in Table 4.1, what is the minimum time needed to complete an assembly? − it is assumed that enough manpower is available to perform tasks in parallel whenever necessary. We can represent this by the oriented graph of Fig. 4.6; here, for

Table 4.1.

Task	Code	Time (hr)	Must follow
Body panels	A	1	—
Chassis	B	2	A
Engine	C	2	B
Transmission	D	3	B
Steering	E	2	C
Electrics	F	5	D, E
Wheels	G	1	C
Doors	H	1	B
Painting	I	2	D, H
Windows etc.	J	1	F, I
Interior	K	4	F, I
Test and check	L	2	J

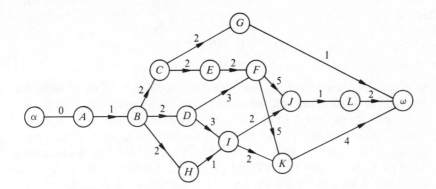

Fig. 4.6 Oriented graph for a task-ordering problem.

example, the arc from A to B shows that A must be finished before B can be started and the number (1) attached to this arc shows that task A takes 1 hour. Two 'notional' tasks have been added: α for the start of the assembly and ω for its completion. The graph contains, in a concise and easily accessible form, all the information necessary for the solution of the problem. The precedence relations, such as C before E, B before C, A before B, link with one another to impose an order that is represented by a path in the graph, in this case $\alpha ABCE$. Finding the minimum time for the assembly is thus equivalent to finding the path from α to ω for which the sum of the arc values is *maximum*: it is the maximum that has to be considered here, because then the other paths having times at most equal to this, it is the maximum that will be associated with the least possible time for the complete assembly. All the tasks must be performed, therefore all the vertices must be visited.

A comment here is that a search for a maximal path in a graph in which all the arc-values are positive can lead to an infinite result: this can happen if there is a subset of arcs $(x_1, x_2), (x_2, x_3), \ldots, (x_{p-1}, x_p)$ with $x_p = x_1$, around which one can travel indefinitely. This is called a cycle in the graph. But it is clear that, unless some mistake has been made in specifying the situation, this can never arise in a real task-ordering problem.

The previous algorithm, which was concerned with finding minimal paths, can be adapted to deal with this problem, taking into account the absence of cycles in the graph; the fact that a maximum, and not a minimum, is being sought makes no fundamental difference to the argument. Again we need consider only elementary paths, that is, paths that traverse each arc only once.

The basic idea is similar to what was done before. A weight $D(i)$ is associated with each vertex and is modified progressively by a relation of the form:

$$D(i) \leftarrow \max_{j \in J} \ [D(j) + L(j, i)]$$

until a stable state is reached; but now it is possible to choose an order for treating the vertices that will give convergence in a single step. This is done as follows. In the graph of Fig. 4.6 the maximum distance from α to A is known, also that from α to B; and knowing the latter, the maximum distances to C, D and H are known also. That is I follows by comparing $D(H) + L(H, I)$ with $L(D, I)$, and so on. Thus the vertices are taken in an order that is such that when any vertex I is reached, all its predecessors have been considered. The process can be started because the following property holds.

> Every finite directed graph without cycles has at least one vertex that has no predecessor.

This can be established by *reductio ad absurdum*. Suppose it is not true; then if x_1 is any vertex, x_1 has a predecessor, x_2 say, and there is a directed arc (x_2, x_1). Again by hypothesis x_2 has a predecessor, x_3 say, and there is arc (x_3, x_2); and so on, giving an infinite sequence of vertices $x_1, x_2, ..., x_k$, which must be distinct because the graph has no cycle. This is impossible because the graph is finite.

We can use this property iteratively. Define a source as a vertex that has no predecessors; then at each stage we remove from the set U of arcs all those that started from the previous source, so as to give a new vertex without predecessors, whose maximum distance from the starting point (α) can be found directly. We have in fact a rather stronger theorem:

Theorem. *A (finite) directed graph G is cycle-free if and only if there is a bijection v of the set X of vertices into the interval of the integers from 1 to n, where n is the total number of vertices in X, such that $\forall (x_1, x_2)$, $(x_1, x_2) \in U: v(x_1) < v(x_2)$*

In other words, the vertices can be numbered, by the bijection v, in such a way that all the predecessors of any vertex have numbers less than its own.

Proof. If G has a cycle $(x_1, x_2, ..., x_k = x_1)$ such a bijection cannot be constructed, for this would require $v(x_1) < v(x_2) < \cdots < v(x_k)$, which is impossible since $x_k = x_1$; so the condition is sufficient.

If G is cycle-free there is a source vertex, which we can number 1. If we remove this and all the arcs that originate from it the remaining graph also is cycle-free and therefore has a source vertex which we can number 2; continuing in this way we can construct the mapping of the form given. So the condition is necessary.

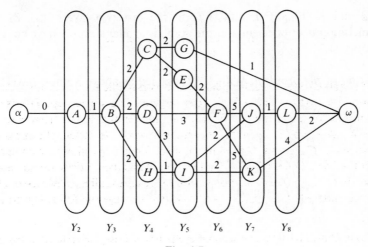

Fig. 4.7.

If at any stage in the process there were an arc (x_1, x_2) of U such that $v(x_1) < v(x_2)$ and x_2 were a source, then x_1 would still belong to the graph remaining after the deletion of x_1, which is impossible; so the function v exists and we have a practical method for constructing it.

Classification of the vertices. The problem is solved with the aid of a rearrangement of the graph (Fig. 4.6) that expresses the precedence relations among the tasks; the rearranged graph is shown in Fig. 4.7 in which the vertices are grouped into 'layers' Y_k. This grouping is done by the following algorithm.

Initialisation. $1 \to p; X \to T; 0 \to k$
Construction. **While** $T \neq \emptyset$ **repeat** k (Y_k = sets of vertices without
$\qquad\qquad\qquad\qquad\qquad\qquad\qquad\qquad\qquad$ predecessors)

$\qquad$**do** $\forall i, i \in Y_k$
$\qquad\quad p \to v(i), p + 1 \to p$
$\qquad\qquad$**do** $\forall j, j \in X, (i, j) \in U$
$\qquad\qquad\quad$**remove** (i, j) **from** U
$\qquad\quad T - Y_k \to T; k + 1 \to k$
$\qquad$**end repeat** k
$\qquad$**end**

The first layer Y_1 is clearly α, the second Y_2 *is* A and the third Y_3 is B. The arcs BC, BD, BH are removed and C, D, H form Y_4. CG and CE, DF and DI, and then HI are next removed; Y_5 consists of the vertices G, E and I. Y_6 consists of the single vertex F; FJ and FK are removed, and Y_7 consists of J and K. Finally L and ω form the tast two layers Y_8, Y_9. The enumeration v is not essential if the graph is available, so we have not given it in Fig. 4.7.

Solution of the problem. With $D^*(i)$ defined as above we now have:

$$D^*(1) = 0, D^*(2) = 0$$

$j = 3$	$D^*(3) = 0 + 1 = 1$
$j = 4$	$D^*(4) = 1 + 2 = 3$
$j = 5$	$D^*(5) = 1 + 2 = 3$
$j = 6$	$D^*(6) = 1 + 2 = 3$
$j = 7$	$D^*(7) = \max[3 + 1, 3 + 3] = 6$
$j = 8$	$D^*(8) = 3 + 2 = 5$
$j = 9$	$D^*(9) = 3 + 2 = 5$
$j = 10$	$D^*(10) = \max[3 + 3, 5 + 2] = 7$
$j = 11$	$D^*(11) = \max[6 + 2, 7 + 5] = 12$
$j = 12$	$D^*(12) = \max[6 + 2, 7 + 5] = 12$
$j = 13$	$D^*(13) = 12 + 1 = 13$
$j = 14$	$D^*(14) = \max[5 + 1, 12 + 4, 13 + 2] = 16$

Thus the length of the longest path is 16, meaning that the minimum time to complete an assembly is 16 hours. The path (i.e. the corresponding task sequence) can be found by noting at each step the predecessor vertex that gives the maximum of D^*. Using this and working back from ω we find the path to be $\alpha ABCEFK\omega$.

The method we have just described in known as the 'method of potentials'; it was first implemented by Bernard Roy in 1960. A better known but more laborious American variant for solving the same problem, PERT (Program Evaluation and Review Technique), was developed at NASA and at RAND in 1954. These methods are in regular use for solving real-life problems efficiently, mainly in the building industry but also in connection with construction work of all types, automobile, naval or aeronautical.

As well as giving the minimum time for execution of a project the methods provide a list of what are called the critical tasks, that is, tasks whose representations in the graph lie on the longest route – the 'critical path'. The importance of these is that, by definition of this route, any increase in the time taken by any of them will delay the completion of the project; and the identification of such tasks provides invaluable information to the person responsible for the project. A further valuable by-product of the algorithm is a work schedule for each of the different groups of people employed on the project.

Given the rearranged graph is in Fig. 4.7 the algorithm for finding the longest path is very simple; it is as follows.

initialisation: $D^*(1) \leftarrow 0$; $D^*(2) \leftarrow L(1, 2)$
repeat for j, $3 < j < n$ $D^*(j) \leftarrow \max[D^*(i) + L(i, j)]$, $(i, j) \in U$
end repeat

The new enumeration, i.e. in the rearranged graph, is such that:

$$(i, j) \in U \Rightarrow i < j$$

Thus any path that arrives at j must pass only through vertices whose numbers are less than j and for which therefore the relevant D^* has already been calculated; which, by recurrence on j, establishes the validity of the algorithm.

Complexity of the algorithm: For each value of j, $(j - 1)$ additions and $(j - 2)$ comparisons are needed; so the total number of elementary operations is of the order of $n(n - 1)/2$, that is, the complexity is $O(n^2)$.

The enumeration of the vertices in the graph of Fig. 4.6 is as follows:

vertex x	α	A	B	C	D	E	F	G	H	I	J	K	L	ω
$v(x)$	1	2	3	4	5	8	10	9	6	7	12	11	13	14

Finally, since the data for problems of this type can never be known exactly, various computational methods have been devised for studying the variations in the critical path and the time for completion of the project as the times for the separate tasks are varied according to known probability laws. We shall not consider these complementary methods in this chapter, the essential aim of which is to demonstrate, by means of examples, the algorithmic approach to problem solving. This consists of the following stages:

1. Analysis of the problem as given, so as to put it into a form that is compact and more readily understandable: a graph.
2. Study of the new problem expressed in this simplified universe, by a method guided by simple and natural ideas derived from an example.
3. Generalisation.
4. Construction and proof of the algorithm for the solution.

Example 8. A topological problem. We now consider the famous 'Eulerian cycle' problem for a graph: to find if in a given graph there is a cycle that, starting from some vertex, traverses every arc once and once only before returning to the starting point. This was first stated by Euler in 1736 in terms of the bridges over the River Pregel in Königsberg: can one take a circular walk that crosses all seven bridges once and once only and returns to the start? – and for this reason is usually known as the Königsberg problem.

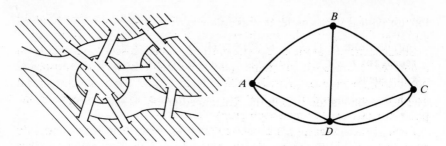

Fig. 4.8 The Königsberg bridges: the Eulerian cycle problem.

Figure 4.8 shows the dispositions of the Königsberg bridges and the equivalent graph. A necessary condition for the existence of an Eulerian cycle is clearly that the graph is connected, that is, that there is a chain of arcs connecting any vertex with any other. Another necessary condition concerns the number of arcs at each vertex: if one is not to leave a vertex by the same arc as the one by which one arrived there, for every arrival arc there must be an associated departure. The condition is therefore:

> *For a connected graph to have an Eulerian cycle there must be no vertex of odd degree.*

where the degree of a vertex is the number of arcs that meet there.

This condition is also sufficient, as we shall show. It gives directly a polynomial algorithm for answering the question of the existence of an Eulerian cycle and in addition provides an algorithm, of complexity of the order of the number of arcs in the graph, for constructing the cycle when it exists.

The necessity of the condition is obvious. Since a cycle that traverses all the arcs must arrive at each vertex by one arc and leave it by another an even number of arcs must meet at every vertex.

The sufficiency is less obvious; it can be established by induction on the number m of arcs of the graph.

Suppose we construct progressively a path through the graph, starting at an arbitrary vertex V and attempting to fulfil the conditions of the problem. Call this path P. To ensure that no arc is traversed twice we remove from the graph each arc after we have traversed it. When F arrives at a vertex X other than V, P can be continued by at least one arc: since an even number of arcs meet at every vertex, after the arrival arc has been removed there must be an odd number left, that is, at least one. Since the departure arc will be removed, the passage of P through any vertex will result in an even number of arcs being removed at that vertex. If the path cannot be continued, the vertex at which it has arrived must be the starting point V; and if at this stage all the arcs have been traversed, the result is proved.

Suppose that is not the case; there must remain a sub-set of arcs that form a number of connected sub-graphs (any sub-graph consisting of an isolated point being, of course, ignored): call these $G_1, G_2, ..., G_k$. Since the original graph G is connected, the path P must meet each of these subgraphs at one point at least, say g_i for the sub-graph G_i.

Each of the sub-graphs is connected and has fewer than m arcs and only even-degree vertices. Assume, on the basis for an induction argument, that each G_i has an Eulerian cycle, E_i. We now construct a new path consisting of:

- the path P from V to g_1;
- the Eulerian cycle E_1 in G_1, starting and finishing at g_1;
- the continuation of P from g_1 to g_2

and so on until V is reached again by the part of P from g_k to V, with vG_k.

The proof is completed by noting that a loop on an isolated vertex is itself an Eulerian cycle. This proof was given by Euler in 1736.

It is very simple to test for this necessary and sufficient condition at each vertex, and the total complexity is $O(n)$, where n is the number of vertices. Further, a practical construction for an Eulerian cycle can be provided; for this we first write a procedure, Euler (W), that will construct for any graph the start of an Eulerian cycle being at the vertex W.

```
procedure Euler (W)
    u ← w; v ← P;
    repeat while V ≠ W{(u, v) is the first unmarked arc starting from u}
            mark (u, v)
            P ← P ∪ {(u, v)}      continue the path P
            u ← v
    end repeat
end Euler
```

The complete algorithm is now easily written; the path is constructed progressively, by a process that follows the proof of the theorem:

```
P ← Euler (S)      {this is this initial path}
repeat while there are still unmarked arcs in G
            {H is a vertex that is on both the path P and an unmarked
            arc}
            concatenate the path Euler (H) with P
end repeat
```

In this algorithm the procedure uses each arc of G at most once; the actual construction of the connected components can be dispensed with, by choosing instead a suitable vertex H as indicated. In the worst case, each arc is considered twice, so if there are m arcs the complexity is $O(m)$ and we have an excellent linear algorithm for the solution of Euler's problem.

Shortly, we shall meet another problem which at first sight seems very close to that of Euler; this, often called Hamilton's problem because he in particular studied it, is the problem of finding a cycle, not through the arcs but all the vertices of a given graph – an example is the Travelling Salesman problem, considered in Chapter 5. Strangely enough, this turns out to be in an entirely different class from Euler's, and centuries of effort by mathematicians, including some of the most famous, have not succeeded in finding a good – that is, polynomial – algorithm; which means that we do not yet have a solution to the general problem of finding a cycle through all the vertices of a graph.

4.2　PROBLEMS FOR WHICH POLYNOMIAL ALGORITHMS ARE KNOWN

We have already noted that if there is an explicit mathematical expression for the solution of a problem, then the complexity of the problem is constant, independent of the data; and this is the ideal situation. Examples are the solution of non-degenerate linear algebraic systems, payroll calculation and the majority of classical physical problems, which reduce to the solution of a system of equations.

We now complete our study with a more detailed discussion of some problems involving other types of data. The first two have been described in detail in the preceding paragraphs.

1. Sorting a set of n numbers　　　$O(n \log n)$.
2. Finding an Eulerian cycle in a graph of m arcs　　　$O(m)$.
3. Finding a given word in a text of length n words　　　$nO(n)$.

An example is the need to search a book or paper for all occurrences of one or more words, such as descriptors, keywords, bibliographical references. It is clear that the obvious algorithm that involves two nested loops, one over the letters of the text and the other over those of the given word, is not practicable, because the complexity, of the order of $n \times$ the number of letters in the word, will be too great. This, however, can be improved so as to give a complexity independent of the word sought, in which each character of the text is examined only once. As so often, the improvement is achieved by trading time for space: unnecessary tests are avoided by storing the word in the memory in the form of a transition diagram.

4. Constructing the minimum cost spanning tree for a graph of
m arcs   O(m log m) (Kruskal 1956, Prim 1957, Tarjan 1977).

An example is the planning of the water supply system for a town. There
are many possible layouts for the piping, with a cost corresponding to each;
every customer (corresponding to a vertex) must be supplied. The source of
the supply will keep the entire network under pressure and if the pipes to
every vertex ('spanning' the network) are not to form any cycles – that is,
are to form a tree – every one must have a supply. The problem is to design
such a tree for which the cost is minimum. There is a trivially simple
algorithm: choose the arc of least cost that does not form a cycle with those
already chosen, and continue in this way until every vertex has been
included. This gives the optimum tree and is also of minimum complexity.

Many other problems in graph theory have polynomial solutions; the
following are the main ones.

5. Shortest path between given vertices in a graph of n vertices and
m arcs   O(mn)
(Ford 1965, Dijkstra 1959, Dantzig 1960, Floyd 1962)

This is complementary to the problem of the longest path and is of the same
complexity; 'shortest' need not refer only to physical distance but to any
'value' or 'weight' attached to the arcs.

6. Connected components $O(n^2)$
(Tremaux 1882, Tarjan 1972)

The problem is to find all the sub-sets of the vertices of a given graph that
are such that any two vertices of the same sub-set are connected by a chain
of arcs. A practical example is to find sub-sets among the separate tasks of a
project that are independent of each other.

7. Transitive closure $O(n^2)$
(Nolin 1964, Warshal 1965, Roy 1965)

The problem is to find, for any given vertex, all those vertices to which it is
linked either directly or indirectly. The algorithm is similar to (vi).

8. Maximum matching $O(n^{5/2})$
The problem is to find the largest possible sub-set of arcs that do not meet in
any vertex; a theorem of Claude Berge gives a necessary and sufficient
condition for such a sub-set to be maximal but it is only recently that Jack
Edmonds has shown that this condition can be tested in polynomial time
and, further, has given a practical method for improving any non-
maximal sub-set. It was in his famous paper 'Paths, trees and flowers' that

he invented the term 'good' algorithm and showed the importance of this. This problem underlies many problems of the assignment or exclusive ordering (tasks that cannot be performed simultaneously) types, staff rostering, scheduling transport fleets.

9. Maximum flow $O(n^3)$
(Ford and Fulkerson 1950, Gondran and Minoux 1978)

Here the 'value' attached to each arc of the graph measures its maximum carrying capacity of some type and the problem is to achieve the maximum flow between two given points. Models of this type are used to find optimum cargo transfers between ports, sometimes for rail and air transport.

There are some problems in graph theory whose complexity has been reduced spectacularly over the years as a return of continued attack by research workers; the following is one example.

10. Testing a graph for planarity $O(n)$

A graph is said to be planar if and only if it can be drawn on a plane surface in such a way that its arcs meet only at the vertices − that is, never cross.

In 1930 Kuratowski gave a method that would decide the question in $O(n^6)$ operations. The order of the polynomial was reduced steadily until an $O(n^2)$ algorithm was found. Then in 1970 Hopcroft and Tarjan produced a method of $O(n \log n)$, and finally in 1974 they reduced this to $O(n)$ and at the same time showed that this was the best possible.

An even stranger case is that of problems for which for a long time no polynomial algorithm had been known but it had not been proved that none existed nor that the problems were necessarily very difficult, because similar problems had been solved. Linear programming was in this class.

11. Linear programming.
The problem is to solve, in $\mathbb{R}^n$, the linear system $\mathbf{A}\mathbf{x} \leqslant \mathbf{b}$ where $\mathbf{A}$ is a matrix of m rows and n columns, with given elements, b is a vector of m given elements and $\mathbf{x}$, to be determined, is a vector of n positive real elements. There may be a further condition, that some linear functional $\mathbf{c}\mathbf{x}$, $\mathbf{c}$ is a given vector of n elements, is to be minimum.

Many problems, often of very large scale and often very important financially, from many fields of activity can be modelled in this form: production management, freight transport, petroleum refinery operation, electricity generation and distribution. It has formed the basis for the success of operational research over the past 25 years, and the success of the method used for the solution of these problems, due to G. Dantzig, rests on this formulation.

Dantzig's algorithm, known as the simplex method, is essentially a heuristic process for deciding the direction in which to continue a search; and whilst, because of the convexity of the space being searched, it guarantees to find the global optimum sought, it may not do so until after passing through a number of points – that is, performing a number of iterations – that is an exponential function of m and n. However, over the past 20 years the algorithm has been improved and extended progressively, and used most effectively almost all over the world; and whilst the theoretical complexity is $O(n^m)$, actual experience, even with problems as large as $m = 1000$, $n = 40\,000$, has suggested a complexity of $O(n^3)$.

Then suddenly in 1979 a paper in Russian, by L. G. Kachian, appeared in Moscow, giving a polynomial algorithm for the linear programming problem, very different from the simplex algorithm. Within a year the paper had been read in Europe and the USA and the algorithm verified and extended; but whilst it perhaps explained the experimental success of the simplex method it has no chance of replacing this, because the latter proves entirely satisfactory for the practical problems that are met.

Kachian's algorithm was front-page news in many American and Canadian journals in 1979; it finally established the convergence in a polynomial number of steps, to a given precision, of a certain family of numerical analysis algorithms. But what is really remarkable is that his discovery has closed the list of problems known to be solvable by 'good' – that is, polynomial – algorithms: there are indeed very few of these. There are of course many variants of each of the general types we have described; and several problems – such as deciding if two arbitrarily given graphs are isomorphic – are in the same case as linear programming was in 1978, with no polynomial algorithm known but no proof of their equivalence to any problem known to be exponential.

It is clear that the class of problems for which no polynomial algorithm is known is very great indeed in comparison with that for which such algorithms are known. If we put on one side the class for which the solution time is known *a priori* to be exponential, that for which there is no theoretical argument against polynomial complexity but no such algorithm has been found so far remains a mystery.

4.3 CLASSIFICATION OF PROBLEMS ACCORDING TO COMPLEXITY

From our individual experience and familiarity with one field of study or another we all form 'intuitive' ideas about which problems are 'more difficult' in comparison with others. This assessment, being personal, is not satisfactory as a measure, but then there is the question, how are we to define the intrinsic complexity of a problem? This is the question we now take up.

At the heart of the discussion of the question lies the difference between mathematics and information science. In the latter it is not sufficient simply to prove the existence of some object, nor even simply to produce a process for constructing that object, that is, an algorithm: the solution must take into account the constraints on space and time imposed by the world in which we live, it must be computable with memory capacity and execution time that are 'reasonable' for both man and machine.

Since any method is normally designed to solve many problems of the same type with different data, whatever measure is used to assess the quality of the method must be based on the performance of the worst case that is likely to be encountered. From a very practical point of view it is the total number of operations necessary for the solution that determines the quality of the method, but for a meaningful comparison to be made this number must be related to the scale of the problem treated, that is, to the size of the input data set; thus we define the complexity of a procedure as:

> the upper bound of the number of elementary operations needed for the solution, expressed as a function of the size of the input data.

The complexity of a problem is then defined as:

> the complexity of the best procedure for its solution, as then known,

and the complexity thus depends on the current state of the art.

Two basic questions now arise:

1. How far can a given algorithm be improved? For certain cases, are methods of optimal complexity known, and are there many problems for which a 'good' solution is known – that is, of low order of complexity like $O(n)$ or $O(n^2)$?
2. Do the complexities suggest a grouping of problems in classes? do they provide methods for moving a problem from one class to another, such as from a 'difficult' problem to an 'easier' one?

We now consider these questions, or rather, groups of questions; the answers, however, give little hope that 'classical' algorithms will solve many types of problem, but at the same time they justify research in artificial intelligence.

4.3.1 Three classes of problem

The best algorithms are the linear ones, that is, those whose complexity measure is of the form $an + b$, written $O(n)$, where n is a measure of the size of the data. Such algorithms do exist; for example, the calculation of the sum of two numbers of $n1$ and $n2$ digits, by the method taught at primary school level, requires the calculation of at most $n1 + n2$ numbers of one digit plus at most $\max(n1, n2)$ carries. The multiplication of two 1-digit numbers is an elementary operation that any machine can perform, as also is the addition of a number and a carry digit. Thus the addition algorithm is of complexity $O(n1 + n2)$, where it is to be understood that this is simply an order-of-magnitude expression and does not take account of constant factors – here, for example, the contribution from the carry digits has been ignored.

Other well-known algorithms, for example for division, square root extraction, solution of quadratic equations, are linear also and therefore fall into the more general class discussed previously, that of polynomial complexity.

1. Polynomial algorithms – class P. This class, the class of 'good' problems, consists of all those problems for which an algorithm is known whose complexity is a polynomial function of the size of the data; the degree of the polynomial must be known, and must be independent of the size of the data. This is usually expressed by saying the complexity is $O(n^r)$, where r does not vary with n.

Other problems are more difficult.

2. Intrinsically exponential problems – class E. Any problem whose complexity is at least of the order of f^n, where f is either a constant or a polynomial in n, is said to be intrinsically exponential; and the same name describes any problem for which the amount of output increases exponentially with the data size n, as for example if the problem is to construct all the sub-sets of a given set, or all the cliques (complete sub-graphs) or all the trees of a given graph: in all these cases the volume of output is of the form (polynomial in $n)^n$.

Some problems are even worse, having a complexity of the form:

$$2^{2^{\cdot^{\cdot^{\cdot^{2^{2^n}}}}}}$$

i.e. repeated exponentiation with the last exponent 2^n; this can be the case for problems concerning the recognition words formed from regular expressions in languages constructed with relatively simple alphabets and grammatical rules.

It can happen that an exponential algorithm is better than a polynomial algorithm for small values of n, but the fundamental difference between the two classes becomes evident when n takes large values.

We now come to the heart of the question: the existence of problems that cannot, *a priori*, be classed as either P or E. There are in fact innumerable such problems; nothing in the statement of these problems suggests that they are essentially exponential in nature, but so far (1989) no polynomial algorithm has been found for any of them.

3. Problems not classifiable as either P or E – class III. The following problems are in this class:

- Solution in integers of systems of algebraic equations (the Diophantine problem).
- Finding a cycle that passes through every vertex of a given graph once and once only (Hamilton's problem).
- The existence of a set of logical values that will give the value TRUE for a given logical expression (Cook 1971).
- Optimisation of the travelling salesman's journey (cf. Chapter 5, Section 12).
- Deciding which files to consult in an unstructured database so as to find a particular item at least cost.
- Deciding the locations of service-providing centres (e.g. telephone, television, fire) so as to maximise the population served and minimise the number of centres.
- Optimal packing of equipment (in a rucksack, train, boat, aeroplane) at least cost.
- Optimal subdivision (with respect to given criteria) of e.g. paper, metal sheets or bars, aeroplane flights, investment portfolios, machine tools, information processing systems.
- Diagnosis (medical, equipment breakdowns, printed circuit board faults).

The list could be greatly extended.

This class is a mystery: not only have tens, in some cases hundreds, of years of effort failed to produce a polynomial solution of any of the problems, even then there is no reason to believe that none exist, but all the problems are equivalent in the sense that if any one is found to have a polynomial solution it will follow that all have polynomial solutions.

We shall reflect on this strange situation in the rest of this chapter and bring in some considerations that apply both to class P – polynomial – and to class 3 – the mystery.

The polynomial problems are the easiest to handle and have been considered in Section 4.2; but as we have seen, there are very few of them.

At the present time the formal problems for which we know 'good' algorithmic solutions form a very small family; all the others are difficult, and all, by definition, concern artificial intelligence.

A final comment here is that even when it is known that a polynomial algorithm exists for a certain type of problem, recognising this in the case of a given problem, constructing the algorithm and adapting the statement of the problem so as to make it amenable to the algorithm – is itself a non-polynomial problem!

4.4 NON-DETERMINISTIC POLYNOMIAL PROBLEMS – CLASS NP

4.4.1 Turing machines

When we have neither an explicit formula for the solution of a problem nor a recursive expression of acceptable complexity there are two methods of attack available to us: construction of an algorithm, and enumeration of cases.

To say that a problem is of polynomial complexity is to say that its solution can be obtained in a polynomial number of steps, without any enumeration. The abstract model for the algorithm that accomplishes this is a black box that can perform only a given set of elementary operations: $+$, $-$, $*$, $/$, **and, or, read, write, if ... then, repeat**. It is an *automaton* and at any instant is in a precisely defined state; it performs a single action that depends on that state and passes into another state, when the process starts again. Such an automaton is called a Deterministic Turing Machine, DTM.

But in some cases the only possibility is enumeration, in effect, trial and error, for which the appropriate model is another abstract machine, the Non-Deterministic Turing Machine, NDTM. This has the same set of instructions as DTM and in addition a special instruction **choice** [S] which creates as many copies of the current state of the machine as there are elements in the set S. By convention, the machine stops when one of these copies arrives at the instruction **stop**. We illustrate the use of this new language with non-deterministic algorithms for two simple problems.

Problem 1 – Feasibility of a logical expression. A logical expression consisting of the logical operator symbols $\lor$, $\land$, $\neg$ and the logical variables $q_1, q_2, ..., q_n$ is said to be *feasible* if there is a set of truth values for the variables that will give the expression the value TRUE. For example, if:

$$E(q_1, q_2, q_3, q_4) = (q_1 \lor \neg q_2 \lor \neg q_3) \land (q_1 \lor q_2 \lor q_4) \land (q_3 \lor \neg q_4) \land (\neg q_1)$$

then: $E(F, T, F, F) = T$, and E is feasible.

The algorithm for investigating feasibility with an NDTM is simple to write:

```
repeat for i ← [1 : n]
        qi ← choice [T, F]
end repeat
    if E(q1, q2, ... qn) then SUCCESS;
                        else FAIL
```

The algorithm creates 2^n copies of itself; for the above expression it creates $2^4 = 16$ copies, of which the 12th gives SUCCESS.

Problem 2 – Colouring a map with 3 colours. On a plane map are regions $R1, R2, ..., Rn$; the problem is to colour these regions with only three colours so that countries with a common boundary are coloured differently. The non-deterministic algorithm is as follows:

```
colour (R1) ← c1      {colour a region and the adjacent regions}
repeat for i ← [1 : n]
    if R1 adjacent to Ri then find a colour for Ri
end repeat i
repeat for k ← [1 : n] while there is a region not coloured
    if Rk is colourable only with colour j then colour (Rk) ← j
end repeat k
if all regions are coloured then stop
else Rmin is region with lowest index for which colours j1 and j2 are
    available
        colour (Rmin) ← choice [j1, j2]
```

This shows the ease with which enumeration programs can be written for an NDTM. The programmer is freed from all the tasks of backtrack management and everything proceeds as though all the copies – which are in effect deterministic Turing machines – work in complete parallelism, raising no technical problems of feasibility. The number of such deterministic machines is arbitrary: it 'explodes' very quickly because, as these examples show, it is essentially exponential. Putting that on one side, we have come to an important point and there are two comments to be made:

1. In each of the above examples every one of the copies is deterministic and its complexity (that is, the number of steps it requires) is polynomial (linear in these examples). This leads to the term non-deterministic polynomial, abbreviated to NP, to describe an algorithm that can be executed in polynomial time on a non-deterministic Turing machine. It is important to

note that NP does not mean non-polynomial, but non-deterministic polynomial.

An immediate corollary is $P \subset NP$.

The set of problems that are polynomial on a DTM belongs to NP, because a DTM is a particular case of NDTM.

2. It can need only a very small change in the parameters to go from NP to P. Thus in the second problem, if there are only two colours the algorithm gives the response (possible/impossible) without ever using the loop **repeat** in which the crucial instruction **choice** appears. The solution is therefore reached in $O(n)$ steps, without any backtracking, and the NDTM has become a DTM.

In the first example, the set of possible values is already restricted to two elements, but what sets the limit to the amount of enumeration is the number of logical variables inside one set of parentheses. Suppose there were at most two and that the expression to be evaluated were put into the normalised form:

$$\bigwedge_{i=1}^{m} (r_i \vee s_i)$$

in which r_i, s_i stand for either a q_j or a $\neg q_j$. Then when the value of the first term is fixed, say the r_i in the ith parenthesised expression, either this expression takes the value T immediately and attention moves to the $(i + 1)$th, or this is not the case; but then the form of the second term, s_i, say, shows immediately, meaning without any use of **choice**, the value that the associated variable must take. If the process can be continued as far as $i = n$ without meeting any contradiction it gives a vector $(q_1, q_2, ..., q_n)$ which establishes the feasibility of the original expression; otherwise that expression is not feasible.

These examples show that the change from P to NP can occur very suddenly, in these cases between $n = 2$ and $n = 3$ for instance, and the question of whether this is inevitable arises. Put another way, the question is: are non-deterministic machines intrinsically more powerful than deterministic machines, in the sense of being able to solve more problems? Or again, is P the same as NP? – which is the situation (Fig. 4.9)?

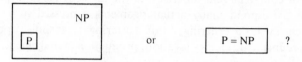

Fig. 4.9 The answer today is: *we don't know.*

4.5 LIST OF NP PROBLEMS

Such a list is easily given; here are some of the NP problems.

1. Feasibility of the logical expression.
2. 3-colouring of a graph.
3. Finding a clique of k vertices in a non-directed graph.
4. Finding a covering set for a given set; that is, given a family F of sub-sets E_i of a set E, to find a sub-family G of F such that:

$$\bigcup_F E_i = \bigcup_G E_i$$

5. Partition of a set: as (4), but with the additional constraint:

$$E_i \cap E_j = \emptyset \quad \text{for all} \quad E_i, E_j \, (i \neq j) \text{ in } G$$

6. Existence of a Hamiltonian cycle in a non-directed graph.
7. The 'knapsack' problem: to find binary variables x_i that satisfy the equation

$$\sum_i a_i x_i = b \text{ where } a_i, b \text{ are given integers.}$$

More generally, to solve any Diophantine problem, that is, to find integer solutions to a system of algebraic equations.

8. Binary partitioning: given a set S of n integers y_i to partition this into two sub-sets S_1, S_2 such that:

$$\sum_{i \in S_1} y_i = \sum_{i \in S_2} y_i$$

9. Existence of a travelling salesman's route through a directed graph of cost less than a given quantity.

The list could be extended considerably: most known problems are in fact NP.

It must of course be remembered that the list is of *types* of problem: to each there correspond many actual problems expressed in a variety of terms, such as task ordering, staff rostering, transport optimisation, petroleum refinement, factory location, production management, electronic or architectural design.

To show that a problem in the above list is in the class NP it is sufficient to give a non-deterministic algorithm that will solve the problem in polynomial time. Take for example problem 9:

Hamiltonian cycle, cost $\leqslant b$, in directed graph G.

$V_1 \leftarrow 1$ starting vertex
$S \leftarrow (2, 3, ..., n)$ vertices to be visited
$\text{cost} \leftarrow 0$ total cost
$nv \leftarrow 1$ no. of vertices already visited

repeat while successor $(v_{nv}) \neq \emptyset$ (successor (v) denotes set of vertices
                                   that can be reached from vertex v)[1]

$v_{nv-1} \leftarrow$ **choice** (successor(v_{nv}))
$nv \quad \leftarrow nv + 1$
$\text{cost} \quad \leftarrow \text{cost} + \text{cost}(\text{arc}(v_{nv-1}, v_{nv}))$

end repeat

if $nv = n$ **and** $\text{cost} \leqslant b$ **then** SUCCESS **stop**
                               else FAIL

Whatever the value of b, each copy of the algorithm will involve a polynomial number of steps, in fact exactly n; so the problem is NP.

The problem of finding an optimal Hamiltonian circuit is not, however, NP: it involves as a sub-problem proving that there are no cycles with cost greater than b, which is not NP. This is complementary to problem 9, meaning that it is the problem of finding cycles that are not solutions of 9; and in general it is not true that if a problem is NP the complementary problem also is NP.

The corresponding result is true for problems of class P, but not, in general, for NP. But for NP the move to the complementary problem amounts to interchanging all the associated SUCCESSes and FAILs in the non-deterministic algorithm. A final SUCCESS for a problem Q indicates FAILs in all the other branches of the algorithm, and therefore a response will not be obtained for the complementary problem $\bar{Q}$ until all the DTMs have completed their tasks; since the number of these is not necessarily polynomial, there is no guarantee that $\bar{Q}$ is NP.

To take the particular case of the Hamiltonian cycle, we do not know how to write an algorithm to decide whether or not there is such a cycle with cost $> b$, so we cannot say that the problem is NP; and this, essentially, is because there is no *a priori* limit to the difference between the actual cost of a cycle and the value b – this is not bounded by a polynomial function of the number of vertices to be visited. Thus the problem of finding an optimal route for the travelling salesman is not NP.

The same conclusion applies to most optimisation problems; only the search for a solution of given cost is NP, the class of the optimisation problem has not yet been settled.

---

1. i.e. there are no circuits that do not pass through all vertices.

4.6   STUDY OF NP PROBLEMS BY
EQUIVALENCE CLASSES

We first show that many NP problems, whilst stated in different terms, are in fact equivalent; and then that, because of the size of the NP class and the amount of effort that has been expended on it, there is little chance that $NP = P$.

The meaning of 'equivalent' is made precise by the following definitions.

Definition 1

A problem Q is **reducible** to a problem R if and only if for any solution s of R there is a function $g(s)$, polynomially computable, such that $g(s)$ is a solution of Q.

Q is then called a particular case of R, and we write $Q \to R$: this means, in effect, that if we can solve R we can solve Q also.

Definition 2

If $Q \to R$ and $R \to Q$ then Q and R are **equivalent**.

Definition 3

A problem is NP-hard if and only if any NP problem can be reduced to it.

NB: NP-hard does not imply NP.

This last, surprising, definition is justified by the following theorem, which provides a point of departure for the proof of many equivalences among problems.

4.7   THE FUNDAMENTAL THEOREM

Theorem. *The feasibility problem for a logical expression is NP-hard.*

This means that the solution of any NP problem (that is, of any problem that can be solved in polynomial time by a non-deterministic Turing machine) can be derived, by a transformation that is itself polynomial, from the solution of the feasibility problem. In other words, if we can solve the feasibility problem we can solve any NP problem, i.e. all NP $\to$ feasibility.

The result was obtained by Cook in connection with work on automatic theorem proving; in most formal systems it gives sharper results than the classical theorems concerning undecidability, e.g. Church 1932, Godel 1931 (cf. Chapter 3). The proof, which we now give, is rather long because we must first make precise the formal model of a non-deterministic Turing machine (NDTM).

An NDTM is characterised by having a reading/writing head, a tape (of arbitrary length) marked off into squares in any of which any one of a finite set of symbols $\sigma_1, \sigma_2, ..., \sigma_r$ can be written, a finite set F of internal states and the following set of properties:

1. The head has access to one square only at each instant.
2. At any instant, every square contains a single symbol.
3. The machine is in only one state at any time.
4. Only the square under the head can be modified.
5. Other actions: head movement, change of internal state, can be brought about only by a function Def_M that defines the machine M.
6. The initial state is one of the possible states.
7. The state associated with the first SUCCESS, or the last FAIL, is called the final state.

Suppose now that a problem Q, of size n, can be solved by an NDTM M; we construct a logical expression $E_{M,Q}$ such that:

$$E_{M,Q} \text{ is feasible} \Leftrightarrow Q \text{ can be solved by } M \text{ in polynomial time}$$

The important point in the proof is that the feasibility of a logical expression can always be decided in polynomial time.

The solvability of Q on M means that there is at least one sequence of states $(e_0, e_1, ..., e_m)$ such that:

- $e_i \in Def_M(e_{i-1})$ (i.e. e_i is a 'legal move').
- e_0 is the initial state.
- e_m is the final state, and $m \leqslant p(n)$ where p is some polynomial function of the size n of the problem.
- no other sequence $(e_0, e_1, ..., e_k)$ of legal states uses more than $p(n)$ squares, that is, has more than $p(n)$ states.

The expression $E_{M,Q}$ which we shall construct will simulate the sequence $e_0, e_1, ..., e_m$; it will involve certain variables and each assigning of values to these will correspond to at most one sequence of legal states. Finally, $E_{M,Q}$ will take the value T if and only if there is an assignment that corresponds to a sequence that leads to a SUCCESS.

The variables used here are those that enable an exact description to be given of the NDTM that is being considered; they are of three kinds:

$t(i, \theta) = 1$ if and only if the head is over square i at time θ

$$(1 < i < m, \ 1 < \theta < m)$$

The machine changes from one state to another at each instant, one square is modified at each change and the total number of squares used by the end of m steps does not exceed m.

$u(j, \theta) = 1$ if and only if M is in state e_j at time θ ($1 < j < f$, where f is the number of possible states in F and $1 < \theta < m$)

$v(i, k, \theta) = 1$ if and only if at time θ the ith square on the tape holds the symbol σ_k ($1 \leqslant i \leqslant m$, $1 \leqslant k \leqslant r$, $1 \leqslant \theta \leqslant m$)

The number r of symbols being fixed and independent of n, it follows that the number of logical variables in $E_{M,Q}$ is of the order of m^2, and is therefore a polynomial function of the size n of the original problem.

We now construct seven logical expressions, to correspond respectively to the seven propositions 1–7 above.

A. The head has access to only one square at each instant.

$$\forall \theta, \ 1 \leqslant \theta \leqslant m; \ \sum_{i=1}^{m} t(i,\theta) = 1, \quad \text{so} \quad \prod_{\theta=1}^{m} \sum_{i=1}^{m} t(i_1\theta) = 1$$

This expression has exactly m terms, so (A) is expressed by means of m^2 terms.

B. At any instant, every square contains a single symbol. If i is the number of the square,

$$\forall \theta, \ 1 \leqslant \theta \leqslant m; \ \forall i, \ 1 \leqslant i \leqslant m; \ \sum_{k=1}^{v} v(i, k, \theta) = 1$$

Since r is independent of n, (B) is expressed by means of m^2 terms.

C. The machine is in only one state at any time.

$$\forall \theta, \ 1 \leqslant \theta \leqslant m: \ \sum_{j=1}^{f} u(j, \theta) = 1$$

Since the number f of states depends only on the machine M, (C) requires m terms.

D. Only the square under the head can be modified.

$$i, 1 \leqslant i \leqslant m; \quad k, 1 \leqslant k \leqslant r; \quad 1 \leqslant \theta \leqslant m:$$
$$(v(i, k, \theta) = 1) \Leftrightarrow ((t(i, \theta) = 1) \vee (v(i, k, \theta + 1) = 1))$$

i.e. if the ith square is under the head, with symbol k, then either the head reads the ith square at time θ, or the ith square still contains the kth symbol at time $\theta + 1$. This is consistent with the conditions already translated into expressions, in particular with A and B.

Since r is constant, (d) can be expressed with $O(m^2)$ symbols.

E. A change of state can be brought about only by the function Def_M, *at time* θ

    if the ith square contains the symbol σ_j
    and the head reads the square i
    and the machine is in state k
    then the next state is one of the states $\text{Def}_M(i, j, k)$

We write this proposition, which is of the form $x \Rightarrow y$, in the form $\neg x \vee y$. Translation of the three premises, with h denoting one of the states of $\text{Def}_M(i, j, k)$, we have:

$$(v(i, k, \theta) = 0) \vee (u(j, \theta) = 0) \vee (t(i, \theta) = 0)$$
$$\vee \ [v((i, k_h, \theta + 1) = 1) \wedge u(j_h, \theta + 1) = 1) \wedge (t(i_h, \theta + 1) = 1]$$

Since M is non-deterministic there will be several $\text{Def}_M(i, j, k)$ for any given triplet (i, j, k), but the number will be finite; so for given (i, j, k) the length of this proposition has an upper bound that is independent of n, and since the number f of states is fixed the condition (e) is expressed with $O(m^2)$ terms.

F. The initial state is a legal state. If we label the state at instant 1 as e_1, and the leftmost square as $i = 1$, then:

$$(u(1, 1) = 1) \wedge (t(1, 1) = 1)$$

Further, the squares from 2 to $n + 1$ contain the statement of the problem Q and the remainder are blank; so if we code the blank symbol by 1 we have:

$$\left(\bigwedge_{2 \leqslant i \leqslant n+1} (v(i, j_i, 1) = 1) \right) \left(\bigwedge_{n+2 \leqslant i \leqslant m} (v(i, 1, 1) = 1) \right).$$

The length of state F is thus $O(m)$.

$F \equiv ((u, 1, 1) = 1) \wedge ((t, 1, 1) = 1)$

$$\left(\bigwedge_{2 \leqslant i \leqslant n+1} v(i, j_i, 1) = 1 \right) \left(\bigwedge_{n+2 \leqslant i \leqslant m} v(i, 1, 1) = 1 \right).$$

G. (g) asserts that there is a state, e_λ say, which is the state sought, equal to SUCCESS. If we assume that M reaches this state at time $m = p(n)$ and remains in that state we have:

$$u(\lambda, m) = 1$$

Combining these expressions we have the condition for the solvability of the problem Q by the machine M:

if $H = A \wedge B \wedge C \wedge D \wedge E \wedge F \wedge G$, then H is feasible if and only if machine M solves problem Q.

By construction, H can be expressed in at most $O(m^3)$ terms.

If a sequence of states $e_1, e_2, ..., e_m$ leads to e_λ then this defines a set of assignments for the variables t, u, r which will give $H = T$; and conversely, if such a set of values is known, these correspond, through the function Def_M, to a sequence of legal states.

We have imposed no constraints on the NDTM M used in this proof, so we have shown that any problem that can be solved by M (i.e. any language recognisable by M) is polynomially reducible to the problem of deciding the feasibility of a logical expression.

4.8 THE NP-COMPLETE CLASS

Cook's theorem, together with the definition of NP-hard, tells us that

$Q \rightarrow$ *feasibility applies to all Q NP.*

Further, the reducibility relation is transitive, so if we can show that, conversely, a feasibility problem is reducible to a problem Q_1, that Q_1 is reducible to Q_2, and so on, we have set up a class of equivalent problems. This suggests that we should be more specific about the 'mystery' class of problems, class 3, and divide it into two parts according as we can or cannot prove that a problem does or does not belong to NP; and this leads to the definition of the class NP-complete.

Definition
A problem is said to be NP-complete if and only if it is NP-hard and it is in NP.

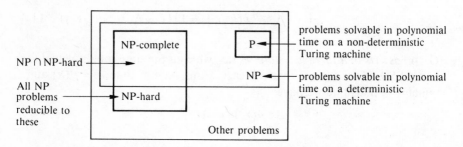

Fig. 4.10.

Figure 4.10 will make the position clear. The general result P = NP is most unlikely to be true, because classical problems, difficult to handle in practice, have been proved to be NP-hard. But what is still more surprising is that almost all these problems are NP; they are therefore NP-complete, and therefore are all equivalent in the sense that if we could solve any one in polynomial time we should be able to solve all problems in this class, also in polynomial time.

Two other properties characterise NP-complete problems:

1. We cannot say that they are not polynomial.
2. We do not know a deterministic algorithm that will solve any of them in polynomial time.

The concept of equivalence is important because it is a matter of transferring a problem from one class to another; the snag is that, in the end, we do not have a good solution for the key problem, that is feasibility. However, the principles of modelling and of transformation of problem specifications can serve as well in actual cases. Further, we must never forget that even though it may have been proved that a certain *class* of problems is NP-complete, a particular case, with particular data, may well be solvable in polynomial time.

We now give a few examples of equivalence to illustrate the general concept.

4.9   SOME PROOFS OF EQUIVALENCES

Equivalence among a large family of problems has been established: problems that, as first stated, were NP have been shown to be reducible to Cook's problem either directly or indirectly through transitivity relations, as shown in Fig. 4.11.

To show that a problem Q is NP-complete we must prove that:

1. Q in NP.
2. Q is NP-hard: but as Cook has proved, $Q \rightarrow$ feasibility, what remains to be proved is feasibility $\rightarrow Q$.

This means that it is necessary and sufficient to find a polynomial transformation from 'feasibility' to Q, such that a solution of 'feasibility' can be made to correspond to every solution of Q.

We first show that to prove the feasibility of a logical expression, even if formally much simpler than those used in the proof of Cook's theorem, is equivalent to the general case.

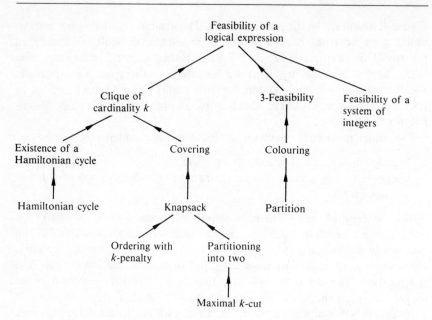

Fig. 4.11 Some reductions established among NP-complete problems.

Example 1.

1. The feasibility problem for a logical expression in conjunctive normal form (CNF) is NP-complete.
2. The feasibility problem for a logical expression in conjunctive normal form, with at most three literals per clause, is NP-complete.

An expression is in CNF when it is written as the logical product ($\land$) of a number of logical sums ($\lor$) of elementary quantities called literals; a literal is either a q or a $\neg q$, where q denotes some logical variable.

The expression H used in the proof of Cook's theorem can be put into CNF; the sums

$$\sum_{i \in I} t(i, \theta) = 1 \qquad (I \text{ being the set of integers over which } i \text{ ranges})$$

can be written, by setting $1 \leftrightarrow T$ and $0 \leftrightarrow F$,

$$\left(\bigvee_i t(i, \theta) \right) \bigwedge_{i \neq j} (\neg t(i, \theta) \lor \neg t(j, \theta))$$

The first parenthesised expression (clause) expresses the fact that at least one of the expressions is T, the second that in none of the (i, j) couples are two variables T simultaneously.

This gives the CNF for A, B, C directly. That for D is obtained by replacing every occurrence of the symbol $\Leftrightarrow$ by its equivalent CNF:

$$x \Leftrightarrow y \equiv (\neg x \vee y) \wedge (x \vee \neg y)$$

This will, at worst, double the length of the expression.

Finally, E, F, G are transformed by replacing the Boolean variables $(0, 1)$ by logical variables (T, F).

The total effect is that H becomes longer by a constant factor; and Cook's result remains valid for expressions in CNF; and in what follows we shall confine ourselves to this form.

The simplest of the CNF expressions that are candidates for membership of the CNF 'clan' are those with at most three literals in any clause, denoted by 3-CNF. We have the following results:

1. That the feasibility problem for a 3-CNF is NP follows from the fact that an NDTM algorithm can be written with a constant number of steps, equal to 3:

    repeat while there is still a clause C_i that is not satisfied
    $$\{C_i = f(x, y, z)\}$$

    $x \leftarrow$ **choice**$[T, F]$
    $y \leftarrow$ **choice**$[T, F]$
    $z \leftarrow$ **choice**$[T, F]$
    if $C_i = F$ **then** FAIL
    end repeat
    if all clauses are satisfied **then** SUCCESS **stop**

2. feasibility $\rightarrow$ 3-feasibility
    Proof: any clause consisting of literals can be transformed into a 3-clause as follows: If the original clause is $(x_1 \vee x_2 \vee \cdots \vee x_i)$, then if we introduce $(i - 3)$ new variables y we can write this

    $$(x_1 \vee x_2 \vee y_1) \wedge (x_3 \vee \neg y_1 \vee y_2) \wedge (x_4 \vee \neg y_2 \vee y_3) \wedge \cdots \wedge (x_{i-1} \vee x_i \vee \neg y_{i-3})$$

    The equivalence of this to the original expression can be proved by recurrence on i.

Suppose we have a solution in terms of x for the original clause, and that $x_{i0} = T$. Let

$$y_j = T \quad \text{for} \quad j \leqslant i_0 - 2$$
$$= F \quad \text{for} \quad j > i_0 - 2$$

The new expression in x and y has then the value T.

Conversely, if there is a set of values for the y_j that makes the expression T, at least one x_i must be T; and since the first clause must be T we have the following:

> **if** $y_i = F$ **then** x_1 or x_2 is T **stop**
> $\quad$ **else** $\{y_1 = T\}$ **if** $y_{i-3} = T$ **then** x_i or $x_{i-1} = T$ **stop**
> $\quad\quad$ **else** $\{y_i = T, \ y_{i-3} = T\}$
> $\quad\quad$ **then** $\exists i_0 (1 \leqslant i_0 \leqslant 4)$: $y_{i0} = T$ **and** $y_{i0+1} = F$
> $\quad\quad\quad\quad\quad\quad\quad\quad\quad\quad$ so $x_{i0+2} = T$
> $\quad\quad$ **end if**
> **end if**

For example, with $i = 4$ the transformation gives the equivalence of:

$$(x_1 \lor x_2 \lor x_3 \lor x_4) \quad \text{and} \quad (x_1 \lor x_2 \lor y_1) \land (x_3 \lor x_4 \lor \neg y_1)$$

Since the new expression has exactly $(i - 1)$ clauses of three literals each, where $i \leqslant 4$, for each clause in the original, the total number of terms is multiplied by 3 at most.

Finally, we now have a way of reducing, in polynomial time, any feasibility problem to a 3-feasibility problem in CNF.

Example 2. The problem of deciding the existence of a k-clique in a given graph is NP-complete.

NB: a clique is a set of vertices with an arc between every pair; a k-clique is a clique with k vertices.

We prove this in two steps, as follows:

1. The problem is NP because, whatever the graph, there are $\binom{n}{k}$ sub-sets of k vertices, which is polynomial in the total number n of vertices of the graph; and for each of these the existence of an arc joining any pair of vertices has to be tested, and therefore $O(k^2)$ tests have to be made.
2. We next prove that the feasibility problem is reducible to the k-clique problem.

Let E be any CNF expression containing k clauses:

$$E = (C_1 \land C_2 \land \cdots \land C_k), \text{ where } C_i = \bigvee_j x_{ij}, \ x_{ij} = \text{(variable) or } \neg\text{(variable)}$$

We now specify a graph, as follows:

(a) Each vertex corresponds to a couple (x, i) where x is a literal in C_i.
(b) An arc joins (x, i) and (y, j) if and only if $i \neq j$ (the two vertices correspond to different clauses); and $x \neq y$ (the two literals are not the negations of each other).

It will be helpful, before going further, to visualise this graph. If E is

$$(x_1 \lor \neg x_2 \lor \neg x_3) \land (x_1 \lor x_2 \lor x_4) \land (x_3 \lor \neg x_4) \land (\neg x_1)$$

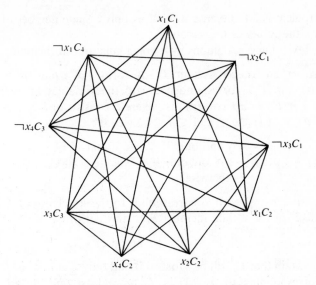

Fig. 4.12 Graph for a k-clique problem.

the graph has nine vertices, because there are nine literals; and an arc joins vertices corresponding to literals from different clauses, which could therefore be T simultaneously. This is shown in Fig. 4.12. Thus the existence of a k-clique in this graph corresponds to the existence for E of a set of k literals belonging to k different clauses – that is, to all the clauses – that can all take the value T simultaneously.

Conversely, if the expression is feasible – that is, if there is a set of truth values for the variables for which every clause is T – then in each of the k clauses at least one literal is T. By construction, there corresponds to this set a set of k vertices in the graph that are completely linked, because these literals are all associated with different clauses and no pair consists of contradictory literals; this is a k-clique.

With the above expression E we find the 4-cliques:

$$(\neg x_3 C_1 \cdot x_2 C_2 \cdot \neg x_4 C_3 \cdot \neg x_1 C_4)$$

and

$$(\neg x_2 C_1 \cdot x_4 C_2 \cdot x_3 C_3 \cdot \neg x_1 C_4)$$

because $\neg x_1 C_4$ is necessarily part of every clique.

Example 3. The existence of a solution of a system of Boolean inequalities is NP-complete.

1. The problem is NP, because it involves only a finite number of different choices, the values of the variables.
2. Feasibility $\rightarrow$ integer solution, by a polynomial transformation.

We construct an integer system IS of form $Ax \geqslant b$ with n Boolean unknowns x_j in $1:1$ correspondence with the variables of E: $(x_j = 1$ in $IS \leftrightarrow X_i = T$ in E) with k constraints, where E consists of k clauses. For the elements a_{ij} of A $(1 \leqslant i \leqslant k, 1 \leqslant j \leqslant n)$ we take

$$a_{ij} = 1 \text{ if and only if } x_j \text{ is a literal of } C_i$$
$$= -1 \text{ if and only if } x_j \text{ is a literal of } C_i$$
$$= 0 \text{ otherwise}$$

Then the ith constraint of IS corresponds to the ith clause of E provided that we take for the second member b_i of this constraint

$$b = 1 - |\{j/x_j \text{ is a literal of } C_i\}|$$

It is then certain that C_i will be satisfied if and only if at least one 'positive' literal (corresponding to $a_{ij} = 1$) is T, or at least one 'negative' literal ($a_{ij} = -1$) is F. This double condition is written in IS:

$$\sum_{j \in J_i^+} x_j - \sum_{j \in J_i^-} x_j \geqslant b_i$$

where

$$J_i^+ = \{j/x_j \text{ is a literal of } C_i\}, \quad J_i^- = \{j/\neg x_j \text{ is a literal of } C_i\}$$

Now

$$(E \text{ is satisfied}) \Rightarrow (\text{at least on } x_j \text{ of } J_i = 1)$$

or

$$(\text{at least one } x_j \text{ of } J_i = 0) \quad \text{for all } i, 1 \leqslant i \leqslant k$$

Thus $x_{j0} = 1$, with $j0$ in J_i, implies (1) since in all cases $\sum_{j \in J_i} x_j$ is less than $|J_i^-|$. In the other case, $x_{j0} = 0$ with j_0 in J_i, suppose first that $J_i \geqslant 1$; then since the sum of the x_j for $j \in J_i^+$ is positive, the inequality (1) holds since then $|J_i^-| - 1 \geqslant \sum_{j \in J_i^-} x_j$.

Thus a solution to the feasibility problem can be made to correspond to any solution of IS by means of the polynomial transformation given.

To take the particular case of the previous expression E:

$$E = (x_1 \vee \neg x_2 \vee \neg x_3) \wedge (x_1 \vee x_2 \vee x_4) \wedge (x_3 \vee \neg x_4) \wedge (\neg x_1)$$

the corresponding integer system is

$$x_1 - x_2 - x_3 \geqslant -1 \quad \text{(clause } C_1)$$
$$x_1 + x_2 + x_4 \geqslant 1 \quad C_2$$
$$x_3 - x_4 \geqslant 0 \quad C_3$$
$$-x_1 \geqslant 0 \quad C_4$$

This can be solved by a direct method. From C_4 we get $x_1 = 0$, and from this, together with $C_1 + C_4$, $x_4 - x_3 \geqslant 0$ which together with C_3 gives $x_4 - x_3 = 0$. Then

$$-x_2 - x_3 \geqslant -1 \quad (C_1)$$

and

$$x_2 + x_3 \geqslant 1 \quad (C_2)$$

whence taking the two possible, $0/1$, for x_2 we get the two solutions

$$(0, 1, 0, 0), \quad (0, 0, 1, 1)$$

which can clearly be put in correspondence with the 4-cliques of the previous problem.

Chapter 5

SOLUTION OF PROBLEMS BY PROPAGATION AND ENUMERATION

It is to enumerative methods – the Type D methods of the introduction to Chapter 4 – that we have to turn for the solution of most problems. A significant amount of this chapter and of Chapter 6 is therefore given over to such methods, and the whole of Chapter 7.

5.1 ENUMERATIVE METHODS: COMBINATORIAL PROBLEMS

A combinatorial problem is a problem of the following general type:

Find an element x belonging to a set X that satisfies a set $K(x)$ of constraints, where X is finite and discrete.

This is a type of problem that is encountered very often in real life, and concerns all cases in which we have to deal with elements that are essentially discontinuous: logical puzzles, ordering items so as to maintain a stock at some planned level, making one decision when several possibilities are open, choosing the location for a new factory, traversing a graph, proving theorems. In all such problems the important feature is that the space X to be searched is *finite and discrete*.

'Discrete' means that there is a finite separation between any pair of points of X: in particular, X is discontinuous. Enumerative methods can be used to attack such problems.

Explicit enumeration – the British Museum algorithm. The name embodies the idea that one method of finding a particular book in the British Museum library (which contains several million) would be to ask for each book in turn until the desired one appeared. In more abstract terms the method is to number all the points of the set (possible because this is finite), examine each one in turn and retain only what satisfies the constraints. The method is certain to succeed whenever success is possible, is simple to implement and is entirely satisfactory when the size of the set does not exceed 10^3 for the hand processing or 10^9 for a computer. The procedure is as follows:

1. Take the first x_0 of X that has not yet been examined.
2. Evaluate the constraints $K(x_0)$.
3. If any constraint is not satisfied, return to (1).
4. Otherwise x_0 is a solution. Return to (1) if all solutions are wanted.

A simple improvement is that it may be possible to reach a decision by evaluating $K(x)$ for only a part of x_0 rather than the complete element.

E. Lucas in his *Récréations Mathématiques* (1891, re-issued 1960) applied this principle to give a systematic solution to the problem of running a maze, such as that of Fig. 5.1.

1. From whichever square one is on, take any path not yet followed.
2. If all the paths have been explored, go back one square along the path by which the present square was reached.

By this process, instead of generating all the possible sub-sets of the set X of squares of the maze, only those are considered that are part of possible paths; and a path is followed until either a dead end or the outlet is reached. A very general method, that of *implicit enumeration*, for solving combinatorial problems can be based on this principle; circumstances are particularly favourable when a gradient can be defined, as we consider next.

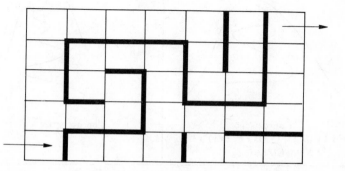

Fig. 5.1 Route through a maze.

5.2 GRADIENT METHODS

A gradient is a variation (gradus = step). Gradient methods are known also as hill-climbing methods from the analogy of reaching the top of a hill by always going in the direction of steepest slope; the general strategy is to try to reach a global optimum via a succession of local optima. Experience has shown that this is a good method, even though it can fail if the space to be searched is not convex.

The general method is that in any actual problem an appropriate numerical value function is defined which takes its extreme value (maximum or minimum) at the goal sought, and to construct a sequence of actions by choosing at each step that action that will give the greatest change in the value of this function. Put in rather more formal terms, the method has given rise to several families of algorithms: the simplex method in linear programming (Section 5.3), the A^* procedure (Section 5.6), successive approximations in numerical analysis, 'alpha–beta' tree pruning (Section 6.4), dynamic programming (Section 5.9), 'branch and bound', separation and evaluation algorithm (Sections 5.11 and 5.12) (Fig. 5.2).

Example 1 (Fig. 5.3). There are six arrows in the initial position S_0 and the problem is to move them into the final position S_F, the only legal moves being the simultaneous reversal of any pair of adjacent arrows. Thus at any step there are five legal moves, the reversals $(1, 2)$, $(2, 3)$, $(3, 4)$, $(4, 5)$, $(5, 6)$. If α denotes any of these actions, α^2 is the identity and therefore we need only find a sequence in which no action is repeated.

Let us take for the value function $f(S)$ for a situation S, $f(S) = $ number

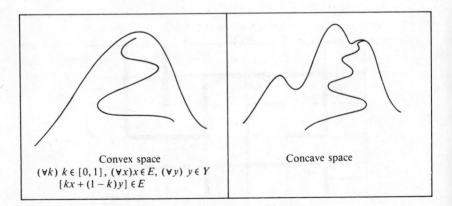

Convex space
$(\forall k)\ k \in [0, 1]$, $(\forall x)x \in E$, $(\forall y)\ y \in Y$
$[kx + (1 - k)y] \in E$

Concave space

Fig. 5.2 Gradient method.

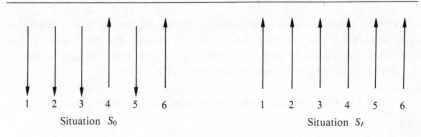

Fig. 5.3 The arrows.

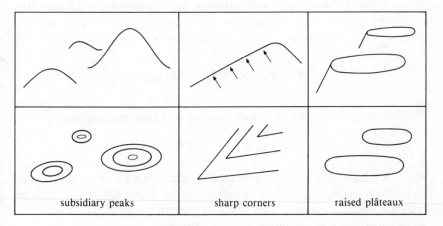

Fig. 5.4 Circumstances where the gradient fails.

of arrows in the right position; so $f(S_0) = f(000101) = 2$,
$f(S_F) = f(111111) = 6$. Calling the moves a, b, c, d, e respectively,
$a \cdot S_0 = S_1 = (110101)$, $f(S_1) = 4$. $d \cdot S_1 = S_2 = (110011)$, $f(S_2) = 4$; so
$c \cdot S_2 = S_F$. It is clear that the order of the moves is immaterial.

Notice that we have had a cross barrier, $f(S) = $ constant, at the second
step. The path, however, is very much affected by the value function and
the process would have gone differently if we had chosen:

$f(S) = $ maximum distance between two wrongly-oriented arrows

for then $f(S_0) = 4$, $f(S_1) = 2$, $f(S_2) = 1$.

Thus the method is not guaranteed to give a solution, and in fact requires
the image (value function) space $f(S)$ to be convex: three types of feature
in this space can cause it to fail – secondary summits, ridges and plateaux
(Fig. 5.4).

Very many problems exhibit this third feature: the approach to the
solution is rapid at first, but then an enormous plain is reached and,

effectively, no further progress is made, so one has to reconsider the value
function; but if this function has been well chosen and the space $f(S)$ is
convex, the method can give rapid and elegant solutions. The algorithms of
Section 4.2, for example, are of this type, with

$f(S)$ = minimum distance to the origin by the shortest path

and

$f(S)$ = number of elements sorted

A particularly favourable and valuable application is to Linear Programming.

5.3　LINEAR PROGRAMMING

A linear program, as we have seen, is a set of linear inequalities:

$$\mathbf{Ax} \leqslant \mathbf{b}, \qquad \mathbf{x} \in \mathbb{R}^n$$

where $\mathbf{A}$ is an $m \times n$ matrix of given real elements, $\mathbf{b}$ a $1 \times m$ vector of given
real elements and $\mathbf{x}$ a $1 \times n$ vector of unknowns. Generally, $m < n$ and the
system is underdetermined, and solutions have to be found that maximise a
given value function, or minimise a cost function.

Example. A small furniture-making workshop receives on the same day two
orders. One is for items each of which will require 11 units of materials and
3 hours of work per item, and will give a profit of 14 (fr., £, $) per item; the
other, 4 units of materials and 5 hours of work and a profit of 7 (..) per
item. In the time available the manager can allocate a total of 46 units of
materials and 32 hours of work to the two orders; how should he distribute
his resources to maximise his profit?

If he makes $x1$, $x2$ items for the first and second orders respectively, then

$$
\begin{aligned}
11 \cdot x1 + 4 \cdot x2 &\leqslant 46 && (1) && \text{(materials constraint)} \\
3 \cdot x1 + 5 \cdot x2 &\leqslant 32 && (2) && \text{(manpower constraint)} \\
Z = 14 \cdot x1 + 7 \cdot x2 &= \max && (3) && \text{(profit to be maximised}
\end{aligned}
$$

This is a mathematical program of the type $\mathbf{Ax} \leqslant \mathbf{b}$, with $\max[\mathbf{cx}]$. $\mathbf{A}$ is a
given matrix, $\mathbf{b}$, $\mathbf{c}$ given vectors, $\mathbf{x}$ the vector to be found.

Since equalities are easier to manipulate than inequalities it is usual in
such problems to introduce auxiliary variables, called slack variables, to
transform the given system into a set of equations. For this example we

introduce variables $y1$, $y2$ and write the system:

$$11 \cdot x1 + 4 \cdot x2 + y1 = 46$$
$$3 \cdot x1 + 5 \cdot x2 + y2 = 32$$
$$\max[14 \cdot x1 + 7 \cdot x2]$$

or in matrix notation

$$\max \begin{bmatrix} 11 & 4 & 1 & 0 \\ 3 & 5 & 0 & 1 \\ 14 & 7 & 0 & 0 \end{bmatrix} \cdot \begin{bmatrix} x_1 \\ x_2 \\ y_1 \\ y_2 \end{bmatrix} = \begin{bmatrix} 46 \\ 32 \\ 0 \end{bmatrix}$$

The method is to start with the obvious solution $x1 = 0$, $x2 = 0$, $y1 = 46$, $y2 = 32$ and improve this by increasing as far as possible the variable that will give the greatest increase in the profit function Z. The 'gradient' to be used is given by the fourth line, and it is clear that in the first instance $x1$ will give the greatest improvement; so we write the first equation as:

$$x1 = 46/11 - 4/11 \cdot x2 - 1/11 \cdot y1$$

and substitute in the matrix to get:

$$\begin{bmatrix} 1 & 4/11 & 1/11 & 0 \\ 0 & 5 - 12/11 & -3/11 & 1 \\ 0 & 7 - 56/11 & -14/11 & 0 \end{bmatrix} * \mathbf{x} = \begin{bmatrix} 46/11 \\ 32 - 3.46/11 \\ -644/11 \end{bmatrix}$$

where $\mathbf{x}$ is the same right-hand side vector as before.

Thus if $x1$ is given its greatest possible value ($46/11$) the profit function has the value $644/11$; when $x2 = 0$ and $y2 = 32 - 3 \cdot 46/11 = 214/11$. What we have done, in effect, is to make a simple translation along the $x1$-axis which shows that Z can be further increased if now $x2$ is increased, the gradient being $7 - 56/11 = 21/11$.

At this stage the coefficient of $x2$ in the second constraint is $5 - 12/11 = 43/11$; hence:

$$\begin{bmatrix} 1 & 0 & 1/11 + 4.3/11.43 & -4/43 \\ 0 & 1 & -3/43 & 11/43 \\ 0 & 0 & -14/11 + 3.21/11.43 & -21.43 \end{bmatrix} * \mathbf{x} = \begin{bmatrix} 46/11 - 4.214/11.43 \\ 214/43 \\ -14.46/11 - 21.214/11.43 \end{bmatrix}$$

This new translation, together with the linear combinations to which it leads, shows, by the last row of the above matrix, that all the gradients and all the relative gains in Z are negative or zero, so the maximum has been reached; the value is:

$$Z^* = \max \cdot Z = 14.46/11 + (21.214/11)/43 = 68.033$$

corresponding to $x1 = 102/43 = 2.371$, $x2 = 214/43 = 4.977$

The method, involving the specification of a space to be searched and an

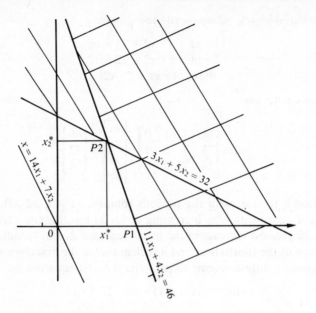

Fig. 5.5 Simplex method for linear programming.

interpretation of the gradient algorithm, is due to G. Dantzig (1959) and is called the simplex method. For a 2-dimensional space a geometrical representation is immediate, as in Fig. 5.5 for the example given. Following the process in this diagram, we start from 'sea level' at the origin O with $x1 = x2 = 0$ and move first to $P1$ and then to $P2$, in each case in the direction of greatest increase of $Z = 14 \cdot x1 + 7 \cdot x2$. The 'summit' is reached at $P2$, which satisfies the constraints and, within those constraints, gives the maximum distance of the line $14x1 + 7x2 = Z$ from the origin.

The solution, of course, is valid only if the real (i.e. not necessarily integer) numbers $x1$, $x2$ are acceptable, and therefore provides a solution to the manager's problem only if the orders in question are repeated often enough for it to be reasonable to use the integer approximations $x1 = 2$, $x2 = 5$. If this is not the case then there is the additional constraint that $x1$, $x2$ must be (positive) integers, and this is an entirely different problem, because the space that has now to be searched, $\mathbb{N}^n$ in general, is not continuous and not necessarily convex. In Chapter 8 we describe the entirely different methods that are needed to solve such a problem.

In matrix notation, the simplex method is easily extended to deal with any number of variables and of constraint. The procedure reduces to a sequence of linear combinations, with the choice at each step decided by a study of the values of the gradients; the process stops when all these are negative.

5.3.1 Formalisation of the simplex algorithm

This algorithm, the complexity of which is not polynomial, is based on a number of simple properties derived from working hypotheses for linear problems:

1. Inequalities of the form $a1 \cdot x1 + a2 \cdot x2 + \cdots + an \cdot xn \leqslant b$ define closed convex sub-spaces of $\mathbb{R}^n$ bounded by hyperplanes.
2. The intersection of a finite number of such sub-spaces is a convex body called a polyhedron if it is bounded or a polytope if not.
3. Every point of a polyhedron can be expressed as a linear combination of its vertices (its extreme points), which are the intersections of the initial hyperplanes and are finite in number; if there are m hyperplanes, expressing the m inequalities, there are $\binom{n}{m}$ vertices in $\mathbb{R}^n$.
4. The optimum cannot be attained at a point strictly within the polytope because, given any interior point, a point on the boundary can be constructed, by linear combinations, at which the value function Z is greater. Provided that the problem is not degenerate – that is, rank $[\det \mathbf{A}] \neq m$ – this value can be further increased by following the 'hyper-edge' to the nearest vertex.
5. A *base* of $\mathbf{A}$ is any sub-set of the indices $[1 \ldots m]$ to which there corresponds a square matrix $\mathbf{B}$, extracted from $\mathbf{A}$, of rank n. The previous statement is equivalent to 'the optimum for a linear program $\mathbf{A}x \leqslant b$ can be reached only as a solution of a base of $\mathbf{A}$'. The matrix $\mathbf{A}$ is partitioned into two sub-matrices $\mathbf{B}$, $\mathbf{N}$ and the system written

$$\mathbf{B} \cdot \mathbf{x}_B + \mathbf{N} \cdot \mathbf{x}_N = \mathbf{b}$$

and a base solution, defined by $\mathbf{x}_N = 0$, is found by solving the Cramer system $\mathbf{B} \cdot \mathbf{x}_B = \mathbf{b}$.

The algorithm scans only the realisable bases, that is, those for which $\mathbf{x}_B \geqslant 0$, which it does by going from one vertex to the next, using the gradient method to guide the choice. At each step one index is removed from the base (one variable becomes null) and another enters (has the possibility of taking a non-null value). Convergence is ensured by the finiteness of the number of vertices.

5.4 THE GRADIENT METHOD IN GRAPH THEORY

The gradient method can be relied upon to give a solution not only to the LP problem but also to the following graph-theoretic problem, which models many practical problems such as the design of a telecommunication or distribution network, questionnaire analysis and automatic classification. The problem is, given a weighted connected graph $G = (X, U)$, construct a partial tree $A = (X, V^*)$ of minimum total weight. Recall that a tree is a cycle-free connected graph; if it has n vertices then, by Euler's formula, it has $n - 1$ edges.

The first solution to this problem was given by Kruskal in 1956; it uses the gradient concept, which suggests considering the arcs of G in order of increasing weight.

Minimum-weight tree algorithm.
> put the arcs of G in order of increasing weight: V
> $V \leftarrow \emptyset$
> **while** there are still arcs not yet considered
> > **if** the first of these does not form a cycle with V **then** add this to V
> **end**

If G has n vertices ($n = |X|$) the algorithm requires exactly n steps.

5.4.1 Proof of Kruskal's algorithm

Let L be the total weight of the tree (X, V) obtained at the final step in the above algorithm; we shall show that there cannot be a tree with total weight strictly less than L.

Suppose this is not so, and that there are trees of total weight less than L; among these there will be one, (X, V^*), of least weight, L^* say. (X, V^*) and (X, V) each have ($|X| - 1$) arcs; let v_i be the first of these that is in the set V but not in V^*: if there is no such v_i the result is proved. Adding v_i to V^* will create a cycle, which must include an arc v_0 which is not in V.

The graph $(X, V^* + v_i - v_0)$ is then a tree, with $(n - 1)$ arcs (and of course no cycle); but the addition of v_0 to $(X, \{v_1, v_2, ..., v_{i-1}\})$ cannot create a cycle because this is a sub-tree of (X, V^*) which is cycle-free, and therefore v_0 must come after v_i in the list of arcs; so weight(v_0) > weight(v_i) (we can assume, without loss of generality, that all the arc weights are different).

It follows that the weight of $(X, V^* + v_i - v_0)$, i.e. $L^* +$ weight(v_i) $-$ weight(v_0), is less than L^*; which is a contradiction.

An algorithm of this type, which deals with objects in an order given by some value function, is called a 'glutton'. Its success is guaranteed whenever the problem can be reduced to finding the intersection of two families of independent parts of the same set, called matroids (cf. Gondran and Minoux 1979).

An example would be to find the minimum-weight spanning tree (i.e. tree that includes all the vertices) of the graph of Fig. 5.6 (which in fact

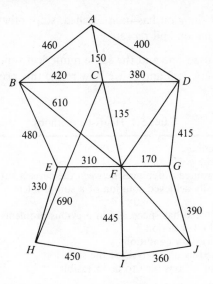

Fig. 5.6 Weighted graph, for determination of minimum-weight spanning tree.

represents the French HT electricity distribution network, and the 'weights' are distances). The order of the arcs in increasing weight is:

$$AC, FG, EH, IJ, CD, GJ, AD, DG, BC, CF, FI, HI, AB, BE, FJ, FD.$$

Kruskal's algorithm allows us to keep, in succession, first AC and then FG, EF, EH, IJ, CD, GJ; AD is rejected because it would form a cycle with AC and CD; DG and BC can next be added, and at this stage all the vertices have been included so the minimum spanning tree has been constructed.

An extension of this method to deal with searches of more general type has led to what are known in AI as heuristic methods of search. We now consider these.

5.5 HEURISTIC SEARCHING

A very general class of problems can be solved, formally, in the following way:

Step 1: Choose one action from among those that are possible.
Step 2: Carry out this action, thus changing the current situation.
Step 3: Evaluate the new situation.
Step 4: Reject any unfavourable situations.

Step 5: If the goal situation has been reached, stop; otherwise choose a new
       starting situation and repeat.

So far we have used one and the same numerical function as a basis for
the decisions in Steps 1, 3 and 5; we now refine this procedure, and Table

Table 5.1 Heuristic methods.

Step 1 Choice of action
- for relevance to the goal
   - reducing unwanted differences between the current situation and the goal
   - known or easily achieved solution of a sub-problem
- from experience
   - repetition of what has succeeded in previous problems
   - identifying the key action
- fulfilling some necessary condition
   - choice dictated by an analysis of the situation
   - elimination of actions seen to be infeasible
- random choice
   - preference for variety

Step 3 Evaluation of the situation
- by analogy
   - recognition of the problem as one previously solved
   - recognition of a sub-problem
   - measuring the distance to the goal
      - from the initial situation
      - in terms of the effort needed
- by some mathematical criterion
   - construction of properties necessary and/or sufficient for the solution
   - construction of a numerical value function
   - finding upper/lower bounds
   - summing the values of acceptable features
- by hope of progress, based on past experience of
   - the simplicity of the situation
   - the rate at which the search progresses
   - any other criterion, e.g. difficulty of the problem

Step 5 Choice of the next move
- continual progress towards the goal
   - development of the situation generated
   - working in parallel
   - take the actions one after the other for all situations simultaneously
- return to the most promising situation
   - as measured by the value function
   - because of the small number of actions it has involved
- by a compromise between
   - the depth of the search
   - the evaluation of the situation

5.1 gives some details of the concepts and heuristic methods used by human workers and by existing computer programs. If we follow the steps of Table 5.1 in constructing a minimum-weight tree and decide:

1. to add another arc at each step;
2. (step 1) to choose always the arc of least weight among those available;
3. (step 5) to start again always from the tree that is being constructed;

we shall reproduce Kruskal's algorithm, and in addition some variants on this which can be shown also to lead to the solution. Thus we can decide either to add or to delete an arc, and in step 1 there is no longer any need to sort the arcs – the choice (b) makes this unnecessary; in step 3, if V contains a cycle we delete from this the arc of greatest weight; and in step 5 we return to the tree (X, V) in course of construction.

Other variants can be obtained by taking connectivity into account. Whilst all these variants converge, they do not, of course, all require the same number of elementary operations; in fact the complexity of the original form (Kruskal's) is $O(n^3)$ (n = number of vertices in the original graph), as is also that of the first variant which avoids the sort. The best algorithm known is $O(n^2)$.

The simplex algorithm also belongs to the class of methods defined by Table 5.1. Here an action corresponds to adding one index to the base and removing another; in step 1 the index giving the highest gradient is selected for addition, and in step 2 the index to be removed is chosen so that the solution will still belong to the polyhedron; and in step 5 the return is again to the current solution.

In a search of this type there is in general no guarantee that a previous path will not be travelled again, nor that the algorithm will converge to a solution even when one exists. Answers to both these implied questions are given by a refinement of the general gradient method, due to Hart, Nilsson and Raphael (1968, 1972), known as the 'A^* algorithm'.

5.6   THE A^* ALGORITHM

A problem starts with some initial situation S_0 and progresses through a sequence of situations S as a result of some sequence of actions, the aim being to reach a certain goal or final situation, the solution of the problem. In this algorithm a numerical value $f(S)$ is assigned to each situation, consisting of two terms:

$$f(S) = g(S) + h(S)$$

where $g(S)$ is the known cost incurred in reaching S and $h(S)$ is a heuristic

Table 5.2.

Algorithm A^*
Step 0   construct the graph $R = (E, A)$ to be searched, setting

> $S_0 \leftarrow E$ (initial situation)   {to be partitioned into two subsets, O of
> $f(S_0) \leftarrow O$ 'open' and C of 'closed' situations respec-
> $O \leftarrow S_0, \quad F \leftarrow \emptyset$ tively, meaning open/closed to further
> search}

while $O \neq \emptyset$ **do**
Step 1   choose in O a situation S such that $f(S)$ is minimum:

$$O \to O - S; \; C \leftarrow C + S$$

   if S is a solution **then stop**
Step 2   **else** develop S by constructing the situations S_i ($0 \leqslant i \leqslant n_S$) generated by
   the possible actions starting from S
Step 3   compute $f(S_i)$ for each i:

$$f(S_i) = g(S_i) + h(S_i), \qquad \text{where } h(S_i) \leqslant h*(S_i)$$

Step 4   put in O, together with their values, those S_i that are in neither O nor C
   for all S_i already in either O or C put

$$f(S_i) \leftarrow \min[f(S_i)_{\text{old}}, f(S_i)_{\text{new}}]$$

   if S_i is in C **then** also **do** $C \leftarrow C - S_i, \; O \leftarrow O + S_i$
end while
end A^*

---

function that estimates the cost of reaching the solution from S by the best possible sequence of actions. Thus $f(S)$ is an estimate of the cost of any solution that is 'constrained to S' – that is, has the same initial actions as S.

$g(S)$ is easily computed if the basic costs are known, that is, the cost $c(S_1, S_2, a)$ of going from S_1 to S_2 by action a; it is simply the sum of the costs of the actions involved in going from the initial situation to S. In what follows we shall assume that all costs are positive, and that $g(S)$ is strictly additive (Table 5.2). Algorithm A^* is characterised by a fundamental property of the heuristic function h: if $h^*(S)$ is the true minimum cost of going from S to the solution by whatever sequence of actions, $h(S)$ is a lower bound for $h^*(S)$; therefore, since $h^*(S)$ must be positive:

$$0 \leqslant h(S) \leqslant h^*(S)$$

If now $g^*(S)$ is the least cost of reaching S from the initial S_0, then $f^*(S) = g^*(S) + h^*(S)$ is the least cost solution that passes through S, and $f(S)$ is an estimate of $f^*(S)$ (and a lower bound).

Theorem. *Algorithm A^* terminates if there is a finite sequence of actions leading from the initial situation to the solution.*

We preface the proof with a simple comment: if only a finite number of actions can be taken in each situation and there are only a finite number of possible situations, then A^* will converge. Each iteration removes one vertex from the set O and adds a finite number of new vertices; the graph remains finite and its scanning requires only a finite number of iterations.

Suppose that, whilst the hypothesis of the finiteness of the action sequence remains valid, the graph to be scanned is not finite; arguing by *reductio ad absurdum*, suppose A^* does not terminate. This can happen only if O grows indefinitely; we shall show that this implies that the smallest value of $f(S)$ is infinite also and that therefore there cannot be a solution attainable by a finite sequence of actions.

For any situation S, let $v^*(S)$ be the number of actions needed to reach S from S_0: this is not necessarily the route that A^* would take and is therefore not known. But whatever the value, since the cost of any arc is strictly positive we have: $g^*(S) > k \cdot v^*(S)$ with g^* defined as above and k some constant. The actual value $g(S)$ as found by A^* thus satisfies:

$$g(S) \geqslant g^*(S) > k \cdot v^*(S)$$

and since the heuristic function $h(S)$ is itself non-negative:

$$f(S) \geqslant G(S) > k \cdot v^*(S)$$

Therefore if $v^*(S)$ becomes infinite so does $f(S)$ and A^* does not terminate.

However, we can prove also that at any stage in the progress of A^* there is always a vertex S_2 in O such that $f(S_2) \leqslant f^*(S_0)$.

If there is a finite sequence of actions and situations from S_0 to the goal, let S_2 be the first of these situations that is also in O; we know that S_2 exists, provided that A^* has not terminated. In any situation $f(S_2) = g(S_2) + h(S_2)$, and here $g(S_2) = g^*(S_2)$ because, by definition of S_2, all the situations previous to S_2 are in C. Further, because of the way A^* is constructed, $h(S_2) \leqslant h^*(S_2)$, so finally

$$f(S_2) \leqslant g^*(S_2) + h^*(S_2) f(S_2) \leqslant f^*(S_2)$$

If the sequence of actions is optimal, then $f(S_2) \leqslant f^*(S_0)$. This contradicts the assumption that f is not finite, and therefore A^* is finite even if the graph is locally infinite, provided that there is a solution that can be reached with a finite number of actions.

Thus A^* will give a solution when one exists; and further, the solution will be optimal. If the algorithm terminated at a vertex S_3 such that $f(S_3) > f^*(S_0)$ then the above proof shows that at the previous step there was a vertex S_2 such that $f(S_2) < f^*(S_0)$ and that therefore S_2, not S_3, would have been chosen in step 1. In fact, every vertex developed by A^* has a cost that is at most equal to $f^*(S_0)$, since otherwise S is either a solution or is not chosen.

The function $f(S)$ must of course take values as close as possible to, but always less than, $f^*(S_0)$. The greater the value of $h(S)$ the more efficient the algorithm will be; it is easily shown that if $h_2(S) < h_1(S)$ every vertex developed by S_2 will be developed by S_1 also. If h is monotone with respect to local costs, that is if $h(S_2) \leqslant h(S_1) + c(S_1, S_2, a)$, it can be shown also that A^* constructs an optimal sequence to every vertex that it develops, that is (S is developed) $\Leftrightarrow (g(S) = g^*(S))$.

The sequence of vertex costs developed must be non-decreasing, so the convergence will be rapid. In this case (monotony) A^* is simply a variant of the Moore–Dijkstra (1957) algorithm for finding the shortest path through a graph: cf. Section 4.2. The most serious defect of the algorithm is its handling of cases where there is no solution.

Example 1. Applications of Algorithms A^*. Following Nilsson we consider the famous puzzle devised by Sam Loyd, the sliding tile puzzle: eight square tiles numbered 1 to 8 are held in a 3×3 frame, leaving one square empty, any of the neighbouring tiles can be slid horizontally or vertically into the empty space, so creating a new space. The problem is to go from a given initial configuration S_0 to a given final S_F in the least number of such moves; for example, with:

$$S_0 = \begin{array}{ccc} 2 & 8 & 3 \\ 1 & 6 & 4 \\ 7 & \Delta & 5 \end{array} \qquad S_F = \begin{array}{ccc} 1 & 2 & 3 \\ 8 & \Delta & 4 \\ 7 & 6 & 5 \end{array}$$

where Δ is the empty square.

Let us specify the functions g, h, etc., as

$$g(S) = \text{number of moves taken in going from } S_0 \text{ to } S$$
$$h(S) = \text{number of tiles in } S \text{ in the 'wrong' position}$$

Then

1. $g(S) \leqslant g^*(S)$, by definition of g.
2. $h(S) \leqslant h^*(S)$, by the nature of the problem.

There is no guarantee that $h(S)$ behaves monotonely. Figure 5.7 shows the tree developed by A^*, with $f(S) = g(S) + h(S)$; here $[x, y]$ means $g = x$, $h = y$ for that situation.

Variants on A^* have been suggested; Pohl (1970) uses a more general form of the function $f(S)$:

$$f(S) = (1 - \alpha) \cdot g(S) + \alpha h(S)$$

where α is a real-valued parameter, $0 \leqslant \alpha \leqslant 1$. This varies the relative

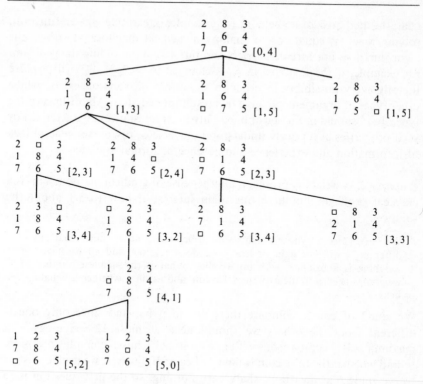

Fig. 5.7 Solution of the sliding-tile problem by Algorithm A^*.

weights given to the rigorous part $g(S)$ and the heuristic part $h(S)$; $\alpha = \frac{1}{2}$ corresponds to the A^* algorithm, $\alpha = 1$ to the pure gradient method and $\alpha = 0$ to what we have called the 'British Museum' algorithm. But there is no reason why α should remain constant throughout a search, and indeed its value can be decreased as the progress is made and the heuristic part becomes less important; for any given problem a post hoc study can be made, to give the value that will minimise the number of vertices developed.

Lastly, the search can be conducted in both directions: from the initial situation towards the goal and also in reverse, the actions being reversed at each iteration. The process stops when the two processes give the same situation.

A^*, like all the other gradient-based algorithms described in this chapter, is a strictly numerical algorithm in the sense that it involves no formal analysis of the successive situations but relies solely on the values of a cost function. There are, however, many problems for which such an attitude does not make sense – because, for example, the need is to find a solution when one is not known in advance, rather than an optimum route to a given goal: the method is of no help in, for example, integrating a given function, solving a set of equations or making a medical diagnosis. Further, the algorithm does not foresee barriers and pitfalls: in the sliding tile problem, for example, if the first row in S_0 is changed to (8 2 3), A^* will explore literally every possibility in order to show that no solution exists, whilst other types of argument can give this result immediately. Algorithms of the type of A^* should in fact be applied only in circumstances characterised by such properties as a poorly-understood universe of discourse, general lack of information and experience and absence of formal arguments.

Example 2. A weighing problem: another case of gradient method. This is a classical problem, but here our main interest is how to set about the solution.

> We have 12 coins whose weights should be equal, but we know that one is different – whether light or heavy we do not know, and all we have for weighing is a balance, with no weights. What is the smallest number of weighings needed to identify the false coin and to show whether it is light or heavy?

We could of course compare the coins in pairs, and since only one is different from the others we should need at most 12 weighings – a maximum of 11 comparisons with one arbitrarily chosen coin plus one more to find whether the false coin is light or heavy. If, instead, we decide to start by weighing 6 against 6 we shall learn nothing; so the first question is to determine the number to be placed in each pan as to gain the maximum amount of information. It is clear that no information is gained by putting unequal numbers in the two pans.

We can answer this question with the help of a value function and a measure of its gradient. We want each weighing to reduce the mathematical expectation of the number of coins remaining of unknown weight: we must use the expectation because we do not know this number until the final step. If there are N coins in total and we put m in each pan, where $2m \leqslant N$, then either the balance beam stays horizontal, showing that there are $N - 2m$ coins of unknown weight, or it does not, showing that $N - 2m$ are of standard weight and either one of the sets of m is heavy or the other is light, these last two possibilities being mutually exclusive. We want our value function $f(m)$ to measure the benefit we shall get from weighing m against m, and a natural choice is the number of coins of unknown weight after any particular choice of $2m$ coins, multiplied by the probability of making that choice. Since there are $\binom{n}{r}$ ways of choosing r objects out of a group of n, it follows that the probability that the balance will be level (the two groups of m are of equal and therefore correct weight) is:

$$\binom{N-1}{2m} \bigg/ \binom{N}{2m}$$

for then the irregular coin has not been picked. This is $(N - 2m)/N$ = $1 - 2m/N$, and the probability of the only other possibility, that the beam swings to one side or the other, is therefore the complement of this, $2m/N$.

Thus the expectation of the number of coins of unknown weight after the weighing is:

$$f(m) = (N - 2m) \cdot (1 - 2m/N) + m \cdot 2m/N = (6m^2 - 4Nm + N^2)/N$$
$$= [6(m - N/3)^2 + N^2/3]/N$$

which is minimum when $m = N/3$. Thus for our problem of 12 coins the optimum procedure is to weigh 4 against 4.

The result is not intuitive, but it leads to a solution in 3 weighings; what is remarkable is that the details of the weighings can be specified without knowing the outcome of any of the three: labelling the coins A to L, the weighings are:

1. A B C D against E F G H
2. A B C E D I J K
3. B E G I C H K L

which will distinguish between the $12 \times 2 = 24$ possibilities.

It is easily seen that the problem cannot be solved with fewer than three weighings: for since any one weighing has three possible outcomes, two can distinguish between $3 \times 3 = 9$ possibilities, which is not sufficient. Thus the method has given the optimum solution.

5.7 IMPLICIT ENUMERATION BY PROPAGATION OF CONSTRAINTS

In Section 5.1 we described briefly Lucas's method for finding a route through a maze; we now illustrate this with another classical problem, not stated as a maze problem. This is the 'N queens' problem: on an $N \times N$ chess board place the maximum number of queens in such a way that none can be taken by any of the others.

Since the queen can capture along a row, a column or a diagonal it is clear that it should be possible to place N queens in this way on an $N \times N$ board: but can such a configuration be constructed? As a first attempt, consider a 4×4 board and take the rows one at a time, placing the first queen on the first square of Row 1 (Fig. 5.8). It is clear that with this placing, and under the conditions of the problem, there can be no solution with a queen in the first column on the second row – one of the constraints $K(x)$ would not be

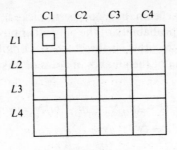

Fig. 5.8.

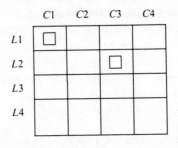

Fig. 5.9.

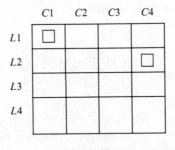

Fig. 5.10.

satisfied; and similarly for the second column of the second row. Thus the first choice for the second row is the third column, as in Fig. 5.9.

Considering the rows in order, the situation now is that the third queen cannot be placed in either column 1 or column 4 of the third row because of the first queen, nor in the second or fourth column because of the second queen; and therefore this partial solution, with only two queens, cannot form part of any complete solution. We therefore abandon the second assumption and place the second queen in the fourth column of the second row, giving Fig. 5.10.

Placing the third queen in column 1 is not allowed, so we place her in column 2; but then placing the fourth queen in any of columns 1, 2, 3, 4 of row 4 is against the conditions, so we must reconsider once more the placing of the second queen. However, there is now no remaining choice for her in the second row, so it is the placing of the first queen that we have to reconsider: we place her in the second column of the first row. This eliminates the first, second and third columns of the second row for the second queen, so we place her in the fourth, giving Fig. 5.11.

For the third row, if we place the third queen in the first column this eliminates columns 1 and 2 for the fourth, and column 4 is already eliminated by the second queen; thus there is only one choice, column 3, giving Fig. 5.12.

This gives a solution to the problem: in fact, we have found all the solutions. We have considered all the possibilities with the first queen in columns 1 or 2 of row 1, and all those with her in columns 3 or 4 can be deduced from these by symmetry about a vertical axis through the middle of the board. Thus there are only two solutions on the 4×4 board.

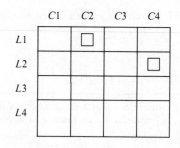

Fig. 5.11.

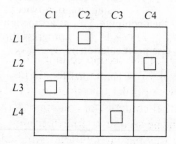

Fig. 5.12 The solution to the four queens' problem.

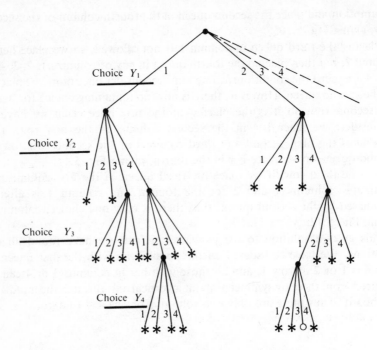

Fig. 5.13 Search tree, with implicit enumeration.

Table 5.3.

ENUM: enumeration of the elements of a set X where X is a Cartesian product of
       sets Y_i, $i \in [1, N]$ and the Y_i are taken in the order $1, 2, ..., N$
  $i \leftarrow 1$; compute Y_i;
  repeat while $i \geqslant 1$ {scan X}
        repeat while $Y_i \neq \emptyset$
              choose an element y_i of Y_i
              $Y_i \leftarrow Y_i - y_i$ {y_i is removed from Y_i so as not to consider the
                                         same situation twice}
              if $i < N$ **then** compute Y_{i+1} as a function of $K(x)$
                          $i \leftarrow i + 1$ {progress through X}
                        else print solution $y_1, y_2, ..., y_N$
              end if
        end repeat Y_i {backtrack}
        $i \leftarrow i - 1$
  end repeat i
end

We now introduce a notation that will help in extending this method to other problems. At each row (i.e. at each level in the assumptions) we have, *a priori*, N possible choices, each corresponding to a column of our chess board; and we can represent any partial solution with k queens by a vector.

$$\mathbf{v} = (y_1, y_2, ..., k_k)$$

where y_i is the number of the column in which the queen on row i is placed. What we have done in finding a solution to the four queens' problem is to scan the tree of possibilities, as in Fig. 5.13. The tree was searched systematically 'depth first' and then from left to right, descending the levels as far as possible before meeting an impasse and back-tracking. The tree can be used either to find only a single solution – ending the search when that is found – or to find all solutions.

We can use a tree search of this type to solve any problem $[x?, x \in X, K(x)]$ for which the space X shares with the chess board the key property of being representable as a Cartesian product: thus the board has been considered as the union of N identical rows, so the space X of that problem is simply the product $X = Y_1 \times Y_2 \times \cdots \times Y_N$ where Y_i denotes the ith row, itself consisting of N squares. The Implicit Enumeration Algorithm is then a matter of executing the procedure given in Table 5.3.

5.7.1 The eight queens problem: version 1

The board is treated as a Cartesian product of the eight rows Y_i, $i = 1$ to 8, and the search conducted in this order of increasing i. At any instant, for all i, column (i) denotes the current element of Y_i, that is, the first (Table 5.4). We now show how two successive improvements can be made to this solution.

5.7.2 Implications related to a choice of placing

It may happen that among the set $K(x)$ of constraints are some that are sufficiently simple – that is, involve sufficiently few unknowns – for a knowledge of the first few values $y_1, y_2, ..., y_k$ $(k < N)$ to suffice to decide whether or not they can be satisfied, given those values. Thus in the problem of the 4×4 board $y_1 = 1$ (first queen placed on the first square of the first row) implies $y_2 \geqslant 3$ (second queen cannot be on either the first or second square of row 2 and then y_3 cannot be either 1 or 3. Choosing $y_2 = 3$ implies that y_3 cannot be either 2 or 4, so there is no possible value for y_3 and an impasse has been reached. This approach leads to the first improvement to the version 1 algorithm, as follows.

Table 5.4.

{column not yet tested in row i}
$i \leftarrow 1$ {index of row}
$\mathrm{col}(i) \leftarrow 1$ {index of row}
repeat while $i \geqslant 1$
*test: **repeat while** $[\mathrm{col}(i) \leqslant 8]$
                  $\mathrm{col}(i) \leftarrow \mathrm{col}(i) + 1$
                  {test for possibility, with regard to previous placings}
                            repeat for $i_p \in [1, 2, ..., i-1]$
                                if queen $(i, \mathrm{col}(i))$ en prise with queen $(i_p, \mathrm{col}(i_p))$
                                    then go to *test {partial check, try next column}
                                end if
                            end repeat i_p
                            if $i < 8$
                                then $\mathrm{col}(i+1) \leftarrow 0$ {partial success}
                                else print solution $\mathrm{col}(i)$ {complete success}
                            end if
                  end repeat col.
                  {backtrack}
$i \leftarrow i - 1$
end repeat i
end 8 queens

If we are to avoid performing unnecessary tests we must take into account such implications, by updating, after each new choice of placing, the set of values available for the kth variable y_k in its set Y_k; but at the same time we must preserve the possibility of backtracking. This can be achieved very conveniently by setting up a vector corresponding to each Y_k which keeps account of both the possible and the forbidden values for y_k, and which gives also for each forbidden value the number of the first choice that has caused the embargo.

Let $\mathbf{L}_k$ by the vector for Y_k; we use the notation:

$\mathbf{L}_k(j) = 0$ means that j is a possible value for y_k (the kth queen can be placed on the jth square of row k)

$\mathbf{L}_k(j) = i > 0$ means that j is a forbidden value for y_k, and that this placing was first embargoed by choice i

Initially $\mathbf{L}_k(j) = 0$ for all k, j since all squares are available. For the 4×4 problem

$$k = 1$$
$$\mathbf{L}_1 = \mathbf{L}_2 = \mathbf{L}_3 = \mathbf{L}_4 = (0, 0, 0, 0)$$

Choice 1:

$$y_1 = 1 \qquad \text{(first queen on first square of row 1)}$$
$$\mathbf{L}_1 = (1, 1, 1, 1)$$
$$\mathbf{L}_2 = (1, 1, 0, 0)$$
$$\mathbf{L}_3 = (1, 0, 1, 0)$$
$$\mathbf{L}_4 = (1, 0, 0, 1)$$

Choice 2:

$$y_2 = 3 \qquad (\mathbf{L}_2 \text{ shows } y_2 = 1, 2 \text{ forbidden by choice 1})$$
$$\mathbf{L}_2 = (1, 1, 2, 2)$$
$$\mathbf{L}_3 = (1, 2, 1, 2)$$
$$\mathbf{L}_4 = (1, 0, 2, 1)$$

$\mathbf{L}_3$ now shows that there is no value available for y_3 (no place for the third queen on row 3), so we must backtrack. This is done without difficulty by, on the one hand, returning to choice 2 with $\mathbf{L}_2 = (1, 1, 1, 0)$ and on the other deleting the implications linked to this old choice ($y_2 = 3$).

$$\mathbf{L}_3 = (1, 0, 1, 0)$$
$$\mathbf{L}_4 = (1, 0, 0, 1)$$

Note that $\mathbf{L}_2 = (1, 1, 1, 0)$, for we now know that everything takes place as though the assignment $y_2 = 3$ were forbidden as a consequence of choice 1 alone.

All this is easily organised and can be checked on the board by, for example, associating embargoes with numbered counters. The vectors $\mathbf{L}$ are the rows, with counters placed on the embargoed squares and available squares left blank.

We can now construct the second version of the algorithm.

5.7.3 The eight queens problem: version 2

The essential difference from version 1 is that the scheme of feasibility testing is changed after each new choice of placing has been made, to take account of the implications of that choice. All squares *en prise* still free become forbidden and are recorded in a vector of 'freedoms' together with the number of the choice.

We use the notation described above, and also, abbreviating 'freedom' to fr, $fr(u, v)$ to denote the state of availability of square v of row u: $fr(u, v) = 0$ thus means that this square is free (Table 5.5). We thus have a method for attacking the queens problem that is very similar to Lucas's for finding a route through a maze (Fig. 5.14).

Table 5.5.

$\forall u \in [1:8], \ \forall v \in [1:8] \ fr(u, v) \leftarrow 0$ {all squares free}
$i \leftarrow 1$
  repeat while $i \geqslant 1$
    repeat while $\text{col}(i) \leqslant 8$
      $\text{col}(i)$ is the first element of Ei such that $fr(i, \text{col}(i)) = 0$
      $\text{col}(i) \leftarrow \text{first\_zero\_of } fr(i, j) \ \text{col}(i) \leftarrow 9$ if there are none
      $j \leftarrow \text{col}(i)$ {test for possibility replaced by embargoes}
      $fr(i, j) \leftarrow 1$
      repeat for $k \in [1 + 1 : 8]$
          repeat for $i \in [1 : 8]$
            if $fr(k, i) = 0$ **then**
            if square (k, i) en_prise with square(i, j) **then** $fr(k, i) \leftarrow 1$
          end repeat i
      end repeat k
      if $i < 8$ **then** $i \leftarrow i + 1$ {partial success}
                  else print solution $[\text{col}(i)]$
    end repeat $\text{col}(i)$
{backtrack}
    repeat for $k \in [i + 1 : 8]$ {restore freedoms}
      repeat for $i \in [1 : 8]$
        if $fr(k, i) = 1$ **then** $fr(k, i) \leftarrow 0$
        end if
      end repeat i
    end repeat k
    $fr(i, \text{col}(i)) \leftarrow i - 1$
    $i \leftarrow i - 1$ {square $(i, \text{col}(i))$ now embargoed by the choice
                                        $(i - 1)$}
  end repeat i

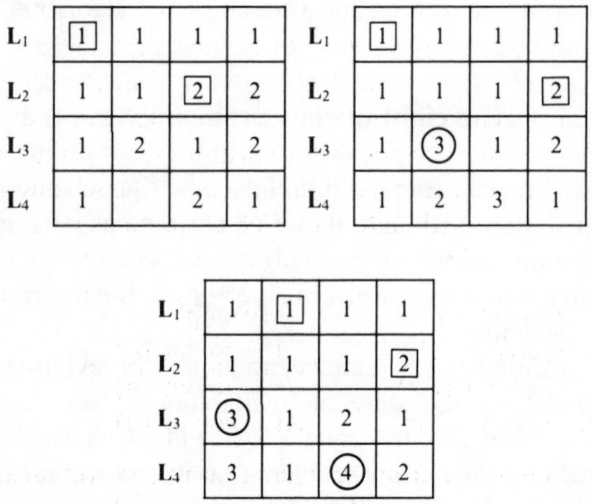

Fig. 5.14 Four queens' problem: second version of the solution.

5.8 CHOICE OF THE ORDER OF THE CHOICES

When we look at this modified algorithm we see that there is no reason why the order $Y_1, Y_2, ..., Y_N$ in which we have taken these sets should be optimal. Clearly, there may be some Y_i with $i > k$ in which there are no available elements even though the solution can be taken as far as k. The first thing to recognise is that the term 'choice' should not be used where in fact there is no choice: all the implications have been treated so far as embargoes, but some may be enforced assignments of particular values to certain variables, of this type:

> Whatever the values of i, if there is only one zero in L_i then the number of the square (i.e. the column) containing this zero must be assigned as the value of y_i, and new implications drawn. A corollary to this is: if the 'degrees of freedom' of Y_k – the number of zeros – is not 1 but 2, then Y_k is a good candidate for continuing the search.

A generalisation of this approach forms the basis of the second modification of the original algorithm.

The basic idea is always make that choice, from among those available, over which there is least freedom of choice. That is, at each step choose the Y_i containing the smallest number of available elements. This is incorporated into the third version of the algorithm (Table 5.6). As before, the states of the elements of each set Y_i are recorded in the vectors L_i, but now the choices are not made in the 'natural' order $i = 1, 2, ..., N$ but in whatever order seems appropriate in the prevailing circumstances; the order chosen is recorded in a vector *choice* and the location y_k for the successive Y_k are recorded in a vector $\mathbf{V}$. Account is taken of forced assignments, that is of situations in which all the positions in a row are embargoed except one; this can have a ripple effect on future assignments. All the assignments are recorded in a stack (called *stack*), a vector, initially empty, in which the locations are recorded as they are made; the depth of the stack at any instant – the number of elements it contains at that instant – is recorded in a variable m. When backtracking has to be done the previous availabilities are restored and the stack emptied as far as the level it had before the choice that led to the backtracking.

With this third version the performance of the algorithm is improved to the extend that the complete solution for the normal board can be worked out by hand in a few hours. The following example will show the speed with which the search can be conducted.

Example of a hand-worked solution. There is no reason to assume that the first queen has to be placed in the first row, so let us suppose that, perhaps after some preliminary thought, we have decided to start with the fourth

Table 5.6.

```
n ← 0                          {number of choices made}
m ← 0                          {number of queens placed}
    ∀j ∈ [1:8] col(i) ← 0      {column chosen in row i}
    ∀j ∈ [1:8] fr(i, j) ← 0    {sets all freedoms to 0}
    i ← 1
    repeat while i ≥ 1         {new row}
    il ← index__of__row for which the vector of freedoms contains the
    fewest zeros
        if nz(il) ≥ 1 then          nz(il) = number of zeros in row (i)
            if nz(il) ≠ 1 then i ← i + 1, choice(i) ← il {new choice}
            end if
            m ← m + 1          {one more queen is placed}
            col(il) ← first zero of fr(i, j)        {possibly the only one}
            fr(il, col(il)) ← 1          {follows from the choice}
            repeat for k ∈ [1:8]
                if col(k) = 0 then
                    repeat for i ∈ [1:8]
                        if fr(k, i) = 0 then
                            if square(k, i) en__prise with square (i, j) then
                                fr(k, i) ← 1 {record according to last choice}
                            end if
                        end if
                    end repeat i
                end repeat k
                if m = 8 then print solution [col(i)] end if
                else        {back track: at least one row has no zeros}
                repeat for k ∈ [1:8]
                    if col(k) = 0 then
                        repeat for i ∈ [1:8]
                            if fr(k, i) = 1 then fr(k, i) ← 0 end if
                        end repeat i
                    end if
                end repeat k
                fr(i, col(i)) ← i − 1, i ← i − 1
        end if
    end repeat i
end 8 queens
```

row and to place the first queen on the third square and then the second on the sixth square of the third row. Labelling the rows 1 to 8 and the columns a to h we then have the situation shown in Fig. 5.15, in which the previous convention is used for the embargoed squares. The degrees of freedom for the successive rows are now $(4, 3, 0, 0, 3, 4, 5, 4)$ and for the columns $(3, 4, 0, 4, 4, 0, 4, 4)$. Row 5 is one of the three most constrained so let us put the third queen there, in the first available square, column a; this gives Fig. 5.16. Row 2 has now only two free squares, so we could consider

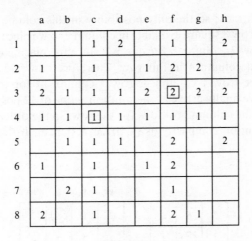

	a	b	c	d	e	f	g	h
1			1	2		1		2
2	1		1		1	2	2	
3	2	1	1	1	2	[2]	2	2
4	1	1	[1]	1	1	1	1	1
5		1	1	1		2		2
6	1		1		1	2		
7		2	1			1		
8	2		1			2	1	

Fig. 5.15.

	a	b	c	d	e	f	g	h
1	3		1	2	3	1		2
2	1		1	3	1	2	2	
3	2	1	1	1	2	[2]	2	2
4	1	1	[1]	1	1	1	1	1
5	[3]	1	1	1	3	2	3	2
6	1	3	1		1	2		
7	3	2	1			1		
8	2		1	3		2	1	

Fig. 5.16 Position after the third queen.

putting the fourth queen there. But for the implications of any a choice we must consider the columns also: d and e also have only two free squares, and in the end we have to place one and only one queen in each row and one and only one in each column. Thus in this problem in particular we see how the constraints $K(x)$ can act indirectly and enable appropriate assumptions to be made: choosing column d is seen to impose more constraints than choosing row 2.

If we continue with column d, putting the fourth queen in row 7 would embargo the two remaining squares in column e and therefore lead to an

immediate backtrack; so the only possibility in this column is row 6; this
leaves only the row 8 square available in column e so we place queen 5 there,
which forces row 2, column b for queen 6 since the placing of queen 4 has
already blocked column h in this row. There are now two and only two
squares left free (row 1 column g, row 7 column h) for the two queens
remaining, so we finally arrive at the solution – one of 12 possible – on Fig.
5.17. If we list the column positions for the rows in the order 1 to 8 we can
express this solution compactly as (g, b, f, c, a, d, h, e). It depends on only

	a	b	c	d	e	f	g	h
1	3	6	1	2	3	1	⑧	2
2	1	⑥	1	3	1	2	2	4
3	2	1	1	1	2	☐2	2	2
4	1	1	☐1	1	1	1	1	1
5	☐3	1	1	1	3	2	3	2
6	1	3	1	☐4	1	2	4	4
7	3	2	1	4	4	1	6	⑦
8	2	4	1	3	⑤	2	1	5

Fig. 5.17.

	a	b	c	d	e	f	g	h
1	3		1	2	4	1		2
2	1	3	1	④	1	2	2	3
3	2	1	1	1	2	☐2	2	2
4	1	1	☐1	1	1	1	1	1
5	2	1	1	1	☐3	2	3	2
6	1		1	3	1	2		
7		2	1	4	3	1	3	
8	2	3	1	4	3	2	1	3	←

Fig. 5.18.

the first three choices; if we want all the solutions we must consider the possibilities for these three one after the other.

To explore the possibilities to some extent, let us first return to the third choice in the above solution. We embargo square (5, a) by marking it 2, since it is now linked to the second choice. The next square is (5, e); in marking the embargoes we can state that (2, d) is now a forced choice and that there is no available square in row 8: this is shown in Fig. 5.18. Given the present first two choices, the only remaining possibility for the third queen in row 5 is column g; there are then several rows with only two free squares and if we place the fourth queen on (2, b) then the fifth queen on (7, a) is a forced choice and these last two choices embargo all the free squares in column h. The other possibility in row 2 is (2, h), which implies the sequence of choices (6, b), (1, a), (7, d); all the squares are then embargoed, so there is no solution. The situation is shown in Fig. 5.19.

What we have just shown is that one and only one solution is determined by the two first moves chosen, (4, c) and (3, f); the compact representation of this partial solution is (*, *, f, c, *, *, *, *). These initial moves were chosen completely at random. We can give a value for the amount of effort needed to find all the solutions. If the first queen has been placed on a square at either end of a row there are six possibilities for the next queen in the adjacent row, five otherwise. Taking into account the symmetry of the board, and therefore of the solutions, about a vertical axis through the centre we need consider only the four cases in which the first queen is to the left of this axis, which means that to exhaust the possibilities we have to conduct a search roughly equivalent to the one we have just shown a number of times $6 + 5 + 5 + 5 = 21$, which is a surprisingly small number.

	a	b	c	d	e	f	g	h
1	⑥	5	1	2		1	3	2
2	1	4	1	3	1	2	2	④
3	2	1	1	1	2	☐2	2	2
4	1	1	☐1	1	1	1	1	1
5	2	1	1	1	2	2	③	2
6	1	⑤	1	4	1	2	3	3
7	5	2	1	⑦	3	1	3	4
8	2	4	1	3	7	2	1	4

Fig. 5.19 End of the search after two choices.

Knowing that the first three choices determine the solution, and that after the first two queens have been placed there are only three possibilities for the third, we see that the total number of situations we have to consider is $3 \times 21 = 63$; and almost every one will give a solution. A crude search would involve $8! = 40320$ cases, so our reduction to 63 has gained a factor of 640.

If we wish to keep only the basic solutions we must eliminate all those that can be derived from others by left/right or rotational symmetry; this gives 12 solutions, only one of which is fully symmetrical.

The final form of our algorithm performs an implicit enumeration of a space Y that has to be searched, which is factorised into components $Y_1, Y_2, ..., Y_n$, by making choices in which the successive Y_i are taken in an order not decided in advance. This algorithm has the important property of being completely general and can be applied to any combinatorial problem whatever: nothing specific to the eight Queens problem enters into its specification. Later in this book we shall apply it to such differently stated problems as optimal colouring of a graph, the travelling salesman's journey, mechanisation of reasoning and playing chess.

5.9   DYNAMIC PROGRAMMING

Dynamic programming is a method for solving optimisation problems. The term programming must not, of course, be taken in the sense of computer programming; it is derived from 'mathematical program', meaning a system for which one seeks a solution that satisfies given constraints. The essential idea is to consider the unknowns of the system as decision variables for which values are chosen *sequentially*; and if two different sequences of decisions lead to the same solution, only the better – according to some criterion – is kept. In the search all relevant values for each variable are studied in parallel, so the process is one of depth-first implicit enumeration.

Example 1. A workshop manager has accepted an order for four items of the same product, to be delivered within the three following months. Taking into account the costs of setting up and running the machinery, the pay of the workers, the costs of materials and of storage, and other overheads, he calculates the total costs of making x_j items ($0 \leqslant x_j \leqslant 4$) during month i ($1 \leqslant i \leqslant 3$) for all possible pairs (i, x_j), and tabulates these as follows (Table 5.7):

How should he plan the manufacture so as to complete the order on time at least cost? The meaning of the table is that if, for example, he decides to

Table 5.7.

Number of items made		0	1	2	3	4
Month of manufacture	1	10	12	15	20	—
	2	10	14	16	19	23
	3	10	12	17	19	—

make one item in the first month, three in the second and (therefore) none in the third the total cost will be $12 + 19 + 10 = 41$ units.

The obvious way to solve the problem is simply to list all the possibilities and find the cost of each; but the amount of effort can be reduced by proceeding month by month. The first row of the table gives directly the cost at the end of each month of the four possibilities – making 0, 1, 2, or 3 items; and adding the appropriate costs from the second row gives the total cost at the end of the second month for each of the five possibilities $(0, 1, 2, 3, 4$ items made). But clearly, whatever is done next, only the decision that gives the minimum cost for each of these possibilities need be considered: that is, for the manufacture of s items by the end of month 2 $(0 \leqslant s \leqslant 4)$, the minimum for varying r of [cost(r at end of month 1) $+$ cost($s - r$ during month 2). So these minimum costs at the end of the second month are:

$$s = 0: \quad 10 + 10 = 20 \tag{1}$$
$$1: \quad \min(12 + 10, 10 + 14) = 22 \tag{2}$$
$$2: \quad \min(15 + 10, 12 + 14, 10 + 16) = 25 \tag{3}$$
$$3: \quad \min(20 + 10, 15 + 14, 12 + 16, 10 + 19) = 28 \tag{4}$$
$$4. \quad \min(20 + 14, 15 + 16, 12 + 19, 10 + 23) = 31 \tag{5}$$

The case $s = 0$ can be ignored since the table shows that 4 items cannot be made in the third month; so adding the costs of making 3, 2, 1, and 0 items in the third month we have for the minimum total cost:

$$\min(22 + 19, 25 + 17, 28 + 12, 31 + 10) = 40$$

and from the way the values have been arrived at it is easy to see that this corresponds to the decision $x_1 = 1$, $x_2 = 2$, $x_3 = 1$.

The 'graph of decision' of Fig. 5.20 gives a picture of the process of solution.

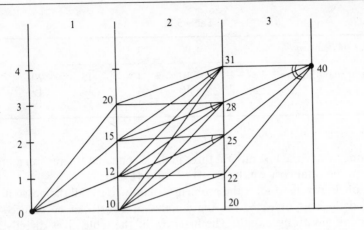

Fig. 5.20 Graph of decisions for a dynamic programming problem.

5.9.1 Theory of dynamic programming

The sequential optimisation process that we have just illustrated can be applied to a whole family of problems; only some very general conditions need be satisfied by the function to be optimised.

Definition
A function f of three real variables u, v, w is **decomposable** if

1. there are functions g, h such that f can be written

$$\forall (u, v, w) f(u, v, w) = g(u, h(v, w))$$

2. the function g above is monotone non-decreasing with respect to the second variable

$$\forall (u, y_1, y_2): y_1 > y_2 \Rightarrow g(u, y_1) \geqslant g(u, y_2)$$

All of dynamic programming depends on the following:

Theorem. The optimality theorem. *For every real function of the real variables u, v, w such that*

$$f(u, v, w) = g(u, h(v, w))$$

$$\operatorname*{opt}_{u,v,w} [f(u, v, w)] = \operatorname*{opt}_{u} \left[g\left(u, \operatorname*{opt}_{v,w} [h(v, w)] \right) \right]$$

This theorem reduces the computing of the optimum of a function of three variables to that of the successive optima of two functions of two variables; a proof is given in Laurière (1979). It is often used for functions of n variables of the form:

$$z(x_1, x_2, ..., x_n) = R_1[r_1(x_1), z_1(x_2, x_3, ..., x_n)]$$

where R_1 is decomposable and z_1 is of the same type as z. We can then write

$$\text{opt}_{x_1,...,x_n} z = \text{opt}_{x_1}\left[R_1\left[r_1(x_1), \text{opt}_{x_2}\left[R_2(r_2(x_2)), ..., \text{opt}_{x_n}\left[(r_n(x_n)) \right], ... \right] \right] \right]$$

This gives a direct expression of the dynamic programming process, which is thus an optimisation procedure based on recurrence equations. The hypotheses of the optimality theorem hold in particular when z is the sum of basic 'costs', each associated with a single variable, as in Example 1.

The method has been applied successfully to stock management, automatic guiding of [military] vehicles, control of industrial processes (especially chemical), economic planning and the theory of games and of stochastic phenomena.

5.9.2 Importance of dynamic programming

A picturesque statement of the basic theorem is: 'every sub-strategy of an optimal strategy must itself be optimal'. Figure 5.21 is a representation of this. The gains that follow from the use of the method are due to the fact that at each intermediate stage all the strategies that lead to a given situation are compared and only the best – or, rather, the value given by the best – is retained for continuing the process. Thus suppose each decision variable x_i can take X_i values; exhaustive enumeration of the possibilities then requires $\prod_i X_i$ situations to be considered. With the dynamic programming approach, if S_i is the number of possible situations before the choice of x_i, the total number to be considered is: $\Sigma_i S_i \cdot X_i$.

The numbers S_i are most often limited by the nature of the problem; for

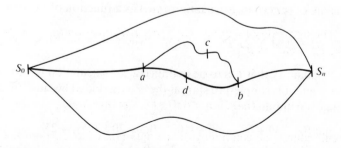

Fig. 5.21 Optimal strategy: sub-strategy (a, c, b) cannot be better than (a, d, b), for otherwise (S_0, a, d, b, S_n) would not be optimal.

example, in Example 1 $S_i = 5$ for all i, with the result that the complexity of the calculation here is of the order of $\Sigma\ X_i$. In some cases the complexity is a polynomial function of the data, for example for the shortest path and knapsack problems, and for certain task-ordering problems. One great advantage of the method is that it can be applied equally well to systems that evolve over time in a non-deterministic way; the future is then specified only in terms of probabilities, yet an optimal strategy has to be found. Stock control to meet uncertain future demands is such a problem, and is illustrated by the following example.

Example 2. Stocks of certain items have to be ordered and held over three periods of time so as to maximise the expectation of profit. Initially the stock is zero. At the start of period i a decision can be taken to buy x_i items at a price of a_i per item. During that period there is a probability $p_i(y_i)$ that y_i items will be ordered, which can be sold at v_i per item; no penalty is incurred if the stock has fallen too low to meet this demand in full. At the end of the third period any remaining stock is sold off at a price of r per item.

Suppose $x_i = 0, 1$, or 2, $y_i = 1$ or 2 for each i and that a_i, v_i and estimates of $p(y_i)$ are as in the following table (Table 5.8):

Table 5.8.

Period i		1	2	3
Purchase price	a_i	10	10	30
Sale price	v_i	30	30	50
Probabilities	$p_i(1)$	0.6	0.6	0.5
	$p_i(2)$	0.4	0.4	0.5

The total number of items in stock can vary from 0 to 4, so five possible states can evolve. Between each pair of decisions (to buy stock) there is a period of uncertainty during which the state can change from s_i to $\max(0, s_i - y_i)$ with probability $p(y_i)$. If the profit in the situation s_i, after the decision x_i, is $c(s_i)$ its expectation $\bar{c}(w_i)$ as a function of the demand is:

$$\bar{c}(w_i) = c(s_i) + \sum_{y_i=1}^{z} p(y_i) \cdot v_i \cdot w_i \quad \text{where } w_i = \max(0, s_i - y_i)$$

This is the quantity that has to be optimized; the calculation has to be done recursively and it is simplest to start at the end (period 3) because from there everything is computable.

$\bar{c}_3(0) = \max[0, -30 + 50, -60 + (100 \times 0.5 + 70 \times 0.5)] = 25$

$\bar{c}_3(1) = \max[50, -30 + (100 \times 0.5 + 70 \times 0.5),$

$\qquad\qquad\qquad\qquad\qquad -60 + (120 \times 0.5 + 90 \times 0.5)] = 55$

$\bar{c}_3(2) = \max[85, -30 + (120 \times 0.5 + 90 \times 0.5),$

$$-60 + (140 \times 0.5 + 110 \times 0.5)] = 85$$

Continuing backwards from here:

$\bar{c}_2(0) = \max[25, -10 + 30 + 25,$

$$-20 + (30 + 55) \times 0.6 + (60 + 25) \times 0.4] = 65$$

$\bar{c}_2(1) = \max[30 + 25, -10 + (60 + 25) \times 0.4 + (30 + 125) \times 0.6,$

$$-20 + ((30 \times 85) \times 0.6 + (60 + 55) \times 0.4)] = 95$$

because the stock at the end of the first period is at most 2 items and the demand at least 1. Finally, with an initial stock of 0 we have for the first period:

$\bar{c}_1(0) = \max[65, -10 + 30 + 65,$

$$-20 + ((60 + 65) \times 0.4 + (30 + 95) \times 0.6)] = 105$$

Thus the optimal strategy is to buy two items in each of the first two periods and 2, 1 or 0 items in the third period according as the stock then is 0, 1, or 2 respectively. The way the stock varies during these three periods will depend on how the sales occur, but the optimum profit of 105 will be gained in every case.

5.10 COLOURING THE VERTICES OF A GRAPH

We introduce this problem by first considering the problem of colouring a graphical map (Fig. 5.22): what is the least number of different colours needed for colouring the countries of a map drawn on either a plane sheet or a sphere so that no two countries with a common frontier have the same colour? This problem is justly famous, for, though very simple to state, it defeated mathematicians for a century. It has long been conjectured – a conjecture being a statement believed to be true and supported by all the evidence available, but of which no proof has been found – that any map whatever, on a plane or a sphere, can be coloured with at most four colours. This is the four colour problem; it was finally solved, and the conjecture proved true, in 1976 (Appel & Haken 1976), by a purely combinatorial method in which a computer was used to search through an enormous number of typical configurations.

The first step in the attack on the problem is to simplify the statement by putting it in the form of a non-directed graph – compare, for example, the problems in Chapter 4. One way to do this is to select some representative point inside each country, its capital for example, take these as vertices and

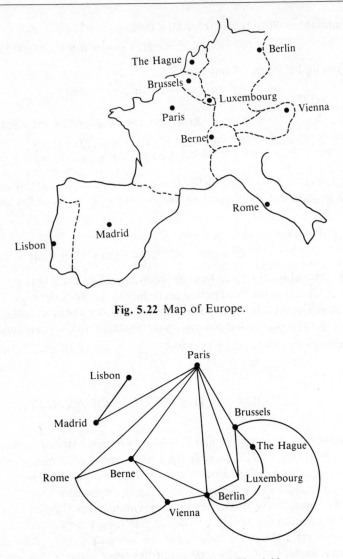

Fig. 5.22 Map of Europe.

Fig. 5.23 Graph equivalent to Fig. 5.22.

join by an arc any pair when the countries they represent have a common frontier. The problem then becomes that of colouring the vertices so that no two extremities of the same arc have the same colour (Fig. 5.23). The problem of finding the least number of colours for the graph is a complete generalisation of the map-colouring problem, for the graph can be of any form whatever: it is not necessarily planar, that is, there need not be a way of re-drawing it so that no arcs cross. In this graphical form it is met in contexts quite different from the original; the following is an example.

5.10.1 An example: organising meetings

The problem is to organise a number of meetings of members of a committee or working group, with constraints related to the wishes of certain members to take part in certain meetings.

Suppose nine meetings $a, b, c, ..., i$ are to be held, each lasting half a day and involving some sub-set of the members. The members have let the secretary know which meetings they wish to attend, and this information shows that the following groups of meetings cannot be held simultaneously: *ae, bc, cd, ed, abd, ahi, bhi, dfi, dhi, fgh*. Also there is at least one member who wishes to attend every meeting. Given that there will always be enough rooms available for whatever number of simultaneous meetings are desired, the problem for the secretary is to find the least number of half-day meetings needed.

The problem is reduced to one of graph colouring by representing the meetings by vertices and joining a pair by an arc to indicate that those meetings cannot be held simultaneously. This is shown in Fig. 5.24.

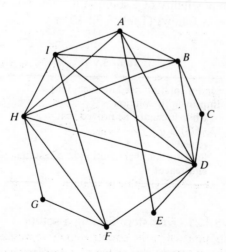

Fig. 5.24 Graph for the committee meetings problem.

5.11   ALGORITHM FOR OPTIMAL COLOURING OF A GRAPH

The minimum number of colours needed to colour the vertices of a graph G so that no two vertices joined by an arc have the same colour is called the chromatic number of the graph, written $\gamma(G)$. Finding this for a given graph is a combinatorial problem; if we define:

S the set of vertices of G

U the set of arcs of G – the set of couples (i, j) of the Cartesian product $S \times S$, such that i is joined to j

$[1, q]$ the set of the first q integers, representing the q colours used

the problem can be stated:

find a function colour: $S \to [1, q]$ such that for all $(i, j) \in U$, colour $(i) \neq$ colour (j) and q is minimum.

We can proceed as we did for the problem of the eight queens: colour one vertex, note the implications of this and continue by implicit enumeration so long as there are uncoloured vertices. There is a difference, however, in the way the optimisation is done; we now stop well before we have exhausted all the possibilities, as soon as we can show that there cannot be a solution better than the best one then known. The criterion is thus linked to the proof of the impossibility of a solution for a certain sub-problem.

The procedure is as follows (Table 5.9):

Table 5.9.

Find a solution needing q colours
Improve this solution
   while it cannot be proved that
   $\gamma(G) \geqslant q$
   repeat $q \leftarrow q - 1$
   look for another solution in q colours
   end repeat

5.11.1   First step: finding a solution

Finding a first solution is easy, for all that is necessary is to use a different colour for every vertex: formally, $\forall i \in S$, $colour(i) = i$. This gives a number $\bar{q}$ of colours, $\bar{q} = $ card (S).

When we attempt to improve this solution we meet an existence problem exactly analogous to that of the eight queens: each vertex (the analogue of a row of the chess board) has initially q degrees of freedom (instead of 8), where $\bar{q} > q$. Thus the ENUM algorithm can be used here also, and we have only to specify

(a) how the choice is to be made when there are 2 equal degrees of freedom;
(b) how the implications of the choices are to be handled.

Point (a) is dealt with by heeding a principle that has already proved its value and which would have applied in constructing the availability diagrams: always make the choice that gives the most information. This implies that one should always select for treatment the vertex that is included in the greatest number of constraints. Here there is only one type of constraint:

$$\text{for all } (i, j) \in U: \text{colour}(i) \neq \text{colour } (j)$$

so the most constrained vertex is the one at which the greatest number of arcs meet – the arc of maximum degree. So in the case of equal degrees of freedom the rule is to choose from among those vertices not yet coloured the one of greatest degree. As usual, the rule is neither rigid – it can be changed – nor indispensable – the algorithm remains valid without it; it is applied only to increase efficiency.

Point (b) is particularly easy to deal with, because the data defining the arcs enable a clear record of the embargoes to be kept. Of course, as for the queens problem, it is advisable to take account of implications in chains, of forced assignments (only one colour admissible) and impasses that require back-tracking with all its consequences.

It should now be clear that it is actually possible to construct a better solution to the problem than the trivial one with each vertex coloured differently. We need only consider the criterion concerning the degrees of the vertices given for (a) above; the degrees of freedom are all equal a priori and the criterion concerning these is not relevant. The algorithm for constructing a good solution, known as the 'greedy algorithm', is as follows (Table 5.10):

Table 5.10.

---

while not all vertices have been coloured **repeat**
    colour vertex joined to maximum number of non-coloured vertices
    deduce consequential embargoes

Example 1. For the graph of Fig. 5.23, corresponding to the map of Europe, we have:

vertex	L	M	P	Br	LH	Bn	Lx	V	Be	R
degree	1	2	6	4	2	6	3	3	4	3

Vertex P is one with the greatest degree (6), and we mark this with the first colour available:

$$I \rightarrow \text{colour } (P)$$

The effect of this is to embargo colour I for any of the six vertices joined to P and at the same time to reduce by 1 the degree of each of these; this gives the second row of Table 5.11.

The next vertex to be taken is Bn, and since colour I is not allowable:

$$II \rightarrow \text{colour } (Bn)$$

with the consequences shown in row 2 of the table. Next, III is allowable for V:

$$III \rightarrow \text{colour } (V)$$

and the rest of the solution follows immediately. The assignments are, in this order:

vertex	P	Bn	Br	V	L	M	LH	Lx	Be	R
colour	I	II	III	I	I	II	I	IV	III	II

Thus we have a solution in four colours; but there is nothing to tell us that this is the least number possible and all we can say is that $\gamma(G) \leqslant 4$, as of course is given by Appel and Haken's theorem.

Example 2. 'Meetings' problem. The first row of Table 5.12 gives the degrees of the vertices of Fig. 5.24. Assigning first colour I to vertex d,

Table 5.11.

	L	M	P	Br	LH	Bn	Lx	V	Be	R
	1	2	6	4	2	6	3	3	4	3
Residual	1	1	0	3	2	5	2	3	3	2
degrees	1	1	0	2	1	0	1	2	2	2
	1	1	0	0	0	0	0	2	2	2
	1	1	0	0	0	0	0	0	1	1
		I		I		I	I		I	I
Colours				II	II		II		II	
embargoed									III	III

Table 5.12.

	a	b	c	d	e	f	g	h	i
	5	5	2	7	2	4	2	6	5
Residual	4	4	1	—	1	3	2	5	4
degrees	3	3	1	—	1	2	1	—	3
	—	2	1	—	0	2	1	—	1
	—	—	0	—	0	2	1	—	1
	—	—	0	—	0	—	0	—	0
	I	I	I		I	I		I	I
Colours	II	II				II	II		II
embargoed		III			III				III
			IV						IV
							III		

because that has the highest degrees of freedom, we find we can assign in succession II, III, IV, III to h, a, b, f respectively; all the degrees of freedom are now reduced to zero, so finally II, II, IV are assigned to c, e, g, i respectively and the conclusion is that for this graph $\gamma(G) \leqslant 5$.

These examples show how we can complete the first step of Algorithm 5A, giving a value q for which we can say that $\gamma(G) \leqslant q$. We cannot say that $\gamma(G) = q$ so we must continue with 'replace q by $q - 1$ and look for a new solution with this new number of colours.'

5.11.2   Second step: search for the optimum solution

Knowing that the number of possibilities for each vertex does not exceed a known number q we continue as in the queens problem and introduce vectors $\mathbf{L}_i$ of q components. But we can move rather more quickly, by noting that any solution is defined only to within a permutation of the colours, a colour such as the I, II, ... we have used being only, for this problem, a name to be used for reference. Thus the first assignments we made:

Example 1	Example 2
I $\rightarrow$ colour (P)	I $\rightarrow$ colour (d)
II $\rightarrow$ colour (Bn)	II $\rightarrow$ colour (h)
III $\rightarrow$ colour (Br)	III $\rightarrow$ colour (a)

do not represent real choices but are merely conventions for the names of the colours of the first vertices, which all have to be coloured differently. The reason for this different colouring is simply that these vertices are all

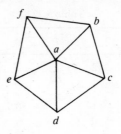

Fig. 5.25 A counter-example

joined in pairs: in Example 1 P is joined to both Bn and Br, which latter is itself joined to Bn; in Example 2, d is joined to h, a and b; h to a and b; a to b. These sub-sets of the vertices are thus joined in all possible ways, or in other words they form complete sub-graphs or cliques. This leads to the following property:

Exactly p colours are needed for a clique of p vertices

We can now say that for the graph of Example 1:

$$3 \leqslant \gamma \leqslant 4$$

because the vertices P, Bn, Br form a clique of cardinality 3. But if we look a little closer we see that the only vertex that has needed a fourth colour, Lx, has done so because it is joined to each of these three, so that the sub-graph P, Bn, Br, Lx is thus a new clique, of cardinality 4. We can therefore conclude that for this example the minimum number of colours is 4: $\gamma = 4$. In the second example a similar line of reasoning shows that there is a 5-clique $a\ b\ d\ h\ i$, so that our colouring of this non-planar graph is optimal and $\gamma = 5$.

These two successes may lead us to wonder if we are attacking the right problem: is it, in fact, that the minimum number of colours is equal to the cardinality of the largest clique? An immediate response is that even if it were, that would not solve the problem: how can we tell if a given clique is the biggest? We shall see later that this is as difficult as the colouring problem.

Further, does a counter-example exist? The simple assembly of triangles – 3-cliques – of Fig. 5.25 provides one: a, b, c must be coloured differently, say by I, II, III respectively; keeping to three colours we must then use II for d and III for e, leaving no possibility for f. Denoting the cardinality of the maximum clique by C_{max} we have $C_{max} = 3$ but $\gamma = 4$. Figure 5.26 is a second, rather less obvious, counter-example; here the only cliques are simple arcs, giving $C_{max} = 2$, but a complete working through of Algorithm 5A, which requires many returns to previous choices, gives $\gamma = 4$.

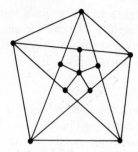

Fig. 5.26 Second counter-example.

Table 5.13 Graph colouring algorithm.

[search for a large clique Φ]

$$\Phi \leftarrow \emptyset \quad C \leftarrow 0 \ \{C \text{ is the cardinality of } \Phi\}$$

while there are vertices of G not yet examined
    examine vertex s of greatest degree
    if s is joined to every vertex of ϕ **then do** $\Phi \leftarrow \Phi \cup \{s\}$
    delete from G all vertices of degree strictly less than C
continue the search in the new graph:
while the graph thus obtained from that at the previous iteration **and** there are at
    least $C + 1$ vertices of degree equal to or greater than C
{colouring the clique}
for all vertices s of Φ **do** colour$(s) \leftarrow p$; $p \leftarrow p + 1$
{initialisation of colouring the whole graph G}
$n \leftarrow$ (number of vertices of G); $m \leftarrow p$; $\{m =$ number of coloured vertices$\}$
                $k \leftarrow 0$; $\{k =$ number of choices made$\}$
$L_i \leftarrow (0, 0, ..., 0)$; choice $(i) \leftarrow 0$, **for** all $i \in \{s\} - \Phi$: colour$(i) \leftarrow 0$;
while $k \geqslant 0$ **repeat**: **if** $m = n$ **then** print
               else $k \leftarrow k + 1$
               choose vector L_i which has the fewest zeros and such that colour
               $(i) = 0$
while L_i has at least two zeros **repeat**: choice $(k) \leftarrow i$; level $(k) \leftarrow m$;
    choose a colour y_i such that $L_i(y) = 0$
    record choice: colour $(i) \leftarrow y$; stack $(m) \leftarrow i$; $m \leftarrow m + 1$;
    delete y_i from possible choices: $L_i(y_i) \leftarrow k$;
    embargoes: **for** all non-coloured vertices joined to s **do** $L_,(y_i) \leftarrow k$
{implications}
for all non-coloured vertices i **do**:
    if L_i has a single zero **go to record**
    if L_i has no zeros **then**
{backtrack}:
{restore freedoms}
$\forall j, \forall i$ **do** if $L_i(j) = k$ **then** $L_i(j) = 0$; $L_k($colour$($level$(k))) \leftarrow k - 1$
release colours: **for** $q =$ level (k) to m **do** colour$($stack$(q)) \leftarrow 0$;
                        $m \leftarrow$ level(k); $k \leftarrow k - 1$

With even such simple graphs and such small numbers we have produced differences of up to 2 units between the two measures; the general situation is that graphs can be constructed for which γ exceeds C_{max} by any integer chosen in advance. The one certain result is:

$$\gamma \geqslant C_{max}$$

Thus C_{max} is a lower bound for the optimum that we are seeking. The algorithm we give establishes the optimality either by showing, by implicit enumeration, that no q-colouring can be constructed even though q is strictly greater than C_{max}; or, in favourable cases, by exhibiting a colouring with $q = C_{max}$ colours.

Before attempting the first provisional colouring it is always useful to look for a clique whose cardinality is as great as possible. We cannot of course be certain of finding C_{max}, but we can say with certainty that $C_{max} \geqslant C$, so we have a lower bound. The problem of finding this clique is in some sense a dual of the colouring problem and the degrees of the vertices play a role again; it can be an advantage to look among those of highest degree. Having found a C-clique we can attempt to improve it, just as in the colouring problem; the principle to use being that no vertex of degree less than C need be considered.

The final algorithm for the colouring problem is as follows (Table 5.13). With the method now developed we can make a successful attack on a new problem, that of the travelling salesman.

5.12   THE TRAVELLING SALESMAN PROBLEM

This simply-stated problem is one of the most famous problems of Operational Research:

> A commercial traveller has n customers, all in different towns; he wishes to visit them all in turn, starting and ending his journey at the same town and not passing twice through an intermediate town. Knowing the distances between every pair of towns, in what order should he make the visits so as to travel the least possible total distance?

It seems that the first studies of this problem were provoked by a puzzle due to the Irish mathematician Hamilton in 1959: to find all the different paths that pass once and only once through every vertex of the graph of Fig. 5.27, returning to the starting point.

The puzzle was stated in terms of a journey round the world, the sphere being represented by a dodecahedron which is opened into the net of Fig. 5.27. The general problem – to find a closed path passing once and only once through every vertex of a given graph – is called the Hamilton cycle

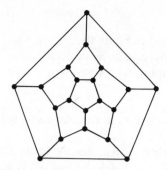

Fig. 5.27 Hamilton's 'tour around the world'.

Table 5.14 Inter-town journey cost for the travelling salesman $(A \rightarrow B = 27,$ $B \rightarrow A = 7)$.

	A	B	C	D	E	F
A	—	27	43	16	30	26
B	7	—	16	1	30	25
C	20	13	—	35	5	0
D	21	16	25	—	18	18
E	12	46	27	48	—	5
F	23	5	5	9	5	—

problem; it has links with group theory and, more unexpectedly, with the four colour problem just discussed. (As was stated in Section 4.1, the problem is of a higher order of complexity than the apparently similar problem of the Eulerian cycle, to find a closed path that traverses every arc once and once only.)

The problem is stated in terms of distances, but any other weighting of the arcs can be used; we use the term 'cost', and in the general case we do not assume that the cost of going from i to j is the same as from j to i: we shall base an example on the cost matrix of Table 5.14 which has this asymmetry. The total number of different cycles starting and ending at a given town is equal to the number of permutations of the remaining $n - 1$, that is $(n - 1)!$; and as with the graph colouring problem, this problem is simple to state but difficult to solve because of the great extent of the field that has to be searched. But again as with the colouring problem, finding a solution, without regard to optimality, is trivial: here we simply go from one town to another in an arbitrary order, for example *ABCDEFA* in Table 5.14. The general procedure, again analogous to that for graph colouring, is thus as follows:

Find some solution and compute the cost, q say
while it cannot be proved that the optimal cost q^* is at least equal to q
look for a better solution, with cost $q = q - 1$

5.12.1   First step: finding some solution

With the six-town problem represented by Table 5.14 we could start with the journey $ABCDEFA$, for which the cost is 124 and on which we would have to improve. We might think that a good method would be to start from one town and progress by always taking the route of lowest cost, but this does not give the minimum and can give very poor solutions. What happens is that the constraints, in this case to generate a Hamiltonian cycle, restrict the choice of the next move more and more severely so that the initial choices of the arcs of lowest costs can lead to later enforced choices of the highest costs.

Suppose, nevertheless, that we adopt this strategy. An obvious first stage would be C to F, with zero cost; returning immediately from F to C is not allowed so we choose the first available least cost path from F, to B at a cost of 5. BC is forbidden so we continue to D (cost 1), then to E (cost 18) and from E to A (cost 12), finally returning to the start, C, by AC at cost 43, the high cost of this last leg of the journey illustrating the general point just made. This gives the cycle $CFBDEAC$ of total cost 79, which is an improvement over 124 for $ABCDEFA$.

In constructing this solution we have limited ourselves to developing the cycle progressively, starting each new leg at the termination of the one just traversed. There is no reason why we should proceed in this way, and as in the queens problem we are free to make the choices in any order whatsoever provided only that we finish with a cycle with the Hamilton property. With this in mind, together with the outcome of the previous experiment, a better strategy would be, not to always choose the arc of least cost, but the negative one of not choosing from those of too high cost. This, however, leads to the question of what is meant by 'too high cost', and that is a relative concept. Since one arc has to be chosen from each row of the matrix and one from each column we can make this rather more precise by saying that we should not choose an arc whose cost is something greater than the minimum in its row and column; as a working hypothesis, perhaps to be questioned later, let us decide not to choose an arc whose cost is more than 10 units greater than the minimum in either its row or its column.

If we apply this to Table 5.14 we eliminate a number of the arcs and get the matrix of Table 5.15. Clearly it is optimistic to assume that the

Table 5.15 Elimination of highest cost arcs.

	A	B	C	D	E	F	Row maxima
A	—	—	—	16	—	—	26
B	7	—	—	1	—	—	11
C	—	13	—	—	5	0	10
D	21	16	25	—	18	18	26
E	12	—	—	—	—	—	5
F	—	5	5	9	5	—	15
	17	15	15	11	15	10	Column maxima

minimum cost route uses only these arcs, and we have no grounds for this. Even so, we can arrive at a solution. It could of course have happened that all arcs except one in each of two rows were eliminated by this process, and that those two were in the same column; the traveller would then have only one route by which to leave each of these towns and both would lead to the one town corresponding to the column. Clearly the Hamilton problem would then have no solution.

Well, have we been too optimistic? The new table tells us that the first row has only 1 degree of freedom – the only route from A leads to D, when DA, leading back to A, must be eliminated, and as we have arrived at D the arcs BD and FD, which would lead to there again, must also be eliminated. The table is now as in Table 5.16. In the second row BA is now obligatory and has the effect of eliminating EA and DB, which latter closes the parasitic cycle BAD. So far we have the partial solution shown on the left in Fig. 5.28. Next, EF is obligatory and eliminates FE, at which stage the remaining degrees of freedom in rows and columns are all 2. Therefore we have a choice for the next arc: let us take that of least cost among those of greatest cost; the latter are all in row D, and we choose DE, eliminating DC and FE and forcing the choice then of FC and CB. This has given us a Hamilton cycle $ADEFCBA$ of cost 64, which is less than the best we had

Table 5.16.

	A	B	C	D	E	F
A	—	—	—	$\boxed{16}$	—	—
B	7	—	—	—	—	—
C	—	13	—	—	5	0
D	—	16	25	—	18	18
E	12	—	—	—	—	5
F	—	5	5	—	5	—

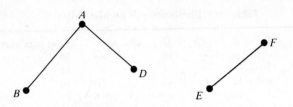

Fig. 5.28 Partial solution to the travelling salesman problem.

found by our previous method. Moreover, we have developed a quick method for finding a good route for the salesman.

If the initial elimination, based on costs, had proved so drastic as to prevent us from constructing a cycle all we should need to do would be to relax the newly introduced constraint – that is, retain arcs of higher cost above the minima. Having shown how to complete the first step successfully we can now turn to the question of optimisation.

5.12.2 Second step: finding the optimum

The previous step has given us an upper bound for the optimum we are seeking; as with the graph colouring problem, or indeed with any physical measurement, it is valuable to have a lower bound also, so as to put the required value between known limits. Thus we need some concept, analogous to that of the clique, that will enable us to say that the cost of any solution will be at least equal to some known quantity: the concept we use is that of a sub-problem of the original problem with the properties (a) we can solve it or at least put a lower bound to the cost of the solution; (b) we can be certain that the solution cannot cost more than any solution of the full problem.

To apply this principle we consider the towns one by one, noting that the traveller must *leave* each town at some time or other; so if we take the sub-problem as 'find the minimum cost of leaving town x' a lower bound is the minimum cost in the corresponding row of the matrix. Thus for town A (Table 5.17):

Table 5.17.

	A	B	C	D	E	F
A	—	27	43	16	30	26

we have a minimum cost of 16; and we can reduce all the costs by this amount without affecting the optimum circuit since the function to be optimised is simply a sum of inter-town costs (because there is only one cost in each row). Thus we can rewrite the costs of leaving A as (Table 5.18):

Table 5.18.

	A	B	C	D	E	F
A	—	11	27	0	14	10

Reasoning in the same way, we subtract 1 from row B, nothing from C, 16 from D and 5 from both E and F; this gives the following (Table 5.19):

Table 5.19.

	A	B	C	D	E	F
A	—	11	27	0	14	10
B	6	—	15	0	29	24
C	20	13	—	35	5	0
D	5	0	9	—	2	2
E	7	41	22	43	—	0
F	18	0	0	4	0	—

This has concerned the traveller *leaving* each town, but equally he must *reach* each one once and once only, and these arrivals correspond to the six columns. All these arrivals can now be achieved by taking an arc in each column whose cost has been reduced to zero, except for column A where the least-cost arc is 5; we can now subtract this from the entries in column A, and thus solve the sub-problem of the least-cost arrival at A. The resulting costs are now (Table 5.20):

Table 5.20.

	A	B	C	D	E	F
A	—	11	27	0	14	10
B	1	—	15	0	29	24
C	15	13	—	35	5	0
D	0	0	9	—	2	2
E	2	41	22	43	—	0
F	13	0	0	4	0	—

In this process we have subtracted a total quantity q' where:

$$q' = 16 + 1 + 0 + 16 + 5 + 5 + 5 = 48$$

so we can say that if we calculate the cost of a journey using these latest values we must add q' to that cost in order to get the real cost of that journey; and since the optimum cycle with these reduced costs must cost at least 0, the optimum cost q^* that we are seeking must satisfy $q^* \geqslant q'$. Then since the previous step has given us an upper bound, q'' say, for q^* we have now put q^* between upper and lower limits:

$$q' \leqslant q^* \leqslant q''$$

We can continue with the reduced-costs matrix, again taking up the idea of eliminating those arcs that are too costly; but this time we can do this quite rigorously. The difference $q'' - q'$, which is 16 here, is the greatest allowable excess cost of any cycle in the original matrix over the optimum q^* that we are seeking; so any cycle in the reduced matrix that costs more than 16 cannot be optimum because it gives a higher cost solution than the best we know already (of cost 64) and therefore can be rejected immediately. It follows that all arcs of cost greater than or equal to $q'' - q'$ ($= 16$) can be eliminated, and if this is done the matrix becomes (Table 5.21):

Table 5.21

	A	B	C	D	E	F
A	—	11	—	0	14	10
B	1	—	15	0	—	—
C	15	13	—	—	5	0
D	0	0	9	—	2	2
E	2	—	—	—	—	0
F	13	0	0	4	0	—

We have to find, if possible, a cycle in this matrix with cost less than q' and to repeat the search until we can prove optimality.

Use of the degrees of freedom again as criteria would suggest starting with row E; but as such an approach would be inefficient for a matrix of larger order we shall use a different one based on a measure of the relative importances of the lowest cost arcs – those of zero cost. These arcs are not in fact all equivalent to each other. It would be ideal if there were a cycle that used only these, but there is no reason why such a cycle should exist: here, for example, we cannot start from both A and B to reach D – which, incidentally, shows that $q^* \geqslant 49$, although we shall not use this result directly.

We shall have to forgo taking some of the zero cost arcs, so the question is, for which of these arcs is the cost of not taking them least? Any given zero lies in a certain row and a certain column; and since the town at the head of column has to be left by one of the arcs whose costs are in that column, the least cost of not taking that particular zero cost arc is the sum of the minima in the row and the column, excluding that zero. A corresponding quantity occurs frequently in optimisation problems and is usually called the penalty; it measures the least amount one will have to pay if one forgoes the ideal choice.

This gives immediately the heuristic rule: always choose the option carrying the highest penalty. If in our problem we write $r(i, j)$ for the penalty associated with the zero cost arc linking i and j we have

$$r(i, j) = \min_{k, k \neq j} c(i, k) + \min_{i, i \neq j} c(i, j)$$

Thus with the above matrix we have:

$r(A, D) = 10 + 0 = 10$

$r(B, D) = 0 + 1 = 1$

$r(C, F) = 5 + 0 = 5$

$r(D, A) = 0 + 1 = 1, \quad r(D, B) = 0 + 0 = 0$

$r(E, F) = 2 + 0 = 2$

$r(F, B) = 0 + 0 = 0, \quad r(F, C) = 0 + 9 = 9, \quad r(F, E) = 0 + 2 = 2$

AD carries the highest penalty so as a first attempt let us take this. The sequences are that all of row A and column D are eliminated from further choices, also the arc DA which would give a 'parasitic' cycle; the matrix thus becomes as on the left below (Table 5.22):

Table 5.22.

	A	B	C	D	E	F	A	B	C	D	E	F
A												
B	1	—	15		—	—	0	—	14		—	—
C	15	13	—		5	0	15	13	—		5	0
D	—	0	9		2	2	—	0	9		2	2
E	2	—	—		—	0	2	—	—		—	0
F	13	0	0		0	—	13	0	0		0	—

Given this choice, the cost of any route from B is at least 1 so, as before, we can subtract this from all the costs in row B and add 1 to the previous lower bound q'; writing $q'(AD)$ to indicate that this follows from the choice of AD, $q'(AD) = 49$. The result of this subtraction is given in the matrix on the right above.

Continuing, we have

$$r(B, A) = 16, \quad r(C, F) = 7, \quad r(D, B) = 2, \quad r(E, F) = 2, \quad r'(F, B) = 0,$$
$$r(F, C) = 9, \quad r(F, E) = 2$$

requiring the arc BA to be taken: if it were not, the cost of any cycle would be at least $q^*(AD) + r(B, A) = 49 + 16$, which exceeds the known upper bound of 64.

Taking BA eliminates row B and column A, and also DB, giving the matrix on the left below (Table 5.23) and subtracting 2 from row D gives that on the right, with $q'(AD) = 51$.

Table 5.23.

	A	B	C	D	E	F	A	B	C	D	E	F
A												
B												
C	13	—			5	0	13	—			5	0
D	—	9			2	2	—	7			0	0
E	—	—			—	0	—	—			—	0
F	0	0			0	—	0	0			0	—

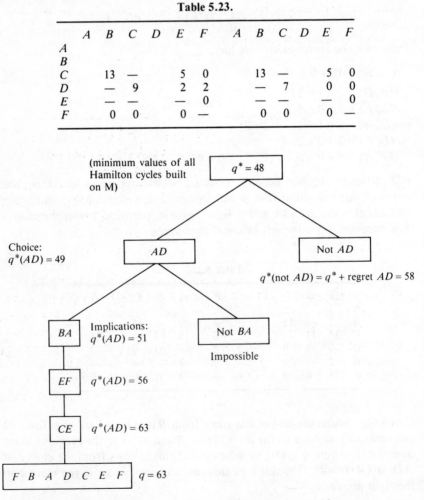

(minimum values of all Hamilton cycles built on M) $q^* = 48$

Choice: $q^*(AD) = 49$

AD Not AD

$q^*(\text{not } AD) = q^* + \text{regret } AD = 58$

BA Implications: $q^*(AD) = 51$ Not BA

Impossible

EF $q^*(AD) = 56$

CE $q^*(AD) = 63$

$F \; B \; A \; D \; C \; E \; F$ $q = 63$

Fig. 5.29 Solution to the travelling salesman problem.

CB can be eliminated because any cycle that includes this arc would cost at least $51 + 13 = 64$ and so would be no improvement. From now on there is no choice; EF must be taken because it is the only arc in its row, and this eliminates EF, after which the only candidate is CE and at this stage we have a total cost of $51 + 5 = 56$ (there is no point in reducing the costs in row C). The remaining arcs are necessarily DC and FB, giving the cycle $FBADCEF$ with a total cost of 63. The tree for this search is given in Fig. 5.29.

We have no guarantee that this is the optimum solution, because there is the unexplored branch '$\neg AD$', corresponding to all cycles that do *not* include AD. We can reconstruct the original matrix to take account of this, performing the appropriate reduction for row A; but as we have now incurred the penalty of not taking AD, which is 10, q^* is now $48 + 10 = 58$ and we must eliminate all arcs of cost at least $63 - 58 = 5$. This gives the reduced matrix (Table 5.24):

Table 5.24.

	A	B	C	D	E	F
A	—	1	—	—	4	0
B	1	—	—	0	—	—
C	—	—	—	—	—	0
D	0	0	—	—	2	2
E	2	—	—	—	—	0
F	—	0	0	4	0	—

Row C and column C shows that both arcs CF and FC must be taken, and this is not allowable in a Hamiltonian cycle for a graph with more than two vertices; so no solution better than 63 can be found by following this branch, and therefore the solution we have found is optimal. It can in fact be shown, with little difficulty, that this optimum is unique: all we need do is to restore the single arc of cost 5, CE, to the reduced matrix; then FC and CE become forced choices, followed then by BD, after which a cost not exceeding 63 can be achieved only by taking zero cost arcs and the cycle is completed by EF, DA and AF. The final result is that the least-cost route costs 63, and only the route $FBADCEF$ has this cost.

5.13   GPS – A GENERAL PROGRAM FOR PROBLEM-SOLVING

GPS – 'General Problem Solver' – is the name of a famous program developed by Newell, Shaw and Simon in the late 1950s and taken up again by Ernst and Newell in 1957. It was one of the very first Artificial Intelligence programs able to solve problems in fields as different as formal integration, logical puzzles, theorem-proving in predicate calculus and grammatical analysis of sentences, not by procedures developed specially for each type but by a single unified procedure.

   All problems put to GPS have the form: initial object – final (goal) object – set of operators; the operators enable transformations to be applied to the objects discussed, with the aim of starting with the initial object and, by a sequence of transformations, gradually reaching the goal. Thus GPS is in a better position than a human solver sitting in front of a blank sheet of paper, because it was already, explicitly, the list of operations available to it whilst the human has to retrieve these from memory or even invent them in the course of the solution.

5.13.1   The general procedure in GPS: sub-problems and plans

The basic approach in GPS is top-down, trying always to break down a given problem into simpler sub-problems. To guide this procedure it uses the difference between the current object and the goal object, where a 'difference' means any feature possessed by one of the objects but either absent from or present with some variation in the other. The program selects only those operations that will reduce the difference found at that stage in the solution; its behaviour is thus very much goal-directed, based on 'means–ends' analysis, and in this respect is very much like that of a human solver.

Goals. GPS has three main goals:

$A(O, x)$ apply an operator O to an object x

$F(O, \Delta, x, y)$ find an operator O that is likely to reduce some difference Δ between the objects x, y

$T(x, y)$ transform object x into object y

Thus all problems have at the start the goal:

   T(object(initial), object(final))

Methods. For each of these goals the program has built-in methods of the form (Table 5.25):

Table 5.25.

if goal is $A(O, a)$ **then** compare argument of O with object a
      let difference be Δ
      if $\Delta = \emptyset$ **then** success **end**
      else create new goal $F(Q, \Delta, a, b)$ **and** put goal $A(O, a)$ aside temporarily
if goal is $F(O, \Delta, x, y)$ **then** try the operators one after another to find if any reduces Δ
      if YES **then** create new goal $A(O, x)$
if goal is $T(x, y)$ **then** let Δ be the difference between x and y
      if $\Delta = \emptyset$ **then** success **end**
      else create new goal $F(Q, \Delta, x, y)$
            if Q cannot be applied **then** check
            else let x' be new object obtained
               create new goal $T(x', y)$

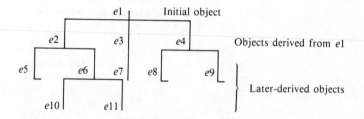

Fig. 5.30 Search tree in GPS.

In order to improve performance, and even where this is not essential, the authors of GPS give an indication of the relative importance of possible types of difference, in the sense of the relative difficulty of reducing these. Also they suggest which operators are best suited to reducing which type – as in the following examples. Starting from the initial object and using the methods just described, GPS looks for one or more suitable sub-goals, to which it applies such operators as can be applied, and so on until either the goal object is obtained or there are no objects left that can be developed further. The procedure followed is readily represented as a tree structure, as in Fig. 5.30; at any instance GPS selects the most promising vertex, that is, the one for which the difference from the goal object at least.

5.13.2 Example 1: The monkey and the bananas

This was proposed by John McCarthy in 1963 (Table 5.26). The statement is as follows.

> On the floor of a room are a monkey and a box, and a bunch of bananas is hanging by a string from the ceiling. The monkey can move around the floor, place the box anywhere and climb on to it; it can reach the bananas only when the box is directly under these. How should it get the bananas?

The problem is entirely trivial for an adult human, but to describe the detailed behaviour of GPS in solving it requires a certain amount of effort of reasoning; it has been discussed already in the section on 'Applications of the Unification Algorithm' (with a robot rather than a monkey) and treated by the resolution principle (Section 3.10.8).

Table 5.26.

---

1. *The environment*

Part A: General   elements: monkey M, box (chest) C, bananas B
locations: $p1$, $p2$, on-C, under-B,

Part B: Operators $O1$:   CLIMB

		condition:	$\text{loc}(M) = \text{loc}(C)$
		action:	$\text{loc}(M) = \text{on-}C$
$O2$:	WALK	condition:	variable x is a location
		action:	$\text{loc}(M) = x$
$O3$:	MOVE	condition:	variable x is a location
			$\text{loc}(M) \neq \text{on-}C$
			$\text{loc}(M) = \text{loc}(C)$
		action:	$\text{loc}(M) = x$
			$\text{loc}(C) = x$
$O4$:	GET	condition:	$\text{loc}(C) = \text{under-}B$
			$\text{loc}(M) = \text{on-}C$
		action:	contents(hand M) $= B$

Part C: Differences
$D1 = \text{loc}(M)$
$D2 = \text{loc}(C)$
$D3 = \text{contents(hand } M)$

Part D: Order of differences $D3$ more difficult than $D2$
$D1$ more difficult than $D2$

Part E: Connection table (reduction of differences)

	$D1$	$D2$	$D3$
$O1$	x		
$O2$	x		
$O3$	x	x	
$O4$			x

2. *Specific task*

Main goal   Transform initial object into final object
Initial object $\text{loc}(M) = p1$, $\text{loc}(C) = p2$, contents(hand M) $= \emptyset$
Final object   contents(hand M) $= B$

Input to the problem. GPS has no *a priori* knowledge concerning any of the problems put to it, so as well as a statement of the problem, information has to be supplied about the universe in which it will have to work. Thus there will be two main divisions in a problem statement, one defining this universe and valid for a family of tasks, the other stating the particular task to be performed on this occasion.

Comments. The statement given above of the monkey-and-bananas problem is input to the problem in almost exactly this form. The 1-variable predicates loc and contents have as their values the location and contents respectively of the variable given. Part D gives the relative difficulties of changing the location of monkey M, the location of the box C and the contents of the monkey's hand (hand M), whilst a cross in the table of part E indicates the choice of operator most likely to reduce the corresponding difference. As already mentioned, these last two parts are not essential, but can help to speed up the solution process.

Solution. The program aims continually to reduce the difference between the initial object (OB_i) and the final object (OB_f), attacking these differences in the order in which they have been given. It does this by constructing a set of intermediate goals and objects, linked to one another in a natural way by parent–child relation so as to form a 'genealogical tree', as in Fig. 5.31. Here the numbering of the sub-goals gives the order in which these are created. Three differences between OB_i and OB_f are detected at the start; the main aim is to reduce $D3$, so the first sub-goal created is $G1 = F(O, D3, OB_i, OB_f)$. Only $O4$ can reduce this difference so the next goal is to be able to apply $O4$ to the initial object: $G3 = A(O4, OB_i)$. This cannot be done at once because the conditions under which $O4$ can be applied are not satisfied: neither the box nor the monkey is in the right place (differences $D2$, $D1$ respectively); so the program creates a further new goal, that of reducing the difference which it considers the more important, $D2$ here. This is $G4 = F(O, D2, OB_i, OB_f)$, with the aim of achieving loc(C) = under-B and leading to $G5$ when a suitable operator has been found.

Again only one operator is suitable, here $O3$, and again this cannot be applied immediately because now $D1$ must be reduced to zero; this is the purpose of $G6$ and $G7$, to give loc(M) = loc(C). In $G7$, $O2$ is applied to OB_i to give a new object OB_1:

$$OB_1: \text{loc}(M7 = p2, \text{loc}(C) = p2, \text{contents(hand-}M) = \emptyset$$

The program now goes back through its list of goals and notes that it has been able to reduce $D1$; the first goal that has not been achieved is $G5$ and here OB_1 can be substituted for OB_i and $A(O3, B1)$ performed, giving a

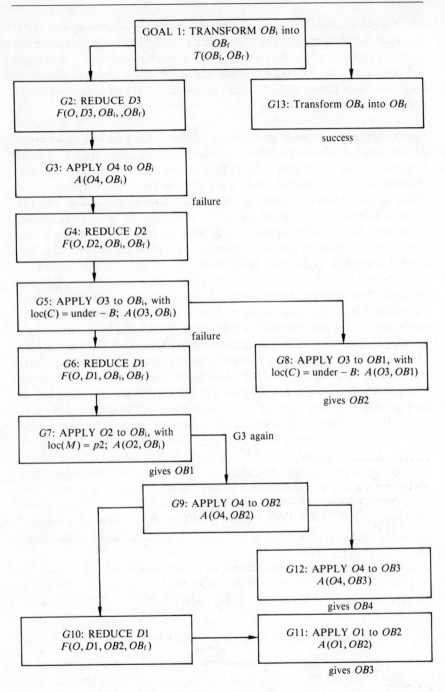

Fig. 5.31 GPS search tree for 'monkey and bananas' problem.

second new object OB_2:

$$OB_2:\ \mathrm{loc}(M) = \text{under-}B,\ \mathrm{loc}(C) = \text{under-}B,\ \mathrm{contents}(\text{hand-}M) = \emptyset$$

Similarly, the return to $G3$ gives rise to three further sub-goals, $G9, 10, 11$, in the last of which the difference $D1$ is reduced to zero by the one operator then relevant, $O1$; and finally, in $G12$, the monkey gets the bananas.

The value of this example is that it shows in full detail how a rather simple everyday type of reasoning can be broken down completely into a sequence of elementary actions. The goal is reached with the help of a mechanism that is extremely simple and is easily implemented; the search is guided efficiently by the concept of differences between objects of the universe of discourse, the need to reduce unwanted differences generating new sub-goals in a perfectly natural way.

It can of course happen that in unfavourable cases the program drives itself into a blind alley, creating a series of sub-goals in direct genealogical descent and finding that the last of these cannot be achieved because no operator can be applied. Further, there is nothing to prevent the same sub-goal from appearing more than once in different search lines; if this occurs there is no need to keep more than one copy and all risk of looping can be avoided if the following procedure is followed.

In the GPS approach, as just summarised, choices are made with the help of a connection table for reducing differences between objects together with an ordering of these differences (Table 5.27). This is completely general: we shall now study its application in a very different context, one that involves theorem proving.

Table 5.27.

```
    OBᵢ: set of goals not yet considered
while there is a goal that has not been studied
      choose a goal G not yet studied
      if  G is the main goal then success end
      end if
      while there is a method that has not been applied to G
      choose a method M
      if M cannot be applied to G then choose another method
                              else if M achieves G
                                    then G ← parent (G)
                                    else if M generates a new goal G'
                                          then if G' has been generated already
                                                    then delete G'
                                                end if
                                          end if
      end if
end while
```

5.13.3 A problem in formal logic

Whilst this application is in the field of first-order propositional logic, no knowledge whatever of this field is required; the exercise can be regarded as a mere game in which strings of characters are to be manipulated according to given rules. Problems of this type had in fact been put previously to students by the American psychologists O. Moore and S. Anderson (1954) in an attempt to understand how humans will act in such circumstances: the unification algorithm (Section 3.7) was not known at that time.

The general problem is to find a sequence of transformations, all belonging to a given set, that will transform one given string of symbols into another. As a particular case, let the initial and final strings be:

$$\text{initial: } (R \supset \neg P) \wedge (\neg R \supset Q) \qquad \text{final: } \neg(\neg Q \wedge P)$$

and the set of legal transformations as in Table 5.28. Here $r0-r12$ are merely reference numbers and do not form part of the respective rules. The symbol $\mapsto$ between two strings $C1$, $C2$ is read 'can be re-written' and means that $C1$ can be transformed into $C2$ without further question. The double

Table 5.28.

(r0)	$\neg\neg A \mapsto A$
(r1)	$A \wedge B \mapsto B \wedge A$
	$A \supset B \mapsto B \vee A$
(r2)	$A \supset B \mapsto \neg B \supset \neg A$
(r3)	$A \wedge A \leftrightarrow A$
	$A \vee A \leftrightarrow A$
(r4)	$A \wedge (B \wedge C) \leftrightarrow (A \wedge B) \wedge C$
	$A \vee (B \vee C) \leftrightarrow (A \vee B) \vee C$
(r5)	$A \vee B \leftrightarrow \neg(\neg A \wedge \neg B)$
	$A \wedge B \leftrightarrow \neg(\neg A \vee \neg B)$
(r6)	$A \supset B \leftrightarrow \neg A \vee B$
(r7)	$A \wedge (B \vee C) \leftrightarrow (A \wedge B) \vee (A \wedge C)$
	$A \vee (B \wedge C) \leftrightarrow (A \vee B) \wedge (A \vee C)$
(r8)	$A \wedge B \to A$
	$A \wedge B \to B$
(r9)	$A \to A \vee X$
(r10)	$\left.\begin{array}{c} A \\ B \end{array}\right\} \to A \wedge B$
(r11)	$\left.\begin{array}{c} A \\ A \supset B \end{array}\right\} \to B$
(r12)	$\left.\begin{array}{c} A \supset B \\ B \supset C \end{array}\right\} \to A \supset C$

arrow $\leftrightarrow$ means that both $C1 \mapsto C2$ and $C2 \mapsto C1$ hold. When applying re-writing to a rule, any letter can be substituted by any other provided that the same substitution is made on both sides of the $\mapsto$ symbol. A letter preceded by the symbol $\neg$ can be replaced by any letter whatever. But no substitution can be performed on any symbol that is not a letter, e.g. on $\neg$ or $\wedge$.

Finally, a rule can be applied to a string provided that, possibly as a result of one or more substitutions, some part of that string has been made strictly identical with the left part of the rule, that is, the part preceding the $\mapsto$ symbol: with the reservation that in the case of rules $r8-r12$ the complete string must have been brought into coincidence, not simply some part. Thus by $r8$ we can rewrite $(P \vee Q) \wedge R$ as $(P \vee Q) \rightarrow (P \vee Q)$, $(P \vee Q) \rightarrow R$ but the same does not apply to $(P \wedge Q) \vee R$.

In this formalism the letters play the same role as variables do in classical algebra; and a substitution is equivalent to a change of variables.

To illustrate this, if we are given the string $(P \supset Q) \wedge S$ we can apply $r2$, substituting P, Q for A, B respectively, getting $(\neg Q \supset \neg P) \wedge S$; and then apply $r6$, substituting $\neg Q$ for A and $\neg P$ for B, to transform this into $(\neg\neg Q \vee \neg P) \wedge S$.

Using these substitution rules and conventions we can construct a connection table that is the exact analogue of that for the operators of the Monkey and Bananas problem; this is given in Table 5.29. Here again a rule transforms one object of the universe of discourse into another, according to a certain law and subject to certain conditions. The table shows which rules are suitable for reducing which differences, but now the differences are

Table 5.29 GPS connection table for the logical problem.

Operators	r0	r1	r2	r3	r4	r5	r6	r7	r8	r9	r10	r11	r12
Differences													
D1 adding a letter				x			x		x	x			
D2 deleting a letter				x			x	x				x	x
D3 changing number of symbols $\neg$	x		x		x	x							
D4 changing number of other connectives						x	x	x					
D5 parenthesis				x			x						
D6 changing order of letters	x	x											

more varied than before: for an arbitrary pair of strings they can concern:

1. Different numbers of letters; $D1$ indicates a difference to be reduced by adding one or more letters, $D2$ to be reduced by deletion.
2. Different numbers of $\neg$ symbols ($D3$).
3. Different numbers of other connectives ($D4$).
4. Different parenthesising ($D5$).
5. Different ordering of the letters ($D6$).

These form the basis of the connection table (Table 5.29). We shall assume here that there is no ordering of the differences according to difficulty of reduction.

Solution of the problem by GPS. The formal statement is:

$$T(OB_i, OB_f)$$

where

$$OB_i \equiv (R \supset \neg P) \wedge (\neg R \supset Q)$$
$$OB_f \equiv \neg(\neg Q \wedge P)$$

The first difference registered by the program is that the 'variable' R has been eliminated in the passage from OB_i to OB_f, suggesting the first sub-goal REDUCE $D2$ with R as parameter. The connection table shows that this might be achieved by means of any of the rules $r3$ ($\mapsto$), $r7$ ($\leftarrow$), $r8$, $r11$, $r12$; only $r8$ can be applied immediately, first to the left-most part of OB_i, giving a new object: $OB_1 \equiv R \supset \neg P$.

It is useful to recall that here, in contrast to what happens to the world generally and in particular in the world of the previous problem, the application of a rule to an expression does not destroy that expression − it simply adds a new object to the universe. This simplifies the task of theorem proving because it removes the need for back-tracking when a return has to be made to a previous state: all the objects considered exist all the time − whilst in the first example the monkey cannot be in two different places at the same time.

The left sides of $r3$, $r7$, $r11$, $r12$ do not, as things stand, coincide with OB_i; GPS notes the difference and creates a group of sub-goals $F(O, \Delta, OB_i, \text{left\_side\_}r_j)$ with $j = 3, 7, 11, 12$; it notes also that $r8$ can be applied to OB_i in a different way.

GPS's general strategy for choosing which goal to attack next consists in developing the one at the deepest level in the search tree. Here it is OB_1, which has differences D_1 and D_2 from OB_f, because it is not the desired letter R that has been lost in going from OB_i to OB_1, but Q. However, GPS considers the simultaneous reduction of the two differences to be a more difficult task than that presented by the original problem and therefore abandons this sub-goal in favour of the deepest sub-goal that has not yet been developed, that corresponding to the application of $r8$ to the right-hand part of OB_i; but this does not get rid of R so the search continues with OB_i and $r7$.

The beginning and the end of the GPS solution are given in Tables 5.30 and 5.31, with comments in square brackets; as will be seen, it generates a total of 65 intermediate goals before reaching OB_f at G66. The search tree is shown in Fig. 5.32.

It will be clear from these two examples that there is no fundamental difference between GPS's method of solution and the way a human solver would go about the task. To argue in terms of differences between the objects considered, and to characterise the legal operators according to the differences they can reduce, is obviously a good and generally applicable idea. Of course, we as humans will often have a better awareness of the

Table 5.30.

Goal 1 TRANSFORM OB_i, OB_f
   $G2$ REDUCE $D2$ (variable R)
      $G3$ APPLY $r8$ to left side OB_i
                 gives $OB_1 = R \supset \neg P$
         $G4$ TRANSFORM OB_1 OB_f
            $G5$ REDUCE $D2$ (variable Q)
            $G6$ REDUCE $D1$ (variable R)
                   RETURN [too expensive compared to $G1$]
                        [return to $G2$]
      $G2$ $G7$ APPLY $r8$ to right side OB_i
                 gives $OB_2 = \neg R \supset Q$
         $G8$ TRANSFORM OB_2 OB_f
            $G9$ REDUCE $D2$ (variable P)
                  REDUCE $D1$ (variable R)
                        RETURN [too expensive compared to $G1$]
      $G2$ $G10$ APPLY $r7$ ($\leftarrow$) to OB_1 [not possible, generate new goal]
            $G11$ REDUCE $D4$ on left of OB_1 (connective $\vee$)
               $G12$ APPLY $r6$ to OB_i [preceding reduction not possible]
                       gives $OB_3 = (\neg R \vee P) \wedge (\neg R \supset Q)$
         $G13$ APPLY $r7$ ($\leftarrow$) to OB_3 [new attempt]
            $G14$ REDUCE $D4$ on right of OB_4 (connective $\vee$)
               $G15$ APPLY $r6$ to OB_3
                       gives $OB4 = (\neg R \vee \neg P) \wedge (\neg \neg R \vee Q)$
            $G16$ APPLY $r7$ ($\leftarrow$) to OB_4 [new attempt]
               $G17$ REDUCE $D3$ on left and right of OB_4 (connective $\vee$)
               $G18$ APPLY $r6$ to right of OB_4
                  RETURN [OB_3 re-created, return to $G2$]
   $G2$
      $G19$ APPLY $r3$ to OB_i

Table 5.31.

*G*53 APPLY *r*12 to OB_2 check
        condition: find $OB_{10} = A \supset \neg R$
  *G*54 TRANSFORM OB_i OB_{10}
  *G*55 TRANSFORM OB_1 OB_{10} [equivalent, judged to be easier]
    *G*56 REDUCE *D*3
    *G*57 APPLY *r*2 to OB_1
        gives $OB_{11} = \neg\neg P \supset \neg Q$
  *G*53 [taken up again]
    APPLY *r*12 to OB_{11} and OB_2
        gives $OB_{12} = \neg\neg P \supset Q$
*G*8 [taken up again]
    TRANSFORM OB_{12} OB_f
    *G*58 REDUCE *D*3 (variable *P*)
      *G*59 APPLY *r*0 to OB_{12}
        gives $OB_{13} = P \supset Q$
    *G*60   REDUCE *D*4 (connective $\supset$)
      *G*61 APPLY *r*6 ($\rightarrow$) to OB_{13}
        gives $OB_{14} = \neg P \vee Q$
    *G*62 REDUCE *D*4 (connective $\vee$)
      *G*63 APPLY *r*5 ($\rightarrow$) to OB_{14}
        gives $OB_{15} = \neg(\neg\neg P \wedge \neg Q)$
    *G*64 REDUCE *D*3
      *G*65 APPLY *r*0 to OB_{15}
        gives OB_{16}
    *G*66 REDUCE *D*6
      *G*67 APPLY *r*1
        gives $OB_{17} = \neg(\neg Q \wedge P)$ *success*
end

universe of the problem that will enable us to find a more direct route to the goal; but equally we may give up when the task is heavy, where GPS works on and in the end succeeds.

5.13.4 Other problems put to GPS

The final version of GPS, due to Ernst and Newell (1967) worked on 11 different tasks; running on the IBM 7090 at Carnegie Mellon University, it took about 20 seconds for each goal generated and thus solved the monkey-and-bananas problem – which, as we have seen, involved 13 goals – in about 4 minutes. The following are brief accounts of these various problems.

1. Formal integration. The first problem in this field given to GPS was to

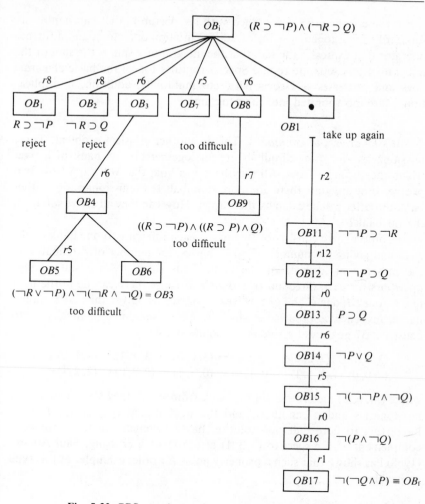

Fig. 5.32 GPS search tree for a problem in formal logic.

integrate te^{t^2} (with respect to t, of course). The result $\frac{1}{2}e^{t^2}$ was given after 3 minutes and the creation of 11 goals. The expression $\sin^2 at \cos at + t^{-1}$ was integrated, to give $\log t + \sin^3 at/3a$ in about twice that time and with about twice the number of goals.

We should note that in this field the final object is not so well defined as is usual; in fact, the only property it must possess is that it contains no integration symbol. This does not make it a more difficult problem; all it does is to impose a strict order of priority among the differences, with the removal of the integration symbol at the head of the list.

For these tasks GPS is provided with six operators that can handle six standard forms, together with four differentiation operators, and a further operator that expresses the fact that the integral of a sum is the sum of the integrals of the separate terms. Special routines for all the basic algebraic laws and processes – associativity, commutativity, addition, multiplication – are incorporated into the program.

2. *'Missionaries and cannibals'*. This is another classical problem. Three missionaries and three cannibals are all together on one bank of a river which they want to cross. All they have is a boat that will carry only two people. If at any time there are more cannibals than missionaries on either bank the latter will be eaten by the former. How can they all arrive safely on the far bank?

An 'object' here consists of two parts, each referring to one bank of the river and giving the number of missionaries, the number of cannibals and the presence or absence of the boat. Thus there are five state-change operators for each direction of crossing, because there can be in the boat one C, one M, one C and one M, two C or two M. Given this, GPS applies its means–ends approach – which is easily simulated manually – to construct 57 goals and arrive at the solution:

$$(3, 3, 1) \to (2, 2, 0) \to (3, 2, 1) \to (3, 0, 0) \to (3, 1, 1) \to (1, 1, 0)$$
$$(0, 0, 0) \leftarrow (1, 1, 1) \leftarrow (0, 1, 0) \leftarrow (0, 3, 1) \leftarrow (0, 2, 0) \leftarrow (2, 2, 1)$$

where (m, c, b) means that on the bank from which they start there are m missionaries and c cannibals, and the boat if and only if $b = 1$. It is interesting to note that this solution has a symmetry in the form of a complement with respect to $(3, 3, 1)$ after the sixth crossing; Saul Amarel (1968) has shown that such a property holds for other examples of this type of problem.

3. *The Towers of Hanoi*. This is a puzzle due to the French mathematician Edouard Lucas. Three vertical rods A, B, C are fixed to a board and on A are four discs in decreasing order of size, the largest at the bottom and the smallest at the top. The problem is to transfer the discs from A to C so that they are in the same order on C and a legal move consists in transferring the top disc from any rod to any other, but a larger disc may never be placed on a smaller.

As in all the preceding problems, certain conditions must be fulfilled before any of the six possible operators can be applied; but here the universe of discourse is very simple and the method of differences is particularly suitable. GPS goes straight to the solution in 46 steps, generating no unnecessary goal.

4. The three coins. There are three coins in a row on a table showing head–tail–head; if a legal move is to turn over any two coins the problem is to produce either H–H–H or T–T–T is exactly three moves.

Here a counter is incorporated into the description of each object so as to record the number of moves; GPS finds the solution after generating only ten goals.

5. The seven bridges of Königsberg. This is the famous Euler problem, already described in Section 4.1, example 8. Figure 5.33 shows the two islands and seven bridges of the River Pregel at Königsberg (now Presburg); the question is, is it possible to start from one point and return there after crossing every bridge once and only once? The operators correspond to the 14 different bridge crossings. As Euler showed in 1736, there is no solution; GPS has no method adapted specifically to the problem and all it can do is attempt to exhaust all the possibilities, but it failed because it had used all the available memory space of the machine in finding several ways of crossing only six bridges.

6. Pouring water. Given two jugs that hold 5 and 8 litres respectively and a tank with an unlimited amount of water, how do you get 2 litres in the small jug?

GPS solves this in 24 steps; it makes several trial-and-error moves because there is a great difference between the two extreme situations, (5, 8) and (2, –).

7. The father and his sons. A father and his two sons want to cross a river; the father weighs 80 kilos, each son weighs 40 and the only available boat will carry only 80 kilos.

GPS solves this with 33 goals.

8. Continuing a sequence (of letters). The particular problem was to find the next two letters of the sequence *BCBDBE*..., which, like all problems of

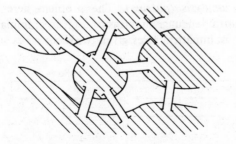

Fig. 5.33 The seven bridges of Königsberg.

this type, raises the fundamental question of the measure of the simplicity of the answer. Here *BF* and *BC* are equally admissible: *BF* would probably be thought the better, but *BC* is based on the idea of starting the sequence over again, and there is nothing to say which is right. The way in which such a problem is expressed to GPS is particularly important; it will be less of a direct transcription than in the previous examples, because the objects are not complete series of letters but partial series with certain relations between letters. A relation between two letters can be either SAME, meaning identity, or FOLLOWS, meaning that the second follows the first in alphabetical order.

The final object is defined by three conditions that it must satisfy. The first is that the blanks in the initial object must have been removed – the two blanks are replaced by the special letters x, y. The second is that the set of relations that enable the final string to be described must be as simple as possible: if two descriptions have the same relations then the simpler is the one whose operands are separated by the smaller number of letters of the sequence. The third condition is that every letter must appear in at least one relation.

Two operators can be applied; one corresponds to giving a relation between a pair of letters of the sequence, the other to assigning a value to a letter. A third causes the sequence to be scanned from left to right. Using these, GPS discovers and records, one by one, the properties present in the sequence. It does not make any provisional assignment of values to x and y, on the contrary it deduces logically the values they must take so that they satisfy the same relations as the letters to which they correspond. This examination of the initial object leads GPS to generate the description shown in Fig. 5.34. In scanning the sequence from left to right GPS sees that there is the relation SAME between the first and third letters and between the third and the fifth; it therefore asserts that the same relation will hold between the fifth and the seventh and so assigns $x = B$. It treats the remaining part of the sequence similarly and arrives at the solution *BF* by this inductive process in 27 steps.

9. Grammatical analysis (parsing). The problem here is to analyse a sentence in a natural language in terms of a given grammar. The following are some of the grammatical rules given to GPS.

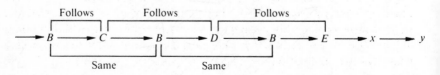

Fig. 5.34 Sequence of letters to be continued.

*R*1. A sentence consists of a noun group followed by a verb group followed in turn by another noun group.

*R*2. A noun group can be an adjectival group followed by a word that can be used as a noun.

*R*3. A noun group can be a word that can be used as a noun.

*R*4. An adjectival group is a word used as an adjective.

Another rule states that the word 'flies', for example, is used sometimes as a noun and sometimes as a verb, 'cold' as an adjective and as a noun. Thus a main goal could be to recognise that the string 'the cold weather kills the flies' (initial object) is a sentence (final object). Knowing that 'weather' can be only a noun, GPS infers that 'cold' must be used here as an adjective and 'flies' as a (plural) noun. In an actual test, GPS parsed the sentence 'free variables cause confusion' in 19 steps.

This example illustrates the importance of a heuristic approach in algorithms such as those used in syntax analysis.

10. Theorem proving. As well as manipulating propositional calculus expressions GPS can prove theorems in first-order predicate calculus, using in particular the method of 'resolution' discussed in Section 3.10. Thus the classical theorem of Church (1965):

$$\exists u \exists y \forall z [[P(u, y) \supset (P(y, z) \land P(z, z)] \land [P(u, y) \land Q(u, y)]]$$
$$\supset [Q(u, z) \land Q(z, z)]$$

was put to GPS, after skolemisation and putting into the form required by resolution, that is, in conjunctive normal form with no quantifiers in the predicates. At the 59th goal the program arrived at the contradiction that proved the theorem.

5.13.5 Conclusion

Whilst it may not be very fast and may generate an excessively large number of intermediate goals, GPS shows that it is possible to produce a single, unified system for solving a variety of non-trivial problems, based on a strategy of identifying differences between objects and using such means as are available for reducing these differences. The ideas behind GPS were taken up later by Slagle (1963) and Quinlan (1969) who improved the performance considerably by making adaptations of the connection tables and the difference orderings that were particularly well suited to two specific fields: formal integration by Slagle (the SAINT program) and logical processing by Quinlan. But whilst the question of performance is not very important, three serious objections can be levelled at GPS.

First, the problems that it has dealt with are not a very representative set; there is something of a family resemblance among them all and none are really difficult. If GPS can solve them it is to some extend because it 'knows' that it can solve such problems and therefore 'knows' that it will be able to reduce the search space to a very small number of elements.

Second, it seems that the method of differences is not appropriate when a global view of the task is necessary for the finding of a solution. The method takes a short-range view, assuming a certain continuity in the path to the solution, that no wide detour is needed and that the problem can be broken down into a sequence of elementary steps, all of which are effectively equal in importance. But there is a large class of problems for which this is far from the case, even among the formal problems and logical brain-teasers similar to those put in GPS. We shall meet many of these in the three chapters that follow.

Third and last – and what I regard as the most serious objection – it is not at all easy to state a problem in a way that can be put to GPS. In fact, the statement prejudges the solution: in every case the system has to be given an appropriate set of differences, the connection table and other information. Further, considerable intellectual effort is required in describing a situation in terms of a set of operators – as, for example, in the case of the Königsberg bridges or the letter sequence to be continued. Nevertheless, to have thought of such a program over 25 years ago is something to be admired.

Chapter 6

GAME-PLAYING PROGRAMS, PSYCHOLOGY OF PROBLEM-SOLVING

In any intellectual game between two players each in turn has to make a decision without knowing how the other will reply. The standard method adopted by human players for overcoming this difficulty is for each to think out in advance a number of possible moves both for himself and for his opponent. Thus player A argues that if he makes a certain move then his opponent B has a choice of a certain set of moves in reply, to each of which A in turn has another set of possible replies, and so on; so a tree structure of possible moves, and therefore of possible situations, is generated as in Fig. 6.1 where the turn to move changes at each change of level. The human player, going through such a process, will envisage the situation that will result from each possible sequence of moves and then make the move that he judges will have the most favourable outcome for himself; and programs for playing games on computers do just the same. The purpose of this chapter is to describe the method most commonly used to achieve this goal.

We discuss first the importance of this tree structure and the way in which a program can construct it; and then consider how to assess the relative values of the situations that are generated. This last, the subject of Section 6.2, is done with the help of what since 1950, following Claude Shannon, has been called an evaluation function. All these calculations have to lead to a choice of move: Sections 6.3 and 6.4 describe the basic method and an improvement on it. It will become clear that the whole procedure is very similar to what we have already described in connection with problems concerning graphs.

Finally in this chapter we study the limitations and the failings of this approach and in Section 6.8 we develop a fundamentally different method.

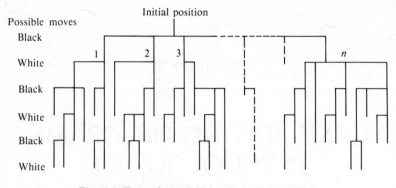

Fig. 6.1 Tree of possibilities for a chess move.

6.1 THE TREE OF LEGAL MOVES

The only reason why the tree is necessary is that we do not know how to evaluate the initial situation properly; in chess, for example, no-one can say at the start whether White or Black will win if each plays faultlessly. Thus the tree is useful as an aid to reducing this level of ignorance. In chess again the ideal would be to envisage a number of moves large enough to generate, at the end of each sequence, positions that could be evaluated exactly – one king checkmated, one side able to apply perpetual check, one king in stalemate, and so on; unfortunately this is seldom possible.

At the start of a chess game each side has 20 available moves, so there are already 400 different possible positions after the first exchange and certainly none of these can be evaluated exactly. Continuing, the number of moves open to each side increases to 50 towards the middle game. Suppose this number were constant, K say, throughout the game; then after n moves the tree generated would have K^n terminal nodes (leaves); taking $K = 40$, after six moves this is 40^6, or about 4×10^9, which is already very large and is multiplied by K (here 40) at each subsequent move. The increase is exponential (roughly K^n) with the depth to which the search is taken, and the time to conduct the search and to evaluate the positions so as to decide the next move would increase similarly. This *combinatorial explosion* prohibits any development of the tree to depths sufficient for reliable evaluation of the positions to be possible: if a supercomputer, able to evaluate ten terminal positions per second, had worked thus without stopping since the formation of our solar system, estimated as 4.6×10^9 years, it would have dealt with only:

$$10 \times 3600 \times 24 \times 365 \times 4.6 \times 10^9$$

or about 15×10^{18} positions. This is about 40^{12}, and so corresponds to only 12 moves, or six exchanges – in all this time the machine would have looked ahead only a dozen moves. When one reflects that a real game usually lasts for about 40 moves on each side one understands the fascination this game has for humans.

It is because the study of games in general, and of chess in particular, leads to the discovery of methods for reducing the combinatorial explosion that it has often been undertaken in support of research in artificial intelligence; and the goal is not so much to produce a program that plays well as to find general methods that can be applied in other fields to solve different problems. The games that have this relevance for artificial intelligence are those for which the tree of possible situations is small enough to be analysed fully by existing computers, suitably programmed: for example, tic-tac-toe, end-game chess problems ('mate in 2' with few pieces on the board) and games such as Nim for which a definitive evaluation function can be constructed; the game with matches popularised in Alain Renais's film, *Last Year at Marienbad*, is in this last class.

Let us consider tic-tac-toe from this point of view. This is played on a 3×3 square as shown in Fig. 6.2; each player has three counters (black and white, say) and in the first phase of the game each in turn puts a counter on whichever vacant square he chooses. The second phase begins when all six counters have been placed; each player in turn can move any one of his counters to a neighbouring vacant square – he can move one step horizontally, vertically or diagonally. The winner is the one who first has all his counters in a straight line – again, in any direction.

For any game there is no problem in generating the legal moves according to the laws of that game; this is always an algorithmic type of procedure, the general principle of which we now indicate for the many games in which two opponent players move pieces on a chess board. Taking the squares of the board one after the other, when we are considering the next move by one side we are interested only in those squares occupied by pieces belonging to

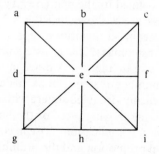

Fig. 6.2 The tic-tac-toe board.

Table 6.1.

occupation (i, j)	the state of the square at that instant; vacant, occupied by one's own piece or by the opponent's
piece (i, j)	the piece on (i, j) when this is not vacant
ndirections	the number of possible directions for the move
directions_allowed	the number of these directions allowed for the piece in question

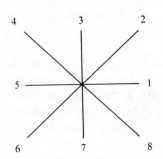

Fig. 6.3 Possible directions in tic-tac-toe and chess.

that side and for each of these squares we envisage the possible displacements of the piece in the directions allowed by the rules. Thus for the square (i, j) we have Table 6.1. Thus in tic-tac-toe, and in chess, there are in general eight possible legal directions (Fig. 6.3).

In tic-tac-toe all the pieces are of the same type and all directions are allowable to each piece – we deal later with moves that, if made, would take the piece off the board. In chess we can consider a total of 12 directions: the above eight plus the (in effect) four directions for the knight; whilst there is only one direction allowed for a pawn and eight for the queen. Each direction is defined by the pair $(\Delta x, \Delta y)$, giving its slope; with the above numbering these are as shown in Table 6.2. A piece p can move a number of steps not exceeding a quantity nstepmax(p) in any one of the legaldirections(p): thus nstepmax$(K) = 1$, nstepmax$(Q) = 8$ in chess and nstepmax$(p) = 1$ for all p in tic-tac-toe. A move in a legal direction and of not more than the legal number of steps can be made, provided it ends on a vacant square, or on an enemy-occupied square with a capture of the enemy piece, or would not take the moving piece of the board.

In chess further technical complications arise in connection with castling, capture *en passant*, pawn promotion and the prohibition of putting oneself in check, but the essence of the procedure for generating moves is as shown

Table 6.2.

	1	2	3	4	5	6	7	8
Δx	1	1	0	-1	-1	-1	0	1
Δy	0	1	1	1	0	-1	-1	-1

Table 6.3.

```
repeat for all squares (i, j)
        if occupation (i, j) = self then p ← piece (i, j) {type pf piece on (i, j)}
            repeat for all directions ∈ (1, ndirections)
                if direction ∈ directions_allowed(p) then x ← i, y ← j
                    repeat for all steps ∈ (1, nstepmax(p))
                        x ← x + Δx, y ← y + Δy {direction}
                        if (x, y) ∈ board and occupation (x, y) ≠ self
                            then record move ((i, j) ← (x, y))
                        end if
                    end repeat steps
                end if
            end repeat directions
end repeat squares
```

in Table 6.3. Using this schema, the simplest way to restrict the growth of the tree is to confine the study to a single step ahead, that is, to depth 1. The procedure is then: (i) generate all the legal moves; (ii) evaluate these; (iii) make the move of greatest value. Taking into account the possibility of the game ending immediately as a result of a gain or a loss, a possible way to play is as follows (Table 6.4).

Table 6.4.

```
if there is a winning move then play this; end
    else consider one's possible legal moves: let c be one's next move
        if the opponent has a winning move after c then delete c
        else find how many opponent moves there are after c
            [call the move generator again]
        end if
        play the move that gives the opponent the least number of replies
end if
```

A 'first-level' strategy. Let us apply this 1-level strategy to tic-tac-toe; suppose the position is as in Fig. 6.4 and it is Black's move. The

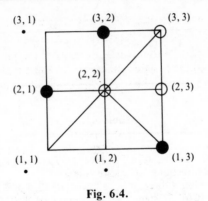

Fig. 6.4.

move-generation algorithm gives the four legal moves for Black:

1. $(3, 2) \rightarrow (3, 1)$
2. $(2, 1) \rightarrow (3, 1)$
3. $(2, 1) \rightarrow (1, 1)$
4. $(1, 3) \rightarrow (1, 2)$

There is no directly winning move, but (4) would lead to Black losing at the next move, so we eliminate this. Of the remaining three, (1) would allow four replies and (2), (3) each three; both of these are in fact winning moves, as will be seen by continuing to apply the same strategy. A study of other positions shows that the strategy is entirely playable; but two things arise that should be noted.

First, the strategy can in principle be applied at any level. Whenever it is found to be impossible to develop the complete tree of moves the possible next moves at the level reached can be compared among themselves on the basis of some numerical value associated with the position resulting from each move – for example, the number of different moves then open to the oponent. This replaces the logical value WIN or LOSE, which can be determined only after a complete enumeration of the possible positions.

Second, the strategy is independent of the particular game. It gives good results for tic-tac-toe and removes the need to remember the complete tree; and at chess it is useful at the start of the game and to certain other stages. At noughts-and-crosses it is equivalent to choosing a vacant square at random – but clearly can be improved in this and other special contexts. Basically, it can be used in any game between two players.

Restricting the search: breadth or depth. The tree shown in Fig. 6.5 summarises the proof by exhaustion for tic-tac-toe: the first player can be sure of winning if he puts his first counter on the central square, whatever moves the opponent may make. Because of the symmetries of the board, once this move (Black here) has been played only squares *a* and *b* are essentially different for White's first move: *a* is equivalent to *c*, *g*, and *i*; *b* to *d*, *f* and and *h*; noticing this enables us to reduce the tree to a quarter of its original size. The complete enumeration is easily generated but for

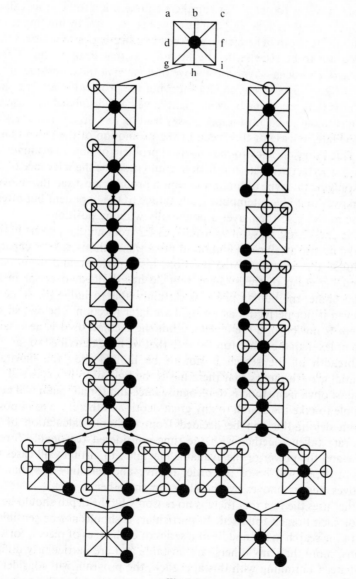

Fig 6.5

brevity we have shown only the best move for Black at each stage, this is, the move that is certain to give him victory. Notice that after his first move all White's moves up to the eighth are forced, and at that move his choice is irrelevant and Black is certain to win.

However, for many games — chess, go, bridge, poker, for example — either no satisfactory evaluation function can be constructed or the number of possible moves is too great for complete enumeration to be practical; so the tree has to be restricted. This can be done in two ways, by limiting either its breadth or its depth. The first is achieved by rejecting certain moves that are judged not to be relevant to the situation at that instant: thus if in a chess game one's queen is *en prise* a move of a pawn at the other side of the board is unlikely to be of any significance; but the problem in making such judgement is that occasionally what might have been dismissed as a useless move can turn out to be advantageous, say leading to a discovered check or a fork, the later release of the queen or the promotion of the pawn that is moved. This brings us back to the unsolved problem of how to evaluate the position — a perfect evaluation function would describe the relevance of the move. Applying this type of limitation would prohibit most sacrifice moves, that is, moves that give a temporary advantage to the opponent but after a few more moves give the player a potentially winning position.

Existing chess programs, on the whole, differ from human players in that they make no use at all of limitation in breadth. With his greater capacity for a global appreciation of the position, his experience and memory of chess and his grasp of the strategy that he has decided to adopt in the particular game, the human player is certainly able to judge the situation better, even if not perfectly; as we shall see later (Section 5 below) such a judgement is not beyond the machine, but the method used is necessarily more complex than the brute-force search that we have described so far. But if the breadth of the search is not to be limited then the inevitable exponential growth means that there has to be limitation in depth.

The most obvious method is to recognise once and for all that it will never be possible to take the search to any great depth and therefore to impose a maximum depth; this can be decided from a simple calculation of the growth rate taken together with the time considered reasonable for the response and the power of the available machine. In virtually all cases this maximum depth will be of the order of five and certainly less than ten half-moves, that is, moves by one player or the other.

Another uses the fact that there is no reason why the depth should be the same for each branch followed. In particular, it should not be sensible to interrupt the search in the middle of a series of exchanges of pieces, for such positions, more than any others, are unstable and are particularly difficult to evaluate. Continuing with this approach, the program will consider the effects of possible checks to the opponent king and the subsequent captures to which these could lead; the search will be continued until the position is judged to be stable for each side, then the possible legal moves are generated and the resulting positions evaluated.

It is a striking fact that all this was conceived for the first time by the English mathematician Alan Turing in 1951, who put them into practice in a hand simulation of the working of such a strategy.

6.2 EVALUATION OF A POSITION

What is wanted is a numerical function $F(S)$ of the position S such that a negative value corresponds to the opponent having the advantage and the greater that advantage the greater the absolute value. There is of course no theory of chess from which a precise definition of such a function can be derived; the most we have is the sign of the function for certain openings, and for all other situations it is a matter of empiricism. An inappropriate choice of function can result in a negative value when that side has the advantage, which is one basic reason why such a program does not play perfectly. Whenever such a program does play badly the reason in the form of $F(S)$ should be sought and the function changed to remove the defect.

We can consider $F(S)$ as the sum of a number of terms, each representing some feature of the position. The most important is always the material on the board, so we take the first term as proportional to the abgebraic sum of the values of the pieces – positive for one's own side, negative for the opponent – called the balance, B; the standard values adopted by human players are used: pawn = 1, knight = bishop = 3, rook = 5, queen = 10. Thus if the evaluating side has an advantage of one bishop ($+3$) but the opponent has an advantage of 1 pawn (-1) then $B = 2$.

The form of F we take is:

$$F(S) = a \cdot B + b \cdot R + c \cdot M + d \cdot C + e \cdot P + f \cdot A$$

where R, M, C, P, A are measures corresponding to other features, roughly in decreasing order of importance, and a, b, c, d, e, f are numerical coefficients whose values have to be decided by the programmer. The meanings of the terms are as follows:

R: The relative safeties of the kings: this is the greater the better one's king is protected behind the rook. The coefficient b can vary during the game, becoming zero when the major pieces have been removed from the board and the kings have to support their pawns or help the attack by protecting their own pieces.

M: The mobility of the pieces, measured by the number of squares to which each piece can move: this number will be weighted by a factor depending on the type of the piece.

C: Control of the centre, meaning, in the algebraic notation shown in Fig. 6.11 and following illustrations, the squares $d4$, $d5$, $e4$, $e5$. The coefficient e takes a low value except in the opening and middle games.

P: Pawn structure. Positive contributions come from protected, advanced and passed pawns and also from the opponent's doubled, isolated and unprotected pawns.

A: This is a measure of the relative possibilities for attack, taking account of pieces advanced beyond the fourth rank, rooks on open files, doubled rooks, possibilities for exchanges against more mobile pieces, attacks of squares close to the opponent king, possible checks or pins.

This list is not exhaustive, some programs taking still other features into account.

It requires patience and perseverance to arrive at a satisfactory set of values of the weighting coefficients $a-f$, and there is no reason why these values should not change in the course of the game, according to the number of moves made and/or the pieces remaining on the board. This form of function can allow sacrificial moves, that is, moves that will give a position for which B is negative (an advantage of one piece to the opponent) but the weighted sum is positive because of the compensation of the other terms. Equally, the values can be modified by the program itself, depending on the results obtained – see Chapter 9.

If F were perfect all that would be necessary would be to generate all the legal moves, evaluate the corresponding positions and play the move that gave the highest value; but in actuality we are far from knowing how to construct such a function. Further, since in addition we cannot develop the tree far enough to reach positions for which there is no doubt about the advantage to one side or the other, we have to find a compromise between the two extremes of depth of search and quality of the evaluation function: the time needed for the calculation increases as the demands of either of these criteria are increased.

Whatever is done, there is another problem to be solved, that of deciding, on the basis of the evaluations of the positions reached when the search has been taken to the maximum depth allowed, which move to play from the starting level; the method invariably used ever since computers have been programmed to play chess is called the *minimax* principle, which we now describe.

6.3 THE MINIMAX AND THE CHOICE OF MOVE

A point to note first is that, simply because we know that our evaluation will not be perfect, no purpose would be served by evaluating intermediate positions in the search before the specified maximum depth, n say, is reached; there is a great risk of these positions being unstable and difficult to evaluate. When the depth n is reached all captures should be taken into account, ordered according to the values of the pieces captured, also the checks: this is called the quiescence mechanism. Thus in Fig. 6.6 the final branches of the tree are not all of the same length, for this varies according to the number of moves needed to reach a quiet, stable position. It is only when we work back through the tree of moves that we assign values to the vertices that precede, in time order, the positions corresponding to the leaves. But the question remains, how are we to do this? It was John von Neumann and Oscar Morgenstern who in 1945 proposed a method that could be employed in any game in which a strategy was needed.

Von Neumann and Morgenstern made the fundamental assumption that the same evaluation function is available to both players in the game; therefore whilst player A will choose his next move so as to maximise the value to him of the resulting position, player B will aim to minimise that same value, and A must assume that B will play in this way whenever it is his move. After A has moved B will reply with the move that will minimise the value of A's position after that (i.e. B's) move; so A should look ahead to this position and choose his move so as to maximise the possible minima

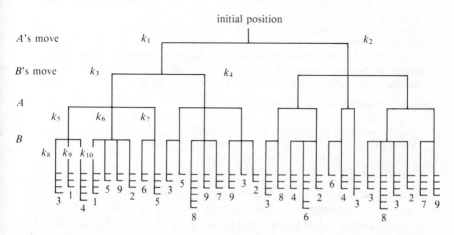

Fig. 6.6 Tree of legal moves, with values of stable positions at different depths.

that B can enforce: and hence the name minimax given to the procedure.

To carry out this procedure all the intermediate nodes are evaluated in succession, finishing at the maximum depth; then, moving back up the tree, each node in turn is given a value that is either the minimum or the maximum of the values of its immediate descendants, according to the parity of its level. The move to make from the initial position (the root of the tree) is then the one that maximises the value thus found for the first level down. Notice that this has nothing to do with the value found by simply calculating $F(S)$ for the initial position: what we have is a value corrected by taking into account the possible later moves.

Figure 6.7, a development of Fig. 6.6, illustrates the procedure. Only two moves, k_1, k_2, for A from the initial position are shown. At the position resulting from k_1 B has two possible moves, k_3 and k_4, and after k_3 it is A's move again with possibilities k_5, k_6, k_7. Consider first k_5. Then B can reply with k_8, k_9 or k_{10}, and if this (depth 4) is the depth at which we have decided to end the search we evaluate the resulting positions, getting the values 3, 1, 4 respectively – these values will take account of any possible checks and captures.

We can state the minimax algorithm (see Table 6.5) as follows:

MINIMAX: go to the lowest level and evaluate the position, finding either the maximum or the minimum according to the order of the level; continue with the next move on the same level, if there is one; otherwise move to the next level above.

To implement this as a computer program, we need a number of service procedures as follows:

Moves (board, player): generates the legal moves for the player to move, for that board position; puts these moves on to a stack, movestack(board, side).
Player (board, move): updates the position after the move.
Restore (board, move): the inverse of *player*, restores the position to what it was before the move.
Value (board, depth): the numerical value assigned to the position; to simplify the algorithm we multiply the values at odd-order levels by -1, so that we need consider only maximum values, whatever the level.

Other definitions are as follows:

Depth: the depth at the stage being studied.
Value (board): the value of the position being studied.
Eval (depth): the best value at that level.
E(depth): a list of the legal moves being studied.

Since these last moves are B's he will play so as to minimise the value of the position, and therefore A sees that if he plays k_5 at the level above he can expect only a value 1 at his next turn. Proceeding similarly he finds that by playing k_6 he can expect only 1 again and by playing k_7, 5. Thus the

Table 6.5.

MINIMAX: INPUT: (board, side)

        OUTPUT: (value of the position = minimax)

        depth ← 1; side ← 1; $E(1)$ ← movestack(board, side);

        eval(1) ← $-\infty$

repeat while $E \geqslant 1$

    repeat while E(depth) ≠ empty

        move ← stackfront $(E$(depth))

        board ← player (board, move)

        if depth ≠ maxdepth **then**

        depth ← depth + 1

        side ← $-$ side

        E(depth) ← movestack(board, side)

        eval(depth) ← $-\infty$

        else {maxdepth: evaluate the position and compare}

        eval(depth) ← MAX [eval(depth).side, value(board)]

        move ← unstack(E(depth)) {cancel previous move }

        board ← restore(board, move) {remain at this depth so long as there are

        moves}

        end if

    end repeat E

    {backtrack}

    if depth = 1 **then** minimax ← eval(1) **end if**

    side ← $-$ side

    depth ← depth $-$ 1

    move ← unstack(E(depth)) {cancel last move at this depth}

    board ← restore(board, move)

    eval(depth) ← MAX [eval(depth), $-$eval(depth + 1)] {minimax evaluation}

end repeat depth

end MINIMAX

---

nodes corresponding to these three moves by A are assigned values $1, 1, 5$ respectively; A seeks to maximise his expectation so he will choose k_7, and assign the value 5 to the next node above. The remaining values shown in Fig. 6.7 are arrived at by the same procedure, with choices alternating between maximum and minimum, until the root (initial) position is reached; the conclusion is that A should play k_1; the sequence of moves is shown by the heavy line in Fig. 6.7. The value of the initial position (obtained at the end of the process $F(S)$) is 5.

Notice that in following this procedure, as in the problem of the eight queens, we have to 'play' the moves when descending the tree and 'unplay' them when ascending; but all we need keep in memory is the updated position on the board and, at each level, the moves that have already been examined. Whilst the execution time can be considerable, for as we have

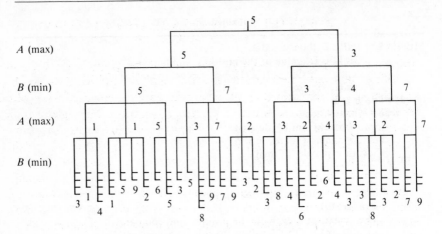

Fig. 6.7 Minimax evaluations for the tree of Fig. 6.6

seen it grows rapidly with increasing depth, the memory demands remain moderate; there is no need to hold any of that part of the tree, and the board positions, that do not correspond to the one sequence of moves being studied at the time, only the best numerical value at each level is necessary. It is for this reason that even cheap microcomputers can perform well here.

There is an alternative procedure that is strictly equivalent to minimax, because it gives precisely the same results, but is significantly faster because it allows whole areas of the tree to be eliminated without the need for detailed examination. This is called the alpha–beta method because the basic idea, first put forward by John McCarthy in 1961, uses two variables which he called α and β; we describe this in the next section. But this too, like the minimax, suffers from the fundamental defect of playing one move at a time without any overall plan; the strength of the human player lies in his capacity for conceiving and developing a strategy and adapting this to the particular game being played.

A different type of procedure, closer to that of the human player, can be programmed; this uses the approach of present-day work in artificial intelligence and, for the particular case of chess, attempts to give the program the deep knowledge of the game that has been built up over centuries and is expressed in the accepted chess language by terms such as pins, pincer-attacks, open files, etc. Programs of this type, based on knowledge rather than brute force, are beginning to be written, not only for chess but also for problems in other fields, for example in chemistry, in medical diagnosis and in mathematics. Section 6.8 below describes such a chess program ('Robin') and Chapter 8 on Expert Systems gives a general treatment.

6.4 THE ALPHA–BETA METHOD

The basic principle is the same as that used in the graph colouring and travelling salesman problems: to use the best values found from the branches of the tree studied up to the present so as to compare these with the best expected from those not yet studied, it can be shown, under certain conditions that we shall discuss, that there is no need to explore some possibilities because their outcome can have no effect on the result. Minimax is an explicit enumeration of the space of the moves; alpha–beta makes only an implicit enumeration, with the help of a pruning procedure.

A situation in which this pruning can be done is shown in Fig. 6.8. Continuing in the context of chess, suppose that at position S it is White's move, that one of his possible moves will result in position A and another in Y, and that A is analysed fully and its value α found. The study of Y is started, and the first move found, by minimax, to give a position Z of value z.

Suppose now that $z \leqslant \alpha$. If y is the value of Y then although this is unknown at this stage we can say that $y \leqslant z$, for as it is Black's move at Y if any other move gives a greater value he will not choose it. If s is the value of S we know that $\alpha \leqslant s$, so we have $y \leqslant z \leqslant \alpha \leqslant s$. These inequalities show that the fact that the true value y of Y is not known is of no consequence, and that therefore there is no point in examining any of the other possible moves from Y. Thus all the branches below Y, apart from Z, can be pruned away; this is called an α-cut.

The corresponding reasoning can be used if the first move is with the opponent, Black; if now the position corresponding to A (A' say) has value β and at Y' White has a move giving position Z' of value $z' \geqslant \beta$, the rest of

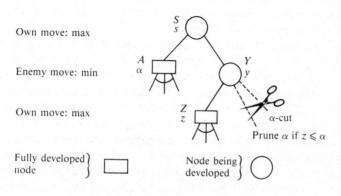

Own move: max

Enemy move: min

Own move: max

α-cut

Prune α if $z \leqslant \alpha$

Fully developed node

Node being developed

Fig. 6.8 Alpha–beta pruning: —— cut.

the tree below Y' can now be pruned: this is a β-cut. However, the same argument applies if A and Z are at different depths in the tree, provided these have the same parity: this is shown in Fig. 6.9.

In Fig. 6.9, A and U are two possible positions resulting from White's move at S; A has been analysed and its value α found; the analysis of U has been started and after an odd number of moves (here 3) a position Z reached, of value z: suppose $z \leqslant \alpha$. At the level Y immediately above, the value y will, as we have seen, satisfy $y < z$, this being Black's move; we want to show that here again the other branches descending from Y can be pruned. At the parent node V of Y two possibilities can arise: either the maximum v there is strictly greater than y or it is equal to y. In the first case, since we know already that $y \leqslant z$ and that an analysis of the other possible moves at Y can result only in reducing y still further, it is clear that analysis can be omitted without affecting the evaluation of V; and in the second we have $v = y$, whence $v \leqslant z \leqslant \alpha$. In either case, V is assigned a value less than or equal to that of A and we have the situation of Fig. 6.8 again. Finally, therefore, in either case the value s assigned to the root node S is independent of the descendents of Y other than Z, so these can be ignored.

By recurrence on the depth, the argument can be applied to derive the same result for such a node Z at any depth that has the same parity as S; and correspondingly, when it is Black's move at S, a β-cut can be made when a node at any level of the same parity as S is found to have a value greater than β, where β is defined as before. Thus at any stage in the search we compare the value at an even-depth node with the best even-depth value (α) we have, and at an odd-depth node with the best odd-depth value (β). Thus these two values, initially $\pm\infty$, suffice to enable us to return up the tree to the initial position and to decide the move to play there.

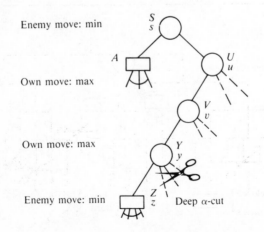

Fig. 6.9 Cut at a deeper level.

The rule can be summarised in Table 6.6. The procedure is shown in Fig. 6.10. Since the cuts can be made at any number of depths provided only that these are all of the same parity, the only values that need be stored are the current best upper bound (α) at the even-parity depths and the best lower bound (β) at the odd-parity depths, where the counting of levels starts from zero at the initial position, the root of the tree. No pruning is done so long as there are at least two terminal nodes that have not been evaluated by means of the function F. In the execution of the procedure the values of α increase with increasing depth whilst those of β decrease, the end being signalled by their becoming equal.

This procedure is exact and is faster than the minimax for the same result. It gives good results when the evaluation function is reliable and the search is taken to reasonably large depths, but these criteria can be met only at considerable computational cost. It is clearly successful for 'mate in n moves' types of problem with $n < 6$ at present, for here the evaluation is correct and the search can be taken to the maximum depth in an acceptable time. With current microcomputers the level of play ranges from average to good.

An interesting effect is that the procedure prunes the more drastically –

Table 6.6.

Move	Present best value	Type of node	Value	
White	α	White	z	$z \leqslant \alpha \rightarrow \alpha$-cut
Black	β	Black	w	$w \geqslant \beta \rightarrow \beta$-cut

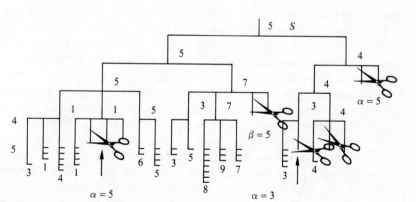

Fig. 6.10 $\alpha - \beta$ pruning for the tree of Fig. 6.6.

and is therefore the faster – the better the nodes are ordered for each cut. The ideal classification, which is of course unknown, would arrange the cuts at each level in order of decreasing value; to approximate to this some programs, before initiating $\alpha-\beta$ pruning to depth 6, say, will first carry this to depth 2 and classify the cuts on the basis of the results and repeat the process with depth 3 and a reclassification. This new classification is then recorded in memory and used as the basis of the depth-6 procedure. The two trials involve only few nodes and are therefore very fast, and the speed-up of the final depth-6 procedure is great enough for the total time to be less than would be taken if this alone had been run.

6.5 FUNDAMENTAL DEFECTS OF SYSTEMATIC TREE DEVELOPMENT

The disadvantages of exhaustive enumeration are many and serious – so much so that one can only marvel that programs based on this principle can play so well. The two main drawbacks are described in the next sections.

6.5.1 First disadvantage: absence of any strategy

It is inherent in this approach that each position is a new one: these programs play not a game but a succession of independent moves. It is clear that the method does not allow an overall plan or strategy to be propagated: all of whatever judgement is exercised is contained in the evaluation function, which gives a numerical assessment of the quality of a position as the sum of a number of easily calculated terms expressing such attributes as development potential, lines of attack, supported and passed pawns. But these terms can never express a long-term view of the game nor enable any reasoning to be conducted about some distant goal that may seem to offer advantages. This is best illustrated by the simple examples often met in the end game; consider for example the position of Fig. 6.11, where White, to move, has two pawns against Black's three: here and throughout we use the algebraic or Continental notation, with the ranks numbered 1 to 8 from White's side and the files a to h from the left, so that d1 is the White queen's square and e8 the Black king's. Any amateur can see that White has a certain win, but this will result from forming and carrying out the long-term plan of promoting the pawn on a2 to queen; the move a2–a4 ensures White's victory. This move would be made at once by a human player. It results in Black giving up the struggle, for his king will not be able to enter the square a4–a8–e8–e4, and the pawn can proceed to queen without

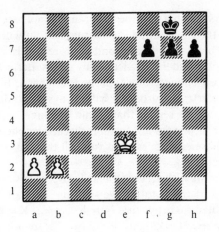

Fig. 6.11 End game, White to move.

needing the support of the white king. Since no black pawn can be the same, Black is certain to lose.

Even though it is very simple, such an analysis of the position cannot be conducted by programs of the type just described – more than five moves by each side, including a forced move by White's king to avoid an intermediate check, are needed to promote the pawn to queen: the program's conclusion is clear – advantage to Black, with three pawns against two. Only brute force, the enormous computing power of the machine, is used, and nothing of its capacity for formal reasoning and manipulation of concepts. It is only our anthropomorphic tendencies that sometimes make us think that in the course of a game the program has 'had the good idea' of such-and-such an attack – an idea, incidentally, that it abandons two moves later as though it had never had it.

The strength of such a program is measured solely by the number of moves it can develop per second, and the only difference between a microprocessor and large mainframe in this context is that the former, today, runs at about a thousand moves per second and the latter (the CYBER) about half a million. But if the approach is by exhaustive development of legal moves, even this latter enormous speed will not suffice.

6.5.2 Second disadvantage: the 'horizon' effect

The need to specify in advance the maximum depth to which the search is taken – to only a few moves by either side, in fact – has itself two main drawbacks. The first is obvious: the program cannot 'see' – and therefore cannot evaluate – those consequences of a move that will become manifest at depths below the cut-off. The second is more subtle and more sinister, and has been emphasised in particular by Hans Berliner, former world champion for correspondence chess, in his 1974 thesis. It is an inescapable consequence of the first: the program will always try to drive unfavourable developments out of the region that it can examine – that is beyond its limited-depth horizon; it does not 'want' any catastrophe to occur, and will sometimes make senseless moves so as to push this out of sight. Hence the term 'horizon effect'.

We can illustrate this with an example from Berliner's excellent thesis, but first an explanation of the notation we shall use here and in what follows. The pieces are identified by the initial letters: K = king, Q = queen, R = rook, B = bishop, N = knight, P = pawn; × denotes a capture (e.g. Q × R means queen takes rook) and + a check (Q × R + means that this capture results in the queen putting the enemy king in check). Pawns are not identified unless there is some special reason for doing so. The squares are labelled as explained in Section 6.5.1. Thus 1 e5 means that on move 1 the pawn in file e is moved to the square e5 (the starting square is not given); 3 N × Be7 + means that on move 3 the knight takes the bishop on e7 and gives check (Fig. 6.12). The white bishop on a4 is hemmed in by the three black pawns and is doomed. The strategy for the good White player is to accept the inevitable loss and get what he can in return; there is the possibility of winning a pawn and attacking another – White will then have a very good position, with one knight ahead. But a program that simply considers single moves will not proceed in this way: it will try to arrange

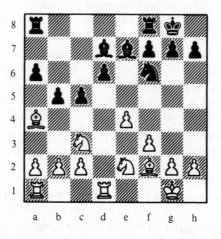

Fig. 6.12 Horizon effect: White to move (H. Berliner 1974).

matters so that the capture of the white bishop is pushed out of its field of vision, and will therefore play as though the capture never took place. This is inherent in the logic of the $\alpha-\beta$ method, to find enough moves, with forced replies, to drive away the capture by the opponent. If the maximum depth is fixed at 5 the best move as found by $\alpha-\beta$ is P − e5, corresponding to the following safety play:

1	e5	d6 × e5	(otherwise P × Nf7)	
2	N − d5 and if	N × Nd5	then 3 R × Nd5	(a)
		Be7 moves	then 3 B − b3	(b)
		B5 × Ba4	then N × Be7 +	(c)

In case (a) the quiescence mechanism gives, before evaluation, b5 × Ba4 but also R × Bd7, a move which Black will prevent by 4 Be6; altogether, the outcome is the capture of a pawn rather than a bishop.

In case (b) the program moves the white bishop to b3 before evaluating the position; the two knights are protected and, apparently, the bishop is safe, but in fact is lost because 4 c4.

Finally, in case (c) the capture by Black is premature and White gains with a knight ahead. In this example the correct initial move would not be found until the search had been taken to depth 7, which would involve examining 168 800 different positions.

The havoc that can be wrought by this horizon effect is considerable, but there seems to be no way to avoid it; the effect is inherent in the basic approach of the method. It can have some very strange consequences for the way the program plays, and it is these that make its play so different from that of a human. Watching it play can be very testing for the writer of the program. In one game in which it had been playing well the Chess 4.4 program had a passed pawn on the seventh rank, which it valued highly but which could not be protected and was effectively lost. The program did not 'want' to lose this pawn and therefore fended off the capture, consequently losing its advantage after a series of unfavourable exchanges. Finally the opponent took the pawn, whereupon Chess 4.4 recovered, began to play well again − and won.

6.6 PSYCHOLOGICAL STUDIES OF PROBLEM-SOLVING BY HUMANS

It is not easy to say just when psychologists first began to study problem-solving. In France, Alfred Binet wrote a paper in 1894 on 'The psychology of calculating prodigies and chess players' in which, great pioneer that he was, he considered the relative importances of memory, imagination and knowledge. He was interested in the abstract representations used by the mental calculators and chess players who were willing to offer themselves as subjects for his experiments, in which he had them calculate (mentally) or play chess blindfold and asked them to say out loud what they were doing.

Binet's studies were repeated and extended by several psychologists including Adrian de Groot, Herbert Simon and John Baylor, especially for chess players. In 1902 Bergson, the first commentator on Binet's work, made the crucial observation that it seemed that the mental representations involved fewer images of the physical world – pieces on the chess board, for example – than indications of directions to be followed.

In the 1920s Otto Seiz, a psychologist of the Wurzburg school, developed a model in which thought processes were described as linear strings of elementary operations; he identified these operations and gave detailed descriptions of processes that he considered valid for all human beings. He drew attention also to the importance of problem solving to the general intellectual personality of the solver, the strength of his determination to solve the problem and the special characteristics of the problem being tackled. The driving force behind the development of these strings of operations seemed to Seiz to be 'the general law of anticipation of results' – that is, reasoning conducted with the help of plans and sub-goals, together with the appropriate amount of abstraction.

Present-day research in artificial intelligence has the merit of testing, with the aid of computer programs, the relevance of such ideas – and the good fortune of being able to do so. But Binet and Seiz's anticipation of this is clear: they were the first to view thinking and reasoning as experimental phenomena, susceptible of scientific investigation. At the beginning of the twentieth century they had already shown that our intellectual powers are related to and conditioned by two entirely tangible phenomena, memory and perception.

6.6.1 Memory

The biggest computers today (1989) have main memory capacities of the order of 1000 million binary units of information: main or central memory meaning that the information there is available to the computer at all times; the human analogy is what we hold in our heads. The term is used in contrast with the auxiliary memories, disks, tapes, cassettes, the roles of which correspond to the books in our libraries – secondary sources of information, less easy of access.

The average time of access to a binary unit of information in a modern machine is of the order of a thousand millionths of a second, a nanosecond; consequently computers can perform very quickly actions that they 'know'.

On the other hand they do not surpass humans in central memory capacity: the average human brain contains some hundred thousand million *neurons*, each of which is connected to between one and ten thousand others, so there are some hundred million million sites (*synapses*) at which information can be exchanged. The amount of information that a neuron can store is at present unknown but there is no doubt at all that it is a great deal more than one binary digit, that is, one yes/no item. Possibly a neuron can hold a thousand or a million such items, perhaps the same piece of information is coded and held at more than one neuron at the same time; whatever the situation, we have been built with an enormous memory capacity, certainly in comparison with the biggest contemporary computers. The existence of such a capacity suggests that we have also been provided with elaborate and efficient access mechanisms, so it is not surprising that experiments show that we are continually structuring our knowledge: we construct multiple reference points, we give names to new entities, we code them, we select – and we forget.

Experiments have shown also that one part of our memory is used in a very special way; this is the *short-term memory*. The collection of neurons that constitutes this is in continual and direct communication with our organs of sense – of sight, hearing, touch and so on – and all new information must be received by these neurons and transmitted by them to the rest of the memory, the long-term memory, for storage there. Information deteriorates very quickly in the short-term memory; it is lost completely after about 5 seconds unless it has been reactivated meanwhile; but it can persist in the long-term memory for hours, days or years without any reactivation except by unconscious processes which are perhaps the source of our dreams. Correspondingly, a much longer time is needed to register a piece of information in the long-term memory than in the short term, several seconds against a few hundredths of a second.

6.6.2 Perception

These few but important facts will perhaps make it easier to understand our attitudes to and difficulties in solving problems. The organisation of our memory into two levels shows that a vital part of our brain works in direct contact with certain organs, our *receptors*, which have conditioned the development of the brain throughout the course of evolution. The visual system has from the earliest times played a specially important role; in the process of inputting spatio-temporal information to the brain it has caused structures to be developed for the efficient coding of such information. Konrad Lorenz has no hesitation in claiming that it is because one species of the great apes, finding that life was becoming harder and hunting more difficult, began to need to imagine, doubtless in a very imprecise way, certain dangerous actions rather than actually perform them in the real world, that this species eventually developed into the human race; for this established the dominant importance of spatial representations. In fact, we use real space as a model to describe all other relations in our internal representations; language makes particularly frequent use of spatial concepts – for example, 'Do you see that clearly?'

One very important, and very surprising, point remains to be made, concerning the size of our short-term memory. Experiments indicate that this is very small: in man, only about seven elementary items, plus or minus two – we shall shortly consider what we mean by 'elementary items'. It is easy to convince ourselves that the capacity cannot be very great: we can give the product 7×8 more or less instantaneously; 72×8, because of the carry, gives the feeling of needing a small amount of memory management which takes rather more time; for 72×89 almost all of us will resort to the pencil and paper that forms part of our usual external memory. If we are not allowed such resources this last task will take much longer since, as we have seen, much time is needed for the exchanges between our internal short-term and long-term memories.

With a capacity of only seven items there is no possibility in problem-solving of holding images of past situations in the short-term memory; every new item destroys one already there, and it is this that makes back-tracking in a line of reasoning quite difficult.

We must now say more about the term 'elementary item'. This corresponds to a block of information that we can recognise, code and store immediately and is to be treated as an entity. What counts as 'elementary' will depend on the field and on the individual. Thus if a sequence of 0s and 1s is read out aloud most people will find it difficult to remember more than half a dozen; but a computer expert is likely to have had some experience of working in octal and therefore of coding blocks of three binary digits by a single octal digit; so he will be able to remember six or seven octals, corresponding to about 20 binaries (Table 6.7). Similarly, a professional musician stores a tune as he hears it played because he has in his long-term

Table 6.7.

Binary	1 0 1 1 0 0 1 0 1 0 1 1 0 0 0 0 1 0 1 1 1						Coding
Groups of 3	101	100	101	011	000	010	111
Octal coding	5	4	5	3	0	2	7

Coding:
000: 0   001: 1
010: 2   011: 3
100: 4   101: 5
110: 6   111: 7

Number to be remembered	5 453 027

memory a large amount of relevant high level information; whilst someone with an untrained ear will do well to recall the first 20 notes.

The conclusion is that the information in the short-term memory consists of pointers to larger blocks, of possible relevance, already stored in the long-term memory.

6.7 PSYCHOLOGICAL STUDIES OF CHESS PLAYERS

The work of de Groot, of Simon and of Winikoff has been concerned with two different aspects of chess playing, perception and reasoning respectively. de Groot in particular has been able to investigate these aspects in some quite outstanding subjects: he studied the approaches and methods of six Grandmasters (including two former world champions), four International Masters, two champions of the Netherlands and ten Experts.

6.7.1 Perception

In these experiments a board was placed in front of the subject with a position from a genuine game, usually from the middle game. It was exposed to him for a time $t1$, during which his eye movements were recorded, in some cases automatically by means of a camera fixed to his forehead. The pieces were then removed and after a further time $t2$ he was asked to reconstruct the position he had just seen. The observations of greatest interest were the order in which he replaced the pieces and number replaced correctly.

The first thing noticed was the small number of fixations of the eyes per second, never more than four. Each fixation gave a lateral vision of $2°$, corresponding to about nine adjacent squares. Further, fixations were repeated, even by the Grandmasters. With all the subjects the board was scanned, not in some geometrical or raster-like order, but in a logical order that depended on the particular position. The eyes hesitated over and returned to a certain critical square, from which they would move along a rank or a diagonal; the king's and the adjacent squares were always in this group. In contrast, certain pieces or configurations – for example, the White grouping f2, g2, h2, Rh1 – were 'photographed' only once; apparently such groupings constitute elementary items of information for an expert player and are stored by him as such. It was only over the less familiar configurations, particularly pieces in advanced positions or badly defended, that longer times were spent in the scan.

The actual conditions were that the board was shown for $t1 = 5$ seconds, the 'thinking' time was $t2 = 30$ seconds and the average number of pieces was 24.

All these expert players reconstructed the board in essentially the same way: after one piece had been placed it was followed by all those in some logical relation to it, by direct or indirect protection or by attack. In carrying out this process the player would, in cases of equality, consider first those pieces whose characteristics were the most unusual.

With the positions visible for such short times perfect reconstructions were scarcely to be expected, but the Grandmasters did in fact achieve this in 5 cases out of 14. Table 6.8 brings out the difference between players of master class and others. The score is evaluated from a function defined by de Groot, which takes account of the number of pieces correctly placed. 'Class C' players are of good club standard.

In these experiments it was seen that the Grandmasters in particular often did much more than merely reconstruct the position: they had already *analysed* it. They could not really do otherwise, because it is only by doing so that one can properly take it in – it is the 'lines of force' of the actions that direct their eyes. They already know the important moves that start from the given position or a few moves later.

These results reported by de Groot all concerned real chess positions, taken from actual games; when this was not the situation, but the pieces were placed on a board at random, all the players, from Grandmaster to club amateur, performed equally badly – none could memorise the board in the 5 seconds allowed.

One of those who took part in these tests were the Grandmaster and mathematician Euwe. Of the position of Fig. 6.13, which he had studied for 5 seconds, he said: 'I remember that my first thought was that Black had a very bad position.' He reconstructed the group of pieces around the black king: black queen, two knights, pawn on e6, white queen and lastly the black bishop on f8; then White's castling was done without any hesitation. The time interval between placing successive pieces was noted in these experiments; de Groot considered that if it were less than 2 seconds the separate pieces must have belonged to the same block of information in the player's memory. It seems that Euwe must have held images of two groups

Table 6.8 Reconstruction of positions shown briefly.

	Grandmasters	Masters	Experts	'Class C'
Perfect reconstructions out of 14	5	4	0	0
Score, out of 264	217	217	158	119

Fig. 6.13 A position to be reconstructed after being seen for 5 seconds (Black to move).

in this way. He commented that the general type of the position reminded him vaguely of the game between Flohr and Fine – but this could not be checked; however, it seems certain that this memory greatly helped him to memorise the position.

Continuing, the joined pawns a2, b2 and then the pawns h7, g6 and the rook h8 were placed as a group, whilst the remaining pieces were placed separately: e5, Nb5, Rb4, a7. Concerning this last pawn Euwe said: 'I didn't look at Black's right, but there must have been a black pawn on a7' – the logic of the game, with the pawns still on a2 and b2, dictates this. Clearly identifying himself with the player (Black) to move, he said he noticed other significant features. 'White's attack is pressing hard on Black, but I am two pieces ahead. What should I sacrifice? The White knight is very strong, so R × N would be a good move – that odd rook on b4 won't be missed. Now I think Black has a win – I shouldn't have said that a minute ago.'

We can see from this the stage at which perception becomes linked with reasoning; which brings us to the second object of our study.

6.7.2 Reasoning

In another series of tests a position, again taken from a real game, was put before each of the experts, who was asked to say what in his opinion was the best move, and to conduct his reasoning out loud. Figure 6.14 gives one of these positions, which was studied by de Groot with particular care: it was from one of his own matches. Here, White has no fewer than 56 legal

Fig. 6.14 White to move: what is his best move? (de Groot 1935).

moves. All the participants came to the immediate conclusion that the problem was essentially one of tactics: there was no need to look for a long term plan, but rather to solve the pressing problem of which of the many possible captures to make. Before giving a detailed analysis of the answers arrived at by the participants, let us give the very clear conclusions that can be drawn concerning their reasonings.

1. The search conducted is very selective. The tree in the Grandmasters' reasoning had between 20 and 56 nodes, a remarkably small number in view of the exponential rate of increase of the number of legal positions. On average, fewer than five initial moves by White were considered, Keres in particular studying only three, two of which (the best moves) he analysed completely. The entire group of 20 players considered a total of only 22 different moves out the 56 possibilities.

2. The search does not go very deep. The truth of this is supported by other evidence also. Contrary to what is often believed, the great players seldom think more than five or six moves ahead; and here four will suffice. No difference in this respect was found between the different classes of players.

3. Back-tracking in common. A move or even a whole episode is reconsidered several times, from which de Groot distinguished three phases in the players' analyses: exploration–elaboration–verification. The player will study the position afresh from a different point of view in each of these phases. A move is worked over several times and the study becomes steadily more serious. The problem that the player puts to himself is repeatedly re-defined in terms of the current working hypothesis, which itself evolves continually until the solution is reached; and at any stage all moves that do not have some relation to the hypothesis then in force are simply ignored. The player must have some means of measuring the distance he is from his hypothesis and from any goal he has set himself – that is, he must have a function for evaluating the position. Table 6.9 summarises some of the numerical observations.

4. Human players use a very concise form of evaluation. Phrases that occur often are of the type 'White now has a winning position, with a good passed pawn', 'Black has an open rank', 'The pressure of the attack is crushing'. Further, very few positions are actually evaluated. Evaluation is not relevant so long as a stable position has not been reached or the problem of the moment has not been solved by some means or other. In the end evaluation, like all analysis, is based on global concepts, far removed from a bald description of the position. It involves concepts such as open or closed positions, control (of a square, a piece or an area), strengths, weaknesses and relative safeties. Abstract moves such as 'Black queen's move', 'bishop's retreat', 'protection of the king', 'empty move', 'keeping up the pressure', 'retreat without losing any time' serve both to judge the position and to formulate and develop goals.

Let us now look in some detail at the choices made by the participants in this test, and at the reasons they gave for their decisions. The best move is B × Nd5 and many players gave this either first or second place; but surprisingly, often for the wrong reason. It is easy to see that this is a good move but the tree that must be searched in order to justify it fully is quite extensive; the search would bring problems of management of the short-term memory, so the experts tend to simplify the study by making rough evaluations. Thus Alekhine said at once: 'I should be very happy to have White here ... B × N is certainly very strong ... let's check ... but if time were running out I should play B × d5.' Building up the tree took him several minutes: keeping one's bearings in a big tree structure is difficult for

Table 6.9 Averages over all participants of observations made in the study of Fig. 6.14

	Different initial moves studied	Total positions studied	Maximum depth of search	Time	Number of backtracks
Grandmasters	4.8	35	6.8	9 min 6 sec	6.6
Experts	3.4	30.8	6.6	10 min 8 sec	6.4

everyone and even a Grandmaster can get lost. Flohr, for example, made a plain mistake in this test; considering among many possibilities the variant

1. N × Bc6   b7 × N
2. B × Nd5   c6 × B
3. B × Nf6   B × B

he said that 4 Nd7 would be a fork on the black queen and rook: but he had confused the position with the memory of another, for the knight on e5 was no longer there to move to d7.

There was certainly one feature common to all the responses: all these experts drew on a considerable knowledge of chess. Thus Alekhine said straight away that the position reminded him of a recent game of Botwinnik's, that the opening must have been Queen's Gambit Accepted and the position that at the 16th move; he even thought he could reconstruct the whole of the opening game. It is clear that it was his knowledge of very many games either played or studied that enabled Alekhine to categorise this position and locate it correctly on the tree held in his memory. The same knowledge, which also enabled him to reconstruct the game, directed his analysis of the position: White, with the advantage of a very open position and the advantage of the attack, had harassed Black from the start, whilst Black had to resist to the end of the game; so Black's only chances depended on his having a better pawn structure.

It is just here that differences in chess culture between different players come into effect. A well-known heuristic rule says, in effect, that a bishop is slightly more valuable than a knight, especially in the end game when it can move freely over the board; relying on this the less strong player will reject the move B × d5, since this will result in the loss of the bishop with 'only' a knight in return. But the master player knows that he must mount the decisive attack before the end of the game, so there is no need to take this rule into account. For him the essential features of the position are: the White attack, which must be kept up; the strength of the knight on e5, threatening Nd7; the relativeness of Black's castling; the undefended white pawn b2, with possible capture by the black queen; and the captures N × d5, B × f6, B × d5, N × f6. These dictate where White moves should be examined in detail; further, the order in which they should be considered is crucial and the best players arrive at this, and then at the solution, by carrying out the developments in parallel.

Table 6.10 gives the development as far as the fourth move of the tree starting from White's initial B × Nd5. The effects of these four moves overlap a great deal and the important thing is to have all four in mind. Since in the given position the white knight could have very strong forks from d7 or e7 it is natural for White to remove the black knights from the board whilst retaining his own. The exchange with the bishop at a2, which is not doing very much, is soon considered and given high priority because this corresponds best to the spirit of the attack. Thus the analysis represented by Table 6.10 is carried out only very partially, even by the Grandmasters.

Three important conclusions concerning chess players follow very clearly from these psychological studies:

1. It is not computing power that makes the great players but their ability to choose the best moves to study.
2. This ability is related to remarkable powers of assimilation of the position, considered as a whole.
3. The acuity of this perception is a function of the breadth of the player's chess knowledge and in particular of the large number of high level concepts that he must carry in his head and be able to recognise in any position confronting him.

Table 6.10 Tree for testing the move B × Nd5 in the position of Fig. 6.14.

1	White			B × Nd5					
1	Black	B × Bd5		N × Bd5		e6 × Bd5			
2	W	B × Nf6		N × Nd5		Qf3 (b)	Ng4 (b)	Ne4 (b)	Re1 (g)
2	B	B × Bf6	Qd8		e6 × d5				
3	W	Nd7 (a)	N × Be7 + (c)		B × e7 (e)				
3	B	Q moves	K moves						
4	W	N × Rf8 (b)	N × c8 (d)						

Notes:
(a) fork on Q, R
(b) ultimate gain in position
(c) fork on K, R
(d) gain of piece and in position
(e) gain of a piece: if 2 ... B × Nd5 3 B × Nf6
(f) Black's N on f6 is now very weak and White has a strong attack
(g) Black's B on e7 threatened by a discovered attack

The fact that White has four possible responses after e6 × B is enough to show that that is not a good move for Black. It is easily shown that White gains in every variant, but the pressure is great enough for all the master players to be satisfied with this depth of analysis.

Psychologists have also studied human problem-solving behaviour in fields other than chess. For example, Newall and Simon (1982) investigated the way students went about solving problems in propositional logic (cf. Chapter 3) and cryptarithmetical puzzles (cf. Chapter 8); the strategies developed by these students and the knowledge they called on were expressed in the form of production rules (cf. Chapter 7), enabling their general approach to be modelled with reasonable fidelity. Mathieu and Thomas (1985) have reported studies made with the game GO, with analyses of electrical circuits and with mechanical problems.

All these observations confirm the conclusions just given: the basic faculty brought into play by the solver is that which enables him to detect in the situation facing him the important groupings of the objects concerned – meaning objects linked by the maximum number of significant relations. This faculty is related to experience in the field of the problem, to knowledge of the subject and to the quality of structuring of this knowledge.

6.8   ROBIN: AN INTELLIGENT CHESS PROGRAM

In Section 6.1 we studied a first type of program for playing chess, and noted that the characteristics of programs of this type were very different from those of human players. Since a human performs better than a program in this difficult field, it is of prime importance for researchers in artificial intelligence to understand how it is that the human gets better results by developing a search tree a thousand or ten thousand times smaller than that needed by the machine. The best way to gain this understanding would be to write a program based on some principle different from exhaustive enumeration of moves, and it was this challenge that Jacques Pitrat, a research worker at the CNRS in Paris, took up in 1972.

The crucial observation is this: if there is such a difference in scale between the trees used by the human player and the machine respectively, then they cannot be the same tree.

The work of Binet, de Groot and Simon has shown that the expert player sees very quickly the features that characterise a position; he literally 'sees' the possible moves that must be given priority in consideration. Thus the good player starts his search with a very deep analysis of the initial position; a very precise vocabulary enables him to describe its potentialities in fine detail and its strong points and the weaknesses of each possible move are perceived and registered. The entire search for the best move is guided by this analysis, both in breadth – by restriction to those moves that the analysis has shown to be relevant – and in depth – by going down through the levels until a stable position is reached after the instabilities caused by the intermediate moves.

Another difference between the machine and the human player is that in the mind of the latter the moves are not played in the order in which they would be played on a real board: impossible moves are envisaged, a move is considered several steps before it can be played; in sum, plans are formed, developed, questioned, abandoned, taken up again and completed, right up to the final choice of the move.

Thus what the human player considers is a tree of plans, and not the huge unintelligent tree of moves of the naive program. Most of the moves found by Jacques Pitrat's program would be missed completely by these other programs – and sometimes even by good human players. We have come now to a second family of game-playing programs, far removed from the first and alone of interest in artificial intelligence because the underlying principles can be applied in many other human activities.

Pitrat's program is called ROBIN; before describing it in some detail we give an example to illustrate its behaviour.

6.8.1 An example of ROBIN's analysis (Fig. 6.15)

The program starts by making a deep analysis of the position; it constructs plans for possible actions by its side, White, among which are:

B1 direct attack on the enemy king, starting with Qh7+
B2 attack on both king and queen by Re1.
B3 capture of the unprotected Black Queen, Q × Q.

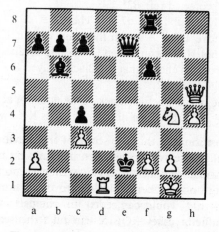

Fig. 6.15 White to move (position E42).

These plans are for sequences of moves, determined in each case by a definite goal to be attained; each goal here is the capture of either the king or the queen. The goals are often very ambitious, sometimes unattainable, but in developing the plans the program will try to make possible those moves that are not, initially, actually impossible, to create threats, disturb the enemy's position and finally either to attain the goal or at least to gain some advantage.

In this process the program works not forwards as the moves would be played in an actual game but backwards from the goal, arguing from there to the starting position in order to decide the correct first move. The move played as a result of this may seem surprising and unnatural to anyone who is not aware of the goal being aimed at.

In this example the program develops $B1$ and $B2$, but in the end it is $B3$ that will succeed when the possible Black replies are taken fully into account. We give below only the plan that finally succeeds; the program examines many variants.

- The program envisages capturing Black's queen by $Q \times Qe2$.
- Therefore the white knight on g4 must be moved.
- But Black could reply $Q \times Qh5$.
- Therefore in moving Kg4 a black piece of value at least equal to the queen must be attacked: the only possibility is Black's king.
- Therefore the sub-goal 'use Kg4 to put Ke7 in check' is created.
- This cannot be done directly, the only relevant squares to which the knight can move being e5 and f6.
- Therefore another sub-goal is 'move the black king'.
- The only piece that can be of any use in this is the rook on d1; any moves of the queen are ruled out by possibility $Q \times Q$.
- Square e1 is not protected (cf. $B2$).
- Therefore the only possibility is d7 with check.
- Hence the key move 1 Rd7 + ! with the main variant 1 Rd7 +, K × R; 2 Nf6 + (certainly not Ne5 because then $Q \times N$ and escapes capture), R × N.
- 3 $Q \times Qe2$; the program checks that the Black reply ... B × f2 + or ... R × f2 gives no advantage to Black.
- There remains the possibility that Black's king does not accept the poisoned chalice offered by Rd7; but then his only move is Ke6, when 2 Qd5 mate.

Admittedly this position is within the scope of the previous programs, the maximum depth of the search being seven half moves; but it shows very clearly the possibility of needing only a very sparse tree to be constructed in order to find the best move – here only 305 moves are considered, whereas 40^7 or another 16×10^{10} would be needed for exhaustive enumeration. As we shall see, in difficult cases ROBIN can take the search down to 20 half-moves or more.

6.8.2   Different types of plan in chess

The analysis of the initial position here is oriented entirely towards detecting favourable configurations; it is these configurations that give rise to the plans, that is, to sequences of goals (which themselves are generalised moves) that in the end will result in some significant advantage. Thus the program concerns itself with such configurations. For ROBIN there are four types of plan, the simplest being just the capture of an enemy piece.

Type 1 plan – simple capture. The program lists for each piece the number and value of every piece that either attacks or protects it: this is a straightforward algorithmic procedure and is fast; 'discovered' (i.e. masked by another piece) attacks and protections are included. A balance sheet is then drawn up and every piece that is less defended than attacked is registered as open to capture and becomes the source of a plan.

In the position of Fig. 6.15 the black queen is virtually *en prise*; for Black, White's rook on d1 and pawn on a2 are immediately *en prise* whilst the pawn f2 and the knight g4 can be captured either by a further attack or by removing at least one of the defending pieces.

Type 2 plan – the double attack. Here a single piece attacks several enemy pieces (usually two) simultaneously; it is clearly more promising than simple capture. The enemy having only one move in reply can save only one of his threatened pieces.

The enemy king can always be one of the pieces attacked in a fork; it is never directly defendable.

Here the program puts the question to its move generator; 'Is there a square to which one of my pieces can move so as to attack two enemy pieces from there, both open to immediate capture?' The generator would be allowed some liberties, thus either the target square could be occupied already and therefore a sub-goal created to remove the occupying piece, or an intervening square could be occupied and would have to be freed. For the position of Fig. 6.16 the analysis shows that White's king e1 and pawn a2 could be threatened simultaneously by the black queen on e6; this square is at present occupied by a black pawn which must first be removed, as must also the pawn d5 which masks a2.

Type 3 plan – attacking the king. At some stage in any chess game particular attention must be given to the special role of the king: if this were unable to escape capture, then everything would be ended, and this fact can be a rich source of enemy plans.

All moves that give check are the beginning of plans, certainly when the attacking piece is not itself attacked or, if it is, the only move open to the

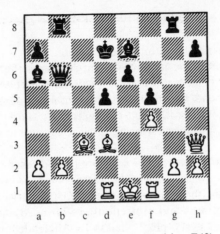

Fig. 6.16 Black to move (position E42).

attacked king is to take the piece. Thus in the position of Fig. 6.15 the move
Rd7 + does not introduce a plan whilst Qf7 + does because in the second
case there is no square to which the king can retreat and the attack is much
stronger. However, the plan must be developed further so as to find if it is
possible on the one hand to remove the black rook from f8 and on the other
to protect the white queen on f7.

Type 4 plan – pawn promotion. As well as the king there is one other piece
that plays a special role – the pawn: for when a pawn reaches the eight rank
it can be changed into any other piece – a queen, for example, although it
would not be sound to plan that any arbitrary pawn should be promoted to
queen. In the middle game, therefore, the program identifies the passed
pawns (pawns with no enemy piece on their own or immediately adjacent
files) and constructs plans for those already on the sixth or seventh ranks.
The simplest plan is to progress the pawn to the eighth rank, provided that
the balance remains favourable; if a friendly piece blocks the way then
ROBIN considers:

either removing that piece

or   causing an enemy piece to move to an adjacent square so that the pawn
       can move diagonally to capture it.

All these initial plans are generated by the program, in parallel and for
both sides. In order to restrict the subsequent search to plans that have a
good chance of succeeding against any defence, it retains only those that
require at most two modifications to intermediate squares.

6.8.3 A language for expression and execution of plans

1. The language. Just as it is convenient to have a standard coding for moves, for example Rd7, b2 × c3, 0–0, as an aid to generating and manipulating these, it is useful for a program that generates a tree structure of plans to have a language in which to express the actions or 'super-moves' that enter into these plans.

A typical action is a request to modify a square that has already been encountered; the state of a square, at the time of consideration, is coded as follows: *V* – vacant (empty, unoccupied); *F* – occupied by a friendly piece; *E* – occupied by an enemy piece; in the two latter cases the name of the occupying piece is given, so that, for example, QEe2 means that the square e2 is occupied by the enemy queen. The actions are then as follows:

QE.e2 → V   remove the enemy queen from square e2

E.a4 → ¬E   change the enemy occupation of a4 to either vacant or friendly occupation

V.a8 → E ⩾ N   cause an enemy knight or stronger piece to occupy a8 which is at present unoccupied

NF.g4 → V*   move the friendly knight from g4: the star ⋆, which can be attached to any action, means '... and keep up the attack'

Thus for Fig. 6.16 the plan for the fork by the black queen is expressed:

F.d5 → V*   move the black pawn d5, keeping up the attack

F.e6 → V*   similarly for e6

QF.b6 → e6   move the white queen from b6 to e6

QF.e6 → e1 **or** a2   consummation of the fork

2. Developing the plans. The program studies the plans one after the other and specifies each action by stating one of the moves to bring it about; thus a single initial plan can give rise to several derived plans. Actions that cannot be performed directly are completed by other means. Thus the program 'knows' that 'remove a piece' means:

- If it is friendly, simply move it:

    In Fig. 6.15 NF.g4 → V* will first be interpreted as
        NF.g4 → h2 **or** f2 **or** e3 **or** e5 **or** f6 **or** h6.

- if it is enemy, either capture it
        or attack it
        or give it something to capture.

In Fig. 6.18 again, none of the knight's moves listed above meet the requirement, indicated by the star, of keeping the initiative, so the program must create the new action

KE.e7 → V* because having the initiative here means 'removing' the king.

We have just seen, as does the program, that the knight can neither capture nor attack nor be taken, so there remains to be considered the rook on d1; with this the new action is interpreted

RF.d1 → R × K*   capture of the king

or

RF.d1 → T + *   attack the king

or

RF.d1 → Rd6 or d7 or d8*   giving the king something to capture

There is of course no chess move corresponding to the first of these actions, so this is ignored; the second requires Rd7 which is possible and fulfils also the third possibility; so the development of this plan is pursued:

1. Rd7   K × d7
2. N × f6 +   K moves
3. Q × Q

It is by proceeding in this way that the program builds up a repertoire of sub-goals on which it can draw in order to achieve any type of action. Take another example: to prevent a capture – a frequent need – the threatened side must either displace the capturing piece or interpose a piece, which can be either friendly or enemy, between that and the threatened piece. In Fig. 6.16 a possible plan for Black involves Qe3 +, but White would reply immediately Q × Q; the idea of interposition suggests

V.g3 → ¬V (cause anything to occupy g3)
QF.b6 → e3 +

A particular interpretation of the 'anything' of the first action is a white pawn (here White is the 'enemy', as it is Black's move that is being considered); and the pawn on h2 can move to g3 if it is given something there to capture. So V.g3 → ¬V is rewritten PE.h2 → g3 and a black piece must be removed to g3 – for the sole reason that this is what the plan requires. The only possibility is the rook on g8, so we have now:

1. Rg3   h2 × g3
2. Qe3 +   Be2

The last move here is generated by the program, which is devising plans for the enemy (White) at the same time, using the same idea of interposition. But the simple capture Q × e2 + is possible for Black, who gains by this.

Another idea for White to remove the threat R × Q by the rook on g3 is of course Q × R; but then the white queen (who must move, in view of the success of the initial plan) has moved to another square. A legal move can make her move again: this is Bh4, found at once by the program with the help of its stock of sub-goals; and as a result Black gains White's queen.

The program constructs and rejects very many plans in the course of this investigation; it can happen that:

- A move that is vital to the plan proves impossible to make: for example, because of captures.
- The balance of material would turn out to be highly unfavourable, or at any rate worse than the stated requirements, even if the plan succeeded.
- A logical impossibility would be encountered, such as the need for the same sequence to be both empty and occupied by one of one's own pieces.
- A constraint could not be satisfied: for example, because there was no suitable move.
- The plan is rejected by an optimistic simulation: even if all goes well, the final material advantage is negative.

Finally, as plans are being made and modified continually the program must keep a record of the basic idea underlying each one. This can be done by means of a special action that expresses the requirement to check some condition at a given instant: for example, if the aim is to free a particular square so that a certain piece can be displaced, a check must be made after further moves have been added, and possible interferences considered, to ensure that the square is indeed empty at the instant required.

6.8.4 Optimising the defence:
the idea of the dangerous move

The method of working of the ROBIN program is such that at any instant it is considering the play of one player only, the one who will lose if the current plan succeeds; at each stage he is aiming for a gain that the other is aiming to deny him by constructing his own plans and may regain the advantage. Thus the program's attention may alternate between the two sides until finally one can find no way to save himself and becomes the loser.

With this approach the program's development of the search tree seems very similar to the way the human player goes about it, essentially following the most promising looking path first and investigating how far, in the worst case, the opponent can defeat the aim. If a potential defeat is found

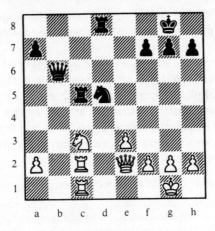

Fig. 6.17 Black to move.

then another line of play, at the level above in the tree, is considered; if this in turn runs into difficulties then the first is taken up again and developed to a deeper level, and so on. Thus the entire play is concerned with finding ways to counter 'dangerous moves' – a term that will be defined later in this section. The aim of each side is to avoid the worst fate by making it impossible for the opponent to play a planned dangerous move or at least to reduce the effects by means of dangerous moves of his own.

A plan that will confound the enemy's plan must defeat all his planned dangerous moves. To achieve this the underlying idea is to react differently to the different types of dangerous move encountered; four types can be defined, and an appropriate response given for each type.

The definition of a dangerous move for ROBIN is related to the concept of evaluation and of ascending the tree by the minimax procedure; the value assigned to a leaf node is taken simply to be the material balance there.

Suppose the program is looking for a plan for player A that will give him a value $v(A)$; a dangerous move by the opponent is then any move that will result in A's value being less than the goal $v(A)$.

Consider the example of Fig. 6.17. One of the plans generated by the program involves getting the black rook d8 to d1, where it will control all the squares to which the white king can move; this plan is expressed:

NF.d5 → V	remove the knight
RF.d8 → D1	bring the rook to d1
RF.d1 → R × K	

With the balance advantageous to Black (capture of the king) this move is dangerous for White so the program, which now takes White's side, seeks to

counter it and at once finds Q × Rd1 and R × Rd1. But Black's move
NF.d5 → V could be NF.d5 × Nc3 which also is dangerous for White;
however the balance is again quickly restored by R × Nc3, and Black has no
further dangerous moves: all threats have been removed and the program
considers again White's play. The three White moves just noted are of
course dangerous from Black's point of view.

Later we shall complete the program's analysis of this position so as to
show how it classifies the dangerous moves and counters possible replies.

The four classes of response to a dangerous move are: new captures,
logical destruction of the move, interferences, local plans. We consider
these separately.

1. New captures. Every move in chess, apart from castling and capture *en
passant*, changes the content of precisely two squares, so at any stage the
last enemy move and the friendly move immediately preceding this will have
modified four squares. At every stage the program looks to see if these four
changes have created possibilities for captures – resulting, of course, in
values greater than that of the dangerous move that is to be countered.

In a standard chess position this first class of responses very quickly
enables those plans to be rejected which, from this point of view, do not
lead to the gains that are sought.

2. Logical destructions. This is simply a matter of removing the dangerous
move from the list of legal moves available to the opponent.

The effect can be achieved by acting on either the square from which the
move would start, or on which it would end, or on an intermediate square.
Thus if the move would consist of a piece X on square p moving to square q,
causing this piece to leave p corresponds to the action:

$$XE.p \rightarrow \neg E$$

whilst if the friendly piece Y is on q the action:

$$YF.q \rightarrow \neg F$$

frustrates the dangerous move. The third action involves causing some
piece, on whichever side, to occupy one of the originally empty squares (*u*
say) on the line between p and q:

$$V.u \rightarrow \neg V$$

3. Interferences. Here attack is considered as one of the possible defensive
actions. The program allows the enemy to carry out its plan but takes
advantage of the resulting changes to the board to lay down a counter-plan
that will be triggered later.

This type of defence is very deceiving; in this context ROBIN has had to 'correct' some analyses made by famous players – cf. the position of Fig. 6.20 below. The possibility of proceeding thus arises from two reasons:

(a) The actions that constitute the plans are not necessarily legal on a real board; they are therefore not affected by certain changes and the plans can remain viable during several subsequent moves.
(b) Since the plans of both sides are generated in parallel by the program, if danger threatens for the enemy it is simple for the program to take its side and try out the plans.

When the first action of such a defensive plan becomes a possibility it is placed, together with the corresponding plan, in the list of actions to be considered in response to the last enemy move.

4. *Local plans.* This refers to building an indirect attack on the piece that could make a dangerous move, such as a fork, a threat of mate or of a capture. This analysis is very similar to that carried out at the start for all the pieces on the board; here it is restricted to a single square.

6.8.5 Some results

This completes the account of the main elements of Pitrat's ROBIN program; the difference from brute-force programs built around alpha–beta pruning is clear: this program genuinely reasons about the game, following a plan that it itself has generated.

There is no *a priori* limit in either depth or breadth to the program's search. The tree that it develops is a tree of plans, that is, of sequences of actions or 'meta-moves' that can give rise to groups of legal moves. This tree is very much smaller than the trees of real moves generated by the previous programs and further, only those actions are developed that are relevant to the plans that are actually studied. An important point is that the investigation does not proceed according to the order in which the moves would be played on a real board but according to the logical sequence in which the actions of the plan should be performed.

The program's performance in analysing real chess positions is broadly up to human players: it has found combinations that had escaped such outstanding players as Euwe, Lasker or Smyslov or analysts such as Mont, and has shown that certain combinations given by Mont and Tarrasch are not valid. We shall now consider some examples.

Example 1 (Fig. 6.18). This is a very difficult position; but going down to a depth of 23 half-moves the program will show that White, if he makes the

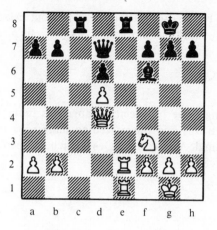

Fig. 6.18 White to move.

best moves possible, can gain at least a rook against any defense.

The idea underlying the plan is to attack Black's king by R × Re8 +, when the king has no means of escape; the plan will succeed because the black queen on d7, who has to protect both c8 and e8, has too much to do. Thus the plan, P1 say, is:

P1: R × R.e8
     R × K.g8

The second move of P1 is dangerous for Black − it could not be more dangerous! − who will resist by capturing the threatening piece. Either of two black pieces, the queen or the rook, is available to take Re8 and so destroy White's plan; this is therefore changed to P2:

P2: QE.d7 → ¬QE
     RE.c8 → ¬RE
     P1

Black's queen has to be moved from the vital square d7; we have already seen that the program has several strategies for such a purpose, one of which is to sacrifice a piece whose capture will have the effect of moving a defending piece. Here, one possible plan among several is P3:

P3:   QF.d4 → g4
       ¬QE.d7   achievable by either QF × Qd7 or QE × Qg4
       P2

At this point the program sees that Black still has a dangerous move: if he moves his queen to b5 she can still control e8 without risk of capture. White must therefore deny Black this move, and can do so by means of a new plan P4, which is a sub-plan of P3:

P4: QE.b5 → ¬QE
     P2

From the beginning there has been a dangerous move for Black in P2: Rc8 × e8, and both this and the preceding dangerous move Qb5 can be prevented by the single White move Qc4, which can be followed by either Q × Qb5 or Q × Rc8:

P5:   QF.g4 → c4
      QF × Qb5
      ¬QE.b5
      P2

It is by continually pursuing the black queen, with the original aim in mind, that White finally succeeds in carrying out the plan; the main variant is:

1. Qg4!   Qb5
2. Qc4!   Qd7
3. Qc7!   Qb5
4. a4   Q × a4
5. Re4   Qb5
6. Qb7   black queen is captured, otherwise Re8 mate

There are several other possibilities for Black; for example, 5 ... R × e4 followed by 6. Q × c8, R × e8 but then 7. Q × e8 +

Altogether, to prove that the first move is the right one and will win Black's queen whatever he does the analysis has to be taken down to 23 half-moves; in one variant, at depth 11 Black has no fewer than 26 moves to choose from. We see from this that the program can find the perfect play, and can prove that it is perfect; this last feature is not necessary to the human player, who needs only to convince himself that a move will not bring him a loss and in most variants will bring a gain. For this example we do not have the space to give the proof that 1. Qg4 is the best move: the program showed that at least 2454 variants would have to be examined in order to establish this.

Example 2 (Fig. 6.19). Berliner gave this position in his thesis to show how it was that in some cases the tree had to be continued to very great depths.

Berliner's own program found the correct move in this way: Black's king is in danger because it cannot move to any of the surrounding squares, so Qh5 + could be fatal. A program based on exhaustive enumeration quickly

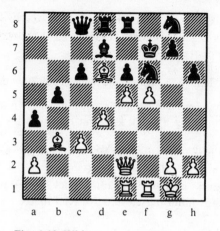

Fig. 6.19 White to move (H. Berliner).

rejects this move after one or two exchanges because it does not 'see' how to recover the white queen after N × Qh5.

ROBIN, on the other hand, taking White's side, looks for a way to counter this dangerous Black move, N × Q. A local examination of the threatening knight's square reveals the possibility of a counter-attack – a fork – on the same piece: this can be exerted by the rook on f1, provided that the (friendly) pawn on f5 can be removed. This is easily achieved by the legal move f5 × e6, but the program sees that this would allow the Black move Re8 × e6, which would be dangerous for White and moreover would frustrate the plan by opening an escape route for Black's king.

However, Qh5 followed by f5 × e6 remains playable because this second move gives check (in fact, double check after N × Q) and the king has only one square to retreat to; so the plan is developed further, in parallel with several others, although the program knows that it must recover at least a Queen after the first exchange:

1. Qh5   N × h5

Restricting the analysis to the squares occupied by the black king gives the following sequence:

2. f5 × e6 + +   Kg6
3. Bc2 +   Kg5
4. Rf5 +   Kg6   Other plans are studied, but this one leads to 5, with the strength of the new double check

5. Rf6 + +   Kg5

6. Rg6 +	Rh4	The rook on g6, protected by the Bishop c2 and the white king, can now advance towards the enemy
7. Re4 +	Nf4	
8. Rf4	Kh5	The second white rook now enters

So far all Black's moves have been forced, allowing white to carry out his plan unopposed, pursuing a black king cut off from his troops: no Black piece can play.

The rest is easy. It is premature for White to deliver the death blow Rh4 because of the danger of Black's reply K × Rh4; this is prevented by the simple move of the white pawn: 9. g3 (any Black move); no black piece can intervene, the King is immobilised and 10. Rh4 mate.

Example 3 (Fig. 6.20). In his book Tarrasch shows the gain of a pawn by the following:

   1. B × h2 +   2. K × h2   Qh4 +   3. Kg1 followed by Q × Ba4!

This is based on a planned fork on h2 and Ba4; but a program that generates plans for White at the same time will see a possible interference by means of a White fork on c7 and Rf8 after freeing the square c5, which last is brought about by the first move of Black's plan. Thus White's plan is put into action after the above moves by:

   4. Qe7!

One possible reply for Black is to protect the two threatened pieces by the one move 4. ... Bd7. But a White plan to attack either Black's bishop or his

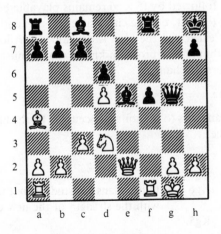

Fig. 6.20 Black to move.

queen, which alone protect each other, and another to attack the badly defended pawn d7, both give Rf4, then Rh4, with an advantage to White that cancels that of Black's pawn capture.

Thus ROBIN showed that Tarrasch's analysis was incomplete.

Chapter 7

EXPERT SYSTEMS

As time goes by, computers will be used less and less for handling numerical information. Until recently most software consisted of algorithms for working with complete information, but in this chapter we shall be considering a class of programs – expert systems – intended as aids to human reasoning in well-defined fields, whose characteristic features are manipulation of symbolically expressed knowledge, reasoning with uncertain and incomplete knowledge and communication with the human user in a modular, non-procedural language. The chapter is in three parts: the first, 7.1–7.4, deals with the formal concept of such systems and describes some realisations, the second, 7.5, discusses further the idea of an expert system and studies several methods for representing knowledge, whilst finally the third part, 7.6, describes work now being done on future programming languages of this kind.

Much of the early work in AI had ambitious goals and aimed to attack very broad fields, for example automatic translation from one natural language to another with any subject matter whatever, general problem solving (cf. GPS), theorem proving in any field (cf. resolution principle). In our own human case, however, it is very clear that an individual can be a master in one field but perform very badly in another; and this is because, in any particular field, man has accumulated a vast body of knowledge over the centuries on which the expert draws, but usually can do so in only one field. AI systems have developed considerably during the last few years as a result of taking note of this; it is now (1989) seen that very good performance can be obtained only by confining the program to a narrow, well defined field, the relevant knowledge of which it 'knows' how to learn, to structure and to manipulate. Such programs already exist: they are called Expert Systems and their aim is to equal the performance of the best human expert in the particular field. This chapter will be concerned with the methods used in such systems for representing large bodies of knowledge.

A particularly important point is that these systems are intended as aids to humans; therefore, to be useful they must be able to conduct a dialogue with a human specialist in a language that is natural to him. It follows that the system must be fully understood by the expert and when necessary must be able to explain and justify its reasoning to him. This implies that the knowledge items used by the system are kept separate from the methods of using them and are accessible to the system itself; and that the method of reasoning is both simple and robust so as to be easily explainable when the need arises.

Finally and above all it must be easy for the expert to transfer his knowledge to the system. The latter will be all the richer if each of several experts gives it his own specialist knowledge, and for this to be a realistic aim it must be possible for the knowledge items to be provided as a sequence of statements in any order, with no pre-judging of the way in which they will be used (in contrast to the fixed order required by classical algorithmic procedures) and for the system itself to structure the knowlege, compare each new item with what it has already and so update its model of the field.

We start our study of expert systems with two actual dialogues with a famous medical system, MYCIN; these concern respectively a diagnosis and an explanation by the system of how it reached its conclusions. A conversational correction of the system's knowledge base is given in Section 7.2.5.

7.1 EXAMPLES OF DIALOGUE WITH AN EXPERT SYSTEM

7.1.1 A medical diagnosis

MYCIN: My therapeutic recommendations will be based on the probabilities of infection by the following potentially infectious
organisms:

1. *pseudomonas aeruginosa*   2. *klebsiella pneumoniae*
3. *escherichia coli*   4. *bacteroides fragilis*
5. *enterobacter*   6. *proteus non mirabilis*

Please tell me the seriousness of Mr. Smith's illness on a scale
increasing from 0 to 4.

User: 3.
MYCIN: Does he show allergic reactions to any microbial agent?
User: No.

MYCIN: What is his weight in kilograms?
User: 70.
MYCIN: My first recommendation, to cover the points ⟨123456⟩, is to give
          clindamycine, dose 595 mg for 14 days.
          Would you wish not to administer certain drugs?
User: Yes, clindamycine.
MYCIN: To cover ⟨23456⟩ give chloramphenicol 1 g for 14 days.
          • Monitor the patient's white corpuscle count
          To cover ⟨1⟩ give gentamicine 119 mg for 10 days
          • Change the dose if there is any renal weakness.

7.1.2 Explanation by the system of its own reasoning

MYCIN: Was the patient's infection contracted in hospital?
User: Why?
TEIRESIAS   (Why it is important to know this)
                This will help to decide the category to which the responsible
                organism belongs.

                • it has already been established that: 1. it is Gram negative
                  2. it is rod-shaped 3. it grows either in or out of air
                • thus if the infection was not contracted during the
                  patient's stay in hospital it is almost certain (prob. 0.8)
                  that the organism is of the category enterobacteriacae; it
                  could be (prob. 0.1: Rule 37) pseudomonas aeruginosa

User: Why haven't you considered the possibility that it is a
                streptococcus?
TEIRESIAS: Rule 33 would have to be used to identify the organism as a
                streptococcus, but the second clause 'morphology of type
                coccus' is already known to be false so Rule 33 is not
                invoked.

7.2   THE MYCIN–TEIRESIAS SYSTEM

MYCIN, together with the supplementary programs TEIRESIAS and
BAOBAB, is a typical expert system that makes active use of a large body of
knowledge given in the form of declarative statements; in this section we
describe its aims, its method of working and its importance.

7.2.1 The aims

MYCIN was conceived as an interactive system that would help a doctor in diagnosing and treating bacterial infections of the blood. It conducts a consultation, in English, with the doctor, who gives it all available relevant information about the patient and the results of any laboratory tests; this information is usually incomplete since, for example, the results of bacterial cultures are commonly not known for 24–48 hours. Accepting this absence of complete information, MYCIN's reasoning is based on a set of knowledge items given to it in the form of production rules – defined and explained in Section 7.3.1; the system can explain its reasoning when requested. The knowledge can be augmented or changed in any other way and at any instance MYCIN has a model of this knowledge, and in a sense 'knows what it knows'.

7.2.2 The importance of MYCIN

MYCIN is one of the most fully developed systems in AI. It is important for two reasons: the techniques that it employs are of general application, and the program is fully operational in its special field, giving high quality results that are of practical use.

The system originated in Shortliffe's PhD thesis at Stanford University (1974). It is the main link in a chain of studies carried out by John McCarthy's group as part of the Stanford Heuristic Programming Project, and was developed in close collaboration with the doctors in the Infectious Diseases Group in the Medical School. However, the same AI researchers – mainly Buchanan and Feigenbaum – using the same methods had already built an organic chemistry expert system, DENDRAL (with METADEN-DRAL), in 1968; and since 1974 this multi-disciplinary group, interested in different aspects of the automation of scientific reasoning, has completed MYCIN by adding a knowledge-acquisition system TEIRESIAS, written by R. H. Davis (1976), described in Section 7.2.5, and BAOBAB (Alain Bonnet, 1980), for the automatic construction of the facts base for a patient from the medical history.

Subsequently this group has turned its attention to other fields, as varied as treatment of meningitis, diagnosis of pulmonary infections, genetic manipulation, mineral prospecting and automobile repair: which shows the power and generality of the methods. Here is a suitable place to note that the problem of diagnosis, even when restricted to so well-defined a subject as microbial infection, is complex; thus in that field:

1. There is no universal panacea that will treat all infectious illnesses.
2. It has been found that every year penicillin is given to one out of four people, whilst it is known that this is ineffective in nine cases out of ten; therefore the seriousness of any infection should be checked before any treatment is prescribed.
3. It follows further from 2 that as much information as possible should be obtained concerning the organism responsible for any serious infection; but this is difficult, because the laboratories need 48 hours or even longer for tests that will give precise enough information.
4. It often happens that the infection is so serious that some treatment must be given before any laboratory results become available, and sometimes – in the case of virulent bacterial infection after heart surgery, for example – in the absence of any specialist advice.
5. To complicate matters still further, incompatibilities can arise between the patient and certain treatments – allergic reactions, raised blood pressure, effects of age, ...

Any diagnostic system, whether human or a computer program, must have all possible information on these points, must know how these may interact with one another and must be able to make a decision in a very short time – a decision based on incomplete information and necessarily a compromise between the best possible treatment and the time needed to determine this. Nevertheless, the problem, though complex, is well defined; it is not necessary to have a general medical knowledge, beyond a theoretical model of bacterial infection or of bacterial resistance to antibiotics.

We shall see later that the representation of knowledge in declarative form, with the help of production rules, is well adapted to the diagnostic problem; further, it eases the generation of a dialogue with the user in natural language, enabling the program to explain its reasoning. Finally, such a system, kept always up-to-date, can act as a good teacher and can help the specialist to keep abreast of new developments.

7.2.3 The structure of MYCIN

The essential components of MYCIN are a knowledge base – a set of given rules – and four main programs, all of which co-operate as shown in Fig. 7.1.

7.2.3.1 The rules

The main source of MYCIN's knowledge is a base of about 400 'production rules', each of which consists of a set of premises describing a particular

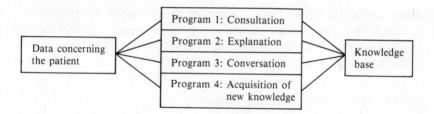

Fig. 7.1 Principle of MYCIN.

situation and a set of actions to be undertaken if all the premises are satisfied. Thus each rule is of the form:

if P_1 **and** P_2 **and** ... **and** P_i **then** a_1 **and** a_2 **and** ... **and** a_j

where the P_i are the premises and the a_m the actions. In MYCIN the predicates all have the form of quadruplets:

⟨predicate⟩⟨object⟩⟨attribute⟩⟨value⟩

Examples are:

Rule 85:   **if**   1. the site of the culture is the blood
            and if 2. the organism is Gram-negative
            and if 3. the organism is rod-shaped
            and if 4. the patient is a host at risk
            then   it is probable (0.6) that the organism is pseudomonas aeruginosa

Rule 217:

            if   1. the organism is a bacteroid
            and if 2. the site of the culture was sterile
            then   the therapy should be chosen from the following:

            chloramphenicol, clindamycine, tetracycline,
            lindomycine, gentamycine

MYCIN has a standard set of 24 predicates (e.g. 'is', 'the_same', 'known', 'belongs_to', ...), 11 objects (e.g. 'organism', 'culture', 'medicament', ...) and 80 attributes (e.g. 'identity_of_organism', 'sensitivity', 'site') which together serve to describe the case being studied. The rules are given in natural language; some are for diagnosis, others for prescription.

A weighting coefficient with value between 0 and 1 is given with each action, to express the level of certainty felt by the expert who has provided the rule in the conclusion he has given: in a field such as this knowledge is never absolutely certain. Further, since the observations – the symptoms – are usually non-independent, Bayesian methods of analysis cannot be used; we shall see that MYCIN uses certain likelihood or plausibility coefficients in its reasoning, which are not in fact probabilities.

7.3.2.3 MYCIN's approximate reasoning

The facts of MYCIN's universe are stated as triplets, each with a likelihood or plausibility coefficient with value between -1 and 1: thus
An example of a MYCIN triplet is:

identity organism	*E. coli*	0.7
identity organism	*Klebsiella*	0.4
sensitivity organism	penicillin	-0.9

Indicating this likelihood coefficient by V, suppose a new fact F is deduced from a rule R whose own likelihood is $V(R)$; then:

$$V(F) = V(R) \times \min_j V(P_j) \qquad \text{where } P_j \text{ is the } j\text{th premise of } R.$$

Since it may be possible to derive the same conclusion from each of two or more different rules, different values may be reached for the same coefficient. If two different rules give the same conclusion with likelihoods $V1$, $V2$ then the value adopted is:

$$V = V1 + V2 - V1 \cdot V2$$

Any fact for which $|V| < 0.2$ is considered to be of insufficient credibility and is eliminated, by the system, from the facts base.

These computational procedures have been criticised by some writers, who have proposed alternative methods: cf. Friedman 1981, Doyle 1979, Swartout 1981.

7.2.3.3 The inferential mechanism

The reasoning process does not start from the given symptoms and look for possible causes but proceeds in the opposite directions, from possible causes of infection to the observed symptoms; and does this by constructing an AND–OR tree.

For any given goal the system considers all those rules whose conclusions relate to that goal; the left side (the AND node) of each such rule is evaluated if that is possible, giving a likelihood coefficient V equal in absolute value to that of the premise of minimum value. If $|V| \geqslant 0.2$ the right side of the rule is constructed and given a likelihood coefficient equal to the product of $|V|$ and the weighting coefficient assigned to the rule. If

$|V| < 0.2$ the rule gives no information, although this does not of course negate the initial assumption.

If any premises cannot be evaluated at the stage reached, these are stored as intermediate sub-goals (OR nodes) and the system proceeds by iteration: this is described in Section 3.1 below.

If no conclusion can be reached the system asks for further information about the patient. It is to avoid putting too many questions at too early a stage to the doctor – who would not like this – that MYCIN adopts this backwards-proceeding exhaustive enumeration; and having tried all the possibilities it is then better able to ask the right question. This enumeration over the production rules, which are rather like rewrite rules, makes MYCIN something of a theorem prover working in a relatively restricted search space.

A few modifications give improvements over the standard procedure:

1. MYCIN generalises the goals; thus 'Is the organism *E. coli*?' is changed to 'What is the identity of the organism?'. Such a change costs the system little extra effort and can avoid the need to put further questions.
2. When considering each goal MYCIN uses literally all the rules, together with their weighting factors, because in this field it is advisable to consider and assess every possibility. Only when an inference is found to be certain (shown by $V = 1$ everywhere) is the search discontinued earlier.
3. In the interests of accuracy MYCIN always retains the right to question the doctor concerning any attributes for which he has not given values but knows that these are current laboratory data.

Further, the system keeps a record of all the steps it has taken and all the knowledge items it has used, for three reasons:

1. To avoid useless calculations such as getting into a loop, searching for information that cannot be obtained.
2. To be able to explain to the expert how and why any conclusion was reached (cf. Section 4)
3. To know what question to ask the expert when it is found the certain needed information is lacking.

7.2.3.4   The metarules

The system has access to its own representation of the knowledge items and possesses a certain amount of intelligence concerning these provided by (1) profiles (2) metarules.

1. A *Profile* is attached to each of the 24 predicates and tells the system which attributes control the predicate in question. This speeds up the calculation by showing if a particular attribute is involved many times in different

premises in different rules, and thus makes possible quick and rough preliminary evaluation of the premises. With the aid of some simple logic this evaluation will show if a rule is immediately applicable, or should be considered later or is inapplicable in the current situation.

2. *Metarules* are symbolic data items structured similarly to the rules, that enable the system to steer its search. They express strategies for avoiding the need for exhaustive enumeration, by showing how best to use the rules themselves in order to reach a given goal: that is, they are rules about the rules, hence their name.

The metarules are numbered; the first concerns the general goal 'Suggest a therapy for a patient' and is as follows:

If a therapy is required, consider in this order the rules that make it possible to:

1. Acquire more clinical information concerning the patient.
2. Find which organisms, if any, could have caused the infection.
3. Identify the most likely organisms.
4. Find all the potentially useful medicaments.
5. Choose the most appropriate and smallest number.

Two other examples are:

Metarule 2

> **if**   1. the patient is a host at risk.
> **and if** 2. there are rules that mention pseudomonas in one of their premises.
> **and if** 3. there are rules that mention klebsiellas in one of their premises.
> **then**   with probability 0.4 the first should be used before the second.

Metarule 25

> **if**   1. the site of the culture is not sterile.
> **and if** 2. there are rules that mention in their premises an organism already found in the patient and which could be the same as the one whose identity is sought.
> **then**   it is certain (prob. 1) that none of these rules will be of use.

(The explanation is that an infection temporarily cured may reappear and therefore it is usual to consider bacteria that have been found previously in the patient; but this will not help if the site is not sterile.)

The precise internal form, in LISP, of the above metarule is:

premise   ($AND(MEMBF SITE CONTEXT)
                (NONSTERILESITES)
                (THEREARE OBJRULES)
                (MENTION CONTEXT PREMISE SAMEBUG))
action   (CONCLIST CONTEXT UTILITY YES TALLY-1)

The metarules are scanned when each sub-goal is considered; they can rearrange the order in which the rules are considered, and reduce the number, so guiding the search and pruning the tree. Since all the available information is available at each node, the metarules are closely tied to the nodes and result in the search process being adapted to the particular context. Thus the control structure and the heuristics are expressed in the metarules instead of being buried in the body of the program.

Finally, since the program calls the rules by content and not by name, any additions to, deletions from or modifications of the knowledge base can be made and the system will adapt itself to these.

7.2.4 MYCIN's explanations and natural-language dialogue

An important requirement built into the design of MYCIN was that it should always be able to explain why it did what it did, so that the doctors would then understand this – and, it was to be hoped, would agree. Thus conversational facilities were provided to enable the user to query the system at any stage. A simple interpreter program handles the questions and provides the explanations, making use of keywords and fixed input/output formats. Its working is greatly eased by the standard form in which the knowledge items are expressed – production rules – and by the very simple type – combinatorial – of the search process used.

As with TEIRESIAS to be described next, we shall not go into the details of the natural language because this is not the main concern of this book.

7.2.5 Acquiring new knowledge: TEIRESIAS

TEIRESIAS is an interactive program whose purpose is to help the expert develop a system that operates on a large body of knowledge: the name is that of the blind oracle in Sophocles's *Oedipus Rex*. It has an interface that enables the user to conduct a dialogue with the program in natural language, so avoiding the need to descend to the low level of the implementation. The system can not only use its knowledge directly but can

Table 7.1.

TEIRESIAS: The following investments seem to be the most appropriate now:
            Varian Corporation and AT&T. Is that right?   1
Expert: No
T: Are there any missing?
E: Yes, Digital Equipment and Data General
T: Are there any that should not be included?
E: Yes, AT&T
T: Would you like me to show how I made that mistake?
E: Yes
T: Let's start with AT&T   2
   I got this by using Rule 27: since

   1. The field in which investments are to be made is not specified very precisely.
   2. The expected return is over 10%.
   3. The investment is to be a long-term one.

   AT&T is a plausible choice (0.4)
   Is this rule right?
E: Yes
T: Is there a premise that should have been checked?
E: Yes, 1   3
T: I have not reached any conclusion about the field of the investment; should I have
   looked for something more precise?
E: Yes, advanced technology
T: All attempts to find a rule that would suggest advanced technology failed because
   in no case were the relevant premises satisfied; this leads me to question these two
   rules: (the system displays the rules on the screen): Are they right?
E: Yes
T: Should I have used one of them?
E: No   4
T: Is there a rule missing?
E: Yes
T: OK, so I need a rule that will tell me that the field should be advanced technology;
   can you give me one?
E: If the client's top tax rate is 50% and if he is following the market trends
   carefully, then (0.8) the investment should be made in the field of high
   technology   5
T: The new rule will be Rule 383; this is how I understand it: if

   1. The client is paying tax at 50%.
   2. The market has been following an upward trend recently.
   3. The client manages his assets carefully.

   then (0.8) the investment should be in high technology. OK?
E: No   6
T: Should I change any of the premises?
E: Yes, change 2
T: If I change 2 to 'the client is following the market carefully', will that do?
E: Yes   7
T: Then you would want to remove 3 – yes?
E: Yes   8
T: (repeats the modified Rule 383, then) I don't like to criticise, but don't you know

the rules about investments that mention the client's tax position and the way he follows the market generally mention also his experience in investing? Should I try to frame a third premise?

E: Yes   **9**

T: What do you think of this: 'The client is a moderately experienced investor'?

E: OK   **10**

T: Most rules of this kind give some conclusion about the level of risk; should I try to give something of this kind?

E: No

T: (repeats Rule 383 with the final modification, then) Will you tell me briefly why you have added this rule?

E: The system had not understood that it could specify the investment field precisely, which is why it applied Rule 27 wrongly

T: Rule 383 is now added to the knowledge base and we repeat the consultation to make sure that the new rule is sound: sit down comfortably, this may take a little time

   Results: Investments suggested: Varian Corporation, Digital Equipment, Data General.

   Everything seems to be OK, doesn't it?

E: Yes

---

1. It is here, after results have been provided by MYCIN, that TEIRESIAS appears on the scene. The first sentence will reveal the error.

2. Heuristics drawn from experience have been given to the program in the form of metarules; one of these says that it is advisable

   (a) to deal with one problem at a time
   (b) to start, preferably, with a conclusion that should not have been reached.

3. The expert points out that this rule should not have been applied. Had it been invoked TEIRESIAS would no doubt have commented that a rule was missing, which would have excluded AT&T.

4. This would have been the case if there had been an error in the value of a premise given as false by another rule.

5. The tracking down of the error, steered by the precise and very pertinent questions put by the system, has been remarkably rapid. In the steps that follow the system interprets the new rule.

6. TEIRESIAS'S error results from a very rudimentary word-for-word analysis of the statement of a rule – not even a syntax analysis. This associates the predicate 'is' with the object 'market'; The system 'thinks' first of a premise of the type 'the tendency of the market is ...'.

7. The error is now easily corrected. The 'second choice' is correct. Clause 3 is deleted because it cannot be assumed, as previously, that the sentence falls into two independent premises, as the system knows in particular that 'carefully' cannot be used twice. All this works because we are dealing with small pieces of text that admit of few alternative analyses, and also because it is easy to test for correctness.

8. A test to establish that a text has been properly understood by the system is as follows:

   read in the original English text
   convert this to the internal representation
   translate back into English and submit this for approval

   When this stage is reached the expert is satisfied; the system now checks that it too is satisfied.

9. See the next paragraph for an explanation of the means whereby the system creates a new rule.

10. The rule must always be applied to the current situation: 'moderate experience' (cf. Waterman's poker program, Section 7.3.2).

also examine this knowledge, select from it and reason about it, so that the dialogue can be conducted as between two specialists.

The original purpose of TEIRESIAS was to extend MYCIN to any infections of the blood whatever (cf. R. Davis Ph.D. Thesis, Stanford 1976); however, by helping the construction of the knowledge base it eases the transfer of the application of the system from one field to another, as has been done several times subsequently (cf. Section 7.4 below). The only important prerequisites are that the knowledge base (as production rules) and the concepts are in the right form and that all that has to be done is to add to or change the database. Everything proceeds as though a teacher, after giving a course, sets his pupils new problems, observes carefully how they deal with these and corrects their mistakes.

7.2.5.1　TEIRESIAS at work: an annotated example

The dialogue given as Table 7.1 illustrates the working of the system. It is due to Davis who, for reasons of readability, replaced *manually* the medical vocabulary with one based on the stock market; thus the equivalences are *E. coli* → AT&T (American Telephones & Telegraph), infection → investment, taking a drug → buying a stock, etc. TEIRESIAS can take account, interactively, of the expert's advice after each consultation. The numbers on the right of the table refer to the notes that follow.

7.2.5.2　TEIRESIAS's method of working

The system asks the expert to judge the validity of its reasoning and he can do so only because

1. The reasoning is based on a simple search procedure using simple given rules and not on a program of the usual type.
2. The system has kept a record of the results of all its actions and can find those that have prevented it from reaching the right conclusion; it is thus able to construct all the possible hypotheses whose adoption would remove the error, and also the effects to be expected in each case.
3. The system, far from putting vague general questions, asks 'In this precise situation, what is it that you know and I don't?'

Through the intermediary of models of the rules TEIRESIAS, in effect, knows what it knows and also, provided that there is some regularity in the knowledge, what it will meet in the course of its search.

The models of the rules. These are concise statements in a high level language, each summarising the essential features of a sub-set of rules all of which relate to some general concept. There are four parts to a model, as follows:

1. A list of examples: this is simply the sub-set of relevant rules.
2. A description of a characteristic member of the sub-set: premises and conclusions characterised by the attributes that appear frequently.
3. Correlations between the attributes; this information is obtained by means of a statistical analysis.
4. Two lists of rules, one of the more general and the other of the more specific.

These models are constructed by TEIRESIAS itself as the knowledge base grows and a single field becomes referred to by several rules. The complete set of models is organised as a tree with the most general concept as its root.

The following is an example.

Model: '*x* is_a_field_of_investment'
Examples: R116, R80, R95, ...
Description: premises: return is/term is/tendency is
            correlations: (return, term)/(tax position, experience, care)
Conclusions: field/risk
More general: 'field_of_investment'
Less general: 'public_services_enterprises_are_a field_of_investment'

When TEIRESIAS is expecting to be given a new rule (cf. at 3 in the example of 2.5.1) it scans the tree of models, starting at the root, to find what it knows already that is relevant to the rule. In this particular case the most specific model that enables it to conclude that high technology is a suitable field for investment is just the one given above by the expert.

The understanding of the statements input to the system in natural language is made possible by relative frequencies with which the predicates appear in models, whilst the correlations between the occurrences of these predicates make it possible to check that the expert has not overlooked anything important. Further, it is the use of these models that compensates for the rudimentary nature of the linguistic analysis; it constitutes also an important characteristic of the system, to tend not to understand just what it expects to understand.

Another benefit of the tree of models is that it enables TEIRESIAS to make some estimate of what it does not know, for example, fields in which there are few reliable rules or few rules at all. It thus knows what further information is needed most urgently and so can ask the most pertinent questions – but it has no means of estimating what still remains to be known nor of assessing the plausibility of a new fact given to it. Finally, the tree enables the system to organise a body of knowledge given to it by the expert in unstructured form, to the benefit of the expert himself.

7.2.6 An evaluation of MYCIN–TEIRESIAS

The system was written in LISP to run on a PDP 10. A critical study has been made by a group of five specialists, none of them involved in the team that wrote the system, using 15 cases and assessing the value of the therapies recommended, the pertinence of the questions put by the system and the numbers of important questions that should have been raised and were not. These experts agreed with 72% of the systems's conclusions; in the majority of the remainder they did not agree among themselves.

Section 7.3 includes a review of a number of expert systems. Many systems provide evidence of the importance of a knowledge-gathering program such as TEIRESIAS: thus with such an aid PUFF, a system for diagnosing pulmonary infections, required less than 50 hours of collaborative work with the experts and under 10 man-weeks for the implementation. There is no doubt whatever that, in certain fields at least, systems using rules and metarules provide an entirely satisfactory solution to the problem of transfer and use of large quantities of knowledge.

A general discussion of the averages, disadvantages, characteristics and underlying assumptions of systems of this kind is given in Section 7.7; meanwhile we note the following limitations of the MYCIN–TEIRESIAS system.

1. The weakest part is the handling of the natural language statements; this has been improved by Alain Bonnet with the BAOBAB program (Bonnet 1980) as regards both the understanding of the rules and the input of the medical history of the patient, the latter thanks to the use of 'frames' analogous to those due to Bobrow and Winograd (Bobrow 1975) (cf. Section 7.6). Even so, not all the problems have been solved.
2. If in some situation MYCIN fails because two or more rules should be modified simultaneously, or because two or more new rules should be added, then TEIRESIAS will fail in turn because the possibility has not been foreseen.
3. When a new rule is introduced, TEIRESIAS always assumes that this may not be reliable but that the knowledge base is correct. The opposite may be the case, and this will lead to problems.

However, the system taken as a whole certainly works, and is useful. It manages a body of specialised knowledge, put into the system in no particular order; it has a model of this knowledge, created and kept up to date by itself, that enables it to conduct a dialogue with the expert and to improve this knowledge in the light of experience. Altogether, it is one of the best systems ever produced, basically simple in design and implementation, easily understood, and the soundness of its conclusions is easily checked by the expert.

7.3   PRODUCTION-RULE SYSTEMS

This section is in two parts: in the first we define an expert system more precisely and show how such a system can be programmed; in the second we list and comment on a number of existing systems.

A *production rule* is an expression of the form:

$$LS \rightarrow RS$$

where LS, the left side, describes some situation in a suitable formalism and RS defines an action to be considered if that situation is found to obtain. Such a rule is very much like a theorem, with LS the premise(s) and RS the conclusion(s), and a chain of rules linked by their LSs and RSs is like a syllogism. The basic method of reasoning used by systems whose knowledge base is in the form of production rules is *modus ponens*, p and $p \supset q \rightarrow q$; but it is not the only one, as will be shown in Section 7.4.

Whilst in practice computing with production rules is set in contrast to procedural systems (cf. Section 7.5) the two are formally equivalent. The former was first suggested by E. Post (Post 1936) and has been used especially to define formal languages and grammars (Chomsky 1963). Since 1974 it has formed the basis of many programs that became called 'expert systems', specialised to particular fields in which the solving of problems required simple reasoning but with a very cognitive approach. All the knowledge required for the solution was expressed as production rules and therefore, since it was not embodied in the program, could be input in modular fashion and easily modified. Figure 7.2 gives an example of the derivation of a result in such a system. Here the premises, $A, B, \ldots$ could be simple logical propositions that are TRUE or FALSE, as in MYCIN, or predicates with variables or in fact relations of any type; of course, the richness of the language and the possibilities for representing knowledge increase with the power of the formalism used (cf. Section 7.4 ff).

	(a)		(b): H, K	
(R1)	$A \rightarrow E$			
(R2)	$B \rightarrow D$		$H \rightarrow A$	(R3)
(R3)	$H \rightarrow A$		$A \rightarrow E$	(R1)
(R4)	$E \wedge G \rightarrow C$		$E \wedge K \rightarrow B$	(R5)
(R5)	$E \wedge K \rightarrow B$		$B \rightarrow D$	(R2)
(R6)	$D \wedge E \wedge K \rightarrow C$		$\cdot\, D \wedge E \wedge K \rightarrow C$	(R6)
(R7)	$G \wedge K \wedge F \rightarrow A$			
			(c)	

Fig. 7.2 Derivation by forward chaining: (a) rules, (b) given facts base and (c) derivation chain.

What is particularly interesting is that production systems have been used by psychologists in attempts to model certain human intellectual processes: for example, Newell (1972) considers this to be the correct formalism for expressing the transfers of information between our short term and long term memories, and that such systems provide a correct model of our handling of knowledge. Thus it is not just a coincidence that such systems are used in AI.

7.3.1 General description

Apart from the set of rules that constitute its knowledge base a production system consists of a working space (the facts base) and an interpreter program.

The working space at any instant contains all the facts that the program

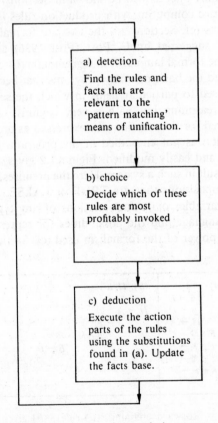

Fig. 7.3 Basic cycle of the rule interpreter.

has been able to deduce (from those given initially) up to that instant; at the start it contains only the statement of the problem to be solved. This space plays the role of a short-term memory holding simple assertions that form part of a static description of the universe of discourse, in contrast to the long-term memory represented by the dynamic knowledge base containing the transformation operators in the form of production rules. These rules can involve variables whose values are set ('instantiated') by the interpreter each time the rule is executed, so as to make them consistent with the facts as then known, by a process of 'semi-unification' or 'filtering' (Fig. 7.3).

Unification is thus the fundamental mechanism that makes it possible for such a system to work; in its most general form it enables the system to find if there is a set of substitutions that will make two given logical formulae identical. There is a fully specified algorithm for this, cf. Section 3.7.

It follows that the interpreter is a key component of the system, in complete control of the order in which the successive deductions are made; each deduction involves the same cycle of basic steps, as shown in Fig. 7.3. The crucial problem here is how to decide which rule to invoke; we study this in Section 7.3.3. Systems differ accordingly as the new information resulting from the deduction is simply added to the facts base or over-writes an existing item; see, for example, Post (1936) or Newell (1971).

The search for attaining a goal is carried out in a natural manner, as in the case of theorem proving, and is conveniently represented with the help of an AND–OR tree as in Fig. 7.4. This can be constructed and traversed in either direction, from the given facts to the conclusion or from the conclusion, considered as a conjecture, towards the facts: these are the forward chaining (Fig. 7.2) and backwards chaining (Fig. 7.4) strategies respectively. Backward chaining is usually preferred since the facts are not independent and many of them will not be relevant to the particular problem; it thus avoids the potential combinatorial explosion by eliminating most of the possible conclusions. MYCIN and DENDRAL (see Section 7.3.4) use this method, a LISP interpreter, making recursive calls of the rules, performing most of the work of the evaluation.

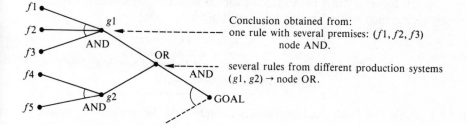

Conclusion obtained from:
one rule with several premises: $(f1, f2, f3)$
node AND.

several rules from different production systems
$(g1, g2) \rightarrow$ node OR.

GOAL

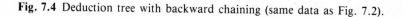

Fig. 7.4 Deduction tree with backward chaining (same data as Fig. 7.2).

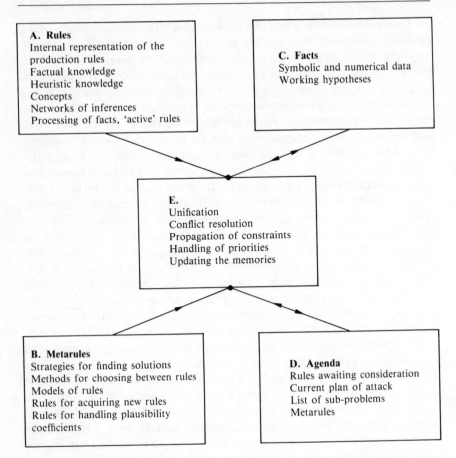

Fig. 7.5 General structure of a production-rule system.

Figure 7.5 gives the general structure of a production-rule system using backward chaining; however, for obvious reasons a good interpreter should be able to work either backwards or forwards, according to the needs at the stage reached and of the type of reasoning used.

7.3.2 Underlying assumptions and fields of applicability of production-rule systems

A number of hidden assumptions are implied by the method for entering and using the knowledge that has just been described.

7.3.2.1 The role of the specialist

The first need is that a specialist in the field to be studied must be able to describe the state of knowledge in that field, and for this the relevant science must have been developed far enough for the right concepts to have been formulated. Otherwise so much detail will have to be given that the knowledge base grows to a prohibitive size (Nilsson 1980).

7.3.2.2 Structure of the field studied

Rules have to be stated; this implies that any interaction between parameters is weak, otherwise the left sides will become impossibly long and inextricable interwoven. The field must therefore be only loosely linked, so that any action involves only elementary knowledge items and brings in only a small number of parameters.

Even so, a single rule may summarise a large amount of knowledge. Thus 'A blood organism that is Gram negative and rod shaped is probably *E. coli*' is a rule based on both physiological and clinical experience.

7.3.2.3 Inference schemas

Reasoning in the field must be possible by means of simple inferential procedures, of the type of *modus ponens* (p and $p \supset q \rightarrow q$) or its variant *modus tollens* ($\neg q$ and $p \supset q \rightarrow \neg p$). The goal must be defined precisely (thus making backward chaining possible) and the variables involved must vary discretely rather than continuously so as to avoid explosive growth of the facts base. The problems to be solved must not involve large numbers of sub-goals that are strongly and sequentially linked; otherwise, a sequential method should be used.

7.3.2.4 Immediate consequences of the assumptions

Systems of this type are not suitable for solving problems for which either the statement or the solution is complicated – problems of a combinatorial nature, for example. By their nature they are oriented more towards modifications of the field of study than towards invariant properties: tautologies and formal definitions and relations do not seem to be matters for the basic mechanisms of production systems, being better handled by other inferential schemas such as 'demons' (Hewitt 1972), 'priority interrupts' (Gascuel 1981), 'similitude classes' (Bundy 1979) (cf. Section 7.4).

7.3.3   Variants on the basic design

The two important considerations are the representation of the knowledge
and the structure of the control.

7.3.3.1   The knowledge base

The nature of the entities involved can vary from one system to another
according to the field of study; usually, to make it possible to adapt the same
system to different fields, a fixed format is chosen for the rules and the
parameters are typed so that the unification process can be suitably
restricted in any particular application. Thus in DENDRAL the left side is
the name of a 'skeleton' – a graph of a part of a molecule – and the right
side gives the changes that can be made to this in the spectrograph. An
example of a rule of this form is

oestrogen → break((14–15), (13–17)) and hydrogen transfer (1, 12)

This convention gives both conciseness in expression and efficiency in use of
the rules.

   Further, whilst in some cases the premises and conclusions of the rules are
basic facts that can be checked and if necessary modified, many systems
now incorporate into their rules procedures called by the rules together with
an evaluation of the results.

7.3.3.2   The control structure

The problem with which the control structure has to deal is that of conflict
resolution – deciding which rule(s) to invoke when there are several
candidates. The choice of strategy is certainly of vital importance, not only
for efficiency but even more for the system's ability to understand its own
actions and to improve its performance.

   The literature of the subject distinguishes three main families of control
structures which we consider in turn:

1. Exhaustive search.
2. Choice by evaluation.
3. Control by means of metarules.

Exhaustive search. MYCIN in particular uses this method, as described in
Section 7.2 (and works backwards from the conclusions to the given facts).
The method is well suited to the situation in which the reply to a precisely
framed question is arrived at by making a weighted judgement, taking all
the responses possible into account. It is satisfactory when the universe

concerned is small enough for there to be no risk of combinatorial explosion.

Choice by evaluation. The crudest strategy is to take the first applicable rule that comes to hand – see for example Waterman (1978) or Moran (1973) in applications in psychology. The efficiency here depends on the order in which the rules have been stored; but the method destroys the most fundamental quality of production-rule systems, the ease with which the knowledge base can be modified.

The alternative is to evaluate every candidate rule according to some criterion and choose the 'best'; possible bases for choice are as follows.

1. The importance of the conclusion of the rule, at the time of the evaluation, in relation to the current goal.
2. Relation to the given facts: choice of the rule that can be unified with the fact considered the most important.
3. Specialisation: choice of the rule giving the most specific conclusion (this is the one used by the LISP interpreter).
4. Choice determined by a graph, either expressing a partial ordering of the rules (DENDRAL) or constructed by the program (Gascuel 1981).
5. Choice of the rule most recently used.
6. Choice of the rule that mentions the most recently used fact.

Control by means of metarules. Of the three methods this is by far the one to be preferred since the logic of the choice, instead of being implicit in the body of the interpreter, is now made explicit in a form similar to that of the rules themselves. At any instant the program's behaviour depends closely on the current state of the search, and the purpose of the metarules is to say which rule should be given priority in each particular situation. The underlying idea is the same as that in the advice given by PLANNER in theorem proving (Hewitt 1972).

Whatever method is chosen, the very nature of the control structure requires that all communications within the system are made via the facts base; the production rules are such that no rule can call another directly – in complete contrast to current practice with classical-style programming, a comparison discussed in more detail in Section 7.5. The important feature of the metarule strategy is that with this rules can be added, modified or deleted and the system itself will made the necessary consequential changes.

7.3.3.3 Computational demands and efficiency of production-rule systems

As a first approximation the time taken by an application is proportional to the product of the number of rules and the number of entries in the facts base. The most important consideration is the number of attempts to invoke a rule that prove fruitless. Schemes have been devised for filtering out useless rules and facts before unification is embarked on; J. McDermott (1978) has given four, together with formulae for the corresponding execution times. A method adopted by several writers is to propagate, after a rule has been used, the facts thereby deduced and then to consider only those rules whose premises mention these facts. Another approach, built into the design of certain interpreters, is to evaluate any sub-expressions common to several rules only once per cycle (see Fig. 7.3), or to save the values from one cycle to another so long as the facts to which they relate are not changed (Gascuel 1981) (Ghallab 1981) (Forgy 1981). Simple heuristics, with low computational costs, give a very good return here; they very quickly reduce the amount of work needed to match the rules with the facts.

Another method is to devise an automatic process for assembling elementary facts into more complex structures or into high-level representations: the probability of successful unification decreases with increasing richnesses of the objects considered and the useless unifications decrease in step with this. It was for this reason that Minsky (Minsky 1975) put forward the idea of prototypes or *frames*, and these are used by many systems (see Section 7.5).

The problem − of reducing the number of unnecessary unifications − is relatively simple when the rules contain no variables. But when there are variables and both the number of rules (several hundreds) and the number of facts (several thousand) are large the problem remains unsolved, and there seems no way to overcome the combinatorial explosion except by the use of meta-knowledge (see Section 7.7).

We shall now look at a number of existing expert systems.

7.3.4 Expert systems based on production rules

7.3.4.1 DENDRAL

Subject: To find the structural formula for an organic compound, given its molecular formula and its mass spectrograph.

Origin: Stanford University. Buchanan, Feigenbaum and Lederberg (Lederberg was awarded the Nobel prize for medicine in 1958). Sutherland & Co. and the Massachusetts Spectrum Laboratory.

DENDRAL developed from work started by Lederberg in 1964 to help elucidate the structure of organic molecules, taking into account the constraints imposed by topology. Originally it was a procedural program of standard type (Davis 1977a) but it was completely rewritten in 1967 because it was becoming unmanageable – for the first time, the need to locate the experts' knowledge in the data part of the system became evident to the programmers.

Features: The type of method used is enumerative search, a combinatorial program generating all the possible structures that satisfy the constraints set by the data; this program is very efficient, and much faster than any chemist could work. When a plausible structural formula has been obtained rules of the form

atomic configuration such-and-such
$\rightarrow$ mass spectrograph fragmentation such-and-such

enables the mass spectrograph to be predicted and compared with observation.

The basic representation used by DENDRAL, both within the rules and for communicating with the expert, is the graph of the structural formula of the compound being analysed.

In any analysis it is usual to stack the sub-tasks in an 'agenda', a data structure whose elements are assigned priorities or, more generally, have predicates associated with them that decide the order in which they should be called. This is because either several rules can be invoked and all but one must be made to wait or a single rule requires several tasks to be executed.

DENDRAL is in daily use by the Stanford chemists; it has given rise to 25 papers in the specialist chemistry journals.

7.3.4.2 META-DENDRAL

Subject: Efficient automatic derivation of the molecular fragmentation rules used by DENDRAL, using as data typical fragmentations observed with samples of relatively simple compounds.

Origin: The bottleneck in DENDRAL was the specifying of the rules, which were provided by the chemists in a very piece-meal manner (Buchanan 1978). It was essential to find a quicker method that would give a better set.

Features: Here again a combinatorial method was used: the graphs for all the data compounds were combined in all possible ways, each resulting configuration becoming the left side of a new rule. The right side gave what was considered, as a result of a statistical analysis of the samples, to be the important peaks to be expected in the mass spectrum.

Rules thus obtained are tested for validity and treated as follows:

1. Redundancies are removed.
2. Rules with the same left side are grouped together.
3. If a rule has a negative premise an attempt is made to make that rule more specific so as to remove that premise.
4. An attempt is made to generalise the rules, keeping the same positive premises and the same conclusions.

META-DENDRAL has produced a set of rules that rival those obtained more laboriously by the experts; in a sub-field that has been little studied it provided new rules that were considered excellent by the experts and which were reported in an international chemistry journal. The system has been extended to deal with nuclear magnetic resonance spectra, in which field it has used very voluminous data, input in random order, to infer more complex rules than it had been possible for the experts to frame (Buchanan 1978).

7.3.4.3 Waterman's program (1970)

Subject: Learning the heuristics of poker.

Origin: Waterman's aim was to write an experimental intelligent system in which the separation of the program and the heuristics would be clear. Further, the program should be able to increase its stock of heuristics, and correct any that proved invalid, during the course of the play.

Features: The heuristics are given in the form of production rules, which are corrected in small steps; the program is able to form new rules.

A position in the game is represented as a vector of 7 components: value of the hand, size of the pot, size of the raise, opponent's bluff (Yes or No), ratio of pot to raise, swap (Yes or No), opponent's style of play. The heuristics are expressed in terms of this vector.

Waterman's program achieves its decision taking and its learning with the aid of a special control structure. The rules are arranged, not at random, but in a specified order and the decision is arrived at by the first successful unification obtained in following this order. This has the effect of making error correction a rather complicated matter, and the effects of any change or addition difficult to foresee. Waterman deals with this difficulty by forming a new rule that describes the precise situation concerned, with a right side that corrects the faulty decision. Then either there is already a rule that can be changed so as to have the same effect as the new rule, or there is not. In the latter case the learning process is very simple: the new rule is placed immediately before the faulty rule. The former case falls into two parts according as the modifiable rule occurs before or after the faulty rule. If before, the field of definition of the symbolic values of the parameters entering into its left side is extended to include those of the new rule, so that the old rule has been generalised. If after, the program restricts the field of the parameters of the faulty rule and all those between this and the modifiable rule, so all unifications attempted before that rule is reached will fail.

There are many dangers in such a control scheme: it is difficult to check by hand calculation the effect of a set of rules, redundant rules are created and have to be eliminated periodically by the system, the program behaves in an unstable manner in the learning phase. However, its author has reported several sets of experiments, with and without a teacher, that have shown its learning capabilities to be effective and to have given good results with, in the end, only about 20 rules.

The program has a changing style of play which is difficult for the opponent to cope with; whilst this may be valuable in poker it could be a grave disadvantage in other fields.

7.3.4.4   The MYCIN–TEIRESIAS family

Subject: Aid to diagnosis and prescription in cases of blood infection; aid to input of expert knowledge.

Origin: E. Shortliffe (1974), R. Davis (1976), Stanford University: Buchanan–Feigenbaum team.

Features: The system is described in Section 7.2. It 'knows' what it knows and what it does, which enables it to explain its reasoning, to answer questions, to learn and to advise the expert, all in the accepted medical jargon. It is a useful system and has been used to good effect.

GUIDON. This, aimed at medical students at Stanford, teaches the principles of MYCIN's reasoning. The knowledge represented by MYCIN's rules is tested against a set of pedagogical rules; whilst MYCIN conducts its search exhaustively and blindly, someone new to the subject needs to be taught these rules a few at a time. Some strategy for diagnosis has to be chosen – toothache is less serious than meningitis; so the medical information scientists at Stanford have been led to examine the rules so as to construct a hierarchy among the clinical entities and to explain the relationships between these. The outcome has been the creation of a new system oriented towards teaching, NEOMYCIN (Clancey 1981).

ONCOCIN. This was written by Shortcliffe as an aid to the treatment of cancer. Its philosophy differs from that of MYCIN in several respects:

- The medical histories of the patients have to be followed, with a clinical profile defined for each one and kept up-to-date. Thus time enters as a basic parameter and the attributes are no longer constants but are variables; this requires fundamental changes in the inference engine, the evaluation of the premises being no longer immediate (see Section 7.5).
- The field is so wide that the rules have to be classified according to the application.
- For the same reason, the system must always check the rules for consistency and completeness.
- So as to avoid long and costly sessions, the rules will where possible assign default values to parameters when no value is given.
- The search strategy is no longer exhaustive but takes the goal into account.

7.3.4.5 SU/X and others

SU/X (Nii 1978). The aim is to find the identity and location of objects in space that are emitting signals. It originated in an attempt initiated by Feigenbaum and Nii (1976) to follow a situation in which the knowledge was changing with time: this time-variation does not vitiate a production-rule system as it would a procedural system.

A 'blackboard' is used to record the facts obtaining at a given instant, as in the Carnegie Mellon HEARSAY system (Erman 1975). The right sides of the rules specify actions that are in fact procedure calls, such as to re-evaluate a certain parameter or to replace one certain assumption by another; thus the main function of the rules is to control the combinatorial explosion.

VM (Ventilation Monitor) (Fagan 1980) is a system for monitoring patients in intensive care units. It receives signals from a variety of clinical measuring devices, keeps a record of how they vary with time and gives an alarm if anything seriously untoward seems to be occurring.

CRYSALIS (Engelmore 1979): derived from SU/X, attempts to infer protein structures from 3-D electron density maps obtained by X-ray crystallography. The molecules are sufficiently complex for the exhaustive search method of DENDRAL and MYCIN to be infeasible, and a richer control structure is needed.

MOLGEN (Friedland 1979): this also originated with the SU/X group. The subject is molecular biology and the aim is to predict the genetic effects of manipulations of the ADN molecule. The main difficulty here lies in bringing about collaborative interworking between rules representing knowledge from different fields, here biology, chemistry, genetics, topology and manipulative techniques.

RITA (Anderson 1976): written at Rand, to provide an aid to design.

PROSPECTOR (Duda 1980, Konolidge 1979): geological system, to guide prospecting for minerals; uses production rules and Hendrix's partitioned semantic networks (Waterman 1978), the set of rules compiled as a graph (cf. Section 7.5.4). With its aid a molybdenum deposit was discovered in British Colombia in 1983, estimated to be worth a million dollars.

DIPMETER (Davis 1981): written in Schlumberger's research department this analyses signals recorded in drilling operations, representing the physical properties of the sub-soil (the 'logs'). As well as rules of the type of those of MYCIN the knowledge base gives methods for extracting significant features from the raw signals. The main problem is to correlate the results obtained from the measurements so as to define the positions and geological structures of the layers traversed.

LITHO (Bonnet 1982, Ganascia 1983): also from Schlumberger and like DIPMETER concerned with the interpretation of geological logs.

DRILLING ADVISER (Hollander 1983): for oil prospecting, written for Elf Aquitaine; this is based on the KS300 inference engine of Texknowledge.

CASNET (Kulikowski 1976): a medical system for the diagnosis and treatment of glaucoma, something of an advance on MYCIN in that it also follows the course of the illness and adapts its recommendations accordingly. Similar systems are HEADMED (Feigenbaum 1977) for psychopharmacology and INTERNIST (Pople 1982) for internal medicine. For the latter, several dozens of specialists have coded rules covering many human illnesses; the system is planned to contain several thousand rules grouped into about 80 special fields.

SACON (Michie 1980) for mechanical engineering advice; SOPHIE (Anderson 1979), a computer aided teaching system concerned with detection of failures in electrical circuits; and EL, NASL (Sussman 1975, McDermott 1978) for design of electrical circuits all include simulation routines for testing their assumptions.

NUDGE (Goldstein 1977): a work-scheduling system, of particular value when the problem is not well formulated.

Several rule-based systems for playing games, such as Waterman's for poker, described above, have appeared recently: PARADISE (Wilkins 1979) for chess and those due to Quinlan (1979), to Popescu (1984) and to Faller (1985) for bridge.

All the above systems are concerned essentially with diagnosis; in the following systems production rules are used to serve other ends.

(QUID) (Kayser 1981): understanding written texts; the detail into which the inference engine goes in conducting its reasoning is variable and can be controlled by the user.

HEARSAY III (Erman 1981): understanding continuous speech.

RESEDA (Zarri 1981): analysis of French historical documents from the Middle Ages; the system attempts to find the motivations and intentions of the individuals concerned.

GARI (Descottes 1981): planning sequences of factory operations. Some of the rules in this system's knowledge base will simply express advice given by experts, and different experts may give conflicting advice; the system then has to have a way of resolving the contradiction.

SAM (Gascuel 1981): for treatment of hypertension, cerebral vascular accidents and lyrangeal cancer.

TOUBIB (Fargues 1983, for IBM France): medical diagnosis in urgent cases.

SPHINX (Fieschi 1981, 1984): originally written for dealing with epigastric illnesses, later oriented towards diabetes and jaundice; communicates with the user in French (Joubert 1981). The system has teaching capabilities (Fieschi 1984).

PROTIS (Soula 1986): diabetes and jaundice; this system's tentative reasoning is particularly effective.

TOM (Cognitech 1986): derived from MYCIN, for diseases of tomato plants.

CESSOL (Ayel 1984): for land surveying.

CRIQUET (Vignard 1985): for classification of galaxies.

R1 (McDermott 1983), XCON: for configuring computer systems. This was designed by Digital Equipment Corporation (DEC) to propose VAX 780 installations that would meet the customer's requirements and satisfy various engineering constraints such as locations of units, lengths of cable runs. It was written in the OPS language (see below) by a team of about 15 people and has about 2000 rules; it is fully operational and is used routinely by DEC to respond to orders.

S39XC (Bartlett 1987), VCMS (Small 1987): AI-based systems used routinely by International Computers Ltd (ICL) to configure ICL Series 39 mainframe systems and to assess computer capacity management.

7.3.4.6 Some general systems

The following systems are distinguished either by the generality of their coverage or by their learning capabilities.

EMYCIN (van Melle 1979): 'essential' or 'empty' MYCIN. It can be used to construct the rule base for a consultant-type of expert system in any field; SACON and DART, for example, were built with its aid.

DART (Bennet 1981, for IBM): for diagnosis of hardware and system faults in computer systems; it was written in 8 months by a team of five computer maintenance specialists. There are some 200 rules, essentially expressing communication protocols and their possible anomalous behaviours.

OPS (Forgy 1977, Carnegie-Mellon University): this has similarities to EMYCIN but differs in allowing the use of variables (OPS works in first-order logic rather than in propositional logic) and in the criteria it uses for rule selection.

TANGO (Cordier 1984): this is essentially a first-order logic inference engine, whose special feature is that it can work without a facts base. New rules are formed after each deduction and the goal, with backwards chaining, used to guide the search.

PECOS (Barstow 1979): this produces LISP programs for algorithms in symbol and graph manipulation, sorting, arithmetical processing, given in abstract form. Object representation and programming techniques are chosen with the aid of some 400 rules; several different versions may be given for the same program, and are evaluated and implemented by means of a more general automatic programming system PSI.

APE (Barstow 1979): also for automatic production of LISP programs for abstract specifications which can include lists, files, stacks, arrays and trees. The programs (for, e.g., sorting, binary search) can have about 60 lines of code. The authors of this system hope to develop a new theory of programming, based on a modular formulation of the basic principles of programming.

TROPIC (Latombe 1977): a program for aiding design in the fields of architecture and electrical transformers. It has an efficient mechanism for handling advice and for back-tracking when checked.

AGE ('Attempt to Generalize') (Nii 1978): this includes an algorithm for generalizing a rule input to the system.

ARGOS-II (Cayrol 1976b, 1979a; Farreny 1980): a general system for simulating the decision-making of a robot in solving a given problem.

Particular attention is paid to the logical aspects of the control [of the robot]; rules can be inhibited or reactivated as required through the use of formal objects and a novel and effective linking of attributes.

CAMELIA (Vivet 1984): a mathematical system, for discovering theorems in integral calculus, finding limits, doing algebra and arithmetic, etc. It is written in LISP and uses REDUCE for its basic operations. Its special feature is the use of meta-rules to construct a plan for the solution of each problem put to it. Further, it can evaluate the premises of rules when necessary: for example, in

```
if ...
if positive (f) = TRUE
if ...
then ...
```

where f is any formal expression and in particular can involve an unknown parameter; the premise *if positive* (f) is treated as a new sub-goal to be evaluated by recursion. Currently, Vivet is looking into the use of meta-knowledge to modify the rules so as to adapt them to new situations.

GOSSEYN (Fouet 1986): a 2000-rule system for designing metal pressings and engine crankcases.

MUSCADET (Pastre 1984): for proving theorems in pure mathematics; it has proved difficult theorems in set theory and topological vector spaces. The knowledge base contains basic mathematics and general proof strategies as well as the rules that are specific to the field being studied; the same inference engine interprets all the types of knowledge, rules, meta-rules and meta-actions, all of which was provided by established mathematicians. In the process of assembling this knowledge it became clear that the experts could not frame the rules from cold, so to say: they reasoned from example, from particular cases, from diagrams; they could need a lot of time to get started, and might not be able to explain why they had chosen a particular method.

7.3.4.7 Systems that can learn

First, we may mention the PONTIUS-O system of I. Goldstein, which simulates the behaviour of a man when learning to fly an aeroplane.

Next, Lenat's AM (Lenat 1975, 1977) for discovering mathematics has had a certain amount of success. Given a few elementary concepts it generates new ones from these and assesses their interest with the help of evaluation functions applied by the rules. By this means it has rediscovered multiplication, in four different ways: iterated substitution, repeated addition, analogy with enumeration of the elements of a Cartesian product and by studying the cardinal number of the set of sub-sets of a given set. It has rediscovered the concept of a prime number and the fundamental theorem of arithmetic, that any integer can be expressed as a product of primes in one and only one way. Table 7.2 gives AM's statement of the concept 'Prime Numbers'; this is the standard structure used in the system, which is able to fill in the entries (facets, or 'slots' cf. Section 7.5) itself, by degrees as it progresses. It creates new concepts by generalising or specialising concepts already formed. The right side of each rule in AM includes an explanation giving the reason for which the rule can be invoked. The system progresses by means of examples which it constructs and generalises itself; it brings into play many heuristics derived from human behaviour and its method of reasoning is inductive.

Lenat has written a new system EURISKO (Lenat 1983), a generalisation of AM that can use meta-knowledge to construct its own rules for any field of study.

BACON (Langley 1979), whose field is physics, is somewhat similar to AM; it has rediscovered Kepler's laws of planetary motion and Ohm's and Coulomb's laws in electricity.

Table 7.2 Example of Lenat's AM: 'prime number' concept.

NAME: Prime Numbers
DEFINITIONS:
    Origin: number-of-divisors$(x) = 2$
    Predicate: Prime$(x) = (\forall z)(z \mid x \rightarrow z = 1$ or $z = x)$
    Iteration: $(x > 1)$ for i from 2 to $x - 1 \neg (i \mid x)$
EXAMPLES: $2, 3, 5, 7, 11, 13, 17, 19$
    Particular cases: $2, 3$
    Boundary-failures: $0, 1$
    Number-of-counter-examples: 12

GENERALISATIONS:	Number. Number with even number of divisors. Number with odd number of divisors.
SPECIALISATIONS:	Unique factorisation. Prime pairs. Sums of primes.
CONJECTURES:	Goldbach. Extreme divisors.
ANALOGIES:	Duality: numbers with small number-of-divisors and divisors of a number
INTEREST:	Relation to multiplication and division and all operations related to these

VALUE: 800

APS ('Adaptive Productions Systems') (Waterman 1975) consists of general models for performing arithmetical operations, learning words, completing series. The rules are ordered and learning is a matter of inserting new rules in suitably chosen places. However, this decreeing of an order goes against the purely declarative nature of rule-based systems and against what is known of human psychology – our knowledge of special and well-defined fields may be ordered but taken as a whole it is not.

Mitchell, Banerji *et al.* (Mitchell 1981) have written a system for formal integration that can improve its performance as a result of experience. Having found a primitive for a given function it extracts from its resolution tree the path(s) it has followed; it then particularises the general rewrite rules it has used by specifying the context in which they were applied, thus turning them into production rules in the usual sense. It then generalises the result by replacing each specific function by the class to which it belongs, so that for example a sine becomes any trigonometric function. Rules that have been used wrongly are marked to be deleted from any future occurrence of the same context. Premises, which can become either too general or too particular, are modified in the light of succeeding exercises; the authors report considerable improvements in performance as a result of these measures.

ANA (McDermott 1979) can learn and remember the way to perform a new task by reasoning by analogy with methods already known. It simulates a robot which manages a shop (of a paint dealer); it generates new rules continually by transferring previously met situations to the new ones it meets, so long as there are no glaring inconsistencies. The importance of this work is that it has shown that very simple mechanisms – here, learning mechanisms – can be easily and effectively grafted on to rule-based systems.

ACT (Anderson & Kline 1979), written by two psychologists at Carnegie Mellon University, deserves special mention because it is both general and able to learn. Its aim is to simulate human behaviour, using the results of classical psychological experiments on concept formation. ACT's knowledge is in two forms: a declarative part consisting of a graph of propositions, similar to the semantic networks of AI; and a procedural part consisting of a set of production rules. Additions to and changes of the rules are obtained by four different means, designation, reinforcement, generalisation and discrimination respectively.

PS ('Production System') (Rychener 1976): with the aid of this a wide variety of AI programs have been rewritten as production-rule systems; examples are:

1. STUDENT (Bobrow), for solving problems in algebra, stated in English.

2. EPAM (Feigenbaum) answers test questions involving series of letters.
3. GPS (General Problem Solver) of Newell, Shaw and Simon can perform tasks in a variety of fields.
4. SHRDLU of Winograd solves problems and conducts dialogues in English in a universe consisting of rectangular blocks; and a similar program of Moran.
5. A program due to Perdue and Berliner for playing chess end games.

We next consider a family of expert systems based on first-order predicate logic and the particular method of inference known as the resolution principle.

7.4 EXPERT SYSTEMS BASED ON FIRST-ORDER LOGIC

A language designed specially for modelling human reasoning has existed for a long time: the language of mathematical logic. A production rule 'situation → possible conclusion', although expressed in a slightly different formalism, is essentially a theorem of this subject, that is, a logical statement concerning assertions whose interpretation may be either true or false. The only difference is that the rules given by the expert are treated as given truths – that is, axioms – even when they cannot be proved to be true; so these rules are very similar to the mathematical rules of rewriting expressions – formal manipulations and grammars, Markov algorithms, monoids. There is thus good reason to think of an expert system in terms of formal logic.

The majority of systems we have discussed so far operate in propositional logic (cf. Chapter 3), in which all the entities concerned are constants; we now consider two systems, PROLOG and SNARK, based on first-order logic, meaning that they admit variables, and some of their applications. PROLOG, due to Alain Colmerauer (1971) was in fact designed with the understanding of natural languages in mind, before the idea of an expert system had been conceived.

7.4.1 PROLOG

PROLOG is a programming language whose basic units are not, as in classical programming languages, instructions but theorems of first-order logic (cf. Section 3.10). The description 'first-order' means that these theorems involve variables, that is, parameters quantified universally and therefore replaceable by any well-formed expression in the language. The statement $P(x_1, x_2, ..., x_n)$, where $x_1, x_2, ..., x_n$ are variables, is a predicate (of order n), and is interpreted as meaning '$P(...)$ is true' (Colmerauer 1971, Roussel 1975). Predicates themselves cannot be quantified in first-order logic: systems in which they can be are known as logics of order 2, 3, ... (Huet 1978).

PROLOG is in effect a particular interpreter of formulae in first-order logic; it acts on clauses, expressions that are disjunctions of predicates (cf. Section 3.10.2). The standard ('normal disjunctive') form of a clause is

$$(\neg h_1 \lor \neg h_2 \lor \cdots \lor \neg h_i) \lor (C_1 \land C_2 \land \cdots \land C_j)$$

which is interpreted as

$$h_1 \land h_2 \land \cdots \land h_i \supset C_1 \land C_2 \land \cdots \land C_j$$

A special feature of PROLOG is that it works only with Horn clauses, that is, clauses in which there is only one positive literal, which is of course on the right, and therefore only one conclusion, C_1 say. Thus disjunctions of conclusions, such as $C_2 \lor C_3$, are not allowed.

Several implementations of PROLOG have been made since the first version, in Fortran (described in Roussel 75), which was followed by a portable interpreter (Battini 1973); the language has been taken up mainly in Portugal (Coelho 1980), Britain (Warren 1977), Hungary (Szeedi 1977) and Japan where it is central to the 'fifth generation' project. Very efficient hardware interpretation is provided by the EPILOG machine of Sansonnet and Alii.

All PROLOG interpreters are in fact theorem provers based on the Resolution principle described in Section 3.10 (Herbrand 1931, Robinson 1965); as explained there, this works by *reductio ad absurdum*, proving $p \supset q$ by showing that $p \land \neg q$ entails a contradiction. Whilst the method is in principle completely general in the sense that it enables any theorem in any formal system to be proved, in practice it is combinatorially heavy, and it is rather unnatural – we seldom reason in this way: but computer programs do this kind of thing better than we do.

A PROLOG clause can be interpreted on either of two different levels: procedurally via an interpreter or declaratively as the statement of a logical theorem in the universe of discourse.

Example. Concatenation (Gallaire 1981). The concatenation of a string X with the empty string NIL is X itself, written

$+ \text{CONCAT(NIL}.X, X)$

If $U = X \cdot W$ where the point means that W is the last character of the string U, the concatenation of U with the string Y is $X.Z$, where Z is the string 'W concatenated with Y':

$$+ CONCAT(X.W. \ X.Z) - CONCAT(W.Y.Z)$$

The importance of PROLOG as a programming language is thus threefold:

1. The clauses translate directly into usable assertions (theorems).
2. The interpreter provides a ready-made unification algorithm.
3. The search tree, representing attempts to unify the clauses two at a time, is handled automatically (back-track LIFO).

Further, the resolution process can be steered by a strategy that assigns priorities to the clauses and to the literals considered for unification (Kowalski 1979, Chapter 3: 'Lush Resolution'): the clauses are scanned in the order in which they are presented and within each clause the literals are scanned from right to left – this will deal with all cases. The version implemented at Marseilles uses depth-first search together with program-mable back-tracking, this latter controlled by the use of the / character, which prohibits any return to the literal on its left: this restricts the scope of the procedure but makes it more efficient.

To summarise, PROLOG provides a simple formalism with which the user can both state and solve his problems; all he has to do is to construct suitable predicates that describe the problem.

7.4.2 An expert system written in PROLOG: PEACE

This, written at Toulouse (Dincbas 1979), synthesises and analyses such electrical circuits as shown in Fig. 7.6. The circuit consists of resistances, inductances and capacitances of given values, and contains no energy source.

The problem of, say, finding the impedance between the two points A and D reduces to proving the theorem

$$\neg \ impedance \ (A, D, {}^{*}X)$$

The result, obtained by *reductio ad absurdum*, will be given by the final value of the variable $^{*}X$, by the resolution principle.

The circuit is described by means of predicates 'equal', 'branch' and 'multiple-node' combined into clauses of the type

'branch(A, B, L_1')' with 'equal$(L_1', L_1\omega)$'   (ω the frequency)
'equal$(C_1', 1/C_1\omega)$'
'multiple-node$(B, 5)$'

The circuit rules needed by PEACE are those concerning the following four transformations (Fig. 7.7):

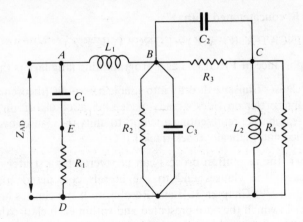

Fig. 7.6 Electrical circuit analysed by PEACE.

1. Impedances in parallel.

$$Z_1 Z_2/(Z_1 + Z_2)$$

2. Impedences in series.

$$Z_1 + Z_2$$

3. Delta → star.

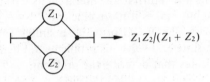

$$Y_i = Z_j Z_k/(\sum Z_i)$$

4. Star → delta.
The inverse of (3): $Z_i = \sum Y_j Y_k)/Y_i$

Fig. 7.7.

PEACE needs also to be able to manipulate complex numbers: PROLOG initially 'knew' only the positive integers; its knowledge has been extended, first to include the negative integers, then the rationals, then the reals (with the precision as a parameter) and finally to the complex numbers. Thus addition when negative integers are allowed is performed with the help of the clauses

$$\text{plus}(-u, v, -w) \Leftarrow \text{less-than-or-equal}(v, u) \wedge \text{minus}(u, v, w)$$

meaning

$$v \leqslant u \quad \text{and} \quad u - v = w \Rightarrow v - u = -w$$

The circuit transformations are expressed in terms of the predicates; thus for (2) above, impedances in series, the predicate is:

$$\text{series } (Z_1, Z_2) \Leftarrow \text{branch}(x, t, Z_1) \wedge \text{branch}(t, y, Z_1) \wedge \text{different}(t, y)$$
$$\wedge \text{simple-node}(t) \wedge \text{suppress}(\text{branch}(x, t, Z_1))$$
$$\wedge \text{suppress}(\text{branch}(t, y, Z_2)) \text{plus}(Z_1, Z_2, Z)$$
$$\wedge \text{add}(\text{branch}(x, y, Z))$$

PEACE's strategy is to apply the above transformations to the circuit to be analysed, in the order given, which corresponds to the minimum number of nodes of the circuit that are involved. Finding the allowable transformations at any stage is done by the unification algorithm and is performed by PROLOG; and the database can be modified after each transformation. It can be shown that the process always converges to a circuit reduced to two points. Thus the solution is obtained purely algorithmically.

In a system such as PEACE all the knowledge involved – basic facts, the Resolution procedures, control schemas – is expressed solely as conjunctions of clauses; this is the characteristic feature of the next system also that we shall describe, MECHO.

7.4.3 MECHO: a system for solving problems in mechanics

This was developed at Edinburgh by Bundy and his collaborators (Bundy *et al.* 1979). Using predicate calculus and PROLOG it solves problems concerning point masses, inclined planes, strings and pulleys, stated in English. It can control its search procedure and develop rules for itself, the latter by using meta-knowledge concerning the rules themselves.

The first task the problem has to undertake is to understand the problem put to it in natural language. A simple word-for-word substitution will not suffice because the field is too wide (Bobrow 1975, Charniak 1978, Gelb 1965); there is no general method and here a full understanding of the physical situation is needed in order to express the problem.

The second task is to learn what is not usually taught in lessons on mechanics, how to solve a system of equations, how to construct a model, how to control a search. What differentiates the expert from the non-expert is the former's ability to make better use of his knowledge, and in this context the Edinburgh group could draw on two excellent resources: a study by D. Marples of the way Cambridge engineers went about setting up the equations for a system, and by Bundy of how people solved systems of linear and quadratic equations. From these Bundy had been able to deduce a set of strategies – 'grouping', 'isolating', 'attracting', all expressible in PROLOG. What remained to be done was to find the right inference rules that could construct the long chains of reasoning from the English statement of the problem to its solution.

7.4.3.1 An example of a problem solved by MECHO

The natural language statement is:

> Two particles of masses b, c are joined by a fine string passing over a smooth pulley. Find the acceleration of the particle of mass b.

The fairly simple syntactic/semantic analysis, using 'schemas' or 'scripts' of mechanics (cf. Section 8.6.2) gives the following set of 22 unitary clauses:

is(particle, $p1$)	mass($p2$, $m2$, time_1)
end-right($S1$, $e1$)	measure($m1$, b)
is(pulley, $pl1$)	given($m1$)
midstring ($S1$, $mi1$)	is(string, $S1$)
mass($p1$, $m1$, time_1)	contact-fixed($e1$, $p1$, time_1)
friction($pl1$, 0)	contact-fixed($e2$, $p2$, time_1)
acceleration($p2$, accel. $90°$, time_1)	contact-fixed($pl1$, $mi1$, time_1)
is(particle, $p2$)	mass($S1$, 0, time_1)
end-left($S1$, $e2$)	acceleration($p1$, accel. $270°$, time_1)
is(period, time_1)	given($m2$)
measure($m2$, c)	sought(accel.)

Marples method looks for an equation expressing the quantity sought, 'accel', in terms of the quantities given, $m1$, $m2$ and the gravitational constant g, this last being added by the MECHO system itself. In the first instance it keeps only those equations that involve the forces acting on, for example, the particle $p1$ and deduces from these:

$$m1 \times g + \text{tension\_1} = m1 \times \text{accel.}$$

The introduction of the new unknown, tension_1, is made necessary by a special rule; but the program knows that this is a tension and also that it needs another relation in order to solve the problem. It then shows that the tension acting on $p2$ is the same, constructs the corresponding equation for $p2$ and arrives at the result by eliminating tension_1. Other problems, considerably more complicated, have been solved by MECHO.

7.4.3.2 The MECHO system

In this account we pass over many points so as to concentrate on those most relevant to the subject of the chapter:

1. representation of knowledge of the physical world.
2. logic for controlling the deduction and resolution procedures.
3. execution of these procedures.

1. The knowledge base − the laws of physics
The system has a simple view of the world, based on Newtonian mechanics. It knows only about objects, of 0, 1 or 2 dimensions and each object is identified uniquely by a name. A point is an object of dimension 0; it can be a particle having a mass, or simply refer to a location in the plane. A line is a 1-dimensional object that has two distinguishable ends. Given these, many objects can be described by means of simple predicates: thus a weight, a pulley and a man are all particles, a string and a rope are lines as are also a bar and a beam, but with different physical properties.

Relations between objects are given as predicates; the name of the predicate specifies the relation and the arguments state the objects between which the relation holds; the order in which the arguments are given, and other conventions such as signs, depend on the parameters of the procedure call. Figure 7.8 is an example. Here AC labels a call that initiates a calculation of the type 'create' (see (B) below) by the module that searches for the named quantities; here the basically recursive nature of the knowledge base becomes evident, since 'force-sum' for example is given by another formula.

2. The control logic
This is written in PROLOG but is peculiar to MECHO because it inhibits the usual Resolution strategy built into PROLOG. Every action is broken down progressively into sub-goals by one of the 150 rules in the knowledge

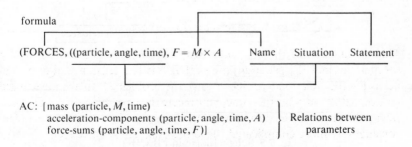

formula

(FORCES, ((particle, angle, time), $F = M \times A$ Name   Situation   Statement

AC: [mass (particle, M, time)
     acceleration-components (particle, angle, time, A) } Relations between
     force-sums (particle, angle, time, F)]   parameters

Fig. 7.8.

base, and each sub-goal, when it is created, is labelled D ('direct'), *AC* ('with creation') or *SC* ('without creation') as appropriate. The different labels initiate different types of action, as shown in Fig. 7.9.

The search proceeds depth-first, taking the rules in a fixed order; MECHO's clauses allow new objects to be created if they are essential to the solution, but keep the number under control.

Similarity classes. MECHO 'knows' the properties of the predicates it uses, for example whether they are transitive, symmetric or reflexive. Those that are their own resolvents are grouped into 'similarity classes', isomorphic with the trees represented by the set of PROLOG clauses. The root of the tree represents the class uniquely and it alone can be unified; thus for 'equality' we have the axiomatisation:

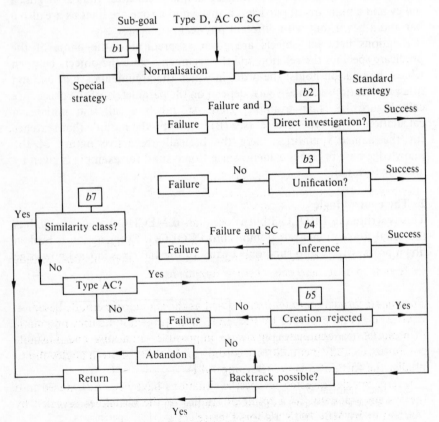

Fig. 7.9 Subgoal logic in MECHO.

$$\text{equal}(a, b) \leftarrow \text{representative}(a, \text{root}) \land \text{representative}(b, \text{root})$$
$$\text{representative}(a, a) \leftarrow \text{is}(a, \text{root})$$
$$\text{representative}(a, \text{root}) \leftarrow \text{arc}(a, b) \land \text{representative}(b, \text{root})$$

which enables all equal elements to be put in the same tree.

Three other predicates also are handled by the same mechanism: 'same-position', 'units-of-measurement', 'time-period', concerning respectively point objects that occupy the same spatial location at the instant considered, quantities of the same nature expressed in different units and time intervals having some part in common.

3. Execution

First-pass. MECHO considers only those relations or equations that do not require any new objects to be created, that is, only those labelled D or SC. This constraint is removed in later stages.

Prediction. MECHO uses information about the physical world to decide if a sub-goal is acceptable, or to predict the nature of the solution: thus a table length must be a positive number, an angle in the context of an object such as an office table must be less than $180°$. This kind of knowledge is used also in manipulating equalities and in discussing solutions.

Marple's method. To find an unknown quantity, x, MECHO:

1. describes it: i.e. states its physical nature (a mass, for example) and the entities related to it (e.g. acceleration, direction, time);
2. looks for relevant relations, i.e. lists all possible formulae;
3. looks for the right equation, i.e. scans this list to find the formula that best represents the current situation, given the known parameters;
4. checks to see if this formula is independent of the other equations already found, so as to determine the new unknown.

Formal algebraic manipulation. As well as the standard methods based on rewrite rules and provided by PROLOG itself, this module uses pragmatic information to eliminate physically impossible situations and unstable equilibria, to study inequalities according to the value of given angles and to predict the form of a curve (Borning 1981).

Inference rules directed to specific situations have been introduced into the system gradually, as a result of studies of the principles revealed by Marples or by MECHO's authors themselves.

7.4.3.3 Results

MECHO runs on a DEC 10 machine, using 80K words of 36 bits. The part of the system that handles natural language has 900 clauses, that for finding the equations has 600 and the algebraic manipulation has 200. The PROLOG interpreter takes 20K.

The system has been applied mainly to three classes of problem: pulleys, particles moving with constant acceleration, particles moving on complex trajectories. So far only certain problems have been entered in English, the rest directly in predicate form. At the time of writing (1985) problems under study concern levers, frameworks, projectiles, moments of inertia, relative velocities, hydrostatics.

Example (Fig. 7.10). A particle starts from rest at *P*. Given *R*1, what is the smallest value of *R*2 such that the particle makes a complete turn of *C*1? The circles *C*1, *C*2 touch the horizontal line at *Q*.

To state this problem in first-order logic the circles are divided into three geometrically related parts, and the figure is represented by a set of about twenty unitary causes.

MECHO's authors have given the complete solutions provided by the system of a number of complex problems; when expressed in usual form these could cover more than a page.

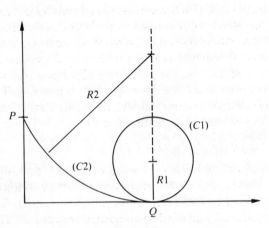

Fig. 7.10

7.4.4 Significance of PROLOG and predicate calculus

The main advantage of writing expert systems in PROLOG is the resulting uniformity of representation: facts, rules of inference, procedures and control structures are all expressed by conjunctions of clauses, which themselves are disjunctions of literals. There is a single computing mechanism, related to the Resolution principle, which simplifies both programming and the semantics of programs, which are consequently easy to check. Experience has shown that the efficiency of PROLOG compares favourably with that of LISP, and for this reason MYCIN has been completely rewritten in PROLOG, with an increase in efficiency (Warren 1977). Further, PROLOG offers the possibility of access to the proof tree, to the inputs and outputs, to different parts of the clauses and of the literals and to the back-tracking mechanism used in the proof.

The real importance, however, lies in the fact that the control of the execution – that is, the deduction process that operates at the meta-knowledge level – can be written in PROLOG itself; writing this becomes the major problem when the knowledge base is large. In effect, PROLOG makes it possible to use clauses as arguments of predicates and so provides some of the features of a second-order logic; new knowledge can be generated or existing knowledge items deleted by means of the commands ADD, SUPP respectively.

7.4.4.1 A control language for PROLOG

Gallaire and Lasserre (1979) have proposed a metalanguage for the control of the deduction in which two types of metarules are introduced into PROLOG and incorporated into the normal strategy. Rules of type Meta-L are used to find the literal to be unified in a given clause; those of type Meta-C to find the ancestor clause among a set of possibilities. Meta-L rules make use of a local, contextual evaluation to 'freeze' certain candidate clauses or to force a back-track, the underlying idea being that if a useful instantiation has not been found there is no point in continuing. The aim of the Meta-C rules is to assign a priority to each candidate clause that depends on certain conditions related to the unification, thus:

$$\text{Meta-C}(P, L, k, R) \Leftarrow C_1 \wedge C_2 \wedge \cdots \wedge C_n$$

states that every ancestor clause, being unified with $\neg P \vee L$, has priority k provided that R is unified with the literal considered in the previous step and that $C_1, C_2, ..., C_n$ are all T. These meta-rules give the user great freedom in designing a strategy specially adapted to his particular problem. The system METALOG written by Dincbas at CERT, Toulouse, provides the user with a set of strategic commands in the form of meta-clauses; these increase PROLOG's effectiveness and turn it into a true problem solver.

7.4.4.2 PROLOG's predicate calculus compared with production-rule systems

The Horn clauses used by PROLOG are clearly similar to production rules but on closer examination several differences appear, all due to the fact that in PROLOG the control structure is pre-programmed (cf. Section 7.4.1): the resolution principle, with its rigid linear strategy, dictates the kinds of trial to be made and the order in which they are to be made. It is however possible to modify this strategy, when the advantage of PROLOG becomes:

1. its benefitting from a general unification algorithm, ready programmed;
2. its benefitting also from a mechanism for managing the AND–OR search tree, this also provided ready-made by the interpreter.

PROLOG differs from production-rule systems in that as each resolution adds a further clause (a rule), the number of rules increases continually during the solution process until the empty clause is reached. This is a characteristic of all systems in which everything occurs at the same level; in particular, the assumptions and the conclusions play the same role and the search process can start as well from one as from the other, the actual direction being set at each resolution and thus variable from one to another. This is an advantage over production-rule systems of classical type, for which in general the rules operate in only one direction.

Whilst the possibility of introducing likelihood or plausibility coefficients into the reasoning was not forseen when PROLOG was designed, their use can easily be incorporated into the interpreter, as for example in MYCIN. However, PROLOG clauses are ordered and modularity and the ease of adding new knowledge items are less than in production systems. PROLOG is in fact a high-level programming language of procedural type: it cannot be read by the first 'expert' who picks up a program.

Of course, PROLOG is not the only means for interpreting the language of first-order logic: another is the use of natural deduction:

$$\textit{modus ponens:}\ \text{given}\ p\ \text{and}\ (p \supset q),\ q\ \text{follows}$$
$$\textit{modus tollens:}\ \text{given}\ \neg q\ \text{and}\ (p \supset q),\ \neg p\ \text{follows}$$

contrasting with both MYCIN which works by backwards chaining and with PROLOG which works in both directions at the same time. Partial backwards chaining is essential for guiding the search towards the goal, but reasoning as usually understood by the expert is mostly by *modus ponens*.

We next give a short account of another system based on first-order logic,

SNARK – Symbolic Normalized Acquisition and Representation of Knowledge (Lauriere 1988) – with examples of its application to formal mathematical manipulation.

7.4.5 SNARK: a first-order logic language

In conjunction with first-order logic SNARK uses a relational form for the expression of knowledge. In contrast to MYCIN which is restricted to propositional calculus it uses variables, which being universally quantified are open to any substitution; thus in SNARK the statement nature $(x) =$ human ... means 'for any x that is human ...'. The famous syllogism is thus written:

if nature$(x) =$ human **then** mortal$(x) = T$

and given nature(Socrates) = human SNARK deduces mortal(Socrates) $= T$. The same rule would be invoked for every x such that nature$(x) =$ human.

By convention, SNARK uses only binary relations; in the written form of these the variables are put in parentheses.

Properties can be nested, as in the relation:

age(roof(x)) = min(150, age(wall(y)))

Objects are usually referenced only by their properties, and need not be given names; thus a geological entity G, of the nature of a 'rift', lying under a layer C and of age greater than 100 years can be defined:

below$(C) = (G)$
nature$(G) =$ rift
age$(G) > 100$

Relations that are of purely mathematical nature can be translated into SNARK; thus the transitivity property of 'below' becomes:

  if under$(x) = (y)$
 and under$(y) = (z)$
then under$(x) = (z)$

These features make SNARK a language of the same family as PROLOG, but it escapes some of the restrictions of the latter: thus neither the order of the premises nor that of the rules is of any significance, and as it uses natural deduction rather than Resolution it is not limited to Horn clauses. But this freedom to input the knowledge in any order is paid for by the threat of combinatorial explosion: at any instant, any variable in whatever rule is then invoked is substitutable by many objects in the facts base, so there may be a very large number of n-tuples for each evaluation. The threat can be countered by a strategy of dynamic evaluation of the rules, based on the principle of starting from what is known at the particular instant and propagating this symbolically (cf. Section 8.3).

Thus SNARK has the characteristics of declarative languages and of expert systems – modularity, declarations of knowledge items – and of problem-solvers – ability for formal manipulation, admission of assumptions, back-tracking, normalisation and unification of expressions. It is currently used in geology, archaeology, medicine, anthropology, mathematics, physics, control of nuclear power stations and for computer-assisted teaching in several of these fields; and to attack combinatorial optimisation problems in bridge playing. To give a little more detail we describe its application to find the primitive – the formal integral – of a given function.

Finding primitives. The knowledge base here is a set of heuristic rules for the strategy to be adopted when faced with a particular problem. For example, if the expression to be integrated is a sum, or a sum raised to some power, a good approach is to separate the terms; this is written in SNARK:

> **let**   expression-to-integrate(i) = (e)
> **if**   sum(e) = T
> **then** $i \leftarrow$ integration(first-term(e)) + integral(second-term(e))

If e involves an inverse trigonometric function (written arctrig) a change of variable should be considered:

> **let**   expression-to-integrate(i) = (e)
> **let**   term(e) = (t)
> **let**   operator-head(t) = arctrig
> **then** change-variable(e) = (t)

Note that:

1. Rules are called only when needed, that is, when at least one of the premises corresponds to one of the conclusions that has been reached as a result of invoking the previous rule.
2. The variable (e) plays the role of a global variable; all the objects dealt with are referenced and described in relation to this. This corresponds to a favourable case that is not found in all applications.
3. Those premises beginning with **let** act as definitions; the evaluation starts with this part and the **if** parts are tested only if their arguments are known.
4. The facts base can contain variables, in the mathematical sense of the word.
5. Some properties in the 'action' part serve to pass parameters; thus the expression 'change-variable(e) = (t)' is recorded as such in the facts base

and may have the effect later on of invoking the rule for change of variable, which states:

to change the variable from x to $y = f(x)$, it must be possible to express (e) dx as a function of y and dy only

in SNARK:

if   change-of-variable$(e) = f(x)$
then calculate $dy =$ derivative $f(x)$ dx
      unify(e, y, dy) (a)
      check not-appears(e, x) (b)

where the actions (a), (b) are:

(a) Apply to the expression (e) the rules:

$$y \to f(x) \quad \text{and} \quad dy \to f'(x)\, dx.$$

(b) Check that after this has been done the expression to be integrated no longer involves the variable x.

Comparing the SNARK to a program of classical type we see that

1. There is no need to order the rules
2. The rules are independent: they communicate only through statements concerning the single global variable (e) – the expression to be integrated – and this can change in the course of the solution. This possibility, for instance case *i*: $\int k \cdot e = k \int e$, or $\int (e_1 + e_2) = \int e_1 + \int e_2$ is taken into account by the system.
3. Several rules can relate to a single primitive and one is selected according to a given set of priorities, depending on the complexity of the expression; another will be chosen if the first choice does not lead to success.
4. The full set of rules for integration consists of 86 for strategies and 368 for handling trigonometric, exponential and logarithmic functions.
5. Compiling such a set of rules demands considerable effort, and experience has shown that some can be forgotten and others are stated with insufficient precision. Modification of rules is easily done, the SNARK language being reasonably close to that of mathematics and thus readable: one scarcely dares to think of what the task would be like in a classical algorithmic language.
6. SNARK enables us to state both very general rules such as those given above and very specific rules such as those in Table 7.3, for integrating a fractional power of a rational function, e.g. $1/(px^2 + qx + r)^{1/2}$.

Role of the variables in SNARK. The instantiated variables refer to entries in the facts base; they play four different roles, each corresponding to one

Table 7.3 A SNARK rule.

if	nature(e) = fraction
let	denominator(e) = d
if	power fractional(d) = T
let	(t) = first-term(d)
if	degree(t) = 2
then	identify(t, $ay^2 + b$)
if	($a < 0 \wedge b \neq 0$)
then	change-of-variable(e) = (t)
	expression(t) = (b/a)cos θ

of four familiar programming processes:

1. Indexing the information items (list chaining).
2. Parametrising the rules (argument passing).
3. Directing attention to a goal (calling a sub-program).
4. Managing the search tree (updating a stack).

We consider these in turn.

1. Indexing. Every variable in the facts base is instantiated, by definition; it corresponds to a value that refers to an object defined only by relations known at that time and possibly having neither a name nor any characteristic property. Further, all the entries bearing on the same property, and so on the same value, are directly accessible: this is the same as in a relational database (Fig. 7.11).

2. Parametrising. The variables in the rules are formal variables, freely substitutable; and the rules are theorems that hold for any object that satisfies the hypotheses. The calls (of the rules) and the passings of parameters are made by value (rather than by name) because it is the values of the objects in the facts base that decides which rule is to be invoked.

3. Sub-program call. Because of the variables a particular conclusion of a rule can associated with the setting of a new goal. Thus the entry

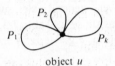

object u object v

Fig. 7.11 An object in SNARK's facts base.

'change-of-variable(e)' enables the possibility of a change of variable in (e) to be recorded, which may be returned to later by another rule which will carry out the procedure. This is a novel type of procedure call, because at any instant there may be goals, each with associated procedures, in competition with each other; the choice must be made by a higher-level rule (metarule) which evaluates the relative difficulties of the competing goals.

4. Managing the tree. By their very nature the problems require there always to be the possibility of back-tracking – for a variety of reasons, such as an unfortunate combination of variables or a rule having been invoked too early, an insoluble problem may be encountered and therefore other possibilities must be examined. This is the classic problem of tree management, sometimes dealt with by recursive programming. In this case the depth to which the recursion has to go is entirely unknown, and can be very great; but the management can be performed simply with the aid of the indexing by variables: the choice of rule can be used to parametrise the indexing of all the facts deduced as a result of its application. For example, if v denotes a change of variable made to the expression e, then afterwards this e is marked ev; if this is found later to lead to an impasse then all the information relating to ev is deleted and the search restarted with the original expression. The strategy for traversing the tree can be expressed by metarules: the preference could for example be given to the least complex of the expressions being considered at that instant. Thus the tree management is controlled from outside the program (Nilsson 1980, Farreny 1985).

Using SNARK's interpreter it has been found possible to construct and implement within only a few days a body of rules for formal integration, with which the average time to integrate a given function is of the order of a few seconds on an IBM 370/168, for example:

$$\int x^3 \arcsin(x)/(1 - x^2)^{1/2} \, dx$$

The improvement over classical procedural programming is clear; a thousand new facts can be inferred in a few tens of seconds.

An important feature of the system is that the line of reasoning – that is, the order in which the rules are used and which can vary from case to case – can always be followed easily. Further, if asked it will always display the sub-tree it has used in order to establish any new fact whatever, starting from the initial information; this property makes expert systems excellent choices as tools for computer-aided teaching.

We have now given several examples that illustrate the declarative approach of expert systems – that is, the use of a knowledge base independent of the program. We shall next compare this approach with that

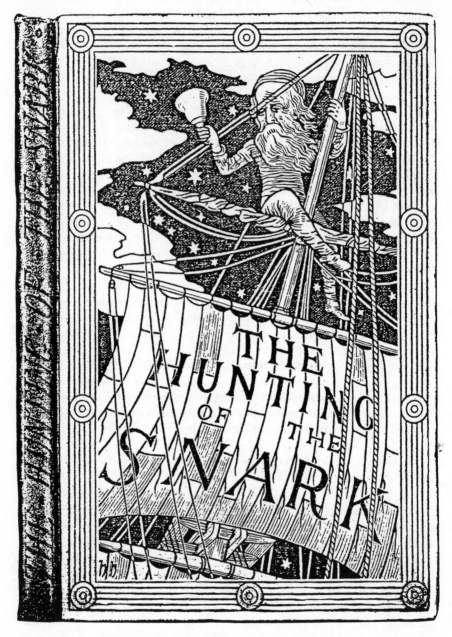

Fig. 7.12 *The Hunting of the Snark* book jacket.

of the classical procedural approach. In the following section, we consider the power and efficiency of declarative languages and indicate the lines along which research is now being pursued. The relative advantages of the declarative and procedural approaches are discussed in Section 7.6 and the control process in Section 7.7: it is the use of meta-knowledge that distinguishes expert systems fundamentally from systems based on rewrite rules.

7.5 THE DECLARATIVE/PROCEDURAL CONTROVERSY

This controversy arose out of the first successes of expert systems using a knowledge base consisting of production rules of the type:

Left side   →   Right side
incompletely described situation   possible conclusion

Thus the item of information:

all Ruritanian politicians are liars

would be entered into the base as:

if nature(x) = politician
if nationality(x) = Ruritanian
then liar(x) = T

There has been a corresponding controversy within classical programming, that between applicative and imperative styles, between recursive and iterative, operational and denotational, static and dynamic, functional and descriptive – the antithesis, in sum, between procedures and specifications. The ideal certainly is simply to specify something, a problem, a program, a knowledge item, a piece of know-how; with the declarative approach of production rules and expert systems, access to information is then gained through unification or the limited form of unification called pattern matching or filtering (Waterman and Hayes-Roth 1979, Nilsson 1980, Farreny 1980).

In the above example the reply to the question 'Is X a liar' is found by two enquiries of the facts base, whilst the assertion 'X is an honest politician' leads by unification to 'X is not Ruritanian'. By contrast, the procedural approach requires every question to be foreseen and a procedure written to deal with each one: if someone is stated to be a politician then his/her nationality is examined to find if he/she is honest. Thus a procedure expresses a flow of information, showing syntactically how knowledge is conveyed, whilst declarative statements simply express factual knowledge in a manner that is independent of use to which this might be put, is completely modular, requires no particular ordering to be observed and gives the semantics of a relation. They answer questions of the type 'What ...?', a point we emphasise because it is of prime importance.

7.5.1 The procedural approach in information science: 'programming languages are not really languages'

The word 'order' has several meanings, two of which are relevant here: one expresses the requirement that something specific shall be done, a command or an instruction or the corresponding verbs; the other, some kind of regularity or succession, a sequence or series. These correspond to two basic features of present-day programming languages – more precisely, to the idea of an algorithm; for these languages enable us to express algorithms, which:

1. consist entirely of instructions (first meaning of 'order').
2. must be given as a precisely defined sequence of these (second meaning).

It is clearly impossible to express in such languages facts such as 'the dollar is high to-day on the Paris Bourse' or 'Lake Geneva is very pleasant in good weather', because they do not correspond to any executable order; and in the absence of further information they are independent of each other.

Some information scientists have sought to relax one of these formidable restrictions, the one concerning the ordering of the instructions, by introducing new primitives. They have shown that in certain types of sequence the instructions can be permuted without affecting the algorithm; the programming languages embodying this idea are said to be 'assignment free' (or 'functional' or 'applicative'), the same variable never being used twice. Present work on parallelism, on Petri nets (see Section 8.4) and on program schemas is concerned with the same problem.

This, however, is to miss the real problem: we find it difficult to write algorithms because the very idea is foreign to us. When we are writing a program we are putting together a jig-saw puzzle of which we know only a few scattered pieces; our knowledge is modular and at any stage is confined to a few, say four to six, lines.

Consider now how we might make a computer use a piece of information such as Ohm's law for electrical circuits: the current I, voltage V and resistance R are related by $V = RI$. If this is entered in the database in this form the key question is how to make the machine recover the statement and interpret it 'intelligently'; this means:

1. Only when appropriate.
2. Making use of the fact that whilst the statement gives V as a function of R and I, it also gives by implication R as a function of V and I, and I of V and R; whatever was known about the values of V, R or I any reasonable person would obtain for two resistors in parallel $I1/I2 = R2/R1$.

We can see from this that when this rule is used it must invoke others, which in this particular case are the laws of algebra, concerning simplification and normalisation of expressions; and this brings to light a fundamental feature of existing programming languages, their implicit assumption of complete information. All the data for which the need has been foreseen in an algorithm must be available if it is to run; no parametrising or other freedom is allowed. But this does not correspond to the way a doctor goes about making a diagnosis, an engineer a design, a mathematician seeking to prove a theorem. Each starts with an incomplete description of the situation, makes whatever deductions are possible, then if necessary sets up more hypotheses in order to continue. Every situation is new: there is no pre-formed schema of universal applicability to guide their deliberations, and their methods are entirely different from the algorithmic approach.

This illustrates the fact that great areas of information processing are not amenable to classical programming. These are the fields in which humans handle factual information, mutually isolated rules, strategies and incomplete knowledge. All the knowledge here is non-algorithmic; it is certainly good to have an algorithm, but this rarely happens. Real needs, first in biology and chemistry, and the difficulties encountered in writing programs in the classical way led to the devising of a radically new approach and so to what we now call expert systems.

7.5.2 The control structure in an expert system

There is a fundamental difference between the control structure of an expert system and that of a procedural program. That of the former is what we may call open: a rule may be invoked at any instant, with no effect on anything but those entries in the facts base that describe the situation then being dealt with; the process goes in cycles, each cycle consisting of the selection of a rule followed by its execution, and after each cycle everything is re-evaluated and the order of the rules recalculated dynamically. In the latter the control is highly localised; the sequentially executed orders and the commands **if-then-else, do, repeat-while** affect only a very small part of the parameter field at any one time. Also the flow of instructions depends very little on the data, so that a small change in the input will usually have only a small effect on the execution

Table 7.4 Features of procedural and expert system approach.

	Knowledge	*Control*	*Reasoning*
Procedural programs	Coded (instructions)	Coded (instructions)	Black box
Expert system	Data rules and facts	Data in form of meta-rules	Accessible, explicit, visible

of a procedure – quite the opposite of the case for an expert system. Again, all the information in an expert system is easily available and the way this is to be used is not built into the rules but is a matter for the metarules and the interpreter; the converse holds for a procedural program because the control is prescribed and the knowledge is dispersed throughout the procedures and the representations used. Thus the two methodologies are in strong mutual opposition.

Whilst the expert system approach is needed when large knowledge bases are involved, the procedural approach is better in the case of specific and well-localised tasks. There is of course no reason why the right sides of certain rules should not be in effect procedure calls; to keep to the spirit of the expert system and to retain its advantages all that is necessary is that those procedures should only be placed in these right-hand parts and should never call each other.

The differences between the two approaches are summarised in Table 7.4.

7.5.3 Examples of production rule systems

The two examples are intended to illustrate the general working of production systems; they show in particular that it is always possible, though at the cost of introducing supplementary variables, to separate the operations into elementary modules having the form of conditional rules. In the light of the second example, in which, in contrast to the first, the rules and the control have been made completely separate, we give finally the fundamental characteristic of a well designed production system.

Example 1. Markov's algorithm for inverting a character string. Table 7.5 gives the rules; the symbols $\neq$ and % are control characters and cannot be substituted by anything else, whilse x, y can be replaced by any non-empty string. The list of rules is ordered as shown. Rule 6 has an empty 'condition' part and can be applied in any situation. Rule 5 has an empty 'action' part and signals the end of the procedure.

The use of these rules to reverse a character string is shown in Table 7.6.

Table 7.5. Rules for
Example 1.

R1:	$\neq xy \mapsto y \neq x$
R2:	$\neq \neq \mapsto \%$
R3:	$\% \neq \mapsto \%$
R4:	$\% x \mapsto x\%$
R5:	$\% \mapsto$
R6:	$x \mapsto \% x$

Table 7.6.

$MOT \mapsto \neq MOT$	(R6)
$\mapsto OT \neq M$	(R1)
$\mapsto \neq OT \neq M$	(R6)
$\mapsto T \neq O \neq M$	(R1)
$\mapsto \neq T \neq O \neq M$	(R6)
$\mapsto \neq \neq T \neq O \neq M$	(R6)
$\mapsto \% T \neq O \neq M$	(R2)
$\mapsto T\% \neq O \neq M$	(R4)
$\mapsto T\% O \neq M$	(R3)
$\mapsto TO\% \neq M$	(R4)
$\mapsto TO\% M$	(R3)
$\mapsto TOM\%$	(R4)
$\mapsto TOM$	(R5)

Example 2. There are three rules that operate on symbols $C1, C2, C3$, each standing for a string of any number of points, including zero.

R1:	$//C1/C2/$	$\to /C2/$
R2:	$/C1/C2/$	$\to /C1/C2//$
R3:	$/.C1/C2/C3/$	$\to /C1/C2/C2C3/$

The symbol $/$ is not substitutable.

If the input strings $C1$, $C2$, $C3$ are of p, q and 0 points respectively the system produces a string $C2$ of pq points, so in effect multiplies p by q; with $p = 3$, $q = 4$ this goes as follows:

```
by R2   /.../....///
   R3   /../..../..../      (C3 being empty)
   R3   /./..../......../
   R3   //..../............/
   R1   /............/
```

The rules can be unified with the input strings in any order; they are considered as productions and the unifications must be made with the entire left sides (cf. Section 3.4).

Some comments. From the start of information science we have been accustomed to thinking in terms of procedures rather than of rewrite rules, so it is not surprising that production systems should seem unfamiliar: but doesn't Example 2 correspond better to the way young children calculate?

The mechanisms used in these two examples may seem cumbersome: the formalism of current programming languages will quite rightly be preferred for such algorithmic situations. On the other hand, that of production rules together with bodies of discrete knowledge items assembled in no particular order becomes important when one has to handle sets of independent statements as is the case with factual assertions, heuristics and decision rules. Mathematical theorems, Chomsky-type grammars, strategies for medical diagnosis, engineering design and know-how come into this category (cf. Section 7.4.2). There is no reason why, after a number of similar cases have been treated, a package of rules should not be kept as such and used as a procedure – as no doubt happens in the human mind.

7.5.4   Efficiency of expert systems

The visible formalism of production rules is only the external representation of the knowledge: most systems translate the rules thus stated into an internal form for the sake of efficiency. This internal form structures the knowledge by grouping the rules and their premises into lists in the LISP sense. We shall describe two systems in which this is done: POLITICS (Carbonell 1978), which uses a nested rule structure that is richer than the external formalism, and PROSPECTOR (Dudas 1980) which works with a multigraph. The inference engines OPS and TANGO optimise the rule-invocation phase by other means, using an internal representation that gains efficiency by trading memory for speed; here interpretation is replaced by compilation, which results in easier invocation of the rules. An important point is that the structuring of which we are speaking is left to the system because it can require major changes if, as is common, the rule base is changed.

Recently, some information scientists have made a practice of using Petri nets (Petri 1962) as modelling tools; the analogy between these and the internal representations used by expert systems is very close, in particular Petri nets with predicates are only a rediscovery of systems of production rules based on first-order logic (cf. Section 7.4).

A final comment at this stage is that the inherent modularity of systems of production rules is itself a contributor to efficiency. Since a rule is activated as a result of an association and not because of an ordering fixed by a procedure, each new conclusion invokes only those rules that are relevant to this; some of these rules will be executed, and will activate other rules in turn, and so on.

In general, tasks that are to be performed are held waiting in an *agenda*, either because several rules can be executed at a particular instant and all but one must be made to wait, or because the action part of the rule executed requires a number of tasks to be performed. An agenda is a set of data items to which relative priorities are assigned, or more generally predicates that decide the order in which the items should be extracted. There is no need to consider any except those that relate to the situation at that instant, and only these are called (cf. test instructions in classical programming). Thus the sequence of inferences and the process of solution can be very different for different given data – which seems to be essential for efficiency. It is not by chance that we humans do not work by following through algorithms: even in the most trivial cases, such as multiplying two numbers together, we use a method adapted to the data, for multiplication using the shorter number as multiplier unless the longer is mainly of small digits and especially if it consists of 0s and 1s only.

Experience has shown that implementing a set of rules is quick and not at all tedious; if an error is found when a rule is executed only a few minutes are needed to correct the rule or to add a new rule. In contrast, an error detected in a procedural program may be difficult to correct because of the side effects that result from the sequential nature of the program, and the task may take several hours; it may also require the expensive and distracting involvement of a professional programmer.

The POLITICS program. The rigid **if-then** rules structure used so far in this chapter can be extended to **if-then-else**, which is well adapted to a nested **if** structure. This is what we describe here, and it has the great advantage of bringing the conditions under which a rule is invoked into closer agreement with the result and also of economising the writing of premises that are common to several rules. Systems of this type have been proposed by Goldstein (1977) and by Carbonell (1978).

Carbonell's POLITICS invokes the rules according to their context, using the idea of a script (Schank 1977), which arose out of research into the understanding of natural languages; consequently, the same rule may be invoked several times. The aim of POLITICS is to simulate human behaviour, with its beliefs and prejudices, when faced with political events. The rules have the internal form illustrated by Table 7.7.

Semantic network of PROSPECTOR. This system, due to SRI and intended as an aid in mineral prospecting, uses an internal representation somewhat different from and more efficient than the one just described. The inference engine constructs a graph whose vertices are elementary propositions and a rule is a sub-set of arcs joining certain vertices. A sub-set is marked AND for the premises of a single rule and OR for the same conclusion given by a number of different rules: this is shown in Fig. 7.13. Starting with the given facts, the successive deductions are made very simply by propagating the pointers through the graph. The optimisation of the process of reaching the goal – the vertex with no successor – is achieved with the aid of standard AI methods – e.g. the A^* algorithm, cf. Section

Table 7.7 A complex rule in POLITICS.

if Y deploys its troops close to or in X and	(script)
if X is a small country and Y a large country and	(trigger 2)
if X is already involved in a military conflict	(trigger 3)
and is in need of help	
and a victory by X would help Y in gaining its	
own ends	
then Y's goal = military aid to X	
else if Y's main aim is to extend its own	
political dominance	
then Y's goal = invade X	

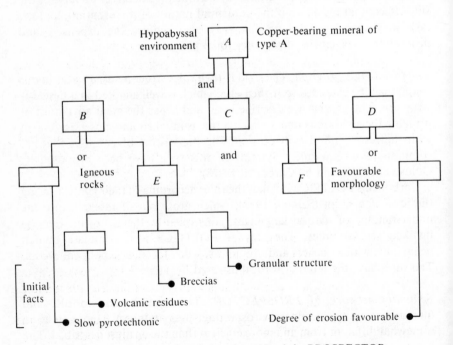

Fig. 7.13 Example of an inference network in PROSPECTOR.

5.6. (Nilsson 1980). This form of representation is very similar to the *semantic networks* and *frames* used in work on understanding natural language (Minsky 1975, Winograd 1982, Pitrat 1983): cf. Section 7.6.2.

Petri nets. In 1962 C. A. Petri suggested a general form of representation of processes as graphs, which was extended by A. Holt in 1970 who gave it the name of Petri nets. These nets are directed graphs whose vertices are either 'places', indicated by circles, or 'transitions', indicated by vertical bars. The places can contain tokens and if all those immediately preceding a transition do contain tokens then that transition is said to be 'active'. An active transition takes place, removes the token from each of its predecessor places and deposits one in each successor. Figure 7.14 is an example.

It will be clear that both transition graphs and finite-state automata are particular cases of Petri nets, and that the form has the advantage of representing not only the process but also its control. They thus enable problems of parallelism and synchronisation – which lie at the heart of information processing – to be modelled elegantly, in particular production rule systems. In these connections Petri nets can be important in these ways:

1. They can bring to light potential conflicts between rules, such as the possibility of two or more being invoked at the same time.
2. They can give the internal representation of the interpreter's rules, and so help in improving the solution time.

Zisman (1978) has suggested the following modification of the rules given in Table 7.5 for inverting a string of characters (Table 7.8); the right side of each rule gives the net rule to be considered after the execution of the current rule. Notice that one of the control characters (%) has been eliminated and that there are now only four rules instead of six. The

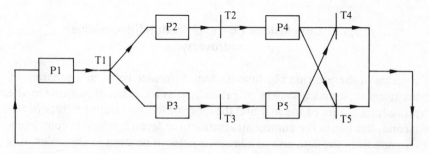

Fig. 7.14 Example of a Petri net; if T1 is triggered, P2 and P3 are loaded. This leads to the triggering of T2 and T3 and hence the loading of P4 and P5, of which only one can be in the active state: the system then returns to its initial state.

Table 7.8 Zisman's modification of
the rules of Table 7.5

P1:	$\neq$ $\neq$ $\rightarrow$	($P4$)
P2:	$\neq$ xy $\rightarrow$ $\neq$ x	($P2$)
P3:	$\rightarrow$ $\neq$	($P1$)
P4:	$\neq$ $\rightarrow$	($P4$)

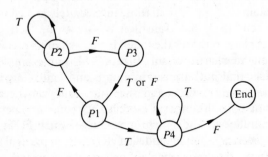

Fig. 7.15 System of production rules represented as a Petri net; for the sake of simplicity the transitions are not shown. There are two kinds of token, T(true) and false(F), according to the truth value of the left part of the rule.

representation for the interpreter, shown in Fig. 7.15, follows immediately; here the arrows correspond to the sequential control of the usual procedures and it will be clear that such a representation must be restricted to the interpreter: it departs from the true spirit of production systems, that is, their modularity. This has proved to be an excellent form of internal representation and, with a few modifications, has been used under the name of Augmentation Networks (ATN, Woods 1972) for the analysis of written texts: see for example Kayser 1981.

7.5.5 Conclusions on the procedural/declarative controversy

It seems in the end that the fundamental difference between a program of the usual type and a system of production rules is not that between the procedural nature of the first and the more or less declarative nature of the second, but lies in the control structure of the second, which is completely separate from the data and so allows the latter to be input in any order. It is this last property – freedom to input the data in any manner – that distinguishes the truly declarative language, whether it is based on production rules or some other type of formal logic. The importance of these languages derives from their complete modularity: the use of independent knowledge items, all communication between different parts of the program via the facts base, removal of the need for any ordering of the knowledge or facts, absence of imperative-type instructions and the possibilities of back-tracking in the solution process and of querying any rule.

7.6 THE DIFFERENT KNOWLEDGE TYPES, AND THEIR REPRESENTATION

The present aim of researchers in artificial intelligence is to create systems that on the one hand use large quantities of knowledge supplied by experts and on the other can conduct a dialogue with a user and explain their own reasoning. Success in this requires there to be an efficient system for managing a large and well-structured knowledge base, a rigorous distinction between the different levels of knowledge (cf. Section 7.6.1), appropriate representation of the knowledge (cf. Section 7.6.2) and a well-defined process for exchanging information between the various sources of knowledge.

It is essential also that the system 'knows what it knows'. With humans, use of such meta-knowledge is a common feature of daily life: thus we may find ourselves unable to name someone we meet in the street and yet know that we do know the name but have forgotten it for the moment, and equally we may know that we have never known the name of someone we meet. Further, we are continually using heuristic rules based on meta-knowledge, such as 'if that were so I should know it'; such rules depend on two basic parameters, the importance to us of the particular fact and the level of our own competence in that field. With humans each item of knowledge carries with it meta-knowledge implications related to the way in which we arrange this item along with the others that we hold, how we rate it, for what purpose it could be useful, to what family of knowledge it belongs. We consider all these points in the following paragraphs, in connection with real-life information systems.

7.6.1 The different types of knowledge

There seem to be eight main types, as follows:

1. Basic elements, real-world objects. These are derived from our perception of the physical world; we do not question their validity and we add them as we encounter them to our facts base.

2. Assertions and definitions. These bear on the basic objects; we accept them as certain.

3. Concepts. These are groupings or generalisations of the basic objects, constructed separately by each of us in our own way. Like MECHO (Bundy 1979) and AM (Lenat 1977), they rest on examples, counter-examples, particular cases and analogous or more general concepts.

4. Relations. These express the fundamental properties of the basic elements and equally the cause-and-effect relations between the concepts; they carry with them assessments of their level of plausibility and of their relevance to a given situation. Further, we must emphasise again that the representation of knowledge in an expert system is very similar to the models used in relational data-bases; the generalised relational model underlies for example OPS, PROLOG, SNARK and TANGO. The 'relationship–entity' couples, familiar in semantic nets, frames and scripts are no more than simple expressions of binary relations. Some expert systems (INTERNIST, BAOBAB, SPHINX) use existing data as their facts base.

5. Theorems and rewrite rules. These are particular cases of production rules, with the special features unquestioned. Theorems are useless without rules (expressing expertise) for using them. It is the presence of theorems in expert systems that makes all the difference between these and standard database management systems, where they are either lacking or have to be specially programmed. In these latter the modification of a theorem or the addition of a new theorem is a difficult matter, even though it may be necessary as much for the structure of the management system as for optimising the response to queries (Gallaire 1978).

6. Algorithms for problem solving. These are essential for the performing of certain tasks; they may or may not have been learned by the system. Here we meet a special type of knowledge: an algorithm is a sequence of actions that constitutes a unit, and in contrast to other types in which the order in which the items are memorised is irrelevant, here it is vital. We humans seem unable to hold in our minds long procedures involving many different actions, and our use of algorithms is limited to very special cases, mostly numerical. However, we have to handle many other types of information, and we find that the computer is of much greater help than a simple calculator in situations where an algorithmic approach has to be made.

7. Strategies and heuristics. These are rules of behaviour, either innate or acquired, which enable us to envisage the actions to be undertaken in a given situation. They use raw information in a sense that is opposite to that in which it was learned: if I know (cf. (4) above) that a certain action will have a certain effect, then if I wish to produce that effect I should consider performing that action. Humans are constantly using this principle, in perception, in forming concepts, in solving problems and in formal reasoning; it was the need to take into account this fundamental type of

human knowledge that stimulated research into expert systems and artificial intelligence.

8. Meta-knowledge. This enters on several levels, and in successive stages. It is a matter first of knowing what is known, what confidence to place in the knowledge, what degree of importance to attach to an item of knowledge in relation to a whole body. It also concerns the organising of bodies of knowledge of different types and knowing when and how each can be used. Section 7.7 deals with this question and how existing systems respond to it.

7.6.2 Knowledge representations in existing systems

Here we give briefly the present most commonly used methods. The relative advantages are mainly technical, the basic differences between the methods concerning the ease with which the knowledge can be modified. Table 7.9 gives an ordering of the representations which although rather crude is nevertheless useful in fixing ideas; the order is from the most procedural (most rigid, most highly structured) at the top to the most declarative (most open, most free-form) at the bottom.

Finite state automata, programs, predicate calculus and production rules are theoretically equivalent (cf. Section 7.5.2) in the sense that in principle they can all be reduced to a universal Turing machine; but they differ greatly in their convenience in use.

'Frames', 'scripts', 'semantic nets' and *ad hoc* formalisms developed to meet the needs of artificial intelligence; they are much used in understanding natural language (Charniak 1978, Cordier 1979, Pitrat 1982).

Table 7.9 Knowledge representations.

Procedural 'closed'			
	1. Finite state automata	Section 7.5.1	Markov 1954
	2. Programs	5.1	Meyer 1978
	3. Scripts (schema)	5.4, 6.2	Schank 1977
	4. Semantic nets	5.4	McCarthy 1977
	5. Frames (prototypes)	5.4, 6.2	Minsky 1975
	6. Graphs, networks	5.4	Petri 1962
	7. Formal specifications	6.1	Germain 1981
	8. Predicate calculus	4.1	Kowalski 1979
	9. Theorems, rewrite rules	6.1	Huet 1978
	10. Production rules	2.3	Shortliffe 1976
	11. Natural language		Pitrat 1981
declarative 'open'			

Frames, or prototypes, are complex data structures proposed by Minsky in 1975; they are representations of typical real-life situations such as waiting at an airport or participating in a family dinner. Each frame consists of a number of 'slots' for the objects that are involved in the situation, with the possibility of a slot referring to another frame; in addition it holds information on how it is to be used – how the slots are to be filled, default values, how the frame is to be activated – and what should be done in untypical situations.

A script, or schema, describes a stereotype scenario and the actions of the people involved; scripts reflect present-day culture and are essential for understanding sentences like 'I went into a restaurant and the waitress brought me the menu' (Schank 1975). They can call other scripts and, more than frames, are concerned with the dynamic aspects of knowledge.

Semantic nets are graphs, often collections of frames and scripts, whose purpose is to describe the elements of the universe of discourse and the relations between these. They have many points in common with models of relational databases.

Graphs and diagrams have been used effectively with computers to prove theorems (Buthion 1975, Pastre 1978; also Section 7.7); they help the proof process by short-cutting steps, memorising the problem efficiently and in an overall sense, and steering the introduction of new elements.

7.6.3 Access to the knowledge, method of use

There are four ways of using a simple piece of information of the form:

$$p \supset q \qquad \text{(e.g. all humans are fallible)}$$

The most obvious is the direct use:

1. An entity is proved to be fallible if I can prove that it is human.

An inverse use involves meta-knowledge:

2. If my goal is to prove that an entity is fallible then a possible subgoal is to prove that it is human.

Both these employ *modus ponens*; the duals use *modus tollens* with the negation of q:

3. If an entity is infallible it cannot be human.
4. If my goal is to prove that an entity is not human then I can try to prove that it is infallible.

The resolution principle, and in particular PROLOG, which uses this in a fundamental way, builds these four types of inference into its special formalism.

In practical work the use made of an item of information will depend on the parameters that measure its reliability, and any information processing system must be able to answer questions such as:

1. What part of statement A is true?
2. What trust would an expert place in this conclusion?
3. What, on average, is the probability of achieving the goal by using A?
4. To what extent should A be preferred to something else?

There are already several working production rule systems, using approximate reasoning, that take into account such parameters.

Production-rule systems have already been described in this chapter, in Sections 7.2 and 7.3; and Section 7.4 discussed the differences between the two of these and of first-order logic in attacking the same problem. In the next paragraph we draw up a balance sheet of the advantages and disadvantages of the production-rule representation.

7.6.4 Advantages and disadvantages of production-rule systems

We start with the disadvantages, of which, mainly, there are three, all stemming from a certain rigidity underlying the formalism used and concerning respectively the design, the statement and the use of the rules. These points are discussed further in Section 7.8, which forms the conclusion to this chapter.

Disadvantages

1. Difficulty of designing a production rule to correspond to a knowledge item. The field of application must have been studied in sufficient depth for the true basic concepts to have been identified, and for the working degree of detail to be not too fine. Otherwise a special rule has to be formulated for every situation encountered, implying the provision of an enormous volume of information, and it is hard to see how this could be achieved.

2. Difficulty of stating a rule. The standard **if-then** form entrains some heaviness in the form of the left sides of the rules and some repetition of the same premise to cover similar situations; also it is ill adapted to complex rules. On the other hand (cf. Section 5.4) there are advantages in this rigid syntax. Capturing the knowledge is always the real problem in writing an expert system.

3. Difficulty of using the rules. This arises not so much from the rules themselves as from the means for communicating between them, which is solely via the facts base; this base plays the role of a short-term memory, which it actually simulates in Newell's GPS (General Problem Solver) (Newell 1975), a 'cognitive psychology' system. This arrangement prevents the rules from calling one another directly and consequently is inconvenient in the execution of algorithms, but at the same time forms the means by which the system knows what it knows at any instant.

If we now look at the intrinsic advantages brought by production rules we shall see that these disadvantages are their necessary accompaniments.

Advantages

1. Modularity. Any item of information can be changed in any way or deleted, or any other added, without effect on any other; so the knowledge can be input in any quantities and in any order, as to a dictionary or an encyclopedia. Experience has shown that this is the way that is natural to the expert providing the knowledge. It is a curious fact that many American workers, in particular Davis, Newell, Quinlan, Stefik and Waterman, dissent from this, and consequently have difficulty in modifying their systems.

2. Ease of modification. This is a corollary to the above. If a rule is modified, or a new rule added, everything continues as before so long as the situation under consideration does not involve the new or changed rule: every change is local and additive. The system has different, and greater, knowledge as a result of the change; its body of knowledge increases continually. This contrasts with procedural systems, in which any change is difficult to make and can have unforeseeable repercussions.

3. Readability. For us: it is undoubtedly because, as we have already emphasised, our own knowledge is modular that production rule systems seem familiar and easy to read. This is not a negligible advantage, for such systems are intended for use by, for example, doctors, biologists and architects, for whom the 'added value' brought by an easily usable set of rules is very real. This applies equally to systems for computer aided teaching (CAI).

For the machine: final automatic checking of the consistency of a knowledge base is simpler when this is expressed as rules than when the form is procedural. Contradiction and redundancy are easily detected by syntax analysis:

$A \wedge B \rightarrow C$ and $A \wedge B \rightarrow \neg C$ cannot hold simultaneously

$D \wedge E \wedge F \rightarrow G$ entrains $E \wedge F \rightarrow G$ by 'subsumption': if both rules are given, only the second is retained. Semantic inconsistencies also can be revealed: thus $A \wedge B \to C$ cannot hold if the definitions of A and B are such that $A \to \neg B$.

4. *Possibility of self-explanation.* This results from the combination of the rules themselves and the control structure. The system can easily work backwards through the chain of rules it has used in order to reach a certain conclusion, and also any meta-rules employed. The uniform representation of the knowledge, related to the format laid down, makes it possible to construct profiles and models of rules which in turn enable questions to be answered and many possible needs for corrections to the data-base to be foreseen.: cf. Sections 7.1, 7.2 and 7.7.

5. *Efficiency.* Experience has shown – and experts have confirmed – that systems such as MYCIN, PROSPECTOR and R1 are powerful and flexible. They are not mere laboratory toys but genuinely operational products and, as Rychener (1978) in particular has shown, have proved adequately efficient and can stand comparison with procedural systems. Their control structure allows them to take account of many parameters that may be needed to characterise a situation; a fundamental reason for their efficiency is that any particular rule will use only those data items that relate to the case then being treated.

7.7 THE META-KNOWLEDGE

Generally speaking, the meta-knowledge is all that is known about the knowledge; it is of fundamental importance to those systems that not only use their knowledge base as such but are required also to be able to reason about this knowledge, to structure it, to abstract it, to generalise it and to decide in which circumstances a particular item will be useful. Whilst it is for the experts in the particular field to provide the knowledge, it is for the system to manage it. We now consider first the basic elements of meta-knowledge and then the strategies and methods for reasoning with these.

7.7.1 Meta-knowledge of the objects of the universe of discourse

Attacking a problem that involves a large volume of knowledge generally requires complex and very varied data to be manipulated, as concerns both the content of the items and the relations between these and the other elements of the system. It is not sufficient for the relevant information simply to exist in the mind of the designer of the system nor even as comments in the program; it must be accessible to the system itself. Thus the elementary objects must have concepts attached to them which, as in MECHO and MYCIN, provide further information, as follows:

- A precise description of the features of the associated data item.
- Pointers to all known examples of the concept.
- Relations with other concepts.
- A pointer to the group of concepts belonging to the same family in the hierarchy of the schemas.

If a word or group of words in a new rule is not known to the system it is analysed in terms of the different concepts recorded, making use of the context and of the other words in the rule. And if a certain concept is used when a particular case is being studied and certain properties are known for other examples of that concept, the system is about to ask the user if those properties hold for the case under consideration. Finally the system can detect violations of relations between concepts.

These systems have the further ability to impose on all concepts on the same level in the hierarchy a modification made by the expert to one or two of these; and to indicate the scales of the changes that would have to be made to the data-base if a new example were added to some structure.

As was described in Section 7.2.3, the rules can be characterised by models; these are created and managed by the system and reflect regularities observed in the rules. They also make it possible to test a new rule for consistency with the existing set, and can indicate to the expert – even if he was not already aware of this – the general direction his rules are taking. Some models become richer as the set of rules grows: in MECHO for example a form of meta-knowledge is associated with the actual statements of the problem, the system seeking to recognise a standard situation in a statement and, if it succeeds, adding to the facts base all the physical laws and assumptions that would normally hold in that situation.

7.7.2 Meta-knowledge of strategies

In production systems strategies also are expressed by means of rules – called meta-rules because they are rules about rules. They are separate from the rules proper and can be manipulated by the system; and the heuristics that guide the search act through these meta-rules in a qualitative and declarative way, rather than quantitatively through an evaluation function. The latter approach, apart from its poorer readability, has inherent risks: the resulting partial order is obtained by a complex computation, and consequently any modification is risky. By contrast, the meta-rule approach, as well as being more readable, is safer; the conclusions reached through a meta-rule indicate possible actions in the situation then existing and thus concern the likely usefulness of certain rules. There is a twofold effect:

1. On the one hand, they remove from consideration rules that are not relevant to the situation, thus pruning the tree.
2. On the other, they construct a partial classification of the remaining rules, thus creating a partial ordering of the branches of the tree.

Of course, successively higher levels of knowledge can be constructed, each resting on the one below and adding to the system's self knowledge. Generality increases at each step upwards, for the same interpreter can work at all levels, also robustness because the models used in the higher layers are unaffected by changes in the elementary knowledge base. The CRYSALIS system (Engelmore 1979), for example, has three distinct levels of rules. This system deals with protein analysis and its potential search space is too great for the normal approach (cf. Section 7.2.3) to be suitable. The rules are therefore grouped into sub-sets, possibly overlapping, each corresponding to a particular processing that is suitable when the associated conditions are satisfied. The level above this (the meta-rules) consists of what are called task rules, which associate classes of physical possibilities with the sub-sets of rules and indicate how a given task might be accomplished. The third and last level, the meta-meta-rules, gives the sub-goals to be attained, expressed in terms of the task rules. An example of a CRYSALIS meta-rule (Engelmore 1979) follows:

if two possible units a, b of the protein have already been located, each with likelihood coefficient at least 0.4
and if the number ...
then activate the rules that mention the task XXX

Here the system, after calling this particular meta-rule, will go next to one of the task rules of the premises of the task XXX, which in turn will say which rules should be used.

CRYSALIS's method of grouping the rules into families has one advantage and one disadvantage. The advantage is that control can be exerted within the body of the rule itself, each rule carrying its own reasons for being applied (cf. the AM system of Lenat, 1977); and the same idea can be applied to a complete family of rules, to give a plan of action. The disadvantage is that as a consequence of this provision the premise part of the rules can become very voluminous.

The problem that is solved by the introduction of meta-rules is of fundamental importance in connection with efficiency and readability;

another solution is to allow more and more complex forms as premises of the rules. Table 7.7 is an example, and the related question of compilation into an internal representation is discussed in Section 7.5.4.

The work of Robert Wilensky (1981) on 'meta-planning' is central to the forming of plans of action, whatever the field of application. Wilensky proposes meta-strategies for solving problems of conflicts between plans, of recurrent plans and of concurrent plans. The same knowledge is given to two different programs, PAM and PANDORA, in declarative form; one constructs plans to solve problems, the other has to understand a story and make plans concerning the people concerned, so as to interpret their actions.

7.8 CONCLUSION

Systems that use declarative data-bases, production rules, prototypes, schemas or semantic nets to represent and manipulate knowledge open the way to an entirely new concept of programming. What is concerned here is the transfer to the machine, in bulk and in as simple a way as possible, of human expert knowledge in a well-defined field; a declarative language, interpreted by the inference engine of an expert system, is basically a structure for the reception of knowledge. This type of approach to programming seems essential in artificial intelligence, where it has already produced effective and efficient systems, as described in Sections 7.2 and 7.3 above.

Sections 7.4 and 7.5 have shown that the two fundamentally necessary requirements are complete independence of the separate elementary knowledge items, and a single and strict syntax for the expression of these items. Given these, systems can be constructed that have a global awareness of the knowledge they contain, which they can analyse and restructure as required by means of (meta-)rules, clauses or schemas.

This very considerable simplicity of representation of the knowledge does not impose any irksome restrictions on either the programmer or the expert – rather, it seems to match very well our natural way of thinking. It has many advantages, in particular, as we have seen in Sections 7.6 and 7.7, bringing together the ideas contained in current work on problem solving on the one hand and understanding natural language on the other.

Taking a different point of view, it is clear that not the least of the benefits of expert systems is their keeping up to date, for us to use, bodies of expert knowledge; for example:

PROSPECTOR, for the geologist.

MYCIN, which is used in medical teaching.

PECOS, from which any programmer can benefit.

Finally, these systems bring out the fact that an essential component of our own intellectual behaviour is our ability to handle large volumes of elementary information. In this context it seems that three fundamental problems, already considered to some extent in production systems, will continue to need special attention in artificial intelligence for a long time to come; these concern the basic actions involved in any handling of knowledge:

> express it – memorise it – use it

Expressing knowledge. We are continually meeting new situations and the experience we build up derives above all from our capacity for abstracting the essence from these situations so as to be able to describe them in terms of general symbols. These symbols will often be those of our normal language, but there are many fields in which this will not suffice, for example because it is too imprecise or because it brings in too many references to contexts that are not relevant to the particular situation. Every specialist gradually develops the proper concepts for his subject, and his own jargon.

Badly written books most often fail by going into too much detail and not making effort enough to generalise the actions they are proposing. Results, not given with principles that would enable reasoned use to be made of them, have to be learned by heart and the knowledge is effectively unusable.

It is certainly not impossible for useful general concepts to be formulated as a result of studying simple situations, because a few gifted individuals have done this; but bearing in mind the difficulty we humans have in doing so, it is not something to be expected of artificial intelligence in the near future.

Memorising knowledge. Memorising any information is subject to technological constraints and is strongly linked with the question of the efficiency of the information system. Whilst, for important reasons of convenience, the knowledge items may be entered into the system independently, as to a dictionary, it is essential that they are stored in some organised way. The rules, grouped into a tree structure, then form a network in which the principal nodes are models containing general descriptions of the rules they represent.

Further, the system must be able to invert the rules, that is, to be able to determine in which situations a given rule will be useful. This is not a simple operation; it involves a generalisation, and makes possible the learning of concepts, summary descriptions of all the situations that are amenable to a certain processing. A certain amount of redundancy is allowable, to avoid the possibly high computational cost of the process: it is clear that if a system is to be both intelligent and efficient the same item of information may need to be given in several different forms.

Using knowledge. Gaining access to information raises a problem of pattern recognition; this will have been eased if, as just discussed, the knowledge has been structured as a tree and provision made for both direct and inverse use of the rules. Meta-rules will help to control the search process, as, more generally, will models of higher level knowledge which both enable strategies related to the context to be used and allow final choices to be delayed as long as possible.

Several expert systems based on production rules have already made some progress in attacking these three questions: for example, CRYSALIS, ARGOS-II, POLITICS, OPS, TANGO, SNARK. It is predominantly the clear distinction between the knowledge itself and the processing of this by iterative interpretation that has made possible the identification and analysis of the problems.

Expert systems thus provide a fundamentally new approach to programming. Of the two main control structures of traditional programming, test and iteration, they keep only the first and with this alone are able to put the entire burden of invoking rules and subsequent processing on to a single interpreter, easily written once and for all. This avoids the two great disadvantages inherent in traditional programming, the ordering of the operations and the imperative nature of the instructions; with the advantages that the knowledge can be entered as independent items in any order and in any quantity and there is no need to prejudge the use to which it will be put. And even more, they remove the need to use any particular programming language: the expert himself, providing the knowledge to the program, defines his own concepts and his own specialist terminology, working at a level of detail that is familiar to him and is best adapted to his problems.

A disadvantage of current programming languages that is especially serious in artificial intelligence research is that they are still at too low a level. A simple action or an elementary item of knowledge can be spread over a large number of coded instructions, so that making any change is difficult and dangerous. AI researchers take the view that the languages of the future will be of the expert system type, complete modularity, complete separation of the knowledge from the control, and consequential greater readability; and that this will contribute to the solving of important problems in knowledge engineering, to communication between humans and programs and to the design and writing of large scale software, not necessarily algorithmic in form.

A number of tasks remain to be accomplished if these systems are to become reliable tools, useful outside the laboratories. Two in particular need to be attacked strongly. The first is the formal study of the languages in which rules and meta-rules are expressed, considering their syntax and semantics, the underlying logic, the primitives of the reasoning process; this corresponds to what has been done for traditional programming languages, but now must not be tied to any existing interpreter or machine.

The second task is to get the results of AI research out of the university laboratories. For expert systems in particular there is a need for general interpreters to be provided that are efficient, have powerful inference mechanisms and are properly documented; it must be made possible for such products to be handled with confidence by the new users, as has become the case for compilers.

The systems already existing have established the feasibility of a radically new approach in information science, with knowledge expressed formally in independent declarative units and structures such as production rules, frames, scripts and semantic nets defined with precision. This leads to elegant solutions to problems of knowledge representation that are simple to comprehend and easy to use, and, by allowing every user to communicate with the system in his own words, avoids the difficulties associated with the traditional programming languages.

7.9   A DO-IT-YOURSELF EXPERT SYSTEM KIT

This is limited to the case in which all the entries in the facts base FB are of the form $a \; R \; b$ where a, b are any words of the universe of discourse, input to the system independently, and related by the relation R; this relation, given by the expert, can be, for example, 'is', 'belongs to', 'equals', 'contains', 'has the value', and so on. The 'fact' $a \; R \; b$ thus corresponds to a logical proposition that can be interpreted as either true (T) or false (F), e.g.

the anemone is a dicotyledon
the organism is of type Gram positive

Correspondingly, every entry in the rule base RB is of the form $\wedge p_i \rightarrow \wedge q_i$ in which the premises p_i and consequents q_i are propositions, with the form (word, relation, word).

We shall not allow variables, which means that our system is one of

1. Find the facts and rules that are pertinent to the situation
2. Choose one of these rules and try to invoke it
3. Invoke this rule if possible, record the consequence

Fig. 7.16 Basic cycle of an expert system.

propositional or zero-order logic. Starting with the initial facts the inference engine, also of level zero, derives new facts by invoking all those rules in *RB* whose premises are satisfied, the consequences being simply added to *FB*. As given in Section 7.3.1 (Fig. 7.4), the kernel of the engine is the cycle of Fig. 7.16. There are two general strategies (cf. Section 7.3):

Forward chaining. We start with the known facts and invoke all those rules whose premises are satisfied, adding the consequents and so getting an enlarged facts base from which to start the process again, continuing until no further facts can be derived – to 'saturation'.

Backward chaining. Here we start from a goal and work back to the facts. Suppose we want to answer a question put by the expert, to which there is a finite number of possible replies; we choose one of these and take this as the goal. We then look for any rules that have this goal as the consequent and if there are any look to see if any of their premises are satisfied; if all the premises of at least one rule are satisfied the goal is attained, otherwise the premises of one rule are taken as a new goal and the process repeated. If no rule has the required consequent we choose another of the possible replies.

The system can put a question to the expert whenever, in the course of its reasoning, it needs a fact that has not been given and cannot be deduced from those that have. The procedure is recursive, because a fact is established by means of a test applied to the rules that lead to that fact, and this test involves establishing that the premises of the rules are satisfied.

Let us therefore construct a recursive function VERIFY, to be called by the main program thus:

result = VERIFY(b, *FB*, *RB*)

where b is the goal sought and *FB*, *RB* the facts and rule bases as before. The syntax of a rule is as follows.

$$\begin{array}{ll}
\langle \text{rule} \rangle & = \text{if } \langle \text{premises} \rangle \text{ then } \langle \text{consequent} \rangle \\
\langle \text{premise} \rangle & = \langle \text{fact} \rangle / \langle \text{fact} \rangle \langle \text{premise} \rangle \\
\langle \text{fact} \rangle & = \langle \text{word} \rangle / \langle \text{word} \rangle \\
\langle \text{consequent} \rangle & = \langle \text{premise} \rangle
\end{array}$$

Table 7.10 gives the text of the function VERIFY.

VERIFY finds the truth value of b by backward chaining, returning T or F according as b is established or not; it calls the procedure PROVE, also given in Table 7.10, to test for the achieving of a set of goals. PROVE in turn calls VERIFY in doing this.

The objects manipulated by these procedures are of three types: PROPOSITION, set_of PROPOSITION and RULE; and to any object r of type RULE there correspond two attributes, PREMISES(r) and CONSEQUENTS(r), both of type set_of PROPOSITION.

Table 7.10 Basic inference engine for propositional logic.

```
function VERIFY return boolean
global constants   RB              set__of RULES
                   AVAILABLE set__of PROPOSITIONS
data               GOALS, FB  set__of PROPOSITIONS
      {the goal is deduced recursively from FB and RB, with possible questions to the
      expert}
variable           OK boolean; OK ← F
if b ∈ FB then OK ← T {b already established: trivial first success}
end if
      {otherwise possibility of deducing b is explored}
repeat for ∀r ∈ RB with b ∈ consequents(r) while OK = F
           OK = PROVE(premises(r))
      {call to PROVE, which checks for truth of premises; possible second success}
end repeat
      {otherwise test to see if b is AVAILABLE}
if OK = F and b AVAILABLE then put question
  OK ← response(b)
end if
      {in case of success record in FB}
if OK = T then FB ← FB∪{b}
end if
return (b, OK)
end VERIFY
function PROVE return boolean {same global constants}
data B set__of GOALS
OK ← T
repeat for ∀b ∈ B and while OK = T
OK ← VERIFY(b)
end repeat
      {all goals in B must be established}
return OK
end PROVE
```

Finally, certain propositions belong to the set AVAILABLE and can be the object of a question put directly to the expert. The function QUESTION(p) puts the question p and returns T or F according to the expert's reply. Thus there are three ways in which a proposition p can be shown to have the value T:

1. by examination of *FB*.
2. by recursive deduction using *RB*.
3. by direct questioning when p is AVAILABLE.

Set notation and high level primitives (Meyer 1978) are used in the text given in Table 7.10 so as to give a clear and concise presentation.

Now, gentle reader, put this zero-level inference engine on to your micro and run it with the rules of Table 7.11: here the propositions a R b are expressed as simply as possible, so that 'the plant has a flower' is reduced to

Table 7.11 A simple set of rules.

(a)	if	flower ∧ seed	then	phanerogam
(b)	if	phanerogam ∧ naked seed	then	fir
(c)	if	phanerogam ∧ 1-cotyledon	then	monocotyledon
(d)	if	phanerogam ∧ 2-cotyledon	then	dicotyledon
(e)	if	monocotyledon ∧ rhizome	then	lily of the valley
(f)	if	dicotyledon	then	anemone
(g)	if	monocotyledon ∧ ¬rhizome	then	lilac
(h)	if	leaf ∧ ¬flower	then	cryptogam
(i)	if	cryptogam ∧ ¬root	then	moss
(j)	if	cryptogam ∧ root	then	fern
(k)	if	¬leaves ∧ plant	then	thallophyte
(l)	if	thallophyte ∧ chlorophyl	then	algae
(m)	if	thallophyte ∧ ¬chlorophyl	then	fungus
(n)	if	¬leaves ∧ ¬flower ∧ ¬plant	then	*bacillus coli*

the one word 'flower'. Let the facts base FB be rhizome, flower, seed and 1-cotyledon. If the goal is 'fungus', VERIFY produces: QUESTION: thallophyte? because (case 3 in VERIFY) 'thallophyte' cannot be deduced from the given facts, so the direct question has to be put. If the expert replies F then VERIFY will return F for the goal.

If the goal is 'lily of the valley' VERIFY calls PROVE so as to test the premises of the one rule (e) that would give a decision. This would then call VERIFY to test the first sub-goal 'monocotyledon', which can be established only through rule (c). PROVE is therefore called again to test the premise of this rule, 'phanerogam and 1-cotyledon'; 'phanerogam' is established by rule (a) since both its premises are in FB, thus giving the first success; and '1-cotyledon' also is known, so 'monocotyledon' and 'phanerogam' can be added to FB. The second premise, 'rhizome' of (e) is now tested; this is already in FB, so the final response is T.

Notice that it is the precise manner of implementing the operation 'b belongs to the set of goals' ($b \in B$) that finally determines the way in which the tree of possible positions is searched: if B is organised as a stack the search is 'depth first'; *Byte* for September 1981 (see also Farreny 1985) gives a microcomputer program of about 400 lines in BASIC.

The efficiency of the recursive function VERIFY is easily improved by changing the parameters B and FB to global variables, to be manipulated explicitly by an iterative program.

Finally, so as to avoid unnecessary repetition of tasks, there must be a means for distinguishing between 'false facts' and 'unknown facts'. Negative conditions in the rules can be tested by making them correspond to facts known not to be true; and it is not difficult to make this inference engine work equally in forward chaining so that the tree is traversed according to the successive conclusions reached until no more deductions can be made.

Chapter 8

ALICE: A LANGUAGE FOR INTELLIGENT COMBINATORIAL EXPLORATION

The real difference is not between the natural and the artificial, but between systems that are programmable and those that are not.
Herbert A. Simon 1977

ALICE is an information processing system that combines a high level language for expressing problems and a general problem solving module that uses the methods of artificial intelligence. Its design and construction were stimulated by two realisations.

A. Traditional programming is expensive. For each new application the information scientist must, in effect, write a new program. Further, any change to the specification once programming has started can incur very high costs: the US Department of Defense in 1972 estimated the cost of a program to be $75 per new instruction but $4000 per correction. There are two reasons for this:

(a) Side effects are difficult to control, because with current procedural languages, even employing the best methodologies such as structured or modular programming or use of abstract types, any correction can have unforeseen consequences.
(b) There is the risk that a change in specification will entail a radical change to the data structure and to the algorithm developed for the solution: the textbooks may provide standard examples but any real-life application will depart from the standard and changes will require continual rethinking and reprogramming.

B. All present programming languages are imperative. This means that the machine has to be told exactly what to do at each step. All that the user is interested in is the statement of the problem and its solution, and specifying every intermediate step is not a task he wishes undertake: in other words, what he wants is an information system in which the statement of a problem is completely separated from the process of solution. Thus we should be envisaging an ideal system to which the user presents his problem in a conversational way, using a descriptive language not too different from natural language; and the machine, working in real time, gives a solution which the user can study and if necessary make changes to the original statement and initiate a new run. This is the approach of ALICE; it can reduce the time for a solution from several weeks, or even months, to a few minutes.

Taken together these arguments, A and B, provide the basic specification for a descriptive (declarative) language in which any problem can be stated in purely formal terms; and a solution system that is general enough to be able to interpret any request made by the user and to take into account all relevant considerations, given in the formal statement of the problem or concerning the orders of magnitude of any numbers involved or the computational resources available. The first point (the language) corresponds to current work on specification languages (Abrial 1974, Guttag 1977, Liskov 1977, Meyer 1978); the second to programming methodologies and the solving of problems in general (Arsac 1977, Nilsson 1980, Pair 1977, Simon 1979).

ALICE can interpret the specification of a problem and take it to the complete solution; in Section 8.9 we show how it can solve certain types of problem expressed in normal English.

We have found it advisable to divide the description of the ALICE software into two parts. First, in Section 8.1 and 8.2, we show the types of problem that the system can deal with, give the input language, describe briefly and in general terms the methods of solution and give three examples. Then Sections 8.3–8.5 describe in more detail the procedures and representations used, the criteria applied, and the handling of choices and constraints. Results are discussed in Section 8.8 and the final Section 8.9 considers the input of problem statements in natural language.

8.1   GENERAL DESCRIPTION OF THE SYSTEM

What we are discussing is the design of a system that on the one hand will accept purely declarative statements of problems, meaning that no algorithm, instruction or advice need be given to it; and on the other can solve problems of acceptably general type, possibly difficult and of significant size.

The input language is required only to allow the problem to be specified; it will be based on standard mathematics. Two choices are available for the solution system: either a compiler that simply takes the input statement and translates into an algorithm constructed by the system for the particular problem, or an intelligent interpreter that considers the problem together with the data, using a general module. The second is better, provided that it can be programmed, for then the system will behave as we ourselves do, taking account of all the features of the particular problem and continually adapting our actions to these: there is no pre-specified algorithm, but the most suitable procedure is used at each step.

What is surprising is that this general program has often been found to perform better on difficult problems than the best available specialised programs – a point taken up and explained in Section 8.8. Over a hundred problems, of a great variety of types, have been successfully solved by the system so far; Section 8.7 gives many of these, together with the times for the solution on an IBM 4331.

8.2 THE ALICE LANGUAGE

The backbone of the language is the vocabulary of set theory and classical logic, with the addition of some useful concepts from graph theory, in particular those of path and successor. The use of sets, functions, Cartesian products and matrices enables the objects that are fundamental to the application to be described; and the relations between these objects can be stated with precision by means of the standard operators, e.g.

$$\in, \forall, \exists, \Rightarrow, \Leftrightarrow, \text{and}, \text{or}, \neg, \neq, =, \geqslant, \leqslant, +, -, *, /, \Sigma, \text{modulo}$$

The following general statement defines the class of problems that ALICE can accept:

> Find $x \in X$, where X is a given finite set, such that x satisfies a given set of constraints $K(x)$.

This is an exceedingly general class; it includes all the standard algorithmic problems such as sorting, updating and managing files, accounting, solution of algebraic systems; the problems of operational research and optimisation such as the travelling salesman, the knapsack problem, resource allocation; and many less well-defined, less classical problems. The only restriction is that the vector of unknowns x must belong to a finite set X.

The reader should not be deterred by the mathematical aspect of the often difficult problems given later: simpler problems are simpler both to state and to solve.

An ALICE problem statement consists of four parts:

1. Definition, beginning with the key-word LET; describes the objects with which the problem is concerned, giving their types.
2. Goal(s), beginning with the key-word FIND; specifies the goal(s) to be attained, the unknown values to be found.
3. Constraints, beginning with the key-word WITH; gives all other relevant features of the problem and its solution, including all relations that the objects must satisfy; any optimisation, or minimisation of a cost function, is given here.
4. Data; all the numerical or formal values needed to complete the specification of the problem.

Example 1. N tasks of known running times are ready for execution on a multiprocessor computer; there is no restriction on which task is to be run on which processor but it is required that all shall be completed within a time L at most, using the minimum number of processors. Find how the tasks should best be ordered.

The first requirement is to translate this natural-language text into ALICE.

Let T be the set of tasks, which we can number from 1 to N; we have to find for each task t of T the processor on which it should be run: let the number of this be $p(t)$. Several tasks can be run in succession on the same processor; assuming that the processors are numbered from 1 upwards as

Table 8.1.

LET	
CONSTANTS N, L	number of tasks, time limit
SET $T = \{1, N\}$	tasks numbered 1 to N
COEFFICIENT d ON T	N, L, values of d will be read
FIND	
FUNCTION $p: T \to T$	N processors could be needed
WITH	
$\forall r \; r \in T$	all processors r
$\sum_{t \in T, \; p(t) = r} d(t) \leqslant L$	
WITH	
$\min_{p} \max_{t \in T} p(t)$	minimum number of processors used
END	

each new one is allocated, the problem is to minimise $p(t)$ over all the tasks t, while respecting the condition that all the tasks must be completed within a time not exceeding L. This is equivalent to minimising max $p(t)$ for $t \in T$, subject to the constraint that no processor is occupied for a total time exceeding L: that is, if $d(t)$ is the duration (running time) of task t, $\Sigma\, d(t) \leqslant L$ where the sum is over all tasks run (in succession) on the same processor, that is, for any processor r over all those tasks for which $p(t) = r$.

The ALICE statement of the problem is shown in Table 8.1. This is the formal statement of the problem. ALICE, as we have said, works with numerical data and these are read in the fourth part of the specification in the order given in the text – N, L and then the vector of running times, d. In actual applications of the program the number N of tasks has been several hundreds (cf. Section 8.7) but here we take as an example only 9, with times as below and $L = 18$; the program then concludes:

9, 18	values of N, L respectively
6, 2, 8, 3, 6, 15, 6, 9, 13	running times
END	

We shall show how ALICE solves this problem in Section 8.3.3.2. It will be seen that a change in the running times can change the solution drastically, in particular a change of the time for task 1 from 6 to 7. Thus, far from developing a method for solving the general formal problem the system adapts its treatment strictly to the data.

Example 2. Mathematical programming, linear or non-linear, can lead to numerical problems in Boolean arithmetic such as the following. Find all the solutions of the set of Boolean inequalities:

$$0 \leqslant x_1 x_4 + 3 x_2 x_5 - x_1 - 2 x_3 - x_4 x_5 - 1$$
$$0 \leqslant 2 x_1 + 5 x_3 - 2 x_4 - 3 x_5 - 2$$
$$0 \leqslant x_2 x_4 + x_1 x_4 + 2 - 5 x_1$$

General programs have been written to solve problems of type; but we shall see in Section 8.3.1 how powerful is ALICE's non-algorithmic approach and how efficient is its manipulation of symbolic expressions. The ALICE statement is shown in Table 8.2 and there are no numerical data.

Example 3. The problem is to find the optimum locations for the emergency services – ambulance, fire, etc. – to cover an urban area. Figure 8.1 gives the possible locations and the area that can be covered from each centre with an acceptable delay, together with the cost associated with each. All the regions have to be covered and the total cost minimised.

Table 8.2.

LET
    SET $I = [1, 5]$
    SET $B = [0, 1]$
FIND
    FUNCTION $x = I \rightarrow B$
WITH $0 \leqslant x(1)*x(4) + 3*x(2)*x(5) - x(1) - 2*x(3) - x(4)*x(5) - 1$
                $0 \leqslant 2*x(1) + 5*x(3) - 2*x(4) - 3*x(5) - 2$
                $0 \leqslant x(2)*x(4) + x(1)*x(4) + 2 - 5*x(1)$

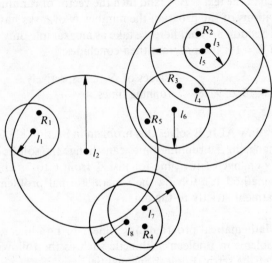

Fig. 8.1 Locations of emergency service centres.

The same problem can arise without any function to be optimised. We have sets $L = \{l_i\}$ of locations l_i, of costs $C = \{c_i\}$ where c_i is the cost associated with l_i, and $R = \{r_j\}$ of regions r_j to be covered; here $i = 1, 2, ..., 8$, $j = 1, 2, ..., 5$, and we take the costs c_i to be $3, 7, 5, 8, 10, 4, 6, 9$.

We have to find a function F that, applied to each region, associates at least one centre with that region, that is, $F: R \rightarrow E$; but Fig. 8.1 shows that only some sub-set of E will suffice for each region. The ALICE language enables this last restriction to be expressed by including the option 'successor' in the declaration of F: thus for example the successors of r_5, meaning the possible images of r_5 under F, are l_2, l_4, l_6. Using this notation

Table 8.3.

```
LET
    CONSTANTS  NR, NL                          numbers of regions and locations
    SET          R = [1, NR]
                 L = [1, NL]
    COEFFICIENT C on E                         costs associated with locations
FIND
    FUNCTION    F: R → E SUCCESSOR
WITH
    ∀r, r ∈ R: F(r) = l ⇒ ∀s, s ∈ R, l = SUCCESSOR(s), F(s) = l
                                               if region s has for successor a
                                               location l already agreed, then
                                               it also is covered by l
    WITH
        min Σ c(l)
        l ∈ L, r ∈ R: F(r) = l
END
    5, 8                                       values of NR, NL
    3, 7, 5, 8, 10, 4, 6, 9                    costs
    1, 2
    3, 4, 5
    4, 5, 6                                    successors
    7, 8
    2, 4, 6
END
```

---

the formal statement of the problem is as shown in Table 8.3. Other formulations could be used; one in terms of 2-valued variables as in Example 2 would serve, but would be more prolix.

ALICE's solution is give in Section 8.3.3.2. The solution, as for the other examples, takes a very short time and the response is almost immediate even when, as in real-life problems, the volume of input data is considerable.

Further keywords enable a wider range of constraints to be expressed; the system 'understands' the concepts of surjection, injection and bijection, of a tree, a path, a cycle, and all the standard logical symbols. The language has been designed so that the statements are as concise and as easily comprehensible as possible, and reasonably close to their expression in normal language.

Table 8.4 gives the full list of ALICE words, with their meanings; the 'rank' of a word or symbol is the number of terms that it involves. Any symbol that does not occur in the dictionary is considered to be the name of a new object and must be declared in the definition part of the statement by the word LET.

The syntax rules are given in Table 8.5, in BNF. Prefix Polish notation is

Table 8.4 Dictionary of the ALICE language.

Symbol	Meaning	Comments	Rank
LET	Definition (part 1)	possible data	2
FIND	Goal (part 2)		1
WITH	Constraint (part 3)		1
END	End of formal statement		0
CST	Constant		1
SET	Set	all these words are	
COE	Vector of numerical coefficients	followed by their definition, given by the user and applying	
COA	Vector of alpha-numerical coefficients	to objects just defined	
MAT	MATRIX		2
FUN	Function		2
INJ	Injection		2
SUJ	Surjection		2
BIJ	Bijection		2
SUC	Successors	followed by list of objects (see text)	0
PRE	Predecessors	as SUC	0
SYM	Symmetry of successors		0
DIS	Disjunction imposed	i, j in disjunction means $i \neq j \Rightarrow f(i) \neq f(j)$	0
VAL	Cost associated		0
DMA/DMI	MAX/MIN degrees in image space		0
PTH	Path, route		2
TRE	tree		0
CYC	Cycle (in graph)		0
MIN/MAX	Minimum/maximum		?
$>, <, \geqslant, \leqslant, =, \neq, +, -, *, /$		usual meanings	0
MOD	Modulo		2
OBJECTS	Definition of a set in terms of its members		n
ON	Relates coefficient/set		1
PDT	Cartesian product		2
INC	Included in		1
BLG	Belonging to		2
$\rightarrow$	From … to	definition of a function	1
ALL	For all, $\forall$		2
EXI	There exists, $\exists$		2
NOT	Logical negation		1
UN	Union		2
IN	Intersection		2
AND, OR, $\Rightarrow$, $\Leftrightarrow$		usual meanings	2
SIG	Sigma, Σ		2

Table 8.5 ALICE language syntax.

⟨statement⟩	⟨phrase⟩ ∗ ⟨data⟩
⟨phrase⟩	⟨declaration⟩ | ⟨constraint⟩ | END
⟨declaration⟩	LET CST ⟨name constant⟩ | LET SET ⟨definition set⟩ |
	LET ⟨vector⟩ ⟨name vector⟩ ON ⟨name⟩ |
	LET MAT ⟨name matrix⟩ PDT ⟨name⟩ ⟨name⟩
	FIND ⟨function⟩ ⟨name function⟩ : ⟨name⟩ → ⟨name⟩
	⟨option⟩∗
⟨definition set⟩	[⟨name constant⟩, ⟨name constant⟩] OBJECT ⟨name
	object⟩∗ | UN ⟨name⟩ ⟨name⟩ | IN ⟨name⟩ ⟨name⟩
⟨vector⟩	COE | COA
⟨function⟩	FUN | INJ | SUJ | BIJ
⟨option⟩	SUC | DIS | DMI | DMA | CYC | TRE | SYM | VAL
⟨constraint⟩	WITH ⟨logical expression⟩
⟨logical expression⟩	⟨binary operator⟩ ⟨logical expression⟩ ⟨logical expression⟩
	| NOT ⟨logical expression⟩ |
	⟨algebraic operator⟩ ⟨algebraic expression⟩ |
	MIN ⟨expression⟩ | MAX ⟨expression⟩ |
	⟨quantifier⟩ BLG ⟨name⟩ ⟨name⟩ ⟨logical expression⟩
⟨binary operator⟩	⇒ | ⇔ | OR | AND
⟨quantifier⟩	ALL | EXI
⟨algebraic operator⟩	< | > | ⩾ | ⩽ | = | ≠
⟨expression⟩	⟨operation⟩ ⟨expression⟩ ⟨expression⟩ | ⟨number⟩ |
	⟨name⟩ | SIG | BLG ⟨name⟩ ⟨name⟩ ⟨expression⟩
⟨operation⟩	+ | − | ∗ | / | MOD
⟨number⟩	⟨"figure"⟩ | ⟨number⟩ ⟨"figure"⟩
⟨name⟩	⟨"letter"⟩ | ⟨name⟩ ⟨"letter"⟩

used in the system itself, because it is unambiguous and allows constraints to be written in a single line without parentheses, but in the text here we use normal algebraic notation, for the sake of convenience.

Table 8.5 uses the standard convention that $⟨x⟩^*$ represents the symbol x concatenated with itself any number of times and | indicates an alternative.

8.3   THE PROBLEM-SOLVING MODULE

Here we give a general description of this part of the system; a detailed account is given in Section 8.5.

ALICE imitates the way a human goes about solving a problem; this is characterised by these actions:

1. The problem is continually restudied, and at every stage the least difficult sub-goal (where difficulty is estimated on a scale that is continually

revised) is attacked. The next step is chosen according to the current state of the constraints and of the numerical values, rather than in a predetermined order decided arbitrarily by the programmer as in traditional algorithmic procedures. ALICE's approach in choosing the next difficulty to attack is similar to ours; thus whilst we do not have a unique algorithm for sorting we know how to choose from those available the one that best suits the particular data, and moreover can change the method later in the process if that seems desirable.

2. A suitable representation is known in advance for many types of constraint. All simple constraints, meaning those that bear on at most two objects, are built into the system's internal representation in terms of a *hypergraph* (see Section 8.5.1); others are dealt with by the equivalent of standard algebriac notation.

3. A plan is constructed for the solution, based on a deep analysis and interpretation of the initial conditions and depending primarily on the estimated difficulty. The most important variables and constraints are identified; these will be used to set up criteria on which to decide the order of the different stages of the solution.

ALICE performs three main actions when solving a problem:

1. Propagating the constraints. This is a matter of combining all the available items of information in such a way as to derive the maximum amount of new information. This can be anything from a very simple to a very complex process; the shorter the expression of a constraint, the greater the chance that it can be used easily. For constraints involving only two variables the propagation is achieved by means of pointers in the graphical internal representation, and for others by means of the algebraic notation. ALICE will take this process as far as possible before continuing with the next action; but for many types of problem – for example, all those that are NP complete (cf. Section 4.4) – this propagation does not suffice to solve the problem completely.

2. Making hypotheses. In the propagation action ALICE delays as long as possible the making of any choice; if and when it finds that no further progress can be made it tries to make an intelligent choice. Rather than embark on a crude enumeration of possibilities it assigns what it considers to be the most important, and then returns to the process of propagating constraints; and so on. With some problems the 'best' solution has to be found by minimising a given cost function, in which case a third type of action is required.

3. Finding and establishing an optimum. ALICE is able to construct criteria with which it can reduce the cost corresponding to each successive choice. It also has methods for combining and relaxing constraints so as to define an interval within which the optimum value

must lie, and finally, by a further propagation of constraints, to prove that the value found is indeed the optimum.

8.3.1 Propagation of constraints

This phase is based mainly on the unification algorithm (cf. Section 3.7). This algorithm enables formal operations to be performed by machine on expressions, as we ourselves would do by hand; in particular, to perform simplifications, e.g.:

$$4 \leqslant 3 \qquad \text{becomes} \qquad F$$

$$2x - 3y + x \neq 0 \qquad \text{becomes} \qquad 3x - 3y \neq 0, \text{ and then } x \neq y$$

Certain special procedures, described in Section 8.5.2, enable ALICE to deduce conditions that are necessary if given relations are to hold; for example, if the following are required to be satisfied:

$$2 \leqslant x \leqslant 5, \qquad 0 \leqslant y \leqslant 2, \qquad 0 \leqslant z \leqslant 9 \qquad x, y, z \text{ integers}$$
$$0 = 2x + y - z - 9$$

then it can deduce ($x = 4$ or $x = 5$) and ($z \leqslant 3$).

In Example 1 above, on allocation of tasks to processors, we have the algebraic constraint on the total elapsed time:

$$\forall r, r \in R \qquad \sum d(t) \leqslant L \qquad \text{with} \qquad t \in T, p(t) = r$$

From the given numerical values ALICE deduces, by summing over r:

$$\sum_{t \in T} d(t) = 68 \leqslant p^* \cdot L$$

where p^* is the optimum number of processors; with $L = 18$ it follows that $p^* \geqslant 4$.

To fix ideas concerning this phase, we give now the complete solution to Example 2 on the set of Boolean equations, which is found by propagation alone. The problem is to solve the set of equations:

1. $0 \leqslant x_1 x_4 + 3x_2 x_5 - x_1 - 2x_2 - x_4 x_5 - 1$
2. $0 \leqslant 2x_1 + 5x_3 - 2x_4 - 3x_5 - 2$
3. $0 \leqslant x_2 x_4 + x_1 x_4 + 2 - 5x_1$

where each x is either 0 or 1.

ALICE considers the constraints in order of complexity, rating (2) as the simplest, that is, capable of providing the greatest amount of useful information (cf. Section 8.3.2). From this it derives a new inequality (cf.

Section 8.4.2):

2a. $2 \leqslant 2x_1 + 5x_3$ which it simplifies to
2b. $1 \leqslant x_1 + x_3$ from which $(x_1 = 1)$ or $(x_3 = 1)$

(3) is now studied, yielding:

$5x_1 \leqslant 4$ hence $x_1 = 0$ and therefore $x_3 = 1$

The original set is now reduced to:

1c. $0 \leqslant 3x_2x_5 - x_4x_5 - 3$
2c. $0 \leqslant 3 - 2x_4 - 3x_5$
3c. $0 \leqslant x_2x_4 + 2$

The last can be ignored as it is always satisfied; the first gives:

1d. $3 \leqslant 3x_2x_5$ and   1e. $x_4x_5 + 3 \leqslant 3$

It follows from (1d) that $(x_2 = 1)$ and $(x_5 = 1)$ and from (1e) that $(x_4 = 0)$ or $(x_5 = 0)$; and therefore $x_4 = 0$. Thus collecting all the results we have the unique solution (0 1 1 0 1)

8.3.2 Making choices

With simple procedural programs a solution can be found only by exhaustive enumeration, but the cost is often prohibitive. With the more highly developed methods such as backtracking, branch and bound, implicit enumeration (cf. Section 5.4) the search tree is fixed once for all and no attempt is made to avoid useless choices in the course of the search. ALICE in contrast avoids making choices as far as possible, because these are costly: if the search space is divided into two at each choice, then if n choices have to be made the time required will be of order of 2^n. Faced with this exponential growth, ALICE has a two-fold goal: it must make choices that take the context into account, providing much new information and thus helping to reduce the amount of work needed for the remaining search; and it must reduce as far as possible the number of choices to be made. For this second aim it must return to the phase of constraint propagation after each new choice has been made. Further, the control system can interrupt this general schema at any stage.

8.3.3 Types of choice and criteria for choices

The original feature of ALICE is that it is always programming its own activity. Nothing is imposed from outside: the system decides for itself, at

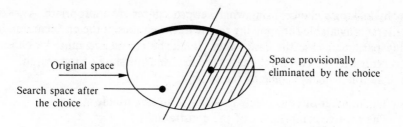

Fig. 8.2 Effect of a choice on the space to be searched.

each step, the best way to proceed. However, two questions must therefore be answered:

1. What kinds of choice are to be made?
2. What criteria enable one choice to be selected from those available?

We consider only the general principles here; the technical details are given in Sections 7.5.1, 7.5.2, 7.5.3.

The choices. Making a choice corresponds to the temporary addition of a new constraint. Intuitively, one would say that the result should be to divide the space to be searched as evenly as possible (cf. Fig. 8.2); a standard way to do this is to fix the value of one of the variables, but this is not what ALICE does except in the last resort, because it tends to concentrate attention on too small a region of the full space. The preferred method is make a less precisely defined choice, for example by setting bounds to some variable or simply setting the parity of an integer variable.

Another method used by ALICE is to work backwards from a goal to a consideration of all its possible antecedents; it will take account of the various costs, as for example by restricting its study to those for which the cost is, on some scale, reasonable. Finally, it uses for preference all the disjunctive constraints that it has been able to discover.

The criteria. ALICE's main strategy is:

   at every step do what gives most information

This is implemented by means of criteria that consider all the asymmetries of the problem: just as it is more rewarding to deal with those constraints, if there are any, that involve not more than two variables, so more information results from making a choice concerning a variable that can take only a small set of values or which is bound to high coefficients. Thus every element, constrained or not, that has some distinguishing feature is a target for study and the system examines it either by constraint propagation or by making a choice, using whatever procedures are appropriate. A set of criteria is available for applying to any of the entities of the problem, but in any particular case the entity that should be considered must be chosen according to the current numerical values and the state of the search.

The following are some of the criteria:

1. The number of constraints in which a given variable appears.
2. The relative complexities of the constraints.
3. The number of different values still possible for a given variable to take.
4. The cardinalities of the sets whose images must be disjoint.
5. Values of the coefficients.
6. Values of the left members in inequalities.
7. The bounds within which a variable must lie.
8. The difference between local optimal cost and the corresponding penalty.
9. The number of possible antecedents.

These all seem simple and natural, and the general approach is to start by considering all of them, but at each step to apply only the one that is most significant. However, one that initially seems excellent may turn out later to reduce the quality of the information, and ALICE is therefore given the capability of changing to another that will enable a useful decision to be made. Also a change of heuristic can be made if the one being used becomes unsatisfactory; this will be desirable when the next goal after reaching a solution is to improve on this: the original evaluation function on which the heuristic was based will no longer apply, because of there being too many cases of ties.

The advantage of this flexible approach over the rigid one of traditional programming will be made clear in the study given in Section 8.6 of a difficult combinatorial problem.

8.3.3.1 General plan for the solution process

ALICE starts by analysing the problem as a whole. First, the statement of the problem is translated into the system's internal representation; the constraints are put into the most convenient form, a pre-compiled graphical form being preferred to the more usual algebraic form because the latter can only be handled by an interpreter. ALICE checks that there are no mutual contradictions in the constraints and estimates the difficulty of the problem; it then tries a few standard sets of values for the variables because of the possibility of there being an immediate solution.

The criteria that could be relevant to the particular problem are then identified. The phase of propagation of constraints is taken as far as possible, and if this does not give a solution the phase of choices is initiated, followed by a return to the first phase. If no optimisation, or minimisation, of a cost function is required this cycle is repeated until either the first solution, or the complete set of solutions, if that is what the user requests, is found. Otherwise ALICE changes to other criteria relevant to this last requirement; here the system has a somewhat pessimistic approach and aims at improving the costs, taking account of the feasibility of doing so and the measured difficulty of the problem and the estimated number of solutions in the working space. Finally, it uses one or other of the following arguments to prove that the solution found is the optimum.

1. A lower bound for the cost is established, and a solution found having precisely this value (cf. Example 1).
2. The original problem with the additional constraint 'total cost less than the best value known' has no solution; from which it follows that this best solution is the optimum (cf. Section 8.6.2, a modification of Example 1).
3. The whole of the search space having been scanned, the optimum solution must have been found. Since the system always makes the right choice the search tree will often be of reasonable size and exhaustive search possible (cf. Example 3).

This general plan is represented diagrammatically in Fig. 8.3.

8.3.3.2   Solutions of the examples of Section 8.2

Here we give simply ALICE's method of attack and the solution obtained; a full justification is given in Section 8.5.3.

Example 1

Plan.

1. Assess the difficulty of the problem.

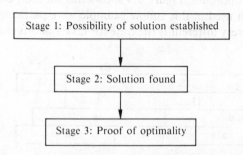

Fig. 8.3 General plan of ALICE solution process.

2. Find an acceptable solution.
3. Prove that this is optimal.

Relevant criteria; durations of tasks – availability of a processor – distribution of tasks over processors.

Stage 1. As soon as the problem is put into the internal form a solution is obvious: since no task takes as long as the limit on the total time (18 units), assigning each task to a different processor will suffice, i.e. $p(i) = i$, giving a cost of nine processors. Thus the problem is judged to be simple, and on a small scale.

Stage 2. ALICE now tries to reduce, as far as possible, the number of processor needed, by this strategy: tasks are assigned to processors in decreasing order of running time and at each step the longest remaining task is assigned to the most heavily loaded processor, provided that the total running time is not exceeded. With the times:

$$\text{task number } i \quad 1 \ 2 \ 3 \ 4 \ 5 \ \ 6 \ 7 \ 8 \ \ 9$$
$$\text{time } d(i) \quad\quad\ 6 \ 2 \ 8 \ 3 \ 6 \ 15 \ 6 \ 9 \ 13$$

and the limit $L = 18$ on the total time, this gives the following allocations:

$p(6) = 1 \ \ p(9) = 2 \ \ p(8) = 3$
                                  (recall $p(i) =$ no. of processor on which task i is run)
$p(3) = 3 \ \ p(1) = 4 \ \ p(5) = 4$
$p(7) = 4 \ \ p(4) = 1 \ \ p(2) = 2$

giving a cost of four processors.

Stage 3. ALICE finds a lower bound for the optimal number of processors as follows. If the optimum number is p^* then $L \cdot p^* = 18p^* \geqslant \Sigma \, d(i)$ over all the tasks i; with the given times, $18p^* \geqslant 68$, so $p^* \geqslant 4$, and the solution obtained is the optimum. Figure 8.4 shows this solution diagrammatically.

NB: The data used in this simple example were particularly favourable; the situation is very different if the time for task 1 or 5 is changed from 6 to

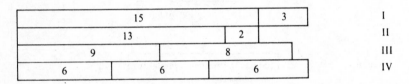

Fig. 8.4 Optimal allocation of processors for Example 1.

7 units. ALICE still finds the lower bound $p^* \geqslant 4$, but with $d(1) = 7$ it can no longer allocate task 7 to any of the four processors already used without exceeding the time limit, and therefore must use a fifth processor. The impossibility of a solution with four processors is shown by returning to the allocation stage, where the only alternative choice is to place task 8 on processor 4 instead of on processor 3: again task 7 cannot be placed on any of the four processors already used.

Example 2. The complete solution has already been given in Section 8.3.1. This makes clear the value of bringing in different criteria: there is no point in trying to optimise too early, when there are no solutions, or at most one. ALICE therefore looks for futher constraints that will give more information, even if these are buried in a large mathematical programming problem. Formal manipulation of the expressions, as here, avoids the heavy numerical processing currently used in such approaches as the simplex and gradient methods.

Example 3. The statement of this problem is 'compiled', on input, into ALICE's graphical representation, in the form of lists equivalent to Fig. 8.5. Here again ALICE finds an obvious solution in stage 1, this time by taking for each region the first location (the first successor) possible. This gives:

$$f(1) = 1, \quad f(2) = 3, \quad f(3) = 4, \quad f(4) = 7, \quad f(5) = 2$$

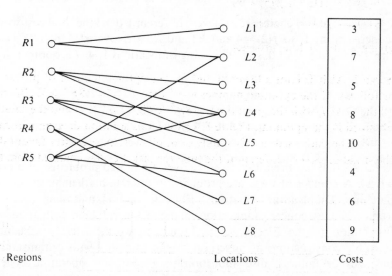

Fig. 8.5 Internal representation for Example 3 (region $R5$ can be served only by $L2$, $L4$ or $L6$).

with a total cost

$$Z_0 = 3 + 5 + 8 + 6 + 7 = 29$$

In stage 2 the criterion is: the cost is smallest for the region that has fewest successors. ALICE thus takes:

$$f(1) = 1, \ f(4) = 7, \ \text{then } f(2) = 3 \text{ and } f(3) = 6 = f(5)$$

with a total cost reduced to $3 + 6 + 5 + 4 = 18$

A lower bound is computed in stage 3. Each region must be covered, and at best this would be done by its least-cost successor. ALICE first considers the most restricted regions, that is, those with fewest successors, thus: $R4$ will cost at least 6, $R1$ at least 3, $R5$ at least 4, $R3$ at least 4; so the optimum cost Z^* must satisfy $Z^* \geqslant 6 + 3 + 4 + 4 = 17$

Further, these minimal costs can be subtracted from the corresponding original costs without affecting the solution; so from here on ALICE works with the reduced costs $(0, 0, 1, 0, 6, 0, 0, 3)$.

Stage 3: the reduced costs of locations 5 and 8, being greater than the difference $Z_0 - Z^*$, are now seen to be too great to be entertained: Z_0 is within a unit of the optimum. We see here that even if optimisation is not required ALICE can give a measure of the distance of its solution form the optimum.

The basic criterion is:

take every arc, not already taken, that gives the greatest reduction in cost

$f(4) = 7$ is a forced choice. If $f(2)$ were different from 4 the total cost would be increased by 1, so $f(2) = 4$ and $R3$ and $R5$ are covered. Finally $f(1) = 1$ with a reduced cost of 0, so the building of locations 1, 4, 7 is optimal, with cost 17.

8.4   RESULTS

So far ALICE has been used to solve over a hundred problems, of a great variety. A number of these are problems in discrete mathematics: optimal matching, Diophantine equations, Eulerian and Hamiltonian cycles in graphs. The rest concern applications in the real world: high-voltage current distribution in the Electricité de France network, delivery schedules, timetable construction, architectural design (possibly with optimisation), diagnosis of failures, disc allocation in a computer operating system, 'travelling salesman' problem and its derivatives, organisation of services.

This last application, which is difficult and can be on a very large scale, is one for which there is no formal solution and shows particularly the strength of ALICE.

Besides such applications – and showing that lighthearted applications are equally possible – ALICE has solved some fifty puzzles and logical brainteasers, such as magic squares and cubes, the Eight Queens puzzle, and those devised by Lewis Carroll, Sam Loyd and Martin Gardner. These illustrate the flexibility of the program and the power of the language. Some of these problems are listed in Section 8.7, with information on the type and scale and machine time required for solution. What is striking here is the small number of choices considered by the program, and the small amount of time needed.

Having experimented with the system over several years and tested it extensively, I have become convinced of its power and robustness. First in order of importance is the practical point, is the speed with which it arrives at a solution, having been given the statement of the problem – from a few seconds to a few minutes. The class of problems amenable to this approach is extremely wide; the only need is to bring the system to the notice of the potential users – service organisations, big companies, operational research centres, software users in general.

However, the second point of importance is theoretical in nature: the system opens a radically new route to programming. It demonstrates the feasibility of a system in which it is necessary only to state the problem, and the system itself will develop a method of solution that is both efficient and well adapted to the particular problem.

8.5   TECHNICAL DETAILS OF ALICE

There are three things to be considered: the internal representation of the problems, the handling of algebraic constraints and the methods of making choices.

8.5.1   Internal representation

Usually, a program is designed with a single application in mind and the representation can be tailor-made to suit; but here we must be able to represent any problem concerning finite sets and any constraints whatever. The ideal would be to translate every statement into a compact form decided in advance and pre-compiled, as in Example 3; but for expressions such as, for example.

$$\forall i, i \in E: \sum_{j \in F} a(i, j) \cdot x(j) \geqslant b(j)$$

there is no representation other than this classical algebraic notation. The ALICE solution is to use a graphical representation – graphs and hypergraphs – wherever possible, that is, for simple constraints involving at most two variables and to leave everything else in algebraic form.

8.5.2 Graphical representation

Figure 8.6 shows the general way in which the information is organised. Essentially it is a bipartite graph: the points on the left, those of the set D, are the initial objects for which values have to be found, whilst those on the right, the set I, are the possible images of these objects.

Unless anything to the contrary is said in the statement of the problem there can be an arc from any $u \in D$ to any $v \in I$. Any information that is provided, such as the values or coefficients, is associated with the relevant arc. As the solution proceeds certain values will become prohibited. Important information, such as admissible extreme values, number of successors of a u in D or antecedents of a v in I, is continually updated.

When the functions sought are of some particular type, such as an injection or a surjection, or the option 'degree imposed' minimum or maximum of the image points, this information is translated locally: two vectors associated with the points give the maximum and minimum number respectively of antecedents allowed – for example, both are 1 for a bijection.

Finally, a hypergraph is constructed with vertices from the set D. This gives the disjunctions, that is, the constraints that require all the points of a family to have different images: for example, in problems concerning permutations, graph colouring, planning. These families are stored in memory: they are hyper-edges, and can involve any number of vertices. After the statement of the problem has been interpreted a special procedure finds the minimum set of disjunctions that will cover D, by constructing the maximal families. This type of 'garbage collector' is of help later in speeding the drawing of inferences from the disjunctive constraints.

8.5.3 Formal representation

The unification algorithm enables the other constraints to be manipulated, the rewrite rules given in Table 8.6 being used to normalise the expressions;

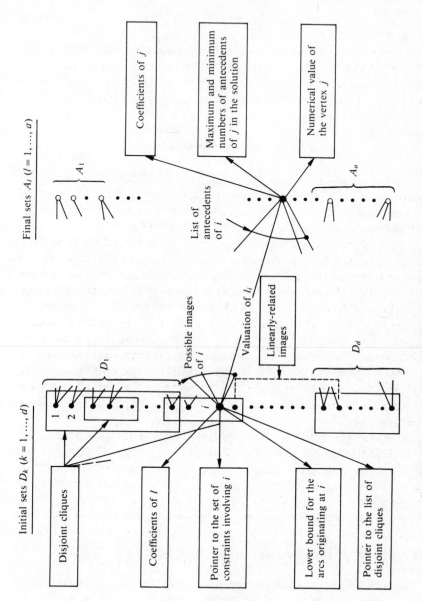

Fig. 8.6 Bipart: graph of the internal representation of a problem.

Table 8.6 Rewrite rules used by ALICE.

$0 * x \rightarrow 0$	$-(x/y) \rightarrow -x/y$
$0 + x \rightarrow x$	$x/-y \rightarrow -x/y$
$-(-x) \rightarrow x$	$x * (y/z) \rightarrow (x * y)/z$
$-x > 0 \rightarrow x = 0$	$x/z + y/z \rightarrow (x + y)/z$
$c * (x + y) \rightarrow c * x + c * y$	$x + x \rightarrow 2 * x$
$-(x * y) \rightarrow -x * y$	$x + (x + y) \rightarrow 2 * x + y$
$x * -y \rightarrow -x * y$	$x + c * x \rightarrow (c + 1) * x$
$x * (y * -z) \rightarrow -x * (y * z)$	$x + ((c * x) + y) \rightarrow (c + 1) * x + y$
$0 \text{ OS2 } c + -x \rightarrow 0 \text{ OS2 } -c + x$	$-x + c * x \rightarrow (c - 1) * x$
$0 \text{ OS2 } c + -x + y \rightarrow 0$	$-x + ((c * x) + y) \rightarrow (c - 1) * x + y$
$\text{OS2} - c + x + -y$	$c1 * x + c2 * x \rightarrow (c1 + c2) * x$
$0 \text{ OS2 } c1 + (-c2 * x) \rightarrow 0$	$c1 * x + (c2 * x + y) \rightarrow (c1 + c2) * x + y$
$\text{OS2} - c1 + c2 * x$	$-(x + y) \rightarrow -x + -y$
$0 = c * fff\, x \rightarrow 0 = fff\, x$	$-0 \rightarrow 0$
$\text{true} \Rightarrow x \rightarrow x$	$1 * x \rightarrow x$
$\text{false} \Rightarrow x \rightarrow \text{true}$	$-1 * x \rightarrow -x$
$\text{true} \Leftrightarrow x \rightarrow x$	$(c1 \rightarrow fff\, c2) \rightarrow (fff\, c2 \rightarrow c1)$
$\text{false} \Leftrightarrow x \rightarrow \neg x$	$(c1 \rightarrow c2 + fff\, x) \rightarrow (fff\, x \rightarrow c1 + -c2)$
$\neg(\forall xy) \rightarrow \exists x \neg y$	$(x \rightarrow x) \rightarrow \text{true}$
$\neg(\exists xy) \rightarrow \forall x \neg y$	$c1 \text{ OS1 } c2 \rightarrow \text{CSP 1 } c1$
$\neg(x \text{ OR } y) \rightarrow (\neg x) \text{ AND } (\neg y)$	$0 \text{ OS3 } c1 \rightarrow \text{CSP 2 } c1 *$
$\neg(x \text{ AND } y) \rightarrow (\neg x) \text{ OR } (\neg y)$	$0 \text{ OS3 } c1 + c2 * fff\, x \rightarrow \text{CSP 3 OS3 } c1\ c2 * fff\, x$
$\neg(x = y) \rightarrow x \neg = y$	$0 = -fff\, x + ggg\, y \rightarrow \text{CSP 4} = fff\, ggg\, x\ y$
$\neg(0 < = x) \rightarrow 0 < = -1 + -x$	$\text{coa } x \text{ OS3 } c \rightarrow \text{CSP 5 OS3 } c \text{ coa } x$
$\text{true OR } x \rightarrow \text{true}$	$fff\, x \text{ OS3 } c \rightarrow \text{CSP 6 OS3 } c\ fff\, x$
$\text{false OR } x \rightarrow x$	$\text{coe } x \text{ OS3 } c \rightarrow \text{CSP 7 OS3 } c \text{ coe } x$
$c \text{ OS4 } c \rightarrow \text{true}$	$\text{mat } c1\ x \text{ OS3 } c2 \rightarrow \text{CSP 8 OS3 } c2 \text{ mat } c1\ x$
$c1 \text{ OS4 } c2 \rightarrow \text{false}$	$\text{mat } x\ c1 \text{ OS3 } c2 \rightarrow \text{CSP 9 OS3 } c2 \text{ mat } xc1$
$x > y \rightarrow 0 \leqslant x + -y + -1$	$0 \Leftarrow c1 + c2 * x \rightarrow \text{CSP 10 } c1\ c2 * x$
$x < y \rightarrow 0 \leqslant -x - y + -1$	$\Sigma\ l \in EQ \rightarrow \text{CSP 11 } l \in EQ$
$x - y \rightarrow x + -y$	$\forall\ l \in EQ \rightarrow \text{CSP 12 } l \in EQ$
$-x \text{ OSO} \rightarrow 0 \text{ OS2 } x$	$\forall\ l \in EQ \rightarrow \text{CSP 13 } l \in EQ$
$(x + y) + z \rightarrow x + (y + z)$	$\forall\ l \in SUC\ jQ \rightarrow \text{CSP 14 } l \text{ / SUC } jQ$
$(x * y) * z \rightarrow x * (y * z)$	$\forall\ l \in PRE\ jQ \rightarrow \text{CSP 15 } l \text{ PRE } jQ$
$x + -x \rightarrow 0$	
$x + (-x + y) \rightarrow y$	
$x * (y/x) \rightarrow y$	
$-x * (y/x) \rightarrow -y$	

the header connectives are always transformed to $\neq$, $\leqslant$ or $=$ and the right side to 0.

Certain unifications can be performed on operators; thus in the table $OS1$ can be taken as $+$, $\times$, or modulo; $OS2$ as $=$ or $\neq$; $OS3$ as $\neq$ or $\Leftarrow$; $OS4$ as $=$ or $\rightarrow$ ('is rewritten'); and fff means 'any function'.

Filters are provided, to reduce the number of attempts at unification. A vector specification of the main features is associated with each expression – header operator, presence of a numerical constant in the left side, number of occurrences of each variable – and the relevant rules are sorted into an order depending on this vector. The code CSPi (i an integer) in the table means that the unification calls a numerical procedure.

8.5.4 Passage of information between the two representations

1. All constraints involving only a single variable are removed from the store of algebraic constraints and recorded in the graph; thus $f(1) = 3$, $f(2) \neq 4$, $f(3) \geqslant 2$ correspond respectively to an assignment, the deletion of an arc and the movement of a pointer in the graph.
2. Linear relations between variables such as $f(4) = f(5) + 6$, inequalities such as $f(6) \leqslant 7$ and disjunctions such as $f(2) \neq f(4)$ are also represented in the graph.

Thus the further the solution process advances, the simpler the constraints become and the more of them are translated into the graphical form; at the end of the process the graph holds all the information.

When any change is made to the graph two particular procedures make the inferences that the context will sustain:

3. When an assignment $f(u) = v$ is made, all the objects in disjunction with u become prohibited from having v as their image; if the degree of v has reached its maximum then all its antecedents are deleted.
4. When an arc is deleted a check is made to see if there are still any possible images, and if there is one then the corresponding assignment is made; similarly when a vertex has reached its minimum degree.
5. When an equality such as $x = y$ is translated, one vertex is deleted; the union of the disjunctive arcs and the intersection of the images are computed and stored.

An impossibility may be detected during the recursive execution of these procedures, such as a contradiction, an empty set of successors, a maximum or minimum degree of a vertex not reached; this information is passed to the monitor program, which takes control, backtracks and restores the situation in the graph and the constraints to what it was before the last choice. Note that the graph has all the information on which the local analysis of the constraints is based: this is what we consider next.

8.5.5 Handling of algebraic constraints

There is one general method and several special methods; we describe these in turn and later will show how ALICE decides the order in which to treat the constraints.

8.5.5.1 The general procedure

This relates to all constraints of the form:

$$T_p - T_n \geqslant 0 \qquad \text{or} \qquad T_p - T_n = 0$$

where T_p contains all the terms having a positive sign, T_n a negative sign.

A special procedure, to be described later, applies when T_p or T_n consists of only a single term. In the general case the constraint is analysed according to the information in the graph, with the aim of generating new constraints that must be satisfied if the original constraint is to be satisfied; these will be simpler than the original and able to provide information that is directly usable.

The main information is summarised in the intervals within which the values of T_p and T_n must lie; and for a constraint(C) to be satisfied these intervals must be located relative to one another in a way determined by the main connective of (C). ALICE always transforms the variables so that they take positive values only; this simplifies the writing of the analysis procedure by giving names to these intervals and to their intersection:

Let $[P, PP]$, $[N, NN]$ be the intervals within which the values of T_p, T_n lie; $A = \max(P, N)$, $B = \min(PP, NN)$, $[A, B] = [P, PP] \cap [N, NN]$

We then have the algorithm shown in Table 8.7.

8.5.5.2 Particular cases

Case 1. Either T_p or T_n is empty, so that (C) is trivially T or F. If either of T_p or T_n consists of only a single term, as many new constraints are generated as there are terms in the other; thus if T_n has only one term ALICE writes for each term t of T_p the new constraint

$$t \geqslant NN - \max t' \qquad \text{where } t' \in T_p, \ t' \neq t$$

Example From $2x_1 + x_2 - 9 \geqslant 0$ we get, if $x_1 \in [2, 5]$ and $x_2 \in [0, 2]$,

$$2x_1 \geqslant 9 - 2, \qquad x_2 \geqslant 9 - 10$$

so $x_1 \geqslant 4$, but no new information is given concerning x_2.

Table 8.7.

---

if $A > B$ **then begin** $(A \cap B = \emptyset)$
   if $A = P$ **and if** operator is $\geqslant$
  then (C) is satisfied trivially; delete (C)
  else (C) cannot be satisfied: **failure**
end
if $A = B$ **then begin** $(A \cap B$ is reduced to a single point)
   if $A = P$ **and if** operator is $\geqslant$
  then (C) is T; delete (C)
  else add new constraints $T_p = A$, $T_n = A$
end
if $A < B$ **then begin**   (the general case)
   if $P < N$ **then** add $T_p \geqslant A$
  else if operator is $=$ **then** add $T_n \geqslant A$
   if $PP < NN$ **then** add $T_n \leqslant B$
  else if operator is $=$ **then** add $T_p \leqslant B$
end

Case 2. Diophantine equations, of the form $ax + by = c$, are treated by a special procedure that uses congruence arguments, for which values marked on the graph as being prohibited are particularly useful. Common factors are found for all the constraints expressing equalities and the congruence equations formed.

Example

From $15x + 18y - 4z - 6 = 0$ we get

$$x \equiv 0 \ (\text{mod } 2), \ z \equiv 0 \ (\text{mod } 3)$$

and these are recorded in the graph by deleting all those arcs that do not satisfy these congruences.

Case 3. Equalities can be used to eliminate variables, but this is done only with linear relations and when each variable appears at least twice in the complete set of constraints — if this second condition does not hold no new information is generated.

Example

From $x + y = 2$, $x + 2y + 3z \geqslant 3$ we get
    $x \rightarrow 2 - y$,   and so $y + 3z \geqslant 1$

Case 4. There is, finally, a type of constraint that we have not yet discussed: the implicit constraint, in which the exact name of the objects is not known.

An example is

$$\forall v, v \in I: \sum c(u) \leqslant b \text{ with } u \in D, \ f(u) = v \tag{1}$$

We have already seen that such conditions can be combined to provide the necessary global conditions; ALICE uses these also as tests for elimination. In general, each constraint of this type, which expresses a condition to be satisfied by a set W of objects w having a property $Q(w)$, is examined after every change to the assignments in W. The constraint is written:

$$\sum_{w\,:\,Q(w)} c(w) \leqslant b$$

where the notation $w : Q(w)$ means that objects w have the property $Q(w)$. If at some given instant there is a w_0 for which it is known that:

$$c(w_0) + \sum c(w) \geqslant b, \ w : Q(w), \qquad w \neq w_0$$

then w_0 cannot have the property Q.

Example. Taking the above case, the inequality (1) is studied after any assignment $f(u_0) = v_0$ and the cost k calculated for those objects that have v_0 as image: $k = \Sigma_u \, c(u)$, where $f(u) = v_0$. The property $f(u) = v_0$ cannot hold for any u such that $c(u) > b - k$, so corresponding arcs are deleted from the graph.

8.5.5.3 Order in which the constraints are taken

The set of constraints in ALICE is dynamic, in two ways. First, as we have seen and in contrast to traditional operational research and numerical computation programs, constraints are being constantly added or removed, or changed from one form of representation to another. Second, at each step the system uses the constraint that it rates the most important, according to a procedure that we now describe.

First, priority is given to the graph; an agenda of tasks is created and until this has been worked through only the inferential procedures on the graph are executed. Control then passes to the algebraic processing and those constraints are analysed that have received most new information since the last time they were considered: in particular, priority is given to those in which at least one unknown has been given a value, and if this has not been done for any constraint the priority is settled by the number of values eliminated by the graph.

In order to classify these constraints ALICE computes for each a measure of difficulty: the more difficult a constraint is to satisfy, the more restrictive it is and the more information it gives. ALICE's measure of the difficulty $d(C)$ of a constraint of the form $T_p - T_n \geqslant 0$ is the empirical formula:

$$d(C) = \max(0, b)/\max(1, S - b)$$

where b is the constant term in T_n and S is the sum of the coefficients of the positive terms divided by the algebraic degree of each, e.g. $5x^2y^3 \to 5(= 2 + 3)$. The greater b and the smaller S, the easier it will be to find a set of values for the unknowns that will satisfy (C).

ALICE also uses the fact that every variable in T_n can provide information concerning some variable of T_p; more precisely, the upper bound of a variable of T_n restricts the upper bounds of those of T_p, and conversely. This idea leads to the use of a diagram, really a representation of a *Grundy function*, to express the logical order of flow of information concerning these bounds.

The lower bounds are considered first, then the upper, and those constraints taken first that act on variables for which no further information is needed. Bounds having been computed for these variables, the values are used for those for which the information is now complete. We can illustrate this with a set of linear constraints, as follows:

$(C1) \quad f(1) + f(2) - f(3) - f(4) - 3 \geqslant 0$

$(C2) \quad f(1) - f(2) \qquad\qquad\quad - 1 \geqslant 0$

$(C3) \qquad\qquad\qquad\quad f(3) - f(4) - 2 \geqslant 0$

Figure 8.7 shows the bounds for the different unknowns. Thus ALICE knows that the lower bound for $f(3)$ provides information concerning the lower bounds for $f(2)$ and $f(1)$. The diagram shows that one vertex, that for $f(4)$, requires no information from any of the others – it has no antecedent; so ALICE first takes the simplest constraint for which $f(4)$ appears in T_n, that is, $(C3)$. If the current known lower bound for $f(4)$ is 5, $(C3)$ gives $f(3) > 7$; the terms of T_n in $(C1)$ then have no unknown antecedents, so this is taken next, giving $f(1) + f(2) \geqslant 3 + 5 + 7 = 15$. If now we have from the graph $f(1) \leqslant 8$, it follows that $f(2) \geqslant 7$.

The constraints have been taken in the right order, to give the maximum amount of information; $(C2)$ can now be used, giving $f(1) = 8$, whence

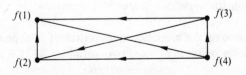

Fig. 8.7 Grundy function.

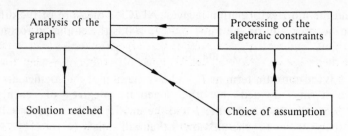

Fig. 8.8 Flow of control in ALICE.

$f(2) = 7$, $f(3) = 7$, $f(4) = 5$. A graph for the upper bounds could be used in the same way, to give the same result.

ALICE spends as long as possible in the inference phase, alternating between the graphical and algebraic representations and delaying as long as possible the need to make any assumption. But when no further new information can be obtained by this means an assumption must be made; this will put a further constraint on the problem and enable the solution to be taken further. ALICE therefore proceeds to the choice of an assumption. Figure 8.8 shows the cycle of events.

8.5.6   Procedures for making the choice

Seven different types of choice are available; these are given below in the system's order of preference.

1. Follow one of the branches in a constraint of the type OR
2. Give a value for the upper or lower bound of a variable.
3. Set a limit to the cost of an assignment.
4. Enumerate completely the solutions of an equation in two or three variables.
5. Perform a global enumeration, provided that the scale of the problem is below some pre-set threshold.
6. Fix the antecedent for a point in the image set.
7. Choose the image for a point in the initial set.

8.5.6.1   Deciding the type of choice

Type 1. Follow one of the branches in a constraint of type OR. Whenever one of the branches involves at most two variables ALICE assumes this to be *T*.

Type 2. Give a value for the upper or lower bound of a variable. Such a choice is made for the variable that appears in the greatest number of constraints, and which therefore has the largest image set; the effect is to divide the image set into two. Such a choice is sensible only when the image set is a set of numbers.

Type 3. Set a limit to the cost of an assignment. This is an optimistic choice and is made when a trivial solution has already been found. The costs are eliminated in order of size until for each point of the initial set D the set of arcs has been halved.

Types 4 and 5. Local exhaustive enumeration of solutions for an equation in two or three variables; global enumeration when the scale of the problem is below some pre-set threshold. These choices involve a consideration of the machine power available. It is not sensible to embark on elaborate formal manipulations when the problem is of a small scale, so the fewer the number of constraints and the fewer the number of arcs from D to I, the greater ALICE's preference for enumeration procedures ALICE knows what it knows and takes this into account in setting the size threshold. Equalities are open to the greatest number of formal methods, whilst inequalities, and even more so constraints of type OR not covered by type 1, are less easily manipulated; the more constraints there are of these last two types, the sooner the threshold is reached at which enumeration becomes preferable.

Types 6 and 7. Fixing the antecedent for a point in the image set, choosing the image for a point in the image set. This is a choice of a couple (object in D, image in I); such choices are made only as a last resort, and therefore when the search space has been considerably reduced. Type 6 is preferred whenever (a) the goal is the entire image set, or (b) there is a point in I with fewer antecedents than the smallest number of successors of any point in D. In either case, ALICE gives priority to the most constraining point, and has a whole battery of criteria for selecting the (object, image) couple that will give most information.

At any stage in the process ALICE will use a criterion only if it can discriminate adequately among the objects to which it refers; and this assessment is made as follows. The criterion must attach some rating to the various objects among which it is required to discriminate; if m is the rating of the best candidate, then the discrimination is adequate if and only if fewer than one-quarter of the field have ratings greater than $m - [m/4]$. This eliminates all criteria that are too flat – all the scores are close and too loose – too many with high scores. The sub-set of best candidates can be

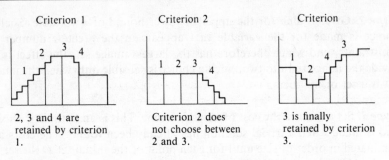

Criterion 1   Criterion 2   Criterion

2, 3 and 4 are   Criterion 2 does   3 is finally
retained by criterion   not choose between   retained by criterion
1.   2 and 3.   3.

Fig. 8.9 Application of three criteria to choose from four candidates.

filtered by a second criterion, and so on until only one remains; this is illustrated in Fig. 8.9

Below we give the criteria used by ALICE, all of which can be applied to both the graphical and the algebraic representation. In the following paragraph we give the production rules that determine the strategy, that is, the order in which the criteria are considered in the various contexts. The terms marked* in the criteria are explained below.

Criteria for choosing a point in the initial set D:

(a) Minimum number of successors.
(b) Maximum number of points in disjunction.
(c) Maximum number of algebraic constraints involving the point.
(d) Minimum global difficulty of the constraints in (c).
(e) Maximum number of coefficients attached to the point.
(f) Maximum of the minimum value of the successor arcs.*
(g) Maximum *penalty*.*
(h) Maximum *interest*.*

Criteria for choosing a point in the image set I:

(α) Number of potential antecedents.*
(β) Number of actual antecedents.*
(γ) Numerical value of the point.
(δ) Values of the coefficients relating to the point.

Notes. The *difficulty* of a constraint is defined in Section 8.5.5.3. The global difficulty of the set of constraints on a point of D is simply the sum of the separate difficulties. The aim of all criteria is to pick out the points of greatest difficulty, so (f) is concerned with those points for which the minimum possible cost is greatest, while (g) enters in optimisation problems.

The *penalty* of a point is the difference between the lowest possible cost and the next lowest: the greater this, the more critical is the point.

(h) concerns algebraic constraints; the *interest* of a variable is defined as the sum over all the constraints that involve x of the changes in the difficulties as x varies from its maximum to its minimum. The interest of x increases as the global difficulty of the constraints on x decreases.

(α) concerns the antecedents $u \in D$ that are still possible at the stage in question for all points $v \in I$; (β) refers to those u that already have v as image.

8.5.6.2 ALICE's strategy: ordering the criteria

ALICE itself chooses the order in which to put the criteria; this will depend partly on the nature of the problem – ALICE will see that certain criteria will not be relevant – and partly on the state to which the solution has been carried (Table 8.8). Two very general meta-heuristics enable the strategy rules to be formulated:

> $H1$: always make the choice that gives most information
>
> $H2$: always make the least costly of the available choices

The order in which the choices should be made is given by the following production rules:

> **if** stage = 0 (reading the problem statement)
> **and** the unknowns are Boolean
>   **then** delete (a)
> **end if**

Table 8.8.

if   no disjunction is imposed
or if all the vertices have the same number of disjunctions
then delete (b)
end if
if   there are no algebraic constraints
then delete (c), (d), (h)
end if
if   all the constraints are algebraic
and all the constraints are linear
then use the simplified formulae to calculate the difficulties
use (h) first
end if
if   the problem is not one of optimisation
or if the D–I arcs do not carry values
then delete (f) and (g)
end if

(Continued)

Table 8.8. (*continued*)

---

if   there are no coefficients associated with D
          then delete (e)
end if
if   there are no coefficients associated with I
          then delete (δ)
end if
if   all the points of I must be reached ($DMI \geqslant 1$)
          then give (α) lowest priority
end if
if   maximum degrees on I are imposed ($DMA = 0$)
          then take as formula for (α): no. antecedents (v) – max. degree (v)
             give (α) top priority
end if
if   the problem is one of optimisation
and   the minimisation of a function $f(D)$ is involved
          then give (β) top priority
          else give (β) lowest priority
end if
if   there are constraints of type $\leqslant$ ($\geqslant$)
and   these bear on the numerical values (coefficients) of points of D
          then give (γ) ((δ)) top (lowest) priority
          else delete (γ) ((δ))
end if
if   stage = 1 (evaluating the feasibility of the problem)
and ifthere is no trivial solution
          then give preference to (a), (b), (c), (d), (e)
end if
if   stage = 2 (finding an acceptable solution)
          then make a choice of Type 3
             give preference to (f), (g), (h)
end if
if   stage = 3
          then if total no. of backtracks $< D$
                then give preference to (f), (g), (h)
             end if
             if total no. of backtracks $< 2.D$
                then give preference to (a), (b), (g), (h)
                else delete all except (a), (b), (c), (d), (e)
             end if
end if

These show that the program starts by being 'distrustful' (of there being a solution), then 'optimistic' when some solution has been found, and then 'distrustful' again as the number of nugatory choices increases and the problem becomes more and more constrained.

It must be emphasised that although the ordering criteria express only heuristic principles, ALICE gives thoroughly rigorous solutions: in other words, there is no necessary contradiction between heuristics and rigour.

We next explain how ALICE proves the optimality of the solutions obtained as a result of heuristic arguments.

8.5.6.3 Proving optimality

Let Z be the cost function that is to be minimised by the solution and Z_0 the value for a solution that has been obtained; the constraint $Z \leqslant Z_0$ is now added to the problem. If Z is a polynomial the new constraint is simply added to the original set of algebraic constraints. The optimality of the solution is established if it can be shown that the problem thus augmented has no solution.

Two particularly common cases are treated differently; these concern the cost functions

$$Z_1 = \min_f \sum_{u \in D} \text{cost}(u, f(u))$$

which arises when the arcs representing the assignments carry values, as in the travelling salesman problem, tournaments and partitioning problems, and

$$Z_2 = \min_f \max_{u \in D} a(u) \cdot f(u)$$

which characterises problems of 'bottleneck' type, in which the controlling quantity is the highest cost, weighted by a coefficient $a(u)$: for examples, problems of ordering, truck routeing, bar or sheet cutting.

Case Z_1. In stage 3 ALICE sets about the cost reduction in the usual way. Each point u of D gives rise to a minimum cost $\min_v \text{cost}(u, v)$; this is subtracted from the cost of every arc starting from u, so that the minimum reduced cost of these arcs is zero. If this zero cost arc is later deleted then ALICE repeats the reduction. The sum of the costs thus reduced gives a lower bound $\mathbf{Z}$ for the solution being developed; optimality is established by eliminating the arcs with costs exceeding $Z_0 - \mathbf{Z}$ until a point has no successor.

Case Z_2. For a solution to be of strictly lower cost than the known solution of cost Z_0 the images v must satisfy:

$$v < a(u) \cdot z_0 \qquad \text{for all } u \in D$$

This inequality restricts the set of possible images for each point; further, a lower bound $\mathbf{Z}$ for the optimum is computed, using all constraints of the

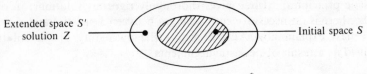

Find $x/K(x)$, solution Z^*

Fig. 8.10 Initial and extended solution spaces.

type:

$$v, v \in D, P(u, v) \Rightarrow Q(u) \leqslant k$$

as in Example 1.

Finally, if the maximum degrees $DMA(v)$ are imposed on the image points ALICE again deduces the lower bound **Z**, here the smallest integer w such that $\sum_{i=1}^{w} DMA(v)$ is greater than the cardinality of D: then every point of D has an image.

The importance of these bounds is greater the sooner they can stop the search for a further solution and can establish optimality. All the computations are based on some necessary condition that the solution must satisfy; they thus involve embedding the space to be searched in some larger space, that is, one subject to fewer constraints: this is illustrated in Fig. 8.10. It follows that any solution lying in S' is at least as good as the best solution in S.

This process of computing the lower bound is thus the dual of the process of choice; together they set limits between which the true minimum Z^* must lie:

$$\mathbf{Z} \geqslant Z^* \geqslant Z_0$$

8.6 EXAMPLES OF ALICE's SOLUTIONS

8.6.1 A logical/arithmetical puzzle

Frank and George play tennis.
Frank beats George 6 games to 3.
In 4 games the server loses.
Who served in the first game?

For the formal statement of this problem we need a vector that says who served in game j ($j = 1, 2, ..., 9$) and another that says who won; define

$FS(j) = 1$ if Frank serves in game j, $= 0$ otherwise
$GS(j) = 1$ if George serves in game j, $= 0$ otherwise
$FW(j) = 1$ if Frank wins game j, $= 0$ otherwise
$GW(j) = 1$ if George wins game j, $= 0$ otherwise

The rules of tennis give:

$FS(j) = 1 - GS(j)$ either Frank or George serves
$GS(j) = 1 - GS(j - 1)$ $j \neq 1$ the players serve in turn
$FW(j) = 1 - GW(j)$ either Frank or George wins

The ALICE statement of the problem is shown in Table 8.9. This problem can be solved without any enumeration of possibilities, and that is how ALICE proceeds. First, the variables $FS(j)$ and $FW(j)$ are eliminated, using (1) and (3); this gives:

$$GW(j) = 3 \qquad (4a)$$

$$\Sigma(GS(j) - 2 \cdot GS(j) \cdot GW(j) + GW(j)) = 4 \qquad (5a)$$

Next, (2) enables all $GS(j)$ to be expressed in terms of $GS(1)$:

$$GS(j) = 1 - GS(1) \quad \text{for all even } j$$

$$= GS(1) \quad \text{for all odd } j$$

Substituting these in (5a) ALICE obtains

$$5 \cdot GS(1) + 4 - 4 \cdot GS(1) - 2 \cdot \Sigma \ GS(j) \cdot GW(j) + \Sigma \ GW(j) = 4 \qquad (5b)$$

and then with (4a)

$$GS(1) - 2 \cdot \Sigma \ GS(j) \cdot GW(j) + 3 = 0 \qquad (5c)$$

Analysing this by congruence modulo 2 shows that $GS(1)$ must be odd, and the graph then translates into $GS(1) = 1$: so the solution is that George serves first.

Table 8.9.

LET	SET GAMES $= [1, 9]$	
	BOOL $= [0, 1]$	
FIND	FUNCTIONS FS, GS, FW, GW GAMES $\rightarrow$ BOOL	
WITH	$\forall j, j \in$ GAMES $(FS(j) = 1 - GS(j))$	1
	$((j \neq 1) \Rightarrow GS(j) = 1 - GS(j - 1))$	2
	$FW(j) = 1 - GW(j)$	3
WITH	$\Sigma \ FW(j) = 6$	4
	$j \in$ GAMES	
WITH	$\Sigma \ [FS(j) . GW(j) + GS(j) . FW(j)] = 4$	5
	$j \in$ GAMES	
END		

NB: Σ $GS(j) \cdot GW(j) = 2$, and as $GS(j) = 1$ is odd, George wins 2 odd-numbered games. Since the last game is won by Frank, there are $4.3/2 = 6$ possibilities for the win of an odd-numbered game by George and 4 for an even numbered, so there are 24 ways in which the situation described in the problem could occur; but ALICE finds the solution without making any choices.

8.6.2 A problem in paper making

A paper manufacturer offers paper of n different qualities; any of his m machines can make paper of any of these qualities, but because of the high cost of changing the raw material and the machine settings from one quality to another there are very strong reasons to plan production so that the total amount required of each quality is made on one machine only. Given the quantities $q(i)$ of each quality i ($i = 1$ to n) over some period, the quantity $p(j)$ ($j = 1$ to m) that machine j can produce in that period and $c(i, j)$ the cost of producing $q(i)$ of quality i on machine j, the problem is to distribute the production among the machines so that the required quantities are produced at minimum cost, and all the paper of any one quality is made on only one machine.

A numerical case from real life has been given by H. Sandl. There are ten qualities ($n = 10$) and four machines ($m = 4$); the requirements $q(i)$, the capacities $p(j)$ and the costs $c(i, j)$ are illustrated in Fig. 8.11.

The ALICE statement of the problem is given in Table 8.10. In the first phase the first task of the program is to find if a solution exists, that is, if

Table 8.10.

LET	SET PAPER = $[1, n]$
	MACHINES = $[1, m]$
	COEFFICIENT q ON PAPER
	p ON MACHINES
	c ON PAPER * MACHINES
FIND	FUNCTION f: PAPER → MACHINES
WITH	$j \in$ MACHINES: Σ $q(i) \leqslant p(j)$, $i \in$ PAPER, $f(i) = j$
WITH	$\min_f \Sigma$ $c(i, f(i))$, $i \in$ PAPER
END	

10,	4								
3	5	10	1	2	3	5	3	8	2
9	10	20	3						
13	9	1	3	14	15	7	9	15	8
13	9	20	6	17	7	9	16	17	1
18	15	11	14	13	8	8	12	17	12
5	4	19	2	6	15	19	4	15	20

	1	2	3	4	5	6	7	8	9	10	
$p(j)$↓	3	5	10	1	2	3	5	3	8	2	←$q(i)$
1	9	13	9	1	3	14	15	7	9	15	8
2	10	13	9	20	6	17	7	9	16	17	1
3	20	18	15	11	14	13	8	8	12	17	12
4	3	5	4	19	2	6	15	19	4	15	20

$$c(i,j)$$

Fig. 8.11.

there is a function f, defining the way the production is organised, that satisfies all the constraints except that of minimum cost. The constraints on capacity $q(i) \leqslant p(j)$ are summed to give:

$$\sum_{i \in PAPER} q(i) \leqslant \sum_{j \in MACHINES} p(j)$$

which is a necessary condition, stating that the total quantity required must not exceed the total production capacity of all the machines. In this example the two sums are equal, both 42; from which the program deduces:

1. A solution is not *a priori* impossible.
2. In the constraint for each j the $\leqslant$ sign must be replaced by = (the full capacity of each machine must be used).
3. Some assignments are forbidden, those for which $q(i)$ would exceed the associated $p(j)$; this is expressed by $q(i) > p(j) \Rightarrow f(i) \neq j$, and gives $f(3) \neq 1$, $f(2)$, $f(3)$, $f(7)$, $f(9) \neq 4$.

No further deductions can be made, so the program has to make some choice. There are no constraints of type OR, so that possibility does not arise; and whilst a choice concerning the small cost numbers could be made, the program eliminates this possibility as a result of judging the search space small enough ($4^{10} = 10^6$ approx.) for a more precise choice of the type $f(i) = j$ to be made.

It is useful to recall here the criteria available to the program – for the antecedent vertex i:

(a) min successors
(b) max disjunctions
(c) max number of constraints with i
(d) max difficulty of constraints
(e) max max coefficients
(f) max min valuation
(g) max penalty
(h) max interest

At each choice the program determines the paper to be considered, in terms of these criteria; but it eliminates three − (b), (c), (d) − immediately because they have no bearing on the problem, the values associated with them being and remaining zero for all i. Then in the first phase the optimisation criteria (f), (g), (h) are ignored, so finally only (a) and (e) remain. The distribution of values for criterion 5 $(10, 8, 5, 5, \ldots)$ is less significant than that for (a): only quality 3 has two successors and the distribution for this criterion is $2, 3, 3, 3, 4, \ldots$. Quality 3 is therefore chosen, because criterion (e) separates it from 2, 7 and 9.

The choice of machine is made with the aid of the second set of criteria − for successor vertex j:

(α) Number of possible antecedents.
(β) Number of actual antecedents.
(γ) Numerical value associated with j.
(δ) Coefficient on j.

The ratings for criterion α are spread over the interval $(6, 10)$, so this has little relevance. For this first choice the ratings for β are all zero, so this is not considered. γ concerns optimisation and is not relevant in this phase; δ concerns a coefficient on j that appears in the set of constraints, and is therefore relevant.

Since each $p(j)$ occurs on the right side of an equality the program chooses the largest so as to increase the possibility of finding a solution and to give the greatest freedom to the choice of the following i. Its first basis for the choice of i and j can therefore be summarised thus: put the paper that is most difficult to assign (criterion (e)) on the most lightly loaded machine (criterion δ), which assigns paper 3 to machine 3 (Fig. 8.12). This

	1	2	3	4	5	6	7	8	9	10	
	3	5	10	1	2	3	5	3	8	2	
1	9	13	9		3	14	15	7	9	15	8 → 9
2	10	13	9	20	6	17	7	9	16	17	1 → 10
3	20	18	15	⊞11	14	13	8	8	12	17	12 → 10
4	3	5			2	6	15		4		20 → 6

Fig. 8.12 Choice 1: $f(3) = 3$.

reduces the available capacity of machine 3 to 10. Nothing more can be deduced.

The relevant criteria are next reconsidered in turn for choice 2, but now the program gives (e) preference over (a) because the distribution has become 8, 5, 5, ...; so paper 9 is chosen; α and δ give equal priorities to machines 2 and 3, and the decision between them is made by applying β: in this first phase it is a good strategy to spread the images as much as possible so as to balance the constraints and thus increase the possibility of getting a solution. Machine 2 is not yet loaded, so we have:

$$\text{choice 2: } f(9) = 2$$

Machine 2's available capacity is now reduced to 2 so the program, taking note of the constraint $\Sigma\ q(i) = p(j)$, must set $f(1)$, $f(2)$, $f(6)$, $f(7)$, $f(8) \neq 2$. Again, nothing more can be deduced, so a third choice must be made. Criterion 1 now has preference because $i = 5$ and $i = 7$ each have only two successors (only machines 1 and 3 are available for either of papers 2 and 7). Criterion 5 cannot distinguish between the two since both demands are 5, and the distinction is made finally by f: the program makes the assignment that maximises the minimum of the costs. Thus:

$$\text{choice 3: } f(2) = 1 \text{ with cost} = 9$$

With the remaining capacity of machine 1 now 4 the program deduces $f(7) \neq 1$, so the only possibility is $f(7) = 3$.

The same criteria give the fourth choice. Paper 6 must next be placed; criterion (f) favours machines 1 and 4 equally since the cost is 15 on either, and the distinction is made by applying the principle of choosing the more lightly loaded machine, in this case 1:

$$\text{choice 4: } f(6) = 1$$

We have seen that all the capacity constraints are equalities. Machine 1 now has a remaining capacity of 1, and for only one quality, paper 4, is the demand 1; so we must set $f(4) = 1$.

For paper 8 the least cost machine is 4 so:

$$\text{choice 5: } f(8) = 4$$

This removes machine 4 from further choices, so we must have $f(1) = 3$.

Two papers remain, 5 and 10, each with demand 2; and criterion f gives:

$$\text{choice 6: } f(5) = 3$$

so $f(10) = 2$.

We have thus arrived at the solution (Fig. 8.13) with a total cost of 99.

Paper	1	2	3	4	5	6	7	8	9	10
Machine	3	2	3	1	3	1	3	4	2	2

Fig. 8.13.

Phase 2. Encouraged by this solution, which was obtained without any back-tracking and after only six choices, the program now becomes more optimistic and looks for a 'good' solution, taking account of the criteria relating to costs which so far it has ignored. If paper 3 is still chosen first, for the same reasons as before, the program now decides to manufacture this on the cheapest machine, 3 (criterion (f)):

$$\text{choice 1: } f(3) = 3$$

which is the same as before; but the lowest-cost criterion next gives:

$$\text{choice 2: } f(9) = 1$$

since machine 1 is the first (in order) that can produce this quantity at lower cost. This assignment entails $f(4) = 1$, and further appeals to criterion (f) give in succession:

$$\begin{aligned}
&\text{choice 3: } f(2) = 2 \\
&\text{choice 4: } f(7) = 3 \\
&\text{choice 5: } f(6) = 2 \\
&\text{choice 6: } f(1) = 4 \\
&\text{choice 7: } f(8) = 3 \\
&\text{choice 8: } f(5) = 3
\end{aligned}$$

and finally

$$f(10) = 2$$

This new solution is (Fig. 8.14) with a total cost of 84, which is a considerable improvement on the first solution.

Paper	1	2	3	4	5	6	7	8	9	10
Machine	4	2	3	1	3	2	3	3	1	2

Fig. 8.14.

Phase 3. So far so good, but can we go on so as to be certain of having found the truly least cost solution? Continuing ALICE's procedure, the cost function:

$$Z = \sum c(i, f(i)) \qquad i \in PAPERS$$

shows that, since every paper i has to have an image (machine) $f(i)$, Z must exceed the sum of the minimum costs of each paper, that is, of the sum over

i of the minima over j of $c(i, j)$; so if $\mathbf{Z}$ has this value:

$$\mathbf{Z} = \sum_{i \in PAPERS} \min_{j \in MACHINES} c(i, j)$$

In using this the program first transforms the costs by subtracting from the values in each column the minimum for that column – that is, the lowest cost of making that quantity of paper of that quality. These transformed costs $c'(i, j)$ are thus (Fig. 8.15):

		1	2	3	4	5	6	7	8	9	10
		3	5	10	1	2	3	5	3	8	2
1	9	8	0		1	8	8	0	5	0	7
2	10	8	0	9	4	11	0	2	12	2	0
3	20	13	6	0	12	7	1	1	8	2	11
4	3	0			0	0	8		0		19
		5	9	11	2	6	7	7	4	15	1

Fig. 8.15.

The sum of the quantities subtracted is $\mathbf{Z}$, here 67; and we now have:

$$Z = \mathbf{Z} + \sum_i c'(i, j)$$

The best solution so far gives $Z = Z_0 = 84$; if the optimum gives Z^* then since the $c'(i, j)$ are all non-negative:

$$\mathbf{Z} \leqslant Z^* \leqslant Z_0, \quad \text{i.e. } 67 \leqslant Z^* \leqslant 84$$

ALICE now deletes all costs that strictly exceed $84 - 67 - 1 = 16$, because any solution that included any of these would necessarily be worse than the one of cost 84 already obtained: the only one here is that of the (10, 4) pair, of reduced cost 19. With no further deductions being possible ALICE proceeds to its first choice, using the optimisation criterion g, that of maximum penalty; so the arc of zero cost, which if it were deleted would entail the highest cost, is chosen. These penalties are simply the second minimum costs in each column (Fig. 8.16). Thus the first choice is again:

Paper	1	2	3	4	5	6	7	8	9	10
Penalty	8	0	9	1	7	1	1	5	2	7

Fig. 8.16.

choice 1: $f(3) = 3$ (the same choice by three different criteria)

with again no further implications. The same criterion next gives:

choice 2: $f(1) = 4$

This entrains $f(i) \neq 4$ for all remaining papers; in particular, the zero reduced costs for papers 4, 5 and 8 are forbidden. ALICE therefore subtracts the new minima (1, 7, 5 respectively) from these columns so as to give new reduced costs and a new lower bound $\mathbf{Z}$ as a result of making choices 1 and 2; this is:

$$\mathbf{Z}(\text{choice 1, choice 2}) = \mathbf{Z} + 1 + 7 + 5 = 80$$

In this context all the new reduced costs exceeding 3 are eliminated because they would give a solution no better than the one available. This leaves Fig. 8.17. These deletions entrain $f(10) = 2$, and similarly the next choice is:

		1	2	3	4	5	6	7	8	9	10
			5		1	2	3	5	3	8	2
1	9		0		0	1		0	0	0	
2	10		0		3		0	2		2	0
3	10					0	1	1	3	2	
					-1	-7			-5		

Fig. 8.17.

is:

choice 3: $f(8) = 1$

which implies $f(9) = 1$, by the capacity constraint. A further subtraction is therefore made in respect of this paper, giving:

$$\mathbf{Z}(\text{choice 1, choice 2, choice 3}) = \mathbf{Z}(\text{choice 1, choice 2}) + 2 = 82$$

and the consequence that now only costs of 0 and 1 are allowed; in particular:

$$f(4) \neq 2 \text{ and therefore } f(4) = 1$$

We now have

Choice 4: $f(7) = 1$, whence $f(2) \neq 1$, $f(5) \neq 1$

so
$$f(5) = 3, \ f(2) = 2$$
It follows from these assignments that
$$f(9) \neq 2, \ f(6) \neq 3$$
so
$$f(9) = 3, \ f(6) = 2$$
giving finally a solution of cost 82.

Proof of optimality. All that remains for ALICE to do is to reconsider these four last choices in turn, either to prove that they are optimal or to produce a better solution.

Choice 4 f(7) = 1. This is trivial: given a solution of cost 82, only a penalty 0 would be an improvement. $f(7) = 1$ is in fact an implication, since its penalty is 1.

Choice 3, f(8) = 1. We have an upper bound of 80 and the penalty of this choice was 3; again this choice is transformed, after returning back up the tree, into an implementation that initiates a new backtrack.

Choice 2, f(1) = 4. The lower bound is 67 and the penalty of this choice is 8; ALICE therefore studies the case $f(1) \neq 4$. This deletion would change Z(Choice 1) to $67 + 8 = 75$. Since there are three other possible assignments for Paper 1, ALICE looks at the situation again. Arcs $(10, 1)$ and $(10, 3)$ are deleted, implying $f(10) = 2$; similarly $(4, 1)$, $(5, 2)$ and $(5, 3)$ are deleted, giving $f(5) = 4$.

The capacity constraint now imposes $f(4) = 4$, saturating Machine 4, so $f(8) \neq 4$; but to satisfy the cost constraint we must have $f(8) \neq 2$ or 3, so $f(8) = 1$ giving $c(8, 1) = 5$ and Z(Choice 1) $= 75 + 5 = 80$.

The solution can now be completed only with arcs of cost less than 2; but we cannot assign $f(9) = 1$ because the remaining capacity on this machine is too small for the demand, and therefore the solution cannot be completed.

Choice 1, f(3) = 3. The only possibility for change here is $f(3) = 2$, giving $Z = 67 + 9 = 76$. All costs exceeding $82 - 76 - 1 = 5$ are now prohibited, necessitating $f(1) = 4 = f(5)$; but these would impose a total load of 5 on a machine of capacity 3 and so cannot assigned simultaneously. Thus $f(3) = 3$ is again the only choice.

It has thus been proved that there is no solution with cost less than 82, so the solution of this cost that has been found is optimal. This solution is (Fig. 8.18):

Paper	1	2	3	4	5	6	7	8	9	10
Machine	4	2	3	1	3	2	1	1	3	2

Fig. 8.18.

The search tree that gives this solution is shown in Fig. 8.19.

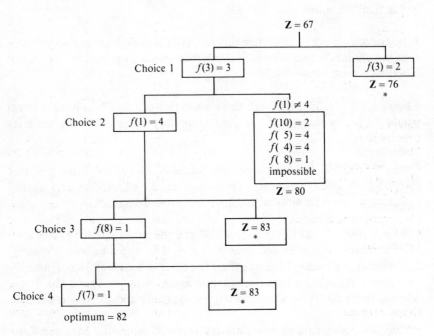

Fig. 8.19 Optimal solution, of cost 82, for the paper manufacture problem.

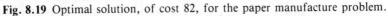

8.7 PROBLEMS SOLVED BY ALICE

In the following list the columns have these meanings:

a number of unknowns (number of vertices of D)
b number of possible values (number of vertices of A)
c number of algebraic constraints
d solution time on IBM 4331 (seconds)
e number of backtrackings

Some of these problems are treated in the text; the figures in brackets (e.g. 8.2) give the relevant paragraphs.

	a	b	c	d	e
Task organisation (8.2)	9	9	1	1	0
Task organisation (8.3.2.3)	9	9	1	2	1
Inequalities (8.3.1)	5	2	3	1	0
Locating services (8.3.2.3)	5	8	1	2	0
Permutations (8.8.2)	9	9	33	4	0
Logic puzzle (8.9.2)	25	25	14	4	1
Flow tree	10	10	1	2	0
Graph covering	5	8	2	3	0
8 Queens (5.7.3)	8	8	1	5	0
5 Queens	64	64	1	1	0
Instant insanity	8	12	20	11	3
False information	10	10	8	1	0
Mike and John at tennis (8.6.1)	19	6	21	3	1
SEND + MORE = MONEY	12	18	7	4	0
DONALD + GERALD + ROBERT (8.8.1)	15	12	9	9	4
LYNDON × B = JOHNSON	16	14	7	4	0
Parametrised crypt-addition	14	12	9	3	0
Crossnumbers	26	10	28	8	0
Multiplication	29	20	23	249	1826
Magic square, order 3	9	9	8	4	0
Magic square, order 4	16	16	10	7	0
Magic cube, order 3	27	27	50	18	0
Magic sphere	26	26	8	6	0
Missionaries and cannibals	80	13	10	11	4
Euler	64	64	0	5	0
Partitioning	15	32	1	4	4
	32	327	1	47	128
	43	327	1	86	628
	45	512	1	91	815
	130	878	1	186	2464
Graph covering	130	878	1	75	429
Linear	9	9	2	2	1
	54	54	2	3	0
	53	53	2	5	7
	647	70	2	41	953
Investment planning	60	2	30	46	0
Linear programming	8	2	4	3	1
	10	2	6	2	0
IBM Haldi test	15	35	1	120	2824
Quadratic programming	6	2	4	4	4
	18	2	4	29	37
	24	2	4	39	98
	32	2	4	92	411
	40	2	4	309	1677
Task organisation	100	250	300	26	0
Disjunctive task organisation	100	250	310	54	27
Shortest path	25	25	56	17	14
Maximum flow	15	65	28	15	16

(*Continued*)

	a	b	c	d	e
Assignment	20	20	0	10	18
Transport	20	10	20	15	10
Minimum tree	60	60	0	6	0
Matching	110	110	0	5	0
Eulerian path	60	60	0	9	5
Dissecting the plane	30	28	22	7	0
	36	26	107	17	0
Travelling salesman (5.12)	6	6	1	1	0
	10	10	1	6	27
	25	25	1	47	433
Hamiltonian circuit	10	10	0	1	0
	20	20	0	2	0
	64	64	0	5	0
	110	110	0	73	1220
	150	150	0	188	2636
Tournament, with constraints	10	10	2	13	18
	25	25	2	67	625
Graph colouring (5.10)	40	40	1	17	1
	99	99	1	71	124
	150	130	1	162	250
	40	4	1	6	0
	110	4	1	12	4
	150	4	1	18	24
Planning	186	27	2	16	12
	186	28	2	4	0
Matching (4.3)	12	2	2	2	1
	32	2	2	2	1
	80	2	2	241	2056
Paper cutting (8.6.2)	4	10	2	6	1
	10	30	2	17	14
Location of services	10	10	2	5	0
	20	40	2	30	98
SNCF timetabling	40	40	2	17	24
	40	40	2	14	47
	53	53	2	31	138

8.8 GENERALITY AND EFFICIENCY OF ALICE

We have already said that ALICE is efficient and, though it is a general program, it can perform better than a good program written specially for the same type of problem. This may seem surprising: we shall explain it by means of some examples. Two basic reasons underlie this success: the power of the formal manipulation of expressions, compared with the attack by numerical computation normally made in solving problems; and the symbolic propagation of constraints that enables the making of choices or assumptions to be delayed as long as possible. This second results in a better informed choice when one has to be made; the set of criteria provided to guide the choice is very complete, having been constructed with a whole family of problems in mind. A specially designed algorithmic program will perform very badly if a case arises that has not been foreseen.

In contrast to an algorithmic program, ALICE studies the context of every problem very carefully, and also, for each choice that has to be made in the course of the solution, the relevant criteria. In the worst case it will perform as the specific program does on all cases. In most cases, at least for certain choices, ALICE will apply an unexpected criterion, one that had been provided with an entirely different class of problems in mind but which proves to be wholly relevant to the current situation. It is this feature that enables ALICE, when attacking problems that can be solved by paper and pencil methods, to solve these with smaller search trees than would be generated by hand. This is illustrated in the following paragraphs.

8.8.1 Example 1: a cryptarithmetic problem

Cryptarithmetic problems are well known, and as they do not require any great mathematical knowledge they provide a good example for comparison. A simple calculation, for example an addition sum, is written with the digits represented by letters; the usual conditions are that the arithmetic is to base 10, so that the digits are from 0 to 9 inclusive, that each letter corresponds to one and only one digit and that different letters correspond to different digits. The problem is to find the correspondence between letters and digits that makes the sum correct.

Problems of this kind can be solved by a numerical program that enumerates the possiblities (cf. Chapter 5). The values for the letters are chosen from right to left so that the carry digits can be dealt with, and the arithmetical operations performed to the extent possible so as to test the validity of the values assigned so far. The general schema is as follows (Table 8.11):

Table 8.11.

begin	$j \leftarrow 1$
	choose (injective) values for letters in column j
	compute jth result
	test for correctness
	if result differs from values already chosen
	then continue
	else return to previous choice
	end if
end	

This program will provide a standard for reference.

Newell and Simon (1978) have made a long study of the way a human solver tackles a problem of this type; they observed the methods of several solvers and sought to model the solution procedures by means of a production rule system. They tested many of their subjects with the example:

$$
\begin{array}{r}
\text{GERALD} \\
+ \text{DONALD} \\
\hline
= \text{ROBERT}
\end{array}
$$

where the letters on the left, G, D, R can all be assumed not to represent 0.

The solutions covered several pages, even when the value of D was given. Reader – try your skill on this problem, and then compare what you achieve with ALICE's solution which we give later. If your search tree has fewer than 20 vertices you will have beaten the best of Newell and Simon's solvers.

This example accentuates a basic weakness of the brute-force enumeration method: very little information is propagated at each choice, and that in an order ill-suited to the needs. The appropriate order depends on the actual operation and can be found only by a symbolic processing of the constraints. Here different values have to be assigned to the six letters D, L, A, N, O, G, so the number of possibilities is $10!/4! = 151,200$; and this is the number of trials that could be needed. ALICE, however, solves the problem with exactly six.

If we denote the carries, from left to right, by a, b, c, d, e the constraints are (Table 8.12): and we know that there is a 1:1 correspondence between the letters and the decimal digits, and that G, D, R are all different from 0.

Table 8.12.

1	$2.D = T + 10.e$
2	$e + 2.L = R + 10.d$
3	$d + 2.A = E + 10.c$
4	$c + R + N = B + 10.b$
5	$b + E + O = O + 10.a$
6	$a + G + D = R$

First inferences in the order found by the system

T is even, by (1)

$(a = 0 \quad b = 0 \quad E = 0)$ OR $(a = 1 \quad b = 1 \quad E = 9)$ by (5)

$R \equiv e \pmod 2$ by (2)

$E \equiv d \pmod 2$ by (3)

Further, none of the carries can exceed 1, since the sum of two letters cannot exceed 17.

Nothing further can be deduced, so the first choice has to be made; a good basis is the OR constraint just derived:

choice 1: $E = 0$, and therefore $a = b = 0$

(5) is now satisfied trivially, and three constraints are affected:

3a. $\qquad\qquad\qquad d + 2 \cdot A = 10 \cdot c$
4a. $\qquad\qquad\qquad c + R + N = B$
6a. $\qquad\qquad\qquad\quad G + D = R$

from which it follows

d is even, by (3a), therefore $d = 0$, $A = 5 \cdot c$

$A \neq 0$ since $E = 0$, so $A = 5$, $c = 1$; (3a) can be ignored subsequently

(6a) now gives

$R \geqslant 3$ since g and D must be different; $G + D \leqslant 9$,
$\qquad$ so $G \leqslant 8, D \leqslant 8$

$G + D$ is now substituted for R in (4a), and the arithmetic module, described in Section 8.4.3.2, deduces two new constraints

7a. $\qquad\qquad\qquad 1 + G + D + N \leqslant 9$

(the maximum value possible for B is 9; and $B \geqslant 7$, because the sum of three different decimal digits, none of which can be 0, must be at least 6). It follows from 7a, (cf. Section 8.5.2.2) that $G \leqslant 5, D \leqslant 5, N \leqslant 5$, and

$$G + D = R \leqslant 7.$$

Constraints (1), (2), (6a) are now reconsidered, since the values of the unknowns have been changed. Since $R \leqslant 7$, (6a) now entails $G \leqslant 6, D \leqslant 6$. (1) gives nothing new but from (2), since $R \leqslant 7, L \leqslant 3$; and since $R \geqslant 3, L \geqslant 1$.

All the constraints have now been studied, so a second choice must be made. There are several candidates – B and the carries – and only two values available; distinction between these can be made by the criterion of difficulty. The carry e, which appears in the two simple constraints, has the greatest interest; hence:

choice 1.1: $e = 0$

We now rewrite the set of constraints:

1b. $2 \cdot D = T$
2b. $2 \cdot L = R$
4b. $1 + G + D + N = B$
6b. $G + D = R$

The graph 'knows' that:

$$4 \leqslant B \leqslant 9, 1 \leqslant N \leqslant 5, 3 \leqslant R \leqslant 7, 1 \leqslant D \leqslant 5, 1 \leqslant L \leqslant 3, 1 \leqslant G \leqslant 5$$

so from (1b) and (2b) it follows that $L = 2$ or 3, $R = 4$ or 5.

ALICE completes the study of this possibility by an enumeration based on (2b), the simplest of the constraints and the one for which the space to be searched is smallest. If $R = 4$ then $L = 2$ and $D + G = 4$, whence $D \geqslant 3$ and therefore, by (1b), $T = 6$ since $0, 2, 4, 8$ are forbidden. Thus $D = 3$, $G = 1$; but now $0, 1, 2, 3, 4, 5$ are assigned and so (4b), $B = 5 + N$ cannot be satisfied, and $R = 4$ must be rejected. If $R = 6$, then $L = 3$, and since $A = 5$ either $G = 2$, $D = 4$ or $G = 4$, $D = 2$; since $T = 2D$ the only possibility is $T = 8$, $D = 4$, $G = 2$. But then $B = 7 + N$ cannot be satisfied, so $R = 6$ and consequently $e = 0$ must be abandoned. The only possibility is therefore:

choice $1 \cdot 2$: $e = 1$.

We now have the new equations:

1c. $2 \cdot D = T + 10$
2c. $1 + 2 \cdot L = R$

R is therefore odd, and in the original context of choice 1, now restored,

$$3 \leqslant R \leqslant 7, \text{ so } R = 3 \text{ or } 7 \text{ since } A = 5$$

It follows from (1c) that $D \geqslant 6$, so from (6b) $R \geqslant 7$, and finally $R = 7$, giving $L = 3$ and $B = N + 8$, so $N = 1$, $B = 9$. Then $D + G = 7$, and we have already $D \geqslant 6$, from (1c); and this would require $D = 6$, $G = 1$, which is not allowed since already $N = 1$. Choice 1 therefore implies that e can be neither 0 nor 1, and must therefore be abandoned.

Choice 2. $E = 9$, and therefore $a = b = 1$ and

3d. $d + 2 \cdot A = 9 + 10 \cdot c$
4d. $c + R + N = B + 10$
6d. $1 + G + D = R$

From (3d), by parity considerations, $d = 1$; hence from (2)

2d. $e + 2 \cdot L = R + 10$

Also from (d), with $d = 1$, $A = 4 + 5 \cdot c$, and since $E = 9$ we must have

$A = 4$, $c = 0$; so

4e. $R + N = B + 10$

(2d) with $L \leqslant 8$, $R \geqslant 4$ now gives $R + 10 \leqslant 17$, so $R \leqslant 7$; and $e + 2 \cdot L \geqslant 14$, so $L \geqslant 7$ or 8

From the other constraints we can deduce $B \leqslant 5$ and $N \geqslant 3$; but for further progress we have to make another choice; we do this for L because this variable has only two possible values, 7 and 8.

$$\text{choice } 2 \cdot 1: \; L = 7,$$

giving

2e. $e + 14 = R + 10$

Since $A = 4$, we must have $R = 5$, $e = 1$; and substituting these values in (4e) and (6d) we have $N = B + 5$, $D + G = 4$; so $D \leqslant 3$, $G \leqslant 3$. Further, from

(1e)
$$2 \cdot D = T + 10$$

we get $D \geqslant 5$, a contradiction. So $L \neq 7$.
Choice $2 \cdot 2$: $L = 8$, giving

2f. $e + 6 = R$
4f. $R + N = B + 10$
6f. $1 + G + D = R$

From (2f), $R = 6$ or 7 and from (6f) $G + D = 5 + e$ so $G \leqslant 5$ and $D \leqslant 5$. Enumeration of the possibilities now gives (Table 8.13):

Table 8.13.

$R = 7$	$R = 6$
$e = 1$	$e = 0$
$G + D = 6$	$G + D = 5$
$2.D = T + 10$	$2.D = T$
$D = 5$	$D = 1$
$T = 0$	$T = 2$
$G = 1$	since 4 and 6 are already assigned
$N = B + 3$	But then $G = 5 - D = 4 = A$, so
$B = 3$	this is not a possible solution.
$N = 6$	

and a solution has been found
$$G \; E \; R \; A \; L \; D \; O \; N \; B \; T$$
$$1 \; 9 \; 7 \; 4 \; 8 \; 5 \; 2 \; 6 \; 3 \; 0$$

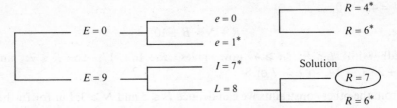

Fig. 8.20 Solution of DONALD + GERALD = ROBERT (a vertex marked *
denotes an impossibility).

It follows from the way this solution has been arrived at that it is unique.
The tree is given in Fig. 8.20; it has six leaves and was developed fully in 9
seconds on an IBM 4331; an enumerative program of the type described in
Chapter 5 took 70 seconds on the same machine.

8.8.2 Example 2: a combinatorial problem

The following problem on constrained permutations, due to M. P.
Schutzenberger, is more complicated. Here $p = p_1 p_2 \ldots p_n$ is a permutation
of the first n integers and the problem is to find all those permutations that
satisfy two constraints defined by binary vectors **m**, **a** of order $n - 1$, as
follows.

By **m** *('monotone')*

$p_{i+1} > p_i$ iff $m_i = 1$; or formally $\forall i, i \in [1, n - 1] m_i = 1 \Leftrightarrow p_{i+1} > p_i$

By **a** *'advance'*

if $a_i = 0$ then $p_i + 1$ is to the left of p_i
if $a_i = 1$ then $p_i + 1$ is to the right of p_i and $p_n \neq n$

Formally

$$\forall i, i \in [1, n - 1]$$

1. $a_i = 0 \Leftrightarrow \forall j, j \in [i + 1, n] p_j \neq p_i + 1$
2. $a_i = 1 \Leftrightarrow (\forall j, j \in [1, i - 1] p_j \neq p_i + 1))$ **and** $p_i \neq n$

The vector **m** gives the directions in which the elements of the permutation vary from one to the next, whilst the vector **a** shows whether the
element ($p_i + 1$) will occur before or after p_i.

Consider first a simple case: $n = 4$, **m** = [0 1 1], **a** = [1 1 0].

Since $\qquad m_1 = 0, \ p_2 < p_1$ $\qquad\qquad$ (a)

$$m_2 = 1, \ p_3 > p_2 \tag{b}$$
$$m_3 = 1, \ p_4 > p_3 \tag{c}$$

Therefore $p_4 > p_3 > p_2$, so

$$p_4 \geqslant 3 \tag{d}$$
$$p_3 \geqslant 2 \tag{e}$$
$$p_3 \leqslant 3 \tag{f}$$

and now from (a)

$$p_1 \geqslant 2 \tag{g}$$

and the only possibility is

$$p_2 = 1 \tag{h}$$

Taking now the constraints expressed by the vector **a**: since

$$a_1 = 1, \ p_1 \neq 4 \tag{i}$$
$$a_2 = 1, \ p_1 \neq p_2 + 1$$

so

$$p_1 \neq 2 \tag{j}$$
$$p_2 \neq 4 \ \text{(known already)}$$
$$a_3 = 0, \ p_4 \neq p_3 + 1 \tag{k}$$

By (f) the only possibility for p_4 is $p_4 = 4$; then from (j), $p_1 = 3$ and finally $p_3 = 2$. The solution is thus the unique permutation $p = [3 \ 1 \ 2 \ 4]$.

This way of conducting the reasoning is exactly what ALICE does; in contrast, a program written specifically for this problem would start by invoking a script 'enumeration' consisting of three phases that can be summarised as follows:

A. Locate one object at a time.
B. Test the partial solution, continue if it is valid.
C. Back-track if a local failure is encountered or a solution has been found.

Phase A concerns the locating of the next element; taking the natural order of $[1, n]$ the process is:

$$A: \ i \leftarrow i + 1 \ \text{and} \ p_i \leftarrow p_i + 1$$

starting with zero values for i and p_i.

Phase B is the critical part, for the efficiency of the program is decided by the order in which the different tests are applied. Three types are needed:

$t1$: is p a permutation?
$t2$: are the m-constraints satisfied?
$t3$: are the a-constraints satisfied?

These should be applied as early as possible so as to avoid trials that will prove useless. $t1$ can be applied immediately after the p_i have been generated and should therefore be made before $t3$. With $t3$, a problem arises when $a_i = 0$, for the elements of p with suffixes greater than i are still unknown; this is resolved by noting that since p is a permutation and therefore a bijection, to say that all p_j with $j \in [i + 1, n]$ are different from $p_i + 1$ is equivalent to saying that either $p_i + 1$ occurs before i, and therefore among the elements already located, or $p_i = n$. So $t3$ can be included in the algorithm.

$t2$ is simple, and on average eliminates more cases than does $t1$; we therefore place it first.

The text is thus as follows (Table 8.14). This program can be improved by

Table 8.14.

---

procedure PERM: generates all permutations of the first n integers, with
                        constraints defined by binary vectors a, m.
$$p \equiv 0; \quad i \leftarrow 1; \quad p_0 \leftarrow n + 1$$
while $i > 0$
        $I \leftarrow$ set of integers $[1, i - 1]$;
        {test the monotonies to see if p_i can be increased}
        while $(m_{i-1} = 1$ **and** $p_i < n)$
            or $(m_{i-1} = 0$ **and** $p_i < p_{i-1} - 1)$
            $p \leftarrow p_i + 1$;
                                            {test permutation}
            if $\forall j \in I, p_j \neq p_i$ **then**   {test successions}
                $q \leftarrow p_i + 1$; OK $\leftarrow$ F   {q present in I or
                                                                                $p_i = n$}
                if $a_i = 0$ **then**
                    if $(p_i = n)$ **or** $(\exists j \in I: p(j) = q)$
                        then OK $\leftarrow$ T;
                    end if
                    else $(a_i = 1$, q not in I and $p_i \neq n)$
                        if $(p_i \neq n)$ **and** $(\forall j \in I: p_j \neq q)$
                            then OK $\leftarrow$ T;
                        end if
                end if
                if OK **then**   {continue with i}
                    if $i = n$ **then** print solution $p_i \leftarrow n$ {forced backtrack}
                    else $i \leftarrow i + 1$
                    end if
                end if
            end if   {return in case of check}
        end while   {backtrack when p_i cannot be increased further}
        $p_i \leftarrow 0$; $i \leftarrow i - 1$
end while
end PERM

---

making special provisions for certain cases, but even so it is a fixed program, written, like all algorithms, without taking account of the numerical data. The permutations are always generated in the same order, whatever the vectors **a** and **m**, and this can be very disadvantageous since the data may forbid certain p_i taking certain values, and these values may be among the last to be assigned: the waste of effort in fruitless trials can then be imagined. Attacked by enumeration, the problem is essentially exponential; but as with other exponential problems, particular data may restrict the number of possibilities to the extent that it becomes of only polynomial complexity.

8.8.3 Solution by ALICE

ALICE takes all these considerations into account. First of all, far from developing a single algorithm, it works with the data. Suppose for example $n = 9$ and the constraint vectors are:

$$\mathbf{a} = (1\ 1\ 1\ 1\ 0\ 1\ 1\ 0)$$
$$\mathbf{m} = (1\ 1\ 0\ 1\ 0\ 1\ 0\ 1)$$

When $m_i = 0$ the constraint is $\neg(p_{i+1} > p_i)$, so $p_{i+1} \leqslant p_i$; but since p is a bijection we must have $p_{i+1} < p_i$. Thus:

i	m_i	constraint
1	1	$p_2 > p_1$
2	1	$p_3 > p_2$
3	0	$p_4 < p_3$
4	1	$p_5 > p_4$
5	0	$p_6 < p_5$
6	1	$p_7 > p_6$
7	0	$p_8 < p_7$
8	1	$p_9 > p_8$

For the *a*-constraints, first $p_i \neq 9$ whenever $a_i = 1$; the other constraints are as follows:

i	a_i	constraint
1	1	$p_1 \neq 9$
2	1	$p_1 \neq p_2 + 1$
3	1	$p_1, p_2 \neq p_3 + 1$
4	1	$p_1, p_2, p_3 \neq p_4 + 1$
5	0	$p_6, p_7, p_8, p_9 \neq p_5 + 1$
6	1	$p_1, p_2, p_3, p_4, p_5 \neq p_6 + 1$
7	1	$p_1, p_2, p_3, p_4, p_5, p_6 \neq p_7 + 1$
8	0	$p_9 \neq p_8 + 1$

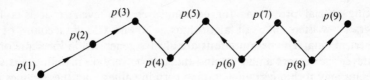

Fig. 8.21 Monotone constraints for Example 2 (permutations) on page 443.

The m-constraints, of type $\leqslant$, are chosen by the system in preference to the a-constraints, of type $\neq$; ALICE takes these in what it considers to be the right order, found as a result of computing a Grundy function (cf. Section 8.5.2.3). This is equivalent to generating in the machine the analogue of the diagram in Fig. 8.21.

The first studied is $p_2 > p_1$; it follows that $p_2 \geqslant 2$, when $p_3 > p_2$ gives $p_3 \geqslant 3$. Similarly $p_5 \geqslant 2$, $p_7 \geqslant 2$, $p_9 \geqslant 2$; $p_4 \leqslant 8$, $p_6 \leqslant 8$, $p_8 \leqslant 8$; $p_2 \leqslant 8$, $p_1 \leqslant 7$.

The $\neq$ constraints are now taken. Some of these can be deleted because they are necessarily satisfied as a consequence of other relations: thus $p_6 \neq p_5 + 1$ must hold because $p_6 < p_5$ and $p_6 \neq p_7 + 1$ because $p_6 < p_7$.

Nothing more can be deduced at this stage, so a choice has to be made. The only possible antecedents for the vale 9 are p_5 and p_9, so, using the criterion of Section 8.5.2, ALICE chooses first a location for this, $p_5 = 9$.

The immediate consequence is the elimination of 15 arcs: $p_i \neq 9$ for all $i \neq 5$, the a-constraints give $p_6 \neq 8 \neq p_7$ and the m-constraints, with $p_3 \leqslant 8$ and $p_7 \leqslant 7$, give

$$p_2 \leqslant 7, p_1 \leqslant 6, p_4 \leqslant 7, p_6 \leqslant 6, p_8 \leqslant 6.$$

Thus only p_3 or p_9 can take the value 8, and the next choice is $p_3 = 8$, giving

$$p_4 \neq 7, p_7 \neq 7.$$

The only possible antecedents for 7 are now p_2 and p_3; the choice $p_2 = 7$ gives

$$p_1 = 6 \text{ or } p_9 = 6.$$

If $p_1 = 6$ then $p_4 \leqslant 4$ and $p_7 \leqslant 4$; so $p_6 \leqslant 3$ and $p_9 \leqslant 5$.

If $p_7 = 4$ then from the only remaining constraint $p_4 \neq p_6 + 1$ the following four solutions are obtained:

$$678192435 \quad 678193425 \quad 678293415 \quad 678391425$$

There are in fact 42 solutions, and all these can be found by making only six binary choices, requiring only 64 cases to be considered, instead of the $9! = 362,880$ by brute-force enumeration.

Still worse possibilities can arise for the algorithmic program. Suppose the data were $n = 100$, $\mathbf{m} = \mathbf{a} = 100 \dots (98$ zeros$)$

The PERM procedure always works in the same way and here would generate in succession 1, 12, 123, 13, 132, 1324, 14, 142, 1423, 143, 1432, 14325, ... ALICE, however, by studying the m-constraints, would find immediately that:

$$p_2 > p_1 \quad \text{and} \quad p_2 > p_3 > p_4 > \cdots > p_{100}$$

and therefore $p_2 = 100$.

Further, all the a-constraints are satisfied trivially, since for all $j \geqslant 2$ and $i > j$ and $p_j > p_i$. Thus the only freedom of choice is the value of p_1, from the set $[1, 99]$, and just 99 permutations will solve the problem. ALICE has therefore solved the problem in a time that is polynomial in n.

Of course, particular data could be catered for in PERM, but the number of possibilities is unlimited: for example, placing the 1 of this example in any other position in $\mathbf{m}$ and $\mathbf{a}$ – when there is no solution – or interchanging 1s and 0s: the program can always be defeated by a new set of data.

The position becomes even worse if, as often happens in real life, a problem is modified slightly by adding constraints. Thus in this example, if the assignment $p_{\frac{1}{3}n} = 1$ is imposed, PERM is very difficult to modify so as to take this new constraint into account at an early enough stage, whereas ALICE can use it immediately so as to restrict the search.

8.9   INPUT IN NATURAL LANGUAGE (FRENCH)

We are now working to make it possible to input problem statements to ALICE in terms as close as possible to natural language, so that the system is accessible to any potential user and is not restricted to computer scientists. The aim is to provide it with a stock of basic knowledge that will relieve the future use of the need to define common objects precisely and to specify their properties; the ideal is that input can be in natural French, read and checked interactively. The main difficulty arises from the huge amount of background knowledge, in all fields, that we call on in all communications: anyone who provides computing support knows that the most difficult part of the task is understanding the questioner.

C. Lopez-Laseica has produced a prototype which we describe below. Just as he has done, we are restricting the universe of discourse in our first attempts, in our case to that of mathematical puzzles. This class is certainly not representative of all possible problem statements but it does present an essential difficulty that has to be overcome – that of getting a deep

446ALICE

understanding of the problem and finding connections between phrases that may be widely separated, so as to be able first to state the problem precisely and then to solve it. The ALICE language is a key component here: it is concise and expressive enough with the help of AI techniques now available – semantic and pragmatic dictionaries, semantic networks – to make the understanding and translation of input statements possible and efficient – a half-page of text can need about 1 to 4 seconds.

8.9.1 Principles of the translation

The major part of the translation program consists of data: the dictionary gives for each word and each use of the word its syntactic forms, its semantic classes and attributes, the other words with which it is usually linked and commonsense inferences that can be drawn from it. For example:

FRANCE
定义 element
group countries
inferences language French
nationality French
constitution republic
relation inhabitant, State

The dictionary, compiled to cover the 50 statements treated, consists of about a thousand words, with the verbs playing a special role. The actions are shown that should be performed so as to express the constraints, so that for the verb 'give', for example, the entry is:

GIVE
definition verb
group person to person
inferences (before):
(subject of GIVE) possesses (thing given)
(after):
(subject of GIVE) possesses (– thing given)
(object of GIVE) possesses (+ thing given)

The entry for EXCHANGE, corresponding to the syntactic construction 'A exchanges with B X against Y' is

EXCHANGE (A B) (X Y)
definition A gives X to B and B gives Y to A

The program arrives gradually at the sense in which a word is used by analysing the text with the help of the dictionary; both syntax and semantics are involved in this understanding.

The verbs are studied first, and give the main structure of the sentence. Next, the short words, the modifiers; these join and relate the different syntactic groups. Any further information that is given in the dictionary but is not useful in the particular context – that is, gives rise to no new constraint – is discarded: thus the adjective 'black' in 'a black cat' is significant if there is later mention of 'a white cat', but not if there is no mention of a cat of any other colour.

In the third state of the process the program generates the translation of the statement into ALICE.

Only when the meaning of the entire text has been correctly seized is the translation complete. Thus according to the context the statement:

John and the teacher read

will be interpreted as either:

activity (John) = activity (teacher) = reading

or simply:

John ≠ teacher

In solving a puzzle the program studies the whole of the problem statement in order to arrive at what seems the appropriate meaning of a phrase. We now give an example: this would be typed in at a terminal keyboard.

8.9.2 Example of translation

Five people, of different nationalities, live in the first five houses in a street. Each follows a different profession and likes a different drink and a different animal; and the houses are of five different colours:

The Englishman lives in the red house.
The Spaniard has a dog.
The Japanese is a painter.
The Italian drinks tea.
The Norwegian lives in the first house on the left.
The owner of the green house drinks coffee.
The green house is on the right of the white house.
The sculptor breeds snails.
The diplomat lives in the yellow house.
They drink milk in the middle house.
The Norwegian lives next door to the blue house.
The violinist drinks fruit juice.

The fox is in the house next to the doctor's.
The horse is next to the diplomat's

Who has a zebra, and who drinks water?

First, the interpreter constructs the various groups in the semantic network. The set of 'persons' has two attributes: 'five' and 'different nationalities'; the verb 'lives in' relates this to the next group, that of 'houses'. This second set is formed, together with its attributes, and so on. All the statements are represented and together complete the semantic network.

The nomenclature is then standardised, so that 'lives in', 'is in', 'is the owner of' all become 'has as a house', and 'on the left of', 'next door to', 'in the middle' are expressed by numerical relations. Finally, the senses in which the words are used is expressed in the semantic network and all that has to be done before handing the problem to ALICE is to set up the following correspondence, which must be preserved throughout the solution:

NAT 1 ↔English	DRK 1 ↔Tea
NAT 2 ↔Spanish	DRK 2 ↔Coffee
NAT 3 ↔Japanese	DRK 3 ↔Milk
NAT 4 ↔Italian	DRK 4 ↔Fruit juice
NAT 5 ↔Norwegian	DRK 5 ↔Water
HOU 1 ↔Red	ANI 1 ↔Dog
HOU 2 ↔Green	ANI 2 ↔Snail
HOU 3 ↔White	ANI 3 ↔Fox
HOU 4 ↔Yellow	ANI 4 ↔Horse
HOU 5 ↔Blue	ANI 5 ↔Zebra
PRO 1 ↔Painter	
PRO 2 ↔Sculptor	
PRO 3 ↔Diplomat	
PRO 4 ↔Violinist	
PRO 5 ↔Doctor	

All the constraints are now expressed in terms of this correspondence and the complete statement handed to ALICE for solution.

The following is the translation of the problem statement into ALICE.

let   SET SNU INT = 1   5[1]
                 SNA INT = 1   5
                 SHO INT = 1   5

1. INT 1   5 means 'the integers 1, 2, 3, 4, 5'. SNU means 'set of numbers'.

```
          SPR   INT = 1   5
          SDR   INT = 1   5
          SAN   INT = 1   5
```

find   BIJ   NAT   SNA   → SS
                HOU   SHO   → SS
                PRO   SPR   → SS
                DRK   SDR   → SS
                ANI   SAN   → SS

with   NAT 1 = HOU 1
                NAT 2 = ANI 1
                NAT 4 = PRO 1
                NAT 4 = DRK 1
                NAT 5 = 1
                HOU 2 = DRK 2
                HOU 2 = HOU 3 + 1
                PRO 2 = ANI 2
                PRO 3 = HOU 4
                DRK 3 = 3
                (NAT 5 = HOU 5 + 1) or (NAT 5 = HOU 5 − 1)
                PRO 4 = DRK 4
                (ANI 3 = PRO 5 + 1) or (ANI 3 = PRO 5 − 1)
                (ANI 4 = PRO 3 + 1) or (ANI 4 = PRO 3 − 1)

ALICE solved this puzzle in 4 seconds, making only one choice. The
solution is:

Nationality	Profession	House	Animal	Drinks
English	sculptor	red	snails	milk
Italian	doctor	blue	horse	tea
Norwegian	diplomat	yellow	fox	water
Spanish	violinist	white	dog	fruit juice
Japanese	painter	green	zebra	coffee

Of course, most real-life problems have statements that are longer, more
complex and more ambiguous. Our aim here is simply to show that a widely
applicable problem solving system can be constructed that is conversational
in nature and can accept problem statements in natural language.

Chapter 9

LEARNING

Learning can be defined as 'improving performance by experience'.

The future of artificial intelligence certainly lies in this field; there is so much to be learned, of such a variety, that the ideal would be an information system that learned, itself, from examples rather than was given items of knowledge, one at a time, by ourselves. But we should be deceiving ourselves if we imagined we knew already how to create such a program, when we scarcely know how a non-learning program should work.

There is also the question of forgetting: for the learning human, he must know what to forget from among the many possibilities presented to him. Here we meet an important technological difference between computers and ourselves, affecting knowledge acquisition in general and problem solving in particular.

Man is pre-programmed to learn. He can do nothing without memorising what he does – sometimes against his wish. The new-born infant already has reflexes and is curious by nature; throughout life man cannot stop himself looking for information, turning his gaze to something that moves, his hearing to an unfamiliar sound. The computer, in contrast, starts with no such program for seeking information and for learning in general; the essays towards machine learning that we shall describe in this chapter have more limited aims.

9.1 DIFFERENT TYPES OF LEARNING

There is a whole spectrum of learning, which we can separate into five levels.

Level 1, the lowest, is simply programmed learning: a code states what is to be done. All the usual computer programs are at this level, as are also the majority of industrial robots – thus once one has been instructed to perform the movements of painting a car it will perform these exactly ever afterwards, whether or not there is a car there.

Level 2 corresponds to rote learning: all the possible situations are memorised, together with the actions appropriate to each. This is the

Fig. 9.1.

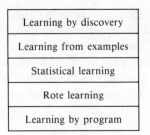

Fig. 9.2 Different types of learning.

Pavlovian type of conditioning: the system confronted with a new situation is 'rewarded' if it performs the right action, 'punished' otherwise.

Level 3 is similar to Level 2 but is improved by a statistical learning process. The situations are now grouped into classes, arrived at by studying many examples, and the system keeps only descriptions of the various classes. This is 'learning without a teacher', and is followed by Level 4, 'learning with a teacher': here, with the help of a teacher, the system can learn from examples, and can generalise.

Finally at Level 5 there is again no teacher and the system itself, by purely inductive methods, can create new situations, new hypotheses and new concepts.

We must emphasise that, whatever the level, there is no suggestion of learning by starting from nothing; it is precisely because at present we do not know what is the minimum amount of knowledge needed to make learning possible that we cannot program a system so that it is truly able to learn (Fig. 9.2).

9.2 THE GAME OF CHECKERS: LEARNING THE PARAMETERS

Checkers is the American name, Draughts the English; A. L. Samuel (1959, 1967), an IBM engineer, wrote excellent programs for this game between 1956 and 1967. It is played on a standard 8×8 chess board; the men can move only forwards, the kings either forwards or backwards, both one square at a time; the branching factor is thus about 8.

9.2.1 Rote learning

Samuel's first program was at Level 2; he gave the program some 180000 positions, taken from the best writings on the game. But since that is a great deal of information – especially for the machines of the period – he used three procedures to reduce the difficulties of memory management:

1. For rapid access the situations were sorted according to:

   - The numbers of men and of kings, on each side.
   - The frequency with which they had appeared in past games.

2. Situations that are symmetrical under the interchange of black and white were treated simultaneously.
3. There was a method for eliminating the positions encountered least often in the most recent games, should the memory be saturated (here, 15 years ahead of the world, Samuel invented an algorithm for changing the pages in a virtual-storage machine).

Further, and nor unrelated to the 36-bit word length of the IBM Series 700 and 7000 machines, Samuel devised a good representation of the board. The black pieces using only the black squares, he enlarged the board and numbered the squares as in Fig. 9.3, the fictitious squares 9, 18, 27, 36 acting as separators. With this representation a position can be expressed as a (binary) vector [1, 36], occupying one machine word, and Black's legal moves, without captures, found by addition of 4 and of 5 (shifting and masking, which are elementary operations for electronic devices).

This first program was only the starting point for the second, an improvement. On the principle that it would be a pity to lose all the

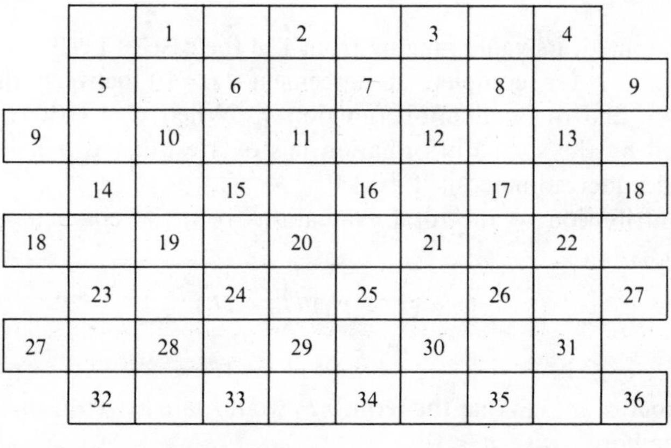

	1		2		3		4	
5		6		7		8		9
9		10		11		12		13
	14		15		16		17		18
18		19		20		21		22	
	23		24		25		26		27
27		28		29		30		31	
	32		33		34		35		36

Fig. 9.3 Samuel's representation of the checkers (draughts) board.

information available when the precise position encountered was not in memory, Samuel introduced a search procedure for studying the position, limited to three half-moves except in the case of a capture at the last move or a Black piece *en prise* – these conditions could sometimes require the search to continue for up to 20 half-moves. Finally, he used a polynomial evaluation function:

$$F = \sum_i p_i P_i$$

with 38 weighting factors p_i and 38 characteristics P_i, among which were the material advantage (P_0), control of the centre, number of pieces exposed, mobility, number of V-configurations (vacant square surrounded by three black pieces), number of threats, relative advances of the two sides.

Samuel was undoubtedly the first to program the alpha–beta procedure described in Section 6.3, later much used in chess programs.

We now consider the use of the program in three different ways.

9.2.2 Learning from the record

Drawing on the knowledge of positions stored in its memory, after each game the program performs a minimax evaluation of the positions encountered, using the function F. In this process it records the number H of moves that, according to F, would have been better than the one stored and the number L of those that would have been worse. If H is small and L large there is good agreement with the stored information; in general, a 'correlation coefficient' (not with the usual meaning of the term):

$$C = (L - H)/(L + H)$$

can be computed, its value ranging from 1 in the case of perfect agreement ($H = 0$) to -1 for complete disagreement ($L = 0$) between the stored information and the evaluation function F. When $C \neq 1$ the evaluation represented by the stored information has over-estimated the situation if $H > 0$ and underestimated it if $H \leqslant 0$.

The contribution to the total evaluation from the characteristic P_i is computed as:

$$C_i = (L_i - H_i)/(L_i + H_i)$$

where

H_i = number of moves that the term $p_i P_i$ would rate as better than the best in the book, with $p_i < 0$

L_i = corresponding number rated worse

Then

if C_i is negative, a positive p_i must be decreased

if C_i is positive, a negative p_i must be increased (i.e. given a positive increment).

Further, the program changes the value of the parameter p_k corresponding to the coefficient C_k of greatest absolute value, setting $p_k = 1$; and then, for all $i = k, p_i = 2^n$ where $n \leqslant |c_k/c_i| \leqslant n + 1$.

Finally, the program keeps only 16 of the 38 original characteristics, 22 of the p_i being set to zero at any time. After each game a black mark is given against the characteristic P_i corresponding to the C_i of smallest value, and when a characteristic has collected three black marks it is deleted from F and replaced by the one that has been in the list of unused characteristics longest.

With these procedures, after about 20 games the program is playing at a high level of skill; but Samuel wanted to do even better.

9.2.3 Learning without a teacher

As this concerns a game, the program can play against itself, and by giving the p_i different values it can be made to learn from its own play.

Let A, B be two versions of the program with evaluation functions Fa, Fb respectively. If A wins then the parameters in Fb are changed slightly; if it loses it gets a black mark and after three black marks Fa and Fb are interchanged and radical changes are made to the parameters of Fb. This is the classical perturbed gradient method for exploring a non-convex space.

Improving on this idea, and combining it with the minimax principle, Samuel produced a fourth program, as follows.

9.2.4 Generalised learning

This is the term with which Samuel himself described the learning capacities of his new program; he had found it distressing that none of its predecessors was able to learn in the course of a game whilst we ourselves see, after a few more moves, that we have made a mistake and take care not to make the same mistake again in the rest of the game.

If a program bases its actions on an evaluation function and uses the alpha–beta method it too can exercise *a posteriori* judgement on all its moves; having met some situation in the course of an evaluation it may well meet this again in the actual play some moves later. This is illustrated in Fig. 9.4. If F gave a perfect evaluation and everything went as predicted, the two

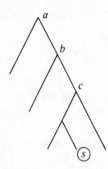
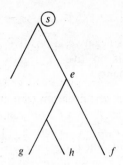

Situation met during the
alpha–beta procedure,
evaluation $F(S)$

Same situation met
in the course of play,
evaluation $F'(S)$

Fig. 9.4 Two evaluations of the same position.

evaluations $F(S)$, $F'(S)$ would be identical; but if it turned out that $F(S) > F'(S)$, then the first evaluation was optimistic and the adversary had proved better than had been reckoned so, as in the earlier version, the program should reduce the positive weights and increase the negative ones. This leads to a procedure similar to the preceding, in which the coefficients $C_i = (L_i - H_i)/(L_i + H_i)$ are recomputed, where now H_i is the number of times since the start of the game that $p_i P_i < 0$ together with $F(S) > F'(S)$. This refers to the case $F(S) > F'(S)$; the case $F < F'$ is treated symmetrically.

Initially the performance of the program thus modified was rather unstable but Samuel now has a record of some 180 000 moves made by it and at night it plays against itself. As a result Samuel is beaten regularly at draughts by his own program. It has reached a level of play that is unprecedented among game-playing programs and some time ago won a game against the Connecticut State champion – K. Nealey – in 1962. It lost honourably in four correspondence games against the world champion, W. Hellman, and also drew against him.

The program plays steadily better and faster – for it becomes increasingly likely that the situation it faces is one that it has met before and that is stored in its memory. Here, however, Samuel has had luck: success in this type of generalised learning depends on the adversary being a good player – if it plays only against poor opponents the program will not learn the best values for the parameters. In fact, the minimax procedure assumes that the opponent plays as well as possible; against a poor player the program will assume, wrongly, that the position has been under-valued and will change its parameters accordingly. Since 'learning' takes place after each move in the same game, 15 moves can suffice to change the parameters completely;

the program will then start to play badly and the opponent has only to start to play well to win the game.

Samuel was the first to introduce into the alpha–beta method the techniques of pruning the tree, in both breadth and depth, and sorting the moves at the first level; but he was concerned above all with the problem he considered the most important:

1. By construction, the evaluation function is linear in each of the characteristics P_i, but some will reinforce each other. Thus if both P_i and P_j give an advantage to Black a term $P_i \times P_j$ will express such a reinforcement.
2. By definition, the most general possible evaluation will be a table; with 38 characteristics taken into account the theoretical ideal is a table of $\mathbb{N}^{38}$ entries.
3. Of necessity, some compromise must be found between the too-crude linear function and the impossible-sized table.

He then developed the idea of tables of *signatures*, hierarchical tables that form a good approximation to the ideal. He classified the 38 characteristics according to type, each type consisting of characteristics that the experts in the game, and Samuel himself, judged to be correlated; and within each type each characteristic is limited to seven different values. A (weighting) coefficient must now be learned for every combination of values within each type: Fig. 9.5 gives the general organisation of these tables of signatures.

Samuel used his 180 000 expert moves to calculate these parameters,

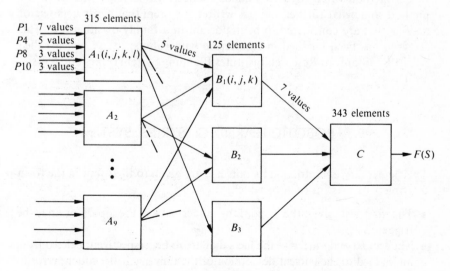

Fig. 9.5 Hierarchy of signatures at three levels.

employing the previous correlation method: he reckoned that stable values had been reached after taking account of some 80 000 moves.

In actuality, everything takes place as though each matrix element were itself a coefficient; there are 315×9 for Type A, 125×3 for B and 343 for C, say 3500 in total, instead of the 16 for the first program. The input to A is the set of values of the characteristics P; to the levels B, the output from A; and to C, the output from B.

Since most of the characteristics are significant only in certain phases of the game, every game is divided into six phases according to the number of pieces on the board and distances they have advanced. This reduces still further the computing time, which is in fact very short because an evaluation is now simply a table look-up: $F(S)$ is given directly by a single instruction:

$$S(S) \leftarrow C(B_1(A_1(P_1, P_2, P_3, P_4), A_2(...), ... A_9(...), B_2(...), B_3(...)))$$

The program became and has remained a true champion in the game. Without any alpha−beta activity, in 68% of cases it finds the best moves in the two first, against 32% for the polynomial evaluation and 16% by random choice; and this is improved significantly by alpha−beta. In addition, it plays consistently well, without a single bad move, throughout the game.

Whilst these programs have the major defect of starting each time from values of the factors p_i that are given, and cannot discover these for themselves, this statistical type of learning is a good principle and is in fact a method often used by humans. One research team has taken the method somewhat further and has written a system that constructs sets of actions that are considered to be important in a family of situations. This research has been pursued in connection with robots; the system is called STRIPS − Stanford Research Institutes Planning System (Fikes and Nilsson 1971).

9.3   ROBOTIC LEARNING: 'STRIPS' SYSTEM

The elementary operators on its universe are given to the robot in the form of triplets of lists, in each of which:

- The first list gives the conditions under which the operator may be triggered
- The second and third give the facts that are to be, respectively, deleted from and added to the current description of the universe if the robot performs the action in question. The consequential changes are propagated in

Table 9.1 STRIPS elementary operator.

OPERATOR 27: move an object in a room	
List C (conditions):	Robot on the floor. Robot in Room X at place $Z1$
	Object on the floor at $Z1$. Object moveable
	Places $Z1$, $Z2$ in Room X
List $-$:	Robot at $Z1$. Object O at $Z1$
List $+$:	Robot at $Z2$. Object O at $Z2$.

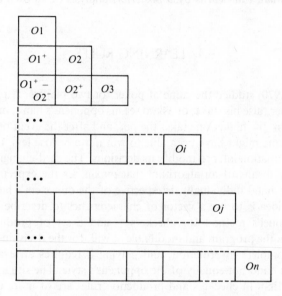

Fig. 9.6 Sequences of operators in STRIPS.

STRIPS with the help of a theorem prover based on the resolution principle (cf. Chapter 3).

Table 9.1 gives an example of such a triplet. 'Learning' occurs each time the system solves a problem; this is a matter of memorising the sequence of elementary operators it has used in arriving at the solution and so acquiring the new information. A plan that has succeeded in n steps constitutes a source of information that could be used to reach intermediate goals, and is a source that STRIPS will exploit in future cases. It first arranges the operator sequence $O1$, $O2$, ..., On in a triangular array as in Fig. 9.6, in which the entry at the intersection of row i and column k gives the facts added by operator Ok that have been retained up to the application of Oi. Then if when attacking a new problem a description matching the goal is found in row j, Oj is the final operator to be applied and by moving up the array the first operator Oi is found whose conditions are satisfied in the new circumstances: the sequence $Oi, Oi + 1, ..., Oj$ will attain the new goal.

The sequence thus found can be regarded as a macro-action, corresponding to a sequence of instructions such as 'pick up the object O, open the door, switch on the light, go up the stairs, put the object O down, switch off the light, end' which the robot will have learned and memorised.

We next consider a game-playing program – poker in this case – developed by D. Waterman, that learns by *a posteriori* analysis of its own experience.

9.4   LEARNING RULES

Waterman (1970) studied the game of poker for two players. A player, in his turn, can either raise his stake, or ask to see his opponent's hand, or quit. If the hands are seen, the higher one takes the pot, and after the event one can work out whether one might have been able to win more or lose less: the program uses this information later to modify its decisions. The card-changing option is dealt with by means of an algorithm that maximises the expectation of the value of each hand individually, irrespective of the opponent's hand.

The basic idea is to use a vector of characteristics to describe the hand – recalling Samuel's method for checkers – and a set of production rules, separate from the program and modifiable at will, for the decisions. Poker is a game of incomplete information, and playing it requires an evaluation not only of one's hand but equally of the opponent's style. The situations are less well defined than in checkers and production rules are of more use than the tables of signatures defined by Samuel; the minimax procedure can no longer be for ultimate protection since every play is unique and will never be met again in the same game.

The characteristic vector has six components, as follows:

1. Value of the hand (VH).
2. Height of the pot (HP).
3. Last raise by the opponent (LR).
4. Number of cards exchanged by the opponent (CE).
5. Probability that the opponent is bluffing (PB).
6. Opponent's style – more conservative or less (CS).

In addition, the program computes various statistics for the games played against the opponent – correlations between stakes and hand values, numbers of bluffs, numbers of quits.

The production rules are of the form:

characteristic vector for the situation → action

The rules are ordered, and Rule i is invoked only if it has not been possible to use any of Rules 1 to $i - 1$.

A rule would be given by an expert as:

> A player holding a hand that is a certain win should make the highest stake he can without risking the opponent's quitting; but if the pot is very high he should see his opponent.

This would be translated by the program as follows, WH denoting 'winning hand': and a $*$ indicating that the corresponding component of the vector is not relevant:

$R1$: $(WH, *, r, *, PB, CS) \rightarrow$ max
$R2$: $(WH, P, r, *, *, *) \quad \rightarrow$ SEE
$R2$ is to be considered before $R1$.

P, the minimum size of the pot for which $R2$ is used, is set in advance, say $P > 100$; the entry r (>0) means that the opponent has previously raised his stake.

The value of max, the greatest stake that will not provoke the opponent's quitting, is given by another rule that takes account mainly of the values of PB and CS. A rule of this type can be refined or modified by the program; learning, at first with the help of a teacher, proceeds by reinforcement, the rules that prove good being favoured and the others having their application restricted.

It is assumed that the teacher provides the information resulting from each play; this consists of:

- The up-dated vector of relevant variables.
- The correct decision.
- The reason for that decision.

Three cases can arise:

1. The right decision was taken by the program for the right reasons; so nothing need be changed.
2. No right-hand side of a rule corresponds to the right decision, and the ith rule was used; the program now inserts after $(i - 1)$ a new rule given by the teacher.
3. Somewhere, either before or after the rule Ri that was used, there is a rule Rj that would have given the right decision; the program therefore changes the parameters of those rules that prevented this from being used.

Example. Suppose the rules at this stage are:

$R1$: $(a1, *, c2, *, *, *) \rightarrow$ raise by 5

$R2$: $(a1, b1, *, *, e1, *) \rightarrow$ increase PB by 0.5 (increased probability
　　　　　　　　　　　　　　 that the opponent is bluffing)
$R3$: $(a2, *, c1, *, e1, *) \rightarrow$ raise by 5
$R4$: $(a1, *, *, *, *, *) \rightarrow$ increase PB by 0.5

and that there are the following constraints:

$$a1 > 8, \quad a2 < 10, \quad b1 > 9, \quad c1 < 3, \quad c2 > 11, \quad e1 = 0$$

with the characteristic vector

$$(9, 4, 5, 7, 0, 5)$$

The value (9) of the hand satisfies the constraints on both $a1$ and $a2$; that of
the pot (4) does not satisfy the constraint on $b1$, nor LR (5) satisfy $c1$ or $c2$;
so only $R4$ is applicable. However, the teacher criticises this decision, saying
the correct action is a raise of 5 because VH (>7) is large and LR (<6) is
small. A new rule is therefore learned:

$R5$: $(a3, *, c3, *, *, *) \rightarrow$ raise by 5, with $a3 > 7$, $c3 < 6$

The program now scans the rules in sequence to see if there is already one
that could have given the same decision. $R1$ is a possibility but is not
suitable because the conditions on $c2$ and $c3$ are contradictory and cannot
be reconciled. $R3$, however, seems to be the right candidate: it gives the
same decision and the constraints on the component values can be modified
so that the given values are acceptable. The modified rule is therefore placed
before the defective $R4$:

$R3'$: $(a4, *, c3, *, e1, *) \rightarrow$ raise by 5; with $7 < a4 < 10$, $c3 < 6$.

The complete learning procedure is given in Table 9.2.

INPUT characteristic vector; correct decision
SCANNING OF RULES

There are two risks, of opposite natures, inherent in this elegant
procedure. The first is over-restrictive rules, as can result from the teacher
being too punctilious; the number of rules then increases without limit, each
one applying to a single case. This can be countered by setting a limit to the
number allowed, the final one, associated with vector $(*, *, *, *, *, *)$, giving
a random decision. All learning, in fact, starts from this single rule.

The other risk is that of redundancy: a rule Ri can make any succeeding
rule Rj redundant because the constraints on the parameters of Rj cause the
value of these to satisfy the constraints for Ri, irrespective of the decisions
of these rules. Conversely, an Ri can render a preceding Rh unnecessary
because the same decision will be taken whether or not Rh exists. The
system looks for such redundancy periodically and deletes any redundant

Table 9.2 Procedure for learning rules.

---

if decision OK **then** end
else construct correct new rule *Rp*
    let *Rd* be rule giving wrong decision
    if there is a rule *Ri* that
        −has the same right side as *Rp*
        −involves inequalities compatible with those of *Rp*
      then if *Ri* occurs before *Rd* in the sequence of rules
        then generalise the definitions of $Ri \cap Rp$
        else (*Ri* occurs after *Rd*)
           restrict the definitions of all the parameters of
           the rules between *Rd* and *Ri* so that they are not
           triggered by the current vector
        end if
    else add the new rule *Rp* immediately before *Rd*
    end if
end if

---

rules; this is done after each game, not after each play, because the rules can be modified very frequently.

Example
    *R*1: (a1, b1, *, *, *, *) → d1
    *R*2: (a2, b2, c2, *, *, f1) → d2
    *R*3: (*, b2, *, *, *, f2) → d3
    *R*4: (*, b1, *, *, *, *) → d3

with

    a1 > 5, a2 > 10, b1 < 9, b2 < 4, c1 < 5, f1 > 15, f2 < 7

*R*1 makes *R*2 (a successor) redundant because a2 < a1 and b2 < b1; so *R*2 is deleted. *R*4 makes *R*3 (a predecessor) redundant because b2 < b1 and f2 is not relevant to *R*4; so *R*3 is deleted.

Notice that all is now provided for learning without a teacher: each time the opponent is seen, if the program loses it constructs for itself a rule that would have given instead a quit, if it wins it constructs a rule that would have raised the last stake.

Waterman completed his study by devising five different poker programs:

1. Random play.
2. Learning with a teacher.
3. Automated learning, without a teacher.
4. Rules provided by a good player.
5. Everything learned by the program itself, the characteristic vector not given.

The number of rules never exceeded 30. Program 3, after a learning period, agreed with experts in 96% of its decisions; it would fairly often respond to very similar situations with different decisions, and bluffed easily – all without making any wrong moves: some opponents found this very disconcerting.

The programs easily beat moderate players, and could almost match experts.

Comments. There are two weaknesses in Waterman's work.

The first is that, as with Samuel's, his program's learning is restricted to numerical parameters; any symbolic information is provided from outside.

The second is that the fixed order of the rules complicates the working of the program and can produce strange unstable behaviour; the ordering makes the set something like a procedure and any change can have uncontrollable side effects, throwing away the advantage of the production rule approach.

The essential problem of machine learning now becomes clear: it is the formulation by the program of the necessary concepts. It must be able to infer, possibly from a single case, the features that determine the situation: this is how we humans learn – no-one needs to learn twice not to put his hand in the fire. We now describe a program that, taking again chess as its subject, attacks the problem by seeking to understand a single example and then to generalise this knowledge.

9.5 LEARNING PLANS

The program is due to Jacques Pitrat. It takes actual games played by masters, attempts to understand the moves and then constructs plans for play, to be used in other (chess) games; initially it knows only two elementary strategies:

1. If a piece is under enemy attack, move it.
2. If one's piece $P1$ is attacking an enemy piece $P2$, consider the move $P1 \times P2$.

Armed with these, the program attempts to understand the attacks and defences of each side; it memorises the sequences of moves that, whether or not any threats are actually carried out, will give an advantage to the initiator if the correct replies are not made.

There are three strategies, as follows:

1. Understanding the position.

Fig. 9.7 Opening moves in the game with White to play.

2. Simplifying and generalising the sequence of moves.
3. Memorising and using the plan constructed.

Understanding the position. Two important cases can arise.

1. The last move was the capture of an enemy piece. Consider for example Fig. 9.7 and the following three moves:

    I. Bb5 × Nc6
   II. d7 × Bc6
  III. Nf3 × e5 (the move to be understood)

To understand (III) we have to understand (I), which was preparing for this, and (II), the counter-move. Therefore, to understand such a capture, the program generates, in any such case, the tree of Fig. 9.8.

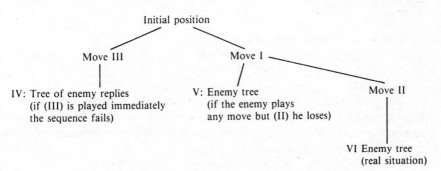

Fig. 9.8 Tree for understanding a chess move.

At the start of the game we are considering we find for IV, by minimax, the Black moves N × Ne5 or a6 × Bb5; for V, Bb7 × c6 (since otherwise White has gained a piece) and for (VI) Black realises that he has lost a pawn. The lesson to be learned – and we shall see later how the program updates and records this – is therefore: 'to capture a pawn protected by a single piece, first displace that piece'.

2. Threats – that is, moves that will gain a piece if the enemy does not make a countering move (Fig. 9.9). The program notes the threat, sees how the opponent parries it and learns from the situation, even if the threat is not carried out. The program constructs and memorises potential actions, learning both attack and defence at the same time; and this even if some combinations are not possible on a real board.

In each of the above cases the minimax procedure accounts for the moves played to the extent that it gives a negative advantage for all other moves.

Simplification and generalisation. What is kept as a result of the above study is the search tree that we have shown, which has been defined by the current game; but since there is very little chance of meeting the same position twice, only the basic characteristics need be kept. This presents a more difficult problem than in checkers or poker because the merest pawn movement can change the situation completely – one has to play quite differently, for example, if in Fig. 9.7 the e5 pawn is moved to e6. Thus a simplification procedure will keep only the best moves of either side, and in fact only those moves that either create or destroy possibilities of captures are kept. Next, the program generalises the tree of moves that it has just constructed together with the positive advantage for one side. In the first place, the colour of the side does not enter and becomes a parameter at the root of the tree; in the second, the squares themselves become the variables: the names of the squares are of no importance; only the relations between them and the constraints on the positions of the pieces are memorised. Thus the initial position

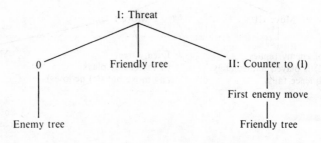

Fig. 9.9 Tree for studying a threat.

White: Kg1, Rf1, d2; Black: Ke8, Ne4 leads first to the tree T1:

$$\text{Rf1}\begin{cases} \diagup\ \emptyset - R \times \text{Ne4} \\ \diagdown\ \text{Ne4 moves} - F \times \text{Ke8} \end{cases} \qquad \text{T1}$$

This tree is generalised by writing:
Initial conditions: R friendly on α. N enemy on γ. K enemy on δ and the friendly R moves to β.

$$\beta, \gamma, \delta \text{ on same rank.}$$

This gives the new tree T2:

$$\text{R}\alpha - \beta\begin{cases} \diagup\ - R \times N\gamma \\ \diagdown\ - N \text{ Moves} - R \times K\delta \end{cases} \qquad \text{T2}$$

which translates the pinning of a knight by a rook.

The names of the pieces also can be generalised, under certain conditions. Any enemy piece captured can be changed for an equal or higher-value piece without destroying the advantage, and conversely any friendly piece can be changed for an equal or lower-value price. T2 is thus generalised to T3:

$$\text{PF}\alpha - \delta\begin{cases} \diagup\ \emptyset - PF \times PE\gamma \\ \diagdown\ PE \text{ Moves} - PF \times KE\delta. \end{cases} \qquad \text{T3}$$

where PF is a friendly piece of value equal to or less than a rook
PE is an enemy piece of value equal to or less than a knight, and KE is the enemy king

The important point here is that the program has identified the concept of a pin by studying a single example.

In certain cases, for example when a piece is captured without playing any part in the game, the generalisation goes further, and the program assigns a completely arbitrary value to the piece, possibly zero, and its square is then considered as unoccupied.

The trees thus generalised are true plans; each corresponds to a gain in material and to sequences of attacks and defences, and can be used equally by either side. But simply learning the plans is not sufficient for using them effectively: a knowledge of how to represent what has been learned is necessary. Many thousands of plans will be created; it is essential to structure them – and in time to forget some of them.

Modification and use of the plans. The generalised trees are stored in memory in a form analogous to Minsky's schemas (Minsky 1975), each schema consisting of three distinct parts: the generalised moves, the squares and the tree itself.

A square is referenced by a formal name, considered as a variable, and a state; the state can be V = vacant (unoccupied), F = friendly or E = enemy and in the F and E cases the value of the occupying piece is given. A generalised move is defined by the (generalised) value of the piece, the starting and finishing squares of the move and possibly the states of the intervening squares.

Example. RFf − d − xEe ⩾ B means that a friendly rook on square f captures an enemy piece, of value a bishop or greater, on e, and that there is at least one empty square, d, between f and e.

Finally, the tree is memorised, each vertex carrying the number of the associated move.

Given an actual position, what has to be done is to find all the schemas that can be applied; but unless care is taken this can be too costly. Suppose for example that the first move recorded on the tree for a certain schema is RF$\alpha - \beta$. If the position in question contains a rook the variable α can be given a value (the identifier of its square) and then β can take any of 14 values. Thus it is advisable to organise the search in such a way that the inapplicable plans are eliminated as quickly as possible and with the minimum of trials; and in the first instance only those plans are considered which could correspond to the material on the board.

The general procedure is to consider first only the least probable of the generalised moves, because these give the most information; for each plan this is found by evaluating a simple function of the form value of the piece × min(values of squares of move). The value of a square is the greater, the less is known about that square; it is 32 for an empty square, 8 if occupied by a pawn, 4 if by a piece, 1 if by the king or queen or if it is a square already completed determined by the system. The least probable move is given by the minimum of this function and the moves are arranged in the schema in the order of the values found.

Thus the tree T2 above gives the following applicable schema (Table 9.3):

Table 9.3.

Squares	Moves	(in order)	Tree
α RF	1. RF	$\beta - \gamma - \times \delta$	(4)
β V	2. E ⩾ N plays		Ø (2)
γ E ⩾ N	3. RF	$\alpha \times \gamma$	(3) (1)
γ RE	4. RF	$\alpha - \beta$	

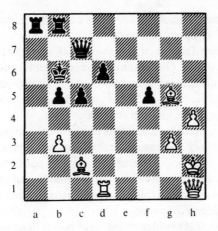

Fig. 9.10 Application of a plan; Black to move.

The position studied is that of Fig. 9.10, with Black to move. In the schema the set 'SQUARES' gives first all the material on the board and then assigns a value to the variable δ, say h2. 'MOVES', if it were ordered according to the real tree, would start with (4) $R\alpha - \beta$ which would lead to 14 trials; but with the ordering given by the evaluation function it starts by examining (1) $RF\beta - \gamma - \times h2$.

In examining the position the rook moves are analysed that will bring it to h2, passing through a square initially occupied by an enemy piece equal to a knight or greater; only (1) $RFa2 - c2 - \times h2$ is kept, since for $Rh8 - h4 - h2$ the white pawn on h4 has too low a value. The values of all the variables in (3) $RF\beta \times \gamma$ are now known, and this move can be only $Ra2 \times c2$. The rook being initially at a8, (4) must now be $Ra8 - a2$.

The unification of the schema with the given position has thus succeeded, so the plan given by the instantiated tree is tried. To find if it could succeed, the program now calls all the plans for possible White responses that are held in its store of schemas; if a minimax procedure gives a positive advantage to the friendly side then the initial plan is put into action, otherwise other plans are tried at the first level of the search tree. The same method is used in another of Pitrat's programs, described in Section 6.3.

Conclusion. This program learns only when it has understood. Its quality is not affected by bad moves that have been played, or by the right move not having been found in an actual game; and if a better move could have been played, no matter − it has learned something. What it learns depends on what it already knows, for in trying to understand a new situation it makes use of the schemas it already holds. It may find itself unable to understand a difficult move at one particular stage in its development but may be able to do so later after playing more games.

Another important feature of this work is that the method can be used for many other games. The plans are very flexible and, in contrast to Waterman's method, are not imperative – they simply indicate such good moves as are possible: final decisions are settled by other considerations such as minimax or some long-term strategy.

At the same time, there is one serious difficulty: the number of schemas in the plans generated is enormous, several tens of thousands in a complete set for a game. This is because there are very many possible variants for any given situation, and very many different situations can arise in chess. The consequence is that although the program learns, it does not know how to use its new knowledge efficiently.

This is a fundamental problem, and has not yet been solved. Essentially, it is not a problem of learning but 'simply' one of managing a huge knowledge base: and it will recall the thoughts we expressed at the end of the chapter on expert systems, and all the problems of meta-knowledge.

9.6 LEARNING CHARACTERISTICS

A very young child learns to formulate concepts and to associate each with a name: he forms the idea of a man, a toy, a tree, a house, ... How do we become able to recognise that a variety of different objects are all examples of the same general concept? – and how do we learn the distinguishing features of that concept? P. H. Winston (Winston 1970) wrote a program that went some way towards answering these questions, and subsequently S. A. Vere (1975) gave a more powerful system which we describe later.

The universe of Winston's system consists of simple objects: cubes, parallelepipeds, prisms, pyramids. A scene is photographed and a program extracts from this what it considers a reasonable representation; each object is identified and the relationships between the objects are stored in the form of a labelled graph in which the objects are the vertices. The relations detected are:

ABOVE, BESIDE, SUPPORTED-BY, ON-THE-LEFT-OF,
IN-FRONT-OF, IS-OF-THE-TYPE-OF.

Thus the scene of Fig. 9.11(a) is represented by the graph of Fig. 9.11(b). As a result of studying many examples and counter-examples with the help of a teacher the system is able to learn the concept that distinguishes a scene.

All learning by experience has something of the reasoning by analogy involved in solving the visual problems used in IQ testing: one has to find a

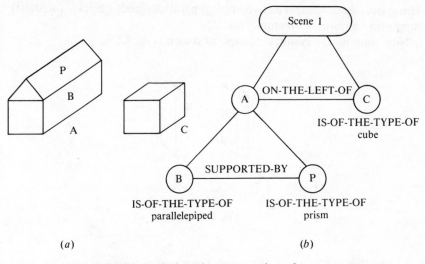

(a)   *(b)*

Fig. 9.11 Analysis and representation of a scene.

rule that relates the first examples; we say in Chapter 3 how part of this task can be done by the unification algorithm, and how Evans's program solved such problems. In Winston's system the sequence of scenes treated starts with a typical situation whose representation is easily memorised; there is then an important change in the conditions of the experiment, in that the teacher shows scenes that are not correct examples of the concept that is to be learned. The system thus learns, as indicated above, by both examples and counter-examples.

An important idea here is that of the 'near-miss'. If the system is shown a scene that is radically different from all the others, there is nothing it can do; but if it is shown one that resembles the others closely but not exactly, then it becomes interested in the differences from its internal model, records these and gradually identifies the secondary characteristics of the concept.

Suppose the first scene shown is (Fig. 9.12):

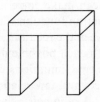

Fig. 9.12.

The system describes this as two vertical parallelepipeds ('bricks' for short) supporting a third, horizontal, brick.

Now suppose the counter example is shown (Fig. 9.13).

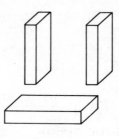

Fig. 9.13.

The system will mark on the graph the essential 'support' relation. A second counter-example is now shown (Fig. 9.14):

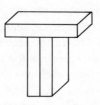

Fig. 9.14.

from which the system infers, and adds to its internal representation, the relation NOT-BESIDE for the vertical bricks. If later on a correct example is shown in which the supported piece is a pyramid the system generalises its representation to allow any object having a plane base – so that it can be supported on the vertical bricks.

Finally, the concept 'arch' is learned, in the form of Fig. 9.15. If a scene is presented which the system can make correspond with the model in more than one way it uses an evaluation function which, by establishing priorities between the objects and between the relations, shows what action should be performed in connection with each possible difference.

The program suffers from two limitations. The first is the poverty of its universe: there are few objects and few relations between them, and these relations all concern objects taken in pairs; the counter-examples are trivial and there is nothing to indicate how to make a good choice.

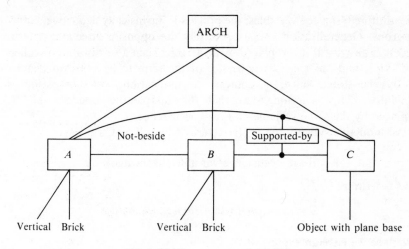

Fig. 9.15 The concept of ARCH.

The second is the purely empirical nature of the learning process: there is nothing to guarantee that it will converge. How could it be made to recognise an object if there were not one but a thousand models? In fact, the system cannot really converge; it keeps only the last model constructed, and none of those that led up to it. There is no possibility of backtracking. If for example it adds the condition NOT-BESIDE it has no means of testing to find if this holds for the preceding examples; other possibilities are ignored by the evaluation function, but it is to these that a return should be made if a contradiction is met.

Vere's work (Vere 1979) makes some improvements in these two respects.

9.7   LEARNING CONCEPTS: VERE's APPROACH

Learning is essentially a matter of extracting a general result by induction on a small number of examples; the process can be accelerated by the use of counter-examples, which can be of any kind whatever, not only 'near misses'. The situations encountered can be complex, requiring representations having several levels, together with disjunctions and negations; such representations make it possible to hold in reserve all the possibilities for resemblances and differences between situations.

We consider first the mechanism for abstraction.

Abstraction and generalisation. Unification in the usual sense consists in substituting terms for variables: the process is intrinsically deductive, and is rigorous. Generalisation goes in precisely the opposite direction, a term becomes abstract if it is replaced by a variable; such a substitution is called inductive, and the specific occurrence of the term to be substituted must always be stated since, in contrast to unification, no substitution is obligatory. There is nothing to say that, for example, the same term shall be replaced by the same variable on every occurrence.

An inductive substitution is characterised by a list of triplets:

$$(\text{term}/\text{occurrence}/\text{variable substituted})$$

and is written:

$$O = (t_1, o_1/v_1); (t2, o_2/v_2); \ldots (t_n, o_n/v_n)$$

Suppose we have an expression E:

$$E = ((\text{work of})\text{Voltaire Candide}) \wedge (\text{French Voltaire}) \wedge (\text{writer Voltaire})$$

The inductive substitution:

$$O = \{(\text{Voltaire}, (1, 3)/x); (\text{Candide}, 1/y)\}$$

will transform this into OE:

$$OE = ((\text{work of}) \ x \ y) \wedge (\text{French } x) \wedge (\text{writer } x)$$

In making inductive substitutions we have to take particular care if we wish to ensure that there will be a corresponding deductive substitution D that can retrieve the original expression from the generalised form: this is made clear by substituting x for Candide also in E above. Since the possibility of return to the original is needed for reasons of consistency, the following constraints are imposed on inductive substitution:

1. The same variable must not be substituted for two different objects.
2. A substitution must not use any of the variables of the expression that it generalises.

Given the definition and these constraints we now have a mechanism for generalisation, expressed as follows:

An expression $E1$ is said to be more general than an expression $E2$ if and only if there is an inductive substitution O such that $E1 \subseteq OE2$

where by convention $E1$ and $OE2$ are in normal conjunctive form and inclusion is understood in the set-theoretical sense that every factor of $E1$ appears in $OE2$. The order of the factors is immaterial.

Thus if the expressions concern ordinary playing cards:

$$E1 = (S \ x) \wedge (H \ y) \wedge (x \geqslant y)$$

is more general than:

$$E2 = (S \ A) \wedge (S \ K) \wedge (S \ 10) \wedge (H \ K) \wedge (H \ Q) \wedge (A \geqslant K) \wedge (K \geqslant Q)$$

because there is a substitution:

$$O = \{A, (1, 2)/x, \ K(2, 3, 4)/y\}$$

such that $E1 \subseteq OE2$.

We shall write $E1 \leqslant E2$ to indicate that $E1$ is more general than $E2$; this is expressed also by saying that $E1$ *covers* $E2$.

For given $E1$, $E2$ and O the part of $OE2$ that occurs in $E1$ is called the *coupling* and the remainder is called the *residue*; in the above example the coupling is:

$$(S \ x) \wedge (H \ y) \wedge (x \geqslant y)$$

and the residue is:

$$(S \ y) \wedge (S \ 10) \wedge (H \ Q) \wedge (y \geqslant Q)$$

For given $E1$ and $E2$ there can of course be several different substitutions O_i such that $E_1 \subseteq O_i E2$, and these can, in particular, give the same couplings but different residues.

Different types of inductive substitution can be thought of as having different political complexions – conservative for those involving the minimum number of changes, liberal if any substitution is allowed; in what follows we shall confine ourselves to substitutions that are *fair*, meaning those that satisfy both the general constraints (1), (2) above and

3. The same term is always substituted by the same variable, in all its occurrences.
4. A term is substituted only when necessary; in particular, a term in the residue may be substituted only if it has already been substituted in the coupling.

It follows that the occurrences of the terms need not be stated in a fair substitution.

It follows from this definition that every expression is its own generalisation and also that of any expression derived from it by simple renaming of variables; but a generalisation $E1$ of $R2$ is said to be *strict* if and only if either $E1 < OE2$ with strict inequality, or $E1 = OE2$ with $O \neq$ renaming. The relation $<$ implies $\leqslant$, but not conversely.

Just as in arithmetic we define the greatest common divisor (or highest common factor) of two numbers, or the maxterm in Boolean algebra, so we define the maximum common generalisation (mcg) E for two expressions $E1$, $E2$ as:

$$E \leqslant E1 \quad \text{and} \quad E \leqslant E2, \quad \exists E': E' < E \leqslant E1 \quad \text{and} \quad E' < E \leqslant E2$$

Thus a concept is a maximum common generalisation of its examples. The examples are taken in pairs, all the possible couplings found and by iteration all the disjoint sub-expressions that generalise all the examples; the mcg finally arrived at may contain disjunctions. The inclusion of counter-examples in the process both refines and complicates the analysis.

Counter-examples clearly result in the description of the concept containing negations; these may be mixed in with disjunctions and the whole put together in any way whatever, so that the final generalisation can be quite complex. Thus:

$$(ON\ x\ y) \wedge (\text{red}\ y) \wedge \neg(((ON\ z\ y) \wedge (\text{cube}\ z)) \wedge \neg(\text{cube}\ y))$$

states

> there is something on a red object and either there is no object that is not a cube on this red object or y itself is a cube

In these descriptions the notation $A \wedge \neg(B \wedge \neg C)$ is preferred to the equivalent $(A \wedge \neg B) \vee (A \wedge B \wedge C)$ because the learning process finds the first form easier to handle. In the process the system is given, once only, a group of examples u_i ($i = 1, 2, ..., p$) and a group of counter-examples v_j ($j = 1, 2, ..., q$). It first constructs the mcg $P1$ for the examples, which will be too broad because it will admit some of the counter-examples. Study of the latter will give a correction term $N1$, expressing what must not be included in the concept; so the current expression $C1$ for the concept is:

$$C1 = P1 \wedge \neg N1$$

The term $\neg N1$ may however over-correct $P1$ and delete some of the examples; so a return is made to the examples and a correction made to $N1$, followed by a return to the counter-examples and so on. Since the number of cases and the descriptive formulae with which the process starts are both finite, the process will end with a finite expression, which in the worst case will be the disjunction of all the cases given. In general it will lead to a compact expression C that gives the characteristics that are found in all the examples but not in any of the counter-examples – which is a description of the concept that is to be learned. The general form of C will be:

$$C = P1 \wedge \neg(N1 \wedge \neg(N2 \wedge \neg(... \neg Nk))...)$$

There is a clear analogy here with the convergent alternating series of classical analysis:

$$S = a_0 - a_1 x + a_2 x^2 - a_3 x^3 + \cdots + (-1)^k a_k x^k + \cdots$$

The successive terms are now symbolic propositions instead of algebraic monomials that can be given numerical values.

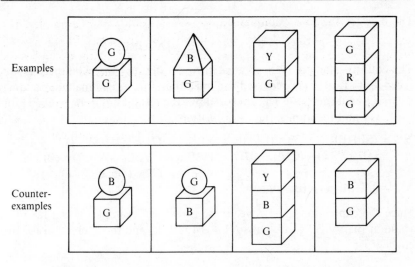

Fig. 9.16 Examples and counter-examples for concept formation.

Example. Figure 9.16 gives four examples from which a general concept has to be inferred and four counter-examples. The descriptions are as follows: for the examples:

$u1 = (O1\ ON\ O2) \wedge (\text{SPHERE}\ O1) \wedge (\text{CUBE}\ O2) \wedge (\text{GREEN}\ O1)$
$\qquad \wedge (\text{GREEN}\ O2)$

$u2 = (O3\ ON\ O4) \wedge (\text{PYRAM}\ O3) \wedge (\text{CUBE}\ O4) \wedge (\text{BLUE}\ O3)$
$\qquad \wedge (\text{GREEN}\ O4)$

$u3 = (O5\ ON\ O6) \wedge (\text{CUBE}\ O5) \wedge (\text{CUBE}\ O6) \wedge (\text{YELLOW}\ O5)$
$\qquad \wedge (\text{GREEN}\ O6)$

$u4 = (O7\ ON\ O8) \wedge (O9\ ON\ O7) \wedge (\text{CUBE}\ O7) \wedge (\text{CUBE}\ O8)$
$\qquad \wedge (\text{CUBE}\ O9) \wedge (\text{RED}\ O7) \wedge (\text{GREEN}\ O8)$
$\qquad \wedge (\text{GREEN}\ O9)$

for the counter-examples:

$v1 = (Q1\ ON\ Q2) \wedge (\text{SPHERE}\ Q1) \wedge (\text{CUBE}\ Q2) \wedge (\text{BLUE}\ Q1)$
$\qquad \wedge (\text{GREEN}\ Q2)$

$v2 = (Q3\ ON\ Q4) \wedge (\text{SPHERE}\ Q3) \wedge (\text{CUBE}\ Q4) \wedge (\text{GREEN}\ Q3)$
$\qquad \wedge (\text{BLUE}\ Q4)$

$v3 = (Q5\ ON\ Q6) \wedge (Q7\ ON\ Q5) \wedge (\text{CUBE}\ Q7) \wedge (\text{CUBE}\ Q5)$
$\qquad \wedge (\text{CUBE}\ Q6) \wedge (\text{YELLOW}\ Q7) \wedge (\text{BLUE}\ Q5)$
$\qquad \wedge (\text{GREEN}\ Q6)$

$v4 = (Q8\ ON\ Q9) \wedge (\text{CUBE}\ Q8) \wedge (\text{CUBE}\ Q9) \wedge (\text{BLUE}\ Q8)$
$\qquad \wedge (\text{GREEN}\ Q9)$

The mcg for the four examples is:

$$P1 = (x \ ON \ y) \wedge (CUBE \ y) \wedge (GREEN \ y)$$

The counter-example $v2$ is eliminated by $P1$ because the cube there is not green, but $v1, v3, v4$ are covered and must therefore be eliminated by adding a correction term $\neg N1$. This must remove the residues $u_i' = \{v_i - O_i P1\}$ for $i = 1, 3, 4$ and the appropriate substitutions:

$u'1 = (SPHERE \quad x) \wedge (BLUE \quad x) \qquad O1 = (Q1/x, Q2/y)$

$u'3 = (Q7 \ ON \ x) \wedge (CUBE \ Q7) \wedge (CUBE \ x) \wedge (YELLOW \ Q7) \wedge (BLUE \ x)$
$\qquad\qquad\qquad\qquad\qquad\qquad\qquad\qquad\qquad O3 = (Q5/x, Q6/y)$

$u'4 = (CUBE \quad x) \wedge (BLUE \quad x) \qquad O4 = (Q8/x, Q9/y)$

Since the expression must cover these three new examples it can take the value of their mcg, so we have $N1 = (BLUE \ x)$ and the expression for the concept is:

$$C1 = (x \ ON \ y) \wedge (CUBE \ y) \wedge (GREEN \ y) \wedge \neg (BLUE \ x)$$

This covers the examples $u1$, $u3$ and $u4$, none of which in fact includes the factor BLUE x; but this does occur in $u2$, which is therefore eliminated by $C1$. To re-admit this example, the factors not covered by either a positive or a negative term of $C1$ form the new residue; here there is only (PYRAM x) which is its own mcg and so provides the further, and last, correction needed. The result is:

$$C = (x \ ON \ y) \wedge (CUBE \ y) \wedge (GREEN \ y) \wedge \neg ((BLUE \ x)$$
$$\wedge \neg (PYRAM \ x))$$

It can of course happen that the process of forming the mcgs gives at one stage not one but several expressions, in which case disjunctions are introduced into the description. Equally, no mcg may be found, either because there is no relation common to the given factors or because of constraints imposed on the unifications; this shows that the only generalising expression is empty, meaning that there is no concept that admits all the examples and rejects are counter-examples. This will result from contradictions in the residues, of the type:

positive residue: $(x \ ON \ y) \wedge (GREEN \ x)$
negative residue: $(x \ ON \ y) \wedge (GREEN \ x) \wedge (RED \ y)$

Vere's program is written in ICECUBE, a dialect of SNOBOL; it produces generalisations in the order of seconds on an IBM 370/158. It is able also to generalise the re-write rules that describe, for example, the stacking and unstacking of the cubes.

More work needs to be done on this program, for example to enrich its vocabulary with descriptions of further relations; but it remains one of the best formalised and most extensible studies of machine learning. The concepts that it arrives at can be of great complexity, possibly beyond what the human mind can formulate and retain.

BIBLIOGRAPHY

Artificial intelligence: general works

Ackoff R. L. (1978) *The Art of Problem Solving*. J. Wiley.

A. I. Software (1984) *The International Directory of A. I. Companies*. A. I. Software, SRL, Rovigo Italie.

Allan J. J. (ed.) (1976) *CAD Systems*. North Holland.

Amarel S. (1968) 'On representations of problems of reasoning about actions'. In *Machine Intelligence*, Vol. 3, Elsevier, 131–71.

Anderson J. R. (1976) *Language, Memory, and Thought*. Lawrence Erlbaum.

Anderson J. R. and Bower G. (1973) *Human Associative Memory*. Winston–Wiley.

Banerji R. (1980) *A. I. A Theoretical Approach*. North Holland.

Bar-Hillel Y. (1964) *Language and Informations*. Addison-Wesley.

Barr A. and Feigenbaum E. A. (1981) *The Handbook of Artificial Intelligence*. W. Kaufmann.

Barstow D. (1979) *Knowledge Based Program Construction*. Elsevier.

Bartlett F. (1932) *Remembering: A Study in Experimental and Social Psychology*. Cambridge University Press.

Bartlett F. (1958) *Thinking*. Basic Books.

Boden M. (1977) *AI and Natural Man*. Basic Books.

Bongard N. (1970) *Pattern Recognition*. Spartan Books.

Bonnet A. (1984) *Artificial Intelligence: promise and performance*. Prentice Hall International.

Brady M. (1983) 'Computational approach to image understanding'. *ACM* Computing surveys, 14 (1), 3–71.

Bruner J. S. Goodnow J. J. and Austin G. A. (1956) *A Study of Thinking*. Wiley.

Bundy A., Burstall R. M., Weir S. and Young R. M. (1980) *Artificial Intelligence: An Introductory Course*. Edinburgh University Press.

Bundy A. (1981) *Artificial Intelligence*. Edinburgh University Press.

Charniak E., Riesbeck C. K. and McDermott D. V. (1980) *A.I. Programming*, Lawrence Erlbaum.

Charniak E. and McDermott D. (1984) *An Introduction to Artificial Intelligence*. Addison-Wesley.

Collins N. and Michie D. (eds) (1968) *Machine Intelligence*, Vol. 1, Elsevier.

Dale E. and Michie D. (eds) (1968) *Machine Intelligence*, Vol. 2, Elsevier.

Dreyfus H. L. (1979) *What Computers Cannot Do*. (Revised ed. Harper (1972).)

Farreny H. and Prajoux R. (1982) 'Les pouvoirs des robots de la 3e génération'. La Science des robots. *Science et Vie.*

Feigenbaum E. (1968) 'Artificial intelligence: themes in the second decade', *Information Processing 68*, Vol. 2, A. J. H. Morrell, ed., 1008–22, North Holland.

Feigenbaum E. and Feldman J. (eds) (1963) *Computers and Thought.* McGraw-Hill.

Feigenbaum E. and McCorduck P. (1983): *The Fifth Generation*, Addison-Wesley.

Gaspar P. (1978) *Problèmes méthodes et stratégies de résolution*, Ed. Organisation.

Gilford J. P. (1967) *The Nature of Human Intelligence.* McGraw-Hill.

Hofstadter D. R. (1977) *Gödel, Escher and Bach.* Basic Books.

Hofstadter D. R. and Dennet D. C. (1981) *The Mind's I*, Basic Books.

Hunt E. B. (1975) *Artificial Intelligence*, Academic Press.

Itzinger O. (1976) *Methoden der Maschinellen Intelligenz*, Springer Verlag.

Jackson P. C. (1974) *Introduction to Artificial Intelligence*, Petrocelli/Charter.

Klix F. (ed.) (1979) *Human and Artificial Intelligence.* North Holland.

Latombe J. C. (ed.) (1978) *AI and Pattern Recognition in CAD*, North Holland.

Latombe J. C. and Lux A. (1979) 'Intelligence artificielle et robotique industrielle', *Le Nouvel Automatisme*, 5, 37–44 and 6, 21–9.

Lighthill M. J. (1973) 'Artificial intelligence: a general survey', *Artificial Intelligence: A Paper Symposium.* Science Research Council.

Lindsay P. H. and Norman D. A. (1977) *Traitement de l'information et comportement humain*, Editions, Etudes Vivantes.

McCarthy J. and Hayes P. (1969). 'Some philosophical problems from standpoint of artificial intelligence', *Machine Intelligence*, Vol. 4, Elsevier.

McCarthy J. (1977) 'Epistemological problems in AI', *IJCAI 5*, MIT Press, 1038–44.

McCorduck P. (1979) *Machines Who Think*, Freeman.

Marr D. (1976) 'Early processing of visual information', *Philosophical Transactions of the Royal Society of London* (Series B) 275, 483–524.

Marr D. (1977) 'Artificial intelligence – a personal view'. *AI*, 37–48.

Meltzer B. and Michie D. (eds) (1969) *Machine Intelligence*, Vol. 4, Elsevier.

Meltzer B. and Michie D. (eds) (1970) *Machine Intelligence*, Vol. 5, Elsevier.

Meltzer B. and Michie D. (eds) (1971) *Machine Intelligence*, Vol. 6, Elsevier.

Meltzer B. and Michie D. (eds) (1972) *Machine Intelligence*, Vol. 7, Elsevier.

Michie D. (ed.) (1968) *Machine Intelligence*, Vol. 3, Elsevier.

Miller, G. A. (1956) 'The magical number seven, plus or minus two: some limits of our capacity for processing information', *Psychological Review* 63, 81–97.

Minsky M. L. (1965) 'Matter, mind, and models', *IFIP.*

Minsky M. L. and Papert S. (1969) *Perceptions: An Introduction to Computational Geometry.* MIT Press.

Newell A. (1973) 'Artificial intelligence and the concept of mind', *Computer Models of Thought and Language.* Roger Schank and Kenneth Colby (eds), W. H. Freeman & Co.

Newell A. (1982) 'The knowledge level'. *AI* 18 (1), 87–127.

Newell A. and Simon H. (1982) *Human Problem Solving.* Prentice Hall.

Nilsson N. J. (1971) *Problem Solving Methods in A.I.* McGraw-Hill.

Nilsson N. J. (1980) *Principles of A.I.* Tioga Pub Co.

Nivergelt J., Craig Farrar J. and Reingold E. M. (1974) *Computer Approaches to Mathematical Problems.* Prentice Hall.

Norman D. A., Rumelhart D. E. and the LNR Research Group (1975) *Explorations in Cognition.* Freeman.

Papert S. (1980) *Mindstorms, Children, Computers and Powerful Ideas*, Basic Books.

Pohl I. 'Heuristic search viewed as path finding in a graph'. *AI* 1(3), 193–204.

Polya G. (1954) *Mathematics and Plausible Reasoning*, Vol. 1 (2), Princeton University Press.

Polya G. (1954) *Induction and Analogy in Mathematics*. Princeton University Press.

Polya G. (1957) *Mathematical Discovery*. Doubleday.

Polya G. (1959) *How to Solve It*. Princeton University Press.

Raphaël B. (1976) *The Thinking Computer*. Freeman.

Rich E. (1983) *Artificial Intelligence*. McGraw-Hill.

Shapiro S. C. (1979) *Techniques of AI*. Van Nostrand.

Simon H. A. (1969) *Science of the Artificial*. MIT Press.

Simon H. A. (1973) 'The structure of ill structured problems'. *AI*, 81–202.

Simon H. A. (1979) *Models of Thought*. Yale University Press.

Simon H. A. and Barenfeld (1969) 'Information processing analysis of perceptual processes in problem solving', *Psychological Review* 5, 473.

Simon H. A. and Siklossy L. (1973) *Representation and Meaning. Experiments with Information Processing Systems*. Prentice Hall.

Simons G. L. (1984) *Introducing Artificial Intelligence*. NCC Publishers.

Slagle J. R. (1971) *A.I. The Heuristic Programming Approach*. McGraw-Hill.

Sussman G. J. (1975) *A Computer Model of Skill Acquisition*. No. 1. Elsevier.

Vidal F. (1971) *Problem Solving*. Dunod.

Von Neuman J. and Morgenstern O. (1944) *Theory of Games and Economic Behavior*. Princeton University Press.

Waterman D. and Hayes Roth F. (eds) (1978) *Pattern Directed Inference Systems*. Academic Press.

Wertz H. (1984) *Intelligence Artificielle*. Masson.

Wickelgren W. (1974) *How to Solve Problems*. Freeman.

Winston P. H. (ed.) (1975) *The Psychology of Computer Vision*. McGraw-Hill.

Winston P. H. (1977) *Artificial Intelligence*. Addison-Wesley.

Wooldridge H. (1963) *The Machine of the Brain*. McGraw-Hill.

Representation of problems

Alem J. P. (1975) *Jeux de l'esprit et divertissements mathématiques*. Seuil.

Bachet de Meziriac (1612) *Problèmes paysans et délectables qui se font par les nombres*. A. Blanchard, Paris (1959).

Berloquin P. (1978) *Jeux mathématiques du monde*. Flammarion.

Berloquin P. (1980) *100 Jeux numériques – 100 jeux géométriques pour insomniaques*. Livre de Poche.

Blanchet J. M. (1976) *Mathématique en liberté*. OCDL.

Chuquet N. (1484) *Jeux et esbatements*. Manuscrit Bibliothèque Nationale, n° 1346.

Deledicq A. (1975) *Mathématiques buissonnières*. CEDIC.

Dudeney H. E. (1967) *536 Puzzles and Curious Problems*. Scribner's NY.

Gardner M. (1977) *Les Casse tête mathématiques de Sam Loyd*. Dunod.

Gardner M. (1979) Les Distracts. *Les Jeux mathématiques du scientific american*. CEDIC.

Gardner M. (1979) *L'Effet haha*. Pour la Science. Belin.

Gerli D. and Girard G. (1976) *Les Olympiades internationales de mathématiques*. Hachette.

Kordiemskii B. (1963) *Sur le sentier des mathématiques*. 2 vols. Dunod.

Kraitchich M. *La Mathématique des jeux*. Dunod.

Loyd S. (1914) *Cyclopedia of Puzzles*. Cf. Garner M. (1960) *Mathematical Puzzles of Sam Loyd*. Dover.

Lucas E. (1960) *Récréations mathématiques* (Nouveau tirage) 4 vols. A. Blanchard.

Sainte-Lagüe A. de *Avec des Nombres et des lignes*. Dunod.

Natural language and the representation of information

Amarel S. (1968) 'On representations of problems of reasoning about actions'. *Machine Intelligence*, Vol. 3, D. Michie (ed.), 131–70.

Anderson J. (1977) 'Induction of augmented transition networks'. *CS*, 125–57.

Ballantyne M. (1975) 'Computer generation of counter examples in topology'. *ATP 24*, University of Texas Press.

Banerji R. B. and Ernst G. W. (1972) 'Strategy construction using homomorphism between games'. *AI* 3 (4), 223–49.

Berge C. (1970) *Graphes et hypergraphes*. Dunod.

Bledsoe W. (1977) 'Non-resolution theorem proving', *AI* (9), 1–35.

Bobrow D. G. (1964) *A Question Answering System for High School Algebra Word Problems*. AFIPS, 26–1, Spartan Books.

Bobrow D. G. (1968) 'Natural language input for a computer problem solving system'. M. Minsky (ed.), *Semantic Information Processing*, MIT Press, 133–215.

Bobrow D. J. and Winograd T. (1977) 'A knowledge representation language'. *CS* 1 (1).

Bonnet A. (1980) 'Analyse de textes au moyen d'une grammaire sémantique et de schémas. Application à la compréhension de résumés médicaux en langage naturel'. *Thèse d'état*. University of Paris VI.

Brown M. F. (1977) 'Doing arithmetic without diagrams'. *AI* (8), 175–200.

Bundy A. (1973) 'Doing arithmetic with diagrams'. *IJCAI* 3, 130–8.

Buthion M. (1979) 'Un programme qui résout formellement des problèmes de constructions géométriques', *RAIRO* Informatique 13 (1), 73–106.

Charniak E. (1977) 'On the use of framework knowledge in language comprehension'. *AI* 1, 255–66.

Charniak E. and Wilks Y. (1976) *Computational Semantics*, North Holland.

Charniak E. (1981) 'A common representation for problem-solving and language-comprehension information'. *AI* 16 (3), 225–55.

Chichetchi B. (1979) 'Compréhension du langage naturel. Traduction paraphrasée d'exercices sur le courant alternatif posés en persan'. *Thèse*. Paris 6.

Chomsky N. (1957) *Syntactic Structures*. Mouton La Hague.

Chomsky N. (1965) *Aspects of the Theory of Syntax*. MIT Press.

Chomsky N. (1982) *Rules and Representation in the Behavioral and Brain Sciences*.

Clancey W. J. (1983) 'The epistemology of a rule-based expert system – a framework for explanation'. *AI* 20 (3), 215–51.

Colmerauer A., Kanoui H., Pasero R. and Roussel P. (1973) 'Un système de communication homme-machine en français'. In *Rapport Groupe d'Intelligence Artificielle*, University of Aix-Marseille, Luminy, France.

Cordier M. O. (1979) 'Commande d'un robot en langage naturel dans un domaine nécessitant des connaissances pragmatiques: les recettes de cuisine'. *Thèse de 3° Cycle*, Paris 6.

Cordier M. O. and Rousset M. C. (1984) 'Interactive operators in expert systems: TANGO'. *ECAI*, 78–9.

Davis R., Buchanan B. and Shortliffe E. (1977) 'Production rules as a representation for knowledge based consultation program', *AI* 8 (1), 15–45.

Desclés J. P. (1982) 'Langages quasi-naturels et catégories grammaticales', *Actes du Colloque: Domaine et objectifs de la recherche cognitive*.

Erli (1983) 'SAPHIR, présentation générale'. *Rapport de la Société d'Etude et de Recherche en Linguistique et Informatique*.

Findler N. V. (1979) *Associative Networks: The Representation and Use of Knowledge by Computers*. Academic Press.

Gelb J. P. (1971) 'Experiments with a natural language problem solving system'. *IJCAI* 2, 445–62.

Gelernter H. (1963) 'Realization of a geometry theorem proving machine'. *Computer and Thought*. McGraw-Hill, 135–47.

Gilmore P. C. (1970) 'An examination of the geometry theorem proving machine'. *AI* 1 (3), 171–85.

Gross M. (1975) *Grammaire transformationnelle du français: syntaxe du verbe*, Larousse.

Gross M. (1977) *Grammaire transformationnelle du français: syntaxe du nom*. Larousse.

Harris L. (1977) 'ROBOT: a high performance natural language data base query system'. *IJCAI* 5, 903–4.

Hayes P. F. (1973) 'The frame problem and related problems in artificial intelligence', In A. Elithorn and D. Jones (eds) *Artificial and Human Thinking*. Elsevier.

Hendrix G. G. (1976) 'Partitioned networks for modelling natural language semantics'. *Dissertation*. University of Texas.

Hewitt C., Bishop P. and Steiger R. (1973) 'A universal modular actor formalism for artificial intelligence', *IJCAI* 3.

Korf R. E. (1980) 'Toward a model of representation changes', *AI* 14 (1), 41–78.

Laurière J. L. (1978) 'A language and a program for stating and solving combinatorial problems'. *AI* 10 (1), 29–127.

Lehnert W., Dyer M. G., Johnson P. N., Yang C. J. and Harley S. (1983) 'BORIS: an experiment in in-depth understanding of narratives'. *AI* 20 (1), 15–62.

Lopez M. (1979) 'Réalisation d'un interface de communication en langue naturelle avec le système TROPIC', *Contrès AFCET*, Toulouse, 25–35.

McDonald D. D. (1980) 'Language production as a process of decision making under constraints'. *Ph.D thesis*, MIT Press.

Marcus M. H. (1980) *A Theory of Syntactic Recognition for Natural Language*. MIT Press.

Merialdo B. (1979) 'Représentation des ensembles en démonstration automatique de théorèmes'. *Thèse de 3° Cycle*. Paris VI.

Nevins, A. J. (1975) 'Plane geometry theorem proving using forward chaining'. *AI* 6 (4), 1–23.

Pastre D. (1978a) 'Automatic theorem proving in set theory'. *AI* 10 (1), 1–27.

Pastre D. (1978b) 'Observation du mathématicien: aide à l'enseignement et à la démonstration automatique de théorèmes'. *Educational Studies in Mathematics* 9, 461–502.

Pitrat J. (1977) 'Formalism for text analysis', Séminaire international sur *Les*

Systèmes intelligents de questions-rèsponses et grandes banques de données. Bonas.

Pitrat J. (1979) 'Réalisation d'un analyseur générateur lexicographique général'. *Rapport n° 79–2 du Gr22.* Paris VI.

Pitrat J. (1980) 'Un interpréteur de contraintes pour la compréhension du langage naturel'. Colloque d'intelligence artificielle, Caen. *Publications GR22 n° 20.*

Pitrat J. (1985) *Textes, ordinateurs et compréhension.* Eyrolles.

Polya G. (1962) *Mathematical Discovery.* Wiley.

Quillian R. M. (1969) 'The teachable language comprehender: a simulation program and theory of language'. *CACM* 12 (18).

Sabah G. (1980) 'Contribution à la compréhension effective d'un récit'. *Thèse d'état.* University of Paris VI.

Sabah G. and Rady M. (1983) 'A deterministic syntactic-semantic parser'. *IJCAI* 8.

Salkoff M. (1973) *Une Grammaire en chaine du français.* Dunod.

Schank R. C. (1975) *Conceptual Information Processing.* North Holland.

Verdejo M. F. (1975) 'Etude du langage naturel'. Simulation d'un robot capable de mener un dialogue en espagnol. *Thèse Paris VI.*

Vilnat A. and Sabah G. (1984) 'How a system may be self-conscious'. *ECAI,* 277–9.

Waltz D. L. (1981) *An English Language Question Answering System for a Large Relational Data Base.* McGraw-Hill.

Wilks Y. (1975) 'An intelligent analyzer and understander of English'. *CACM* 18 (5).

Winograd T. (1972) *Understanding Natural Language.* Edinburgh University Press.

Winograd T. (1980) 'What does it mean to understand language?' *CS* 4, 209–41.

Winograd T. (1983) *Language as a Cognitive Process.* Addison-Wesley.

Winston P. H. (1975) 'Learning structural descriptions from examples'. In *The Psychology of Computer Vision.* McGraw-Hill.

Woods W. A. (1970) 'Transition networks grammars for natural language analysis'. *ACM* 13 (10), 591–606.

Woods W. A. (1975) 'What is a link?' In D. G. Bobrow and A. Collins (eds) (1975) *Representation and Understanding.* SA. Academic Press.

The history of artificial intelligence: early programs

Colby K., Weber S. and Hilf F. D. (1975) *Artificial Paranoia.* Pergamon Press.

Ernst G. and Newell A. (1969) *GPS: A Case Study in Generality and Problem Solving.* New York Academic Press.

Evans T. G. (1963) 'A heuristic program to solve geometric analogy problems'. In *Semantic Information Processing.* M. Minsky (ed.), MIT Press.

Greenblatt R. D. *et al.* (1967) 'The Greenblatt chess program'. *Proc. AFIPS* Fall Joint Computer Conference, 31, 801–10.

Guzman A. (1968) 'Computer recognition of three-dimensional objects in a visual scene', *MAC Tech. Report 59, thesis,* Project MAC, MIT Press.

Moses J. (1967) 'Symbolic integration'. *Rapport Technique MAC-TR-47,* MIT Press.

Newell A., Shaw J. C. and Simon H. A. (1957) 'Programming the logic theory machine'. *Western Joint Computer Conference,* 230–40.

Newell A. and Simon H. A. (1956) 'The logic theory machine: a complex information processing system', *IRE Trans. on Information Theory.* IT-2, 3, 61–79.

Shannon C. E. (1950) 'Programming a computer to play chess'. *Scientific American*.

Slagle J. R. (1963) 'A heuristic program that solves symbolic integration problems in freshman calculus'. Feigenbaum and Feldman (eds), McGraw-Hill.

Tonge F. (1961) *A Heuristic Program for Assembly Line Balancing*. Prentice Hall.

Turing A. M. (1950) 'Computing machinery and intelligence', *Mind*, 59, 433–60, Reprinted in *Computers and Thought*, 11–35.

Weizenbaum J. (1966) 'Eliza: a computer program for the study of natural language communication between man and machine'. *CACM* 8, 36–45.

Winston H. and Brown R. H. (ed.) (1979) *Artificial Intelligence. An MIT Perspective*. Vols I and II. MIT Press.

The LISP language

Cayrol M. (1983) *Le Langage LISP*. Cepadues éditions.

Chailloux J. (1979) 'Le modèle VLISP: description, implémentation et évaluation', *Thèse de 3° Cycle*. Université de Vincennes.

Chailloux J. (1985) *Le Lisp*. Manuel de référence. INRIA.

Farreny H. (1984) *Programmer en LISP*. Masson.

Queinnec C. (1980) *Langage d'un autre type: LISP*. Eyrolles.

Siklossy L. (1976) *Let's talk LISP*. Prentice Hall.

Steele G. L. Jr (1984) *Common LISP*. Digital Press.

Wertz H. (1985) *LISP. Une introduction à la programmation*. Masson.

Representation of non-classical knowledge and logic

Aillo L. and Levi G. (1984) 'The uses of metaknowledge in AI systems'. *ECAI*, 705–19.

Bobrow D. G. and Collins A. (eds) (1975) *Representation and Understanding*. Academic Press.

Boose J. H. (1984) 'Personal construct theory and the transfer of human expertise'. *ECAI*, 51–60.

Borillo M. and Virbel J. (1977) *Analyse et validation dans l'étude des données textuelles*. Editions du CNRS.

Brachman R. J. (1977) 'What's in a concept: structural foundations for semantic networks'. *International Journal of Man–Machine Studies* 9 (2), 127–52.

Buchanan B. G. and Duda R. O. (1982) 'Principles of rule-based systems'. Stanford University Technical Report. *HPP–82–14*.

Carbonell J. G. (1980) 'Towards a process model of human personality traits', *AI* 15.

Chouraqui E. (1982) 'Contributions à l'étude théorique de la représentation des connaissances'. *Thèse d'Etat*. Nancy.

Coelho H. (1984) 'An Introduction to the knowledge representation subfield'. *ECAI* 283–5.

Coulon D. and Kayser D. (1980) 'Un système de raisonnement à profondeur variable'. *Congrès AFCET-TTI*. Nancy, 517–27.

Davis R. (1978) 'Knowledge acquisition in rule-based systems: knowledge about representations as a basis for system construction and maintenance'. In D. A. Waterman and F. Hayes-Roth (eds) *Pattern Directed Inference Systems*, 99–134.

Davis R. (1979) 'Interactive transfer of expertise: acquisition of new inference rules'. *AI* 12 (2), 121–57.

Davis R. (1980) 'Meta-rules: reasoning about control'. *AI* 15 (3), 179–222.

Doyle J. (1979) 'A truth maintenance system'. *AI* 12 (3), 231–72.

Duda R. O., Hart P. E., Nilsson N. J. and Sutherland G. L. (1978) 'Semantic network representations in rule-based inference systems'. In D. A. Waterman and F. Hayes-Roth (eds) (1978) *Pattern Directed Inference Systems*, 203–22.

Ferber J. (1984) 'Mering: an open-ended object oriented language for knowledge representation'. *ECAI*, 195–204.

Fillmore C. (1968) 'The case for case'. In Bach and Harms (eds) *Universals in Linguistic Theory*. Holt, Rinehart and Winston.

Gallaire H. and Lasserre C. (1979) 'Controlling knowledge deduction in a declarative approach'. *IJCAI* 6, S1-S12.

Ganascia J. C. (1984) 'Reasoning and result in expert systems: main differences between diagnostic systems and problem-solvers'. *ECAI*, 31–40.

Goldstein I. P. and Grimson E. (1977) 'Annotated production system: a model for skill acquisition'. *IJCAI* 5, 311–17.

Hayes P. (1973) 'The frame problem and related problems in A.I.'. *Artificial and Human Thinking*. Elsevier.

Hayes P. (1977) 'In defense of logic'. *IJCAI* 5, 559–83.

Hayes P. (1977) 'On semantic nets, frames and associations', *IJCAI* 5, 99–107.

Hayes-Roth F., Waterman D. A. and Lenat D. B. (eds) (1983) *Building Expert Systems*. Addison-Wesley.

Kahn G. (1984) 'On when diagnostic systems want to do without causal knowledge'. *ECAI*, 21–30.

Kayser D. (1984) 'Examen de diverses méthodes utilisées en représentation des connaissances'. *Congrès d'Intelligence Artificielle et Reconnaissances des Formes. AFCET*, Paris.

de Kleer J., Doyle J., Steele G. J. and Sussman G. J. (1977) 'Amord: explicit control of reasoning', Proc. Symp. Artificial Intelligence Programming Languages, Sigplan notices 12. *Sigart Newsletter* 64, 116–125.

de Kleer J. *et al.* (1979) 'Explicit control of reasoning'. In P. H. Winston and R. H. Brown (eds) *Artificial Intelligence: An MIT Perspective* (Vol. 1), 93–116.

Laurière J. L. (1979) 'Représentation et utilisation des connaissances'. *Publications du GR 22*. Programmes d'intelligence artificielle utilisant une grande quantité de connaissances. 3–112. Rouen.

Laurière J. L. (1982a) 'Représentation et utilisation des connaissances. Première partie: les systèmes experts'. *Technique et science informatiques*. Afcet, n° 1, 25–42.

Laurière J. L. (1982b) 'Représentation et utilisation des connaissances. Deuxième partie: représentation des connaissances'. *Technique et science informatiques*. Afcet, n° 2, 109–33.

Laurière J. O. (1988) *Intelligence Artificielle, Vol. 2: Représentation des Connaissances*. Eyrolles.

Levesque H. J. (1983) 'The logic of incomplete knowledge bases in conceptual modelling: perspectives from artificial intelligence'. *Databases and Programming Languages*, Brodie, Mylopoulos and Schmidt (eds) Springer-Verlag.

McCarthy J. (1968) 'Programs with common sense'. In M. Minsky (ed.) *Semantic Information Processing*, 403–9.

McCarthy J. (1980) 'Circumscription – a form of non-monotonic reasoning'. *AI* 13, 27–39.

McDermott D. (1980) 'Non-monotonic logic II: non-monotonic modal theories'. *Rep. n° 174*, Computer Science Dept, Yale University.

McDermott D. and Doyle J. (1980) 'Non-monotonic logic I', *AI* 13 (1 & 2), 41–72.

Minsky M. (ed.). (1968) *Semantic Information Processing*. MIT Press.

Prade H. (1983) 'A synthetic view of approximate reasoning techniques'. *IJCAI* 8, 130–6.

Reiter R. (1978) 'On reasoning by default'. *Theoretical Issues in Natural Language Processing-2*, Illinois, 210–18.

Reiter R. (1980) 'A logic for default reasoning'. *AI* 13 (1 & 2), 81–132.

Rieger C. (1976) 'An organization of knowledge for problem solving and language comprehension'. *AI* 7, 89–127.

Rosenberg S. (1983) 'HPRL: a language for building expert systems'. *IJCAI* 8, Karlsruhe, 215–17.

Rousseau M. (1973) 'Résolution automatique d'exercices d'électricité posés en français', *Thèse*, Paris VI.

Rychener M. D. (1976) 'Production systems as a programming language for artifical intelligence applications'. Ph.D., Carnegie Mellon.

Schank R. C. (1972) 'Conceptual dependency: a theory of natural language understanding'. *Cognitive Psychology* 3, 552–631.

Schank R. C. (1975) *Conceptual Information Processing*. North Holland.

Schank R. C. and Abelson R. P. (1977) *Scripts, Plans, Goals, and Understanding*. Lawrence Erlbaum.

Shortliffe E. H. and Buchanan B. G. (1975) 'A model of inexact reasoning in medicine'. *Mathematical Biosciences* 23, 351–79.

Skolem T. (1967) 'The foundations of elementary arithmetic established by means of the recursive mode of thought, without the use of apparent variables ranging over infinite domains'. In *From Frege to Gödel*. Harvard University Press.

Stefik M. (1979) 'An examination of a frame-structured representation system'. *IJCAI* 6, 845–52.

Stefik M., Aikins J., Balzer R., Benoit J., Birnbaum L., Hayes-Roth F. and Sacerdoti E. (1982) 'The organization of expert systems: a tutorial'. *AI* 18 (2), 135–73.

Szolovits P. and Pauker S. G. (1978) 'Categorical and probabilistic reasoning in medical diagnosis'. *AI* 11, 115–44.

Tabourier Y. (1982) 'Problèmes de normalisation et de décomposition dans les modèles conceptuels de données'. *Informatique et gestion* 133, 72–81.

Van Melle W. (1980) 'A domain-independent system that aids in constructing knowledge based consultation programs'. *Rep. No. 820*. Computer Science Dept. Stanford University. (*Doctoral dissertation*).

Weyhrauch R. W. (1980) 'Prolegomena to a theory of mechanized formal reasoning' *AI* 13 (1 & 2), 133–70.

Wilensky R. (1978) 'Understanding goal-based stories'. *Research Report 140*. Yale University.

Winograd T. (1975) 'Frame representations and the declarative/procedural controversy'. In D. G. Bobrow and A. Collins (eds), *Representation and Understanding*, Academic Press.

Woods W. (1975) 'What's in a link ? Foundations for semantic networks'. In D. G. Bobrow and A. Collins (eds), *Representation and Understanding*, Academic Press.

Zadley L. A. *et al.* (eds) (1975) *Fuzzy sets and their Applications to Cognitive and Decision Processes.* Academic Press.

Zadley L. A. (1979) 'Approximate reasoning based on fuzzy logic'. *IJCAI* 6, 1004–10.

Expert systems and their applications

Abrial J. R. (1974) 'Data semantics'. *IFIP, TC2.*

Aikins J. (1979) 'Prototypes and production rules: an approach to knowledge representation for hypothesis formation'. *IJCAI* 6.

Anderson R. and Gillogly J. (1976) 'Rand intelligent terminal agent RITA design and philosophy'. *R–1809–ARPA.*

Anderson J. and Kline P. (1979) 'A learning system and its psychological implications'. *IJCAI* 6.

Anderson J., Kline P. and Beasley C. (1979) 'Complex learning processes'. In R. Snow (ed.), *Aptitude Learning and Instructions.*

Barnett J. and Berstein M. (1977) 'Knowledge-based systems: a tutorial'. *System Development Corporation.* TM(L) 5903.

Barstow D. R. (1979) 'An experiment in knowledge based automatic programming'. *AI* 12, 73–119.

Bartels U., Otthoff W. and Rawlefs P. (1981) 'APE: a system for automatic programming from abstract specifications of data types and algorithms'. *IJCAI* 7, 1037–43.

Battani G. and Meloni H. (1973) 'Un interpréteur de PROLOG'. Aix-Marseille, *GIA Luminy.*

Bennett J. S. and Engelmore R. (1979) 'SACON: a knowledge-based consultant for structural analysis'. *IJCAI* 6, 47–9.

Bennett J. S. and Hollander C. R. (1981) 'DART: an expert system for computer fault diagnosis'. *IJCAI* 7, 843–5.

Bobrow, D. G. (ed) (1975) *Representation and Understanding*, Academic Press.

Bobrow D. G. and Winograd T. (1979) 'KRL: another perspective'. *CS* I(1), 24–79.

Bonnet A. (1980) 'Analyse de textes au moyen d'une grammaire sémantique de schémas. Applications à la compréhension de résumés médicaux en langage natural'. *Thèse d'Etat.* Paris VI.

Bonnet A. (1981) 'Applications de l'intelligence artificielle: les systèmes experts', *RAIRO Informatique* 15 (4).

Bonnet A., Cordier M. O. and Kayser D. (1981) 'An ICAI system for teaching derivatives in mathematics', *Proc. of 3rd World Conference on Computer Education* (WCCE), Lausanne, 27–31.

Bonnet A., Harry J. and Ganascia J. G. (1982) 'LITHO: un système expert inférant la géologie du sous-sol', *TSI* 1 (5), 393–402.

Bonnet A. and Dahan C. (1983) 'Oil-well data interpretation using expert system and pattern recognition technique', *IJCAI* 8, 185–9.

Borning A. and Bundy A. (1981) 'Using matching in algebraic equation solving'. *IJCAI* 7, 466–71.

Bourgoin D. (1978) 'PARI: un programme heuristique pour résoudre des exercices d'arithmétique'. *Thèse de 3ème cycle*, Paris VI.

Brown J., Burton R. and Boll A. (1975) 'SOPHIE: a step towards creating a reactive learning environment'. *International Journal of Man–Machine Studies, 7,* 675–716.

Buchanan B. and Feigenbaum F. (1978) 'DENDRAL and META-DENDRAL'. *AI* 11, 5–24.

Buchanan B. and Mitchell T. (1979) 'Model directed learning of production rules'. In D. A. Waterman and F. Hayes Roth (eds) (1978) *Pattern Directed Inference Systems.*

Bundy A., Byrd L., Luger G., Mellish R., Milne R. and Palmer M. (1979) 'MECHO: a program to solve mechanics' problems', Dept of AI, University of Edinburgh, *Working Paper* 50, 1–104.

Bundy A. *et al.* (1979) 'Solving mechanics' problems using meta-level inference'. *IJCAI* 6, 1017–27.

Carbonell J. (1978) 'POLITICS: automated ideological reasoning'. *CS* 2, 27–51.

Carhart R. E. (1979) 'CONGEN: an expert system aiding the structural chemist'. In D. Michie (ed.) (1980) *Expert Systems in the Microelectronic Age.*

Cayrol M., Fade B. and Farreny H. (1979) 'Objets formels et attributs dans ARGOS II'. *Actes Congrès AFCET*, Toulouse, 256–63.

Cayrol M., Fade B. and Farreny H. (1979) 'A decision-command function for a general robot'. ARGOS-II, *Tech. Report*, University of Toulouse.

Charniak E. (1978) 'On the use of framed knowledge', *AI* 11(3), 225–66.

Chomsky N. (1965) 'Aspects of the theory of syntax'. MIT Press.

Clancey W. J. (1979) 'Tutoring rules for guiding a case method dialog'. *International Journal of Man–Machine Studies* 11, 25–49.

Clancey W. J. and Letsinger R. (1981) 'NEOMYCIN: reconfiguring a rule based expert system for application to teaching'. *IJCAI* 7, 829–36.

Clocksin W. F. and Mellish C. S. (1981) 'Programming in Prolog'. Springer-Verlag.

Coelho H., Cotta J. C. and Pereira L. M. (1980) 'How to solve it with PROLOG'. Lab. Nat. de Engenharia Civil, Lisbon.

Cognitech (1986) *TOM: Un Système expert en diagnostic des maladies de la tomate.* Cognitech.

Colmerauer A. (1977) 'Programmation en logique du premier ordre'. *Actes Journées 'La compréhension'*, IRIA.

Cordier M. O. (1979) 'Commande d'un robot en langage natural dans un domaine nécessitant des connaissances pragmatiques: les recettes de cuisine'. *Thèse de 3ème cycle*, LRI, Paris XI.

Cordier M. O. and Rousset M. C. (1984) 'Propagation: another way for matching paterns in KBS'. Cyb. and Syst. Res. 2.

Davis R. (1979) 'Interactive transfer of expertise: acquisition of new inference rules'. *MIT 11*, 1–36; abridged version in *IJCAI* 5, 321–8.

Davis R. and Buchanan B. (1977) 'Meta-level knowledge and applications'. *IJCAI* 5, 920–7.

Davis R., Buchanan B. and Shortliffe E. (1977) 'Production rules as a representation for a knowledge-based consultation program'. *AI* 8, 15–45.

Davis R. and King, J. (1977) 'An overview of production systems'. *Machine Intelligence*, vol. 8, 300–32.

Davis R., Austin H., Carlbow I., Frawley B., Pruchnik P., Sneiderman R. and Gilreath J. A. (1981) 'The DIPMETER adviser: interpretation of geological signals'. *IJCAI* 7, 846–9.

Davis R. and Lenat D. B. (1982) *Knowledge Based Systems in Artificial Intelligence.* McGraw-Hill.

Descottes Y. and Latombe J. C. (1981) 'GARI: a problem solver that plans how to machine mechanical parts'. *IJCAI* 7, 766–72.

Dincbas M. (1979) 'PROLOG et un exemple de programme expert écrit en PROLOG'. *Doc. CERT.*, 2/3122.

Dincbas M. (1980) 'A knowledge-based expert system for automatic analysis and synthesis'. In *CAD, Proc. IFIP*, Tokyo, 705–10.

Dincbas M. (1980) 'Le système de résolution de problèmes METALOG'. CERT/DERI *Report N°. 3146, Convention DRET 79, 1216*, Toulouse.

Doumeingts G., Breull D. and Pun L. (1983) *La Gestion de production assistée par ordinateur*. Hermes Publishing.

Doyle J. (1979) 'TMS: a true maintenance system'. *AI* 12, 231–72.

Duda R. O., Gaschning J. and Hart P. (1980) 'Model design in the PROSPECTOR consultant system for mineral exploration'. In D. Michie (ed.) (1980) *Expert Systems in the Microelectronic Age*.

Duda R. O. (1982) 'The PROSPECTOR consultation system'. *Final Report SRI 8172*.

Duda R. O. and Gaschning J. G. (1981) 'Knowledge based expert systems come of age'. *Byte* 6 (9), 238–83.

Engelmore R. and Terry A. (1979) 'Structure and function of the CRYSALIS system'. *IJCAI* 6, 250–6.

Erman L. and Lesser V. (1975) 'A multi-level organization for problem-solving using many diverse cooperating sources of knowledge'. *IJCAI* 4, 483–90.

Erman L., Hayes-Roth F., Lesser V. R. and Reddy D. R. (1980) 'The HEARSAY-II speech-understanding system: integrating knowledge to resolve uncertainty'. *Computing Surveys* 12, 2.

Erman L., London P. and Fickas S. (1981) 'The design and an example use of HEARSAY III'. *IJCAI* 7, 409–15.

Fagan L. M. (1980) 'Representing time dependent relations in clinical vetting.' Ph.D. Stanford.

Fargues J. (1983) 'TOUBIB: Contribution à l'étude du raisonnement. Application à la médicine d'urgence'. *Thèse d'Etat*. Paris.

Farreny H. (1980) 'Un système pour l'expression et la résolution de problèmes orienté vers le contrôle des robots'. *Thèse d'Etat*, Toulouse.

Farreny H. (1982) 'Des puits de science qu'on peut sonder'. In *La Science des Robots. Science et Vie-hors-série*, 68–75.

Farreny H. (1985) *Les Systèmes-experts, principes et exemples*. Cepadues.

Feigenbaum E. (1977) 'The art of artificial intelligence'. *IJCAI* 5, 1014–29.

Feigenbaum E., Buchanan B. and Lederberg J. (1971) 'On generality and problem solving: a case study using the DENDRAL program'. *Machine Intelligence*, vol. 6, 165–90.

Ferrand P. (1983) 'SESAM : an explanatory medical aid system'. *ECAI*, 13–20.

Fieschi M. (1981) 'SPHINX: aide à la décision en médecine: le système Sphinx. Application au diagnostic d'une douleur épigastrique'. *Thèse, Médecine*, Marseille.

Fieschi M. (1984) *Intelligence artificielle en médecine: systèmes experts*. Masson.

Forgy C. and McDermott, J. (1977) 'OPS: a domain independent production system'. *IJCAI* 5, 933–9.

Fouet J. M. (1982) 'Désapprendre à programmer'. Pub. GR 22, n°. 30.

Fouet J. M. (1986) 'Compilation des connaissances dans la machine GOSSEYN'. Cahiers du Laforia N° 60, Paris, 255–69.

Friedland P. (1979) 'MOLGEN: knowledge based experiments design in molecular genetics'. Ph.D. Stanford.

Friedman L. (1981) 'Extended plausible inference'. *IJCAI* 7, 487–95.

Gallaire H. and Minker J. (eds) (1978) *Logic and Data Bases*. Plenum.

Gallaire H. and Lasserre C. (1979) 'Controlling knowledge deduction in a declarative approach'. *IJCAI* 6, S1-S12.

Gallaire H. (1981) 'Le langage PROLOG'. L4, 12R. Lectures, Toulouse.

Ganascia J. G. (1983) 'MIRLITHO. Validation des résultats et détection des contradictions dans les systèmes de diagnostic'. Thèse 3ème cycle Paris Sud.

Gascuel O. (1981) 'Un programme Général d'aide à la décision médicale structurant automatiquement ses connaissances'. *Congrès AFCET RF-IA*, Nancy.

Georgeff M. (1979) 'A framework for control in production systems'. *IJCAI* 6, 328–34.

Germain M. (1981) 'Journée sur les spécifications'. *AFCET-TTI Conference*, Nancy.

Ghallab M. 'Decision trees for optimizing pattern-matching algorithm'. *IJCAI* 7, 310–12.

Goldstein I. and Roberts R. (1977) 'NUDGE: a knowledge-based scheduling program'. *IJCAI* 5, 257–63.

Green C. (1976) 'The design of the PSI program synthesis system'. *Proc. of the Second International Conference on software engineering*, 4–18.

Green O. O. (1976) 'The design of the PSI program synthesis system'. *IJCAI* 2, 4–18.

Hayes-Roth, F., Waterman D. A. and Lenat D. B. (1977) 'Principles of pattern-directed inference systems', 577–601.

Hayes-Roth F., Klahr P. and Mostow D. (1981) 'Advice-taking and knowledge refinement: An iterative view of skill acquisition'. In J. R. Anderson (ed.). *Cognitive Skills and their Acquisition*, Lawrence Erlbaum, 231–53.

Hedrick C. L. (1976) 'Learning production systems from examples'. *AI* 7(1), 21–49.

Herbrand J. (1931) 'Une méthode de démonstration'. *Thèse*, Paris.

Hewitt C. (1972) 'Description and theoretical analysis (using schemata) of PLANNER: a language for proving theorems and manipulating models in a robot'. *Ph.D.* MIT, AI Lab. Report 258.

Hollander C. R. *et al.* 'DRILLING ADVISER'. Trend and application conference. Washington.

Holt A. W. (1971) *Introduction to Occurrence Systems*. Associative Information Technique, E. Jack (ed.). Elsevier.

Huet G. (1978) 'Unification dans les logiques d'ordre 1, 2 ,3, oméga. *Thèse*. Paris.

Johnson T. (1984) *The commercial applications of expert systems technologies.* OVUM.

Joubert M. (1981) 'MEDIUM: acquisition de données medicales en français'. *Thèse*. Marseille.

Kahn K. M. (1981) 'UNIFORM: a language based upon unification'. *IJCAI* 7, 933–9.

Kayser D. and Coulon D. (1981) 'QUID: variable-depth natural language understanding', *IJCAI* 7, 64–6.

Kliber, D. and Morris P. (1981) 'Don't be stupid', *IJCAI* 7, 345–7.

Konolige K. (1979) 'An inference net compiler for the PROSPECTOR rule-based consultation system', *IJCAI* 6, 487–9.

Kowalski R. (1974) 'Predicate logic as a programming language', *Proc. IFIP* 3, 569–74.

Kowalski R. (1979) *Logic for Problem Solving*, North Holland.

Kulikowski C. A., Weiss S., Trigoboff M. and Safir A. (1976) 'Clinical consultation and the representation of disease process: some A.I. approaches'. *Report CEM-TR 58*, Rutgers University.

Kulikowski C. A. and Weiss S. (1982) 'Representation of expert knowledge for consultation: the CASNET and EXPERT projects'. In P. Szolovits (ed.), *Artificial Intelligence in Medicine*, Westview Press.

Lagrange M. S. and Renaud M. (1984) 'Deux expériences de simulation du raisonnement en archéologie au moyen d'un système expert: le système SNARK'. *Informatique et sciences humaines* 59–60, 161–88.

Lagrange M. S. and Renaud M. (1985) 'Intelligent knowledge based systems in archaeology: a computerized simulation of reasoning by means of an expert system'. *Computer and Humanities* 19, 37–52.

Langley P. (1979) 'Rediscovering physics with BACON-3'. *IJCAI* 6, 505–7.

Lasserre C. (1978) 'Rapport de la logique mathématique dans les systèmes de décision en robotique'. *Thèse* Docteur Ingénieur, Toulouse.

Latome J. C. (1977) 'Une application de l'intelligence artificielle à la conception assistée par ordinateur'. *Thèse d'Etat*, Grenoble.

Laurière J. L. (1971) 'Sur la coloration de certains hypergraphes: applications aux problèmes d'emploi du temps'. *Thèse*, Paris VI.

Laurière J. L. (1972) 'Problèmes d'emploi du temps (E. H. R)'. *Actes des journées combinatoires Afcet.*

Laurière J. L. (1974) 'Un programme d'élaboration des emplois du temps scolaires'. *Congrès AFCET 'aide à la décision'*, Paris.

Laurière J. L. (1974) 'Problèmes d'emploi du temps et algorithme de coloration des hypergraphes'. *C.R. Acad. Sci. Paris* 278 *a*, 1159–62.

Laurière J. L. (1976) 'Un langage et un programme pour énoncer et résoudre des problèmes combinatoires'. *Thèse d'Etat.* Paris VI.

Laurière J. L. (1982) 'Applications industrielles des systèmes experts'. 4e Journées Francophones Genève, IMAG, Grenoble.

Laurière J. L. (1983) 'Représentation et utilisation de connaissances'. *TSI* n° 1 et 2.

Laurière J. L. and Vialatte M. (1985) 'Manuel d'utilisation du moteur d'inférence SNARK'. Institut de programmation. Paris VI.

Laurière J. L. and Vialatte M. (1986) 'SNARK: a language to represent declarative knowledge'. IFIP Dublin, 811–16.

Le Faivre R. (1974) 'Fuzzy problem solving'. *Ph.D.* Tech. Rep 37. University of Wisconsin.

Lenat D. (1975) 'BEINGS: knowledge as interacting experts'. *IJCAI* 4.

Lenat D. (1977) 'The ubiquity of discovery', *AI* 9(3), 257–86.

Lenat D. and McDermott J. (1977) 'Less than general production systems architecture'. *IJCAI* 5, 928–32.

Levesque C. (1984) 'Un système expert en paye et gestion du personnel'. *Thèse 3ème cycle*, Paris VI.

Lindsay R. K., Buchanan B. G., Feigenbaum E. A. and Lederberg J. (1980) *Applications of Artificial Intelligence for Organic Chemistry: The Dendral Project.* McGraw-Hill.

McCarthy (1977) 'Epistemological problems in AI'. *IJCAI* 5, MIT, 1038–44.

McCracken D. (1979) 'Representation and efficiency in a production system for speech understanding'. *IJCAI* 6, 556.

McDermott D. (1978) 'Planning and acting'. *CS* 2, 71–109.

McDermott D. (1979) 'Learning to use analogies'. *IJCAI* 6, 568–76.

McDermott D. and Forgy J. (1977) 'Production system conflict resolution strategies'. In F. Waterman and D. A. Hayes-Roth (eds) (1978) *Pattern Directed Inference Systems*, 177–201.

McDermott D., Newell A. and Moore J. (1977) 'The efficiency of certain production system implementation'. In F. Waterman and D. A. Hayes-Roth (eds) (1978) *Pattern Directed Inference Systems*, 155–76.

McDermott D. and Steele B. (1981) 'Extending a knowledge-based system to deal with ad-hoc constraints'. *IJCAI* 7, 824–8.

McDermott D. (1982) 'RI: a rule-based configurer of computer systems'. *AI* 19, 39–88.

Manna Z. and Waldinger R. (1975) 'Knowledge and reasoning in program synthesis'. *AI* 6, 175–208.

Markov A. (1954) *The Theory of Algorithms*. US Dept of Commerce, translated from Russian by J. Shorr-Kon.

Meloni H. (1982) 'Etude et réalisation d'un système de reconnaissance automatique de la parole continue'. *Thèse de Doctorat d'Etat*, University of Aix-Marseille 2, Luminy.

Meyer A. (1980) 'Ten thousand and one logics of programming'. *ILP, MIT 6380*.

Meyer B. and Baudoin C. (1978) *Méthodes de Programmation*. Eyrolles n° 34.

Michie D. (1980) *Expert Systems in the Microelectronic Age*. Edinburgh University Press.

Minsky M. (ed.) (1975) 'A framework for representing knowledge'. In Winston 75, 211–77.

Mitchell T. M., Utgoff P., Nudel B. and Banerji R. 'Learning problem solving heuristics through practice'. *IJCAI* 7, 127–34.

Moran T. (1973) 'The symbolic nature of visual imagery'. *IJCAI* 3, 472–7.

Myers J. D. and Pople H. (1977) 'Internist: a consultative diagnostic program'. In *Internal medicine proceeding of the 1st annual symposium on computer applications in medical care, IEEE*.

Mylopoulos J. (1981) 'An overview of knowledge representation'. *SIGPLAN* 16(1). 5–12.

Newell A. (1976) 'Production systems: models of control structures'. In W. Chase (ed.) *Visual Information Processing*, 463–526.

Newell A. (1982) 'The knowledge level', *AI* 18 (1), 87–128.

Newell A. and McDermott J. (1975) 'PSG manual'. *Report*. Carnegie Mellon University.

Newell A. and Simon H. (1972) *Human Problem Solving*. Prentice Hall.

Nii N. and Allello N. (1978) 'AGE: attempt to generalize'. *Work Paper 5*, Stanford.

Nii N. and Feigenbaum E. (1978) 'Rule based understanding of signals'. In F. Waterman and D. A. Hayes-Roth (eds) *Pattern Directed Inference Systems*.

Nilsson N. (1980) *Principles of Artificial Intelligence*. Tioga Pub. Co.

Pastre D. (1978) 'Automatic theorem proving in set theory'. *AI* 10 (1), 1–27.

Patil R., Szolovits P. and Schwartz W. B. (1982) 'Modelling knowledge of the patient in acid-base and electrolyte disorders'. In P. Szolovits (ed.), *Artificial Intelligence in Medicine*. Westview Press.

Petri C. A. (1962) 'Communication with automata', *Ph.D.*, Bonn.

Pierrel J. M. (1982) 'Utilisation de contraintes linguistiques en compréhension automatique de la parole continue: le système Myrtille-II'. *TSI*, Vol. 1, N° 5, 403–21.

Pinson S. (1980) 'Représentation des connaissances dans les systèmes experts'. *PAIRO Informatique* 15 (4), 343–67.

Pitrat J. (1970) *Un programme de démonstration de théorèmes*, Monographie AFCET 7, Dunod.

Pitrat J. (1985) 'Utilisation de connaissances déclaratives', Cours école d'été AFCET Aix en Provence.

Pople H. (1982) INTERNIST: 'Heuristics methods for improving structures on ill-structured problems'. In P. Szolovits (ed.) *AI in Medicine*, Boulder.

Post E. (1936) 'Finite combination processes'. *Journal of Symbolic Logic* 1, 103–5.

Post E. (1943) 'Formal reductions of the general combinatorial decision problem'. *American Journal of Mathematics* 65, 197–215.

Pun L. (1982) 'Predictive complicate coordinating plannings'. Asia-Pacific conference on operational research, Singapore.

Pun L. (1984) *Systèmes industriels d'intelligence artificielle*. Editions Tests.

Quinlan J. 'Knowledge-based system for locating missing high cards in bridge'. *IJCAI* 6, 705–7.

Roussel P. (1975) 'Prolog: manuel de référence et d'utilisation'. Groupe d'intelligence Artificielle. Marseille Luminy.

Rousset M. C. (1983) 'TANGO: moteur d'inférences avec variables', Thèse 3° cycle. Orsay.

Rychener M. D. (1976) 'Production systems as a programming language for artificial intelligence applications'. *Ph. D.* Carnegie Mellon University, Vols 1 and 2.

Schank R. and Abelson R. (1977) *Scripts, Plans, Goals and Understanding*. Lawrence Erlbaum.

Shortliffe E. (1976) *Computer-based Medical Consultations*: MYCIN. Elsevier.

Shortliffe E., Carlisle Scott A., Bischoff M. B., Campell A. B., Van Melle W. and Jacobs D. (1981) 'ONCOCIN: an expert system for oncology protocol management'. *IJCAI* 7, 876–981.

Soula G. *et al.* (1986) *PROTIS: a fuzzy expert system with medical applications in fuzzy logic in knowledge engineering*. Verlag Tüv, 295–310.

Stefik M. (1978) 'Inferring DNA structures from segmentation data'. *AI* 11(1), 85–114.

Stefik M. (1981) 'Planning with constraints (MOLGEN 1)' *AI* 16(2), 111–40.

Stefik M. (1981) 'Planning and meta-planning (MOLGEN 2)'. *AI* 16(2), 141–70.

Sussman G. and Stallman H. (1975) 'Heuristic techniques in computer-aided circuit analysis', IEEE Transactions on Circuits and Systems, *CAS* 22 (11), 857–65.

Swartout W. R. (1979) 'Explaining and justifying expert consulting programs'. *IJCAI* 7, 815–23.

Szeredi P. (1977) 'Prolog, a very high-level language based on predicate logic'. *Hungarian Conference on Computer Science*.

Uhr L. (1979) 'Parallel-serial productions systems'. *IJCAI* 6, 911–16.

Van Melle W. (1979) 'A domain independent production-rule system for consultation systems'. *IJCAI* 6.

Vialatte M. (1984) 'Introduction de métaconnaissances, de gestion d'hypothèses, de logique d'ordre 0 et 2 dans SNARK'. Rapport institut de programmation.

Vialatte M. (1985) 'Description et applications du moteur d'inférence SNARK'. *Thèse*. Paris 6.

Vignard P. (1985) 'CRIQUET: un outil de base pour construire des systèmes experts'. INRIA. Paris.

Warren D. H. (1977) 'Implementing Prolog: DAI'. *Research Rep. 1 and 2*. University of Edinburgh.

Waterman D. (1970) 'Generalization learning techniques for automating the learning of heuristics'. *AI* 1, 121–70.

Waterman D. (1975) 'Adaptive production systems'. *IJCAI* 4, 296–303.

Waterman D. and Hayes-Roth F. (eds) (1978) *Pattern Directed Inference Systems*. Academic Press.

Waterman D. and Newell A. (1971) 'Protocol analysis as a task for artificial intelligence'. *AI* 2, 285–318.

Weiss S. M. and Kulikowski C. A. (1978) 'Expert: a system for developing consultation models', *IJCAI* 6, 942–7.

Wilensky R. (1981) 'Meta planning', *CS* 5, 197–233.
Wilkins D. (1979) 'Using plans in chess'. *IJCAI* 6, 960–7.
Winograd T. (1975) 'Frame representations and the declarative procedural controversy'. In D. G. Bobrow and A. Collins (eds) (1975) *Representation and Understanding.*
Winograd T. (1982) 'Des machines savantes, mais incultes'. *La Sciences des Robots, Science et Vie-hoprs-série*, 76–83.
Winston P. H. (1975) *The Psychology of Computer Vision.* McGraw-Hill.
Winston P. (1977) *Artificial Intelligence*, Addison-Wesley.
Zarri G. P. (1981) 'Building the inference component of an historical information retrieval system'. *IJCAI* 7, 401–8.

Automatic theorem-proving and program construction

Abrial F. (1974) 'Data semantics'. IFIP TC2 working conference.
Adam A. (1973) 'Gadget: Un programmes de génération automatique de programmes sur les graphes et les ensembles'. *Thèse*. Paris VI.
Adam A. (1978) 'Utilisation des transformations sémantiques pour la correction automatique des programmes'. *Thèse d'Etat*, Paris VI.
Adam A. and Laurent J. P. (1980) 'LAURA: a system to debug student programs'. *AI* 15 (1–2), 75–122.
Aho A. V., Hopcroft J. E. and Ullman J. D. (1974) *The Design and Analysis of Computer Algorithms.* Addison-Wesley.
Arsac J. (1977) *Nouvelles leçons de programmation.* Dunod.
Barstow D. (1979) *APE: Knowledge Based Program Construction.* North Holland.
Bibel W. (1980) 'Syntax-directed, semantic-supported program synthesis'. *AI* 15, 243.
Bibel W. (1982) 'A comparative study of several proof procedures' *AI* 18 (3) 269–93.
Bledsoe W. W. (1971) 'Splitting and reduction heuristics in automatic theorem proving'. *AI* 2, 55–77.
Bledsoe W. W., Boyer R. S. and Henneman W. H. (1972) 'Computer proofs of limit theorems', *AI* 3, 27–60.
Bledsoe W. W. and Bruel P. (1973) 'A man-machine theorem proving system'. *IJCAI* 3.
Bledsoe W. W. (1977) 'Non-resolution theorem proving'. *AI* 9, 1–35.
Bobrow D. G. (ed.) (1980) 'Special issue on non-monotonic logic'. *AI* 13, 1–2.
Bourgoin D. (1978) 'PARI: un programme heuristique pour résoudre des exercices d'arithmétique'. *Thèse de 3ème cycle*, Paris.
Carrière O. (1973) 'Réalisation d'un programme heuristique qui résout des tests psychologiques de mesure de facteur G'. *Thèse*. Paris VI.
Chang C. and Lee R. C. (1973) *Symbolic Logic and Mechanical Theorem Proving.* Academic Press.
Chang C. L. and Slagle J. R. (1979) 'Using rewriting rules for connection graphs to prove theorems'. *AI* 12 (2), 159–78.
Cooks S. (1971) 'The complexity of theorem proving procedures'. *3th ACM symposium on theory of computing.*
Dallard R. (1974) 'Présentation d'un programme de démonstration de théorèmes d'arithmétique'. *Thèse*. Paris VI.

Delhaye J. L. (1970) 'DATAL: un programme de dèmonstration automatique de théorèmes'. *Thèse*. Paris VI.

Doyle J. (1979) 'A truth maintenance system'. *AI* 12, 231–72.

Evans T. G. (1968) 'A program for the solution of geometric-analogy intelligence test questions'. In M. Minsky (ed.) *Semantic Information Processing*. MIT Press.

Faller B. (1984) 'An expert system in symbolic integration', *ECAI* 82–3.

Flavigny B. (1972) 'Sur la détection a priori des erreurs dans les programmes'. *Thèse*. Paris VI.

Gelernter H. (1963) 'Realization of a geometry theorem proving machine'. In E. A. Feigenbaum and J. Feldman (eds) (1963) *Computers and Thought*, McGraw-Hill, 134–52.

Gillet N. (1980) 'Un exemple d'utilisation de connaissances en démonstration automatique'. *Thèse*, Paris VI.

Grandbastien M. (1974) 'Un programme qui résout formellement des équations trigonométriques par des procédés heuristiques'. *Thèse*, Paris VI.

Green C. (1969) 'Theorem-proving by resolution as a basis for question-answering systems'. In B. Meltzer and D. Michie (eds) *Machine intelligence*, vol. 4, Elsevier, 1783–205.

Guttag J. (1977) 'Abstract datatypes and the development of data structures'. Comm ACM 20–6, 396–404.

Hearn A. C. (1971) 'Reduce: a system and language for algebraic manipulation'. In S. R. Pelnick (ed.) *Proc. ACM 2D Symposium on symbolic and algebraic manipulation*.

Hertz A. (1975) 'Programmes de démonstration de théorèmes formulables en logique des prédicats du premier ordre avec égalité'. *Thèse*. Paris VI.

Hewitt O. (1972) 'Description and theoretical analysis (using schemata) of Planner: a language for proving theorems and manipulating models in a robot'. *Ph.D.* MIT.

Huet G. (1972) 'Constrained resolution: A complete method for higher order logic'. Rep. n° 1117. Case Western Reserve University. *Doctoral dissertation*.

Huet G. (1973a) 'A unification algorithm for type theory'. *Iria Laboria*.

Huet G. (1973b) 'A mechanization of type theory', *IJCAI* 3.

Huet G. (1975) 'A unification algorithm for types lambda calculus'. *Theoretical Computer Science* 1, 27–57.

Huet G. (1978) 'Unification dans les logiques d'ordre 1, 2, ... omega'. *Thèse d'Etat*, Paris VI.

Kling R. (1971) 'A paradigm for reasoning for analogy'. *AI* 2, 147–78.

Kowalski R. (1970) 'Search strategies for theorem proving'. *Machine Intelligence*, vol. 5, Elsevier, 181–200.

Kowalski R. (1974) 'Predicate logic as a programming language'. In J. L. Rosenfeld (ed.) North Holland, 569–74.

Kowalski R. and Kuchner D. (1971) 'Linear resolution with selector function'. *AI* 2, 227–60.

Lasserre C. (1978) 'Apport de la logique mathématique dans les systèmes de décision en robotique'. *Thèse*. Toulouse.

Laurent J. P. (1972) 'Un programme qui calcule les limites en levant les indéterminations par des procédés heuristiques'. *Thése*. Paris VI.

Laurent J. P. (1973) 'A program that computes limits using heuristics to evaluate the indeterminate forms'. *AI* 4, 69–94.

Lenat D. B. (1983) 'EURISKO: a program that learns new heuristics and domain concepts'. *AI*, March.

Liskov B. (1977) 'Abstraction mechanisms in CLU'. *Comm ACM* 20–8, 564–76.

Mackworth A. K. (1977) 'Consistency in networks of relations'. *AI* 8, 99–118.

Manna Z. and Waldinger R. I. (1975) 'Knowledge and reasoning in program synthesis'. *AI* 6, 175–208.

Mathiab-Group (1974) 'The Macsyma reference manual'. *MIT lab. for computer science.*

Meyer B. and Baudoin C. (1978) *Méthodes de programmation.* Eyrolles.

Moses J. (1971) 'Algebraic simplification: a guide for the perplexed', *Proc. ACM 2nd Symposium on symbolic and algebraic manipulation.*

Nevins A. J. (1974) 'A human oriented logic for automatic theorem proving'. *J. ACM* 21, 606–21.

Nevins A. J. (1975) 'A relaxation approach to splitting in an automatic theorem prover'. *AI* 6, 25–40.

Nevins A. J. (1975) 'Plane geometry theorem proving using forward chaining', *AI* 6, 1–23.

Pair C. and Gaudel M. C. (1977) 'Les structures de données et leur représentation en mémoire'. Rapport INRIA Rocquencourt.

Pastre D. (1976) 'Démonstration automatique de théorèmes en théorie des ensembles'. *Thèse.* Paris VI.

Pastre D. (1978) 'Automatic theorem proving in set theory'. *AI* 10 (1), 1–27.

Pastre D. (1984) 'MUSCADET. Un système de démonstration automatique de théorèmes utilisant des connaissances et des métaconnaissances en mathématiques'. *Thèse d'Etat.* Paris VI.

Pitrat J. (1970) *Un Programme de démonstration de théorèmes.* AFCET. Dunod.

Post (E.) (1936) 'Finite combination processes'. *Journal of Symbolic Logic 1*, 103–5.

Relter R. (1980) 'A logic for default reasoning'. *AI* 13, 82–132.

Robinson G. A. and Wos L. (1969) 'Paramodulation and theorem-proving in first order theories with equality'. In D. Michie (ed.) *Machine Intelligence*, vol. 4, Elsevier.

Robinson G. A. (1973) 'The generalized resolution principle'. *Machine Intelligence*, vol. 3, 77–98, Elsevier.

Robinson G. A. (1974) 'Mechanizing higher-order logic'. *Machine Intelligence*, vol. 4, 151–98, Elsevier.

Robinson J. A. (1965) 'A machine-oriented logic based on the resolution principle'. *J. ACM* 12, 23–41.

Vivet M. (1973) 'Un programme qui vérifie des identités en utilisant le raisonnement par récurrence'. *Thése.* Paris VI.

Vivet M. (1984) 'CAMELIA: A knowledge based mathematical system'. *ECAI* 603–12.

Wegman M. N. (1978) 'Linear unification'. *Journal of Computer and System Sciences* 16, 158–67.

Wos L. T., Carlson D. G. and Robins G. A. (1965) 'Efficiency and completeness of the set of support strategy in theorem-proving'. *J. ACM* 4 (12), 536–41.

THE PROLOG LANGUAGE

Clocksin W. F. and Mellish (1981) *Programming in PROLOG.* Springer Verlag.

Colmerauer A. (1978) 'Metamorphosis grammar. Natural language communication with computers'. *Lecture notes in computer science, Vol. 63.*

Colmerauer A., Kanoul H. and Van Caneghem M. (1983) 'Prolog, bases théoriques et développement actuels'. *TSI.* 2 (4).

Kowalski R. (1980) *Logic for Problem Solving.* North Holland.

Roussel P. (1975) 'Prolog: manuel de référence et d'utilisation'. *Rapport GIA.* Marseille, Luminy.

Venken R. (1984) 'A Prolog meta-interpreter for partial evaluation and its application to source transformation and query-optimisation'. *ECAI* 91–100.

Warren D. H. D., Pereira L. M. and Pereira F. (1977) 'Prolog – the language and its implementation compared with LISP'. *Proceedings of the Symposium on Artificial Intelligence and Programming Languages (ACM),* SIGPLAN Notices 12(8), and SIGART Newsletter 64: 109–15.

Problem-solving and planning

Abelson R. P. (1975) 'Concepts for representing mundane reality in plans'. In D. G. Bobrow and A. Collins (eds) (1975) *Representation and Understanding,* Academic Press, 280–309.

Berliner H. (1979) 'The B* tree search algorithm: a best-first proof procedure'. *AI* 12 (1), 23–40.

Bitner J. and Reingold E. (1976) 'Backtrack programming techniques'. *C. ACM* 18, 651–6.

Carbonell J. (1978) 'Politics: automatic ideological reasoning'. *CS* 2, 27–51.

Carbonell J. (1981) 'Counterplanning: a strategy-based model of adversary planning in real-world situations'. *AI* 16 (3), 295–329.

Cayrol M., Fade B. and Farreny H. (1979) 'Formal objects and feature associations in ARGOS-II'. *IJCAI* 6, 31–133.

Cayrol M., Fade B. and Farreny H. (1979) 'Objets formels et attributs dans ARGOS-II'. *Congess AFCET, Toulouse,* 256–63.

Cayrol M., Fade B. and Farreny H. (1980) 'ARGOS-II un système de production pour écrire des résolveurs experts'. *Actes du Congrès AFCET Informatique,* Nancy, 351–61.

Edmonds J. (1965) 'Paths, trees and flowers'. *Canadian Journal of Mathematics* 17.

Ernst G. W. and Newell A. (1969) *GPS: A Case Study in Generality and Problem Solving,* Academic Press.

Eastman C. (1971) 'Heuristic algorithms for automated space planning'. *IJCAI* 2.

Eastman C. (1973) 'Automatic space planning', *AI* 4, 41–64.

Ernst G. W. (1971) 'The utility of independent subgoals in theorem proving'. *Information and Control* 4.

Fahlman (1974) 'A planning system for robot construction tasks'. *AI* 5 (1), 1–50.

Farreny H. (1980) 'Un système pour l'expression et la résolution de problèmes orienté vers le contrôle de robots'. *Thèse d'Etat.* Toulouse.

Fikes R. E. (1970) 'REF-ARF: a system for solving problems stated as procedures'. *AI* 1 (1).

Fikes R. E. and Nilsson N. J. (1971) 'STRIPS: a new approach to the application of theorem proving in problem solving'. *AI* 2, 189–208.

Fikes R. E., Hart P. E. and Nilsson N. J. (1972b) 'Some new directions in robot problem solving', In B. Meltzer and D. Michie (eds) *Machine Intelligence*, Vol. 7, Elsevier.

Floyd H. (1967) 'Non-deterministic algorithms'. *J. ACM* 14 (4), 636–44.

Fouet J. M. (1979) 'Conception par ordinateur de mécanismes à une boucle'. *Thèse*. Paris VI.

Garijo R. (1978) 'GPFAR2: Un système d'écriture automatique de programmes pour le calcul optimisé des fonctions récursives'. *Thèse*. Paris VI.

Gelperin D. (1977) 'On the optimality of A*': *AI* 8, 69–76.

Gloess P. (1976) 'GENER: un générateur de programmes'. *Thèse*. Paris VI.

Golomb S. and Baumert L. (1965) 'Backtrack programming'. *J. ACM* 12, 516–24.

Gondran M. and Minoux M. (1979) *Graphes et Algorithmes*. Eyrolles.

Guzman A. (1968) 'Decomposition of a visual scene into three-dimensional bodies'. *AFIPS Fall Joint Conferences 33*, 291–304.

Haralick R. M. and Elliott G. L. (1980) 'Increasing tree search efficiency for constraint satisfaction problems'. *AI* 15, 263–314.

Hewitt C. (1969) 'PLANNER: a language for proving theorems in robots'. *IJCAI* 1.

Hewitt C. (1971) 'Description and theoretical analysis (using schemata) of PLANNER: a language for proving theorems and manipulating models in a robot'. *Rep. No. AI-TR-258*, AI Laboratory, MIT.

Karp R. (1975) 'On the computational complexity of combinatorial problems'. *Networks* 5, 45–68.

Laurent J. P. (1978) 'Un système qui met en évidence des erreurs sémantiques dans les programmes'. *Thèse d'Etat*. Paris VI.

Laurière J. L. (1978) 'A language and a program for stating and solving combinatorial problems'. *AI* 10, 29–127.

Laurière J. L. (1979) *Eléments de programmation dynamique*. Gauthier-Villars.

Lawler E. and Wood D. (1966) 'Branch and bound methods: a survey'. *Opn. res.* 14, 699–719.

Lawler E. (1976) 'A note on the complexity of the chromatic number problem'. *Information Processing Letter*, 5, 66–7.

Lemaitre C. (1974) 'Problèmes de planification et apprentissage dans le cas d'un programme de simulation de robot'. *Thèse*. Paris VI.

Lenat D. B. (1982) 'The nature of heuristics'. *AI* 19 (2), 189–249.

Little J. D., Murty K., Sweeney D. and Karel O. (1963) 'An algorithm for the travelling salesman problem', *Opn. Res.*, 11, 972–89.

McDermott D. (1977) 'A deductive model of control of a problem solver'. *SIGART*, 63, 2–7.

McDermott D. (1978) 'Planning and acting'. *CS* 2, 71–109.

Mackworth A. K. (1977) 'Consistency in networks of relations'. *AI* 8, 99–118.

Mathieu J. and Thomas R. (1985) *Manuel de psychologie*. Vigot.

Meyer B. and Baudoin C. (1978) *Méthodes de programmation*. Eyrolles.

Mitchell T. M. (1979) 'An analysis of generalization as a search problem'. *IJCAI* 6, 577–82.

Pfefferkorn C. E. (1975) 'A heuristic problem solving design system for equipment layout'. *C. ACM* 18 (5), 286–97.

Plaisted D. A. (1982) 'A simplified problem reduction format'. *AI* 18 (2), 227–61.

Pohl I. (1970) 'Heuristic search viewed as path finding in a graph'. *AI* 1, 193–204.

Reinfold E., Nievergelt J. and Dec N. (1977) *Combinatorial Algorithms: Theory and Practice*. Prentice Hall.

Rousselot F. (1975) 'Simulation d'un robot qui comprend et exécute des ordres donnés en français'. *Thèse*. Paris VI.

Sacerdoti E. D. (1974) 'Planning in a hierarchy of abstraction spaces'. *AI* 5, 115–35.

Sacerdoti E. D. (1975) 'The nonlinear nature of plans'. *IJCAI* 4, 206–14.

Sacerdoti E. D. (1977) *A Structure for Plans and Behaviour*. Elsevier.

Siklossy L. and Marinov V. (1971) 'Heuristic search versus exhaustive search'. *IJCAI*, 2, 601–10.

Siklossy L., Rich A. and Marinov V. (1973) 'Breadth-first search: some surprising results'. *AI* 4 (1), 1–27.

Siklossy L. and Dreussi (1973) 'An efficient robot planner which generates its own procedures'. *IJCAI* 3.

Siklossy L. and Roach J. (1975) 'Model verification and improvement using DISPROVER'. *AI* 6 (1), 41–52.

Stefik M. J. (1980) 'Planning with constraints'. Rep. N° 80–784. Computer Science Dept, Stanford University. *Doctoral dissertation*.

Sussman G. J. and Steele G. L. (1980) 'CONSTRAINTS – a language for expressing almost-hierarchical descriptions'. *AI* 14 (1), 1–39.

Tarjan R. (1972) 'Depth first search and linear graph algorithms'. *Slam J. Comput.*, 146–60.

Tonge F. (1961) *A Heuristic Program for Assembly Line Balancing*. Prentice Hall.

Welsh D. J. and Powell M. B. (1968) 'An upper bound for the chromatic number of a graph and its application to the timetabling problem'. *Computer J.* 10, 41–5.

de Werra D. (1974) 'A note on graph coloring'. *Rairo R* 1, 49–53.

Wilkins D. (1980) 'Using patterns and plans in chess'. *AI* 14 (2), 165–203.

Wilkins D. (1982) 'Using knowledge to control tree searching. *AI* 18 (1), 1–51.

Computer-assisted teaching and learning

Anderson J. and Kline P. (1979) 'A learning system and its psychological implications'. *IJCAI* 6, 16–21.

Brown J. S. and Burton R. (1975) 'Multiple representation of knowledge for tutorial reasoning', in D. G. Bobrow and A. Collins (eds) (1975) *Representation and Understanding*. Academic Press, 311–50.

Brown J. S. and Burton R. (1978) 'Diagnostic models for procedural bugs in basic mathematical skills', *CS* 2, 155–92.

Cauzinille E. and Mathieu J. (1982) 'Cognitive processes in the design of an intelligent tutoring system'. Colloque Tübingen, June 1985.

Elcook E. and Murray A. (1967) 'Experiments with a learning comments in a go moku playing program'. *Machine Intelligence*, vol. 1, 87–104, *Machine Intelligence*, vol. 2, 75–88. Elsevier.

Fikes R. E., Hart P. E. and Nilsson N. J. (1972) 'Learning and executing generalized robot plans'. *AI* 3, 251–88.

Hagert C. (1984) 'Introduction to the learning subfield'. *ECAI* 461–3.

Kodratoff Y., Ganascia J. G., Clavieras B., Bollinger T. and Tecuci G. (1984) 'Careful generalization for concept learning'. *ECAI* 483–92.

Kodratoff Y. and Sallantin J. (1983) (eds) *Outils pour l'apprentissage*. Publications du GR 22, Journées d'Orsay.

Langley P. W. (1977) 'Rediscovering physics with BACON 3'. *IJCAI* 6, 505–7.

Langley P. W. (1981) 'Data-driven discovery of physical laws'. *CS* 5, 31–54.

Lenat D. B. (1977) 'The ubiquity of discovery'. *AI* 9 (3), 257–86.

Michalski R. S. and Chilausky R. L. (1980) 'Learning by being told and learning from examples: An experimental comparison of the two methods of knowledge acquisition in the context of developing an expert system for soybean disease diagnostic'. *International Journal of Policy Analysis and Information Systems* 4, 125–61.

Michalski R. S., Carbonnel J. G. and Mitchell T. M. (1983) *Machine Learning: An Artificial Intelligence Approach*. Tioga Pub. Co.

Michalski R. S. (1983) 'A theory and methodology of inductive learning'. *AI* 20 (2) 111–61.

Mitchell T. M. (1983) 'Learning and problem solving'. *IJCAI* 8, 1139–51.

Papert A. (1972) 'Teaching children thinking'. *Programmed Learning and Educational Technology* 9, 5.

Sallentin J. (1979) 'Représentation d'observations dans le contexte de la théorie de l'information'. *Thèse d'état*. Paris 6.

Sallentin J. and Quinqueton J. (1983) 'Algorithms for learning logical formulas', *IJCAI* 8.

Samuel A. L. (1959) 'Some studies in machine learning using the game of checkers'. *IBM Journal of Research and Development* 3, 210–29. (Reprinted in E. A. Feigenbaum and J. Feldman (eds) (1963) *Computers and Thought*, McGraw-Hill, 71–105).

Samuel A. L. (1967) 'Some studies in machine learning using the game of checkers II'. Recent progress. *IBM Journal of Research and Development* 11, 601–17.

Simon H. (1983) 'Why should machines learn'. In R. S. Michalski, J. G. Carbonnel and T. M. Mitchell (eds) (1983) *Machine Learning: An Artificial Intelligence Approach*. Tioga Pub. Co.

Stevens A., Collins A. and Goldin S. (1979) 'Misconceptions in students' understanding'. *International Journal of Man–Machine Studies* 11, 145–56.

Vere S. A. (1975) 'Induction of concepts in the predicate calculus'. *IJCAI* 4, 281–7.

Waterman D. A. (1970) 'Generalization learning techniques for automating the learning of heuristics'. *AI* 1, 121–70.

Winston P. H. (1970) 'Learning structural descriptions from examples'. *Rep. No. TR-231*. AI Laboratory, Massachusetts Institute of Technology.

Winston P. H. (1978) 'Learning by creating and justifying frames', *AI* 10 (2), 147–72.

Game-playing programs

Adelson-Velskiy G., Arlazorov V. and Donskoy M. (1975) 'Some methods of controlling the tree in chess programs'. *AI* (6) 4, 361–71.

Baudet G. (1978) 'On the branching factor of the alpha–beta pruning algorithm', *AI* 10, 173–99.

Berliner H. (1980) 'Computer backgammon'. *Scientific American*, 54–69.

Berliner H. (1980) 'Backgammon computer program beats world champion'. *AI* 15, 205–20.

Botwinnik M. (1970) *Computers, Chess and Long Range Planning*. Springer-Verlag.

Clarke M. (1977) *Advances in Computer Chess*. Edinburgh University Press.

De Groot A. (1965) *Thought and Choice in Chess*. Mouton.

Faller B. (1985) 'Traitement inférentiels de faits conditionnels sur une application nécessitant un pattern-matching efficace: le jeu de la carte au bridge', *Thèse 3° cycle*. Paris sud.

Finkel R. A. and Fishburn J. P. (1982) 'Parallelism in alpha–beta search'. *AI* 19 (1) 89–106.

Frey P. W. (ed.) (1977) *Chess Skill in Man and Machine*. Springer-Verlag. Vol. 1. Vol. 2 (1980).

Knuth D. and Moore H. (1975) 'An analysis of alpha–beta pruning'. *AI* 6 (4), 293–326.

Pitrat J. (1971) 'A general game playing program', in *Artificial Intelligence and Heuristic Programming*. Edinburgh University Press, 125–55.

Pitrat J. (1976) 'A program for learning to play chess'. *Pattern Recognition and Artificial Intelligence*. Chen Academic Press, 399–419.

Pitrat J. (1977) 'A chess combination program which uses plans'. *AI* 8, 275–321.

Pitrat J. (1978) 'Realization of a program learning to find combinations at chess'. *Computed Oriented Learning Processes*, 397–424.

Popesco R. (1984) 'CHELEM: Un système-expert pour trouver la ligne de jeu du déclarant au bridge'. *Thèse de 3° cycle*. Paris VI.

Rosenbloom P. S. (1982) 'A world-championship-level Othello program', *AI* 19 (3) 279–320.

Tricot J. (1975) 'L'ordinateur et les jeux'. Série d'articles dans la revue *L'informatique Nouvelle*.

Wilkins D. (1979) 'Using plans in chess'. *IJCAI* 6, 960–7.

INDEX